Fodor's

GREAT AMERICAN
SPORTS AND
ADVENTURE
VACATIONS

Fodor's Travel Publications, Inc.
New York • Toronto • London • Sydney • Auckland

ISBN 0-679-02598-7

Fodor's Great American Sports and Adventure Vacations

Project Editor: Paula Consolo
Editors: Karen Cure, Caroline Haberfeld, Conrad Little Paulus, Larry Peterson, Melanie Roth
Editorial Contributors: Jonathan Abrahams, Naomi Black, Hannah Borgeson, Fionn Davenport, Erik Fair, Susan Farewell, Catherine Fredman, Rosemary Freskos, Bud Journey, Kristin McGowan, Michael B. McPhee, Peter Oliver, Peter Potterfield, Melissa Rivers, Lee R. Schreiber, Lisa Skriloff, Bill Strickland, Dennis Stuhaug, Michael J. Sullivan, Scott S. Warren, Jonathan Weisel, Sandra Widener, Rena Zurofsky
Creative Director: Fabrizio LaRocca

Cover Photographs: background: John Telford; left spot: Magnus Rietz/Image Bank; middle spot: Glenn Moody/Vermont Bicycle Touring; right spot: Torsten Blackwood/HI-AYH
Design: Tigist Getachew

Special Sales

CONTENTS

You're free-falling through 2,000 feet of perfectly clear Montana air. You're eye-to-eye with a school of Day-Glo fish alongside a reef on the Florida coast. You're scudding along in a sailboat, the New England salt air stinging your lips, or calling out "wagons ho-o-o-o!" from a canvas-topped covered wagon jolting down the Oregon Trail. You're shooting hoops with Michael Jordan, learning to lob on Nick Bollettieri's home turf, roaring down a Grand Prix race track in a BMW 325i at 135 mph.

No, you're not Walter Mitty. You've just joined the growing group of Americans who have learned that a vacation can be more than a trip to the beach—Americans who are taking advantage of the increasing number of trips and sports schools that make it possible for ordinary folks like you to spend a week or two or three learning—and performing—feats that you heretofore only fantasized about.

This guide will turn you on to hundreds of ways to do just that, enabling you to come away from your vacation with a lot more than a suntan. You will have cross-country skied to frozen waterfalls or watched, all alone, as Old Faithful blew off steam. You will have improved your golf swing or mastered the short game; sea-kayaked next to a breaching pod of whales or shot the continent's most awesome whitewater in a rubber raft; or even mountain-biked through the Rockies, gaining an intimate understanding of their name.

Whether you're young or old, an athlete or a wannabe, alone or traveling with your family or friends, you'll find a lifetime of great outdoor vacation ideas inside this book. These are mainly scheduled group trips and courses in the United States that last between 5 and 14 days. Keep in mind that in addition to the trips described here, there are many other scheduled trips: shorter trips, longer trips, trips to other parts of the country, and even trips to other countries. Also, most of the outfitters running these trips can set you up on a special tour, one that's customized for you and your family or a group of friends. Each chapter in this guide contains a comprehensive checklist of questions to help you choose the right trip—from the ones described here as well as from others that you find out about on your own.

If you have special needs, don't forget to query the outfitter before you sign up. If you're traveling with your family, for instance, be sure to ask whether youngsters are allowed. Some trips and courses are just not suited to kids—they're too hard or too dangerous or require too much sitting still—and some trips are fine for 13-year-olds but would be horrible for toddlers.

If you're traveling solo, ask about the single occupancy policy. Most prices we quote are per person based on double occupancy. Almost all companies will charge you a single supplement if you request a single room; some companies charge you the extra fee even if you request a double but end up in a single. If you observe any kind of special diet, ask whether the outfitter will supply food that you can eat, and if you use a wheelchair or need any other assistance, make sure that the outfitter can accommodate you.

Finally, once you've made your decision, get all the details of your trip nailed down. Then ask:

How much of a deposit is required and when is the balance due? Most schools and outfitters require you to put down a deposit by a particular day in order to reserve your spot, then pay in full some time before the departure date.

What is the cancellation policy? You may get a full or partial refund if you cancel your reservation, and then again, you may not. Policies vary from full refunds offered up to 30 days before the trip to partial refunds offered up to 7 days before the trip to no refunds offered ever. Find out how far in advance you must cancel to get a full refund, and ask if any allowances will be made for cancellations due to medical emergencies. If the outfitter

offers cancellation insurance, always take it. You'll receive a full refund if for any reason you can't make the trip.

Are taxes and tips included in the cost? Generally, taxes and tips are not included, and these can add substantially to the cost of your trip. Be sure to ask who customarily gets tipped and about how much that tip should be.

Every care has been taken to ensure the accuracy of the information in this guide. All prices and dates quoted here are based on information supplied to us at press time, but this may change, and the prudent traveler will avoid inconvenience by calling ahead. The publisher cannot accept responsibility for errors that may occur.

Fodor's wants to hear about your travel experiences, both pleasant and unpleasant. When a school or outfitter fails to live up to its billing, let us know and we will investigate the complaint and revise our entries where the facts warrant it. Send your letters to the editors of Fodor's Travel Publications, 201 E. 50th Street, New York, NY 10022.

Readers should also remember that adventure travel and outdoor vacations may entail certain risks. While outfitters, trip operators, and tour guides mentioned in this book have been carefully selected, the publisher makes no warranties regarding their competence, reliability, and safety practices and disavows all responsibility for injury, death, loss, or property damage that may arise from participation in their trips.

Baseball Fantasy Camps

by Michael B. McPhee

What baseball lover hasn't dreamed of a shot at the major leagues? It's the bottom of the ninth, and you're playing in front of a loyal home-team crowd. Runners on first, second, and third eye you tensely as you step up to the plate. The pitcher checks the signals, winds up, and hurls the ball. . . . A moment later the stadium erupts in wild celebration as the ball you've clobbered drops cleanly over the right field fence.

For most of us, this scenario will always remain a fantasy, but those who want to get a little closer to the dream can join one of 22 baseball fantasy camps created by the major league teams. You can go down to your favorite team's spring training facility for one week in the off-season and be coached in the game by some former greats. As best they can, the teams try to re-create the conditions major leaguers train under in the spring.

Want to learn a breaking pitch? Let Rollie Fingers show you how he does it. Or let Gary Carter show you how to catch a breaking ball. Tommy Lasorda or Denny Doyle will show you signals, when to steal, when to swing or when to bunt.

Mornings are spent warming up, stretching and exercising. Together, you're coached in all the fundamentals, then you're given a position and taught how to play it. Lunch usually follows. In the afternoon, the camp breaks into teams, and real games—complete with

umpires, base coaches, and trash talking—are played. It all ends in the locker rooms with showers, beers, and (for the men) banter with the pros about how the day went.

At the end of the week, more pros show up, and you play a team made up of former players. An awards banquet follows that night, with the Most Valuable Player award, the trainer's award (given to the player who spent the most time in the trainer's room), and dozens more.

All the teams emphasize that anyone can play, man or woman, experienced or not. The large majority of participants are men, but women do come. The Red Sox camp, for example, usually gets 4 or 5 women each year. Some come with their husbands, but most are alone. And yes, the women do sometimes play better than the men. Men or women, however, rank beginners may feel a bit awkward around the former college players. People come from all walks of life: carpenters, doctors, shopkeepers, and writers. The minimum age for most teams is 30, but a few allow anyone over 21 to play. The oldest participants are in their late seventies; there's no real age limit. And you don't have to be in great shape, just reasonably able to chase a grounder and run to first base. Some teams, such as the Mets, encourage disabled persons to join. Every team emphasizes fun, and the high jinks and shenanigans that go on all week leave everyone laughing on the plane back home. Guests who aren't playing are

Outdoor writer Michael B. McPhee has contributed to The New York Times, The Washington Post, *and* The Boston Globe.

usually welcome, and many teams have a special package for them.

Players need only bring a glove and spikes (rubber preferred), and the team will supply the rest, including your uniform with your name printed on it and the number of your choice. You also get lots of mementos—autographed baseballs, bats, trading cards of yourself at your position, warm-up jackets, and the like.

Prices are steep—between $3,000 and $4,000 for the week—but the accommodations are usually posh, the food is usually the same as what the major leaguers eat, and the price includes massages, rubdowns, and a few drinks at night.

CHOOSING THE RIGHT CAMP

The vast majority of people pick the camp of their favorite team or the one where a favorite player is supposed to show up, but whether you have a favorite team or not, here are some questions to ask:

How many years has the camp been run? The more years the camp's been running, the more likely it is to be run well.

How large is the camp? The total size doesn't really matter so much as the size of the individual teams within the camp and the number of managers for each. Nine campers per team would be too few; 20, too many. Thirteen is about right, with 2 pro managers.

How many teams are there and how many playing fields? If the camp has more teams than fields, you may end up warming the bench more than you would like.

What pros have actually signed up for the camp? How many days will each of them be there, and how much time will I actually spend with them? In promoting themselves, camps can be loose with the names of pros. Try to find out who has actually signed on the dotted line. You want more than a cameo appearance, so find out how many days the pros will be around, whether they will dine with you, stay at your hotel, or join you after practice in the locker rooms. The biggest

names sometimes fly in for the Saturday game and then fly out again.

Who plays in the big Saturday game against the pros? In some camps, everyone plays; in others, it's just the 2 best teams.

What's the cost and what's included? Unless stated otherwise, all the prices given here are per person, double occupancy, and include accommodations, ground transportation between the hotel and the ballpark, breakfasts, lunches, and one dinner, usually a Saturday night awards banquet; you must fend for yourself for other dinners. Prices do not include airfare unless stated otherwise. If you want a private room, rather than sharing one with another camper, you must pay a few hundred dollars more.

What are the free-time activities? Some teams organize evening programs, with open bars, videos of the day's games, and conversation with the pros; some camps simply leave you at the ballpark after practice with a see-you-tomorrow attitude. At least 2 programs take campers out to local restaurants one night. Don't worry too much about golf, tennis, swimming, and other activities—your days will be full and you'll be dead tired at night. But if you're into golf, it doesn't do any harm to ask if the pros will play with you.

What are accommodations like? Campers stay in generally upscale hotels or resorts. Ask for brochures that list facilities and describe rooms. Ask for the room you want—some face the beach, others the parking lot; some are upper-floor rooms with great views, others are lower down and noisier; some are single rooms, others are suites.

Is laundry service available? This could allow you to pack fewer clothes.

What's the food like? At most camps breakfast and lunch are served. You could be eating hamburgers and fries or lemon chicken and baked potatoes.

Are there any off-season events? Sometimes campers get together throughout the year to socialize or play ball. Sometimes they go to the sponsoring team's games during the regular season, and their presence in the stadium is announced before the game.

Can I bring my spouse or a friend? Almost all week-long camps let you bring a nonplaying guest. Some offer your guest a complete package (usually Thursday through Sunday) that includes everything from rooms and meals to airfare; others have no special package but will help make arrangements. The exception is the Dodgers camp; guests can't stay here unless they play. If you're bringing someone, make sure there's enough for him or her to do.

When does the camp take place, and how early do I need to sign up? Most of the camps are in late January or early February. A few teams, such as the Yankees and Dodgers, have fall camps. As a rule, you need to make reservations 2 months in advance; to play it safe, leave 4 months, particularly for the more popular camps—those run by the Cubs, Yankees, Orioles, and Dodgers.

MAJOR PLAYERS

BASEBALL FANTASY CAMPS This organization operates camps for the Baltimore Orioles, the Milwaukee Brewers, and the Texas Rangers (Twin Lakes Park, 6700 Clark Rd., Sarasota, FL 34241, tel. 813/925–4855 or 800/336–CAMP, fax 813/922–3751).

BASEBALL HEAVEN The camps of the Atlanta Braves, the Cleveland Indians, and the Cincinnati Reds are run by this company (Box 1033, Southampton, PA 18966, tel. 215/938–7311).

DREAM WEEK Dream Week organizes the camps of the Philadelphia Phillies, the Chicago White Sox, the Kansas City Royals, and the St. Louis Cardinals (Suite 203, Huntingdon Valley Federal Building, 2617 Huntingdon Pike, Huntingdon Valley, PA 19006, tel. 215/938–1200, fax 215/938–7746).

MAJOR SPORTS FANTASIES This outfit operates programs for the Boston Red Sox and the Minnesota Twins (RR3, Box 1788, Waterbury, VT 05676, tel. 802/244–4100 or 800/CAMPS94, fax 802/244–5835).

RANDY HUNDLEY'S BASEBALL CAMPS The Chicago Cubs and the St. Louis Cardinals camps, as well as the Field of Dreams camp, are run by this organization (675 North Court, Suite 160, Palatine, IL 60067, tel. 708/991–9595 or 800/766–4004, fax 708/991–9471).

THE CAMPS

ATLANTA BRAVES The Braves' camp is held at the team's training facility in West Palm Beach, Florida, and games are played at the Municipal Stadium there. Former players who have participated in the camp include Darrel Chaney, Ralph Garr, Rod Gilbreath, Glen Hubbard, and Rick Mahler.

Over 90 campers (capacity is 104) stay at the West Palm Beach Airport Hilton Hotel (tel. 407/684–9400), which is not where the Braves stay. The 10-story hotel has a pool, one tennis court, and a basketball court, and there's an 18-hole golf course about 15 minutes away. Breakfast is served at the hotel, lunch at the camp, and you're on your own for dinner. The Braves encourage nonplaying guests to join the campers; they can get together with other guests or join the wives of the former players on several shopping expeditions. Guest packages are available.

There are 2 post-game, locker-room bull sessions a week, which are the stuff of male fantasy: sitting around in towels, drinking beers and chatting with the pros.

During the season, the campers have a reunion at the Fulton County Stadium, and their presence is announced to the Braves' fans prior to the game. *The Atlanta Braves Baseball Heaven, c/o Baseball Heaven, Inc., Box 1033, Southampton, PA 18966, tel. 215/938–7311 or 800/8–BRAVES. Early Feb. in West Palm Beach, FL: 7 nights, $3,595. Price includes airfare from anywhere in the continental United States. Guest package: 3 nights, $595* *(including airfare). Campers must be at least 30 years old.*

BALTIMORE ORIOLES This camp is conducted by Baseball Fantasy Camps, Inc., which also runs the camps for the Milwaukee Brewers and the Texas Rangers. This is one of the most popular, due to steady management and enthusiastic Orioles fans. In the past enrollment has been capped at 130 campers, enough for 10 teams. A high percentage of the participants— more than 40%—are repeats. In any given year, up to 33 former players have signed up to coach the campers, including Al Bumbry and Boog Powell. And Earl Weaver and Brooks Robinson have come in for the big game on Saturday.

Everything takes place at Twin Lakes Park, which the Orioles use for 2 weeks in the spring before giving it up to minor league teams. The park has 5 fields, a field house, and a complete selection of training equipment, including pitching machines and batting cages. The 10 teams play doubleheaders each day, leading up to the big game on Saturday against the former Orioles.

Accommodations are at the Harley Sand Castle Hotel (tel. 813/388–2181) on Lido Beach in Sarasota, Florida, which is where the Orioles stay while in training. It has two pools but no tennis courts; golf is 15 minutes away. Breakfast and lunch are taken at the ballpark, prepared and served by the Orioles' kitchen staff. Campers are on their own for dinner, except for the awards banquet. Spouses are welcome to sign up for a Thursday–Sunday package.

A reunion night is held during the regular season with each player from the fantasy camp, in uniform, announced in Camden Yard prior to an Orioles game. *The Baltimore Orioles Fantasy Camp, c/o Baseball Fantasy Camps, Inc., Twin Lakes Park, 6700 Clark Rd., Sarasota, FL 34241, tel. 813/925–4855 or 800/336–CAMP, fax 813/922–3751. Early Feb.: 7 nights, $3,500. Price includes airfare from Baltimore. Guest package: 3 nights, $695 (including airfare from Baltimore). Campers must be at least 30 years old. Register by Thanksgiving.*

BOSTON RED SOX Both the Red Sox and Minnesota Twins camps are run by the same operator at the same time in the same town, about 20 minutes apart, so you have the advantage of being able to get together several times for rap sessions and autograph parties, as well as for 2 games.

The Red Sox camp is held in Fort Myers, Florida, in Palm Stadium. There are about 130 campers and more than 25 former major leaguers. Bill Lee, Louis Tiant, Rico Petrocelli, and Bob Stanley have all played. Ron Luciano, the umpire crew chief, concurrently runs a minicamp for up to 20 umpire wannabes. There's also a coaching camp for up to 30 participants.

Everyone stays at the Sheraton Harbor Place (tel. 813/337–0300) in downtown Ft. Myers, Florida. The hotel has one tennis court and three pools. A guest package is available. You're on your own for breakfast, but the price includes lunches, which are served in the park, and 5 dinners, including the awards banquet.

Most of the pros eat dinner with you, which is a real plus; it's these sorts of informal gatherings that make baseball camps so memorable. Twice during the week former players such as Gary Bell and Dick Radatz conduct a kangaroo court, fining campers for dumb things they did during the day. *The Boston Red Sox, c/o Major Sports Fantasies, RR3, Box 1788, Waterbury, VT 05676, tel. 800/ CAMPS94 or 802/244–4100, fax 802/244– 5835. Late Jan. in Ft. Myers, FL: 7 nights, $3,500. Price includes lunches and 5 dinners but not breakfasts. Guest package: 7 nights, $750. Luciano's umpire school: 7 nights, $950. Coaching camp: 7 nights, $1,750. Campers must be at least 30 years old. Register by mid-Dec.*

CHICAGO CUBS What is it about those Cubs fans? This camp is so popular they have it 3 times a year, twice in January and once again in April. The campers all come down to train at Fitch Park in Mesa, Arizona, using the same facilities as the Cubs, then play their games in Ho Ho Kam Stadium nearby. Anywhere from 60 to 80 campers show up. Capacity is 88. Roughly 12 major leaguers are on hand, including, in past years, Glen Beckert, Ron

Santo, Billy Williams, Jose Cardenal, and Joe Pepitone.

You stay at the Dobson Ranch Inn (tel. 602/831–7000), which is where the Milwaukee Brewers' campers stay. It's a plush resort on the edge of town, with a top-ranked golf course, 20 tennis courts, and four pools. Nonplaying guests are welcome, but the Cubs don't have a guest package.

You eat breakfast at the hotel and lunch at the ball field. You're on your own for dinner. Videos of your games are shown every night. Many of the pros play golf, and campers are welcome to join them on the links or at the pool.

The Cubs also host a 3-day minicamp in June, held at Wrigley Field and limited to 48 players. Campers have to find their own place to stay; fortunately, most of them live in Chicago. *The Chicago Cubs, c/o Randy Hundley's Baseball Camps, 675 North Court, Suite 160, Palatine, IL 60067, tel. 708/991–9595 or 800/ 766–4004 , fax 708/991–9471. Jan. and late Apr. in Mesa, AZ: 7 nights, $2,995. Campers must be at least 30 years old. Chicago minicamp in June: 3 days, $1,895. Price includes lunches but not accommodations.*

CHICAGO WHITE SOX Details about the White Sox's week-long camp in Sarasota, Florida, were unavailable at press time. For more information, contact *The Chicago White Sox, c/o Dream Week, Inc., Suite 203, Huntingdon Valley Federal Building, 2617 Huntingdon Pike, Huntingdon Valley, PA 19006, tel. 215/938–1200 or 800/888–HERO, fax 215/ 938–7746.*

CINCINNATI REDS The campers use the Reds' facilities in Plant City, Florida, and games are played in the Plant City Stadium. Former Reds who have signed up in the past include Darrel Chaney, Don Gullet, Jim Maloney, Joe Nuxhall, and Pat Zachry. Marge Schott and her dog have been known to drop by, as has Pete Rose.

The Reds take on a maximum of 96 campers, who stay at the Embassy Suites (tel. 813/875– 1555), a 15-story hotel about 2 miles from Tampa Airport and about 30 minutes from the stadium. The hotel has a pool but no tennis or golf. All rooms are suites. Breakfast and lunch are at the stadium. Dinners are not included, but the Reds host a cocktail party at the hotel every night with most of the pros in attendance. Guests not playing are welcome, and there's a good guest package.

Campers leave with an armful of Reds paraphernalia—the usual uniform, bats, balls, and videos. The team announces the campers to Reds fans prior to a regular-season game in Riverfront Stadium. *The Cincinnati Reds Baseball Heaven, c/o Baseball Heaven, Inc., Box 1033, Southampton, PA 18966, tel. 215/938–7311 or 800/755–REDS. Late Jan. in Plant City, FL: 7 nights, $3,595. Price includes airfare from anywhere in the continental United States. Guest package: 3 nights, $695 (including airfare). Campers must be at least 30 years old. Register by mid-Dec.*

CLEVELAND INDIANS The Indians hold their camp at their spring-training grounds at Chain-O'Lakes Stadium in Winter Haven, Florida. It's the complete facility used by the Indians, and all equipment is available to the campers. In the past, about 12 former major leaguers signed up, including Bob Feller, Mudcat Grant, Tito Francona, and Herb Score.

The camp averages about 80 campers but can hold up to 96. You stay at the Grenelefe Golf and Tennis Resort (tel. 813/422–7511) in Haines City, Florida, which is about 30 minutes from Orlando and 15 minutes from the ballpark. Should you bring a partner, or plan to stay on, the resort has three 18-hole golf courses, 20 tennis courts, and 4 pools. Campers stay in villa suites. Breakfast and lunch are served at the ballpark. You're on your own for dinner, except for the Saturday night banquet.

Campers are also treated to a reunion during the Indians' season at the Gateway facility in Cleveland. *The Cleveland Indians Baseball Heaven, c/o Baseball Heaven, Inc., Box 1033, Southampton, PA 18966, tel. 215/938– 7311 or 800/75–TRIBE. Late Jan. in Winter Haven, FL: 7 nights, $3,595. Price includes airfare from anywhere in the continental*

United States. Guest packages: 3 nights, $595 (including airfare). Campers must be at least 30 years old.

DETROIT TIGERS   The Tigers have 2 week-long camps back-to-back at Tiger Town, their own training facility in Lakeland, Florida. Games are played in nearby Marchant Stadium. About 17 former players attend each camp; in the past the roster has included Mark Fidrych, Rocky Colavito, Al Kaline, and Mickey Lolich. Willie Horton, who is loved among the players for his barbecue, has also participated, playing and cooking.

Roughly 80 campers show up each week and are housed with the Tigers at the Holiday Inn-North in Lakeland (tel. 813/858–1411). Guest packages are available. The hotel has a pool but no tennis or golf; when we went to press the hotel receptionist was answering the phone in Japanese. Campers are on their own for breakfast but are fed lunch at Tiger Town and 5 dinners at the hotel.

The Tigers are big on hosting evening social events, such as Willie Horton's barbecue night; a championship night, where top teams are feted; and an autograph night, which features an open bar.

The Detroit camp is unique in that it has a large, very active alumni group. Former campers have games every other weekend during the season at a college in Detroit and sometimes take on the campers from the Cleveland Indians. The Tigers campers have a luncheon every 6 weeks through the year, publish a newsletter, and perform charity work. *Detroit Tigers Fantasy Camp, c/o Sports Fantasies, Inc., 28777 Northwestern Hwy., Suite 290, Southfield, MI 48034, tel. 313/353–5643, fax 313/353–5641. Early Feb. in Lakeland, FL: 7 nights, $2,995. Price includes airfare from Detroit, lunches, and 5 dinners but not breakfasts. Guest package: 7 nights, $1,000 (including airfare from Detroit). Campers must be at least 21 years old. Register by Dec. 15.*

HOUSTON ASTROS   The Astros have a 3-day camp, held in August with about 25 players, who can be as young as 21. Campers stay at the Sheraton Astrodome (tel. 713/748–3221), an eight-story hotel across the street from the stadium with three pools but no tennis or golf. All practices with the veterans and games among the campers are held in the Astrodome. Veterans include Jimmy Wynn, Enos Cabell, and Norm Miller. *The Houston Astros, Budweiser Astros Fantasy Camp, Box 288, Houston, TX 77001, tel. 713/799–9879, fax 713/799–9794. Early Aug. in Houston: 3 nights, $2,295. Campers must be at least 21 years old. Register by June 30.*

KANSAS CITY ROYALS   Details about the Royals's week-long camp were unavailable at press time. For information, contact *The Kansas City Royals, c/o Dream Week, Inc., Suite 203, Huntingdon Valley Federal Building, 2617 Huntingdon Pike, Huntingdon Valley, PA 19006, tel. 215/938–1200 or 800/888–HERO, fax 215/938–7746.*

LOS ANGELES DODGERS   The Dodgers camp is unique in that the club owns its own 450-acre facility, including accommodations, dining room, conference center, 2 golf courses, and all the fitness equipment you would ever need. It's called Dodgertown and it's in Vero Beach, Florida.

There are 2 camps, one in November and one in February. About 15 former Dodgers, including some from the old Brooklyn Dodgers, show up. You meet and play ball with the likes of Ralph Branca, Carl Erskine, Steve Garvey, Clem Labine, and Duke Snider. Tommy Lasorda may show up for the big game on Saturday.

The camps sell out, with 96 campers in each. About 50% of the campers are on their second time around—always a good sign. Because you stay at Dodgertown, you eat and sleep in the same facilities as the Dodgers. Spouses or friends aren't allowed to stay in players' rooms unless they're playing, too, but the Dodgers will help them find a room in town and will assist with transportation.

Nights are spent reviewing films and videos of the day's workout and of Dodgers World Series highlights. Campers are welcome to use all the recreational facilities, including the golf courses and pools.

The campers have a very strong alumni group, which travels and plays around the world. One year they traveled to Russia and played an exhibition game there. *Los Angeles Dodgers Adult Baseball Camp, Dodgertown, Box 2887, Vero Beach, FL 32961, tel. 407/569–4900 or 800/334–PLAY, fax 407/770–2424. Nov. and Feb. in Vero Beach, FL: 6 nights, $3,995. Price includes all meals. Campers must be at least 30 years old. Register at least 3 months in advance.*

MILWAUKEE BREWERS A relatively small number of campers—about 40—and up to 10 pros attend the Brewers' camp at Compadre Stadium in Chandler, Arizona, where the Brewers hold their own spring training. The camp was under new management in 1994, when the roster of former Brewers included George Scott, Charlie Moore, and Rollie Fingers.

Accommodations are at the Dobson Ranch Inn (tel. 602/831–7000), a rather posh resort in a residential area outside Chandler, about a 20- to 30-minute drive from the stadium, and about 20 minutes east of Phoenix Airport. The two-story inn has a pool, and there's an 18-hole public golf course four blocks away. Breakfast and lunch are served at the stadium by the Brewers' kitchen staff. Dinner is on you until the Saturday night banquet. *The Milwaukee Brewers Fantasy Camp, c/o Baseball Fantasy Camps, Inc., Twin Lakes Park, 6700 Clark Rd., Sarasota, FL 34241, tel. 813/925–4855 or 800/336–CAMP, fax 813/922–3751. Late Jan. in Chandler, AZ: 7 nights, $2,995. Price includes airfare from Milwaukee. Guest package: 3 nights, $695 (including airfare from Milwaukee). Players must be at least 30 years old.*

MINNESOTA TWINS The Twins' camp is now under the same management as the Red Sox camp. It's held at the same time, and the teams play two games against each other and visit each other twice. The unannounced shenanigans between the camps is part of the fun.

The Twins' camp is held in the Lee County Sports Complex in Ft. Myers, Florida. Although it's a minor-league facility, it still has all the coaching and training equipment of a major-league camp, such as batting cages, pitching machines, and so on. The Twins also offer umpire and coaching schools.

Among the former Twins that have signed up in the past are Tony Oliva, Mudcat Grant, Frank Quilici, and Ron Perranoski. The 60-odd campers stay at the Ramada Hotel in Ft. Myers (tel. 813/936–4300). The Ramada is on Rte. 41 about 14 miles from the beaches. It has a two-story motel section and a five-story hotel. Facilities include a pool and four tennis courts. *The Minnesota Twins, c/o Major Sports Fantasies, RR3, Box 1788, Waterbury, VT 05676, tel. 802/244–4100 or 800/CAMPS94, fax 802/244–5835. Late Jan. in Ft. Myers, FL: $3,400. Price includes all meals. Guest package: 7 nights, $750. Umpire camp in late Jan.: 7 nights, $950. Coaching camp in late Jan.: 7 nights, $1,750. Campers must be at least 30 years old. Register by Dec. 25.*

MONTREAL EXPOS At the Expos' (and the Atlanta Braves') spring training facility, Municipal Stadium in West Palm Beach, Florida, the likes of Gary Carter, Bill "Spaceman" Lee, Steve Rogers, Ken Singleton, Larry Parrish, and Warren Cromartie teach the finer points of baseball to up to 78 fantasy camp participants. An outside company called PAS*SPORTS operates this program for the Expos. A coaching camp is run simultaneously; for half the price of the regular camp, you can serve as the assistant to a professional coach throughout the week.

After working on baseball techniques all day, campers socialize with the pros during four scheduled group dinners, participate in a trivia contest hosted by two Expos broadcasters, and join in the uproarious laughter at Warren Cromartie's outrageous kangaroo court.

Campers and the pros who don't live in the area stay at the comfortable Holiday Inn on Singer Island (tel 407/848–3888 or 800/HOLIDAY), a modern, 7-story building on beachfront property about 7 miles from the ballpark and 12 miles northeast of Palm Beach International Airport. The hotel has biking, fishing, and an Olympic-size pool; golf and tennis can be arranged at nearby facilities.

Alumni reunite at two Expos games at Olympic Stadium during the following regular season. At one game, they have dinner and watch the game together; at the other, they come out onto the field in uniform in front of thousands of spectators and are introduced by name as their picture flashes on the scoreboard. *Montréal Expos Fantasy Camp, Box 8235, Warwick, RI 02888, tel. 401/785–2637 or 800/989–2267, fax 401/785–2637. Feb. in West Palm Beach, FL: 7 nights, $3,095. Price includes breakfasts, lunches, and 4 dinners. Guest package: 7 nights, $425 (including breakfasts, lunches, and 4 dinners). Coaching camp: 7 nights, $1,600 (including breakfasts, lunches, and 4 dinners).*

NEW YORK METS The Mets play host to some enthusiastic campers in Port St. Lucie, Florida, and no wonder: As many as 30 former players return each year, and many of them stay in the same hotel as the campers. The roster includes Bud Harrelson, Ed Charles, Jerry Koosman, and Gary Carter. Games are played in the Thomas J. White Stadium, about 10 miles from the five-story Holiday Inn (tel. 407/337–2200), where both pros and campers stay. The hotel is on U.S. Hwy. 1 in Port St. Lucie, about 8 miles from the beach. The hotel has a pool and there are several 18-hole golf courses nearby. Guests are welcome, but there's no guest package.

About 100 campers show up each year, and space fills up early. The Mets camp is unique in that it encourages disabled campers to attend. "Playing skills are not necessary—having a good time is," is their motto, and they make sure you get to play, regardless of your ability.

Breakfast is at the hotel, lunch is in the clubhouse, but you're on your own for 4 dinners. One night, everyone eats together at a restaurant in town. *The New York Mets Ulti-Met-Week, 1096 Rainer Dr., Altamonte Springs, FL 32714, tel. 407/788–2222, fax 407/788–3677. Early Feb. in Port St. Lucie, FL: 7 nights, $3,995. Price includes airfare from New York, break-*

fasts, lunches, and 2 dinners. Campers must be at least 30 years old. Register by Oct. 15.

NEW YORK YANKEES At the New York Yankees Spring Training Headquarters in Fort Lauderdale, Yankee legend Mickey Mantle teaches the secrets of his phenomenal success to 90 campers at each of three week-long programs in early spring and fall. Assisting him is a talented crew of baseball stars, which might include Ron Guidry, Jake Gibbs, Bucky Dent, Moose Skowron, Hall of Famers Catfish Hunter and Enos Slaughter, and former Yankee manager Hank Bauer. The organization is planning to add at least one more session, for a yet-to-be-determined weekend in July.

A private room is reserved for every camper at the Palm-Aire Spa Resort in Pompano Beach (tel. 305/972–3300 or 800/2–PALM–AIR), 15 minutes from Fort Lauderdale International Airport. This is where the Yankees stay during spring training. The resort has 5 golf courses, 37 tennis courts, and a state-of-the-art health club.

Both Yankees camps are big on loading campers up with lots of paraphernalia—more than just the standard uniform, balls, and cards. *Mickey Mantle's Week of Dreams, Box 7777, Grayson, KY 41143-7777, tel. 606/474–7771, fax 606/474–8008. Early May and late Oct.–early Nov. in Fort Lauderdale, FL: 7 nights, $3,950. Price includes airfare from New York (or a travel credit toward airfare from elsewhere) and private room. Guests stay free in campers' rooms. Campers must be at least 30 years old.*

NEW YORK YANKEES Former pitching great Whitey Ford runs his own camp for the Yankees each fall. His campers also play and practice at the Yankees' own facility in Ft. Lauderdale, Florida; games are in the Ft. Lauderdale Stadium. In the past such players as Clete Boyer, Graig Nettles, Joe Pepitone, Ron Guidry, and even Yogi Berra have signed up.

About 70 campers are expected each season. The hotel used by campers changes, but they recently stayed at the Marriott-Ft. Lauderdale North Hotel (tel. 305/771–0440), a 17-story high rise in the business district, with a pool but no tennis or golf. Campers get to stay in rooms by themselves, and guests can accompany them for free. There's a small additional charge for guests who attend the Saturday banquet. Breakfast and lunch are at the training facility; for dinner, you're on your own.

Both Yankees camps load campers up with paraphernalia—more than just the standard uniform, balls, and cards. *The Whitey Ford Baseball Fantasy Camp, 74 Palisade Ave., Cliffside, NJ 07010, tel. 201/943–0999, fax 201/943–4166. Early Nov.: 7 nights, $3,795. Price includes airfare and private room. Guests stay free in campers' rooms. Campers must be at least 21 years old. Register by Sept. 1.*

PHILADELPHIA PHILLIES Details about the Phillies' week-long camp in Clearwater, Florida, were unavailable at press time. For more information, contact *The Philadelphia Phillies, c/o Dream Week, Inc., Suite 203, Huntingdon Valley Federal Building, 2617 Huntingdon Pike, Huntingdon Valley, PA 19006, tel. 215/938–1200 or 800/888–HERO, fax 215/938–7746.*

PITTSBURGH PIRATES Campers come down to the Pirates' training facility in Bradenton, Florida, and games are played at McKechnie Field. About a dozen former players spend the week with you, and as many as 25 may show up for the game on Saturday. Possible players include Jim Leland, Jay Bell, Lloyd McClendon, and Bill Mazeroski.

A maximum of 72 campers stay at the Holiday Inn-Riverfront (tel. 813/747–3727) in downtown Bradenton, about 15 minutes from the field. The hotel has an outdoor pool but no golf or tennis. The beach is 9 miles away. Breakfast and lunch are served in the Pirate City cafeteria. Three dinners are taken at the hotel when the team hosts question-and-answer sessions and signs autographs. There's no package for nonplaying guests, but the Pirates will assist with arrangements.

The Pirates host a reunion during the regular season and introduce the campers in their uniforms during a game at Three Rivers Stadium. *Pittsburgh Pirates Camp Bradenton, c/o The Pittsburgh Pirates, 600 Stadium Circle, Pittsburgh, PA 15212, tel. 412/323–5025, fax 412/323–5024. Early Jan. in Bradenton, FL: 7 nights, $2,995. Price includes airfare from anywhere in the continental United States, breakfasts, lunches, and 3 dinners. Campers must be at least 30. Register by mid-Dec.*

ST. LOUIS CARDINALS The Cardinals have a 3-day camp in July, held in St. Louis, with games played in Busch Stadium. Up to 45 campers come to practice and play against 9 pros, including Bob Gibson and Curt Flood.

The biggest difference between this and other camps, other than its short duration, is that no accommodations are provided and most of the campers live in the St. Louis area. The pros usually stay at the Marriott Pavilion across the street from the stadium and may make dinner plans or have drinks with the campers, but nothing is planned by the camp. *The St. Louis Cardinals, c/o Randy Hundley's Baseball Camps, 675 North Court, Suite 160, Palatine, IL 60067, tel. 800/766–4004 or 708/991–9595, fax 708/991–9471. June–Aug. in St. Louis, MO: 3 nights, $1,595. Price includes lunch but no accommodations or ground transportation. Campers must be at least 21 years old.*

ST. LOUIS CARDINALS Details about the Cardinal's week-long camp in St. Petersburg, Florida, were unavailable at press time. For more information, contact *The St. Louis Cardinals, c/o Dream Week, Inc., Suite 203, Huntingdon Valley Federal Building, 2617 Huntingdon Pike, Huntingdon Valley, PA 19006, tel. 215/938–1200 or 800/888–HERO, fax 215/938–7746.*

SAN FRANCISCO GIANTS This popular camp, limited to 78 players, is held at Arizona's Scottsdale Stadium in Indian School Park, where the Giants go for spring training. Campers and pros stay together at the two-story Scottsdale Hilton Resort and Spa (tel. 602/948–7750), which has four tennis courts and a pool but no golf. Veteran pros include Dusty Baker, Bob Bremly,

Orlando Cepeda, and Juan Marichal. There's an almost 60% return rate, so be sure to register at least 6 months in advance. *San Francisco Giants Fantasy Camp, Giants Ticket Office, Candlestick Park, San Francisco, CA 94124, tel. 415/330–2575 or 800/SFGIANT, fax 415/467–3803 or 415/330–2572. Early Feb. in Scottsdale, AZ: 7 nights, $3,800. Price includes airfare from San Francisco. Campers must be at least 30 years old. Register by Aug.*

TEXAS RANGERS This camp died briefly, but was revived in 1994 by Baseball Fantasy Camps, Inc., which also runs the Orioles' and Brewers' camps. Enrollment should be about 40, making this a relatively small camp. Among the pros who signed up for 1994 were Mickey Rivers and Ferguson Jenkins.

All coaching and play is in Pt. Charlotte, Florida, in the Charlotte County Stadium, where the Rangers train in the spring. Campers have full use of all Rangers facilities, including batting cages, pitching machines, weight room, and saunas.

Campers stay at the Palm Island Resort (tel. 813/697–4800), which is on an island accessible only by boat. Campers are ferried to the mainland each morning, then bused to Charlotte County Stadium. The resort has 11 courts and 4 pools, and there's an 18-hole golf course less than 5 minutes away. The island has more than 2 miles of beaches, and the rooms are all up on stilts, within 50 yards of the water.

Unlike most other camps, this one includes 5 hotel dinners. A guest package is available. The first 75 campers to sign up receive tickets to opening day at Arlington Stadium. *The Texas Rangers Fantasy Camp, c/o Baseball Fantasy Camps, Inc., Twin Lakes Park, 6700 Clark Rd., Sarasota, FL 34241, tel. 813/925–4855 or 800/336–CAMP, fax 813/922–3751. Late Jan. in Pt. Charlotte, FL: 7 nights, $3,600. Price includes airfare from Dallas and all meals. Guest package: 3 nights, $795 (including airfare from Dallas and meals). Campers must be at least 30 years old. Register by early Dec.*

TORONTO BLUE JAYS Begun in 1991, the Blue Jays camp is owned and operated by three current members of the Blue Jays organization: first base coach Bob Bailor, minor league manager Garth Iorg, and Ken Carson, director of Florida operations. About 15 former Blue Jays, including John Mayberry, Willie Upshaw, and Buck Martinez, assist in instructing a maximum of 70 campers at the Blue Jays' spring training facilities in Dunedin, Florida, 30 miles west of Tampa International Airport.

The program begins on Superbowl Sunday, so the highlight of the welcome party is the huddle around the TV to watch the game. For the rest of the week, though, the focus is baseball, baseball, baseball.

Accommodations may vary from year to year. Participants in the 1994 program were lodged about 10 miles from the ballpark at the Adam's Mark Caribbean Gulf Resort (tel. 813/443–5714 or 800/444–2326), overlooking Clearwater Beach, on the Gulf of Mexico. In their free time campers can go jet skiing and parasailing at the hotel, and tennis courts and golf courses are a few miles away. Many of the pros stay in the same hotel as the campers. Four nights during the week, special guests, who may include current Blue Jays, show up at the hotel for informal chats; in 1992, World Series MVP Pat Borders made an appearance.

For the past few years participants have been invited to a special reunion during the old timers' game at the SkyDome, the Blue Jays' regular-season home. *Blue Jays Fantasy Camp, Box 957, Dunedin, FL 34697, tel. 813/736–0705 or 800/688–4529, fax 813/734–7661. Late Jan.–early Feb. in Dunedin, FL: 7 nights, $3,600. Price includes airfare, breakfasts, lunches, and two dinners. Guest package: 7 nights, $850 (including airfare but not meals). Campers must be at least 30 years old. Register by Oct. 31.*

NONAFFILIATED CAMP

FIELD OF DREAMS This camp is held each year over Labor Day Weekend in Dyersville, Iowa, using the actual field built for *Field of Dreams*, the popular 1989 baseball film.

Campers play for 3 days in copies of 1919 White Sox uniforms, and they attend the requisite awards banquet. Evening activities include a riverboat gambling cruise. In past years, up to 9 former major leaguers signed up for the camp, including Reggie Jackson, Lou Brock, Curt Flood, and Vida Blue.

The camp is limited to 45 campers, who are broken down into 4 squads. Two squads play an inning, then warm the benches while the other 2 play an inning, until the games are completed.

Everyone stays at the three-story Best Western Dubuque Inn (tel. 319/556–7760), which is 26 miles from the stadium. The hotel has an indoor pool, and there are two golf courses within 3 miles. Breakfast and lunch are served at the field, and a final banquet is held on a riverboat. Guests not playing are welcome, but there is no package for them. *Field of Dreams Baseball Camp, c/o Randy Hundley's Baseball Camps, 675 North Court, Suite 160, Palatine, IL 60067, tel. 708/991–9595 or 800/766–4004, fax 708/991–9471.*

Labor Day Weekend: 5 nights, $2,395. Campers must be at least 30 years old. Register 5 weeks in advance.

TEAMS WITHOUT CAMPS

These are the teams that, as of early 1994, had no camps of their own. You may want to call and ask about their future plans.

California Angels, Box 2000, Anaheim, CA 92803, tel. 714/937–7200.

Oakland Athletics, Oakland Coliseum, Oakland, CA 94621, tel. 510/638–4900.

Seattle Mariners, Box 4100, Seattle, WA 98104, tel. 206/628–3555.

Colorado Rockies, 1700 Bway., Suite 2100, Denver, CO 80290, tel. 303/292–0200.

Florida Marlins, 100 N.E. 3rd Ave., 3rd Fl., Ft. Lauderdale, FL 33301, tel. 305/779–7070.

San Diego Padres, Box 2000, San Diego, CA 92112, tel. 619/283–7294.

Basketball Fantasy Camps

by Michael J. Sullivan

ou know your weekend game of hoops could be better. You know that somewhere deep inside you is a gravity-defying, in-your-face, slam-dunking machine. You know, as you watch your favorite NBA star pull off a lightning fast pick-and-roll and then duck and bob and weave and leap his way to the net, that you, too, could do that. Well, maybe, sort of. If somebody showed you how. With practice.

Well, here's your chance.

At a basketball fantasy camp, usually held in the NBA's off-season, current and former professional players and coaches lead men and woman through some fundamentals of the game in 4 or 5 days of serious workouts, coaching tips, practice drills, and competition—in short, total immersion in all things basketball. This is your chance to improve your game and get some insight into how the pros do it in the bargain.

Basketball fantasy camps are a relatively new phenomenon, not nearly as widespread as their baseball counterparts. They should not be confused with the numerous basketball camps run for high-school players hoping for the attention of college team scouts. These camps are for adults. There are only 3 that have been held every year for several years, although a couple of others are held sporadically. Unlike baseball fantasy camps, which are often sponsored by individual teams, these camps are independently run. NBA teams do, however, sometimes donate equipment and tickets to their games.

All camps follow the same basic format: You're teamed up with other players of similar ability, go through warm-up routines, run individual skill drills, and participate in everything from one-on-one to full-team competitions. Next you learn NBA plays and use them during a league-style series of games climaxing with a big match on the last day. Although none of the schools requires a particular skill level, you'll have a hard time keeping up and will feel out of place if you don't play at least some hoops and aren't already in pretty good shape. All camps have you sign a liability waiver, and one asks for written verification from your doctor that says you're up to the intense workout.

In fact, the word *fantasy* ought to be taken with a few grains of salt. These camps aren't about basketball as a spectator sport—you are expected to work through the same drills and practice moves that the pros do. Your skills and stamina are tested to the limit and improved. Just don't expect to increase your hang-time by too much: Some moves are possible only if you're 7 feet tall.

CHOOSING THE RIGHT CAMP

Because there are so few basketball camps most people won't find one where their

Host of a weekly sports radio show on New York's Long Island, Michael J. Sullivan is a lifelong hoops fan and has written a book for children about Shaquille O'Neal.

favorite team's players are sure to be. And since the instruction is top-notch across the board, you'll probably pick a camp either because of the reputations of the camp leaders or because of the price. When choosing a camp, it's a good idea to ask the following:

What NBA pros besides the camp leaders have signed on as staff? Every year different players help coach the camp teams. There is no guarantee that a particular player will return year after year, so if meeting your favorite basketball star is the only reason you plan to sign up, make sure he'll be there.

How large is the camp? As far as working on your game, the total number of campers won't matter so long as there is at least one coach for each group of players. One of the beauties of basketball is its flexibility: You have only 6 players? Fine, just play 3-on-3. If there are an even number of players up to 10, let the game begin. The size of the camp *will* make a difference, however, in the amount and quality of the time you spend on the court with whichever NBA stars you came to be near.

How much playing time can you expect to get? Get a sense of the ratio of time spent on drills and individual skill instruction, and how much is spent in scrimmages. If you have several hours of free time each day, find out what else there is to see and do in the area.

What's the cost and what's included? Two of these camps cost about the same amount per day, although one is a day longer; the third camp's per-day fee is more than twice that of the other two. This has a lot to do with location—Lake Tahoe and Palo Alto versus Maui—but is also a reflection of the luxuriousness of the camp. Unless otherwise noted, prices are per person, based on double occupancy (which means that you'll be rooming with another player unless you pay an additional fee) and include lodging, dinner, and either lunch or breakfast. T-shirts, shorts, basketballs, and sometimes even basketball shoes are all supplied.

What are accommodations like? Campers stay in generally upscale hotels. Ask for brochures that list facilities and find out which rooms campers are slated for.

What's the food like? Generally, you eat in the hotel restaurant, although the Magic Johnson camp also has a luau.

How far in advance do I need to book? The camps we list require from 1 to 3 months advance booking.

THE CAMPS

THE WEST COAST

CALIFORNIA **Don Nelson Basketball Fantasy Camp.** Golden State Warriors coach Don Nelson leads this camp with the same skill that he uses to coax stellar performances from such NBA stars as Chris Mullin.

Nelson's camp is held over the course of 4 days, usually in August, on the campus of Stanford University, about 20 miles south of San Francisco in Palo Alto. Practice and games are in the school's Maples Pavillion, a sports arena with three full-size basketball courts.

Upon arrival, you and your 50 to 60 fellow campers are evaluated by Nelson and his staff of 8 to 10 current and former Warriors players and coaches who team you up with other campers of similar ability. You spend 17 hours over the 4 days doing skill drills, skill competitions, one-on-one, and 3-point shooting, as well as playing 3-on-3 and 4-on-4 half-court and full-team, full-court games.

One of the bonuses of this camp are the daily Basketball Bull Sessions built into the schedule. These range from the first night's question-and-answer session with the whole group to informal conversations and get-togethers in the hotel bar after the day's playing is done. Nelson and his staff are available to campers for pointers or even a little extra practice. As a player for the Boston Celtics in the 1960s and 1970s, Nelson perfected the one-handed foul shot, so if you're having trouble knocking down your jumper, he's the man to see. Nelson also loves tennis, and campers who play—and have any energy after the day's hoops are over—are invited to test their forehand smash against him.

This may be the least expensive of the basketball fantasy camps, but you won't lack for any creature comforts. Stanford's campus is elegant and refined, designed by renowned landscape architect Frederick Law Olmsted, with pale-colored Spanish-revival buildings on well-tended grounds in the midst of a wealthy suburban community.

Lodging is just off campus, in the Stanford Park Hotel, which has a workout room with a sauna and a Jacuzzi for which you'll be most grateful. Lunch and dinner are included in the price, but not breakfast. Lunches are served on a terrace at the Maples Pavillion. Dinners range from the first night's ordered-in pizza to the next night's group outing at a local restaurant, and a Southwestern-style barbecue on the last evening. An awards ceremony and luncheon are held in the hotel's banquet room after the final game. Many campers' families join them for this.

There are no age limits, although campers do tend to be 30 or older. Most are from the region and are also "weekend Warriors" who play a regular game at their local gym.

Along with your enhanced playing abilities and newfound insight into the game, you come away with such souvenirs as warm-up and practice gear and a video of camp highlights, from both on and off the court. There's also at least one reunion; during the NBA season, you're invited to watch a Warriors' practice, then you and your fellow camp veterans get to play a game on the court of the Oakland Coliseum Arena and attend that night's Warriors match. *Don Nelson Basketball Fantasy Camp, c/o U.S. Sports Development, 919 Sir Francis Drake Blvd., Kentfield, CA 94904, tel. 800/433–6060, fax 415/459–1453. Aug.: 4 days, $1,995. Sign up at least 1 month in advance.*

NEVADA **Cotton Fitzsimmons/Kurt Rambis Fastbreak Fantasy Camp.** Since 1991, this fantasy camp held on the Nevada side of Lake Tahoe for a single 5-day session in early July has attracted a diverse group of 32 basketball fanatics, most of them devoted followers of the Phoenix Suns.

The big draw here is long-time Phoenix coach and local hero Cotton Fitzsimmons. You learn the drills and plays that he created for the Suns. In addition, former Laker Kurt Rambis, and 2 current or former NBA players join the instructing roster. At past camps such greats as Connie Hawkins, Lionel Hollins, and Charles Barkley have participated.

You're on the courts for 5 hours each day, in 2½-hour practice sessions, each packed with passing, dribbling, and shooting drills designed to increase your heart rate, strengthen your legs, and sharpen your eye. You also learn how to fight through picks and master the pick-and-roll. Practice and games take place at the Incline Village High School gymnasium, not far from the hotel.

You stay at the Hyatt Regency Tahoe in Incline Village, an affluent residential community. Breakfast and dinner, included in the package, are served at the hotel's restaurant; for lunch, you're on your own. Among the souvenirs you take home are your practice gear, a new pair of Nike basketball shoes, a team photo, and a video of the final game.

You must be 30 or older to attend, and you need a note from your doctor asserting that you're fit enough to play. *Cotton Fitzsimmons/ Kurt Rambis Fastbreak Fantasy Camp, Box 1369, Phoenix, AZ 85001, tel. 602/514–8246, fax 602/379–7922. July: 5 days, $2,600. Sign up at least 2 months in advance.*

HAWAII

MAUI **Magic Johnson/Jerry West Executive Camp.** Don't get the idea that you come here just to watch a dazzling show of round-ball by two legendary former Lakers. This camp is about improving your overall conditioning and polishing up such basic skills as passing, shooting, and dribbling.

It is also pricey—and more than even the most expensive baseball camp—but look at where it's held and who's leading it! Both Magic Johnson and Jerry West were on several championship Los Angeles Lakers teams—in different eras—and are among the best guards the game has ever seen. They now conduct a couple of 5-day basketball camps each July, on the west end of Maui, in the beach resort town of Lahaina.

You and your 29 fellow campers will be put through your paces by Johnson, West, and the other 5 past and present NBA pros on the staff. You also get personal attention from the stars, and Magic Johnson generally gets to know every camper.

Five hours a day are spent learning and going through the same drills and plays that Johnson and West used when they were with the Lakers. Each day is broken up into 2 on-court sessions—3 hours in the morning, then another 2 hours from 4 PM to 6 PM, allowing time in between to rest up, explore Maui, or practice what you learned before noon. Toward the end of the camp there are 3-on-3, free-throw, and 3-point-shot competitions.

You play on the courts at the Maui Civic Center gymnasium in Lahaina. On the fifth day your squad participates in a final game, with Lakers announcer Chick Hearn calling the play-by-play. There's a luau on the beach the night before the big game, and a closing and awards ceremony at a brunch banquet after it.

Lodging is in the Westin Maui hotel, in Lahaina. Every camper gets his (or her) own room—which at these prices only seems right—and meals at the hotel restaurant are part of the package. The luau and banquet aside, there isn't much organized activity off the court, although socializing between campers and between campers and staff is commonplace. Those who can afford to come here tend to be successful business executives and Hollywood celebrity types. Bring your business cards—everyone else does. Film director Garry Marshall, like many campers, attends almost every year. Still, it's basketball not business that you've come for, and

while schmoozing happens, it doesn't happen on the court and isn't the focus of the camp. Some campers even bring their families. The camp has sold out every year that it's been held, so sign up well in advance.

You take home such mementos as a monogrammed Lakers uniform, practice gear, a new pair of Converse basketball shoes, a sports duffle bag, photos of yourself with your fellow campers and with Magic Johnson and Jerry West, and the video—with Chick Hearn's play-by-play—of your final game. And camp ain't necessarily over when it's over; you are invited to a reunion game at the Lakers' home court in the Los Angeles Forum, where you play in front of the crowd gathered for that night's NBA matchup. *Magic Johnson Enterprises, Inc., 10100 Santa Monica Blvd., Suite 316, Los Angeles, CA 90067, tel. 310/843–9611. July: 5 days, $5,900. Price includes a private room and all meals; sign up at least 3 months in advance.*

SOURCES

There is no umbrella organization for basketball fantasy camps, so information about them can be hard to come by. To find out if any besides those listed above are being held this year, call your local or favorite NBA team and ask if any of its players or coaches are running a camp. Don't bother calling the NBA; its representatives will not have this information.

PUBLICATIONS The NBA's magazine, *Hoop* (355 Lexington Ave., New York, NY 10017, tel. 508/452–6310), sold at every franchise's arena, is one place to check to find out about upcoming basketball fantasy camps. You might also scrutinize the ads in the back pages of *Sports Illustrated* (1271 Ave. of the Americas, New York, NY 10019, tel. 800/541–1000).

Bicycling

by Bill Strickland

See the country by bike and you see it as no one else can. Cycling brings you closer to the landscape, the people, the wildlife—closer even to the spirit of the land. When cycling, you notice hills, dips, rough roads, and breezes; you pay attention to the weather. Bicyclists travel slowly enough to spot rare flowers, birds, and small animals, and quietly enough to happen upon deer and other large mammals. Locals will wave to cyclists, or stop to chat while you're refueling at the country store.

Still, you can travel long distances on a bike: You see more and cover more ground than you could on foot. A laid-back bike tour might cover 150 or 200 miles in less than a week. Big-ride sessions can go 600 miles. Yes, you can do it. Bike touring is easy on the body. Modern bikes are more comfortable than ever and have more gears for easier pedaling. On the right terrain, even an out-of-shape non-cyclist can cover 30 miles or more before lunch. I once toured with a woman who hadn't been on a bike in five years; she rode 130 miles in a week. On another tour, I pedaled alongside a recreational rider who finished a 250-mile trek just one year after hip-replacement surgery.

The existence of commercial touring companies makes it possible for just about anyone to tour by bike. These organizations supply the expertise. There's no need for you to know how to plot a bike-friendly route, arrange food and lodging, customize your bike to carry equipment and luggage, or fix a flat tire. You don't even have to own a bike. You simply choose an area of the country you'd like to see, identify the companies that offer tours there, and ask a few questions to make sure you and the trip are a good match (*see* Choosing the Right Trip, *below*). And, of course, you have to pay: A bike trip with an outfitter can run from $130 to $250 per day, not including bike rental. If you want to cut costs, you can opt for a camping trip instead of an inn trip.

A typical touring company offers a selection of 2- to 10-day trips with preplanned routes. The company will have scouted the most scenic and traffic-free roads, major points of interest, and the best places to eat and sleep. It usually provides at least 2 guides for every trip: One rides with the cyclists, and the other drives a support van along the route. This van transports your luggage to each destination and patrols the route, carrying water, snacks, repair equipment, and even tired cyclists. Most companies also rent bikes.

These organized trips have from 6 to 15 riders and range from day-long pedaling marathons to casual jaunts with many stops, in which the bike is mainly used to travel from one point of interest to another. Will you ride

Managing editor of Bicycling *magazine Bill Strickland hates cars and gas consumption, so he pedals his way to work. In more than ten years of riding he's toured every corner of the United States. Strickland also writes a mountain biking skills column for* Mountain Bike *magazine.*

too fast or too slow to remain with the group? It doesn't matter. Most tours offer multiple options for each day's ride. You can go short or long, flat or hilly, hard or easy.

Whichever option you choose, you won't be alone. Just as there are few atheists in a foxhole, there are few enemies on a bike tour. Sharing physical challenges seems to bond people. I've yet to join a tour on which the participants didn't cheer each other on during the day and gather at night to share tales from the road. It seems that at least one close, lasting friendship is formed on every trip, and it's not uncommon for riders to meet a mate.

Of course, traveling as a group can be a drag. You're tied to a common schedule for everything from waking in the morning to eating dinner. Sometimes your meals must be selected from a limited menu. If the weather stinks, you can't hide in the lodge for another day. If you need a rest day, it's more often than not spent in the back of the support van—not exactly the best way to explore the country. See an inn you'd rather stay at, or enjoy a village so much you'd like to tarry there an extra day? Too bad.

Most tour veterans I've talked with, however, agree that the advantages of commercial trips outweigh these inconveniences. The few bad experiences I've heard about occurred when cyclists chose trips that didn't match their cycling ability. But if you'd still rather gather a group of friends and create your own itinerary, most bike-touring companies will be glad to guide you.

I said that anyone could complete a bike tour, and I meant that. I did not mean that anyone could complete any bike tour. I had a great time one summer on a week-long trip that covered 850 miles. Maybe a 30-mile-per-day bike-and-shop through quaint New England towns is more your speed. Or maybe you're in excellent shape but don't want to grind out 100-plus miles per day—you'd prefer biking yourself senseless with 50 miles of Colorado mountain passes every morning.

It is important to match your physical ability and ambition to the trip. Don't sign up for the toddler trip along the Outer Banks and then complain that you aren't getting enough training miles at your target heart rate. Nor should you let your aspirations outweigh your common sense and land you in a West Coast hammerhead tour with ultrafit riders when you just wanted to spin a few miles between sips of wine.

In the trip descriptions, we've tried to give you an accurate picture of how tough the riding will be. Don't judge toughness by mileage alone. I've been toasted senseless by 20 miles of hilly Pennsylvania roads, and walked away from 65 flat Florida miles whistling and wishing for more. Pay attention to other factors such as terrain description, number of off-bike activities (the more detours, the less strenuous the trip is likely to be), and even the time of year. Rolling Kentucky hills in September? Sign me up. Same territory in summer's dog days? Ugh.

The classic touring areas are New England (especially Vermont and the Massachusetts coast), Pennsylvania, North Carolina and Virginia, and California. They all deserve your consideration, but pay attention to the other listings, too. Tour companies have branched out in the past few years, and some of these gambles have led to the discovery of amazing new areas for bike touring. Any region seems fair game these days.

Also be honest about your level of comfort. Rugged camping trips sound admirable, but it's okay to spoil yourself on a pampered tour of plush resorts. Hey, it's a vacation.

Finally, there's food. Fuel. You burn a lot of calories on a week-long tour—up to 2,000 calories per day—so you must take in a lot simply to replace your energy stores. This means you get to eat and eat and eat and not feel one bit guilty. Gaining weight on a bike tour is almost impossible. Indulge: spicy Mexican meals, fresh seafood, hearty midwestern dinners, heapings of family-style Amish fare, campfire-grilled anything, homemade soups and breads. The secret's out. Sure you must eat to ride, but you can also ride to eat.

See you on the road. And, as the pros say, keep the rubber side down.

CHOOSING THE RIGHT TRIP

To be included in these listings, each touring company had to offer trips along preplanned, established routes; offer at least 2 mileage options each day; offer some type of support (such as motorized route patrols, "sag" service for tired or injured riders, and luggage transport); provide or assist in arranging lodging; provide at least some meals, including snacks for munching while you cycle; and require the use of helmets (you never appreciate a skid lid until you need it).

But before you buy, take some time to learn more about the company and the specific tour you're interested in. Don't be shy about asking questions. Think of it this way: For the cost of a week-long tour, you could buy a trick new bike. And if the organizers seem too busy to respond, that's a kind of response in itself.

How long has the company been in business? You take a trip with an outfitter in order to capitalize on its experience. Make sure it has enough, or at least the people running it do.

Who are the leaders, how old are they, and how are they trained? Sound a little nosy? Hey, you're putting your whole vacation in these people's hands. Make sure they're fit to hold it.

How tough is the trip? Find out as much as you can. Describe your riding experience and physical condition, then ask if the organizer thinks you can do the trip (or if you'll be bored). You'll get an honest answer: A miserable guest is not a repeat guest.

How much can the mileage be increased (or decreased)? Most companies will go beyond their stated limits.

What's the weather like when I want to tour? Some folks like it hot; others think cold is "fresh." In any case, you will have to bring the proper clothes.

What are the accommodations like? Be specific or be surprised. Some impressive bed-and-breakfast inns, for example, require you to share hallway bathrooms or telephone lines.

If it's a camping trip, find out if you'll be in a campground with hot showers or in farmer Joe's field.

What are the meals like? Same idea. Also, most companies skip at least one lunch or dinner. We list these deletions but changes may occur.

Will laundry service be available? This could be the difference between one suitcase or two.

What's the cost and what's included? Costs vary from outfitter to outfitter, depending on the type of accommodations, the quality of the food, or simply the remoteness of the area where you'll be biking. Prices in these listings are per person and include double occupancy, lodging, meals, gratuities, entrance fees to parks and attractions, and, when applicable, camping fees.

Always ask whether there are extras: $75 for that hot-air balloon trip or $50 for the massage that was added shortly before the tour. Airfare, the cost of shuttle service between the airport and the trip starting and ending points, and the cost of renting bikes or other equipment are not included in prices we quote, unless we note otherwise.

What is the makeup of the touring group? You can find out the size of the group and the participants' ages, gender, marital status, and home states. This will keep you from being a third wheel in a couples-only tour.

Is this same tour available for singles (families, senior citizens, women, whatever)? You may prefer to pedal with your peers. Some companies offer reduced rates for kids and families.

How extensive is the support? Some companies make only one or two runs along a route; others patrol constantly. Find out how many guides work each trip. The more the better.

Can the leaders handle minor mechanical repairs (and is there a charge)? Something will break. Something always breaks. If it's just a wheel that needs minor truing, I'd expect a freebie. But be reasonable: If your bottom bracket and hubs must be overhauled, cough up a tip even if the guide doesn't charge you for 2 hours of labor.

What is the rental equipment like? Find out what brands of bikes are used, how many sizes they offer, and how old the fleet is. Between the sleek road bike and thrasher mountain bike lies an ideal touring compromise called a hybrid, or cross bike. These are equipped with flat bars (for an upright sitting position and more stability) and semi-wide tires (for a cushy but easy-spinning ride). Ask if the company has these. If you want special equipment—gel saddles or mixte frames—make sure you can get it. Ditto for camping equipment. Prices quoted in the listings for rentals get you a two-wheeler for the duration of the trip.

Do you offer free helmet use?

What extras are included? Many companies offer T-shirts, sweatshirts, water bottles, and other freebies.

Are any local events happening before or after the tour? I have biking buddies who only take tours when they can piggyback big events such as the Kentucky Derby or wine harvest festivals with their trips.

How far in advance must I book? The most popular trips may fill up a year in advance; others can be booked just a month before. Always call if you want to make a last-minute booking; cancellations are common.

Do you have references from past guests? To be honest, I never call the telephone numbers I get. But if a company ever refused to give me any names, it would make me wonder why.

MAJOR PLAYERS

When it comes to touring companies, bigger is usually better, although many small organizations run fine programs. These are often created by locals who know their region well and offer excellent routes, good value in accommodations, and interesting sights and attractions off the beaten path.

The difference between small companies and the major players is scope. Where the small tour operator offers 6 yearly trips, the large organization runs 30. The small operator works within a state or a small multistate area. The major companies span whole geographic regions, coasts, maybe even the entire country. If one tour is booked, they can offer another (and another) with approximately the same flavor.

Following are descriptions of the 2 major touring companies, the ones with the most consistent quality and widest variety of tours. The service of both is exceptional. If you can't find exactly what you're looking for in our listings, give these touring experts a call and ask about their other offerings.

BACKROADS This is the biggest touring company in the world. In business since 1979, it offers more than 90 different biking trips, each run several times per year. Domestic destinations include California, Washington, Alaska, Oregon, Utah, Arizona, New Mexico, Colorado, Montana, Idaho, Wyoming, Florida, North Carolina, Virginia, Hawaii, Mississippi, Louisiana, Vermont, Maine, and Minnesota. The company has a heavy West Coast and western U.S. bias, although it continues to expand. Foreign destinations include Canada, Europe, China, Mexico, Costa Rica, Thailand, Bali, Australia, and New Zealand.

Backroads is famous for its exquisite lunches, prepared by the guides in the company's fleet of custom-designed trailers. The full menu for trips reads like the bill of fare at a better big-city eatery: smoked salmon, homemade pasta with pesto, and fresh fruit pies. I've never eaten better than on a Backroads trip.

Accommodations on this company's trips are often hostelries on the National Register of Historic Places or comfortable lodges and inns with regional flavor and personality.

Backroads rents its own line of bikes, made by Chimayo. The guides are generally young and knowledgeable about cycling and the area of the tour. I've never talked to anyone who's been disappointed with a Backroads trip, although some cyclists complain that the itineraries are too tame. The company has its own travel agency and also offers skiing, walking, and hiking trips, as well as custom-designed tours for groups (1516 5th St., Berkeley, CA 94710–1740, Suite B122, tel. 510/527–1555 or 800/462–2848, fax 510/527–1444).

VERMONT BICYCLE TOURING This company merged with VCC Four Season Cycling in November 1993, increasing its tour schedule throughout the United States and Europe. Going strong since 1972, Vermont Bicycle Touring (VBT) now runs 17 different tours in Vermont, 22 in other states, and 7 in other countries, serving 7,000 to 8,000 guests each year. In addition to Vermont, tours are run in Florida, Hawaii, Maine, Maryland, Massachusetts, North Carolina, Pennsylvania, and Virginia, as well as in Europe, Canada (Nova Scotia), and New Zealand.

Accommodations on VBT's U.S. trips rival those of the other top-notch companies, and many of the same restaurants are used. Lunch is not included in the price on VBT trips; instead, before you set out, you have the option of chipping in $5 per touring day for the picnic lunch. These plentiful and tasty spreads are not quite as extravagant as those of Backroads, but neither are VBT's prices. Most riders opt to throw in the $30 for the week, and those who don't often change their mind after the first day.

Typical VBT guests are casual cyclists, including lots of older riders, but the company also seems to attract riders who want to hammer, or ride a lot of miles fast. This last quality may be because—as several high-mileage friends have told me—the company is extremely willing to customize its routes. The grapevine has it that former VCC tours attracted more "serious" riders, and I can tell you that I've been on a VCC tour with a triathelete and other riders who kicked my butt all over the street. VBT doesn't plan to tame the routes, but we'll have to wait and see who signs up for the bigger company's trips. VBT has one more plus: Its fleet of rental

bikes is always in top-notch condition (Box 711, Bristol, VT 05443, tel. 802/453–4811, fax 802/453–4806).

Here are quick sketches of 6 smaller but still significant companies:

BICYCLE ADVENTURES Although it specializes in West Coast touring, Bicycle Adventures also offers trips in British Columbia and Hawaii. I like this company because it was founded (in 1984) and is still staffed by Pacific Northwest natives who know the area well. It offers 18 different trips (Box 7875, Olympia, WA 98507, tel. 206/786–0989 or 800/443–6060, fax 206/786–9661).

BIKE VERMONT This company runs 160 weekend and 5-day tours in Vermont, more than any other company. The organizers have run trips in New England since 1977 (Box 207, Woodstock, VT 05091, tel. 802/457–3553 or 800/257–2226, fax 802/457–1236).

ENCOMPASS CYCLING VACATIONS Founded as Bike Wisconsin in 1987, this company has served more than 1,100 guests in a single year on tours in Wisconsin, Minnesota, Michigan, Indiana, Florida, Mississippi, Kentucky, Colorado, and New Mexico. Still, Encompass Cycling Vacations remains focused on the Midwest and gives cyclists in Chicago, Milwaukee, Minneapolis, and St. Louis plenty of options nearby (Box 3461, Madison, WI 53704, tel. 608/249–4490, fax 608/249–7441).

MICHIGAN BICYCLE TOURING This is the Michigan version of Bike Vermont. The company offers 21 different bike tours in Michigan (plus one in China) and skiing tours in the off-season. It's been in business since 1978 (3512 Red School Rd., Kingsley, MI 49649, tel. 616/263–5885).

THE TANDEM TOURING COMPANY Tandem touring is a growing market, and this small company is poised to take advantage of the trend. It caters to twicers with trips in the Rockies, California, and France (3131 Endicott, Boulder, CO 80303, tel. 303/499–3178, fax 303/494–5826).

TIMBERLINE BICYCLE TOURS Aggressive riders like this company's big-mileage and high-altitude tours in the western United States, northern Great Lakes, and Canada. These routes will wear out anyone (#J, 7975 E. Harvard, Denver, CO 80231, tel. 303/759–3804).

FAVORITE TRIPS

THE NORTHEAST

MASSACHUSETTS **From the Vineyard to Nantucket.** This 5-day ride is a classic cycling tour in Vermont Bicycle Touring's home turf. The islands of Martha's Vineyard and Nantucket have been popular spots for pedaling vacations for years: The riding is easy—flat to rolling—and the traffic is never overbearing. These conditions combined with the Atlantic seaside scenery make it easy to understand why so many 2-wheeled tours take place here. This trip begins on the Vineyard, where you have 3 days to explore the harbor and back roads. It's a bit of a huff to get to the bluffs at the southwestern corner of the island, but the spectacular views are worth the effort. Much of the riding is on designated bike paths. You ferry to Nantucket for the final 2 days, cruising on more bike paths, some of which wind right through historic fishing villages.

On both islands you sleep in fine inns. Meals are predominantly fresh from the sea, but there's a variety of gourmet food. Though a bit touristy, this relaxing tour became a classic for a reason. See for yourself. The distance covered daily averages 22 miles. This trip is run about 12 times per year. *Vermont Bicycle Touring, Box 711, Bristol, VT 05443, tel. 802/453–4811, fax 802/453–4806. May–Sept.: 5 days, $999. Price does not include lunches. Road bike rental, $98.*

VERMONT **Connecticut River Valley.** This 5-day ramble follows the Connecticut River, the meandering border between Vermont and New Hampshire. It's one of my favorite Vermont tours, because the river is never far away, and you cross it several times.

You visit New Hampshire's Dartmouth College campus and explore a restored Shaker village. There's even hiking on some mountain trails. Yes, mountains. You have to endure some climbs, but the slopes are more steady than steep. This is an excellent introduction to Vermont cycling.

Nights are spent in historic New Hampshire and Vermont inns, as well as mountain lodges. Take your swimsuit. Daily distances range from 18 to 53 miles. This trip is run about 21 times per year. *Bike Vermont, Box 207, Woodstock, VT 05091, tel. 802/457–3553 or 800/257–2226, fax 802/457–1236. May–mid-June: 5 days, $585. Late June–mid-Sept.: 5 days, $655. Late Sept.–mid-Oct.: 5 days, $695. Late Oct.: 5 days, $655. Road bike rental, $80.*

VERMONT **Middlebury, Lake Champlain, and the Green Mountains.** It seems silly to praise a Vermont tour for its views—all trips in this state have knockout scenery—but this one has received exceptionally high marks from all the Vermont cycling veterans I've talked with. The 5-day tour begins and ends in Middlebury and wanders along the shore of Lake Champlain and into the Green Mountain National Forest. The terrain is rolling, through a landscape of farms, orchards, typical New England towns, and several other lakes. All this is shadowed by the Adirondack peaks on the west and the Green Mountains on the east.

You sleep in an inn built by the family of Ethan Allen and an old stagecoach stop. The food might include smoked salmon over linguini with roasted garlic and garden vegetables offered by the Vermont Marble Inn or Swift House's breast of pheasant with a cherry brandy sauce. Daily distance options range from 13 to 45 miles. Beginners can tough it out; intermediate riders will just cruise and enjoy the views. This trip is run about 18 times per year. *Bike Vermont, Box 207, Woodstock, VT 05091, tel. 802/457–3553 or 800/257–2226,* fax 802/457–1236. May–mid-June: 5 days, $585. Late June–mid-Sept.: 5 days, $655. Late Sept.–mid-Oct.: 5 days, $695. Late Oct.: 5 days, $655. Road bike rental, $80.

VERMONT **From the Capital to Stowe.** Backroads bills this 5-day trip as one of its most luxurious. Coming from a company where plush is the norm, that's saying something. The accommodations—country inns and manors listed among the best by *Vermont* magazine—don't disappoint, and neither does the riding. It's vintage Vermont, with rolling roads through green hills. There are maple sugar houses where you can stop and sample before you buy, ski resorts with exceptional views and accommodations, and a trail-crossed countryside where you meet fellow autoless travelers—hikers and horseback riders.

The trip begins in Montpelier, the state capital, and hits Craftsbury Common, Stowe, and Waterbury. Daily distance options range from 17 to 51 miles. There's an optional rest day in Stowe and an optional tour of Ben and Jerry's ice-cream factory in Waterbury. (You're not doing all that riding for nothing.) About 8 trips are run per year. *Backroads, 1516 5th St., Suite B122, Berkeley, CA 94710–1740, tel. 510/527–1555 or 800/462–2848, fax 510/527–1444. Aug.–Oct.: 5 days, $1,195. Road (with flat or drop handlebar) or hybrid bike rental, $109.*

THE MID ATLANTIC

PENNSYLVANIA **Delaware River Valley.** On this 5-day trip you cross into New Jersey but spend most of the week in the pastoral countryside of Bucks County, Pennsylvania. I do a lot of pedaling in this region, and I can attest to the lack of traffic and rolling hills that make for some of the finest road riding in the country. The scenery includes woodlands, old stone farmhouses and colonial buildings, mills, tiny towns along the Delaware, and even historic sites (you visit the spot where George Washington made his famous crossing). Don't worry, you're not overloaded with history. The historic sites are just another part of the landscape. The entire experience is soothing, and you feel farther from big-city civilization than you really are (New York is less than 2 hours away). The accommodations are bed-and-breakfasts and former private manors built during the 1800s.

I also like this tour company's rental bike: a Bridgestone XO-2, a hybrid with a "moustache" handlebar. Stylin'. Daily distance options range from 25 to 45 miles. Intermediate riders will have the most fun. There aren't any monster climbs, but the hills are steady. The trip is run twice each year. *Northstar Bicycle Tours, 113 Crawley Ave., Pennington, NJ 08534, tel. 609/737–8346, fax 609/737–3787. July–Aug.: 5 days, $780. Price does not include lunches. Hybrid bike rental, $90.*

PENNSYLVANIA **Lancaster County's Farms and Towns.** There are ritzier, plusher tours of this popular cycling area, but I like this one because it allows you to cover more ground. Pennsylvania Dutch country is a patchwork of Amish and Mennonite villages; fields, farmhouses, and barns; grassy valleys; and tourist towns so rich in antiques shops, general stores, and gift shops that the local chamber of commerce invariably advertises them as "quaint."

You traverse the county in 5 days, traveling from inn to inn. Each day's ride is scenic and soothing, with minimum traffic: You're more likely to share the road with horse-drawn carriages than with autos. The route is hilly, though, and even an advanced rider could tire by the end of the week. Still, I wouldn't hesitate to recommend the tour to a beginner, because the roads are cyclist-friendly and the scenery is captivating.

The 19th-century inns where you stay are generally either in the middle of a lot of acreage or in a tiny village. Most meals are Amish family-style spreads of fresh vegetables, poultry or meat, and warm breads. Daily distance options range from 25 to 40 miles. This trip is run 3 times per year. *Northstar Bicycle Tours, 113 Crawley Ave., Pennington, NJ 08534, tel. 609/737–8346, fax 609/737–3787.*

July–Aug.: 5 days, $775. Price does not include lunches. Hybrid bike rental, $90.

VIRGINIA **Historic Sites Along the Colonial Parkway.** This is an underrated touring area that's especially suited for families. The terrain is mild, often flat, and the rich history of the region provides plenty of off-bike experiences. Whenever I've cycled in Virginia, I've been impressed by the lack of traffic and the general respect for cyclists exhibited by most auto drivers, especially on the parkways. This 5-day trip begins in Williamsburg and travels up and down the Colonial Parkway.

Much of the route passes through national parklands, and sometimes it winds through Revolutionary War battlefields. You see plenty of peanut and cornfields, as well as large stands of pine. Sound soothing? It is.

One of the highlights of this tour is the final day's exploration of Jamestown, the country's first permanent English settlement (1607).

Accommodations are in modern inns that provide more convenience than charm. Daily distance options range from 20 to 45 miles. If you're looking to jam out the miles—and you're not a history buff—you may get bored. Special dates for families are available. About 10 trips are run each year. If you have extra time before or after the tour, check out the nearby Busch Gardens theme park. *Vermont Bicycle Touring, Box 711, Bristol, VT 05443, tel. 802/453–4811, fax 802/453–4806. Apr.–Nov.: 5 days, $699. Price does not include lunches. Road or hybrid bike rental, $98.*

VIRGINIA **Challenging the Shenandoah.** This is a completely different Virginia: the Shenandoah Valley, 200 miles of rolling farmland and woodland, with the Shenandoah, Blue Ridge, and Allegheny mountain ranges serving as a backdrop. The terrain is challenging. It's constantly rolling, with a few significant climbs. Vacationers new to bike touring will fare okay on this 5-day trip if they're fit; experienced cyclists can take the longer routes and wear themselves out. Traffic is never a factor.

You sleep in historic inns, the best of which is probably the Jordan Hollow Farm Inn, a 200-year-old restored horse farm next to Shenandoah National Park. Horseback rides are available for an extra fee. Average daily distance is 33 miles. This trip is run about 6 times per year. *Vermont Bicycle Touring, Box 711, Bristol, VT 05443, tel. 802/453–4811, fax 802/453–4806. May–Oct.: 5 days, $899. Price does not include lunches. Road or hybrid bike rental, $98.*

THE SOUTH

FLORIDA **Another Side of the Sunshine State.** Winter cycling doesn't get much better than this, especially for the novice who wants to see just what this cycling thing is all about. Florida riding is generally flat or gently rolling. The only challenge comes from the wind, which never seems to stop. Good tours like this 5-day excursion are planned to keep you riding mostly with a tailwind.

You'll be riding in northern and central Florida, where the terrain is not what you might expect. You begin just north of Orlando and pedal through Mount Dora and Ocala. No beaches and bikinis, just rolling farm country—horses and citrus. There are a lot of roadside lakes, and Spanish moss hangs from oak trees that line the route. I like cycling in Florida: It's an easy spin with fabulous sunsets.

Accommodations are provided at inns with rambling enclosed porches, quiet grounds, and antique furniture. Daily distance ranges from 20 to 45 miles. This trip is run about 5 times per year. *Vermont Bicycle Touring, Box 711, Bristol, VT 05443, tel. 802/453–4811, fax 802/453–4806. Dec.–Mar.: 5 days, $1,055. Price does not include lunches. Road or hybrid bike rental, $98.*

KENTUCKY **Bluegrass Country.** The bluegrass isn't just for hooves. My wheels have galloped through this region, and I can report that the sight of miles of white fences rolling over hills is as beautiful as any canyon vista. This 5-day trip begins in Lexington and passes through Boonesborough State Park, several Appalachian towns, and the Shaker village in Pleasant Hill. Most of the sparsely traveled roads are bordered by distinctive horse-farm fences, and you cycle to Keeneland Race Course, where you can watch the trainers at work.

Obviously this is a trip for horse lovers, but anyone looking for a bike tour beyond the "typical" destinations should consider this tour. The riding is a bit tougher than you'd expect, but there are no major climbs.

The accommodations are in historic hotels and inns, many built to house early horse breeders and traders. The food? Just ask for spoonbread and cornsticks. Daily distance options range from 11 to 55 miles. About 4 trips are run each year. *Backroads, 1516 5th St., Suite B122, Berkeley, CA 94710–1740, tel. 510/527–1555 or 800/462–2848, fax 510/527–1444. May and Oct.: 5 days, $1,045. Road or hybrid bike rental, $109.*

LOUISIANA **New Orleans and the Plantations and Bayous Beyond.** I have to admit that my chief interest in this tour is the food: southern Louisiana Cajun-Creole cuisine. Nearly every meal served by the restaurants and hotels on the route includes cayenne, hot sauce, and crawfish.

Oh yeah, the riding. You spend at least 2 days in New Orleans, enough time to get a feel for the city. Your hotel here is sure to have patios decked with tropical plants, porches overhanging the streets, and fountains in the courtyards. You cycle through the Latin Quarter, which can be either an adventure or a misadventure, depending on the traffic.

Once you ease out of the Big Easy, the roads get more interesting. They travel around bayous, through gently rolling woods, and to small southern towns. There seem to be plantations around every corner, and many of them are open for tours.

Daily distance options are 30 to 50 miles. Beginners will have no problem. This 6-day trip is run about 3 times per year. *French Louisiana Bike Tours, 601 Pinhook Rd. E, LaFayette, LA 70501, tel. 800/346–7989. May,*

Sept., and Oct.: 6 days, $795. Price does not include lunches. Mountain bike (with smooth tires) rental, $89.

MISSISSIPPI **Antebellum Mansions to Civil War Battle Sites.** This is one of my personal favorites, partly because most of the route is on the amazingly cyclist-friendly Natchez Trace Parkway—which has low speed limits, no commercial traffic, and no buildings to blot the southern landscape—and partly because the route passes through scenes of great historic interest.

You begin this 6-day tour in the small Mississippi River town of Natchez, which has more than a dozen antebellum mansions open for tours (and some historic homes waiting to be purchased and renovated). From there you travel along the parkway to Port Gibson, Vicksburg, and other Civil War battle sites. Save your strength for the last day's 20-mile loop through Vicksburg's Military Park, where you tour a battlefield filled with monuments and markers explaining the conflict.

These Mississippi roads are flat or gently rolling—perfect for easy cruising or blow-your-lungs hammering. Where else could you time-trial from Civil War mansion to Civil War mansion? Those mansions, each of which is on the National Register of Historic Places, are where you sleep at night. The food includes catfish and southern barbecued chicken.

Daily distance options range from 20 to 45 miles. At the end of the trip, a hydrojet returns you to Natchez from upriver. About 7 trips are run each year. *Vermont Bicycle Touring, Box 711, Bristol, VT 05443, tel. 802/453–4806, fax 802/453–4811. Mar., Apr., Oct., Nov.: 6 days, $1,195. Price does not include lunches. Road or hybrid bike rental, $106.*

NORTH CAROLINA **Blue Ridger.** This 6-day climbing excursion on the Blue Ridge Parkway is vintage stuff. This road has been designated as one of the country's best cycling routes, and I have to agree: No commercial vehicles are allowed, and the 45-mph speed limit is obeyed by car-bound tourists gawking at the primo mountain overlooks.

You cycle through Pisgah National Forest, Transylvania County (Waterfall Capital of the Country), and miles of fruit orchards. Of course, all this beauty has its price. The first day, for instance, begins with a 10-mile climb from Asheville to Mt. Pisgah. But after you finish huffing, there are 18 glorious downhill miles. Judging from the parts of this route I've ridden, I'd say that your whole trip will be like this. Don't go if this doesn't sound like your idea of a good time.

Some of the entryways onto the parkway are no fun for cyclists, but here's where you benefit from being on a tour: The support van shuttles you through the busiest parts.

The accommodations are found in quiet country inns and hotels, avoiding the seedy tourist dives of the commercial areas. Daily distance options are from 20 to 40 miles, but I wouldn't recommend the area to any cyclist who isn't fit and experienced. The trip is run 3 times per year. *Paradise Pedallers, Box 34625, Charlotte, NC 28324, tel. 800/992–3966, fax 704/335–8686. June–Aug.: 6 days, $790. Free shuttle from Asheville airport. Road or hybrid bike rental, $69.*

NORTH CAROLINA **Novices Take to the Outer Banks.** This is also North Carolina, but it isn't the Blue Ridge Parkway. The lung-busting climbs and killer views are replaced by flat, low-effort terrain and oceanside scenes of the Outer Banks, a chain of barrier islands and peninsulas that is a popular tourist draw. You won't face the parking shortages and lack of mobility that the car-bound can encounter, but you will see almost all of the nature preserves, historic districts, rivers and marshes, and other key animal-watching spots that abound here.

This 6-day spin is good for novices because of the multitude of off-bike attractions and because the pedaling is usually assisted by a tail wind. There's only one climb: a bridge to one of the islands. After cycling to the town of Beaufort, you can take a yacht trip to Carrot Island, famous for its wild ponies. This is included in the cost of the trip.

Accommodations are in historic bed-and-breakfast inns, and the food is fresh from the sea. You average about 40 miles per day, but they're easy miles. This trip is run 2 times per year. *Paradise Pedallers, Box 34625, Charlotte, NC 28324, tel. 800/992–3966, fax 704/335–8686. May and Sept.: 6 days, $790. Free shuttle from New Bern airport. Road or hybrid bike rental, $69.*

THE MIDWEST

MICHIGAN **Mackinac Island Wayfarer.** This region—with its rolling terrain, lakeside routes, and potential island adventures—could become one of bike touring's hot spots. For now, though, the roads are uncrowded and the countryside is still unspoiled, although tourist shops are popping up. Michigan is not known for its good weather, but the moderate temperatures of summer and fall make cycling here ideal. There's little humidity—or rain—to knock you off your bike in summer, and in fall (the best time to go) the colors burst from the trees and the days are cool.

This 5-day tour begins in Charlevoix, a village on the shores of Lake Michigan. You wind northward through hilly countryside that alternates between farmland, forest, and small tourist towns. A ferry takes you to Mackinac Island, which has interesting geological formations, Victorian architecture, and several fudge shops that are famous in the Midwest. Best of all, automobile traffic is banned. The biggest vehicles you encounter are horse-drawn carriages.

This is billed as MBT's most deluxe tour, and riders I've talked with have agreed. The lodging is in luxury-class hotels and inns. You eat at 4 inns, 2 with complete menus and 2 with just 3 choices of entrées. Lunch may be complemented by fresh local cherries, blueberries, or peaches.

Daily distance options range from 23 to 63 miles. Athletic beginners can handle the route, and there are enough side roads to keep even advanced pedalers busy. About 3 trips are run per year. *Michigan Bicycle Touring, 3512 Red School Rd., Kingsley, MI 49649, tel. 616/263–5885. June and late Sept., Oct.: 5 days, $729.*

Late Aug. and early Sept.: 5 days $829. Price does not include 2 lunches. Road bike rental, $80; mountain bike rental, $95.

WISCONSIN **The Waterfront Villages of Door County.** This state's thumb-shaped peninsula, surrounded by Green Bay and Lake Michigan, has always been a haven for nautical folks, but we 2-wheeled types are beginning to feel at home here, too. Beginners are enticed by the flat to gently rolling terrain as well as the waterfront villages—on this peninsula you cannot escape waterfront villages—where the shops and sights provide plenty of diversion for those who tire of cycling. With its lighthouses and small towns, the area has been compared to Cape Cod, with slightly better biking.

This 6-day trip begins at Sister Bay, far north on the peninsula in the tourist mecca of Door County. But don't worry: You move along back roads instead of the car-heavy thoroughfares, cycling south along the Green Bay side, then returning on the more picturesque Lake Michigan side. What makes this attractive for novices is that you cycle from small town to small town, instead of on one long road that stretches for miles. There are plenty of places to bail, and should you decide to, there are plenty of things to do.

Daily distance options range from 25 to 69 miles. Accommodations are provided in inns and hotels built in the nautical style, with widow's walks, fancy weather vanes, and large bay windows. Fish is the usual fare, but full midwestern meals—steak and potatoes—are also popular. This trip is run about 5 times per year. *Encompass Cycling Vacations, Box 3461, Madison, WI 53704, tel. 608/249–4490, fax 608/249–7441. June and late Aug.: 6 days, $795. July and Sept.: 6 days, $850. Hybrid bike rental, $95; road bike rental, $75.*

THE SOUTHWEST

ARIZONA **Going Downhill Through Canyonlands.** If this 5-day tour were run backward, it would be a killer of a climb. But as it stands, the route includes a couple of 10- to 15-mile descents amid a desert panorama that changes daily. It's good stuff for beginners—it's inspiring to ride these roads—with enough challenges to give more advanced spinners fits.

You begin in Oak Creek Canyon, go through Sedona, and stop overnight at Mormon Lake, the largest natural lake in the state. Leading to the lake, the trip is a collection of red-rock canyon eye poppers. After that, it becomes a kind of Tour de Lake. By the third day, you're at the lip of the purple-and-pink painted high desert. Later, on the way from Flagstaff to the Grand Canyon, you hit alpine country.

This is scenery usually reserved for mountain bikers or ultrafit road whippets. There's a detour through Walnut Canyon, which once sheltered the largest Native American cliff-dwelling habitat in the country. I also like the last day's scoot along the eastern section of the Grand Canyon. The road is closed to automobiles in the summer, so you're free to concentrate on the view.

The daily distance ranges from 40 to 80 miles, with about 50 being average. The toughest climb is a mile or so. There are a lot of rolling hills, but about an equal amount of flats or downhills. It's like this: I'd send my mother or my hammerhead buddies. Accommodations range from the rustic (old cabins at Mormon Lake) to the luxurious (bed-and-breakfast inns). At mealtime, don't pass up the spicy Mexican dishes. This trip is run about 2 times each year. *Southwest Cycle Expeditions, Box 30731, Flagstaff, AZ 86003, tel. 602/526–4882. June and July: 5 days, $700. Price does not include lunches and 1 dinner. Road bike rental, $100.*

NEW MEXICO **Pedaling the Peaks.** This is a *rider's* tour—90-plus miles per day in macho territory. But here's the surprise: About half to two-thirds of the cyclists who take the 7-day trip are intermediates extending themselves—and succeeding.

The trip rolls through deceptively tough country. Don't get me wrong. This part of the state has some bonafide killer climbs to as high as 7,000 and 10,000 feet. But most of the terrain is simply rolly, rolly, rolly, and you don't realize how high you're climbing. The first day includes no major ascents or mountain passes, but you still climb about 4,000 vertical feet.

You start in the low flats of Albuquerque and climb to Santa Fe, then Las Vegas (New Mexico, that is), and on to the high mountain desert of Taos. You do the almost-mandatory routes, such as the Enchanted Circle road that rises above Taos, but for me this trip gets stars for its marriage of mileage and spectacular scenery. It's not often you get a chance to unleash yourself and see what you can do on a week-long basis, and it's even rarer that you get to do so in pretty country like this. You can even stretch your workout by taking optional rides on the 2 rest days.

You have to arrange for accommodations yourself. About half the crowd camps, and the others stay in motels that set aside rooms for this trip. The average daily distance is about 75 miles. This trip is run only once each year. *Pedal the Peaks, 2878–H West Long Circle, Littleton, CO 80120, tel. 800/795–0898. June: 7 days, $325. Price does not include hotel, camp fees, or dinners. Rental bikes can be arranged through affiliated bike shops.*

NEW MEXICO **Hill-Hopping from Santa Fe to Taos.** Get out your climbing legs, folks. This is a Backroads trip with bite. You begin at 7,000 feet, on the Alameda mountain in Sante Fe, in the foothills of the Sangre de Cristo Mountains. The first of 5 days is spent tooling through the area in search of ancient adobes, museums, galleries (this entire region has become an arty mecca), and historic cathedrals and homes. Then the hill-hopping begins. I've talked to experienced cyclists who wore themselves out on the High Road climb, a curvy route with plenty of mountain scenery. Beginners will have to shuttle up in the support van or plan to arrive well after dinner.

Taos is your base for the rest of the trip. As you explore the surrounding areas, you'll avoid the biggest ascents (on the Enchanted Circle road, you cycle *around* New Mexico's highest mountain, 14,000-foot Wheeler Peak), but still face some lung-busters in the 9,107-foot Palo Flechado and 9,854-foot Bobcat passes. The payoff for all this effort, of course, is the background of New Mexico peaks and valley vistas—and the big-time descents. The restaurants are classic southwestern eateries, and, as usual, Backroads has found some dandies. The best day on this route is the long climb and descent to Red River, a mountain resort in Carson National Forest, north of Taos.

Daily distance options range from 7 to 81 miles. Most of us could hack 30 to 40 per day and still have enough energy left to explore at night, but this is a surprisingly tough trip for Backroads. On the last day, you ride only 17 miles; the rest of the day is spent on a Class III whitewater raft trip down the Rio Grande, which lands you back in Santa Fe. About 13 trips are run annually. Do yourself a favor: Drink plenty of water. *Backroads, 1516 5th St., Suite B122, Berkeley, CA 94710–1740, tel. 510/527–1555 or 800/462–2848, fax 510/527–1444. May–Sept.: 5 days, $1,185. Road (with flat or drop handlebar) or hybrid bike rental, $109.*

THE ROCKIES

COLORADO **Alpine Meadows in the San Juan Mountains.** The southwestern corner of Colorado is a mecca for mountain bikers, but the road riding is just as sweet. This 5-day trip is a good sampler of what draws so many cyclists to the area. The ride begins with a train ride: A workhorse locomotive chugs up 2,500 feet from Durango to Silverton on narrow-gauge tracks. The engine stops at 9,000 feet. The next 24 miles—over Red Mountain Pass—are up to you. This is the easiest day, but not the most scenic.

Veteran cyclists of this region tell me that honor goes to the second day's ride, which curves and climbs through alpine meadows covered with either wildflowers or yellowing aspen, depending on the season. The trip includes a rest day in Telluride, the historic town where Butch Cassidy pulled his first robbery in 1889. Even if you don't consider yourself a mountain biker, be sure to rent a mountain bike and spend a few hours exploring the trails around here. You may be converted. History buffs should plan to make a side trip to the Anasazi ruins in Mesa Verde National Park.

Can you hack the climbing? Three mountain passes? I'd give an athletic beginner about a 50% chance of pedaling the whole trip. Daily distance options range from 19 to 97 miles. Accommodations are provided in hotels, inns, and lodges plush enough to have hot springs and hot tubs. This route is also done as a camping trip, and there are special dates for singles. About 15 trips are run each year. *Backroads, 1516 5th St., Suite B122, Berkeley, CA 94710–1740, tel. 510/527–1555 or 800/462–2848, fax 510/527–1444. July–Sept.: 5 days, $1,155 inn, $598 camping. Road (with flat or drop handlebar) or hybrid bike rental, $109.*

COLORADO **The San Juan Mountains for the Ultrafit.** Here's a tour of the San Juans for more athletic riders. This 7-day climbing odyssey is one of the reasons Timberline Bicycle Tours is gaining a reputation as a company catering to fit cyclists. The trip covers much of the same area as the Backroads tour listed above, but Timberline cyclists will pedal about twice as much—and twice as high. Every day includes at least one challenging climb, many of them to 10,000 feet and above. The 13-mile ascent to Red Mountain Pass is probably the toughest.

Accommodations are in restored Victorian hotels, national park inns, and mountain lodges. The tour ends with a long downhill back to its starting point in Durango.

Expect to grind out about 55 miles per day. I wouldn't attempt this unless I trained for it. Natural climbers and the extremely fit should have fun. This trip is run 3 times per year. *Timberline Bicycle Tours, #J, 7975 E. Harvard, Denver, CO 80231, tel. 303/759–3804. Late June–mid-Sept.: 7 days, $875. Road bike rental, $95.*

MONTANA **Glacier National Park.** This is a trip that will instill a feeling of real accomplishment in beginner bikers—how many people can say that they cycled to the spine of the Continental Divide?—but it requires more perseverance than pedaling power. At the same time, pedal slammers and hammerheads can choose to knock themselves out on these climbs.

The 6-day trip begins in West Glacier with a day of easy cruising. Then you go up and up and up. The main route is the Going-to-the-Sun Road, generally recognized as one of the most scenic cycling climbs in the country. How far up and how scenic? At times you're cycling above the cloud and fog line. On a clear day, you can stop for water atop 6,646-foot Logan Pass and look down on waterfalls, virgin evergreen forests, and alpine meadows. Don't forget those peaks in the distance, either.

Frequent riders in the area report spotting mountain lions, goats, bighorn sheep, and even the occasional grizzly. The brochures tout these sightings, but in truth you probably won't get that lucky.

The highlight of the lodge-and-inn accommodations is the final night's stay in the Glacier Park Lodge, which has a lobby supported by pillars of Douglas fir. You can cut costs almost in half by choosing the trip's camping option.

Daily distance options range from 15 to a downright scary up-and-down 104 miles crossing the Canadian border. About 9 trips are run each year. Special dates for singles are available. *Backroads, 1516 5th St., Suite B122, Berkeley, CA 94710–1740, tel. 510/527–1555 or 800/462–2848, fax 510/527–1444. July–Sept.: 6 days, $1,092 inn, $598 camping. Road (with flat or drop handlebar) or hybrid bike rental, $109.*

THE WEST COAST

CALIFORNIA **Napa and Sonoma for Two.** What makes this 7-day wine country tour special? It's twice as nice because it's a tandem trip. There's nothing like rolling along with your mate (or a friend). Climbing can be difficult, but cruising on the flats is amazingly easy, and you can talk and share food *and* the effort. Give it a try, even if you're a beginner.

During the trip, you travel the same territory as other wine-country tours—Napa and Sonoma valleys—stopping at wineries along the way. The course begins in Napa and follows the Russian River, from vineyards to redwoods, ending at Bodega Bay.

I have to be honest: The traffic in these parts is sometimes horrendous, and the locals seem to be sick and tired of cycle tourists clogging up their roads even more. Even so, the scenery is gorgeous, and you follow side roads to much better riding; this is another trip that became a classic for a reason.

In addition, a few extra dollars can buy you lots of extras: hot springs, massages, mud baths, glider rides, and hot-air balloon trips. The food is gourmet, and the bed-and-breakfast accommodations are predictably plush.

The riding ranges from up-and-down to gently rolling. A beginner may get worn out but can ride the entire route. This trip is run about 4 times per year. The daily distance average is 45 miles. *The Tandem Touring Company, 3131 Endicott, Boulder, CO 80303, tel. 303/ 499–3178, fax 303/494–5826. Mar., Apr., Sept., Oct.: 7 days, $1,388. Price does not include some dinners and lunches. Tandem bike rental, $32 per day.*

CALIFORNIA **Lassen Volcano Alpiner.** The climax of this 7-day trip is a hike to the summit of the southernmost volcano in the Cascades chain. You climb 4,000 feet in the first day's assault of Mt. Shasta, then spend the second day riding rollers southeast to the northern gate of Lassen Volcanic National Park. The third day begins the ascent of Lassen Volcano; you ride to 8,000 feet, then leave the bikes behind to hike a short trail to the crest.

The rest of the trip is spent exploring the national parks and rolling roads of this part of northern California. The traffic is surprisingly light; there are so many side roads that the tour avoids the main thoroughfares. And this area isn't overtoured; it still feels fresh.

Keep an eye peeled for Bigfoot: This is prime territory for sightings of the beast. Timberline is a company that caters to fit cyclists. Daily distance average is 60 miles. Accommodations

are provided at inns and lodges within the park. This trip is run twice each year. *Timberline Bicycle Tours, #J, 7975 E. Harvard, Denver, CO 80231, tel. 303/759–3804. July and late Aug.: 7 days, $875. Road bike rental, $95.*

CALIFORNIA **Cruising to Microbreweries.** Here's a (hic) fun alternative (burp) to the standard wine tours. Where else could you build up and try to cycle off a beer belly at the same time? This 6-day tour through the northern part of the state takes you to mid- and post-ride tastings at a number of microbreweries, including the Napa Valley Brewing Company, Willett's Brewing, Anderson Valley Brewing, and (my favorite) North Coast Brewing, which is housed in a former mortuary.

You cycle on rolling terrain over a varied route—sometimes along seaside cliffs, sometimes on quiet countrylike lanes, and sometimes in traffic. And because the tour begins and ends in San Francisco, you get a chance to pedal across the Golden Gate Bridge.

Accommodations are Backroads quality—plush, luxurious, and usually historic. Daily distances range from 8 to 53 miles. Beginners and heavy drinkers may need to rely on the support van. This trip is run about 8 times per year. *Backroads, 1516 5th St., Suite B122, Berkeley, CA 94710–1740, tel. 510/527–1555 or 800/462–2848, fax 510/527–1444. June– Oct.: 6 days, $1,090. Road (with flat or drop handlebar) or hybrid bike rental, $109.*

OREGON **Southern Oregon and Crater Lake.** On this 6-day tour beginners are introduced to the fine cycling of southern Oregon by being shuttled to the crest of the toughest climbs and left to enjoy the wooded landscape and rolling riding.

The trip begins in Ashland, just north of the California border, and heads farther into Oregon on a bike path that parallels Bear Creek. You skirt the foothills around Medford, then load the bikes into the van for a gas-powered trip to Crater Lake National Park (about 7,000 feet high). The quiet, little-traveled park roads make a relaxing loop. You cycle out of the park and follow the Rogue River before returning to Ashland.

The scenery includes small towns, historic mining-era villages, thick forests, covered bridges, and the Cascades looming in the distance. You skip the worst climbs, but the unrelenting rolling terrain can be tough. There's a layover day in Jacksonville, where you can explore the National Historic Landmark town or cycle through the Applegate Valley. Be sure to check out Ashland, where the tour begins and ends. It's a college town, site of a Shakespeare festival, and one of the best small cities on the West Coast.

Accommodations are provided in historic inns and bed-and-breakfasts. The daily distance average is 30 miles. This trip is run about 3 times per year. *CycleWest, 75 Bush St., Ashland, OR 97520, tel. 503/770–0359 or 800/831–5016. July–Sept.: 6 days, $898. Free shuttle from Medford airport. Road bike (with drop or straight handlebar) rental, $97.*

WASHINGTON **Island Hopping in the San Juans.** Get lucky with the rain and you won't find a nicer place to ride than the islands in the Pacific Northwest's Puget Sound. Waterfront rambles, thick woodlands, beach cruises, craggy clifftop overlooks, and plenty of island hopping make this a 6-day variety tour.

The terrain can be mildly challenging but is nothing compared to that of the ever-present peaks in the background. While you roll over the islands just north of Seattle, the entire Olympic Mountain Range juts into sight. It's a rare treat for a bike rider to enjoy a view without having to conquer it.

There are hiking options and wildlife cruises. On one of the latter you might spot killer whales navigating the Sound. You spend your time on three islands: Lopez, Orcas, and San Juan. An advanced rider can burn big-time energy on Orcas; novices can keep themselves busy exploring the tourist shops after completing easier routes.

Accommodations are provided in historic inns. Meals are usually fresh from the Pacific. Average daily distance is 33 miles per day.

This trip is run about 36 times per year. Special dates are available for singles. *Bicycle Adventures, Box 7875, Olympia, WA 98507, tel. 206/786–0989 or 800/443–6060, fax 206/786–9661. Apr.–Nov.: 6 days, $1,098. Road or mountain bike rental, $118.*

WASHINGTON **Whidbey Island and the Olympic Peninsula.** This 6-day Backroads jaunt is a slightly different take on Puget Sound. You can keep your mileage moderate because there are extremely low mileage options, so there's more time to check out the area's attractions—"quaint" villages, pier-side taverns, antiques stores, and historic forts.

Hammerhead cyclists won't be happy; the distances are too short, and the groups on this trip tend to be mellow recreational riders or tourists looking for two-wheeled adventure. But the scenery is no less impressive, and the air is no less fresh.

The tour begins and ends with a ferry trip between Seattle and Whidbey Island, and you pedal to other Puget Sound islands and harbors. You stay in inns that are typically Backroads: log buildings, rambling Victorian houses on bluffs, and renovated farmhouses, some with wood-burning fireplaces.

Daily distance options range from 7 to 53 miles. This tour is also run as a camping trip, including one night in a Port Townsend inn. The tour is run about 16 times each year; go for the summer trips if you can. *Backroads, 1516 5th St., Suite B122, Berkeley, CA 94710–1740, tel. 510/527–1555 or 800/462–2848, fax 510/527–1444. June–Oct.: 6 days, $1,195 inn, $598 camping. Road (with flat or drop handlebar) or hybrid bike rental, $109.*

ALASKA

SOUTHEAST **Crossing the Frontier.** Whoa, is this still America? Cycling friends who've crossed this state tell me there is simply no territory for two-wheeled road travel that's more wide-open or wild. This 7-day trip gives you the opportunity to explore the wilderness while enjoying some of Backroads's trademark cushiness. The tour begins and ends in Anchorage. You roll out on the Glenn Highway, following the Matanuska River into the wilderness, and you raft back down the river the next day.

The route traverses spruce forest, alpine meadows, several small mountain passes with gradual upgrades, and even a few glaciers. You pedal by 14,000-foot Mount Wrangell, the state's largest active volcano. There's also a ferry ride into Prince William Sound. Keep your eyes peeled for moose, bald eagles, seals, porpoises, killer whales, and more.

As you'd expect in such a big state, the rides encompass big miles. Three rest days are thrown in, but the week's total could still top 350 miles, including one killer century (100-mile ride) on day 5. Don't panic if you're closer to the beginner side of the cycling spectrum: The rest days and low-mileage options can get you through.

The food is regional—salmon and halibut barbecues, homemade pies—and the accommaditions range from rustic pioneer-style roadhouses to luxurious mountain lodges. Lots of extras are available: horseback rides, flyovers in a Piper Cub, and scenic chair lifts over glaciers. About 8 trips are run each year. *Backroads, 1516 5th St., Suite B122, Berkeley, CA 94710–1740, tel. 510/527–1555 or 800/462–2848, fax 510/527–1444. June–Sept.: 7 days, $1,498. Price includes whitewater rafting but not other off-bike activities. On 2 nights, 3 or 4 people will have to share rooms. Road (with flat or drop handlebar) or hybrid bike rental, $128.*

HAWAII

THE BIG ISLAND **Lava Flows and Snorkeling.** This is one trip where the bike is in danger of becoming just an accessory, but you can scoot around the Big Island of Hawaii on 2 wheels better than on 4, so we'll keep the bicycles, thank you. Tropical rain forests, sugar cane fields, rolling pastures, white and black sand beaches, surf, lava flows, mountain vistas. What more could you ask?

The southern half of the island is your base for 6 days. You pedal from Hilo to Kona, spending 2 days at the base of the Kilauea Volcano, where you can see the live lava flow (check it out at night if you can). You can also hike to the crater one day. At Kona, you spend a day snorkeling.

The riding here is tougher than you might think because of the hilly terrain. There are some climbs, and you should average about 48 miles per day. Accommodations are in inns, where the restaurants serve regional fare—pig roasts and I-can't-believe-it fruit salads. This tour is run about 8 times per year. Special dates are available for singles. *Bicycle Adventures, Box 7875, Olympia, WA 98507, tel. 206/786–0989 or 800/443–6060, fax 206/786–9661. May–Oct.: 6 days, $1,150. Road or mountain bike rental, $126.*

SOURCES

ORGANIZATIONS **American Youth Hostels** (Box 37613, Washington, DC, 20013–7613, tel. 202/783–4943) runs long tours and provides inexpensive accommodations. **Bikecentennial** (Box 8308, Missoula, MT 59807, tel. 406/721–1776) runs long tours, sells cycling maps, and provides information about touring. It publishes *The Cyclists' Yellow Pages* and *BikeReport*. **League of American Wheelmen** (Suite 120, 190 W. Ostend St., Baltimore, MD 21230–3755, tel. 410/539–3399), an organization of cycling enthusiasts, runs events, provides touring information, and publishes *Bicycle USA*. **Rails to Trails Conservancy** (Suite 300, 1400 16th St. NW, Washington, DC, 20036, tel. 202/797–5400) promotes conversion of abandoned railroad land to cycling paths and provides touring information.

PERIODICALS *Bicycle USA,* the magazine of the League of American Wheelmen (*see* Organizations, *above*), is published 8 times per year and is distributed to members. Every issue contains at least one touring feature and lots of rides and events. *Bicycling,* a how-to magazine, features numerous touring articles throughout the year and a special touring issue. It's published 11 times per year (Rodale Press, 33 E. Minor St., Emmaus, PA 18098, tel. 215/967–5171). *Bike Midwest* lists rides and events in this region. It's published 7 times per year (Suite C, 2099 W. 5th Ave., Columbus, OH 43212, tel. 614/481–7723). *The Cyclists' Yellow Pages,* an annual publication distributed to Bikecentennial members (*see* Organizations, *above*), lists sources of touring information and maps. *Northern California Cyclist,* published 11 times per year, lists rides and events for the northern part of the state (Suite 304, 490 2nd St., San Francisco, CA 94107, tel. 415/546–7291). *Southern California Cyclist,* also published 11 times per year, lists rides and events in this region (Box 3571, Manhattan Beach, CA 90266, tel. 213/546–7181). *Sports Etc/Northwest Cyclist* lists rides and events in the Pacific Northwest. It's published 10 times per year (Box 9272, Seattle, WA 98109, tel. 206/286–8566). *Texas Bicyclist,* published 9 times per year, lists rides and events in this state (3804 El Campo, Fort Worth, TX 76107, tel. 800/227–8282).

BOOKS Pick up a copy of *500 Great Rail Trails* (Living Planet Press) to discover the U.S. rail-trail system, a series of abandoned rail lines that have been converted to bike trails. The 162-page guide tells you where the trails are and how long they run; it also gives highlights along the route and tells you where to get a map. Researched and written by long-time cycling writer Dennis Coello, the *Bicycle Touring Series: Arizona, Colorado, Utah* (Northland Publishing) maps out the best routes in each state, pointing out attractions and features worth stopping for. Some of the best touring books available are those in the *Bicycling the Back Roads Series: Northwest Oregon, Northwest Washington, Pacific Coast, Southwest Washington* (The Mountaineers Books). Each book has more than 200 pages compiled by local experts, with detailed route directions, sightseeing tips, and lodging and food recommendations for the area covered. Two other series, *The Best Bike Rides: Pacific Northwest, New England* and *Short Bike Rides: Cape Cod, Central Massachusetts, Connecticut, Eastern Pennsylvania, Long Island, New Jersey, New York City, Rhode Island, Washington, D.C., Western Washington* (both published by Globe Pequot), are comprised of 200- to 300-page comprehensive handbooks to touring the covered area. The routes always include local "secrets" as well as the traditional—and well-traveled—favorites. The maps are clear and the directions precise, and there's information on lodging and dining options.

ALSO SEE There's no need to keep your two wheels on the road: This country has trails where you can lose your inhibitions. The Mountain Biking chapter will put you there.

Canoeing and Kayaking in Flatwater

by Dennis Stuhaug

ere are some of the pleasures of flatwater canoeing and kayaking: Stroking crisply across a remote lake, dipping your paddles deeply into the water and surging forward with every stroke. Drifting across a placid, forest-rimmed pond, the trees reflecting crisp and clear in the morning air. Making camp on the shore of a lazy river, the blue of the sky slowly dissolving into purples and a loon calling into the shadows. These pleasures are accessible to even a novice paddler, lacking the carefully acquired and honed skills of the whitewater paddler, on rivers and lakes nationwide. If you've never done any canoeing or kayaking, you might start with short guided trips on nearby waters. Like it, and the idea of paddling for days at a time? Then sign up for a week-long guided group canoeing trip (these are fairly widely available in the west), or go to one of the hundreds of outfitters that thrive in the country's major flatwater canoeing and kayaking areas—the Adirondacks or the Boundary Waters Canoe Area of northern Minnesota or adjacent Quetico Provincial Park, in Canada—and have an outfitter put together a longer camping-and-canoeing trip for you. Typically, outfitters in such areas can plan a route to suit your tastes and abilities; equip you with map, canoes or kayaks, paddles, personal flotation devices, and all camping gear (including tents, sleeping bags and pads, stoves and cookware, and more); and supply you with an assortment of fresh and freeze-dried food as well as the necessary permits.

Outfitters can also supply you with a guide. Most paddlers shove off without one. After all, on slow, easy-paddling rivers where you can't possibly get lost, a guide seems a needless expense (at about $90 to $130 a day). But especially if you lack basic camping and outdoor experience, there are definite advantages to going with an expert—and these apply whether you go with a scheduled group outing or opt for a custom trip.

Because both canoes and kayaks can carry considerable gear, the level of comfort can range from pleasant to downright luxurious, compared to, say, backpacking trips, so going with a guide is a good introduction to life in the woods for novices in the outdoors. It's also an ideal introduction to the world of good canoes and kayaks.

Under the tutelage of these veteran outdoors people—who may display the knowledge of naturalists and historians on the river, the eye of artists when unveiling the vistas that cry out for photographs, and the soul of a chef when they set up camp on the riverbank and prepare your meals—you learn by example. By copying their economical paddle strokes, you move your canoe more easily through the water. After breaking camp and stowing gear once or twice, you find your own packing becoming quicker and neater. With their expert instruction,

---

Dennis Stuhaug, the managing editor of Canoe Magazine, *is a former whitewater and flatwater instructor and a longtime sport and recreational paddler.*

you learn how to make your craft go where you want it to, and very quickly, you are able to read routes down river channels. The first day is hectic as you learn how to pack the canoe most efficiently, learn new strokes or re-learn old ones, and get accustomed to your paddling partner and to the group. But a rhythm emerges within a day or so, and with it, a sense of confidence on the water. You learn how a 6-hour paddling day feels and how to slice into the wind or deal with crosscurrents, and you ultimately come to feel at ease on the water. When you're not paddling—on layover days, at lunchtime, or after you've beached the canoes and readied your campsite at day's end—you spend your time fishing, hiking, swimming, or lazing around camp.

For both scheduled group trips and custom expeditions, most outfitters start out with a rendezvous at an inn or local paddling center, where they introduce you to your craft, fit you for paddles and life jackets, and discuss what to expect on the journey. On independent and custom outfitted trips, you also discuss your route, your gear, and your food packs. Then it's off to the embarkation site or, in paddling terms, the put-in (the end of the trip is, appropriately enough, called the take-out). Some outfitters shuttle you to the put-in; others ask that you provide your own transportation.

Don't expect smooth going all the way. Nature exacts her own tolls in the form of rapids, beaver dams, shallows, and occasional dry spots that must be hiked over to get to the next patch of water; the boat must be carried around the obstacle, in a maneuver known as the portage, from the French word *porter,* "to carry," used by the French-Canadian voyageurs who first explored the continent's inland waterways. Helping hands are not only appreciated but usually expected—and there are plenty of paddles and packs that need to be transported, in addition to the boats; the sooner they are, the sooner you're back on the water.

More and more flatwater outfitters use kayaks as well as canoes (seldom both on the same trip). Often equipped with seats with adjustable backrests, kayaks are more comfortable than canoes. However, they're harder to portage, since they weren't designed to be carried. While a canoe can be hoisted onto the shoulders of a single schlepper with relative ease, kayaks take two people to carry. Consequently, kayaks are more frequently found on long river trips rather than on lake-to-lake itineraries.

The cost of these excursions usually runs about $100 per person per day for scheduled group trips, about $150 a day for a custom expedition—varying considerably depending on the number of guides and the quality of the provisions, and on whether you camp or stay at one or more inns, whether paid permits are required in the wilderness area where you paddle, and whether the outfitter's price includes shuttle service to and from put-in and take-out.

CHOOSING THE RIGHT TRIP

The river is drawing you like a magnet, and you're all set to slap your money down. Before you open your wallet, open your mouth and start asking questions. The more questions, the better. A reputable outfitter or school will be glad to answer any you put forth.

How long has the company been in business? As a general matter, stick with an outfitter who has been in business for several years. That's not a rap on new businesses, but an acknowledgment that the company with a few years in its wake has already met the questions and challenges that you're liable to throw at them. As you grow in experience and knowledge, you can look to alternative sources. Ask about the outfitter's current operating license, and the professional organizations the company belongs to. At the least, it should be an active member of such professional groups as America Outdoors or the North American Canoe Liveries and Outfitters Association, umbrella organizations that set minimum standards which members must agree to.

How experienced are the guides? The better the guide, the better the trip. Your guide should be certified by either the American

Canoe Association (ACA) or the British Canoe Union (BCU) and able to administer emergency medical aid, including CPR. The certification process ensures that the instructor can teach the right strokes the right way and has the necessary wilderness skills such as route-finding and navigating on a river. A guide's ability to identify plants, animals, and geological phenomena is also a decided bonus.

How strenuous is the trip? Some can be a leisurely float while you're waited upon hand and foot. Others may expect you to help with portages, pitch in while making camp, and grab a paddle to power the boat. Mileage doesn't count as much as hours on the water and paddling conditions, so be sure to ask about wind, waves, and weather. Expect that the more you do, the more fun you'll have and the more rewarding the trip. But don't set yourself up for an experience beyond your physical abilities to enjoy. Be honest with yourself—how strenuous a trip do you want?

How many people are in the group? The more there are, the less sense of wilderness you may have. Ten is common. Still, a group of about 20 can be companionable and offer diverse socializing off-river.

What is the ratio of paddlers to guides? Usually there are 4 or 5 paddlers per guide, but on trips with a support crew to do camp chores and cooking, the ratio may be lower.

What's the cost and what's included? Make sure the costs are precisely spelled out, and that you understand exactly what is and what is not included. Unless otherwise noted, the prices for all trips described below include your guide and basic instruction, canoes or kayaks, life preservers, all meals, and accommodations while you're canoeing—either tents on camping trips or your room on inn-based trips. Unless we specify to the contrary, sleeping bags and pads are included in the cost of custom trips but not in that of scheduled group trips; if they're not, and you need them, find out whether the outfitter will rent them and for what fee.

There is considerable variation as to whether transportation to and from the put-in and take-out and more than basic instruction are included; be sure to find out your outfitter's policy.

What are the meals like? There's enough room in a canoe to pack a cooler, so you can usually expect a good supply of fresh fruits and vegetables and frozen meat or chicken. Breakfasts usually encompass the range of typical camping specialties: hot cereal, granola, pancakes. Lunches "on the paddle" (in which your paddle doubles as a serving platter) are often a smorgasbord including cheese, peanut butter, and fruit. Dinners can be ambitious or fairly basic. If you care, ask to see sample menus.

What are accommodations like? Some canoe trips have you going from lodge to lodge, but they are unusual and none are described here. If you hear of one that interests you, be sure to query the operator as to the style and comfort level of the properties on the itinerary. Most canoe trips involve camping; if you don't supply your own equipment, make sure that the gear you get from the outfitter is up to the conditions. Are the sleeping bags warm enough? Are they made of down, which loses its insulating properties when wet, or of a synthetic that can keep you warm even if it's had a dousing? Are the tents modern and easy to set up? And is their mosquito netting free of holes?

What do you do when you're not paddling? Few river trips involve more than 6 hours or so on the water. Ask what happens the rest of the time, and find out whether hikes, nature walks, wildlife watching, or photography are planned and what the countryside is like off the river. Would this be a good trip for rereading *War and Peace?*

Is the trip suitable for singles? Most canoes are powered by 2 paddlers and a single person may not always be matched with an appropriate partner. If you're traveling solo, find out what the policy is before you sign up. Similarly, most camping trips put 2 people in a tent. If you're without a partner, ask whether you have a choice of having a tent of your own or whether you'll be paired up with another tripper.

How far in advance is booking required? Although it's possible to sign up for a trip at the last minute, most outfitters prefer your booking as much as 90 days in advance or even more. This is primarily so that they can be sure of having enough participants before making the complicated arrangements involved in planning a trip.

If the outfitter you want to go with can't take you, contact local chambers of commerce or the state tourist offices, for recommendations of others in the area. Their addresses and telephone numbers are included in the service information following text describing canoeing areas in which scheduled group trips are uncommon or nonexistent and where most paddlers use outfitters to set them up on independent or custom trips.

Canoe outfitters are an independent lot, and concentrate on serving the rivers near their home base. Operators who offer trips throughout a broad area are unusual.

DVOŘÁK'S KAYAK AND RAFTING EXPEDITIONS

Bill and Jaci Dvořák's family-owned outfit, founded in 1969, is one of the finest in the country; while they offer a considerable number of whitewater rafting trips, they also have numerous flatwater canoeing and kayaking trips. Canoe trip offerings range from a half-day on the Arkansas River to 12 days on the Colorado. On canoe trips, meals tend to be southern-style cooking, and most involve camping rather than overnights in inns. The number of participants ranges from 10 to 25, with 3 guides for every 10 guests. Guides have up to 10 years of experience as well as first-aid and CPR certification; they're known for their energy, enthusiasm, and respect for the environment. Rates are around $150 per day (17921 U.S. 285, Suite F, Nathrop, CO 81236, tel. 719/539–6851 or 800/824–3795, fax 719/539–3378). *See also* River Rafting and Canoeing and Kayaking Whitewater.

LAUGHING HEART ADVENTURES California's federally designated Wild and Scenic Rivers—the Eel, Smith, Trinity, and Klamath—

are the prime paddling grounds of this well-established company, founded in 1987. Most guides have 10 years of experience and all are ACA-certified and have advanced first-aid training; there are usually 2 on a trip, which runs with up to 10 participants. Meals are typically hot and filling, providing the calories you need after strenuous days on the river. You're not expected to help with camp chores unless you wish. Rates average $80 per day, not including tents, sleeping bags, and pads, which are available for rent (Box 669, Willow Creek, CA 95573, tel. 916/629–3516, fax 916/629–2206).

THE NORTHEAST

MAINE **Expedition on the Great Allagash.** The Allagash is Maine's own river, with the state owning the shoreline for the 96 miles of the Allagash Wilderness Waterway. Probably one of the most popular paddling areas in the East, the Waterway extends back 500 feet from the riverbank on each side, creating the illusion of near-wilderness despite its being remarkably accessible—and despite a century of active logging. You see an occasional road end and an occasional camp, but for the main part you canoe through dense stands of balsam fir and spruce, camping in sheltered nooks among the dark trees. Mergansers sail in flotillas along the shore. It's possible to see moose, and an occasional whitetail deer is visible, along with geese, ducks, ospreys, great blue herons, bald eagles, the splash of a beaver, the shadow of a mink, and the blue dive-bomb of a kingfisher. While the best fishing is early in the year, you can still land your dinner as the summer heats the river. Classic northwoods paddling, the river alternates between swift, stony stretches and long, sluggish pools. The riffles and little drops demand your attention as you pick and choose a path down areas of thin water; if you miscalculate, you'll hear a decisive thump as you glance off a submerged boulder. But for the most part, the waters are not beyond the abilities of the beginner with some experience.

On this fully outfitted 9-day trip from Maine Sports Outfitters, you have plenty of time to explore the mud bars, poke into eddies and creek mouths, watch for wildlife, and learn the tips and tricks that let a canoe drop gracefully down a riffle. Maine Sports Outfitters, founded in 1976, usually provides a pair of river professionals for each party of 10. On the river, the guides are naturalists with a broad range of plant, bird, and animal knowledge, and they give you plenty of paddling points and tips. (They're also registered Maine guides, with wilderness first-aid training.) Once ashore, they transform into camp craftsmen—setting tents, laying a fire, and starting dinner with a speed guaranteed to amaze. Their culinary wizardry produces breakfasts of bacon and eggs with fried potatoes or pancakes with Maine maple syrup, soup-and-sandwich lunches, and dinners of steak with onions and mushrooms, barbecued chicken, or sautéed scallops, shrimp, and lobster.

The outfitter's season begins in July, a bit after the first paddlers of the season go down the river, and extends until September, when the weather is excellent and the river uncrowded, and there's still plenty of water to move a canoe downstream. *Maine Sports Outfitters, Box 956, Rte. 1, Rockport, ME 04856, tel. 207/236–8797, 800/722–0826, or, in Maine, 800/244–8799, fax 207/236–7123. Maine Publicity Bureau, Box 2300, Hallowell, ME 04347, tel. 207/582–9300 or 800/533–9595. July–Sept.: 9 days, $849. Sign up 1 month in advance.*

MAINE **Northwoods Paddling on the Machias.** When ticking off the list of Maine's scenic waterways, the Machias has to be near the top of the list—along with the Allagash, Penobscot, and St. John. What does it have to offer? Start with swamps, marshes and lakes, some sporty rapids that throw a bucket of spray in the bow person's face, ledges, portages—the full mix of classic northwoods paddling that defines canoeing's heritage. Free-flowing from Fifth Machias Lake to the sea, about 75 miles, it is flanked by near-wilderness. While logging roads do extend along the river, only a handful of cabins mark human presence. Frosting on the canoeing cake is that the Machias is much less h[...] ily traveled than the Allagash and much m[...] accessible than the St. John.

Trips down the river from Maine Spo[...] Outfitters are scheduled for June, when co[...] ditions are optimum. As on the outfitter[...] Allagash trips, there is at least 1 guide for eac[...] 6 guests, and a typical party is a pair of professionals guiding a party of 10. Only one Machias trip is planned each year, depending on water conditions. Meals are similar to those served on the outfitter's Allagash trip. *Maine Sports Outfitters, Box 956, Rte. 1, Rockport, ME 04856, tel. 207/236–8797, 800/722–0826, or, in Maine, 800/244–8799, fax 207/236–7123. Maine Publicity Bureau, Box 2300, Hallowell, ME 04347, tel. 207/582–9300 or 800/533–9595. June: 5 days, $495. Sign up a month in advance.*

NEW YORK **Quietwater in Adirondack Park.** Less than a century ago the Adirondacks were the nation's chosen destination resort, a network of hundreds of miles of rivers, streams, ponds, and lakes that attracted canoeists from all over the country. J. Henry Rushton, the father of American canoe design, grew up on an Adirondack river and placed his stamp on modern American canoe building from his boat shop just north of the present park. Nineteenth-century author Nessmuk, less well known as George Washington Sears, wrote his incredibly popular woodcraft stories based on cruises in the Adirondacks. The founders of the American Canoe Association camped at Lake George to create the organization in 1880.

McDonnell's Adirondack Challenge puts together paddling vacations throughout the area; one of its most popular trips takes you through the stream-connected Saranac Lakes chain. With its many bays, points, islands, marshes, and ponds, it would take a summer to adequately explore the waters of this area; the lexicon of the canoeist is written on its quiet waters. There are a number of public campgrounds in the area.

Rather than offering a roster of group trips, McDonnell's sets up a special departure for every party, with one guide for about 6 guests.

av-
re

s

mized, prices vary; aver-
per day including guide,
pment, and meals, but the
p or down depending on
e, how many in your party,
en route. If you want to bring
nd camping equipment or just
d directions, McDonnell's will
u. The company operates out of
Outfitters, an umbrella organiza-
ndles reservations for a variety of
ss sports. McDonnell's Adirondack
ge, All Seasons Outfitters, 168 Lake
Ave., Saranac Lake, NY 12983, tel.
91–6159. Visitor Information Center,
t of Webb, Box 68, Old Forge, NY 13420,
315/369–6983. July–Oct.: 2 days–2 weeks,
out $75 per person per day. Sign up a month
advance.

THE SOUTH

GEORGIA **The Okefenokee: Black-Mirror Waters and Trembling Earth.** This 600-square-mile wilderness in the southern part of the state—far from being the smelly, foul basin that the word *swamp* might suggest—provides a paddling experience that's simply not to be missed. The preserve's eastern reaches, where Wilderness Southeast begins its 5-day paddling trips, is made up of expanses of water-based prairie patched here and there by solid and not-so-solid islands known as hammocks. Composed of densely matted floating vegetation bound together by a network of roots, some of these hammocks shiver when trod upon (which is why the Indians who named the swamp called it "the land of the trembling earth"). In the west are dense forests of cypress, whose roots have stained the swamp's pure water the color of dark tea; in shady areas, it is quite black and perfectly reflects the lush green overhanging vegetation and the lacy trails of Spanish moss to magical effect. The Okefenokee's shallows and backwaters shelter thousands of alligators; the preserve is also the territory of deer and otter, dozens of kinds of snakes, and hundreds of species of birds.

While rental canoes are readily available at key visitor areas on the fringes of the swamp, Wilderness Southeast trips are particularly rewarding since they are led by naturalist-guides who give you background about the swamp's fascinating ecosystem.

Moreover, in addition to the some 40 miles of stillwater paddling in the swamp, there's another 10 down the Suwannee River, which begins in the Okefenokee. Camping is within the Okefenokee National Wildlife Refuge, one of the public lands within the swamp; you set up tents on wooden platforms. With savory dishes like vegetarian chili and stir-fried shrimp and rice on the menu, the meals are surprisingly tasty. Usually a pair of guides accompany 14 guests. Wilderness Southeast, founded in 1973, is a nonprofit educational corporation.

If you go in spring, you will find flowers in bloom, nesting birds, the gators at their most active, and a lot of other people. In fall, you can sign up for special photo-workshop trips with lodging in cabins rather than in tents. *Wilderness Southeast, 711 Sandtown Rd., Savannah, GA 31410, tel. 912/897–5108, fax 912/897–5116. Okefenokee National Wildlife Refuge, Rte. 2, Box 338, Folkston, GA 31357, tel. 912/496–3331. Apr. and Nov.: 5 days, $440. Sign up 3–4 months in advance.*

MISSISSIPPPI **Paradise for Paddlers.** Snow-white sand beaches and sparkling clear water reflecting magnolia, cypress, and oak: It sounds like a promotional piece for paradise. In fact, though, the images describe the Wolf River in the southern part of the state, one of the cleanest and least developed rivers in the South, yet one that even beginning paddlers can handle. The water is basically placid, with only a few scattered, easy-to-negotiate riffles marring the surface. A 5-day cruise takes you through lush forests, with a beach around every bend; you share the scenery with the deer, raccoons, owls, and great blue herons. (The beavers along the rivers are timid, and you are more likely to see the stumps left by their gnawing than their actual faces.) Under the surface, you can find bass, catfish, sunfish, and the occasional prowling gar; bring your fishing tackle. If you paddle the full 58 miles from the Mississippi Route 26 bridge, you pass through the Wolf River Wildlife Management Area, a federal reserve where you can see alligators aplenty and have a chance at spotting the rare scarlet king snake.

On this slow and beautiful river, you won't find long, scheduled group trips, and few paddlers feel the need of a guide, but if you do, Wolf River Canoes can supply one, along with your canoe, paddles, personal flotation devices, and shuttle to put-in (camping equipment can be rented). *Wolf River Canoes (Joseph Feil), 21652 Tucker Rd., Long Beach, MS 39560, tel. 601/452–7666. America Outdoors, Box 1348, Knoxville, TN 37901, tel. 615/524–4814. Apr.–Oct.: 5 days, $595. Price does not include food, tents, stove, and cookware, or sleeping bags and pads; sign up 1 month in advance.*

THE MIDWEST

MINNESOTA **Boundary Waters Canoe Area Wilderness.** The lure to paddlers of this 150-mile arc of woodlands across northeast Minnesota is powerful: 1,175 lakes dotting 1.1 million acres of forests inhabited by more than 225 species of birds and 55 species of mammals (moose, deer, bear, coyote, fox, otter, mink, bobcat, lynx, marten, and wolf); and 2,200 campsites, give or take a few, scattered along at least 1,500 miles of canoe routes. There are no roads and no cabins. No airplanes can land, and motorboats are permitted only in a very small area. Abutting the BWCA across the border to the north is Quetico Provincial Park, whose pristine acreage doubles the amount of wilderness beckoning the paddler. A system of permits, in effect on both sides of the border, limits the number of visitors and keeps them widely dispersed, so that you can easily go for days without seeing other paddlers.

Lakes are connected by a system of streams, rivers, and portages; ponds and bogs sparkle among the conifers. It's classic northwoods flatwater canoeing, as good as it gets. There are some challenging, if not downright dangerous, rivers, and most of the rivers have at least riffles. However, well-established trails give you the choice of portaging around difficult spots. You can spend a lifetime in the area and not exhaust its possibilities nor tire of its beauty.

Typically, in this area, you sign up with an outfitter, who provides boats, food, all camping equipment, and the necessary permits and campsite reservations. Tom & Woods' Moose Lake Wilderness Canoe Trips is typical (a frill here is that lodging before and after your trip is included). As is usual among local outfitters, this one also helps you plan a route that suits your paddling ability and camping experience and takes in the waterfalls, wildlife, islands, and other natural features that you travel to the area to experience. The outfitter sets you up with Mad River Kevlar canoes and Eureka tents, plus everything else you need; all you have to bring is your clothing and fishing gear.

Summer is the best time to visit, though if the itinerary you plan takes in a river or stream, you may prefer to travel in late spring or early summer, when water levels are higher, or after the start of the fall rains. *Tom & Woods' Moose Lake Wilderness Canoe Trips, Box 358, Ely, MN 55731, tel. 218/365–5837 or 800/322–5837. Minnesota Office of Tourism, 375 Jackson St., 256 Skyway Level, St. Paul, MN 55101, tel. 612/296–5029 or 800/657–3700. May–Sept.: $185–$195 per day. Sign up 3–7 months in advance.*

MINNESOTA **Another Approach to the Boundary Waters Canoe Area.** One of the favorite trips among canoeists who sign up for Top of the Trail's outfitting services is a relatively easy, laid-back course through the BWCA's northwest corner. But even with plenty of company you won't rub elbows with your neighbors given the vast amounts of space as you loop around Saganaga Lake, skirt the international boundary between the United States and Canada from Saganaga through Knife Lake and on to Birch, then make a left turn through a chain of small lakes and ponds to Thomas Lake. At that point, you swing northeast, crossing Kekebabic and Ogishkemuncie lakes and the Seagull River as you return to Saganaga. The paddling delivers a little bit of everything the BWCA promises—big lakes, ponds, little rivers, great scenery, no matter which way you're looking, and 39 brief portages. (And if this route doesn't sound appealing, Top of the Trail can design any number of others.)

Top of the Trail, a member of the Minnesota Canoe Association and the United States Canoe Association, was established in 1987. Fresh foods mix with freeze-dried foods on your menu, which includes omelettes, French toast, pancakes, granola, and cereal for breakfast; summer sausage sandwiches, bagels, and spaghetti for lunch; and steak, lasagna, and turkey tetrazzini for dinner. While most paddlers opt for an independent trip, guides are also available; they all have extensive paddling experience and first-aid training, and they leave it up to you as to whether you help with camp chores or just go fishing. The total outfitting fee varies depending on the size of your group, when you go, and what kind of canoes you use—several are available, and the lighter, easier-to-portage models nudge your tab to the higher end of the scale. *Top of the Trail Canoe Outfitters, Saganaga Lake, Box 1001, Gunflint Trail, Grand Marais, MN 55604, tel. 218/388–2255 or 800/869–0883. Minnesota Office of Tourism, 375 Jackson St., 256 Skyway Level, St. Paul, MN 55101, tel. 612/296–5029 or 800/657–3700. May–Sept.: $120–$138 per day. Sign up 2 months in advance.*

THE SOUTHWEST

ARIZONA **Canyons and Hot Springs along the Colorado.** As fall slowly drains into the dark hours of the year, it's time to head for the desert. One of the most spectacular, thoroughly enjoyable, and little-known paddle trips in North America is along the Black Canyon of the Colorado River below Hoover Dam. Picture steep canyon walls vaulting up from the big, smooth river, picture bighorn sheep looking down on the canoes, picture yourself stretched back in a bubbling hot spring soaking your paddle-weary muscles. And the best part of the trip is yet to come.

Summertime, traditionally, is vacation time. Most people hoard their free time jealously, and burn it off in a single grand splurge. Summer, though, is not the best time to poke around the Lake Mead National Recreation Area south of Las Vegas and downstream of Hoover Dam. It's hot! Really hot! But if you wait until November is about ready to fall off the calendar, temperatures subside into the comfortable. You can venture out into the noonday sun without sloshing sunblock over each square inch of bare skin. Fish no longer flee to the deepest depths, and are more than interested in trying out the selection of lures or baits you offer.

Best of all, there's another natural vacation break at the tail end of the month—Thanksgiving. Squeeze another day onto the 4 days of Thanksgiving weekend, and you have just enough time for one of Laughing Heart Adventure's fabulous Thanksgiving expeditions, with a multicourse holiday meal—from turkey with all the fixings to sweet potato pie for dessert.

Below Hoover Dam, the Colorado is big but placid and crystal-clear, rolling on its way toward the Gulf of California. This is flatwater canoeing country, with plenty of emphasis on the flat. You definitely earn the miles between each campsite.

Expect a maximum party size of 10 guests, supported by at least a pair of ACA-certified guides. Meals are filling: huevos rancheros, Dutch-oven lasagna, and an assortment of homebaked cakes—all freshly prepared. After dinner, you can relax, since guests are not required to help with camp chores. If you can't make the Thanksgiving journey, try for the similar trip that Laughing Heart mounts over the Easter weekend, with a similar banquet spread on the riverbank. The price of the trip includes round-trip transportation from Las Vegas. *Laughing Heart Adventures, Trinity Outdoor Center, Box 669, Willow Creek, CA*

95573, tel. 915/629–3516 or 800/541–1256, fax 916/629–2206. Thanksgiving and Easter: 5 days, $425. Sign up 2–3 months in advance.

UTAH **Paddling the Green through Red-Rock Country.** With the orange-red sandstone just outside Canyonlands National Park soaring upward from the river's edge, the Green River in Utah can be a photographer's paradise. For those who keep their images in their memories, it's hard to beat this 5-day, 70-mile paddle between Green River, Utah, and Mineral Bottom, at the confluence of the Green and the Colorado rivers—a trip offered by Southwind Kayak Center, founded in 1987. The river's course runs through sheer canyons and past inviting side canyons, and abandoned mines and cabins.

Southwind makes the trip both with canoes and kayaks. With its gentle current, this is cruising country for kayaks—great for beginners—and easy strokes power you across or up the river and build speed downstream atop the current. But while leisurely for kayaks, the stream is strenuous for canoeists, requiring far harder paddling, and you need a fair amount of experience, although it is certainly within the reach of even moderately competent paddlers. Guides have from 2 to 5 years of professional training in instruction and leadership, and all are certified in first aid and CPR; most have advanced wilderness medical training as well.

Paddle rafts accompany the trip, and the support crew of 3 whips up western-style meals such as salmon grilled with herbs, barbecued steak or chicken breast, with fresh salads and vegetables, hot soup, and warm bread. After dinner, the crew sets up comfortable camps on remote beaches while you explore the nearest canyons in the company of your 2 naturalist-guides.

The Green is navigable year-round, but spring and fall are the best seasons, as the water is warm enough for swimming and high enough to move swiftly but not too high to submerge good campsites on the riverbanks and islands. Winter temperatures can dip to the 20°F to 60°F range while summer days top out at 110°-plus (albeit with far cooler nights). Price includes transportation to and from Los Angeles. *Southwind Kayak Center, 17855 Sky Park Circle, #A, Irvine CA 92714, tel. 714/261–0200 or 800/764–8494. Year-round: 5 days, $995. Sign up 3 months in advance.*

THE ROCKIES

COLORADO **Classical Music on the Dolores.** On this 8-day trip down the great Dolores, which surges through the deserts of the Southwest, through alpine forests and past ancient Anasazi sandstone caverns, outfitter Bill Dvořák regularly invites musicians from the Los Angeles Philharmonic, who ride in rafts and provide nightly concerts while you're on the river. Canoers and kayakers are welcome as well as rafters, however, and the outfitter provides your boat. You can portage around the few Class III rapids along the route that you don't want to take on, or you can ride through on a raft while a guide takes your boat through.

The Classical Music Trip is immensely popular, and early reservations are strongly suggested. For specifics on the food and outfitting style, see River Rafting. *Dvořák's Kayak and Rafting Expeditions, 17921 U.S. 285, Suite B-3, Nathrop, CO 81236, tel. 719/539–6851 or 800/824–3795, fax 719/539–3378. June: 8 days, $1,450. Price does not include tent; sign up 9–12 months in advance.*

THE WEST COAST

CALIFORNIA **An Easy Trip down the Gentle Eel.** Back in 1850, explorer Josiah Gregg had a broken skillet and a hankering for fresh food. Bivouacked by a northern California river, a member of his party successfully swapped the broken pan to a party of local Native Americans for a mess of fresh eels. Even though the natives already had a name for the river, *Weeyot,* Gregg immediately renamed it Eel to commemorate the meal.

Today, this gentle stream is California's longest wilderness river. The main Eel rises at the foot of Bald Mountain in the Mendocino National Forest and heads south for 20 miles before turning northwesterly through the Coast Range to the Pacific, wiggling through a land of towering old growth redwood forests, with only a few roads in sight. In the presence of these ancient trees, many paddlers whisper in awe. Deer may gingerly step out onto the wide gravel beaches in search of a drink, or a raccoon may be glimpsed in the water at the mouth of a tributary, watching the canoes pass as he hunts for a meal.

Laughing Heart Adventures' 7-day canoe expeditions on this stream, the longest of several available, usually have no more than 10 guests, supported by at least a pair of guides, sometimes 3. They tend to know much more than just the techniques of shepherding their flock down the river. If you find a track at the river's edge, they can describe the animal and as likely as not show you where to watch for a glimpse of it. They can identify a bird from its song, point out a nearly hidden nest in a tree, and spin a tale about the rich coastal environment. When you encounter the modest whitewater stretches, they provide enough thorough but low-key coaching to help get novices through without a hitch. Off the river, their accomplishments really shine: The guides pride themselves on the ability to whip up a fabulous meal while guests relax on the riverbank. Signature dishes include huevos Mexicanos at breakfast and lasagna made in the Dutch oven at dinner.

The Eel, whose average annual 90 inches of precipitation fall mostly from November through March, shrinks to a thread meandering down the wide gravel banks and bars by April. Riding the boundary between the cool, moist Pacific air and the heat of inland California, the Eel gets strong upriver winds most afternoons; Laughing Heart trips avoid the winds by starting early in the morning and making camp early on the river's beautiful sandy beaches. *Laughing Heart Adventures, Trinity Outdoor Center, Box 669,*

Willow Creek, CA 95573, tel. 916/629–3516 or 800/541–1256, fax 916/629–2206. Mar.–July: 7 days, $700. Sign up 2–3 months in advance.

CALIFORNIA **Splashing through a California Switzerland on the Trinity and Klamath.** The word *alps* conjures up images of rugged mountains, lush meadows, and sparkling streams—and for the paddler venturing into the Trinity Alps of northern California the imagery is fully justified. The Trinity River splashes down through steep-walled canyons, turning and twisting among stands of towering evergreens as it works its way from the spine of California to where it meets the Klamath River and dashes to the sea. This is superb canoeing water, alternating between long, placid pools mirroring the dark needles of the conifers and the rugged rocks and bouncing waves and gleaming whitewater in the easy drops. It's a classic big California paddle.

On this canoeing trip from Laughing Heart Adventures, it takes 6 easy days to paddle the 75 miles from Hawkins Bar near Willow Creek to the mouth of the Klamath River, where it pours into the Pacific Ocean near Klamath Glen in Redwood National Park. The upper stretches of the trip are paralleled by road, but it is a generally unobtrusive road that does not diminish the sense of isolation. The few cabins that pop in and out of view do little to dispel the illusion.

Below the confluence of the Trinity and Klamath rivers, downstream from the Hoopa Reservation, the dense forests of the Coast Range close in, and the river works its way through near-wilderness. Along the riverbanks you might glimpse deer, raccoon, even a shy black bear. Birds of prey glide overhead, especially during the salmon runs.

With a maximum party size of 14 and at least 2 guides (and sometimes 3), there's plenty of time to absorb the guides' knowledge. Want to improve your paddling? Or learn the difference between Douglas fir, hemlock, and pine? Curious about the tiny, clawed footprint in the sand? Want to lean back and enjoy the changing skies at the end of the day, with the smells of food in the air? That's what this trip is all about.

River levels on the Klamath are not as critical as on some rivers; an upstream dam keeps the flow even. However, the upper stretches cross California's interior, and air and water temperatures can be quite warm from mid- to late summer. *Laughing Heart Adventures, Trinity Outdoor Center, Box 669, Willow Creek, CA 95573, tel. 916/629-3516 or 800/541-1256, fax 916/629-2206. May–Sept.: 6 days, $660. Sign up 2–3 months in advance.*

SOURCES

ORGANIZATIONS Membership organizations set standards for river guides and outfitters and are good sources for referrals and for checking references. Among them are **America Outdoors** (Box 1348, Knoxville, TN 37901, tel. 615/524–4814), the association for national river guides, and the **National Association of Canoe Liveries and Outfitters** (Rte. 27 and Catro Rte. 2, Box 2119, Butler, KY 41006, tel. 606/654–4111). Another good source for information about guides and outfitters and listings of local clubs, the backbone of paddling sports today, is the **American Canoe Association** (8550 Cinderbed Rd., Suite 1900, Box 1190, Newington, VA 22122-1190, tel. 703/451–0140), which publishes the "American Canoeist" newsletter. Clubs focus on everything from whitewater to placid river drifts to fierce surf competition to Olympic sprints to long-distance sea kayaking. There are literally hundreds of them in the United States today.

PERIODICALS *Canoe Magazine* (Box 3146, Kirkland, WA 98083, tel. 800/MY–CANOE), another source for an up-to-date list of local paddling clubs, is the leading magazine in North America focusing on the full range of paddle sports—flatwater and whitewater, canoes and kayaks. It runs destination stories as well as articles on trips and techniques. The quarterly *Paddler* (Box 775450, Steam-boat Springs, CO 80477, tel. 303/879–1450) covers a broad spectrum of canoe and kayak trips and runs product reviews and tips on paddling skills.

Foldable kayaks occupy a unique niche in the paddling universe: Those who love them, love them passionately; those who don't, don't. "Folding Kayaker" (Box 0754, Planetarium Station, New York, NY 10024-5069, tel. 212/724–5069), a bimonthly newsletter, keeps readers abreast of what's happening in the folding world with a breezy, informal style that includes a great deal of hard, useful information.

BOOKS *Canoeing*, prepared by the American National Red Cross, is *the* basic book on canoe technique. If you don't have access to a canoe club or other paddling instruction, it is your best source of safety information. *Basic Canoeing* is an abridged version of the full book. *Canoeing Made Easy*, by I. Herbert Gordon, is a manual for beginners with plenty of tips for the most experienced of boaters. *Canoeing & Rafting: The Complete Where-to-Go Guide to America's Best Tame and Wild Waters*, by Sara Pyle, is a state-by-state list of canoe and kayak waters with notes on difficulty and optimum paddling times; it's valuable despite its somewhat dated livery and outfitter information.

In the summer of 1930, a pair of Minnesota teenagers—Eric Sevareid, 17, and Walter Port, 19—paddled an 18-foot canoe from Minneapolis to Hudson Bay, 2,250 miles away. *Canoeing With The Cree*, by Eric Sevareid, describes their 4-month journey on the wilderness waterways made famous by the fur traders. While a great yarn in its own right, Sevareid's narrative also gives a look at the North Woods in the last days of the wilderness, before civilization encroached. *The Complete Wilderness Paddler*, by James West Davidson and John Rugge, is, on the surface, a ripping tale of a great adventure, paddling down the Moisie River in Labrador. But each step of the trip is carefully dissected, giving the reader insights into the skills, techniques, and knowledge needed for paddling a canoe virtually anywhere. A must-read for anyone interested in canoe tripping. *A Guide to Big Water Canoeing*, by David Alan Herzog, is an introduction to the techniques of big-water paddling—big water being, for Herzog, the large lakes, bays, and salt water of North America. An invaluable resource. *Pole, Paddle & Portage: A Complete Guide to Canoeing*, by Bill Riviere, distills the experience and Northeast viewpoint of this respected outdoors writer and former Maine canoe guide into a readable introduction to canoeing. *Rivers Running Free: Canoeing Stories by Adventurous Women*, edited by Judith Niemi

and Barbara Wieser, is an anthology, best read by the fire of a winter's evening, showing that others have gone before you.

ALSO SEE If you like flatwater canoeing and kayaking, you may want to tackle whitewater, either in a canoe or kayak (*see* Canoeing and Kayaking in Whitewater) or on a raft (*see* River Rafting). Or you may want to try canoeing in flatwater under the aegis of a wilderness program such as Outward Bound (*see* Major Players in Wilderness and Survival Schools).

Canoeing and Kayaking in Whitewater

by Dennis Stuhaug

ith a quick draw, the paddler in the bow swings the canoe away from the rock and down the smooth tongue of water flowing out of the glistening whitewater of the rapid. The evergreens arch over the narrow tunnel of the river, and there is a half-shadowed movement in the bankside brush that may have been a nervous deer. A kayak slips through the water after the canoe, its paddler laughing as the boat bursts through the waves in a cloud of spray into a smooth, placid pool.

This is classic whitewater river paddling. Virtually anyone can master the basics in a few lessons under the guidance of a seasoned instructor. The strokes and combinations of strokes that allow a boat to move forward, backward, or sideways, or turn, are simple to grasp. The art of finding a route through a boulder garden is readily acquired. Your kayak is upended? Many people can learn to roll a kayak right side up in a single lesson. Your canoe is swamped? Maneuver yourself around to the upstream side of the canoe and hang on as the canoe runs the rapids.

Instruction is available both on learn-as-you-go group trips down rivers across the country and in organized whitewater paddling schools. Typically, the former involves a classic wilderness camping-trip format, with guides to teach paddling skills and handle camp chores; the cost includes food, equipment, instruction, and lodging (usually a tent) at about $125 to $150 per person per day.

During organized classes, you spend from 3 days to a week in a single location, usually at the school's base camp or headquarters, and learn strokes, reading the river, and ways to get out of the water if you get in (one of them, the Eskimo roll, involves using your paddle to flip your kayak right side up); the cost runs about $75 a day per person, including equipment and lunch but not breakfast, dinner, and lodging. If you wear contact lenses, you may want to bring a pair of swim goggles.

Typically, you meet early in the morning over breakfast and get a brief description of what you'll do during the week, followed by a detailed description of what you'll learn that day. Then it's down to the water for step-by-step demonstrations of the techniques on the docket, and lots of practice. Many schools videotape you in action, and play the videotapes at the end of the day, after you've showered, cleaned up, and had dinner.

You can do whitewater canoeing in either canoes or kayaks. A small number of programs are exclusively for kayakers or traditional canoes, while others use one or the other depending on the preferences of those who have signed up. Instructional programs use canoes and kayaks with equal frequency nationwide. What's the difference, practically speaking, between canoes and kayaks?

Dennis Stuhaug, the managing editor of Canoe Magazine, *is a former whitewater and flatwater instructor and a longtime sport and recreational paddler.*

Canoes are usually open on top; you kneel or sit relatively high in the craft and power the boat with a single-bladed paddle. Kayaks are enclosed, and the paddler sits low and propels the craft with a double-bladed paddle. Unlike long, stable sea kayaks (a.k.a. touring kayaks), which are usually from 15 to 20 feet long, averaging about 17 feet, whitewater kayaks are short, typically under 13 feet, with a low center of gravity so that they respond instantly to the paddler's command—a responsiveness that in the hands of a novice equals extreme tippiness. Whether you learn one or the other is a matter of personal taste; some people don't like the idea of sitting in kayaks because they're enclosed, and opt for the open-decked canoe.

The opportunity to travel in the company of a professional guide who not only knows how to get you down the river but can also point out the natural features of the landscape is reason enough to sign up for a group whitewater trip rather than strike out on your own. Being able to lean back after a day on the river in anticipation of a superb meal, without having to do the cooking, is another. And facing the challenge of a complex rapid—and accomplishing the last mile into camp—are the pleasures that quickly make new paddlers into devotees.

CHOOSING THE RIGHT PROGRAM

Before you leap to sign up, start asking questions—and the more, the better. A reputable outfitter or school will be glad to tell you anything you want to know.

How strenuous is the trip? On point-to-point trips, you may be waited upon hand and foot—or you may be expected to help with portages and pitch in making camp. In terms of sheer toughness, mileage doesn't count as much as the number of hours on the water and paddling conditions, so be sure to ask about wind, waves, and weather. Unless otherwise noted, all the trips described below are available for people of all paddling levels.

Also, familiarize yourself with whitewater classifications, the shorthand code that pad-

dlers use to describe the relative difficulty of rivers. The classification goes in increasing order of difficulty from Class I to Class VI. *Class I* connotes moving water with riffles and small waves, runnable by practiced beginners. Obstructions, if any, may be easily avoided. *Class II* signals easy rapids with waves up to 3 feet. Channels are wide and clear, and the routes may be easily identified from a boat without scouting. Some maneuvering is required. Class II waters are runnable by intermediate paddlers. *Class III* waters contain narrow passages and high, irregular waves capable of swamping an open canoe. Complex maneuvering and scouting from shore may be required. You need experience. *Class IV* rapids are long and difficult, with constricted passages, often requiring precise maneuvering in turbulent waters. These waters are generally impassable for open canoes. A high degree of paddling skill is essential. *Class V* rapids are long and violent, nearly always requiring scouting from shore. Rescue conditions are difficult, and any mishap causes a significant hazard to life. Only a team of experts should undertake these waters. *Class VI* waters approach the limit of navigability; they are nearly impossible, very dangerous, and suitable only for teams of experts and only after close study and with all precautions taken.

Remember when choosing a trip that river conditions are not static. A change in water level and river flow can transform a stream. In some cases, a very challenging rapid may disappear when higher water floods a channel. In others, a simple section of river at low water may turn into a caldron as the volume of water increases.

How long has the company been in business? As a general matter, stick with an outfitter or school that has been in business for several years when you're a beginner. The company with a few years' experience under its belt has already dealt with the challenges that you're liable to throw them. As your experience grows, you will be better prepared to deal with newcomers. Ask about the outfitter's current operating license, and find out which professional organizations the company belongs to. At the least, it should be an active member of such professional groups as America Outdoors, the National Association of Canoe Liveries and Outfitters, or the American Canoe Association (*see below*). These organizations set minimum standards for the profession.

How experienced are the guides and instructors? The better the guide, the better the trip. Instructors and guides should be certified by either the American Canoe Association (ACA) or British Canoe Union (BCU). The certification process ensures that the instructor can teach the right strokes the right way and that the guide knows the necessary wilderness skills. Also ask whether guides are experienced naturalists, and find out how well they know the region. One guide in each group should be able to administer emergency medical aid, including CPR. A knowledge of plants, animals, and geological phenomena is a decided plus.

How many people are in your group? The more there are, the less sense of wilderness you may have. Ten is common on group trips, though a group of about 20 can be companionable and offer diverse socializing off-river.

What is the ratio of paddlers to guides or instructors? Usually, on trips, there are 4 or 5 paddlers per guide, but on trips with a support crew to do camp chores and cooking, the ratio may be higher. In instructional setups, the greater the number of guides, the more personal attention you will have.

How much time do you spend on the water? This is especially relevant when you're signing up for a clinic or school. The usual range is 5 to 6 hours; you may get tired after that if you don't start out in great shape.

What do you do when you're not paddling? Few river trips involve more than 6 hours or so on moving water. Ask what happens the rest of the time, and find out whether there are plans for hikes, nature walks, wildlife watching, or photography.

What's the cost and what's included? Make sure it's precisely spelled out, and that you understand exactly what is and what is not included. Typically, and for the operations described below unless otherwise noted, paddling schools include instruction, equipment, and lunch only, with accommodations, breakfasts, and dinner extra. On point-to-point trips, the price you pay includes instruction and guiding, all meals while you're on the river, boats, life preservers, wet suits if you need them, and camping equipment, including tents but not sleeping bags and pads. Anything you need that is not supplied is usually available for rent if you don't have your own equipment. Find out if you will need a wet suit and ask whether it's included.

What are the meals like? On point-to-point trips, ask for sample menus. In general, because there's enough room in a canoe to pack a cooler, you can usually expect a good supply of fresh fruits and vegetables as well as frozen meat, fish, or chicken. Breakfasts are generally the standard camping fare: hot cereal, granola, pancakes, and the like. Lunches are often a smorgasbord of cheese, peanut butter, fruit, and perhaps something canned. Dinners may stick with simple but satisfying lasagna and pasta—but can aspire to culinary heights; in some regions, there's an informal competition among river guides as to who can produce the more elaborate fare.

What are the accommodations like? If accommodations are not included, ask about what's available nearby; then call the properties themselves and find out about the establishment's rooms and facilities. If the outfitter is providing camping gear, make sure it's of a quality you'll be happy with; you don't want a sleeping bag that isn't warm enough or a tent that you have to wrestle with to set up. Also ask about the campsites and shower and latrine arrangements.

Is this program suitable for singles? Most canoes are powered by 2 paddlers and a single person's luck of the draw may not always match them up with an appropriate partner. Find out what the outfitter's policy is before you sign up. Similarly, most camping trips routinely put 2 people in a tent. If you're without a partner, ask whether you have a choice of having a tent of your own or whether you'll be automatically paired up with another tripper.

Do you have references from past guests? If you have qualitative questions about a program you're considering, there's no better way to get them answered than to chat with someone who's paddled the waters and spent time with the staff.

How far in advance do I need to book? Count on a week to several months ahead, depending on whether you are signing up for a short instructional program in an off-season or a longer river journey in the West.

MAJOR PLAYERS

DVOŘÁK'S KAYAK AND RAFTING EXPEDITIONS

Bill and Jaci Dvořák, well-known for their flatwater canoeing trips and rafting trips, are also well known for their 1- to 12-day whitewater instructional clinics, staged on Class II and Class III waters such as the Arkansas, Colorado, Dolores, Green, Gunnison, Rio Chama, Rio Grande, and North Platte. (Their rafting trips are usually accompanied by several inflatable kayaks.) Clinics are held either at the Dvořák base on the Arkansas River or on another one of the western rivers they run; whitewater kayaking and canoeing trips are offered on a variety of western rivers. Instructional programs, available for beginners, intermediates, and experts, have a 4:1 student-to-instructor ratio. A support raft goes along on kayak trips, which means that meals incorporate lots of fresh fruits, vegetables, and meats, as well as whole grains. The operation was founded in 1969 and has been going strong ever since, growing by leaps and bounds every year (17921 U.S. 285, Suite F, Nathrop, CO 81236, tel. 719/539–6851 or 800/824–3795, fax 719/539–3378). *See also* River Rafting and Canoeing and Kayaking in Flatwater.

NANTAHALA OUTDOOR CENTER

Founded in 1972 and now employee-owned, this member of America Outdoors and the North American Liveries and Outfitters Association is one of the country's top paddling schools and river runners. Both on trips and in schools, groups are limited to 10 with 2 instructors who are ACA-certified with advanced wilderness first-aid and CPR training and 5 years of experience or more. Boats are modern, since the fleet is replaced every year. NOC instruction programs, which run from March through October and cost from $134 to $147 per day, take place on the Chattooga, French Broad, Little Tennessee, Nantahala, Nolichucky, Ocoee, Oconaluftee, and Tuckaseigee; depending on the course's level and length, you may experience up to 4 of these streams. Specialized instruction programs are available for people with mobility impairments, quick learners, timid learners, women, children, and people on tight budgets, among others. Meals, included in prices for both trips and schools, are hearty; during instruction programs, they're served family-style and dinners may star a salad flecked with edible flowers from the NOC garden. Accommodations are available in NOC's modern-rustic bunkhouse, which has a limited number of shared rooms with shared baths, but there are campgrounds and motels nearby (41 Hwy. 19W, Bryson City, NC 28713, tel. 704/488–6737, fax 704/488–2498).

OTTER BAR KAYAK SCHOOL

Routinely lauded in paddling and outdoor publications for its excellent programs and its remote, pristine location in the Klamath National Forest, Otter Bar offers a tempting combination: the comfort of a good resort, the intimacy of a small inn, with ambitious cuisine, and outstanding whitewater instruction and tripping on a variety of great northern California rivers. Week-long programs are offered at beginning through advanced levels and use a fleet of kayaks that is new every year. The school was founded in 1981 (Box 210C, Forks of Salmon, CA 96031, tel. 916/462–4772).

OUTDOOR CENTRE OF NEW ENGLAND

In 1991, nine years after this central Massachusetts school was established on the Connecticut River, *Paddler* magazine recognized founder Tom Foster as "the godfather of contemporary paddling instruction in the United States." The school is very technically oriented, emphasizing Olympic-style techniques that reflect the latest knowledge about the use of the human body to propel a craft through the water. Typically, students spend as much as 6 hours on just a mile of river, working on eddy turns, peelouts, and other maneuvers, and zooming in and out of waves and across troughs. However, the OCNE staff can also teach you wilderness canoe tripping, freestyle canoeing, downriver kayak or canoe racing, and open-water kayaking. Group workshops and private instruction are available at all ability levels. Staffers are all ACA-certified, not only excellent technical paddlers but also experienced teachers, and the student-to-instructor ratio is a low 3:1. OCNE has its own guest house, which can accommodate up to 18 in private rooms with shared baths, and a dorm-style, air-conditioned lodge (bring your own linen). The all-you-can-eat breakfasts and lunch buffets charge you up for the days to come (10 Pleasant St., Millers Falls, MA 01349, tel. 413/659–3926, fax 413/659–3464).

SUNDANCE KAYAK SCHOOL AND EXPEDITIONS

Instruction and paddling facilities are second to none at this school, founded in 1973 and based on the banks of the Rogue River, in southern Oregon's Siskiyou Mountains. Imagine 5 days of personalized kayak teaching, capped with 4 days of paddling on one of the most spectacular of the United States's Wild and Scenic Rivers. That's the basic beginner's kayak school at Sundance, and it's just one of the school's programs. Other offerings range from 4 or 5 days of intermediate and advanced instruction on Oregon's North Umpqua or Illinois River to multi-day trips on the Middle Fork of Idaho's Salmon River or a run down the Colorado through the Grand Canyon. All instructors have worked at Sundance at least 5 years (8 to 12 years is more usual), a year of that as an apprentice to learn the school's teaching techniques. The Sundance Riverhouse, located on the last piece of privately owned property upstream of the Wild and Scenic section of the Rogue River, has a huge skylighted dining room, an oversized living room, and accommodations in both traditional rooms and more unusual digs—jumbo dome tents set up on carpeted decks and fitted out with beds, chests of drawers, and electricity. The outdoor hot tub is

one focal point of student socializing (14894 Galice Rd., Merlin, OR 97532, tel. 503/479–8505, fax 503/476–6565).

ZOAR OUTDOOR PADDLING SCHOOL

Bruce Lessels, a nationally acclaimed paddler and writer who wrote the Appalachian Mountain Club's definitive *Whitewater Handbook,* is the director of this operation on the shores of the Deerfield River in the northern part of Massachusetts' Berkshires, which offers 1- to 5-day whitewater classes and river trips for all levels of paddlers. All instructors are ACA-certified with 5 to 7 years of paddling experience; they're chosen as much for their ability to communicate their love of the sport as for their ability to handle canoes and kayaks. While there's some classroom work, with video presentations to help instructors make their points, 85% of the time is spent on the water. Equipment is state-of-the-art, with new boats purchased every other year. The variety of programs enables the school to put together courses of students with similar goals and experience and to fine-tune the material covered to suit each group. A river rescue course is among several special-interest programs (Mohawk Trail, Box 245, Charlemont, MA 01339, tel. 800/532–7483 or 413/339–4010, fax 413/337–8436).

FAVORITE SCHOOLS AND TRIPS

THE NORTHEAST

MAINE **Kayak School on the Androscoggin River.** Rising in Maine's Rangeley Lakes and looping into New Hampshire before curling back into southern Maine and the sea, this is one of the few rivers in New England with constant whitewater. From its outpost at Errol, the Northern Waters whitewater school offers beginner and intermediate kayakers both an introduction to the pleasures of whitewater and a sound basis in kayaking fundamentals.

The program begins with a brief talk that familiarizes new paddlers with the jargon of the river as well as with an overview of what they will be learning. Starting on a placid section of the river, paddlers learn how to exit an overturned kayak (it's axiomatic that if you're not pushing your limits, you're not learning, and if you are pushing, you'll take an occasional swim). You also learn to rescue yourself and aid in the rescue of others.

Then it's off down a section of river matched to your level of paddling skills. Under the tutelage of skilled instructors, you'll soon learn to maneuver at will across the current, zip in and out of eddies, and read the currents. Each day you expand on what you learned the preceding one. A strong group, with a good grasp of skills, voyages into spicier water; a group moving more sticks to easier stretches. By the program's conclusion on the fifth day, paddlers know how to roll their boats and comfortably run Class III water. Kayak classes are typically limited to 6 boats. Other programs are available for those who want to work with traditional open canoes; 4 boats are the usual maximum here.

A restaurant and motel are nearby; many paddlers stay at the campsites at the paddling school, which have showers, shops, and a rec hall where you can watch videos on river safety and paddling techniques such as the Eskimo roll. *Northern Waters, Saco Bound, Box 119-C, Center Conway, NH 03813, tel. 603/447–2177. May–early Sept.: 5 days, $390. Price does not include food; sign up 2 months in advance.*

MAINE **Playboating on the Kennebec and Penob.** These two streams, located about 5 hours from Boston and home to some of New England's favorite whitewater, are the destination of this Outdoor Centre of New England trip, one of the few that ventures away from its central Massachusetts base. The Kennebec is known for the spectacular, steepwalled Kennebec Gorge, with its Class III and IV rapids; the West Branch of the Penob, for the awesome 2-mile-long Ripogenus Gorge, where the river descends a stomach-dropping 70 feet per mile over Class V rapids with names like the Exterminator, and the whitewater maze called the Cribworks. It takes a good paddler to handle these waters, and this trip is open to experienced paddlers only. Off the river, you can spot wildlife—moose, osprey, bald eagle, and the like. And you can swim in these rivers, despite the latitude, since they drain from shallow lakes and run warmer than those in some other parts of the country. Leaders are OCNE owner Tom Foster, along with Kel Kelly, a national medalist in women's solo freestyle. The student-to-instructor ratio is 3:1; groups usually have about 6 students. OCNE arranges for group campsites. *Outdoor Centre of New England, 10 Pleasant St., Millers Falls, MA 01349, tel. 413/659–3926, fax 413/659–3464. July: 4 days, $295. Price does not include meals; sign up a month in advance.*

MAINE **Canoeing on the St. John.** The great explorer Samuel de Champlain sailed into the mouth of the St. John on June 24, 1604, the feast day of St. John the Baptist, and from the calendar gave the river its name. If he had been there just a month earlier, he might have noted it as one of the great paddling rivers of the Northeast, for in May, the 128 miles of river from Fourth St. John Pond to what is now the bridge at Dickey offers whitewater canoeing that is unparalleled east of the Mississippi. Then, during high water, many of its rapids and riffles are easier to run, with rocks and ledges deeper under the surface. It's certainly easier to pick your way down a stony stretch without a firm thump to remind you that you miscalculated the depth of a boulder. The river banks display mile after mile of vast timberlands managed for timber and pulp, and you often sight deer, moose, loons, and eagles.

The 8-day canoeing trips run by Maine Sports Outfitters, founded in 1976, are fully outfitted, so all you need to bring are your clothes and personal items. Guides double as instructors on the river and cooks ashore, and in their company you rough it in comfort and with great down-home cooking, often with fish just pulled out of the river. The standard ratio is 6 guests per guide; as often as not this means a pair of guides with a party of 10. *Maine Sports Outfitters, Box 956, Rte. 1, Rockport, ME 04856, tel. 207/236–8797 or, in Maine, tel. 800/244–8799, fax 207/236–7123. May: 8* *days, $795. Sign up at least 1 month in advance.*

MASSACHUSETTS **Learning to Kayak on the Deerfield.** Offering some of southern New England's easiest yet most rewarding paddling, the northern Massachusetts sections of this stream are a good bet for beginners. Zoar Outdoor Paddling School kayak classes put in on one of the Class I sections, near the towns of Charlemont and Florida, and gradually move into Class II water as paddlers become more confident. Both a beginner and an intermediate program are offered, each available in 2- and 3-day sessions. For more aggressive paddlers, or quick learners who start with some skills, the second or third day out may be in Class III waters. All classes start at 8 in the morning and last an entire day—take-out is at 5!

Classes are also available for those who want to paddle traditional open canoes. Camping facilities and a number of motels and bed and breakfasts are nearby. *Zoar Outdoor Paddling School, Mohawk Trail, Box 245, Charlemont, MA 01339, tel. 413/339–4010, or 800/532–7483, fax 413/337–8436. Apr.–early Sept.: 2–3 days, $160–$235. Sign up a month in advance.*

MASSACHUSETTS **Paddling Workshop in the Berkshire Foothills.** Even drought years don't cancel workshops run by the Outdoor Centre of New England, since the primary teaching rivers—the Ashuelot, West, Millers, and Deerfield, ranging from Class I to Class IV—are downstream from dams that release water regularly and keep the paddling lively. The 4- and 5-day workshops for beginners and intermediates are a terrific introduction to the world of paddlesports. A good variety of craft is available, with something for every body type, and the enthusiasm of the staff, who live and breathe paddling, is infectious. The first day begins early with gear checkout, and, after an orientation, a trip to a calm-water practice site, where the group is divided by ability levels. Subsequent instruction, which runs from early morning until 5 every day with a break for lunch, addresses appropriate paddling points—effective upper and lower body

movement, boat leans, self-rescue, and more. The point is to help you become an efficient paddler. A variety of shorter workshops is also available, including beginner–intermediate workshops for those over 50, for women, and for those who want to earn an ACA instructor certification. The student-to-instructor ratio is usually 3:1. *Outdoor Centre of New England, 10 Pleasant St., Millers Falls, MA 01349, tel. 413/659–3926, fax 413/659–3464. July–Aug.: 4 days, $189; 5 days, $329. Price includes instruction, boat, meals, and accommodations; sign up a month in advance.*

THE MID ATLANTIC

PENNSYLVANIA **Playing Around on the Youghiogheny.** Just because you can spell it or pronounce it (a hint: *yock-a-GAIN-nee*) doesn't mean you can paddle it. While the Middle Yough is on the mellow side, the Lower is definitely spicy: The 7-mile stretch from the village of Ohiopyle, Pennsylvania, down to Stewarton has hosted 2 Open Canoe National Championships as well as a host of other competitive events, and the swirling, bouncing watercourse lives up to its reputation as one of the Northeast's premiere whitewater playgrounds. But the Youghiogheny is within your grasp with a little careful coaching, a bit of tutelage on rolling, technique, and the opportunity to follow an expert from Riverport School of Paddling in Confluence, Pennsylvania.

First item on the agenda is a trip to a nearby lake, where paddlers learn, relearn, or hone Eskimo-rolling skills. After lunch, it's off to the Yough to put your skills to work on moving water—the destination varies with the strength and goals of the class. The Yough is dam-controlled, with regular releases, so there's plenty of whitewater throughout the year. Summer and fall are the most popular times.

Interested in paddling solo-decked canoes or open canoes? Or slalom racing or squirt-boating, the river equivalent to freestyle mogul skiing? Have a yen to learn more about river and boating safety? Want to instruct? Special-interest clinics are a regular feature at Riversport. Maximum class size is 6 per instructor, and as often as not the number is more like 4 or 5. *Riversport School of Paddling, Box 95, 213 Yough St., Confluence, PA 15424, tel. 814/395–5744. Mar.–Oct.: 1–3 days, $95–$250; 4 days, $325; 5 days, $395. Price includes 3 meals a day and camping; sign up a month in advance.*

WEST VIRGINIA **Kayak School on the New.** This river's name is a misnomer—on a geologic scale it's possibly the oldest river on the continent and perhaps one of the oldest in the world. But age doesn't signify that it's in danger of wearing out. Rising in the Blue Ridge Mountains in North Carolina, it is a fierce whitewater playground as it traverses Virginia, backing off to a Class I with a touch of Class II as it penetrates into West Virginia. And it is in West Virginia that the playground becomes a schoolground for neophyte kayakers.

Novice paddlers in North American River Runners's 4-day kayak school start out upside down in Summersville Lake, 40 minutes north of the New. It's not an exercise in humility, but a confidence builder, graphically illustrating just how easy it is to slip out from under a capsized craft. With no more than 5 paddlers around an instructor (and often fewer than that), everyone gets the personal help needed to give them mobility in the boat as well as confidence to push further.

Once the group has the basics down, paddlers and equipment are shuttled to the New. For most groups, the first section of river is basically Class I water, with a few patches of Class II splash. That afternoon and on subsequent days, instructors show their flocks the mysteries of eddies, how to read the water to pick out a clear channel, and the techniques of ferrying from one side of the river to the other without being carried away by the current. As the class becomes comfortable on one stretch of river, the instructor gradually adds challenges.

The incredible variety of the New River offers a full curriculum of river kayaking, with sheltered areas coddling the rank novice and spicy drops tickling the fancy of more advanced

students. The group's strengths and goals determine what sections you run. Camping facilities are available at the school and motels and bed and breakfasts are nearby. *North American River Runners, U.S. Rte. 60, Box 81, Hico, WV 25854, tel. 304/658–5276 or 800/950–2585, fax 304/658–4212. May–Sept.: $85 per day. Sign up 1–2 weeks in advance.*

THE SOUTH

NORTH CAROLINA **Kayaking Classes on the Little Tennessee.** Like most kayaking programs, the Nantahala Outdoor Center's 7-day intensive river kayaking course starts on placid water—in this case, the warm waters of Lake Fontana. The half- to full-day session, depending on group skills and needs, covers basic strokes and acquaints paddlers with how strokes work and link together to control and move a kayak. Everyone is going to turn over, both to learn how to slip out under a capsized craft and to roll up and continue paddling without the inconvenience of a swim.

Then it's off to the river! During most sessions, the first river to toss a few drops into your face is the Little Tennessee, one of the jewels of the Great Smoky Mountains. Relax for a minute on this Class I stream and look up at the mountains. In spring the banks explode with the colors of blossoming rhododendrons and laurel. The possibility of wildlife lurks around every bend, even though the rivers selected for beginner programs don't descend through wilderness. (Virtually every beginner river over the week has a road winding alongside. In the rare event of a mishap, it's easy to get off the river.)

Don't think this class is just a tranquil drift. Under the watchful eyes of the instructors, group skills are constantly assessed and new adventures planned. Strokes quickly become second nature. Paddlers learn route-finding both by listening to instructors and by following them from eddy to eddy, from wave to tongue of water. Then you move from the gentle Little Tennessee to the bouncy Nantahala, with its outstanding play spots and popular slalom race sites. Crowning the program, for the vast majority of the intensive classes, are runs on the Ocoee River, site of whitewater slalom races for the 1996 Summer Games in Atlanta. While that particular course is not readily accessible (or, for that matter, really within the skills of most fresh-out-of-the-box paddlers), it still offers a chance to claim, truthfully, that you paddled the river the gold medal contenders slalomed. Lodging is in the modern-rustic NOC lodge. *Nantahala Outdoor Center, 41 Hwy. 19W, Bryson City, NC 28713, tel. 704/ 488–6737, fax 704/488–2498. Mar.–Oct.: 7-day intensive course, $915. Price includes NOC lodging and all meals; sign up 1–2 months in advance.*

THE SOUTHWEST

TEXAS **Learning to Kayak on the Rio Grande.** If you're an intermediate or advanced kayaker, the Rio Grande's 90-mile-long Lower Canyons and Regan Canyon section is the place to come in spring to hone your skills for the whitewater season ahead. Bill and Jaci Dvořák run laid-back 7-day instructional seminars here from mid-March through late April, when the desert is blanketed in spring blooms, daytime temperatures range between 70°F and 90°F, and river water is a comfortable 60°F to 70°F.

Starting at La Linda, Mexico, the river's course winds through the lonely, silent chasms, rocky flats, and desert mountains along the Texas–Mexico border. There are some quiet stretches, but you'll bounce through some good rapids as well. After a few hours on the river each day, you'll have plenty of time to hike up the side canyons to explore local landmarks ranging from old homesteads to the mysterious Candelilla ruins. The trip is among the company's most popular for beginners and intermediates, suitable for anyone who has never been in a canoe or kayak before. Starting with the basics of kayak design and how to choose a paddle and a personal flotation device and helmet, you cover types of paddling, carrying methods, water safety and different self-rescue methods, and whitewa-

ter safety techniques such as how to swim in whitewater with and without your boat. *Dvořák Kayak and Rafting Expeditions, 17921-B U.S. Hwy. 285, Nathrop, CO 81236, tel. 719/539–6851 or 800/824–3795, fax 719/ 539–3378. Mid-Mar.–late Apr.: 7 days, $925. Sign up 1–2 months in advance.*

THE ROCKIES

IDAHO **Running Salmon River Whitewater.** Born high in the snowy Sawtooth Mountains of Idaho, the Salmon River today is one of the most sought-after whitewater runs in the entire United States. One of the very first rivers to be protected under the federal government's Wild and Scenic Rivers Act, its 200 miles of fabulous whitewater, ranging from a laid-back Class II to a spray-in-your-face Class V, is one of the longest stretches of unspoiled river remaining on the continent. American explorers Lewis and Clark saw the rapids in the 19th century (and, having seen the waters' fearsome power, continued their epic journey on foot); but people have lived in the area for at least 8,000 years, and when you venture into the wilderness back from the river, you may discover petroglyphs and ancient tools as well as signs of more recent habitation. You'll also discover prime fishing: This is the spawning ground for chinook salmon and Dolly Varden, rainbow, and cutthroat trout— these last known as redsides among locals.

Flowing as clear as the snows from which it springs, the Middle Fork of the Salmon cascades from the confluence of Marsh and Bear creeks and runs for about 125 miles through the rocky canyons and dense woodlands of the River of No Return Wilderness area of the Salmon National Forest to join the Main Salmon. The smooth flow of the river is broken by Class IV–V Velvet Falls, Redsides, and Rubber.

The thrills don't let up once you paddle out into the Main Salmon. From there down to Vinegar Creek—90 miles—there are 65 named rapids up to Class V. And yet, with raft support and 6 guides accompanying each party of no more than 24 people, it is a safe and practical trip for paddlers familiar with big whitewater. You run through the second-deepest gorge in North America on your passage through the mountains (the deepest is Hells Canyon on the Snake River, with the torrents from the Salmon flowing into the Snake and helping it in its massive excavation). The scenery is truly spectacular.

Mackay Bar–Wilderness River Trips' kayak runs offer you a choice of 6 days on the Middle Fork, 6 days on the Main, or 12 days on both. You paddle a vigorous 10 to 15 miles a day, soak away tired muscles in one of the many natural hot springs that line the river, cast a lure out in the peace of the evening as the guides clean up from a dinner of prime rib cooked in a Dutch oven, fresh vegetables, and just-made desserts—there is an informal but very real competition among the guides on this river as to who can put together the best menu and meal.

Guests fly via bush plane from Boise to put-in and back to Boise from take-out when the adventure is over. Guides carefully screen guests who want to kayak; if you lack whitewater paddling skills, you can go along for the ride in the support rafts.

When's the best time to paddle the river? Depending on the weather, the river opens in early May. Melt off from mid-May and into June sends flows soaring, and the river becomes a fierce torrent. Weather in July and August is normally the best, and the river is clear and spunky. Declining flows can reduce the rapids in September. *Mackay Bar–Wilderness River Trips, 3190 Airport Way, Boise, ID 83705, tel. 800/635–5336 or 208/344–1881, fax 208/344–1882. May–Oct.: 6 days on the Middle Fork, $1,165; 6 days on the Main Salmon, $995; 12 days on both, $1,850. Price includes sleeping bags; sign up 4–6 months in advance.*

THE WEST COAST

OREGON **A Learning Trip down the Rogue.** Some rivers achieve a mythic existence, a perceived reality above and beyond the water,

the channels, and the drops. Even their names become legends, and their rapids become catchphrases in the lexicon of river paddlers. Right at the top of this list are the 40 sparkling miles of Oregon's Rogue that have been designated a Wild and Scenic River, which burst from Oregon's warm interior and flow out to the cool, breezy Pacific shoreline. This stretch is so popular that access to the river is by permit only, and long lines form each year as individuals, clubs, and commercial operations vie for the few open slots.

One of the best ways to experience the Rogue is on Sundance Kayak School and Expedition's 9-day combination instruction program–river trip, available for both beginners and more advanced paddlers. The standard beginner's program kicks off with 5 days of top-level kayaking instruction near Sundance's own riverfront lodge near the town of Galice. Neophytes learn basic kayak strokes and braces, the fundamentals of the Eskimo roll, and how to exit from an overturned boat and choose a route through currents and rapids. Such basic techniques as entering and leaving eddies and ferrying across a current become second nature in the warm, quickwater sections of the upper Rogue. By the fifth day, virtually everyone is fairly proficient in their kayaks, and certainly capable of taking on the Class III whitewater waiting in the designated Wild and Scenic sections of the Rogue, 4 miles downstream of the Sundance Riverhouse.

Graduation is definitely the icing on this vacation cake. Up to a dozen students, accompanied by 4 instructors and a pair of raft guides, set off down the Rogue. Days are spent playing in the river, riding waves like a surfboarder in the ocean while instructors glide among the covey of neophytes, offering bits of advice and words of encouragement. Nights are spent camped on the riverbanks under a canopy of unbelievably bright stars. Meals are definitely on the gourmet end of the scale, with a tilt toward the healthful.

If your time is short, you can skip the Rogue run and sign up simply for the 5 days of instruction. *Sundance Kayak School and Expeditions, 14894 Galice Rd., Merlin, OR*

*97532, tel. 503/479–8508, fax 503/476–6565.
Mid-May–mid-Sept.: 9 days (including 5 days
of lodge-based kayaking instruction and a 4-
day raft-supported trip), $1,305; 5 days of
instruction only, $725. Price of all programs
includes lodging during instructional section
of program and all meals; sign up a month in
advance.*

SOURCES

ORGANIZATIONS Setting standards for the
outfitters and guides are several organizations:
America Outdoors (Box 1348, Knoxville, TN
37901, tel. 615/524–4814), the association for
national river guides; the **American Canoe
Association** (8550 Cinderbed Rd., Suite 1900,
Box 1190, Newington, VA 22122-1190, tel.
703/451–0140), which publishes the "American Canoeist" newsletter; and the **National
Association of Canoe Liveries and Outfitters**
(Rte. 27 and Catro Rte. 2, Box 2119, Butler,
KY 41006, tel. 606/654–4111). For lists of paddling clubs, the backbone of paddling sports
today, contact *Canoe Magazine* (tel. 800/
MY–CANOE) or the American Canoe Association.

PERIODICALS *Canoe Magazine* (Box 3146,
Kirkland, WA 98083, tel. 800/MY–CANOE),
the leading paddle sports magazine in North
America, focuses on both flatwater and whitewater canoeing and kayaking, rivers and lakes.
It covers both international and North
American canoeing and kayaking destinations and offers a look into the nooks and cran-
nies of local paddle-sports trips. Regular
columns offer tips and techniques for all levels of paddling. Each bimonthly issue includes
sections listing paddling schools and major
outfitters. The quarterly *Paddler* (Box 775450,
Steamboat Springs, CO 80477, tel. 303/879–
1450) covers a broad spectrum of both major
and easily accessible canoe and kayak trips,
and includes product reviews and pieces on
paddling skills and techniques.

BOOKS *Canoeing & Rafting: The Complete
Where-to-go Guide to America's Best Tame
and Wild Waters,* by Sara Pyle, is a valuable
state-by-state compendium of canoe and
kayak routes, with notes on degree of difficulty and the best time to paddle; the information on equipment rentals is a little dated.
The ultimate reference guide for river running nationwide, *The Complete Whitewater
Sourcebook,* by the Boat People (tel. 408/258–
7971), lists phone numbers, water levels,
regional guidebooks, access points, and permit requirements; the book is a must if you're
planning a trip of your own and a reliable
source for names of outfitters. *Whitewater
Canoeing,* by William Sandreuter, reflects the
author's 35 years of whitewater canoeing.
While he protests that he is attempting to por-
tray the canoe as a "stately lady," he does
describe her as a craft ready and willing for
the thrill and enjoyment of moving water.

ALSO SEE If you love the north woods, look
over Canoeing and Kayaking in Flatwater. If
it's the spray in your face that draws you,
check out River Rafting.

Caving

by Naomi Black

C aving, or spelunking, as it is also called, is not for everyone. It's a dark, dirty, often cold and wet excursion into a fragile, hostile environment. Spelunkers would not even call it a sport. They consider it a science, with rules originated and safeguarded by a small community of serious cavers who will ostracize anyone who caves recklessly. And for good reason: Caving is dangerous. People die or injure themselves in caves every year.

Why do they do it? Because when you're caving, spelunkers say, you enter into a world apart, a dimly lit world of primitive beauty— not at all like the fully illuminated "show caves" most tourists see. In wild caves, you have to look hard for spectacular speleothems (mineral formations), and their subtle colors seem dull compared to their show-cave counterparts. But beyond the geology—and the biology and the history—of the caves lies the excitement of the experience: the adventure of coming to terms with the dark, the cold, the pervasive damp, and your latent claustrophobia.

Caves are not the place for thrill-seekers. Getting around on muddy, uneven ground is slow and slippery; duck walks and belly crawls are common. It's vital to be in good shape; walking a half mile in a squat can be murder on the thigh muscles. If you suffer from a fear of heights or dark water, think again about spelunking. Some of the most interesting caves require technical climbing skills involving equipment, or wading through midriff-high cold water.

No one in his right mind goes caving alone, and anyone who wants to try the sport should get in touch with the National Speleological Society (NSS), which has about 10,000 members (*see* Sources, *below*). This is the organization to join for information on recreational caving, and joining it is, without question, the best way to get started. You can also take a short course in speleology at Western Kentucky University (*see* Favorite Courses, *below*). The NSS, which owns the rights of entrance to many caves, sponsors regional "grottoes," or local chapters. An individual can become a member of a grotto without joining the NSS, but membership facilitates entree to other grottoes throughout the country.

Grotto members are loath to reveal the whereabouts of caves to outsiders, so joining a grotto is virtually the only way to learn about interesting local caves and join group excursions led by members to distant caves. Most caving trips involve a single day or weekend, but many grottoes plan at least one week-long excursion a year, with car-pool transportation. There are also professional guides, but the practice of leading people on caving expeditions for pay is a controversial issue. The NSS and most spelunkers in the grottoes look down on these guides, so commercial trips have not been covered in this chapter.

New York City–based Naomi Black writes frequently about the outdoors. A member of the National Speleological Society, she has caved in the Northeast and in California.

Through the NSS and its grottoes, novices can learn the basics of cave safety and etiquette from experienced members and are able to join not only grotto trips but also other programs led by members. The personality of the grottoes differs from one to the next, and their activities vary from region to region. Typically, however, a grotto publishes a newsletter, offers practice sessions for such skills as knot tying and vertical ascents and descents, gives classes for first-aid certification and rescue training, and organizes cleanups of local caves in addition to scheduling trips for members of all abilities. Grotto activities are normally free or provided at cost to members (whose annual dues are usually under $25).

Underground formations have survived for hundreds if not millions of years, but a single fingerprint can stop the growth of a stalactite or turn it black. Cavers are, therefore, understandably concerned about educating anyone who wants to explore underground. A good leader will insure that you learn conservation, as well as proper technique and the history and geology of the caves.

The time it takes to traverse a cave always varies, depending on the pace of the slowest person and on the activities planned inside (exploring side tunnels, practicing skills, etc.). Even a fairly short beginners' cave takes half a day to get through. That allows for exploration time down small tunnels or up craggy passageways. Leaders also make time for rest and for "black-out" periods when cavers stay still, stop talking, and turn out their lights.

There are wet caves where stalactites and stalagmites grow, like stone icicles and obelisks—made of minerals deposited by the slow drip of water. There are dry caves and mazelike horizontal caves where no climbing is necessary, and three levels might cross over one another in a 3-D network of tunnels; and there are up-and-down caves where vertical drops might be as high as 300 feet. You can expect to see speleothems of all sorts—mineral formations, mostly crystalline, in various shapes: There are gypsum crystals, blood-red gypsum flowers, and selenite needles, as well as stalactites and stalagmites and hefty

columns where the two meet. You might encounter manganese oxide lining some caves, a sticky black goo that's impossible to wash out of clothes. (Don't worry: You wear coveralls.) Honeycomb formations of calcite cover ceilings; huge calcite crystals coat walls, like alligator skin 11 inches thick.

In addition to the richly decorated limestone caves like Carlsbad and Mammoth that are found in many states, there are sandstone cliff dwellings and rare gypsum caves in arid areas of the Southwest, littoral (or sea) caves on the coasts, lava tubes in Hawaii and California, and caves made from fallen boulders and debris. Once you have some experience, you'll be able to enjoy the variety of caves this country has to offer. Grottoes often welcome visiting groups or individual NSS members from other states.

CHOOSING THE RIGHT TRIP

At the beginning, don't be particular about where you go underground. Wherever your grotto is headed, just go. Any cave should make you happy. But choosing to cave with a group or guide who is safety-oriented and aware of cave etiquette can make the difference between a successful trip that's fun and a potentially dangerous or uncomfortable trip. For that reason, you should ask the following questions before going.

Has the leader arranged to give the group's exact whereabouts and anticipated time of departure from the cave to a responsible person aboveground? It's a customary precaution to leave word of a group's location and estimated time of return; in the event of a serious delay, someone will come after you.

Is there an orientation covering etiquette and conservation for this particular trip? The trip will be most rewarding if you are briefed beforehand on the geology of the cave, its biology (will you see bats, small animals, fish?) and what is necessary to protect its ecology.

Does the leader have permission from the landowner to enter the cave? The NSS frowns on groups entering private caves without permission. Sometimes a landowner will give blanket permission to one grotto, but one only; sometimes the owner might close a cave if someone has been injured or if cavers have been careless with human waste or trash (a pee bottle and plastic bags are indispensable accessories on lengthy or overnight cave trips).

Is the leader bringing a carbide, electric, or miner's lamp as a primary light source? Each person brings three light sources on a caving trip: one (or two) attached to the helmet, one in hand, and sometimes a spare. Flashlights are not good enough for a leader, who needs a brighter, more reliable source of light to lead the way and examine speleothems close-up.

Does someone in the group have first-aid training? Rescue training? Will you bring a first-aid kit? Can you rig up a heat tent for emergencies? If the leader of the group has not had first-aid training, make sure another group member has. An emergency first-aid kit is de rigueur, as is a tented enclosure to be used, in case of injury, to prevent hypothermia.

What conditions can I expect? Temperatures in caves hardly fluctuate at all. In the Northeast they typically range from about 50°F to 56°F; in central California, 55°F to 58°F; and in Oregon, as low as 42°F. Caves can be running with water and covered with mud, and there are some crystalline caverns that are nothing but ice, and therefore much colder. The temperature is 55°F in Mammoth Cave, 56°F in Carlsbad.

FAVORITE COURSES

THE SOUTH

KENTUCKY **Basic Speleology.** This 7-day course at Western Kentucky University, taught by spelunker and author (*The Longest Cave*) Roger Brucker, investigates the basics of cave science, delving into geology, biology, chemistry, hydrology, and ecology. The building blocks taught here help cavers discover new passageways wherever they are and teach

beginners to appreciate just how fragile an environment a cave is. At least 60% of course time is spent in the Mammoth Cave system, much of it in undeveloped areas. The caving is rigorous, so students must be fit.

As in the Exploration of Mammoth Cave course, *below,* students are responsible for their own meals and lodging (although the school will help coordinate camping and bunkhouse reservations) and for transport to Nashville, Tennessee. This course can also be taken for credit, at additional cost. *Basic Speleology, c/o Dr. Nick Crawford or Dr. Chris Groves, Center for Cave and Karst Studies, Department of Geography and Geology, Western Kentucky University, Bowling Green, KY 42101, tel. 502/745–4555. June: 7 days, $291. Price includes rental of lights but not room and board. Sign up 2–3 months in advance.*

KENTUCKY **Exploration of Mammoth Cave.** Students in this week-long course, given by Western Kentucky University, study the longest cave system in the world, and the history of its exploration, mining, and commercialization. The passageways at Mammoth cover nearly 330 mapped miles beneath the 52,700 acres of Mammoth Cave National Park. Although it's not as decorative as Carlsbad and other show caves, Mammoth does reveal beautiful rust-colored speleothems, among them classic stalactites and stalagmites, translucent ribbons running along the ceiling, flowstone, draperies, and formations nicknamed Frozen Niagara, Moonlight Dome, and Crystal Lake.

Trips to Mammoth follow tourist trails within the cave (now closed to the public) and historic connecting routes. The class decides which route to take. All students must be in excellent physical condition.

Most activities not in the cave—lectures, meals, and food preparation—take place at Maple Springs Research Center in the Park. Participants make their breakfasts and bag lunches in the big kitchen-and-meeting-room building and then convene around 8 or 9 in the morning to go to the cave. There's an hour or two before each evening's lecture when students can prepare their dinner, take a walk, or just relax.

Lodging is not included but can be arranged, in simple dormitory-style single-sex rooms in the bunkhouse with shared baths and hot showers, or at campsites within 100 yards of the buildings. Camping is free, and the bunkhouse costs $2 a night. Students are responsible for getting there and for their own food. You fly into Nashville, Tennessee; from there on, all transportation is provided by the school. Vans will pick you up at the airport, take you to go grocery shopping, and shuttle you to the cave and back. The course can be taken for credit for an additional fee. *Exploration of Mammoth Cave, c/o Dr. Nick Crawford or Dr. Chris Groves, Center for Cave and Karst Studies, Department of Geography and Geology, Western Kentucky University, Bowling Green, KY 42101, tel. 502/745–4555. June: 7 days, $291. Price includes light rental but not room and board. Sign up 2–3 months in advance.*

SOURCES

ORGANIZATIONS The **American Cave Conservation Association, Inc.** (Box 409, Horse Cave, KY 42749, tel. 502/786–1466) is a national, nonprofit organization founded in 1977 for the purpose of protecting caves, karstlands, and groundwater. It is responsible for the planning and development of the American Cave and Karst Center & Museum in Horse Cave, Kentucky. Membership costs $25 ($15 for students) and includes a year's subscription to *American Caves* magazine.

The **National Speleological Society** (Cave Ave., Huntsville, AL 35810, tel. 205/852–1300), affiliated with the American Association for the Advancement of Science, was founded in 1941. Membership (ages 17 and over) costs $25 and includes a year's subscription to two publications. The **National Caves Association** (Rte. 9, Box 106, McMinnville, TN 37110, tel. 615/668–3925) produces

a brochure that identifies 84 tourist caves in 21 states and Puerto Rico. Some have adventure tours to caves that require scrambling. The nonprofit educational **National Outdoor Leadership School** (288 Main St., Lander, WY 82520–0579, tel. 307/332–6973; *see* Climbing and Mountaineering) teaches such caving skills as route-finding, passage-memorizing, rope work, technical climbing, first aid, and rescue.

PERIODICALS *American Caves* (Box 409, Horse Cave, KY 42749, tel. 502/786–1466), published three or four times a year by the American Cave Conservation Association, covers subjects of interest, archaeological and otherwise, to both academic and recreational spelunkers. *NSS Bulletin,* published semiannually by the NSS (*see* Organizations, *above*) is a scholarly journal with technical articles on speleology. *NSS News,* published monthly, prints articles on recreational caving and provides a forum for such controversial issues as caving for pay.

BOOKS The following are available through Speleobooks (Box 10, Schoharie, NY 12157): *Caving Basics,* by Tom Rea for the NSS; *Adventure of Caving: A Practical Guide for Advanced and Beginning Cavers,* by David McClurg; *American Caves and Caving: Techniques, Pleasures, and Safeguards of Modern Cave Exploration,* by William R. Halliday, MD; *The Longest Cave,* by Roger W. Brucker and Richard A. Watson; *Speleology: The Study of Caves,* by George W. Moore and G. Nicholas Sullivan; *Karst Hydrology: Concepts from the Mammoth Cave Area,* by William B. White and Elizabeth L. White.

ALSO SEE The chapter in this book on Climbing and Mountaineering contains information on programs that can teach you skills you need in some caves, while the Wilderness and Survival Schools chapter covers a couple of programs that include cave exploration among their activities.

Climbing and Mountaineering

by Peter Potterfield

 You don't have to be among the fortunate few to experience the many pleasures of climbing: the satisfying bite of the ice axe as you crampon across a steep glacier beneath towering peaks; the solidity of a smooth rock face as you reach for a hold on its warm granite, adrenaline pumping, confidence high; or the tranquillity you feel when you're deep in the wilderness en route to a remote alpine peak or standing atop a high, quiet summit on a clear summer day.

By taking a course or two on basic rock climbing or mountaineering at any of a dozen quality climbing schools all over the country, almost anyone who is moderately fit can experience the excitement of this sport. For everyone from novices to those whose skills are modest or just rusty, these schools offer a safe way to enjoy different kinds of climbing. In just a couple of days, they can have a beginner climbing pretty well or put a climber of medium abilities on harder routes. These schools offer a range of experiences, from a few days of rock climbing instruction at California's Yosemite or on New York's Shawangunk Cliffs to week-long alpine programs that include ascents of major peaks such as Mount Rainier or month-long attempts on Alaska's Mount McKinley.

Each climbing course concentrates on a different facet of the sport; some address sever-

al. *Rock climbing* can be done in almost all parts of the country, not necessarily in the mountains; many towns and cities have cliffs, quarries, crags, or even indoor climbing walls where beginners can learn and experts can practice. It's an activity that you can pursue after work or on weekends, since you have to travel only as far as the nearest steep rocky surface to be able to do it. When you take a rock climbing course, you learn to recognize hand- and footholds in rocks that may appear quite smooth, and to use these holds to ascend rock faces of anywhere from 20 to 3,000 feet. Many of the skills you acquire in a basic rock climbing course are used in other forms of climbing, including ice climbing and mountaineering. *Ice climbing* involves climbing frozen waterfalls, traveling on glaciers, or ascending steep slopes covered with snow or ice, using special equipment (and additional skills). Snow and ice techniques are a must in Alaska and the higher elevations of the Rockies, the Cascades, and the Sierra. Few beginners start out learning to handle ice; it's a skill that climbers acquire as they gain experience. *Mountaineering* involves traveling on foot to a summit in mountainous terrain, heading into the alpine zone, the area near and above timberline. This may require skills in both rock and ice climbing, so thorough mountaineering courses will cover the basics along with other skills you need to spend extended time in the wilderness. The wilderness

The author of Selected Climbs in the Cascades *and* Chimney Rock, *Seattle-based Peter Potterfield has climbed from Alaska and the Sierra to Nepal. He is the editor of* Pacific Northwest Magazine *and contributes regularly to* Condé Nast Traveler *and* Outside *magazine.*

experience is one of the rewards of moun-taineering—but to get it, you must live near the mountains or travel to them and commit to a block of time.

To choose among America's hundreds of climbing programs, it is best to decide what you want to learn and where you want to learn it. Do you want to stay close to home or trav-el to an area you've always wanted to visit? No two climbing areas are quite alike. The landscape is different, and—more to the point for rock climbers—the terrain is different. In some areas you may have to contend with dif-ficult weather conditions, while others are reg-ularly warm and sunny. The quality of the rock also varies from one rock climbing area to another, requiring you to master different skills. Where you find cliffs of fractured or broken rock, you acquire a whole repertoire of ways to grasp the protrusions. Where the local rock is smoother, you may learn crack techniques, different approaches to sticking your hands and feet into cracks in the rock; or you may concentrate on friction climbing, which involves using your weight and bal-ance to ascend a smooth rock face without holds. Basic skills such as rappelling and belaying are standard elements of the cur-riculum in most locations.

Most U.S. climbing schools operate pretty much in their home region, although some offer courses around the country and a few travel worldwide. Many operate year-round, changing their location with the season and their curriculum with the location. You usu-ally overnight in local motels and camp-grounds and eat meals in local restaurants, except when courses are held partially or entirely in the backcountry; then you camp out or spend the night in a high-country guide hut. Tuition ranges all the way from $50 to $150 per day, with the average course cost-ing about $110 per day.

CHOOSING THE RIGHT COURSE

While there are a lot of questionable opera-tions in the mountain-guiding game, most climbing schools are run by competent

climbers and guides. However, you can't be too careful, since you could be injured or even killed while learning to climb. The schools and courses we list are all quality operations, but they are not the only good ones. Asking a few key questions will help you find the school that's right for you, although you won't know everything you want to about the par-ticular guide or instructor to whom you're assigned until you're actually out on those rocks.

Is the school accredited by the American Mountain Guides Association? It's not nec-essarily a bad sign if it isn't, since accredita-tion is a relatively new function for this or-ganization, which is dedicated to developing and maintaining high standards of mountain guiding and climbing instruction (*see* Sources, *below*). However, AMGA accreditation does assure you that the school's safety practices are appropriate for its activities. If the school you're interested in is not accredited, ask about the safety record.

How long has the school been in business? Longevity provides some assurance that it's not a fly-by-night operation.

What are the instructors' qualifications? If you're serious about acquiring climbing skills, go for a program whose instructors are expe-rienced teachers as well as experienced climbers. If you're told where the instructors have climbed, don't be impressed before you ask: "But can they teach?" If all you want is a taste of the sport, you may prefer to hang out with a hotshot climber who can regale you with sagas of climbs in the Himalayas and other exotic locales.

What's the cost and what's included? Unless otherwise noted, your fee for courses listed below includes instruction, transportation between course venues, and any necessary technical climbing equipment (such as ropes, helmets, harnesses, and the like), but not meals, accommodations in motels or camp-grounds, sleeping bags and pads, tents, camp stoves, and personal gear such as backpacks.

Be sure to ask whether the outfitter provides special rock shoes, crampons, ice axes, and double plastic boots (climbers' standard footwear, resembling ski boots, in snow and ice environments); there is considerable variance from one operation to the next. (When the necessary equipment is not included, outfitters may provide it on a rental basis.) Also find out whether your bunk and food while lodging in guide huts or backcountry lodges is included.

What are food and accommodations like? When you attend most courses, you lodge and dine in establishments available in the mountain town nearest the course venue. Often, motels are simple and restaurant offerings basic—but exceptions exist. On backcountry trips, ask about the menu.

What experience is required for the course? For beginner courses—and all those described below, unless otherwise noted—no previous climbing experience is required, but you should be at least moderately fit. As one wise man observed, climbing would be great, a truly wonderful thing, if it weren't for all that damn climbing. Moreover, once you're in school, it quickly becomes obvious if you're out of shape—and that can be embarrassing.

What is the school's stated purpose or philosophy? Some schools emphasize minimum impact wilderness travel, others teach you to climb using lightweight gear, still others concentrate on pragmatic outdoor skills.

Can you supply references from past students? Call a few. Ask how they liked their instructors, and make sure that the program seemed competently run.

How far in advance do I Need to book? Every school has different sign-up dates, ranging from 2 weeks to 6 months before the course begins.

MAJOR PLAYERS

ALPINE SKILLS INTERNATIONAL For most climbing schools, speed isn't a high priority and the weight of the equipment used isn't a major concern. This AMGA-accredited operation, established in 1979 with a distinctly European flair, is different, teaching a unique style of climbing that empasizes going fast and light. If you're a purist in other endeavors and fit enough to handle the extra challenges that this climbing style demands, go for it. The school offers a full range of mountain experiences year-round, including rock climbing, ice climbing, and mountaineering courses. It's also a good place to see the latest in climbing clothes (Box 8, Norden, CA 95724, tel. 916/426–9108, fax 916/426–3063).

AMERICAN ALPINE INSTITUTE *Outside* magazine called this AMGA-accredited organization, founded in 1975, the best all-around climbing school and guide service in the country. Certainly, the AAI is one of the biggest, offering a variety of rock climbing, alpine mountaineering, and guided ascents in North America, Asia, Europe, and South America; courses in the United States are in Alaska and on its home turf in the North Cascades (1515 12th St., Bellingham, WA 98225, tel. 206/671–1505).

EASTERN MOUNTAIN SPORTS CLIMBING SCHOOL The oldest professional climbing school in the eastern United States, this one was founded in 1968 under the aegis of the Eastern Mountain Sports retail operation. The school's varied courses take place in several eastern locations year-round (at press time, western locations are being considered); guided climbs and programs for women and adolescents are also available. It's accredited by the AMGA (Box 514, North Conway, NH 03860, tel. 603/356–5433, fax 603/356–9469).

EXUM MOUNTAIN GUIDES It was 1931 when Glen Exum made the first ascent of the ridge in Wyoming's Grand Tetons that now bears his name. In the same year, he founded this guide service, now one of the oldest in the United States. Exum guides are the only ones authorized to guide climbs of all routes and all peaks within Grand Teton National Park. They also offer instruction in rock climbing and mountaineering, snow and ice climbing, and winter mountaineering as well as a range of guided climbs (Box 56, Moose, WY 83012, tel. 307/733–2297).

NATIONAL OUTDOOR LEADERSHIP SCHOOL

This private nonprofit operation founded in 1965 is not a climbing school as such. Its courses impart a wide range of outdoor skills and safety practices, with a strong emphasis on minimum-impact wilderness travel; in a NOLS course, you learn climbing as you learn a lot of other things, including general outdoor skills, teamwork, and safety practices. In teaching these topics, NOLS is one of the most respected organizations in its field, enrolling some 2,000 students every year in its huge array of courses staged from the Rockies to the Sierra Nevada, the Cascades, and Alaska. Though most courses last from 2 weeks to 3 months and many are for teens, there is a good selection of shorter courses geared specifically toward adults, and all NOLS climbing and mountaineering courses are accredited by the AMGA (288 Main St., Lander, WY 82520-0579, tel. 307/332–6973, fax 307/332–3631). *Also see* the chapter on Wilderness and Survival Schools.

PACIFIC CREST OUTWARD BOUND
Teaching climbing is just one of the ways that this AMGA-accredited school, based in Portland, Oregon, and founded in 1966, furthers its larger goal: to help students grow spiritually by meeting the challenge of acquiring apparently difficult new skills. Courses are staged up and down the West Coast, from Washington State's North Cascades and California's Sierra Nevada southward to Joshua Tree National Monument (288 Main St., Lander, WY 82520-0579, tel. 307/332–6973, fax 307/332–3631). *Also see* the chapter on Wilderness and Survival Schools.

RAINIER MOUNTAINEERING, INC.
RMI founder Lou Whittaker is a charming raconteur and celebrated climber who holds court on the mountain at some of his courses. His guides have been taking aspiring climbers up Mt. Rainier since 1968 (guided ascents and seminars on the mountain's Disappointment Cleaver route are one of its best-known programs); winter seminars, advanced climbing instruction, and climbing expeditions in other parts of the United States and abroad are among its other activities (535 Dock St., Suite 209, Tacoma, WA 98402, tel. 206/627–6242, fax 206/627–1280; in summer, Paradise, WA 98398, tel. 206/627–6242, fax 503/274–7723).

YOSEMITE MOUNTAINEERING SCHOOL

The sole climbing school and guide service in Yosemite National Park, founded in 1969, this AMGA-accredited operation has taught rock climbing and mountaineering to thousands of visitors to this celebrated California national park. The varied terrain here allows for a wide range of climbing activities, for climbers of all levels of ability and experience. The school, primarily known for its day-long programs, is based in Yosemite Valley in spring and fall, and at Tuolumne Meadows in summer (Yosemite National Park, CA 95389, tel. 209/372–1244 in spring and fall, tel. 209/372–1335 in summer, fax 209/372–1330 in winter).

FAVORITE COURSES

THE NORTHEAST

NEW YORK **Basics on the Shawangunks.** The 'Gunks, a 90-minute drive north of Manhattan, is one of the outstanding climbing venues in the United States thanks to its fractured rock. One of the draws of Eastern Mountain Sports Climbing School's 4-day Basic Rock Program here—actually 4 single-day courses offered consecutively as a package—is the wide variety of rock of different textures and the kinds of holds you are exposed to. It's a thorough introduction to rock climbing that will give you some proficiency fairly quickly. Instructors, one for every 3 students, teach the basics of everything from equipment to knots, and the fundamentals of belaying, climbing, and rappelling. You begin climbing on relatively easy rock faces, then move on to multipitch routes that call for more difficult moves, using more sophisticated techniques. Lodging and meals, including lunch, are up to you; there are campgrounds, bed-and-breakfasts, hotels, and restaurants in the vicinity. *Eastern Mountain Sports Climbing School, Box 514, North Conway, NH 03860, tel. 603/356–5433, fax 603/356–9469. May–Sept.: 4 days, $375–$550. Sign up at least 1 week in advance.*

NEW YORK **Beginning Mountaineering in the Adirondacks.** Adirondack Rock and River Guide Service's 4-day beginning mountaineering course, a comprehensive winter-climbing program held in the mountains of upstate New York, teaches you what you need to know to travel safely and efficiently on hard-packed snow, including techniques for self-arrest, belaying, climbing, and descending, as well as the use of ice screws, dead men, and other devices as protection on snow. The finale is particularly grand: a 6-mile trek to the granite cliffs known as the Gothics, and the ascent, weather permitting, of the Gothics' 1,000-foot North Face. Winter-camping experience is helpful, and basic ice climbing skills are required. The client-to-guide ratio is 4:1 (2:1 during the final ascent). You may need double plastic boots (which can be rented). Climbers have the option of overnighting in local campgrounds or lodging in the school's own comfortably rustic lodges, one of which has an indoor climbing wall. Adirondack Rock and River, which has several other courses on rock climbing, ice climbing, and general mountaineering, has been teaching since 1988 and is accredited by the AMGA. *Adirondack Rock and River Guide Service, Box 219, Keene, NY 12942, tel. 518/576–2041. Mar.: 4 days, $295. Sign up 1 month in advance.*

THE ROCKIES

COLORADO **Rock Camp in Rocky Mountain National Park.** Colorado Mountain School's wide-ranging 7-day course, held in and around Rocky Mountain National Park, takes you quickly from the basics to multipitch rock climbs. Even on the first day, after going over knots, protection, belaying, and rappelling, you get in some climbing. But the climbing is continuous during the next 2 days,

as you develop your skills and learn new ones. On the fourth day, you begin preparing for 2 more days of climbing on big, multipitch walls and an ascent of one of the rock spires in the park's high country. The student-to-instructor ratio ranges from 6:1 at the beginning to 3:1 later on.

Dormitory lodging and some meals are available in CMS's Climbers' Lodge for an additional cost; campgrounds, motels, hotels, and restaurants are in the town of Estes Park, which is where you'll probably buy the fixings for the brown-bag lunch you're asked to bring every day.

Colorado Mountain School, founded in 1982, offers a full program of instruction, from beginner to advanced, in all types of climbing. The school is accredited by the AMGA, and is the concessioned guide service for Rocky Mountain National Park. *Colorado Mountain School, Box 2062, Estes Park, CO 80517, tel. 303/586–5758. May–Oct.: 7 days, $845–$995. Sign up 1–2 months in advance.*

COLORADO **Rock Week in Steamboat Springs.** The off-season charm of the laid-back ski resort of Steamboat Springs is a definite plus for Rocky Mountain Ventures' Rock Week, 6 days of intensive instruction and guided climbing that will make you competent at high-angle rock work; the course covers everything from knots and simple rope systems to complex anchors, hanging belays, lead-climbing skills, and self-rescue. An indoor climbing wall and video are used to practice and analyze your progress, and the student-to-instructor ratio is 3:1 or 4:1.

Unusual among climbing schools, this one provides everything you need, including not only the instruction, technical equipment, and the guided climbing that are part of the course but also a climbing manual, meals, dormitory-style lodging (or other digs at extra cost), even use of a health club. Accredited by the AMGA, Rocky Mountain Ventures offers a full curriculum of rock and ice climbing courses, as well as guided trips into the nearby Mount Zirkel Wilderness of Routt National Forest. Note that in early spring the course is held near Grand Junction, Colorado.

Rocky Mountain Ventures, Box 775046, Steamboat Springs, CO 80477, tel. 303/879–4857. Apr.–Sept.: 6 days, $885. Price includes meals and accommodations; sign up 1–2 months in advance.

WYOMING **Basic and Intermediate Climbing with Ascent of the Grand Teton.** In less than a week, Exum Mountain Guides can put you atop the 13,770-foot Grand Teton, the centerpiece of the national park of the same name and one of those alluring peaks that all climbers want to scale; access to the approaches to the summit is relatively short, and the mountain's granite and gneiss is sturdy. Exum starts you with a basic climbing course, which is held in the park on moderately angled rock faces and covers the fundamentals of rock climbing and mountaineering. Short ascents of varying difficulty on the low-angled slabs expose you to the realities of the sport and let you try out different skills and moves. Then you go on to Exum's intermediate course, to learn techniques for climbing steeper faces and handling multipitch climbs as well as methods of anchoring and placing protection; there's also more rappelling. This instruction prepares you for what follows—a guided ascent of the Grand Teton. The precise route taken to the summit (there are several) varies depending on conditions, weather, and participating students' expertise; usually it includes a boat ride across Jenny Lake and a night at the Exum Grand Teton Hut at the mountain's 11,600-foot Lower Saddle.

Most students take a week to complete the pair of courses and climb the Grand, although the combination can be done in 4 or 5 days with good weather, or stretched out for a longer time. Lodging and meals during the courses are available in Grand Teton National Park and in nearby Jackson. *Exum Mountain Guides, Box 56, Moose, WY 83012, tel. 307/733–2297. June–Aug.: 4–5 days, $425–$570. Sign up 2–3 months in advance.*

WYOMING AND SOUTH DAKOTA **Beginning Climbing in the Black Hills and Devils Tower.** No one who saw the movie *Close Encounters of the Third Kind* will forget Devils Tower, that distinctively shaped plug of rock jutting out of the western plains. It's where you spend the last 2 days of a 5-day introduction to climbing program from Sylvan Rocks Climbing School & Guide Service, founded in 1989. The first 3 days are spent a few hours' drive away, in the forested Needles area of South Dakota's Black Hills, notable for its roughly textured rock and for its low elevations and resulting low incidence of severe storms. Because it's remote, the area is not overrun by climbers as are the Shawangunks and Yosemite. Here you get a solid introduction to basic climbing moves, rappelling, and anchor systems, and then acquire more sophisticated skills, such as handling self-equalizing anchors and ropes, self-rescue, and multipiece hardware placements. This prepares you for the ascent of Devils Tower, where you learn sophisticated crack techniques on the Tower's superb rock and solidify your mastery of the fundamentals. Though most students are beginners, most acquire a very high level of climbing skills. Student-to-guide ratios range from 4:1 to 2:1, and Sylvan Rocks, founded in 1989, is accredited by AMGA. Lodging and meals are available near both sites. *Sylvan Rocks Climbing School & Guide Service, Box 600, Hill City, SD 57745, tel. 605/574–2425. May–Oct.: 3- to 5-day packages, $300–$690. Sign up 2 months in advance.*

THE WEST COAST

CALIFORNIA **Rock Faces of Yosemite.** After 5 days of Yosemite Mountaineering School, you won't be ready to climb El Capitan or Half Dome, but as you make your way through the basics of rock climbing and on to a guided ascent, you will definitely get a feel for the crisp granite that has made this park one of the world's most famous climbing destinations. The 5-day Alpencraft course is actually 5 day-long courses offered as a package.

Your first day, an overall introduction to rock climbing, ends with a short climb on one of Yosemite's distinctive rock faces. Over the next 2 days you progress through basic climbing techniques and equipment to more advanced skills; you learn to use belay anchors, nuts and runners, and more difficult holds and techniques, then set up rappel anchors and rig secure rope positions. The fourth day covers basic snow and ice techniques, including glissading and the use of ice axes and snow belays, and the final day sees you ascending Mt. Dana, Young's Peak, or another summit, depending on the expertise of participating students, under the watchful eye of one of the guides. As if your sense of accomplishment at having reached the summit isn't enough, there's a spectacular view of the Sierra from the top.

You must provide your own meals and lodging. Yosemite is immensely popular—nearly overcrowded in summer—and even a campsite must be reserved many months in advance. Meals are easy to come by at the many food concessions in the valley. The student-to-instructor ratio is 3:1. *Yosemite Mountaineering School, Yosemite National Park, CA 95389, tel. 209/372–1244 in spring and fall, 209/372–1335 in summer. May–late Oct.: 5 days, $250. Sign up 5 months in advance.*

CALIFORNIA **Fast and Light above Donner Pass.** Alpine Skills International's 5-day Rock Skills Seminar teaches you a specific approach to rock climbing: fast and light, with a minimum of equipment. Suitable for experienced as well as novice climbers, the intensive course is carefully planned and covers both face and crack climbing techniques, as well as the placement and removal of protection anchors in multipitch climbing. You also get instruction in direct aid, that is, how to put climbers' hardware directly into the rock to use as hand- and footholds (something that fewer and fewer climbers do nowadays); and you learn the protocol required when you function as the lead climber in a group (something taught only in advanced courses at most schools). At regular intervals, your instructor videotapes you and then analyzes the tape to help you refine your climbing technique. The mountain above Lake Tahoe where much of the climbing is done, Donner Summit, offers more than 300 possible ascents ranging from easy to the most challenging anywhere, as well as weather that stays pleasantly cool even in summer. The area is well-known among climbers, but perhaps more widely famed as the site of the starvation, death, and cannibalism of the ill-fated Donner Party of pioneers, who attempted to cross the pass in the winter of 1846–1847. Present-day visitors are likely to have a happier experience.

Climbing always requires a certain level of fitness; the Alpine Skills approach demands even better physical condition, and the staff will question you carefully about your fitness level before they sign you up. The course is held at Alpine Skills' Donner Spitz Hutte, a favored destination of day-trippers, who often drop in for espresso and wine while they're out on the trail. Breakfast and dinner are served at the chalet, and although most accommodations are in dorms, it's possible to snag a private room, a real luxury when you're in climbing school. The student-to-instructor ratio is 8:1 maximum. *Alpine Skills International, Box 8, Norden, CA 95724, tel. 916/426–9108, fax 916/426–3063. June–Oct.: 5 days, $485. Price includes tents, stoves, and fuel but no climbing gear besides harnesses; sign up at least 3 weeks in advance.*

CALIFORNIA **Mountaineering in the Sierra Nevada.** Pacific Crest Outward Bound's 14-day Alpine Mountaineering Course takes place at and above timberline, from 9,000 to 10,000 feet, at various locations in the High Sierra's Sequoia and Kings Canyon National Park. Focusing on mountaineering, backcountry travel, and rock climbing, it challenges you in a variety of activities and terrain to rise to a variety of physical challenges and master a variety of skills—among them low-impact travel. The ultimate goal is personal growth. A typical day involves many hours on the trail and lots of teamwork, and is physically and mentally rigorous. Although many Outward Bound courses are for teenagers, this one is open only to adults 21 and up. The student-to-instructor ratio is approximately 4:1 or 5:1. Meals are nutritious and wholesome, and unlike many operations that rely on freeze-dried and other prepackaged foods, Outward Bound uses staples such as beans, rice, pastas, and seasonings. *Pacific*

Crest Outward Bound School, 0110 SW Bancroft St., Portland, OR 97201-4050, tel. 503/243–1993, fax 503/274–7723. June–July: 14 days, $1,495. Price includes meals, sleeping bag and pad, backpack, rain gear, and other necessary equipment; sign up 6 months in advance.

CALIFORNIA **Winter Rock Seminar in the Desert.** Joshua Tree National Monument is southern California's equivalent of the 'Gunks: It's close to where large numbers of climbers live; the granite is outstanding; and the weather is good in winter, when cold makes climbing uncomfortable farther north. Wilderness Connection's introductory rock climbing course, which is held here in winter, crams so much information, instruction, and experience into 5 days that even absolute beginners can advance rapidly. You start by covering the basics, including terminology, safety systems, and knots; progress to climbing and rappelling on low-angle faces; and gradually move on to more sophisticated climbing moves, belaying, and hardware placements.

Motels and campgrounds are convenient to Joshua Tree National Monument and to Tahquitz and Suicide Rocks, areas in the San Bernardino National Forest not far from the town of Idyllwild, where the course is held in summer; Suicide Rocks, which has some 200 routes, is in the sun most of the day, and Tahquitz, which has relatively long routes and plenty of crack climbing, remains cool and shady. The Wilderness Connection, established in 1989, is AMGA-accredited, and the student-to-instructor ratio is 3:1 or 4:1. *Wilderness Connection, Box 29, Joshua Tree, CA 92252-0029, tel. 619/366–4745, fax 619/366–9315. Year-round: 5 days, $575. Sign up 2 weeks in advance.*

OREGON **Mountaineering on Mount Hood.** The realm of snow and ice atop this celebrated peak is the setting for this 5-day program, one of several offered by Timberline Mountain Guides. In this course, you immediately travel by Sno-Cat from the grand, WPA-vintage Timberline Lodge at 5,000 feet to the 8,500-foot level; from here, you pack your gear to

9,300 feet, where you set up a base camp at Illumination Saddle. The next day you get some basic snow and ice climbing instruction, which prepares you for the summit attempt on the following day, which you make via the mountain's moderate South Side Route. You then return to base camp to work on intermediate snow and ice climbing and glacier-travel skills, including crevasse rescue. On your last day you ascend Mount Hood for the second time, this time via either the more challenging Leuthold's Couloir or Wyeast routes. *Timberline Mountain Guides, Box 23214, Portland, OR 97281-3214, tel. 503/636–7704. Apr.–July: 5 days, $650. Price includes camping gear and food, as well as Sno-Cat transport; sign up 6–8 weeks in advance.*

OREGON **Mountaineering on Mount Hood, Rock Camp in the Desert.** This Timberline Mountain Guides' program is one of the most unusual in the United States: It includes a day in climbing school at the 5,000-foot level; a day-long climb via Sno-Cat (a multipassenger over-snow vehicle) of 11,235-foot Mount Hood, Oregon's highest summit; and a rock course in the sunny desert of the eastern part of the state. For giving you a taste of varied terrain and conditions, the combination is hard to beat.

The climbing school introduces you to the alpine environment and basic high-altitude climbing techniques, such as footwork, rope handling, and the use of an ice axe and crampons. The second day you ride the Sno-Cat to 8,500 feet, and, using your newly acquired skills, climb to the summit via the South Side Route—challenging but feasible. On the following day, you travel to eastern Oregon's Smith Rock State Park, a climbing area frequently compared with Yosemite Valley for its good-quality rock and long climbing season. Here, you have 2 days of instruction in the fundamentals of rock climbing—including balance, rope handling, belaying, rappelling, and more footwork—and you make several climbs. Lodging and meals are available near both sites.

Timberline offers a full range of other climbing courses, including mountaineering courses and snow and ice climbing instruction on Mount Hood, as well as rock climbing courses in other locations and guided climbs throughout the Cascades and elsewhere. Timberline's instructional program is accredited by the AMGA. *Timberline Mountain Guides, Box 23214, Portland, OR 97281-3214, tel. 503/636–7704. Mar.–July: 5 days, $350–$670. Price does not include transportation to Smith Rock State Park; sign up 4–6 weeks in advance.*

WASHINGTON **17 Days of Mountaineering on Mount Rainier.** This 17-day program, designed for adults, is one of the shorter offerings from the National Outdoor Leadership School (NOLS). Like all those from this organization, it isn't specifically a climbing course—the emphasis is on minimum-impact wilderness travel, camping skills, teamwork, and safety. But you do learn a lot about climbing, because climbing and mountaineering skills are a requisite on Rainier.

Initially the pace is slow as you move through the forests and rivers surrounding the mountain and master the NOLS leave-no-trace camping methods. In a few days, however, you move to the incredible world above timberline, high on the heavily glaciated slopes. There, for the next 2 weeks, you learn map-reading and route-finding as well as safety and emergency procedures, and your days are packed with instruction in glacier travel, rope systems, crevasse rescue, and ice-axe and crampon use. You set up a new camp every 2 or 3 days, but there is plenty of climbing and plenty of time for reflection.

Meals are heavy on grains, pasta, lentils, and beans, and draw on the NOLS trail cookbook; macaroni and cheese, and beans and rice embellished with hot sauce and spices are typical fare. Students do the cooking, with some guidance. *NOLS, 288 Main St., Lander, WY 82520-0579, tel. 307/332–6973, fax 307/332–3631. Aug.: 17 days, $1,950. Price includes meals, group camping equipment, and tents; sign up 3–5 months in advance.*

WASHINGTON **Snow and Ice Climbing Seminar and Mount Rainier Ascent.** This 14,410-foot dormant volcano is the second

highest mountain in the Lower 48 (after California's Mount Whitney). Its terrain is diverse, and its slopes are heavily glaciated, so it is unsurpassed as a site for teaching glacier travel, snow climbing, and even vertical ice climbing, the subject matter of this 5-day program from Rainier Mountaineering, Inc. (RMI). Because the course also includes an ascent to Rainier's summit, it's a strong option if you're training for a climb in Alaska or the Himalayas, or if you know rock climbing and want to get a feel for a big, glacier-covered volcano. Even an ambitious beginner in at least moderately good shape can complete the course.

The seminar generally begins with a trek from the Paradise Visitor Center at 5,000 feet to Camp Muir, a small plateau at 10,000 feet on Rainier's South Side. There's a ranger station here, as well as an open area where climbers not on this RMI trip pitch their tents and a guide hut with a bunkhouse. At Camp Muir, you spend 3 days working on basics—snow and ice climbing techniques, including self-arrest and team-arrest, belays, roped travel, snow anchors, knots, route-finding, crevasse rescue, and technical ice climbing. The terrain here is truly awesome, and the glaciers are huge. Usually by the fourth day everyone has acclimated to the thin air of this elevation, and, weather permitting, the summit attempt begins.

A big plus of the course is the Camp Muir bunkhouse: Basic as it is (4 walls and a roof), it beats squatting at the door to a tent trying to get your camp stove lighted in the wind—especially in bad weather, which can blow in at any time on this mountain. You don't even have to do the cooking; the RMI staff does it for you—oatmeal for breakfast, sandwiches for lunch, stew for dinner, and other plain but nutritious fare. *RMI, 535 Dock St., Suite 209, Tacoma, WA 98402, tel. 206/627–6242, fax 206/627–1280; in summer, Paradise, WA 98398, tel. 206/627–6242, fax 503/274–7723. May–Aug.: 5 days, $555. Price includes bunkhouse meals and lodging; sign up at least 12–16 weeks in advance.*

WASHINGTON **12 Days of Alpine Mountaineering in the North Cascades.** The North Cascades, home turf for the American Alpine

Institute (AAI), offers an array of alpine terrain unmatched in the Lower 48: peaks over 10,000 feet, deep canyons, more than 300 glaciers, varied fauna and flora, and hundreds of mountain lakes and streams. AAI's 12-day mountaineering program is held in the heart of the area, largely above timberline, in the rugged alpine areas of North Cascades National Park and the Glacier Peak Wilderness Area in Snoqualmie National Forest. Up here, among the glaciers, the craggy rock spires, and the hidden meadows, you learn the fundamentals of rock, snow, and ice climbing and how to travel in the alpine environment without harming it. You also learn to identify avalanche hazards and other risks, and acquire self-rescue and minimum-impact camping skills. Although climbing experience isn't required, it's helpful to have done some backpacking. You camp out in tents, usually on snow or glaciers, and prepare meals in camp. Food, which you supply (with some AAI coaching), should be nutritious enough to fuel your exertions without weighing down your pack—something worth considering since the base camp moves several times. Group sizes range from 3 to 5 students with 1 instructor, to 6 to 10 students with 2 instructors. The natural follow-up to the course is a 4- to 10-day AAI expedition in the Cascades or Canada. *AAI, 1515 12th St., Bellingham, WA 98225, tel. 206/671– 1505, fax 206/734–8890. May–early Oct.: 12 days, $1,260. Sign up 3 months in advance.*

ALASKA

CENTRAL **23-Day Mountaineering Seminar and Mount McKinley Ascent.** Every year, hundreds of climbers ascend this mountain, also known as Denali ("the high one"). Yet it's a serious undertaking. Making it as safe and as enjoyable as possible is this program from Alaska Denali Guiding, which has earned a reputation as one of the best guide services on Denali. Along with alpine-mountaineering instruction, the program includes an ascent of the mountain by the East Buttress route. Though the least difficult approach to McKinley, it still involves very high altitude, arctic conditions, crevasses, steep ice slopes, and unpredictable weather.

The climb begins at 7,200 feet, on the Kahiltna Glacier, accessible via a breathtaking bush plane flight from Alaska Denali Guiding's base in the hamlet of Talkeetna. From here, you learn knots, rope care and management, placement of snow and ice anchors, belay techniques, glacier travel, use of ice axe and crampons, and sophisticated snow and ice techniques. A major camp is established at 14,000 feet, and a high camp, from which the summit attempt is made, at 17,000 feet; intermediate camps are put in as required. With 23 days, there is plenty of time for teaching, and with more than 13,000 feet of elevation to gain, plenty of opportunity for practice. On this expedition, you are not just a student but also a key member of an expedition and an integral part of the team.

No previous climbing experience is required, but a very high fitness level is essential to reach the summit, since the work of climbing the mountain is substantial.

Alaska Denali Guiding, founded in 1982, offers many other adventure trips in the state, including mountaineering trips and guided climbs throughout the Alaska Range, guided treks across the tundra, ski-mountaineering trips on the Ruth Glacier, as well as custom guided climbs and expeditions. *Alaska Denali Guiding, Box 566, Talkeetna, AK 99676, tel. 907/733– 2649, fax 907/733–1362. May–July: 23 days, $2,450. Price includes meals, tents, and stoves; sign up at least 6 months in advance.*

SOURCES

ORGANIZATIONS The **American Mountain Guides Association** (Box 2128, Estes Park, CO 80157, tel. 303/586–0571) can provide a list of members and accredited schools and guides and can help you find the guide service to meet your needs. In addition, you can contact local climbing shops in areas where you want to climb.

PERIODICALS The bimonthly *Climbing* (Box 339, Carbondale, CO 81623, tel. 303/ 963–9449) covers this sport exclusively. The monthly magazines *Outside* (1165 N. Clark, Chicago, IL 60610, tel. 303/447–9330) and *Backpacking* (33 E. Minor St., Emmaus, PA 18098, tel. 215/967–5171) regularly run articles on mountaineering.

BOOKS *Climbing in North America,* by Chris Jones, is the best overview of climbing in and around the continent. *Fifty Classic Climbs,* by Steve Roper and Allen Steck, gives you a glimpse of the varied climbing available in the United States and Canada. *Mountaineering, Freedom of the Hills,* edited by Don Graydon, is the standard reference on climbing techniques, equipment, ethics, and more.

ALSO SEE Like the feel of testing your limits and coming to grips with your fears? *See* Wilderness and Survival Schools.

Covered Wagon Trains

by Melissa Rivers

agons, ho-o-o-o!" The call goes out and your wagon lurches forward, canvas cover flapping against the frame. Burly wagon masters bark instructions to the sturdy horses as you're jostled this way and that on the dusty, bumpy trail. Atop a ridge, you forget the dust and saddle sores and take in the beauty of the scenery that beckoned you here. The horizon widens, waving grass ebbs and flows on the warm, sage-scented breeze, and distant pink-and-buff-colored spires reach for the deep blue sky. Here, all appears as it was in the 1800s, minus the roaming herds of buffalo.

Join a modern wagon train to go back in time, to step out of the hectic 20th century and experience, if only for a few days, what the tens of thousands of brave emigrants of the westward movement endured. Most trips are run from June through early September on trails throughout the Southwest and the Rockies. The terrain varies widely—from the dry desert of Arizona and the red-rock arroyos of Colorado to the lushly forested mountains or grassy plains of Wyoming—and should be a major consideration when choosing your trip. Some wagon trains follow historical byways, such as the Pony Express route or the rough Overland, Mormon, and Oregon trails, while others utilize gentler logging roads through protected parklands.

For some outfitters, the authenticity of their wagon train is the most important element: Their wagons are authentic replicas, with wooden- or steel-rimmed wheels and canvas tops that roll up for visibility and down for shade. Other outfitters put comfort first, providing modernized wagons with shock absorbers, rubber wheels, and foam-padded seats to relieve some of the uncomfortable bounce of the trail. They also provide camp amenities such as tents, folding stools, portable potties, and solar showers (as opposed to pit toilets and warm water in a basin for sponge bathing on most "authentic" trips). You're usually responsible for bringing a sleeping bag, water canteen, flashlight, and binoculars.

Trail guides and cooks—most of them professional cowboys with ranching or rodeo backgrounds—can wrangle horses, rattle off cowboy poetry, lecture on the flora and fauna seen along the trail, and rustle up surprisingly delicious campfire meals (heavy on the steaks, stews, biscuits, and cobblers). They are usually between 20 and 60 years old, very amiable, and decked out in jeans, boots, hats, and bandannas.

A typical day on the trail is long. You rise to the sound of the morning bell (usually around 7:30) and gather for breakfast from the chuck wagon before packing and hitching up the teams for the day's journey. Board

---

Melissa Rivers is a freelance writer who has covered areas as near as Mexico and Canada and as far as the Orient. Although she didn't make the trip by covered wagon, Melissa did migrate west and now lives comfortably near the end of the famous Oregon Trail.

one of the canvas-topped wagons or ride the gentle saddle horses for a trek of 6 hours or more, which might cross rivers, prairies, or rocky passes in sight of ghost towns and herds of wild horses and antelope. Stop to take photographs or gather round for historical talks at sites along the route. At "nooning," you get a break for cool water and sack lunches while the teams rest up for the remaining journey.

When you "circle up" the wagons in the late afternoon, the horses are unhitched and tents are set up by the trail hands while you rest, hike, swim, hunt for arrowheads and rocks, or lend a hand with chores (not a requirement) until the dinner bell, when everyone gathers around a crackling campfire to eat and be regaled with stories and songs of the Old West. After your hard day, you'll probably want to take an early leave and head to a tent, tepee, or wagon, or simply stretch out under the stars and drift off to sleep, serenaded by coyotes baying at the moon.

Covered wagon trains appeal to a broad cross section of nostalgic dudes, but there are often young families—college-educated baby boomers and their kids—along for the ride. A trip can cost from $600 to $900, but many outfitters have reduced rates for children. Most people come with little or no riding or camping experience and are here to live out their Western fantasy, or just get closer to nature. The rewards of healthy outdoor fun and the chance to relive pioneer history must be carefully weighed against frustrations such as bug bites, lack of indoor plumbing, and disagreeable weather and dust.

CHOOSING THE RIGHT TRIP

In choosing a trip, consider whether authenticity or comfort is more important to you, as well as what type of topography and scenery you would most enjoy. Here are some questions you should ask about each trip you consider:

How long has the company been in business? Chances are that you're not going to find a fly-by-night covered wagon train operation; however, because you're going to be on the dusty road for up to a week, the more knowledge and experience the guides have the better.

Are the wagons authentic reproductions? Are wheels wooden-rimmed, steel-rimmed, or rubber? Are seats padded for comfort? Try to gauge what your tolerance for discomfort is when choosing a trip. Of course, this is a gritty activity to begin with—all part of the experience—but pads on the seats can make your ride that much smoother.

Is there the option of riding in wagons and on horseback? Is riding experience necessary? Usually, you have a choice of riding in a wagon or on a horse; it's often more interesting to break the trip up by trying both. If you *have* to spend part of the time on a horse, however, it would be wise to learn how good a rider you have to be.

What will the accommodations be like? The choice of accommodations varies from padded bunks in the wagons to tepees and tents (some with foam-padded bottoms).

What kinds of showers and toilets are provided? Just how outdoorsy are you? For some, the thought of communing that closely with nature for a week is too much. For others, a portable toilet would be too representative of the present to enjoy the trip into the past.

What kind of meals are provided? Can the outfitter meet special dietary requirements? A lot of the menus on these trips have meat as the main course. There are usually side dishes and salads as well, but if you are a vegetarian or have other dietary restrictions, it's a good idea to find out what the options are.

What is the maximum group size? The groups range in size from 20 to 45. As people sign up for the trip, wagons, which carry around 8 people apiece, can be added on. The more people on a trip, the more interesting it can be—but more than 45 people might prove too large as the train gets longer.

What chores, if any, are guests required to do? The trail hands generally help set up camp and saddle the horses, but what is expected of you can vary—cooking, caring for horses, pitching tents, and so on. Find out what is required and decide how willing you are to pitch in. Helping out can make the experience even more true-to-life.

What are the free-time options? The areas around the trails that you ride on offer a wide variety of activities, from swimming to fishing to hiking. Make sure that there are opportunities to take advantage of them.

What's the cost and what's included? All outfitters listed below supply accommodations and meals for would-be pioneers. Some supply sleeping bags and pads, but some don't, so be sure to ask. You will have to bring your own boots, binoculars, and canteen. Although occasionally a trip will run in a circle, most covered wagon trains move from a starting point to a different finish point. Outfitters will either transport you back to the starting point or arrange to have your car driven to the finish point; this is included in the trip price.

Do you have references from past guests?

How far in advance do I need to book? Make a reservation as early as possible; a growing interest in covered wagon trains means that, by spring, outfitters are often booked for the year.

FAVORITE TRIPS

THE MIDWEST

NEBRASKA **Oregon Trail Wagon Train.** History buff Gordan Howard's 6-day covered wagon trek couldn't be more authentic. Your group of up to 40 can ride on long, uncushioned benches in traditional wooden wagons that Howard's family constructed. Or, if you get tired of bouncing uncomfortably with 3 to 15 other passengers (wagons vary in size but none has shock absorbers), you can switch to the scout horses or walk alongside as the pioneers usually did. As you travel, Howard—a 58-year-old farmer-turned-trail-guide—shares his extensive knowledge of early American history and the Oregon Trail.

The wagon train starts out at a base camp 2 miles outside Bayard and follows the sec-

tion of the Oregon Trail that cuts through the panhandle of Nebraska, between Chimney Rock—a towering rock spire that was a "sign post" to pioneers heading west—and Scotts Bluff National Monument. The prairie schooners roll through a wide, rolling valley covered in sage, blue stem, and buffalo grass and hemmed in by bluffs to the south and the Platte River to the north. Along the trail, you can walk in worn wagon ruts and search for artifacts such as Indian beads, arrowheads, shards of pioneer crockery, and broken utensils left by those who passed this way in the 1850s. You can learn to load and fire a black powder rifle, square dance on the prairie, and take part in an "Indian encounter." At the end of the day, you sit on stumps around the campfire and chow down on typical trail meals—buffalo hump or ham and beans. Jump in the water tank to cool off. You can lend a hand with the camp chores (though this is not mandatory) or crawl toward sleep in your short-walled tent, similar to those used by the pioneers. The primary concession to comfort is the custom potty wagon with chemical toilet. Otherwise, this trip is so authentic that a Northeastern college will give you graduate credits in history for participating. *Oregon Trail Wagon Train, Rte. 2, Box 502, Bayard, NE 69334, tel. 308/586–1850. May–Sept.: 6 days, $600. Sign up 30 days in advance.*

THE SOUTHWEST

ARIZONA **Wagons Ho Wagon Train.** The spirited 76-year-old Ruth C. Hefner founded Wagons Ho Wagon Train almost 30 years ago in Kansas, and her company is one of the most experienced outfitters in the business. It's also the only outfitter that operates year-round, running during the winter in the Phoenix-Scottsdale area and in the Grand Canyon area throughout the summer months. The winter trip, with temperatures ranging from 45°F to 75°F, runs in the Sonoran Desert, in the foothills of the McDowell Mountains, with no towns in sight. Instead, you're surrounded by saguaro cactus and mesquite, cottonwood, and cedar trees, and you might see gophers, coyote, and jackrabbits along the route. The summer trip takes you up into forested country on an abondoned Indian trail across private ranch land. The heat is tempered by the higher elevations along the route, so it's quite pleasant for you and all the deer, cattle, rabbits, and quail.

Over the decades, Ruth has found a happy medium between authenticity and comfort on her 4-day journeys. A train of 4 to 12 covered wagons, complete with steps and cushioned seats, travels along the summer and winter trails. Knowledgeable guides accompany you and your group of up to 46, explaining the flora and fauna and discussing the historical stagecoach stops. A trail hand shares his Native American lore, a Pony Express rider delivers mail, a stagecoach intercepts your group, and there's always the chance of an "Indian encounter." Your evenings are filled with square- and round-dancing, storytelling, roping demonstrations, and songs of the Old West, sung to the accompaniment of a guitar or accordian. Afterward, you bed down either in a tent or in one of the wagons' padded bunks. Portable restrooms and solar showers are part of the train, and most of the food (pioneer recipes and more modern fare) is prepared in kitchens and trucked to the site. Ruth has thought of everything, down to sunbonnets and prairie dresses for women who want to get into the frontier spirit. *Wagons Ho Wagon Train, Box 60098, Phoenix, AZ 85082, tel. 602/230–1801 or 602/ 977–7724. June–mid-Sept. and Oct.–mid-May: 4 days, $975. Sign up 2–4 weeks in advance.*

THE ROCKIES

COLORADO **Picture Canyon to Black Mesa Wagon Train.** Krikwell Cattle Company's 7-day trip is impressive for the number and variety of sites you visit as you travel along an old Indian trail in the southeast corner of Colorado near the Texas panhandle. The first day is spent transporting the group of about 25, horses, and equipment to the trailhead. The ride, which parallels the famous Penrose Cattle trail, begins in Picture Canyon, named for the Apishipa petroglyphs (Native American pictographs dating to AD 85) that grace sheer rock

walls. Traveling southwest down the canyon, you stop at Crack Cave, where Celtic emigrants inscribed a solar calendar that remains accurate to this day. In nearby Holt Canyon you find a homesteading map etched in stone by a 1903 survey crew, and a burial ground used by early settlers. The wagon train then heads up a steep pass and over a mesa to Outlaw Point, a tremendous vantage spot affording views of Black Mesa (the highest point in Oklahoma), the cedar-covered mesas of New Mexico, the prairies of Kansas, and the Cimarron River and Santa Fe Trail. Still ahead are the ruins of pioneer homesteads, fences, barns, and cemeteries, and a ranch rodeo at Prather Bluff. Cross the Santa Fe Trail Cutoff and you'll be cutting through Black Mesa Pass, with its old quarry and dinosaur tracks—not to mention Robbers Roost in the hill country where outlaws holed up in stone-walled hideouts. This trip is run only once a year and reservations can be made the previous winter. The cost of the trip includes transportation from the nearest airport in Amarillo, Texas (3 hours away) to the Kirkwell ranch in Springfield, Colorado; pre-trip lodging; and post-trip camping at the base ranch. *American Wilderness Experience, Box 1486, Boulder, CO 80306– 1486, tel. 303/444–2622 or 800/444–0099, fax 303/444–3999. Late May: 7 days, $1,000. Sign up at least 2 weeks in advance.*

WYOMING **Along the Oregon Trail.** In 1988, when horsewoman Nona Bates couldn't find an outfitter that provided short covered wagon train tours, she started Trails West, which now specializes in 3-day slices of pioneer life on the Oregon Trail. Four custom-built, steel-wheeled, oak-plank wagons carry you and a small group of 20 people down a 70-mile stretch of trail. (The wagons are extra wide for wheelchair access—Trails West is probably the only operator with wagons built specifically to accommodate travelers with disabilities.) Here the Oregon, Overland, and Mormon trails come together through the South Pass to cross the Continental Divide. During the 8 to 10 hours spent on the trail each day, you try everything from panning for gold and pink garnets in the Sweetwater River to examining rocky eagle nesting sites to drinking pure water from underground springs. You stop at the boomtown of Lewiston, St. Mary's stage stop, and a Mormon graveyard, where the victims of a 1856 blizzard are buried. Evening camp is set up by the trail crew at Diamond Springs, an old Shoshoni campground; here you are treated to hearty campfire meals of 16-oz. steaks and fresh berry cobblers before retiring to photogenic Crow-style tepees with triangular doorways and tall ridgepoles. *Trails West, Inc., 65 Main St., S. Pass City, WY 82520, tel. 307/332–7801 or 800/327–4052 (can also be booked through American Wilderness Experience, tel. 800/444–0099, fax 303/444–3999). June–early Sept.: 3 days, $350. Sign up 6 weeks in advance.*

WYOMING Along the Sweetwater River. Family-owned and operated, Great Divide Tours has been running horseback vacations in Wyoming for eight years. In celebration of the Oregon Trail Sesquicentennial, the firm now offers a 40-person, 6-day trek that covers 150 miles of the famous trail. Under huge blue skies, you follow the grassy high plains of central Wyoming along the Sweetwater River to South Pass, gateway to the "land of opportunity." During the 5 or 6 hours spent on the trail each day, your 8 steel-wheeled wagons, led by knowledgeable guides in period costume, pass through stands of aspen, pine, and cedar, and fields of sagebrush and blooming cacti and wildflowers. Antelope and herds of wild mustangs roam through the area. In the evening, living history programs, cowboy poetry, dances, and raucous musical reviews recreate life among the emigrants of the 1800s. Foam-padded, two-person tents, solar showers, and portable outhouses provide the modern-day touches. Great Divide also offers the Outlaw Trail Wagon Train in the Big Horn Mountains, a week-long trip through outlaw country to the Hole-in-the-Wall made famous by Butch Cassidy and the Wild Bunch. *Great Divide Tours, 336 Focht Rd., Lander, WY 82520, tel. 307/332–3123 or 800/458–1915. Mid-July and mid-Aug.: 6 days, $1,050. Sign up 30 days in advance.*

WYOMING Teton Country Covered Wagon Adventure. The lush Bridger-Teton National Forest and Mt. Leidy Highlands in the northwest corner of Wyoming are the ideal setting for Wagons West's 6-day journeys. The intimate 15-person train is run by a trio of seasoned partners and travels along the forested network of old logging trails with the wagon covers rolled back so you can better view the spruce, pine, and aspen trees; the high country wildflowers; and the deer, elk, moose, and eagles. You spend half of each 6-hour day on the trail in comfortable, converted hay wagons (with rubber tires and heavy-duty shocks) and the other half on horseback (though full-day horseback options are available at additional cost), following the trail as it opens up to panoramic views of the Grand Tetons, the Gros Ventre River, and the Wind River mountain range. After circling up the wagons in the early afternoon, you have time to hike, sunbathe, take pictures, or ride to a nearby stream for a cool dip. The guides share their knowledge of Western history and philosophy, while the cook sweats over the campfire and his old Dutch oven to prepare typical cowboy meals (barbecue, stews, biscuits, and cobblers) that passengers fondly describe as "hearty, ample, and brown." A cowboy crooner entertains later in the evening, before you drift off to sleep in a tepee, tent, or padded bunk. *American Wilderness Experience, Box 1486, Boulder, CO 80306–1486, tel. 303/444–2622 or 800/444–0099, fax 303/444–3999. June– Aug.: 6 days, $675. Sign up at least 2 weeks in advance.*

WYOMING Teton Prairie Schooner Holiday. Nick Wilson was a boy when he first passed through the untamed West into Jackson Hole, Wyoming, in the mid-1800s. As he got older, he rode for the Pony Express and the Overland Stage company, and he was among the first to drive covered wagons over Teton Pass into Jackson Hole. Today, his great-grandson Bill Thomas continues the tradition, leading modern adventurers through the wildlands of northwest Wyoming. Thomas's prairie schooners, modeled after the old Conestoga wagon (with the addition of rubber tires and padded seats), carry you along back-country roads through the pine forests of Targhee National Forest between Grand Teton and

Yellowstone national parks. You learn a little of what life was like for Nick Wilson when the Pony Express delivers the mail and you visit with Indians and a mountain man. Each evening, you roll out your sleeping bags and pitch your foam-padded tents in a new camp, near scenic high-mountain lakes. These are the perfect places for you to fill your free time canoeing, swimming, hiking, and photographing the bountiful wildlife. In the evenings, you sit around the camp fire enjoying Dutch-oven meals and cowboy yarns. *Bar-T-Five Inc., Box 3415, Jackson, WY 83001, tel. 307/733–5386 or 800/772–5386, fax 307/739–9183. Late June–Aug.: 4 days, $545. Price does not include transportation from Jackson. Sign up 3–8 months in advance.*

SOURCES

ORGANIZATIONS You can learn about wagon trains from the **National Trail Ride and Wagon Train Association** (c/o Art Howell,

Box 8625, Gadsen, AL 35902, tel. 800/633–2270).

BOOKS To get a feel for the historical significance of covered wagon train travel, or just get in the mood, you might enjoy reading about life on the Oregon and California trails. Most pioneers kept diaries, many of which were later published. Of particular interest is *The Oregon Trail*, by Francis Parkman, a fascinating account of the route's emigrants in 1846. The *Journal of Travels*, by Joel Palmer, is an interesting picture book with quotes from pioneers' diaries illuminating life on the trail. *On the Oregon Trail*, by Jonathan Nicholas and Ron Cronin, is a coffee table book, filled with distinctive pictures of life on the trail and quotes from pioneers.

ALSO SEE If this type of rough-and-tumble, true-to-life Western experience is for you, check the Working Farms, Ranches, and Cattle Drives chapter for other vacation options in the same spirit.

Cross-Country Skiing

by Rosemary Freskos and Jonathan Weisel

Picture a skier in slick skin-tight leggings with neon-pink stripes racing past you on short high-tech skating skis. Up ahead, an instructor wearing black stretch pants, a nylon windbreaker, and dark goggles digs her metal-edged skis into the snow, accomplishing a nearly perfect telemark turn. Behind her, another skier, dressed in wool knickers and a fisherman's sweater, glides along on machine-set tracks, basking in the sunshine and breathing deep the dry, cold air.

Scenes like this one, which you'll see at cross-country ski areas across the United States, say volumes about how the sport has grown in the past 50 years. With so many ways to enjoy it, cross-country skiing has become appealing to a large assortment of people. It's one of the top sports for low-impact cardiovascular exercise, and a good way to enjoy the wintery outdoors.

You learn about nature while cross-country skiing. You not only see tracks but also see animals; you come to know what the flow of clouds may mean for weather the next day; and eventually you can guess the temperature—close to accurately—based on the sound of your skis gently rubbing on the snow (rule of thumb: The higher-pitched the squeak, the colder it is). Furthermore, when you cross-country ski, you don't make much noise, you don't burn fossil fuels, and you don't really need much money.

A cross-country trip is usually cheaper than a downhill-ski vacation. You can pay as little as $7 for a daily trail pass instead of the $25 to $48 for a lift ticket, and rentals run about $12 as opposed to the $20 you pay to rent alpine skis. Moreover, there are many out-of-the-way lodges and inns with cross-country networks, and these are relatively inexpensive, whereas in downhill-ski areas the price of accommodations tends to be inflated.

To keep costs really low, you can ski cross-country just about anywhere there's enough snow. Rent a pair of skis from a local shop and try them out in your backyard or at a nearby golf course. Or take a few lessons with a professional instructor who can help you outsmart your feet—show you how to move with fluid grace across the flats, ascend the hills, descend the hills, and turn. It's best to learn at a cross-country ski resort, where the trails are machine-groomed with tracks. That means the snow is compacted into a consistent surface and two parallel grooves, or tracks, are cut into it so that your skis can't go anywhere but forward. Tracked trails allow anyone to experience the thrill of speed with confident

Rosemary Freskos, a regular contributor to Fodor's guides, has been writing about snow sports for some two decades. Jonathan Wiesel, cross-country co-chair of the North American Ski Journalists Association, has visited more than 300 cross-country ski areas in the United States and Canada. He's been a ski area operator and an industry consultant, and he now works part-time as a guide and instructor.

control at any pace, and the trail systems are so well marked and signed, it takes both talent and effort to get lost.

But there's a lot more to cross-country skiing than machine-groomed tracks. You can scuttle through the backcountry on virgin snow on wider, more stable skis; speed down hard-packed skating lanes using short skis to step-and-glide forward much as you would on ice skates; or don heavier, metal-edged skis to descend lift-served slopes, lunging forward on one knee in a telemark position.

In this chapter we cover several types of cross-country ski vacations. We tell you about entire areas devoted to the sport, such as Jackson, New Hampshire, and Royal Gorge, California, where there are several connected trail systems; we cover individual hotels and ranches with their very own trail networks; and we add a few organized guided trips by outfitters who will take you from lodge to lodge or hut to hut.

Keep in mind that you can have many different experiences at various cross-country ski areas, which are wildly diverse in size and emphasis. If you choose a large area, you have a large choice of accommodations and your trail pass gives you access to a big network with a wide variety of trails. Individual hotels, lodges, and ranches, on the other hand, may have small trail networks but more personality. Some accept only a dozen overnight guests; others have three score lodgers and hundreds of day skiers. Many include trail fees in multiday packages, but the day visitor pays $10 to $15 for a few hours of skiing. Guided trips with outfitters make it easy: You pay one price and they take care of just about everything. Guide companies generally emphasize service rather than challenging terrain, and they usually offer a combination of track and touring, or even stick just to groomed trails.

Because there's still some confusion about the nomenclature of cross-country skiing, the Cross Country Ski Areas Association, a national organization representing cross-country ski operators and suppliers, has come up with some standard definitions. *Nordic skiing* is an all-inclusive term comprising every kind of skiing other than alpine skiing: track, skating, backcountry, and telemarking—all using skis that are of lighter weight than alpine and boots and bindings that leave your heel free. The organization uses the term *cross-country* more exclusively, to refer to skiing on machine-groomed surfaces—both tracks and compacted lanes—although most people use *cross-country* interchangeably with *Nordic*. *Ski touring* is off-track skiing, from fooling around on skis at a local golf course to treks traversing the Tetons. Ski touring can be variously described as bushwhacking, mountaineering, or backcountry skiing, but it *always* refers to skiing on ungroomed trail.

Note: In most cases, cross-country skiers measure distance in kilometers (km) rather than miles. To convert kilometers into miles, divide by 1.6.

CHOOSING THE RIGHT EXPERIENCE

Cross-country ski areas have a justified reputation for hospitality, comfort, and culinary excellence; guided tours can be either plush or primitive. If you're researching the ideal site or tour, it's helpful to ask the following questions.

How long has the resort or hotel been operating as a cross-country destination? How long has the guide service been in business? Experience gives any business the knowledge it needs to work out problems with its operation and to meet the needs of all its customers.

Are the trails groomed or ungroomed? If you are going on a guided tour, the answer to this question will tell you a lot about the trip. You won't find groomed trails leading to a backcountry hut.

How many km of machine-groomed track are there? Are the tracks single or double and is there a skating lane? Obviously, more track means more skiing terrain to keep you busy. Some individual hotels have only 20 km of groomed track, which is probably enough for a beginner, but more advanced skiers will be happier at a place with 50 km or more. Single-track trails accommodate only one skier going in one direction, which makes them ideal for those looking for solitude. Double tracks are set so that skiers can travel in both directions. Skiers who want to skate will need a skating lane, a wide flat trail of packed snow.

Are all the trails groomed or are there back-country trails as well? Backcountry skiers visiting a resort or hotel should make sure that there are plenty of marked, ungroomed trails where they can get into the wilderness they love.

Is the system connected to other systems, and if it is, does your trail pass cover the connected systems? Some inns and hotels have trail networks that connect with other networks where you are allowed to ski using the same trail pass. This means you get more skiing area for your dollar.

What's the cost and what's included? Is professional instruction included? Guide service? In this chapter, costs quoted for packages and guided tours are generally per person and include double occupancy accommodations, meals (but not alcoholic beverages), and trail fees, unless stated otherwise. Guided trips with outfitters also include the services of a guide, who often gives the group instruction.

Many cross-country ski areas and even individual inns and ranches supply a limited number of group lessons as well as some short guided tours and clinics gratis; others don't. Paying extra for lessons and tours can add substantially to the cost of your trip. In all cases, you have to pay extra for private lessons and longer guided tours. Rental equipment is not included in the prices we quote unless stated otherwise.

Keep in mind that the multiple-day packages that we list are not your only option. At some resorts you can simply buy a daily trail pass (we list the price of this when it's available); at others, the trails are open only to overnight visitors, but you can pay for accommodations and a trail pass, without the meals, lessons, and guide that are included in the package.

What are the accommodations like? Hotel rooms vary tremendously, and guided tours may lead you to primitive huts or comfortable country inns.

What are the meals like? You could be dining in four-star restaurants, or eating beans around a wood stove.

Are the resort or hotel's instructors certified by the Professional Ski Instructors of America? What experience do the outfitter's guides have? Certification by PSIA assures that instructors have both the necessary skiing skills and the communication skills required to teach effectively. If a guide is going to lead you into the backcountry, make sure that guide has been there before. Also make sure at least one guide has first-aid and CPR training.

What kind of equipment is available? Does the rental shop have waxable skis? What type of binding systems are on the rental skis? Lots of skiers bring their own skis, but if you're renting, you want to be sure the resort has the kind of skis you need. If you want to practice skating and it stocks only touring skis, you'll be out of luck. Many ski shops offer only waxless skis, so more advanced skiers, who prefer to choose a wax to match the skiing conditions, may be left unsatisfied. Also, if you bring your own boots but don't want to carry your own skis, you should be sure that your boots will fit on the rental ski bindings. New skiers might want to ask about the latest innovation, the micro ski, which is only three-quarters the length of older models and makes turning and learning a breeze on packed snow.

What is base elevation? What is the highest point on your trip likely to be? People who don't do well at high elevations should not pick ski areas in the mountains, and if you have limited time, you may want to avoid areas with high altitudes, where it's important to acclimate. When traveling from sea level to an elevation of 6,000 feet or higher, you should avoid strenuous exertion the first day or two. Remember that alcoholic beverages affect you twice as fast at higher elevations, and headaches are often a symptom of oxygen depletion.

What other recreation is available on site? Is there downhill skiing nearby? It's always fun to have other options.

What kids' programs and facilities are available? Almost half the adults out on the trails have children under 18. When you bring a child skiing you have to be sure that the kid won't be bored. Ask about day care and baby-sitting, a snow-play area, children's rental equipment, narrowly set tracks for smaller skis and legs, and the availability of insulated sleds that you can use to pull your tiny tot along the trails as you ski.

Are there former guests that you can call as a reference? There's nothing as good as word of mouth to ensure the quality of experience.

How far in advance do I need to book?

FAVORITE TRIPS

THE NORTHEAST

NEW HAMPSHIRE **The Balsams in the Wilderness.** The appeal of this ski resort is more a matter of quality than size. There are few ski establishments that offer the attention to service, architectural character, and culinary accomplishments that you find at The Balsams, a classic Grand Hotel founded in 1866. Set on a 15,000-acre private holding in far northern New Hampshire, it has both a Mobil 4-star and an AAA 4-diamond rating, and it has been named a Historic Hotel of America by the National Trust for Historic Preservation. And to make it easier for you to have a good time here, the management includes just about all activities in the price of the Balsams America Plan.

This is beautiful, rugged country, closer to Montreal than Boston, and because The Balsams sits 600 feet higher than the surrounding area, it gets 250 inches of snow annually, 100 inches more than lower-lying lands. The 76-km groomed cross-country trail system, with both tracks and a skating lane, is complemented by 30 km of backcountry trails. The system provides close to 1,000 feet of vertical change, with trails passing through heavy stands of birch and maple. Trails can generally be skied in either direction, effectively doubling the system's length.

The Balsams also has a small alpine ski area with good telemark instruction. There's ice skating, a snowshoeing trail (equipment and instruction available), and horse-drawn hayrides, too. And yes, it's all included in the cost.

Although the facilities are open to day visitors, you won't find crowds of skiers. In fact, there are very seldom more than 100 people on the trails, even during the busiest seasons.

The hotel's ski shop has a staff of instructors and guides, many certified by the Professional Ski Instructors of America. Guides lead several free tours, including a Thursday luncheon tour that can run from 10 km to 15 km and may or may not head off track, depending on the ability and desires of participants. There's a maximum of 8 people per guide.

Guides will also lead you on a tour that involves a ski lift to 2,700 feet and a rewarding view of Canada, Maine, and Vermont. Also offered is a naturalist tour where participants study the tracks of rare pine marten, moose, and fox. The area boasts a peregrine falcon population, and if you come during the spring nesting season you might get a glimpse of one. Both alpine and cross-country skiers can take advantage of several warming shelters with heaters. Toilets are located at various points along the trail.

Although the hotel has more than 200 rooms, you won't find crowds on weekdays, when the best rates are available. The property has just about everything you need, including a movie theater, ballroom, nightclub, and piano bar with evening entertainment, as well as a recreation staff and a free nursery for infants to 5-year-olds. The atmosphere in the dining room is somewhat formal—men wear sports jackets—but co-owner and chef Phil Learned makes a poached salmon fillet that's worth dressing up for. Sunday-to-Friday ski packages include accommodations, breakfasts, dinners, use of both cross-country and alpine facilities, many guided tours, and 3 group lessons. *The Balsams/Wilderness, Dixville*

Notch, NH 03576, tel. 800/255–0600, fax 603/255–4221. Mid-Dec.–late Mar.: mid-week 5-night package, $400–$650. Trail fee: $7 (included in package).

NEW HAMPSHIRE **Jackson of the East.** Because the elevation ranges from 750 to 4,000 feet, there's an unusually high number of trails rated "most difficult" in this cross-country ski area, but the grooming is first-rate, with a mix of tracks and skating lanes. Back in the 70s, when the town came on hard times, Jackson made a calculated decision to establish a grand cross-country trail system twining through and around itself. It competes with Stowe, Vermont, in the Northeast for Nordic supremacy (although Stowe is better known for alpine skiing).

Jackson has 28 groomed trails totalling 91 km, ranging from a dozen shorties of less than 1 km to one that's 17.8 km. It also has an additional 90 km of backcountry routes. Conditions are variable, typical of the Northeast.

The area is controlled by the Jackson Ski Touring Foundation, headed by long-time director Thom Perkins. The Foundation maintains the trails and organizes lots of events, demonstrations, races, day tours, and clinics. It sponsors a Women's Weekend as well as a 5-km hot chocolate loop. It will also tailor treks anywhere from 3 km to 15 km, an hour to a full day. Groups of up to 10 people are escorted by one guide. There's a guided orientation tour every Monday at 10:30.

The area's Jack Frost Nordic Shop offers group lessons for $10 per person for an hour and 15 minutes, $25 for a private lesson. It also rents skis for $12 for the first day and $7 for additional days.

The town of Jackson is classic New England, complete with covered bridge. It's in the Mt. Washington Valley below the Presidential Range, about 2½ hours north of Boston. No matter what type of lodging you choose in Jackson—inn, hotel, B&B, condo, or motel— you will be able to step out your door onto the trails, which span 3 river valleys and 60 square miles in the White Mountain highlands. Two alpine ski areas, Wildcat and Black

Mountain, are connected to the system, so you can telemark down their runs at no extra cost. If you want to ride the lift, however, you will need to buy a downhill pass, but you'll get that at a discount when you show your cross-country pass.

When you're not skiing, you can linger in the town's taverns, fine restaurants, and galleries or head south to North Conway for a shopping spree in the factory outlet stores. Active visitors can take sleigh rides or try ice skating for free on several small rinks in town or for $5 on Emerald Lake. *Jackson Ski Touring Foundation, Rte. 16, Box 216, Jackson, NH 03846, tel. 603/383–9355 or 800/XC–SNOWS. Jackson Lodging Bureau, tel. 800/ 866–3334. Mid-Dec.–late Mar. Trail fees: $7–$9.*

VERMONT **First of Its Kind.** The first cross-country ski resort in North America, Trapp Family Lodge was founded in 1968 at Stowe, Vermont, a well-known alpine ski area and one of the biggest Nordic areas in the Northeast. There are 3 other cross-country ski centers totalling 135 km of groomed trails around Stowe, but Trapp Family Lodge is the kingpin. It has 55 km of groomed trails, single-tracked with a skating lane, and access to 50 km of ungroomed routes. The elevation change between Skaters Waltz, on the low southern end of the network, and the Slayton Cabin, near the northern end, is more than 1,000 feet. Trails meander through meadows and forests of sugar maple, pine, and birch, with occasional grand views of the Green Mountain peaks.

Trapp's trail network connects with both Topnotch (20 km, groomed) and Mt. Mansfield (35 km, groomed), and Edson Hill Manor (25 km, groomed) is easily accessible by car. All areas honor each other's trail passes when you ski from one area to the next, giving you the greatest concentration of groomed tracks in New England. You can start at the easier trails of, say, Topnotch, and graduate to the more advanced skiing at Trapp's in the same day. Both the groomed and wilderness trails are well mapped.

The fine staff of 6 full-time instructors has been rigorously trained by long-time Nordic director Charlie Yerrick, and in 1990 the ski shop was voted by Ski Industries America the top cross-country retailer in the United States. Naturalist and teacher Dick Smyth leads 1½- to 2-hour nature tours over easy terrain weekdays, studying everything from animal tracks to forest types ($5; sign up at lodge or ski shop). Guided backcountry day treks for groups of up to 6 can run as much as 20 km (prices vary), not necessarily tough skiing but a certain stamina is required. There are no overnight tours.

The original Trapp Family Lodge, built in 1941, burned down in 1980; it was replaced by a less idiosyncratic Tyrolean-style structure that sits grandly on Luce Hill, with an annex and guest houses nearby. The 93 lodge rooms all have a balcony and a view, but they're smaller and slightly more expensive than the 100 guest house apartments, which have kitchenettes and fireplaces and are also offered as time-share units. The lodge, however, is more convenient to dining options.

Hot drinks and snacks are available at the cross-country center; you can get a soup-and-sandwich lunch along the trail at the Slayton Cabin; and the Austrian Tea Room and Bar is open 10:30 AM–5:30 PM for light entrées and sandwiches. The lodge restaurant specializes in Austrian cuisine. Dinner is accompanied by harp, piano, or guitar music. Since both trails and restaurant are open to the public, and Trapp Family Lodge is one of Stowe's best-known sightseeing destinations, staying here is not an intimate experience.

When you're not skiing tracks, you can try the downhill slopes, snowshoe, or go for a horse-drawn sleigh ride. The lodge has a fitness center with indoor pool, massage, sauna, and exercise room, and the charming though touristy town will satisfy the serious shopper. *Trapp Family Lodge, Stowe, VT 05672, tel. 802/253–8511 or 800/826–7000 (reservations). Mid-Dec.–early Apr.: 5-day package for 2, $840. Trail fee: $10 (included in package).*

VERMONT **From Craftbury Common to Stowe.** After 3 seasons of bicycling and hiking tours, outfitter Backroads switches gears

in winter to offer a number of cross-country ski trips. This 5-night trip includes stays in 2 fine Vermont inns near extensive trail networks. Guides lead you on daily tours from the inns, but if you would rather ski your own route you are free to do so. Instruction is offered for less-experienced skiers, and intermediates and experts can polish up on their skating and striding techniques.

The trip begins at the colonial village of Craftsbury Common, where you spend 3 nights at the elegant Inn on the Common, known for its 5-course dining feasts. Guides lead you on trails from the Craftsbury Nordic Ski Center through woods and open fields and around icy lakes. The 100-km system is groomed with side-by-side trails for skating and for diagonal striding. You're shuttled to Stowe, and if conditions are right you ski on the Recreation Path, an 8½-km ungroomed route that runs from the village, along a river, and is part of a 150-km trail system. By day's end you arrive at the Edson Hill Manor, a Georgian colonial-style inn. From here you do day-trips on the 50-km Mount Mansfield network, and if you want to hit the alpine slopes, Backroads will shuttle you back to Stowe.

Situated on 225 acres of rolling countryside, Edson Hill Manor has 25 rooms, 16 in the carriage house and 9 in the main manor house. Backroads groups usually stay in the carriage house rooms, which have pine paneling and raised brick fireplaces. Its restaurant serves innovative American cuisine, including a delicious grilled rabbit with cornbread stuffing and pecan chili sauce.

This tour includes 3 daily meals, lodging, guides, lessons, gratuities, a horse-drawn sleigh ride, and shuttle to Stowe and back to Craftsbury Common. There's a $50 charge for rental skis, and a $50 charge for round-trip van transfer from Burlington (either the airport or downtown). A maximum of 26 skiers are escorted by 2 guides. *Backroads, 1516 5th St., Suite B112, Berkeley, CA 94710-1740, tel. 510/527–1555 or 800/462–2848, fax 510/527–1444. Feb.: 6 days, $1,245.*

VERMONT **Viking Inn-to-Inn Tours.** Inn-to-inn trips used to be a famous pastime of

Vermont winters—leisurely guided jaunts with baggage transported for you, fine food and drink awaiting in century-old hostelries, rooms furnished with antiques, and goose-down comforters spread on old brass beds. Although many of the operators of these tours have long since gone under, the Viking Ski Touring Center has survived. It is one of New England's oldest cross-country ski centers, founded in 1970, and its touring company, Viking Inn-to-Inn Tours, still runs 5-day inn-to-inn trips that combine skiing with hospitality and fine food in the atmosphere of 18th- and 19th-century buildings.

Novice skiers can handle most of these trails, although intermediates are likely to ski—and see—rather more. A mix of groomed and un-groomed paths run through farmland and birch, pine, and maple forest. Terrain is more gentle than at many Vermont resorts, and views look over rolling hills and up to the Green Mountain peaks. A maximum of 8 people accompanied by 1 or 2 guides—depending on the cohesiveness of the party—ski between 4 country inns.

The group starts at Viking's Londonderry guest house, a 4-bedroom B&B converted from an 1860s farmhouse. The first hour is spent with a brief review of technique, with the staff evaluating skiers to make sure side trips match skiers' abilities. It's as little as 5 km, but no more than 10 km, from one inn to the next, but trips on ungroomed routes to downhill play areas and viewpoints can double the distance skied daily.

Other accommodations include the 200-year-old Colonial House, near Weston, which is known for its made-to-order omelets; Rowell's Inn, a former stagecoach stop near Simonsville; the Village Inn, near the tiny town of Landgrove, which offers a sleigh ride and a hot tub; and on the final night, Londonderry's Highland House, the newest of these 4 (built in 1842) and perhaps the most posh, with a lovely post-and-beam dining room and many antiques. Breakfasts at the inns include fresh baked goods. For dinner there's a variety of meat and fish entrées. Lunches, eaten on the trail, include sandwiches, fruit, hot drinks, brownies, and cookies. All meals, baggage

transportation, and a sleigh ride are included in the cost of this tour.

The Viking Ski Touring Center is in south central Vermont, near Bromley, Stratton, and Okemo ski areas. Its own 40 km of trail, which you'll use if you extend your stay, are double tracked but lack a skating lane; grooming is good. Three km of trail are lighted on Saturday nights. *Viking Inn-to-Inn Tours, 287 Rt. 100, Weston, VT 05161, tel. 802/824–6286, fax 802/824–3934. Jan.–early Mar.: 5 days, $535. Trail fee: $11 (included in package).*

THE MIDWEST

MINNESOTA **Boundary Wilderness.** The Gunflint Trail, tucked up in the northeast corner of Minnesota, is about as far north as you can go before entering Canada. It's an uncrowded, wild land of lakes and forest broken by rolling hills. The region is best known for the Boundary Waters Canoe Area Wilderness, long winters, moose, and timber wolves. When snow falls, it stays—and stays dry.

The region also has 4 cross-country trail networks with more than 200 km of ski trails: the 100-km Upper Gunflint Trail connected by the 29-km straight-run Banadad Trail to the 55-km Central Gunflint Trail. And then there's the Pincushion Trail, whose unconnected 25 km are about 25 miles south of the Central Gunflint. The entire system is spread out along the 63-mile highway known as (what else?) the Gunflint Trail. These ski trails lace around or over a half dozen lakes, over hills (300-foot elevation change throughout the system), past impressive cliffs, and by spruce bogs. Most are double tracked, but some combine single track and a skating lane. The Gunflint area has 6 lodges, one B&B, the Ollie Cabin, and the Banadad yurts.

Boundary Country Trekking can help you customize a self-guided, cross-country, lodge-to-lodge, yurt-to-yurt, or lodge-to-yurt trip. You can also choose to stay at just one lodge, from which you can take day-trips. The company makes your reservations, maps out a route for you, and arranges to have your car and luggage driven to each destination. You can take meals at the lodges or yurts or bring your own food. There is no instruction and no guide on these tours, but if you choose at least one night at the Bearskin Lodge, you can take advantage of its free group lessons.

One popular option is a night in a woodstove-heated yurt shared by 4 to 6 persons. A yurt host brings overnight gear and prepares a hearty Mongolian hot pot dinner, with platters of veggies and meat cooked in steaming broth and served fondue-style.

The distance between lodges is generally 8 km to 12 km, but you can take longer routes or even travel part of the way by car. *Boundary Country Trekking, 590 Gunflint Trail, Grand Marais, MN 55604, tel. 218/388–4487 or 800/322–8327, fax 218/388–4487. Thanksgiving–early Apr.: about $115 per day. The larger the group the lower the rate.*

MINNESOTA **Sugarbush and Norway.** With its collection of items as varied as historical depot signs and neon clocks, and accommodations ranging from a remodeled chicken coop to a small lodge, Maplelag is nothing if not eclectic. This is a ski resort with a style of its own, and owners Jim and Mary Richards take pride in the high percentage of repeat visitors they get each year.

Located in rural northwestern Minnesota, 20 miles from Detroit Lakes and about an hour's drive from Fargo, North Dakota, Maplelag is at the edge of a dense forest. Just a few miles west, the prairie begins, so Maplelag is probably the last (or first) cross-country ski area east of the Rockies. The resort has 53 km of groomed trails winding through forest and an excellent telemark practice area about a half mile from the main lodge. Most loops are gentle and groomed only for diagonal stride, with double tracks; Wavy Gravy has a good deal more up-and-down. There are 6 km of skating trail maintained for race training and as a technical challenge, and a new 1½-km lighted loop.

Instruction by 4 staff members, 2 of whom are Norwegian, tends toward the informal. Classes are usually small, sometimes only 2 or 3 in

a group, and cost $7 per person, per hour; private lessons cost $10 per hour. You can request to join a guided introductory tour of the trails, which is offered free. Free mid-week tours to nearby Tamarack Wildlife Refuge and Itasca State Park are also available.

You can spend winter days and nights skiing, snowshoeing, ice fishing, and ice skating, and the 500 pounds of sunflower seeds distributed at feeding stations along the trails annually make for excellent bird-watching. You might also see deer and, occasionally, moose and bobcats, and you will probably come across wolf tracks.

To soothe sore muscles, you can relax in one of the 2 saunas, the Turkish steam bath, or the 30-person outdoor hot tub, then make the plunge into the 8-foot swimming hole cut into the icy lake. As a reward for this feat, you are allowed to buy a T-shirt proclaiming your achievement. On Saturday nights you can dance to a DJ, and if you really want to get away, the Shooting Star Casino on White Earth Reservation is just a half-hour's drive.

The word *Maplelag* reflects the owners' interest in Norway and the fact that this used to be a working maple syrup farm. The Richards collect and display Norwegian folk art, stained glass windows, homemade Scandinavian skis, metal lunch boxes, neon clocks, and railroad signs. There is a range of accommodations for the 180 guests; you might stay in a small lodge with modern furnishings and a private bath, or you could choose a remodelled Finnish sauna or a former chicken coop, which don't have private baths. All guests must either bring linens or a sleeping bag or rent linens for $30 per week.

Meals are served family-style in the main lodge dining area, which is reserved for overnight guests. Dinners often follow an ethnic theme—Italian, Greek, Chinese, or German—and there is always a vegetarian option. The rich desserts include double fudge brownies and hot fudge sundaes. For breakfast you might feast on Swedish pancakes with lingonberries; for Sunday brunch you are treated to a Scandinavian smorgasbord. *Maplelag, Rte. 1, Box 52, Callaway, MN*

56521-9741, tel. 218/375–4466 or 800/654–7711 (reservations). Mid-Dec.–mid-Mar.: 5 nights, $260 (extra nights, $46). Price does not include $30 per week for linens.

THE SOUTHWEST

ARIZONA **Grand Canyon's North Rim.** At this northern Arizona lodge you can have the overwhelming silence, space, and awesome beauty of the Grand Canyon almost to yourself. Although more than 400,000 visitors come to the area in summer, in winter the backcountry Kaibab Lodge has no more than 50 guests. Located just 5 miles north of Grand Canyon National Park's North Rim entrance station, it is accessible only by enclosed tracked SnowVan, a 1½-hour, 26-mile trek south from the Jacob Lake junction, where U.S. 89A and Rte. 67 intersect.

The lodge is home to the North Rim Nordic Center, founded in winter 1988–89, and sits on the 1,500-square-mile Kaibab Plateau, towering a vertical mile over the desert and up to 9,200 feet above sea level. The snow is reliable, and the sunshine abundant.

You ski on the center's 60 km of mostly intermediate trail, groomed with both double tracks and a skating lane, or on the 23 km of forested backcountry trails, which are marked but ungroomed. In addition, you can try telemarking on the groomed telemarking hill and take free group lessons in classic, skate, or telemark skiing from the small ski school staff of 3 certified instructors.

If you're feeling more adventurous, you can join one of the free guided tours, which range from 10 km up, or choose to pay $25 to $60 extra for special tours to canyon overlooks that include meals and, in some cases, SnowVan transportation, snowshoes, and overnight stays in huts. No more than 8 skiers are accompanied by one guide.

If you stay at Kaibab for 5 days, consider taking the overnight expedition to Grand Canyon's Point Imperial. You ski along 23 km of groomed trail to a sleeping hut at the edge of Saddle Mountain Wilderness, just outside the park. The views from Saddle Mountain are incredible: You can see Shiva Temple, Echo Cliffs, and Marble Canyon. To reach Point Imperial, you have to ski 3½ km more—on marked but ungroomed trails through old-growth forest. This trip can be taken by 5 to 8 skiers. Each pays $25, which includes the guide, one dinner, one breakfast, 2 box lunches, and transportation of some equipment.

Back at the Kaibab Lodge, you can choose to sleep in fully furnished cabin rooms with one or two double beds, private bath, and hot showers, or heated yurts with eight bunk beds (bring your own sleeping bag, pillow, and towel) and outhouses. Both are comfortable but far from luxurious. The main lodge has a dining room, where you eat all your meals, and a great room with a fireplace, where skiers socialize. There's also a television room, beer and wine bar, gift shop, hot tub, and ski rental and repair shop.

Keep in mind that the lodge is at high altitude. Children over 5 who can ski will probably have fun, but there's no day care here and no special facilities for kids. *North Rim Nordic Center at Kaibab Lodge, Box 2997, Flagstaff, AZ 86003, tel. 602/526–0924 or 800/525–0924 (outside Arizona), fax 602/527–9398. Dec. 24 and 29: 5 days, cabin for $600 per person, group yurt for $520. Jan.–Mar.: 5 days, cabin for $560, yurt for $480.*

THE ROCKIES

COLORADO **The Green View.** Characterized by good taste and natural beauty, Vista Verde is being transformed from mighty fine to superb. Founded as a working cattle ranch in 1920, the 540-acre spread was purchased in 1991 by John and Suzanne Munn, who have dramatically improved the facilities. They've added to and redecorated the cabins, built a new lodge, and created a lake, but they've wisely kept vital staff, including chef Jacques Wilson, famous for his desserts (try the chocolate raspberry torte).

Vista Verde has 30 km of 2-way trail, groomed by Sno-Cat with a skating lane and double tracks so that you can ski side-by-side with a friend. Although the network is on the small side, it is an unusually gentle and scenic system, which the Munns plan to expand. Trails wind across meadows and through conifer and aspen groves, and offer glimpses of the Continental Divide. The system connects with 50 km of marked trails and virtually unlimited backcountry opportunities in the surrounding Routt National Forest. You can count on more than 300 inches of snow annually.

The ranch is situated at 7,800 feet, 25 miles from Steamboat Springs, and a free shuttle makes runs to the airport and into town. The 8 log cabins and 3 lodge rooms can accommodate 36 guests, but there are seldom more than 20 except at Christmas. The cabins are nestled among aspen on a hillside, only a moment's walk from the ski trails. Deer, elk, fox, and other wildlife are often visible in the meadow below.

There's a telemark area and a sledding course, or you can try snowshoeing or horseback riding if the weather is good. So you won't forget that this is one of Colorado's finest working ranches, you are encouraged to take the sleigh, drawn by 2 black draft horses named Doc and Dillon, out to feed the herd of horses.

The 5-night NordiClass package for novice or expert includes lessons by certified instructors, fun events such as a treasure hunt and an obstacle course competition, moonlight or lamplight skiing, all equipment, lodging, three daily meals, snacks, and transportation to and from Steamboat. *Vista Verde Ranch, Box 465, Steamboat Springs, CO 80477, tel. 303/879–3858 or 800/526–7433. Mid-Dec.–mid-Mar.: 1 night, $135 ($175 for the holiday season). Jan. and Mar.: 5-night NordiClass package, $625.*

COLORADO **10th Mountain Division Huts.** Colorado contains the greatest number of ski-in huts and yurts in North America, but its crown jewel is the 10th Mountain Division trail and hut system—14 huts set in the White River National Forest between Vail, Aspen, and Leadville and connected by 400 miles of trail.

Although it's possible to arrange your own trip to the area by calling the 10th Mountain Division Hut Association (tel. 303/925–5775), you will need at least one experienced backcountry navigator with map and compass skills (and a bit of self-confidence and common sense about backcountry winter travel). Another option is to go with Vail-based Paragon Guides, a company that has been leading groups through the area since 1978.

Paragon's overnight tours run from 3 to 8 days and are rated Level I, Level II, and Level III. When arranging your trip, be very honest about your experience and skiing ability. A maximum of 8 skiers are escorted by 2 guides. Transportation to and from the trailheads, meals, hut fees, backcountry and telemark instruction, sleeping bag, and community equipment are provided. Sleeping bags and food are transported to the huts by Paragon, but be prepared to tote a 20- to 30-pound pack. A pretrip orientation and acclimation day is spent at the Arrowhead Ski Area, near Vail, where participants are given a lift ticket, Nordic skills lessons, use of backcountry ski equipment, and a briefing on the trip, all part of the trip cost.

This is a high and light-filled land of dramatic contrasts, where most of the huts lie above 11,000 feet and the term *dry powder* is an understatement. Aspen groves spill down hillsides, conifer stands and meadow are intermingled, and there are bowls, glades, and endless vistas. Add crisp air that should be bottled for sale on city store shelves, and you have a skier's dream of heaven.

You ski from 6 miles to 8 miles each day, with elevation gains and losses of 700 to 3,000 feet, depending on the group's abilities and the route chosen by your guides. At least one layover day is incorporated into most trips so you can relax, tour, telemark, or summit a nearby peak.

The huts are 2-story log buildings sometimes described as backcountry chateaus. Mattresses line the upstairs bunks, which can sleep up to 16 people. The heating and cooking are done with wood stoves, and water comes from melting snow. Large south-facing solar pan-els provide the energy to light the main areas of the hut, but flashlights are needed to navigate your way to the outhouse at night.

The trail is named after the 10th Mountain Division Army Ski Troop that trained at nearby Camp Hale during World War II. Make your reservation early; hut capacity is limited and booking the precise trip you want can be difficult. *Paragon Guides, Box 130, Vail, CO 81658, tel. 303/926–5299, fax 303/926–5298. Late Nov.–mid-Apr.: 3–8 days, $510–$1,400.*

COLORADO **Welcoming Your Kids.** Here's a cross-country resort that not only accepts children but also caters to them. The kids get their own programs, such as wildlife tracking and ski games, and they even have a winter playground called Knickerknickerland over which they rule (adults are denied entry unless accompanied by a child). Unique among cross-country areas, C Lazy U Ranch hires a certified teacher to tutor children in English, history, math, science, and French, so you don't have to feel guilty if your kids are missing a few days of school.

Since the ranch is at 8,300 feet, you have to take some time to acclimate, but once you do, you can take advantage of nearly 40 km of groomed trail with a single track and a skating lane, as well as an area especially groomed for beginner telemarking. C Lazy U's trails run from 1 km to 8 km, and grooming is good. There are also backcountry routes and hills for advanced telemarking.

Ranch guides lead a series of free tours, including a 5-km round-trip to the top of Baldy Mountain, with 60-mile vistas. One 15-km round-trip backcountry tour for intermediate and advanced skiers winds through a forest of subalpine fir, spruce, and lodgepole pines along the Continental Divide. You may see elk, moose, red fox, coyote, ermine, snowshoe hare, eagles, and hawks. The number of skiers and guides varies with each tour, but there are seldom more than 4 guests per guide. The ranch's rental equipment is generally new, and there are more touring skis than track or telemark, but it's all lent out gratis.

Under new ownership since 1988, C Lazy U Ranch has both AAA 5-diamond and Mobil 5-star ratings. It's a 2-hour drive from Denver's Stapleton Airport via I–70 and Route 40, which continues to Steamboat Springs. You pass over Berthoud Pass, from which you can see paths carved through the mountains by avalanches, through the Fraser Valley, and on to Granby, 6 miles from the ranch.

As many as 100 guests are accommodated in a medley of cabins, none of which has TV or phone. Food is served in the dining room, where 10 guests sit at each table. Two entrées are offered for dinner: a customary hearty western platter, perhaps rack of lamb with fresh rosemary apricot glaze, and a lighter dish, such as turkey with cranberry sage sauce.

Ranch facilities are entirely reserved for overnight guests, so faces become familiar in short order. There's plenty of recreation on the more than 2,000 private acres and 3,000 acres of surrounding national forest: sleigh rides, a ½-mile sled run, daily shuttles to alpine skiing at Winter Park and Silver Creek, snowshoeing, dogsledding, sauna and Jacuzzi, moonlight tours, trap and skeet shooting, skating parties, racquetball, and even bingo and billiards for the more sedentary. *C Lazy U Ranch, Box 379, Granby, CO 80446, tel. 303/887–3344, fax 303/887–3917. Mid-Dec.–late Mar.: 1 night, $95–$160. Ask about minimum-stay requirements.*

IDAHO **Backcountry Trekking.** On this 3-day trip beginning in the Sawtooth Valley you stay in one yurt and one walled tent and tour above the tree line. You pass through a coniferous forest of pines and furs and through stands of aspen. The terrain is alpine rugged, with peaks above 10,000 feet, but you ski along a valley and a ridge on relatively easy trails.

The tour begins in Sun Valley, Idaho, and you are driven by van 1 hour and 15 minutes north to the hut trailhead in the Sawtooth Valley. It's just 3½ miles, about a 3-hour ski, to Fishook Hut, a Mongolian-style yurt in Fishook Valley with views of the Sawtooth Mountains. You enjoy an early afternoon lunch at the hut, then guides take you out on backcountry tours chosen to match your group's skiing abilities.

The next day you ski to Bench Hut, a walled tent at an elevation of 7,500 feet. You cover more than 5 miles of relatively easy terrain with gentle switchbacks that taper off to a low-angle ridgeline from which you can look east across the Sawtooth Valley to the White Cloud Mountains. Red Fish Lake, created by glaciers, is directly below you. You arrive at Bench Hut in time for lunch. The afternoon is spent touring around the hut, perhaps climbing the slopes that rise just behind it. You might tour 2 of the area's lakes or take lessons in telemark technique from the guides.

The trip's highlight is the third day's 4-mile loop around the 5 lakes above Bench Hut. You use climbing skins to scamper up the low ridge behind the hut, and tour across or around the small alpine lakes. At the highest point, you ski out onto the fifth lake and look up at the imposing vertical towers of Mt. Heyburn. You eat a late lunch back at Bench Hut and then ski 6 downhill miles out.

The huts are easy to get to and backcountry sleighs with provisions are pulled by the guides and guests who want to help out, so skiers can spend most of their time on the trail carrying a backpack containing only personal items and a sleeping bag.

The company takes pride in its reputation for good food, which is prepared by a trained chef. Meals may include homemade pizzas, feta cheese salad, or a savory basil lemon chicken dish with rice pilaf. The huts are in the Sawtooth National Recreation Area, where permanent structures are prohibited. The Spartan accommodations have lodgepole pine bunk beds with foam mattresses; the pit toilets are out back. Fishook Hut has the added luxury of a hot tub, and Bench Hut has a sauna.

A maximum of 12 skiers are escorted by 2 guides. Standard tour includes guiding, instruction, meals, transportation to and from trailhead, ski equipment, sleeping bag, and avalanche transceiver. The company supplies a variety of the latest equipment on the tours, so people can try out different skis. The deluxe tour is a little pricier but includes both fancier foods and wines. *Sun Valley Trekking, Box 2200, Sun Valley, ID 83353, tel. 208/788–9585, fax 208/788–9585. Mid-Nov.–mid-Apr.: standard tour, $110 per person per day. Price includes ski rentals.*

IDAHO AND WYOMING **A Tamer Route to the Tetons.** This exclusive 7-night trip run by Bill and Pam Bryan of Off the Beaten Path takes you on several adventures in the Targhee and Bridger Teton national forests of Idaho and Wyoming. There is enough variety to satisfy most winter recreation appetites.

The trip begins in the resort town of Jackson, but 5 days are spent on the sunny side of the mountains at Teton Ridge Ranch, a small and brilliant skiing gem near tiny Tetonia, Idaho. Comprised of 1,600 acres of varied terrain, the ranch has more than 20 km of trail groomed with both double tracks and a skating lane. Trails are designed to be pleasurable rather than challenging, with 2 distinct kinds of terrain. One loop series leads east through conifer and meadow, climbing into Wyoming before returning to the lodge. Routes heading south and west wind gently downhill, following a series of miniature valleys, crossing small intervening aspen-clad ridges. You may spot moose, deer, and coyote tracks but seldom the animals themselves. There's telemark skiing down Teton Pass and backcountry tours in the Big Hole Mountains.

Off the Beaten Path books the entire ranch for its tours. The 10,000-square-foot log lodge accommodates only 10 guests in 5 bedrooms, with a whirlpool, steam shower, and wood stove; meals are superb.

Dana Dewitt, the ranch's guide, naturalist, and part-time chef, joins Bill and Pam in leading you to their favorite places to ski. Your stay usually begins with a relaxing arrival day, but a late-afternoon kick-and-glide session can be arranged before cocktails and dinner. You can also choose to spend a day on the downhill slopes or the cross-country tracks at Grand Targhee Ski Resort (21 miles away) or at the giant Jackson Hole ski area. One morning is set aside for a sunrise ski tour of the ranch and environs. It's the best time to glimpse wildlife.

You return to Wyoming for 2 full days at Spring Creek Resort, which is surrounded by spectacular views. You sleigh ride through the world's largest elk herd, tour Grand Teton National Park with a naturalist, and see bighorn sheep in an area that claims the largest concentration of the species in the Lower 48. A sleigh-ride dinner highlights the final evening. All meals, lodging, guide service, and ground transportation to and from Bozeman Gallatin Airport are included. *Off The Beaten Path, 109 E. Main St., Bozeman, MT 59715, tel. 406/586–1311 or 800/445–2995, fax 406/587–4147. March: 7 nights, $2,500.*

MONTANA **Big Sky, Big Ranch.** Lone Mountain Ranch is a giant of the winter guest-ranch genre, with 75 km of trail groomed with double tracks and a skating lane. Located 15 minutes from burgeoning Big Sky alpine ski area and 40 miles southwest of Bozeman, it's less isolated than other ranches. And since Lone Mountain's trails and dining area are open to the public, you're likely to meet more skiers here than at other ranches, where facilities are restricted to overnight guests.

Skiing begins at 6,700 feet, so you must think about acclimating. Virtually every groomed route gives views of 11,166-foot Lone Mountain Peak, which dominates the region. Most trails involve a fair amount of climbing and turns and are suited to eager intermediates or to less experienced skiers with time on their hands.

Open since 1977, Lone Mountain offers a great diversity of tours. A number of all-day snow-coach trips take guests into Yellowstone National Park, where you ski over mostly gentle terrain. Fawn Pass, on the fringe of Yellowstone, is a delight in spring, when you have a chance of seeing grizzlies. One overnight trip goes by Sno-Cat to a backcountry yurt in the Spanish Peaks and includes guided skiing and meals. On all Lone Mountain tours, group size is usually limited to 7 skiers with one guide, and tour length ranges from about 5 km to 19 km.

Up to 50 guests stay in the ranch's 23 different cabins clustered around a mountain stream right beside the ski trails. These log structures house from 2 to 9 people; they have private baths, western-style furnishings, and electric heat. Some have fireplaces. Dining in the main lodge is headed up by European-trained chef Gerard van Mourik, whose rack of lamb has become a local legend. There is, however, always a lighter option, such as grilled breast of chicken.

Lone Mountain packages include airport shuttle, an on-snow buffet that's a gastronomic and visual treat, and a sleigh ride to the North Fork Cabin. Here, you and 40 to 50 other guests are seated at tables of 8 to 10 and served an elegant, family-style prime rib dinner, cooked on an old-fashioned wood stove, with cheesecake for dessert. You are entertained by such lively acts as the singer and guitarist Walking Jim Stoltz.

Consider making January reservations, when coldest temperatures are offset by driest snow. Keep in mind that the ranch's ski retail shop is top of the line, and its rentals are state of the art. *Lone Mountain Ranch, Box 69, Big Sky, MT 59716, tel. 406/995–4644, fax 406/995–4670. Early Dec.–early Apr.: 7-day package, $1,900 per couple.*

MONTANA **Railroad and Ski Tracks.** Halfway between the towns of East and West Glacier lies tiny Essex, Montana, home of Izaak Walton Inn, the only American cross-country area with doorstep delivery by Amtrak. This is wild country: The inn is a stone's throw from Glacier National Park, trails border the Great Bear Wilderness, and the vast Bob Marshall Wilderness is almost next door. It's a region known for wildlife, including cougar, elk, eagle, moose, and wolf; bears have been known to prowl the trails early on April mornings.

Backcountry enthusiasts have spectacular touring opportunities in Glacier National Park and the adjoining Flathead National Forest. Small groups of 8 to 10 skiers with 2 guides are led on 10- to 20-km tours that include transportation to and from the trailhead and lunch. The Avalanche Creek tour through

Moose Country, on the southern tip of Glacier, is ideal for beginners, and intermediates will enjoy practicing turns on the numerous hills of the Autumn Creek tour, which has awe-inspiring views of the crest of the Continental Divide. The Snyder Lake tour will challenge more advanced skiers.

For those who prefer to stay close to the inn, there are more than 30 km of trails groomed with double tracks and a skating lane on mostly gentle terrain. These run along the Middle Fork of the Flathead River and photogenic Essex Creek at a comfortable altitude below 4,500 feet. There's 1 km of lighted trail for night skiing, as well as a telemark hill that can be skied at night even though it's not lit. Snow around Essex is extremely dependable, with about 450 inches each year.

The half-timbered, 3-story hotel, built in 1939 to accommodate crews for the Great Northern Railroad, has 31 rooms, and additional lodging is in beautifully renovated 4-person cabooses with minikitchens, set on a hilltop overlooking the inn. A 5-night package includes luggage transfer from the train, 2 daily meals, trail privileges, sauna, a lesson, and a tour of Glacier National Park.

The railroad theme is maintained throughout the inn. Lodging is decorated with photos of trains and lanterns, and the Flagstop Bar and the Dining Car have railroad memorabilia on the walls. Be sure to try the succulent huckleberry cheesecake pie. For a change of pace, you can drive an hour from the inn to Big Mountain, an excellent downhill skiing complex. *Izaak Walton Inn, Box 653, Essex, MT 59916, tel. 406/888–5700, fax 406/888–5200. Mid-Nov.–mid-Apr.: 5 nights, $548; 7 nights, $727. Trail fee: $5 (included in package).*

MONTANA **Yellowstone on Skis.** Off the Beaten Path has hired two guides—a naturalist and a Nordic ski specialist—to lead this 8-day trip through Yellowstone National Park, which in winter is the closest you can get to an African game park without crossing the ocean. Bison roam sheltered valleys; elk graze around the steaming geysers and mud pots, where the snow has melted; otter frolic in the icy streams; and bighorn sheep make appearances on the rocky ledges.

The guides recount Yellowstone's history, teaching you about forest regeneration after the great fires of 1988 and discussing park controversies such as destructive grazing caused by elk and bison overpopulation, and the proposed reintroduction of the timber wolf.

The trip starts in Bozeman, and you are transported by van to the park. You spend 3 nights at the Mammoth Hot Springs Hotel, which is surrounded by open country and relatively easy skiing terrain. The first full day ends with a soak in the Boiling River Hot Springs. You are transported by snowcoach 75 miles south along the spectacular Grand Canyon of the Yellowstone to the Old Faithful Lodge, where you stay for another 3 nights in comfortable cabins. Here you ski the Upper Geyser Basin, stopping at Morning Glory Pool and Lone Star Geyser. The snowcoach then takes you another 30 miles to the town of West Yellowstone, where you spend an afternoon skiing the famous Rendezvous Trail tracks. Saturday's lodging is at the handsome and historic Gallatin Gateway Inn near Bozeman.

Plan to ski from 13 to 19 km per day over gentle terrain. Trails are groomed sporadically. A maximum of 8 skiers are escorted by 2 guides. You should have some experience on cross-country skis. All meals, lodging, guide service, instruction, and ground transportation are included. *Off the Beaten Path, 109 E. Main St., Bozeman, MT 59715, tel. 406/ 586–1311 or 800/445–2995, fax 406/587– 4147. Early Feb.: 8 days, $1,950.*

WYOMING **Rendezvous in the Tetons.** You can ski on the sunny, quiet side of the Tetons if you book a trip with Rendezvous Ski Tours, founded in 1987 by Glenn Vitucci and Carole Lowe. The company offers customized tours for both beginner and expert skiers using its own spacious guest house and 3 Mongolian-style yurts located in Targhee National Forest, along the Idaho-Wyoming border and near the Jedediah Smith Wilderness and Grand Teton National Park.

The terrain is typical of the west slope of the Tetons: wide open, low-angle bowls and broad ridges that you can cruise for miles, as well as high-angle powder bowls and relatively easy summit peaks that offer spectacular views. Snowfall is steady and reliable with more than 500 inches of champagne powder between November and April. The skiing is less steep and there are shorter runs than in Jackson, but the region has few of the sub-zero temperature inversions that plague the Jackson side of the Tetons.

Most groups are comprised of fewer than 8 skiers with one guide. Daily distances and level of difficulty varies with each group; however, it's a 3- to 4-mile ski from the base guest house to each of the yurts—light, round structures 20 feet in diameter, with wood stove and propane cook stove—which sleep 8 on bunk beds with sleeping bags. The yurts lie a couple of thousand feet lower than Colorado's 10th Mountain Trail cabins, so there's less time needed for altitude acclimation.

Rendezvous's guest house, with its wonderful canyon views, is near Driggs, Idaho. It can sleep up to 12 skiers and has a hot tub. Package tours include van shuttle from either Jackson, Wyoming, or Idaho Falls airports, as well as accommodations, most meals, instruction, and use of light backpack (10–25 lbs.), climbing skins, and avalanche transceivers, if necessary. The town of Jackson Hole, with its huge alpine ski area, and Grand Teton National Park, are 45 minutes by car over the pass. *Rendevous Ski Tours, 219 Highland, Victor, ID 83455, tel. 208/787–2906, fax 208/354–8489. Late Nov.–early Apr.: 4–7 days, $395–$695.*

THE WEST COAST

CALIFORNIA **Big Daddy on Tracks.** Skiers often argue over which alpine ski resort is the largest, but in the world of cross-country skiing there's no doubt who is Big Daddy. By any criterion, Northern California's Royal Gorge leads the pack by a long kilometer—largest, most famous, and most popular.

Located just off I–80 on the way to Lake Tahoe, Royal Gorge spreads over 9,000 acres; it has 8 track systems with 83 trails and 321 superbly groomed kilometers, the equivalent of skiing from San Francisco to the crest of the Sierras. Annual snowfall here averages 400 inches, but when the snows don't fall, the resort covers up to 15 km with man-made white powder. Trails have double tracks and a skating lane, and changes in temperature and snow type have relatively little effect on skiing quality because the resort's grooming is the best in the business.

Royal Gorge is one of those rare areas that was selected for its aesthetic appeal rather than merely added onto a preexistent facility. Trails slip around ridges, undulate through meadows and along frozen lakes. They are well marked for ability levels and distances and have enough variety to please beginners and challenge experts. From Summit Station views west are dominated by spectacular Devil's Peak (7,704 feet), while craggy Castle Peak looms to the north, reaching almost 10,000 feet. From Point Mariah you can see the precipitous 4,400-foot drop into the Royal Gorge itself, on the North Fork of the American River. Three unique short surface lifts allow you to practice downhill techniques and save you from having to climb from low-lying trails to higher routes (there's 1,600 feet of vertical change).

Instructors certified by the Professional Ski Instructors of America offer a program of group lessons with 6 to 8 skiers and private instruction, including telemark and skating clinics. Guided tours may be arranged at the ski school (fees vary). Ski hosts are stationed at Summit and patrol the trails, giving advice and directions. You can break up your skiing day with stops at the area's 10 warming huts, 4 cafés, and 2 hotels.

If you're not on skis, you have to take a Sno-Cat-drawn sleigh about 6 km to reach the 35-room post-and-beam Wilderness Lodge. Rooms here have wood paneling and quilts on the beds. The restaurant serves French country cuisine. Rainbow Lodge, a 1920s B&B on the Yuba River, is at the far end of the resort's 22-km Interconnect Trail. You can drive your car to this property, which has 32 rooms with old-fashioned furnishings, wood-paneled walls, and chintz comforters. There are no TVs or phones, and some rooms share a bath. The excellent restaurant serves continental and Italian cuisine.

Be aware that the resort's size does have its downside: On weekends and holidays there can be too many skiers around the trailheads, although after the first few kilometers, the crowds thin out. There are 3 alpine ski areas within a 3-mile radius of the resort, and gaming at Incline Village on Tahoe is only 40 minutes away. *Royal Gorge Cross Country Ski Resort, Box 1100, Soda Springs, CA 95728, tel. 916/426–3871 or 800/634–3086 (outside N. California), fax 916/426–9221. Mid-Nov.–mid-May: 5-day ski week (using Wilderness Lodge), $460 (not available on major holidays). Trail Fees: $13.50 half day and $17.50 full day, weekends and holidays; $12.50 half day and $15.50 full day, weekdays (included in package).*

CALIFORNIA **Sierra Tahoe Tour.** On this 5-day Backroads tour you sample 4 different cross-country areas in Northern California—Royal Gorge, Tahoe Donner Cross-Country Ski Resort, Tahoe Nordic, and Squaw Creek. Groups of 12 to 20 skiers are escorted by 2 leaders certified in Nordic ski instruction. Three hotels are used as bases from which the guides lead day trips.

At Royal Gorge you have more choices than at any other resort in North America. You can ski the easy and intermediate terrain around the open meadows of the Van Norden track system or though the woods of the Summit Station track system. You ski the broad, flat meadows of Euer Valley at the Tahoe-Donner Cross-Country Ski Resort, and if you feel ambitious you can try the more challenging slopes. Then you go gliding at Tahoe Nordic along Lake Tahoe's lovely north shore. Time is set aside on the last day of the trip for skiing the gentle trails of Squaw Creek's Cross-Country Center.

Royal Gorge's Rainbow Lodge, the 1873 vintage Truckee Hotel, and the modern Resort at Squaw Creek are your accommodations for this trip. Equipment rental costs $50. *Backroads, 1516 5th St., Suite B122, Berkeley, CA 94710, tel. 510/527–1555 or 800/462–2848, fax 510/527–1444. Jan.–Feb.: 5 days, $1,295.*

WASHINGTON **Topping the Cascades.** The Cascade Mountains of Oregon and Washington aren't precisely a Nordic byword, so why add Methow Valley to your list of places to know? Well, how about 175 km of groomed trail with more in the works, hut-to-hut *and* lodge-to-lodge skiing, lots of cold powder, helicopter skiing, telemarking, and a million acres for touring? Add truly spectacular views (the Cascades may reach up to only 7,000 feet locally, but the valley floor is only 2,000 feet!), negligible altitude acclimation, plus 200 days of sunshine a year and voilá! A Nordic mecca.

This Backroads lodge-to-lodge tour begins just 10 miles outside the town of Winthrop, at the 78-room Sun Mountain Lodge, an AAA 4-diamond resort with 360° views of the valley and the Sawtooth Wilderness. The lodge has outdoor hot tubs to soothe sore muscles, and Backroads guests are treated to a relaxing evening sleigh ride. The gourmet dinner served in the lodge might include hickory applewood smoked duckling or rainbow trout roasted on bamboo leaves with an almond crust.

Sun Mountain Lodge is accessible to the 175-km trail system maintained by the Methow Valley Sport Trails Association and is the centerpiece of the valley. Backroads guides lead you through the mostly flat and rolling farm and woodlands. All skiing abilities, from novice to expert, can be accommodated. You can ski from 3 km to 20 km each day, stopping on the trail to eat the lunch Backroads packs for you. Although you have to pay more for the privilege, try to arrange to take a lesson with Don Portman, one of the lodge's outstanding instructors.

From Sun Mountain you follow the New Methow Trail down the valley into Winthrop, spending the night at the Rio Vista Hotel, which overlooks the Methow River. It's an easy ski through these lower lands before you head to the Mazama Country Inn, a wilderness lodge that's the stopping point for the plows that clear the highway to it.

On the final day of the tour you can choose to ski through rolling woodlands to a warming hut or take a skating lesson. Two certified Nordic instructors lead the group of up to 16 skiers and give daily lessons to those who want them. Rentals cost $50. *Backroads, 1516 5th St., Suite B122, Berkeley, CA 94710-1740, tel. 510/527-1555 or 800/462-2848, fax 510/527-1444. Jan.–Mar.: 5 days, $1,145.*

SOURCES

ORGANIZATIONS The **Cross Country Ski Areas Association** (259 Bolton Rd., Winchester, NH 03470, tel. 603/239-4341) promotes the sport and aims to protect the interests of operators and skiers. It serves as a clearinghouse of information on where to go and how to get started skiing cross-country.

PERIODICALS *The Best of Cross Country Skiing,* a directory published by the Cross Country Ski Areas Association, provides a verbal and pictorial introduction to the sport. Its concise listings cover size of trail system, additional recreation, availability of accommodations, kids' attractions, and more. Published five times per winter, *Cross Country Skier* (1823 Fremont Ave. S, Minneapolis, MN 55403, tel. 612/377-5105 or 800/827-0607) is a wide-ranging magazine, covering U.S. (and a few Canadian) ski destinations, technique, equipment, waxing, and touring tips. *Ski Trax* (2 Pardee Ave., Suite 204, Toronto, Ontario M6K 3H5, Canada, tel. 416/530-1350), a Canadian publication covering both U.S. and Canadian cross-country skiing, was recently changed from a tabloid to a magazine format. It provides much of the same information as *Cross Country Skier* but has a greater emphasis on racing. It's published 4 times per winter.

BOOKS In *Cross Country Ski Inns, Northeastern U.S. & Quebec* (Robert Reid Associates), Marge Lamy describes 37 hostelries and their trail systems. Her pleasant prose is complemented by excellent color photographs. *Gene Kilgore's Ranch Vacations* (John Muir Press) includes a substantial section on ranches with winter operations.

ALSO SEE Once you've learned to ski cross-country, it may be time to work on your downhill technique. The Ski Schools chapter will help put you on the slopes. Or perhaps you'd rather skip the hills and speed things up on the flats: check out Snowmobiling. Or try tripping cross-country behind a pack of yipping huskies—look into Dogsledding.

Dogsledding

by Susan Farewell

Hike!" commands a musher as he releases a brake.

They don't call it mushing for nothing. The word is from the French *moucher,* meaning "to go fast." And the dogs do. On command, a team of surprisingly small, amazingly strong huskies charge off, howling and yowling excitedly. Of all the wild sporting adventures out there, dogsledding may be the wildest—not only because it's exotic, but because you're literally out in the wilds with pack animals, just like a polar explorer.

Dogsledding, like most adventure sports, is not for everyone. For one thing, you have to like the cold. "How cold?" you ask. Let's just say sled dogs start to get uncomfortable when the temperature rises above zero. You also have to like roughing it. Even the nicest accommodations aren't far removed from camping out (here, luxury means a wood stove in your tent), and with camping out comes cooking out—any rib-sticking cuisine that can be cooked in a pot.

Most importantly, you have to like dogs—a lot. Out in the wilderness, with nothing but snow as far as the eye can see, it's you, a handful of other campers and guides, and a pack of 35- to 55-pound dogs. Contrary to the romantic image you may have of sled dogs, they're not all cuddly, clean Siberian huskies. They're often mutts (a little malamute, a lit-tle timber wolf, some Samoyed, German shepherd, you name it), not particularly clean, and, in some cases, downright smelly. Some outfitters maximize your contact with the dogs, having you help with everything from harnessing to feeding to untangling snarled sled lines, while others take care of everything for you. In any case, there's something very special about the experience of working with animals. One week with the same dozen or so dogs and you can't help but get attached.

Your trip will probably begin when you meet the other participants at a central location, often an airport. From there, you move on to the wilderness area you're going to traverse. The first day is usually reserved for general instruction on mushing—learning how to harness and unharness the dogs and getting a feel for the movement of the sled. Expertise is gained on the trail. Most outfitters take you out for a short run the first day to leave you eager to get started in earnest. Cross-country skiing and snowshoeing are combined with mushing on some trips, and some introduction to these sports is included in your orientation.

You'll be mushing through some of the country's most scenic landscapes—from the woods of Maine to the wilds of Minnesota—areas inhabited by birds and beasts most people see only on TV. And traveling by sled, there's

Connecticut-based freelance writer Susan Farewell has traveled worldwide in search of sporting stories. She first learned about dogsledding in Greenland, when she hitched a ride on one to the local airport.

nothing between you and nature's handiwork. Most trips are structured with 2 to 3 hours of mushing in the morning and 3 to 4 hours after lunch.

Meals are always big and fortifying, with lots of carbohydrates to give you energy on the trail, but you'll find everything from beef bourguignon to spaghetti. The level of service—from the amount of work done by the guides to the sophistication of the meals—varies with each outfitter.

The distance covered each day is usually between 15 and 35 miles, depending on the stamina of the group and the trail and weather conditions (heavy snow can slow things down). This may sound arduous, but the dogs do most of the work, and the clean crisp air rushing past you makes 7 or 8 miles an hour feel like flying.

Driving a team of dogs is an experience all ages can enjoy, although some outfitters do set a minimum age. The only requirements are good physical health and a serious sense of adventure. All sorts of individuals are attracted to the sport, including singles, married couples, and families with older children. In some cases, they're very athletic and outdoorsy, but not always. If you want to sample the experience without committing a whole vacation to it, look into the handful of winter resort areas where you can go out for a shorter outing—among them Krabloonik Kennels in Snowmass, Colorado (Box 5517, 81615, tel. 303/923–4342), which offers 2-hour rides.

The following trips are longer, at least 5 days, although some of the outfitters offer shorter and longer trips as well. Prices for the 5-day trips range from $600 to $1,300.

CHOOSING THE RIGHT TRIP

We list just a small sampling of dogsledding trips. If you're choosing between trips we don't list, be sure to ask the following questions.

Will I be driving my own team of dogs? If you're not interested in skiing or snowshoe-ing, make sure you pick an outfitter who gives each member of the party a sled. You may need to consider your level of physical fitness if you're going to be cross-country skiing.

What kind of accommodations are provided? Accommodations on dogsledding trips generally aren't luxurious, but they can vary from tarps spread out in the open to heated cabins. Don't count on privacy.

What is the food like? Expect hearty meals from every outfitter, but ask for more specifics. Some outfitters offer a catered vacation, with each meal prepared by a staff member; others expect participants to plan, prepare, and clean up communally.

How many miles are covered each day? Get a good idea of how strenuous each outfitter's pace is.

What will my responsibilities be on the trip? If you're expecting a relaxing vacation, make sure you don't pick an outfitter who'll have you doing everything from hitching up the dogs to pitching the tents.

What's the cost and what's included? The prices of trips we list include accommodations, meals, and all major equipment—sleds, tents, and cookware. For these trips, sleeping bags and pads are also provided, but on some trips you will need to bring your own. Some outfitters also provide insulated jackets and other cold-weather wear that you might not own.

How long has the company been in business? Generally, a company with several years experience has learned how to deal with all kinds of problems.

Do you have references from past mushers? If you have questions about what the experience is like, there's no substitute for a chat with someone who has been on the trip and dealt with the outfitter.

How far in advance do I need to book? It's often necessary to reserve a spot on a dogsledding trip at least 3 months in advance—but there could be room for you on a trip that leaves tomorrow.

MAINE **Touring the Northern Woods.** There couldn't be a more fitting setting for a dog-sled experience than the northern woods of Maine, home to the Mahoosuc Guide Service. It is an area of unmatched wild beauty, featuring the state's highest peak (Mt. Katahdin), biggest state park (Baxter), and largest lake (Moosehead). Year-round residents include a number of large black bears, moose, bob-cats, and flocks of birds. If you've ever wanted to climb into one of those snowy paper-weights, this is for you.

Your 5-day trip through Rapid River country begins at Mahoosuc's headquarters in tiny Newry, just north of Bethel. The night before you set out, maps and routes are discussed; gear, including boots, parkas, and backpacks, is issued; and a video is shown providing instruction on everything from how to har-ness and handle the dogs to how to set up a winter camp. You spend the first night in a local bed-and-breakfast and then rise bright and early for the 45-minute drive to Rich-ardson Lake, where your journey begins.

Mahoosuc's groups are intimate (4 to 10 peo-ple), and each party is accompanied by 2 or 3 guides. There are enough sleds on each trip to accommodate everyone, with 2 mushers per sled. You take turns driving, and some-times you have to run alongside your sled. There's time for cross-country skiing and snowshoeing at the end of the day and on the one rest day.

Most gear is piled on a sled, but you have to carry a light pack containing your sleeping bag, pad, and clothes. You sled along Richardson Lake and Rapid River onto the frozen Umbagog Lake, taking in a landscape filled with spruce and fir trees, streams and lakes, and a menagerie of wildlife.

Campers take part in preparing meals; you might be asked to chop a hole in the ice for water or gather wood for a fire. Mahoosuc spe-cializes in vegetarian dishes; one favorite, called Rubaboo, is a traditional Maine log-ger's stew, dense with split peas and barley. Home-baked desserts, such as chocolate-chip and oatmeal cookies, elicit "oohs" and "aahs" from campers at the end of each meal.

At night, you retire to your sleeping bag in a canvas tent heated by a wood stove. The dogs sleep outside, under the stars, periodically howling in unison, snouts pointed to the sky.

Mahoosuc Guide Service is owned and oper-ated by Polly Mahoney and Kevin Slater, com-mitted outdoorspeople, former Outward Bound leaders, and state-registered Maine Guides. They offer sledding trips in Maine, New Hampshire, and Canada that range from day trips to 10-day expeditions. Their phi-losophy is as fresh as the snowy landscape their sleds traverse: "To respect and accept the wilderness, not to compete against it." Most equipment (including the ashwood dog sleds) is handmade, using techniques devel-oped by Native Americans; some of the trips are conducted by Native American guides. Many of the dogs were raised in Alaska, and several are veterans of the 1,049-mile, Anchorage-to-Nome Iditarod sled race.

All equipment is provided, including camp-ing gear, parkas, snowshoes, extra-warm boots, and skis with special bindings to accommodate those boots; serious Nordic skiers may want to bring their own equip-ment. *Mahoosuc Guide Service, Bear River Rd., Newry, ME 04261, tel. 207/824–2073. Dec.– May: 5 days, $500–$600. Book at least 3 months in advance.*

THE MIDWEST

MINNESOTA Following the Voyageur's Highway. One week with Boundary Country Trekking in Minnesota's Boundary Waters Canoe Area and you'll be thinking about buy-ing yourself a team of huskies and a sled. Arleigh Jorgenson, one of North America's leading mushers and racers, heads up this dogsledding program, and you'll be driving your own team. His unflagging enthusiasm and knowledge of dogsledding make these trips especially worthwhile.

This 5-day trip begins in Ely, Minnesota, with an evening orientation session, when you watch a video filmed from inside a sled and get an excellent feel for movement on the trail. The first day is spent getting familiar with the dogs and sleds. After you learn the basics of harnessing the team, using the brakes, turning the sleds, and understanding the dogs, it's time for a short ride. For your first run you use a small team (3 or 4 dogs) that you are able to physically reign in if you have problems commanding them. By the end of the trip you'll be able to handle a full team of 7 or 8.

The first 2 nights are spent in modern cabins with indoor plumbing. Then, in the company of your guide, you're off to explore the historic Voyageur's Highway on the border of the United States and Canada. The Highway is actually a series of lakes connected by portages. It was used for centuries by Native Americans who traveled between lakes to trade and hunt. In winter the frozen lakes are prime dogsled terrain.

Each day, you and as many as 7 other mushers and a guide spend an average of 6 hours on the trail, covering between 20 and 40 miles a day. Much of the time, you ride on the runners of the sleds, which requires good balance and a workout for muscles you may not generally use. In some areas, you have to run alongside and guide the sleds: While it's usually pretty smooth going over the frozen lakes, some of the portages can get a little rough. You stop often to give the dogs time to catch their breath or for some advice from your guide on upcoming terrain.

At the end of the day you settle in camps set up in advance by the Boundary Country staff. Sleeping quarters include basic tents and cabins that sleep 2 to 4 as well as yurts—canvas structures that look like huge marshmallows with a plexiglass skylight on top. All accommodations are furnished with mattresses, tables, chairs, and wood stoves; yurts also have gas lights. Meals on the trail are high in carbohydrates and protein, but the staff outdoes themselves to concoct palatable entrées in the rough and rugged environment of the trail. Grilled rainbow trout, beef bour-

guignon, and shish kebabs are a few of the dinner specialties.

Other Boundary Country destinations include the Gunflint Trail on the north shore of Lake Superior and the wilds of the Canadian Arctic. Trips range from 2 days to 2 weeks in length. Boundary Country provides everything but personal clothing. *Boundary Country Trekking, 590 Gunflint Trail, Grand Marais, MN 55604, tel. 218/388–4487 or 800/322–8327. Mid-Nov.–late-Apr.: 5 days/6 nights, $1,385. Sign up 2 months in advance.*

MINNESOTA **Outward Bound in the Boundary Waters Canoe Area.** The intensely scenic Boundary Waters Canoe Area, 2 million acres of forests scattered with more than 100 lakes, is the setting for a dogsledding and cross-country skiing expedition sponsored by Outward Bound, known for its wilderness education program. The course, which takes place in December or January, is not only a physically challenging adventure but also an inspiring emotional experience; meeting the challenges of the wilderness and working together with others results in personal growth.

The group assembles in Duluth, Minnesota, then moves on to the base camp in Ely for an orientation. A "sleeping warm" seminar on the first afternoon teaches you to use insulated sleeping bags and pads to conserve body heat and survive Minnesota's bitterly cold nights, a lesson you quickly put to good use. The 3 instruction sessions on the second day have you out cross-country skiing, running sled dogs, and performing ice rescues: The trip traverses frozen lakes and rivers, and it's important to be prepared for emergencies. How much time you spend in Ely depends on the group; with Outward Bound, you never move faster than the slowest person. Once everyone is ready, you head for the woods and spend the next 6 days alternately mushing and cross-country skiing across frozen lakes and portages, 3 to 15 miles a day.

On the trail, you begin every day with breakfast at 6 and stop for snacks every couple of hours—but never for long, since your body temperature drops when you stop moving. When skiing, you travel ahead of the sleds, learning to navigate the trails, reading the safety of the ice, and breaking trail for the dogs. At 3 or 4, you stop and set up camp for the night. You cook meals communally over an open fire, usually simple but filling dishes such as spaghetti, macaroni and cheese, chili, or vegetarian casseroles. You sleep under a tarp on one of the frozen lakes.

Outward Bound provides everything but personal clothing, though a parka and wind jacket can be supplied on request. Participants are encouraged to go on the trip individually, rather than with a friend or relative, as group dynamics are a big part of the experience. You must also be open to new experiences and in good physical condition; a medical exam within the year is required. Minimum age is 16, and most participants are in their 20s and 30s. *Voyageur Outward Bound School, 10900 Cedar Lake Rd., Minnetonka, MN 55305, tel. 612/542–9448 or 800/ 328–2943. Dec.–Jan.: 8 days, $895. Sign up 2 months in advance.*

ALASKA

NORTHWEST **Exploring the Gates of the Arctic National Park.** Sourdough Outfitters will take you mushing through this park, which, with 8,300,000 acres above the Arctic Circle, is one of the last great wilderness areas in the world. Within its boundaries, the 600-mile-long Brooks Range weaves between glassy rivers and scattered lakes. The area teems with wildlife, including the Western Arctic caribou, the black bear, Dall sheep, moose, wolves, wolverines, lynx, grizzlies, eagles, falcons, and many migratory birds.

Sourdough Outfitters offers several 6- and 8-day sledding trips here between mid-February and mid-April. This is one of the most beautiful times of year in Alaska; the days are 14 or 15 hours long and the Northern Lights dance at night. Daytime temperatures generally are in the teens or twenties, although it can drop well below zero at night.

Your trip begins with a day of orientation in Bettles, where you start by learning about the history of dogsledding from its origins as a means of commerce to its use for recreation. Next is a thorough familiarization with equipment: how to set the brake, tie the reins, load the sled, and keep the runners clean of ice. Then it's time to get to know your dogs. Going beyond harnessing them and giving commands, you learn to perceive the pecking order of each team—which dog is the leader and which are the followers. On a short ride around Bettles, your team follows the guide's lead team, allowing you to get a feel for driving. (By the end of the trip you'll take a turn as the leader.) Upon your return, you get a lesson in unharnessing and feeding the teams.

In the morning you're off and running, driving your team over 15 to 30 miles (in 4 to 8 hours) of trail a day, stopping periodically for photo opportunities or to give the dogs a rest. At day's end, you help set up the tent camp, gather firewood, melt snow for water, and unharness, feed, and care for the dogs. Nights are spent in large, army-style canvas tents that sleep 3 or 4 and are heated with wood-burning stoves. Meals are basic, consisting of anything that travels well and can be easily cooked in a pot or pan: spaghetti with Italian sausage, lasagna, meat loaf, stews, and chili.

Sourdough provides all camping gear plus special boots, heavy-hooded parkas, insulated wind-proof mittens, and snowshoes. *Sourdough Outfitters, American Wilderness Experience, Inc., Box 1486, Boulder, CO 80306, tel. 303/444–2622 or 800/444–0099, fax 303/ 444–3999. Feb.–Apr.: 8 days, $1,800; 6 days, $1,530. Sign up 3 months in advance.*

SOURCES

ORGANIZATIONS The **International Sled Dog Racing Association** (Box 446, Nordman, ID 83848, tel. 208/443–3153) provides information on races and other dogsled activities and publishes a magazine called *Info* ten times a year. Membership is $20 a year.

PERIODICALS *Mushing* is a bimonthly magazine that covers all aspects of dogsledding, including how-to information and articles on health, ethics, and news (Stellar Communications, Box 149, Ester, AK 99725, tel. 907/ 479–0454).

BOOKS *Cold Nights, Fast Trails,* by Dave Olesen; *Dog Driver: A Guide for the Serious Musher,* by Mike and Julie Collins; *The Joy of Running Sled Dogs: A Step-by-Step Guide to Training and Enjoying Sled Dogs,* by Noel Flanders; and *Travelers of the Cold: Sled Dogs of the Far North,* by Dominique Cellura provide detailed information on the how-tos and experience of dogsledding.

ALSO SEE If you think you need some survival coaching before you tackle winter camping, turn to the Wilderness and Survival Schools chapter.

Fishing Camps and Fly-Fishing Schools

by Bud Journey

he reason for all the fly-fishing schools scattered around the country is simple: *It is not easy* to cast a bulky line, a flimsy leader, and a feather-light fly between trees, against the wind, away from the back of your neck, and into position just in front of a fish's nose. The fly must land without frightening the fish and must look natural, or the fish will see it for what it is: a deceitful attempt by an antagonist to entice it into ingesting a bundle of feathers, fraught with peril, containing no food value at all.

Therein lies the allure of fly-fishing: It's a challenge that's rewarding when you succeed and that teaches you humility when you fail. Spin-casting, trolling, and bait-fishing have a similar attraction, and the type of angling you choose has nothing to do with a right method or a wrong method. It has more to do with personal preference and what's available.

If you'd like to spend a week's vacation learning to fish, a fishing school like those we list here can teach you the rudiments, supply the equipment, and see that you get a chance to practice your newly developed skills on nearby streams or ponds—for a price. A 2-day course can run from $95 to $500. If you're a seasoned angler, you can sign up for an advanced class, or choose one of the camps, charter boats, or guide services.

Fishing schools and fishing camps are not always discrete entities; in fact, their elements often overlap. The operators of most fishing schools also usually offer guide service for a day's fishing or can recommend local guides, who will show you where, when, and how to fish specific bodies of water. On the other hand, although most fishing camps don't offer formal instruction, their guides are usually willing and quite able to provide what brief, on-the-spot tips the novice or intermediate fisherman will need during the trip. Though you can fish by yourself, the guides know all about the local waters and the best ways to extract their inhabitants; sometimes they even provide equipment. They charge hefty sums per day ($75–$350) for their expertise, but many anglers feel they are worth it.

Camps often house and feed you, but usually do not supply equipment; most anglers prefer to use their own. It is common for fishing schools to furnish all or most of the necessary gear while you're in class, and they frequently provide lunch, but for other meals and lodging you're usually on your own—though the operators will help you make arrangements. Guide services and charter boats, which usually charge by the day, can put together a 5-day or week-long package for a vacation, but you often have to forage for nearby food and lodging.

Almost all fishing camps are independently run, as are most fishing schools, although

Bud Journey, a freelance writer and photographer who lives in Montana with his wife and two children, has been fishing since he was six. He has won regional and national outdoor writing and photography contests and claims to have caught a 10 lb. 9 oz. walleye.

some are set up in conjunction with a manufacturer or a merchant such as Orvis or L.L. Bean. Bigger is not necessarily better, nor is the instruction superior or more personalized. It makes more sense to book a school in an area you want to visit than to go out of your way to attend a school with a big-name sponsor.

If you're working on a limited budget, it might be best to forget the school altogether and look for a fishing camp that can provide a few minutes of instruction before you go out onto the water. Some camps cost less than $100 per day. Be forewarned, however, that if you're fly-fishing, those few minutes of instruction are not likely to make you more than barely competent. If it's what you can afford, though, go for it; a crash course in the fishing camp may be enough.

No matter what method of fishing you prefer, and whether you're at a school or camp, you soon become familiar with the concept of catch-and-release. Because the populations of some species have been diminished by over-fishing, short growing seasons, low reproduction, loss of habitat, and other factors, most schools and camps encourage the practice of carefully releasing uninjured or slightly injured fish. At some, this practice is mandatory.

Although fly-fishing skills are generally considered the hardest to master, you must know a few basics for any kind of fishing. Consider the following: You must (1) get a lure in front of a fish and (2) entice that fish to take the lure into its mouth. The fish will do so because (1) it wants to eat the lure or (2) it wants to attack the lure. Sometimes both.

A fly fisherman almost always tries to simulate food for the fish. A bait fisherman actually offers the fish real food. Anglers who cast artificial lures (cast-and-retrieve) or who troll, slowly dragging a lure behind a boat, are trying to imitate food *or* provoke an attack. It's the same with jiggers, who sit over their quarry in a boat or on a bank and bounce their lures up and down, and also with little children who fish with safety pins on the end of a string. Their varying degrees of success

depend on their skill and on the willingness of the fish to take the lure. As all anglers learn, the disposition of the fish can be affected by weather, barometric pressure, water temperature, pH factor, fishing pressure (the number of people fishing a particular area), the food supply, and just plain cussedness.

For some, the allure of fishing is in the challenge. Making a perfect cast into a tiny pocket of open water, amid weeds, willows, and overhanging limbs; fooling a wily game fish into striking; then deftly guiding it to the net through an underwater labyrinth of weeds, roots, and rocks is the ultimate satisfaction. For me, however, fishing is renewal. It recharges me after the pressures of the modern world have sucked the vigor from me. Sometimes I catch fish; sometimes I don't. But it's not the catching that counts, it's the process: a renaissance that only a fisherman knows. You'll have to try it to understand. And with apologies to the anonymous person who first said it, I would like to remind you that if you're too busy to go fishing, you're too busy.

CHOOSING THE RIGHT OUTFIT

You can never be absolutely sure you'll be satisfied with a school or camp until you've been there yourself. No matter how well you check it out, it may not meet your expectations. You can minimize that possibility, however, by asking the right questions.

On which species do you focus? Trout? Walleye? Salmon? Bass? Northern Pike? Different fish inhabit different parts of the country, and anglers have their preferred species. If you want trout, you might go to the Rockies; for bass, try the South. Northern pike lurk in Minnesota lakes and in much of the West and Midwest; salmon stay on the coasts.

What method do you teach? Ask schools whether they teach just fly-fishing or can also instruct you in other methods, such as jigging, spin-casting, and trolling. Remember that learning a method of fishing is just the beginning. A school can give you a glimmering of these skills, but you must go fishing again and again to refine them. A school can teach you to read water—to recognize the kinds of places fish like to stay and feed—but only by hunting a species time after time do you discover its ways and habits.

Do you provide actual on-site fishing opportunities for real fish in natural conditions? That's a question that's essential to ask any fishing school you're considering. Casting and fishing on a stocked or sterile pond is a far cry from fishing in the wild for wild fish on a swiftly moving stream, surrounded by vegetation and other obstructions.

What's the cost and what's included? Unless otherwise noted, the cost of camps includes food and lodging but not guiding; schools' prices include instruction only; and guide services provide guiding only. All prices are per person unless otherwise noted.

Tackle is provided at schools unless otherwise noted, but not usually for the time you spend fishing on your own after completing the school. Camps and guides seldom provide tackle, but may be able to lend or rent it to you. Boats may or may not cost extra.

When accommodations are not provided, most outfits can steer you to a variety of accommodations in a range of prices. The cost of your fishing license is almost always extra.

How do I get there? Some fishing camps are very remote, and getting there can be not only pricey but also time-consuming. Some operators have shuttles; in remote areas you'll often be transported by river boat, airplane, float plane, horseback, and the like. Sometimes the cost is extra, sometimes it is included in the rate.

What are accommodations like? The best surprise is no surprise, so be sure you know what you're paying for. If you're staying at a fishing camp, ask what the guest quarters and public spaces are like; they could be stylishly rustic and sturdy or they could be cheap motel rooms with paper-thin walls. If you're camping, find out about the campsites and the shower and latrine arrangements. Before you sign up to use the outfitter's tents or sleeping bags, make sure they are suited to the location.

What's the food like? Although ambitious cuisine is unusual, plain American fare, which you are most apt to find, can seem extraordinarily tasty when your appetite is sharpened by a day in the fresh air. Still, some outfitters and camps do better in the kitchen than others. If what you eat matters to you, make sure you know what to expect.

Is a guide available? What is the fee? How many guests per guide? Guides' fees can often be split by as many as 3 people, although with fly-fishing, 2 anglers per guide is the most you want.

What equipment is required? What else will I need? Make sure your equipment matches the requirements of the camp or school you are considering. For fly-fishing in streams you probably need waders, which are not always provided, although in hot weather in some waters, you can wade in sneakers and shorts or jeans.

In a fly-fishing camp, are fly-tying facilities available? You might want to try to "match the hatch" of insects that are emerging while you are there.

What is the weather like? Is it buggy? The weather can range from snowstorms in the Rockies in June, though they're rare, to hot and humid in Florida, which is usual. Mosquitoes are always around in woods and swamps, but some seasons are worse than others.

What is there for non-fishing companions to do? Many schools and camps are near cities large enough to have the usual complement of amusements; at those in the wilderness, you'll have to be content with such rural pursuits as hiking, bird-watching, identifying wildflowers, and other nature studies. There's often riding, swimming, and exploring ghost towns or historic sites.

How long have you been in business? Can you provide references? Longevity should not necessarily be the deciding factor. Everybody has to start sometime, so if other things are favorable, don't let the operator's lack of experience discourage you. It's best to get a word-of-mouth recommendation from an independent source, but if none is available, calling people on a list provided by the operator is better than nothing. Chances are that if the anglers you call are satisfied, you will be too.

How far in advance must I book? You can ordinarily sign up anywhere from a month in advance to a year ahead. The more famous and the more remote locations tend to fill up faster. If you have your heart set on a specific location or program, however, give a call and you may snag a cancellation.

MAJOR PLAYER

ORVIS This long-established Vermont fishing-tackle manufacturer sponsors mid-priced fly-fishing schools in Vermont, Wyoming, New York, Virginia, Massachusetts, Pennsylvania, and California. Most of the courses are shorter than 5 days, but virtually all Orvis schools can help you round out a week's vacation by arranging guided or unguided fishing trips for the remainder of your time. The schools provide Orvis equipment and all follow the same formula for successfully teaching all levels of angler—as individuals or in groups—how to hook, land, and release a fish. The courses are often booked by companies as corporate entertainment for clients or executives, and classes are noncompetitive; each student progresses at his or her own pace. Orvis publishes a newsletter and a pamphlet describing the various schools (Historic Rte. 7A, Manchester, VT 05254, tel. 800/235– 9763, fax 802/362–3525).

FAVORITE TRIPS

THE NORTHEAST

MAINE **Colonial Sportsman's Lodge.** Variety, economy, and home cooking set this fishing lodge apart. Owner-operator Pat Takach believes her camp in rural northeastern Maine is unique: Here, guests can fish for land-locked salmon from the front yard on the bank of Grand Lake Stream. Pat also cooks and serves the meals, in which she takes

great pride. Guests can take a full American plan and eat at the lodge or choose basic housekeeping cabins. There are cooking facilities in 5 of the 6 cabins.

Besides land-locked salmon, you can fish for lake trout, smallmouth bass, brook trout, white perch, and several varieties of panfish, including crappie. But you must bring your own equipment; rentals are not available. You can fish from the bank or rent a boat for $35 per day. The fishing guides charge $120 per day for 2 people and use locally manufactured 20-foot-long Grand Lake canoes to get to the best fishing waters. Fly-fishing is a major activity at this site, but you can cast lures, troll, and bait-fish, if you prefer. Catch-and-release fishing is encouraged but not required. Free-time activities include swimming and tennis. *Colonial Sportsman's Lodge, Grand Lake Stream, ME 04637, tel. 207/796–2655. May–Sept.: 5 days, $175 housekeeping units; $375 with meals. Sign up 2 months in advance.*

NEW YORK **Tightlines Charters.** Nobody knows trolling with downriggers better than John Oravec. He fishes for species that spend their time suspended between the surface and the bottom. A 10- to 12-pound lead ball tied to his line keeps the bait at the proper depth, and the line releases when the fish takes the lure. Oravec is a full-time charter captain who fishes for king salmon, steelhead trout, brown trout, lake trout, coho salmon, and Atlantic salmon in the western basin of Lake Ontario. Oravec also writes articles and conducts seminars for fishing enthusiasts, so instruction is one of his fortes. He provides hands-on learning for his fishing clients, both beginners and experienced anglers, but does not house or feed them.

The intriguing aspect of Oravec's operations is that he also goes for muskies and walleyes in the St. Lawrence and Niagara rivers with downriggers, which is a departure from the traditional methods. People usually cast-and-retrieve for muskies, and go jigging, bait-fishing, and trolling without downriggers for walleyes. There's also fly-fishing in local streams and the Niagara River for brown trout, king salmon, and steelhead, and Oravec will set up a variety package or "safari" for you, using all these different methods for different species in different waters. He uses a state-of-the-art, 33-foot charter boat for his downrigger fishing, as well as smaller boats for shallower waters, and provides all the necessary equipment for up to 6 guests. Children fish free.

Oravec's base of operations is Point Breeze, in the Lake Plain region of upstate New York, which is an apple-growing area between the Finger Lakes and Niagara Falls. Local lodging runs from pricey waterfront motels to budget-oriented bed-and-breakfasts, and meals range from fast food to fine dining on the water. Free-time activities include swimming, jet-skiing, golf, camping, shopping, and a variety of other pursuits. *Tightlines Charters, 913 Sunset Beach Rd., Waterport, NY 14571, tel. 800/443–2510, fax 716/682–3037. Mid-Apr.–mid-Sept.: 5 days, $625 per person with small boat (2 person min.), $500 with large boat (4 person min.). Price includes equipment but not food and lodging; sign up 3–6 months in advance.*

NEW YORK **Beaverkill Valley Inn.** This family-oriented inn sits in an undeveloped area of Catskill State Park, within a stone's throw of the Beaverkill and near other classic trout streams, surrounded by eastern hardwoods and flowering shrubs. Whitetail deer, foxes, raccoons, bears, coyotes, and other animals also live in the area.

The Victorian lodge, built in 1893 and now renovated, has 20 rooms, 12 with private baths. It has an indoor swimming pool, a self-serve ice-cream parlor, children's playroom, and 2 private tennis courts, along with a casting pond stocked with trout. Breakfast and lunch are buffets, and dinner has a set menu. You might have corn chowder, loin lambchops, fresh vegetables, bread baked on the premises, and black-and-white chocolate mousse. Guests hike and mountain-bike on 17 kilometers of maintained trails, and photography is also popular.

You fish free in the casting pond, on a 3¹/₂-mile stretch of the Little Beaverkill that's exclusive to guests, and in numerous other public waters in the vicinity. The inn contracts with several local fishing guides, whose fees vary from $75 to $200 per day. The famous Wulff School of Fly-fishing, which offers top-quality 2-day schools, is less than a mile away. *Beaverkill Valley Inn, Lew Beach, NY 12753, tel. 914/439–4851, fax 914/439–3884. Apr.–Sept.: 5 days, $825 ($700 shared bath). Sign up a month in advance.*

VERMONT **Orvis Fly-Fishing School.** The Orvis Company's main school is in Manchester, the site of its manufacturing plant. This is a scenic, rural region of southern Vermont, between the Green and the Taconic mountains. Continuity and longevity are two of the school's hallmarks: It has been around for nearly 30 years, and Rick Rishell has been at the helm since 1978. Much of its business comes from word-of-mouth recommendations.

You can take either of the two sessions that are given each week: Friday, Saturday, and half of Sunday; or Tuesday, Wednesday, and half of Thursday. A parent-child program runs for two weekends in April. The focus is on casting, fly selection and entomology, knots, equipment, and reading water. And casting for trout in Orvis's stocked ponds gives you a chance to put your skills to work on real fish. The school handles classes of up to 36 students and keeps the student to instructor ratios at reasonable levels for the various aspects of the course—3:1 or 4:1 on the casting ponds; 18:1 for fly-selection lectures; and about 8:1 for knot-tying seminars.

After completing the course, students fill out their vacations by fishing sections of the Battenkill through Orvis-owned access points. The school can also lend you equipment to use and provide guides, if you want. The area is oriented toward tourism, and besides fishing, you can play golf or tennis, go shopping, visit museums and antiques shops, and go to summer theater.

Orvis can arrange lodging at the plush Equinox Hotel or at other local hotels and B&Bs. *Orvis Fly-Fishing School, Box 798, Manchester, VT 05254, tel. 800/235–9763, fax 802/362–3525. Early Apr.–late Aug.: 5 days, $395. Sign up 2 months in advance.*

VERMONT **Streamline Fly-Fishing School.** Peter Cammann is so into fly-fishing that he runs a fly-fishing school, sells equipment, and broadcasts and writes about fly-fishing as well. In keeping with the technical aspects of the sport, he limits his classes to a maximum of 3 people per instructor. His young but experienced crew (some have appeared on ESPN fly-fishing shows) believes in hands-on instruction in a real setting, so you learn on an actual stream, where such variables as wind, changing currents, and streamside vegetation complicate the mechanics of convincingly getting a fly in front of a fish. Fees for classes include lunch and a handbook, *Fly Fishing for Trout,* and all equipment except waders during the course.

A good 5-day vacation is to take 2 days of fly-fishing instruction with Cammann or one of his instructors, then go on day-trips by canoe, armed with a copy of his *Fishing Vermont's Streams and Lakes,* to try out your new fishing skills on one of the many nearby bodies of trout water. For fishing on your own, Cammann can put you in touch with a local canoe-rental service (and a guide, if you wish). The staff can also help you arrange accommodations: The varied local lodging ranges from B&Bs to motels and condos, and the dining runs toward fine restaurants, with a few pizza places thrown in.

The school is in the rural, forested Mad River Valley of northern Vermont, where a convenient mixture of 6 first-class trout streams, numerous tennis courts, a famous golf course designed by Bobby Jones, horseback riding, hiking, canoeing, and other sports can make a lively vacation. *Streamline Fly-Fishing School, Box 1218, Waitsfield, VT 05673, tel. 802/496–5463, fax 802/496–5463. Early Apr.–late Oct.: 5 days, $420. Price includes lunch; sign up 1–2 weeks in advance.*

THE MID ATLANTIC

PENNSYLVANIA **Fishing Creek Outfitters.** In the foothills of the Endless Mountains of northeastern Pennsylvania, Allen and Iris Johnson offer one-day fly-fishing schools at two levels, and a guide service for trout fishing along Fishing Creek. The basic school for beginners is made up of 6 students and 2 instructors; the next level is a custom-tailored course with 1 or 2 advanced students per instructor.

The basic class focuses on fly-casting technique, with additional instruction on the bugs fish eat and the whys and hows of equipment. The first 2 casting sessions take place on a spacious grassy area where instruction can go on with a minimum of extraneous complications, but the third round is under real fishing conditions: on the creek's slippery rocks and uneven terrain, amid hook-catching vegetation in the pine and deciduous woods. The casting sessions are punctuated with classroom instruction, and equipment is provided. The advanced class concentrates on any of the myriad aspects of fly-fishing that the student chooses: casting technique, reading the water, fly selection, appropriate equipment, or any other.

Combining a class with 4 days of guided fishing ($150 per day, $225 for 2) on private stretches of several area streams makes a nice vacation. The Johnsons can recommend local motels and B&Bs. *Fishing Creek Outfitters, RD 1 Box 310–1, Benton, PA 17814, tel. 717/925–2225, fax 717/925–5644. May–June and Oct: 5 days, $750. Price includes lunch; sign up 3–4 months in advance.*

VIRGINIA **Orvis Roanoke.** Robert Bryant runs his operation on 800 acres of mountainous private land with 2 casting ponds fed by springs. Guests spend 2 days in fly-fishing school and 3 days (or as many as they wish) on guided trips on the Smith and Jackson rivers, fishing for rainbow trout, brown trout, and smallmouth bass. Both the Jackson and the Smith are tailwater streams: They're below dams, which makes for the good, cold water the fish need. The Jackson runs through mountainous terrain, and the Smith flows in the Piedmont area. Your guide will arrange transportation.

The school covers casting mechanics, proper equipment, knots, entomology, reading water, and the other basics of fly-fishing. The instructors, led by Lou Barlow, all have 5 years or more experience, and the student-to-teacher ratio is 4:1. The school can take a maximum of 13 students, preferably older than 12, though younger children who can handle a full day of fishing are accepted. Equipment is provided.

The guide service (catch-and-release fishing only) provides float-fishing for bass and wading for bass and trout, with no more than 2 anglers per guide and equipment provided, though you're welcome to bring your own ($150 per day, $225 for 2).

Bryant can help you find lodging and meals; there is a wide variety of each in the Roanoke area. *Orvis Roanoke, 19 Campbell Ave., Roanoke, VA 24011, tel. 703/345–3635. Late Mar.–early Sept.: 5 days, $750. Price includes lunch and guide service; sign up 1 month in advance.*

THE SOUTH

FLORIDA **Gypsy Guide Service/Suncast Fly-Fishing College.** Captain Pete Greenan uses fly-fishing equipment and other light tackle to fish for tarpon, snook, redfish, sea trout, and a few other species in the Charlotte Harbor area of southwest Florida. He concentrates on the mild backwaters for most of the action but will venture farther out for the hard-fighting tarpon. His busiest time is in winter, but the fishing is better in the spring and fall—even in the summer, if you can put up with the heat and humidity.

Captain Greenan finds that even experienced anglers are often unprepared for the special requirements of saltwater fly-fishing. He is willing to help with on-the-spot instruction, but too much of it cuts into the fishing time; consequently, he now runs a 3-day school in October and April to properly prepare his saltwater clients, and combines it with 2 days of guided fishing. Greenan normally takes out only 2 fly-fishermen or 3 spincasters at a time, but he can accommodate larger groups with the assistance of another guide. The fee per day is $350 for up to 3 people, and all equipment is provided. Children are welcome if they are truly interested in fishing.

The setting is typical of southwest Florida, with white sand beaches and mangrove islands

where eagles, ospreys, and other wildlife are often in evidence. Free-time activities include swimming, beaching, bicycling, shopping, and sightseeing in and around Sarasota. There's a wide assortment of lodging and dining options, and Greenan can put you in contact with an affordable motel or make reservations for you. *Gypsy Guide Service/Suncast Fly-Fishing College, 2416 Parson Lane, Sarasota, FL 34239, tel. 813/ 923–6095. Oct. and Apr.: 5 days, $1,195. Price includes lunch; sign up 1–2 months in advance.*

TENNESSEE **McClintock's Guide Service.** Fred McClintock has set up his low-key, one-man operation to accommodate 1 or 2 serious adult anglers who are up for long, hard days of fishing primarily for trophy fish. He uses a 20-foot bass boat to go after smallmouth bass, walleyes, and rainbow trout in Dale Hollow Lake and striped bass in the Cumberland River—both in north central Tennessee, in a rural mountainous region of mostly hardwood forest, with some cedar and poplars.

A typical day would run 8 to 12 hours on the water, casting lures and trolling, so free time is limited. Most guests simply relax when they're not fishing, but country music fans might make a beeline for Nashville, just 100 miles southwest.

Most guests bring their own fishing equipment, but loaners are available if necessary. There's a wide variety of lodging, from modest motels to expensive houseboats, and you eat at small, family restaurants or fast-food places. When you're fishing on the lake, you can buy lunch at an island restaurant, but a bag lunch is needed for the river. *McClintock's Guide Service, Rte. 3, Box 272, Celina, TN 38551, tel. 615/243– 2142. Year-round: 5 days, $1,000 (1 or 2 people). Sign up 3 months in advance.*

THE MIDWEST

MINNESOTA **Fish Tech Institute.** This is one of the all-time great fishing opportunities for kids. Director Reggie Thiel orients his 6-day residential schools so that kids are taught to fish while getting lots of opportunities to try out what they've learned. Open to kids age 10 to 17, the school is run at 4 different levels. Levels 1 to 3, for the youngest and least skilled, have classroom seminars and 7 to 8 hours each day on the water. Level 4 students go on fishing trips in Canada or Minnesota's Boundary Waters Canoe Area—a vast wilderness of lakes and forests along the northern border of the state. (Thiel also offers a 4-day parent-child school.)

The school takes a broad approach, teaching kids about all methods—fly-fishing to bait-fishing and everything in between. It also covers at least 8 different species, including walleyes, bass, northern pike, and trout. It takes 32 to 36 students, and the pupil to teacher ratio is a very low 3:1. Corporate sponsorship permits Thiel to charge pupils less than it actually costs to teach and house and feed them.

Students sleep in large lodges with porches (bring a sleeping bag and pillow), and the food is healthy plain cooking. All fishing equipment is provided, though kids can bring their own if they prefer. They spend so much time learning to fish that they have only about 1½ hours of free time in the afternoons to swim, fish, visit, or nap.

The school is at Leech Lake, the third largest lake in Minnesota, about 4 hours north of Minneapolis on Highway 371. The region is rural and heavily forested. *Fish Tech Institute, Box 807, Walker, MN 56484, tel. 218/547–1882, fax 218/547–3364. Mid-June–mid-Aug.: 6 days, $325 (level 1), $425 (level 2), $475 (level 3), $495 (level 4); 4-day adult-child sessions, $495. Sign up 4 months in advance.*

SOUTH DAKOTA **Custom Caster.** Larry and Jan Weeks arrange guided fishing trips in the Black Hills region of western South Dakota for people who want to catch rainbow trout, brown trout, brook trout, northern pike, smallmouth and largemouth bass, crappies, bluegills, and perch.

The method of fishing is your choice: fly-fishing, casting, and bait-fishing are all available.

If you need help with your technique, Larry and Jan can provide impromptu instruction for $20 per hour. That won't get you on the professional fishing tour, but it will acquaint you with the basics of fishing in western South Dakota. The Weekses have enough guides at their disposal to accommodate 12 anglers in the summer and 6 in the winter. The angler-to-guide ratio is 2:1, and the guides use canoes, float tubes (an inner tube with a suspended seat), and wading to exploit the wide variety of fishing waters in the region. If you don't have your own fishing equipment, rentals are available. Kids 10 and over are welcome, provided they are avid anglers and don't need supervision; those under 13 fish free.

The Black Hills are actually fair-sized mountains, covered with pine and aspen forests and drained by many streams, including spring creeks. Free-time activities include hiking, mountain biking, swimming, and golf. If you want bright lights, you can go gambling in Deadwood, 3 miles away.

Lodging choices range from campgrounds and RV parks to expensive and inexpensive motels, and you can go in for fine dining or settle for fast food. *Custom Caster, 316 W. Main, Lead, SD 57754, tel. 605/584–2217, fax 605/584–1183. Year-round: 5 days, $500. Sign up 90 days in advance.*

THE SOUTHWEST

NEVADA **Reno Fly Shop Fly-Fishing School.** This small, informal operation offers 1 or 2 2-day classes per month of basic instruction in fly-fishing, after which you go on guided fishing trips for such trout species as rainbow, brown, cutthroat, and brook. After classroom work, Dave Stanley and Dave Bryeans conduct the casting segments of these courses in schoolyards and parks, which have none of the brush, rocks, and other hazards of streams.

The school is basically a custom weekend class for up to 20 students, with the instructors focusing on individual needs and each teacher handling no more than 6 students. Equipment is provided if you need it. All aspects of fly-fishing, from knot-tying to equipment and fly selection, are covered, but at least half of each day is spent on casting. After completing the course, you can take Reno Fly Shop's guided fishing trips for as many days as you wish, to a variety of waters, including the Truckee River and Lake Tahoe ($185 per day for 1 or 2 people).

The unique feature of this school is that it takes place in Reno, Nevada, with all that that implies in terms of gambling and high-powered entertainment, not to mention lodging and dining choices. The school can help you arrange your accommodations. Camping, hiking, swimming, sightseeing, and water skiing are other popular activities. *Reno Fly Shop Fly-Fishing School, 294 E. Moana La., No. 23, Reno, NV 89502, tel. 702/825–3474, fax 702/825–5610. Mar.–July: 5 days, $650. Price includes lunch on guided trips; sign up 1 month in advance.*

TEXAS **Lake Fork Marina.** Keith and Darla Blair run a fishing camp for serious anglers at their marina on the shore of Lake Fork Reservoir in northeast Texas. Many consider this the prime bass lake in the state: It has produced 37 of the top 50 bass ever taken in Texas, averaging more than 14 pounds each. The marina is in a rural setting of gently rolling mountains with forests of mixed hardwoods and pines.

The Blairs provide lodging in motel-style rooms with small fridges and set you up with experienced full-time guides. The family-style meals in the restaurant are not included in the cost, but the price is moderate: breakfast, lunch, and a dinner with fried catfish, quail, hamburgers, or chicken-fried steak run no more than $20 per day.

The guides take you out in comfortable, well-equipped 19- and 20-foot bass boats, 1 or 2 guests per guide. Most of them can provide equipment, but they prefer that you bring your own. The favorite kinds of fishing are cast-and-retrieve, jigging, and bait-fishing for bass and crappie. You can buy bait and any supplies you might need at the marina. The best, and busiest, months are February, March, and

April (during the spawn), September (during the bass-fishing tournament), and October.

There's not much to do except relax and swap fishing stories during the few waking hours that you're not on the water. Because the reservoir is full of stumps, it's good for fishing, but awful for swimming. *Lake Fork Marina, Unit One, Box 2, Alba, TX 75410, tel. 903/765–2764, fax 903/765–3369. Year-round: 5 days, $1,375 (1 or 2 people). Price includes lodging but no meals; sign up 8 months in advance.*

THE ROCKIES

BRITISH COLUMBIA **Elk Valley Bighorn Outfitters.** This camp, run by Bob Fontana, is beside the Elk River in the southeast corner of British Columbia, near the Alberta line. It's about 40 miles by gravel road north of Elkford, but within a day's drive for many residents of Idaho, Washington, and Montana. Because the high-mountain cutthroat trout populations are fragile, all fishing is catch-and-release, and only artificial lures are used, since they are easier to release and thus less damaging. You do your fishing from the bank of streams and lakes.

Fontana's camp, easily the wildest in this chapter, is surely in the most awe-inspiring territory. His guiding area, hundreds of square miles in size, lies just south of Banff National Park. Here, as in Banff, high rocky peaks dominate the landscape, and coniferous forests and meadows cover the lower mountains and valleys. Natural high-mountain lakes dot the region, drained by pure, clear streams.

Fontana and a wrangler use horses to transport guests and supplies to the backcountry, which is accessible only this way or on foot. The outfitter has several camps set up with small cabins, bunks, and cook shacks, and he supplies all your needs except sleeping bags and fishing equipment. He usually accommodates between 4 and 10 people, including children (ask about family rates), and 1 or 2 guides do the work. Food is cooked over a campfire or a portable wood cookstove, but it is plentiful and of high quality: You might dine on turkey, vegetables, salad, and strawberries.

You're likely to see elk, mountain goats, bighorn sheep, moose, coyotes, wolves, deer, black bears, grizzly bears, wolverines, mountain lions, water fowl, or grouse—not all species on every trip, but you will always see lots of wildlife.

Fontana can also set up a 7-day combination trip that includes both backcountry fishing and lower-elevation float fishing in the Elk River and the North Fork of the Flathead River. *Elk Valley Bighorn Outfitters, Box 275, Cranbrook, BC V1C 4H8, Canada, tel. 604/426–5789. Late June–late Aug.: 5 days, $660; 6 days, $775; 7 days, $875. Sign up 6–12 months in advance.*

BRITISH COLUMBIA **Fernie Wilderness Adventures.** Kim Sedrovic's camp in southeastern British Columbia lies within a day's drive of most of Montana and Idaho. You fly into Kalispell, Montana, or Cranbrook, British Columbia, and Kim picks you up from either airport. The lodge, a large, old log building in a secluded wooded setting, accommodates 12 people. All meals are provided, including excellent shore lunches while you're on float trips. Children are welcome.

Sedrovic uses platform rubber rafts and MacKenzie River boats (a standard hard-sided design that accommodates a guide in the middle and an angler on each end) to float the North Fork of the Flathead River and the Elk River for Westslope cutthroat trout and bull trout, a close relative of the Dolly Varden trout. (This is one of the few places you can still catch trophy bull trout.) He prescribes a cast-and-retrieve technique for both species, and when the conditions are right he switches to fly-fishing. The guest-to-guide ratio is 2:1.

The guided float trips go through extremely wild and scenic country, including the Flathead Valley, which skirts the west side of Waterton National Park. Competition from other anglers is light or nonexistent, and photo opportunities abound. It's not unusual to see

deer, moose, elk, black bears, grizzly bears, wolves, and coyotes while floating the rivers.

It's best to provide your own fishing equipment, but Kim has some loaners and can help you with lure selection. He can also, at no extra cost, provide fundamental instruction on how to fish these rivers. In addition, he runs a 7-day trip that includes 3 days of float-fishing and 3 days of backcountry horseback riding, camping, and fishing. *Fernie Wilderness Adventures, 9 Ridgemont Ave., Fernie, BC VOB 1M2, Canada, tel. 604/423–6704. Mid-June–late Sept.: 5 days, $659; 6 days, $800; 7 days, $900. Sign up 4 months in advance.*

IDAHO **Cougar Country Lodge.** Here is an opportunity to combine fishing with adventure in Hell's Canyon, the deepest gorge in North America. Steve Wieber takes you in jet boats through some spectacular whitewater on your way to great fishing for rainbows, steelhead, smallmouth bass, catfish, and that dinosaur of the water, the sturgeon.

Wieber runs his service in the Hell's Canyon National Recreation Area, which encompasses 67½ miles of the gorge separating northeastern Oregon from western Idaho. In your free time you can go hiking, swimming, visit historic pioneer and Native American sites, and watch for wildlife. Mule deer and bighorn sheep are seen almost daily, as are waterfowl and birds of prey.

Guests use their own equipment for fly-fishing and cast-and-retrieve to catch trout and bass, and use cut-bait and worms for catfish and sturgeon—the lodge supplies equipment for the latter. Children of all ages are welcome, and those under 50 pounds pay half price. Catch-and-release is required for sturgeon and recommended for bass and steelhead.

The outfitter can accommodate up to 22 people at the lodge, and takes them out in its 4 boats in groups of 4 to 6 to fish for the day. If you're after sturgeon, which live at the upper end of the gorge, 2½ hours away, you charter a boat ($1,000 for up to 4 people) for an overnight at a tented camp, which is set up for you by the boat driver, who also cooks.

for you by the boat driver, who also cooks. Most guests do this as part of a 5-day package.

The log-cabin lodge, on the Snake River 40 miles south of Lewiston, has a deck, 7 rooms, and 2 baths, and the carpeted rooms have doubles, singles, and bunks. The home-cooked food is excellent and plentiful, and the campers, too, eat well: salads, barbecued chicken, rib steak, game hens, halibut, and such.

In your free time you can play volleyball, pitch horseshoes, swim at the big river beach, or go hiking. The lodge also offers drop-off service: For $450 it will transport as many as 12 anglers with their own food, camping gear, and tackle to the upper gorge or another fishing site, and pick them up whenever they specify. *Cougar Country Lodge, 805 Snake River Ave., Lewiston, ID 83501, tel. 208/746–3546 or 800/727–6190. Mar.–Dec.: 5 days, $775 at lodge, $750 at lodge and camp (plus boat charter). Sign up 1 month in advance.*

MONTANA **Montana River Outfitters.** Owner Craig Madsen likes to give his clients a variety of fly-fishing options on 3 of the greatest trout-fishing streams in the world. You can fish for rainbows, browns, and cutthroats on day-trips in drift boats on the upper Missouri or choose 5- to 7-day float trips in inflatable rafts on the Smith River for rainbows and browns or on the South Fork of the Flathead River for native cutthroats.

Fishing equipment is available for rent on all trips, each guide takes care of only 1 or 2 guests, and children are welcome. On the Missouri River day-trips, the fishing is good despite the fact that the river winds through farming and ranching country near Wolf Creek, and you're never far from civilization. The Smith River trip is more remote, but you are driven to the put-in and from the take-out. The trip to the South Fork, in the heart of the huge Bob Marshall Wilderness Area, is about as remote as it gets in the lower 48 states; you ride in 20 miles on horseback. The scenery on these remote trips run from spectacular to breathtaking.

On the Missouri trips, groups as large as 20 can stay in the outfitter's cabins and motel units at Wolf Creek and eat at a local restaurant (at extra cost). On the trips into backcountry, where the groups are 4 to 8 people, everything is included except your sleeping bag and fishing equipment. The guides set up tents and cook the meals on a campstove. The food is fresh—you might have salad, potatoes, steak, and strawberry shortcake. *Montana River Outfitters, 1401 5th Ave. S, Great Falls, MT 59405, tel. 406/761–1677 or 406/235–4350. Mar.–Oct.: 5 days on the Missouri River, $1,425 ($1,575 for 2 people); 5 days on the Smith River or South Fork, $1,775; 6 days, $2,075; 7 days, $2,375. Prices include lodging but no meals; sign up 2–4 months in advance.*

MONTANA **Catch Montana.** John Adza and John Talia's camp is strictly for those who want the best fly-fishing and the best accommodations available. You don't have to be an advanced fly-caster to fish with Catch Montana, but it caters only to people who take fly-fishing seriously, fully appreciate the sport, and respect Montana's fragile trout fisheries by practicing catch-and-release.

Adza and Talia and the other guides help you work out the glitches in your technique—assistance you probably need before you can properly fish the sometimes fickle waters of western Montana. They use platform rubber rafts to fish for rainbows, browns, cutthroats, and brook trout in the fabled waters of the Bitterroot River, Clark Fork River, and Rock Creek. A stone fly hatch on the Bitterroot in late March or early April provides a unique early spring dry-fly fishing opportunity for those who can't wait until summer.

The secluded lodge is in wooded land on the bank of the Bitterroot River, a few miles north of Hamilton. The valley is flanked on both sides by mountains, and the Selway-Bitterroot Wilderness in the Clearwater and Nez Perce National Forest lies only a few miles west. Whitetail deer, water fowl, beavers, grouse, ospreys, and other wildlife are in evidence on all sides. The lodge has luxurious accommodations (including a hot tub) and good home-cooked meals. Though you could go hiking or wildlife watching, after a long day place in the spacious, comfortable living room telling each other lies.

Accommodations at the lodge are limited to 6 people, but you can also fish with Catch Montana while staying at a motel in Hamilton, 10 miles south, and the outfitter can transport you. It's best to bring your own fishing equipment, but loaners are available. Guides work with a maximum of 2 guests per boat. Young people age 16 and up are welcome, if they've come to fly-fish. *Catch Montana, Box 428, Hamilton, MT 59840, tel. 800/882–7844. Late Mar.–mid-Oct.: 5 days, $1,550 ($1,250 for guided fishing only for 1 or 2 people). Sign up 6 months in advance.*

THE WEST COAST

CALIFORNIA **Clearwater House.** Dick Galland runs this fly-fishing school and camp out of a refurbished turn-of-the-century farmhouse next to Hat Creek, a prime trout stream in a sparsely populated part of northern California.

The school generally runs from Wednesday to Sunday, but shorter sessions are available. All classes take place on Hat Creek in natural fishing conditions, and video cameras are used to help fine-tune your skills. The beginners' class covers equipment, knot-tying, casting fundamentals, reading trout habitat, fly selection, and tips on how to play a trout. Intermediates learn how to catch large trout using sinking line and underwater flies called nymphs, and also how to make long casts and natural-looking floats with dry flies. The advanced class covers the technical fine points, teaching the most versatile and refined casting skills.

Clearwater House is in Cassel, in a scenic mountainous area between Burney and Fall River Mills, less than 40 miles from Lassen Volcanic National Park. It's a great place to spend a fishing vacation. You can go sightseeing and hiking in your free time, and Clearwater also offers guide service ($250 per day) and accommodations to other anglers. *Clearwater House, Box 90, Cassell, CA 96016, tel. 916/335–5500 (off-season 415/381–1173), fax 916/335–5500. Late Apr.–mid-Nov.: 5*

days, $795 beginners and intermediates, $895 advanced. Prices include room and board; sign up 3 months in advance.

CALIFORNIA **Lewiston Inn.** In the high mountains of northwest California, 30 miles west of Redding and a short skip east of Weaverville, lies the historic mining town of Lewiston. The inn, at the headwaters of the Trinity River, where it flows out of Lewiston Lake, is surrounded by great fishing country in the heart of Bigfoot territory. Don't worry: There has never been a verified case of Bigfoot eating a fisherman.

The inn's 7 rooms are in 2 restored mining buildings of the handful left in town; the main one was built in 1875. Connor Nixon, the owner, caters to anglers, especially fly-fishermen, and 40% of his guests are typically return customers. The rooms are furnished with antiques, all have baths, and some have private entrances and decks. Fifteen guests can be accommodated; children of all ages are welcome. Fishing packages of different lengths can be arranged, with guides or without, but all include food and lodging. A full breakfast is usually served on the back deck, overlooking the Trinity River; lunch is packed for your day of fishing; and dinner is taken at the Lewiston Hotel, a former stagecoach stop in town.

Lodge guests are free to do unguided shore fishing and wading fishing, and many of them bring their own float tubes. If you choose to fish with a guide ($200 per day for 1, $250 for 2), the maximum number of anglers is 3. All the guides give casting instruction for an additional charge, and though some have loaner fishing tackle, it's best to bring your own. Guided trips include fishing from a drift-boat on the Trinity River and from a power boat on Lewiston Lake; the craft used range from aluminum boats and platform rafts to float tubes and a 13-foot Boston Whaler.

The setting is coniferous forests, drained by many streams and rivers, and the inn is only 10 minutes away from the Trinity Alps. Free-time activities might include hiking, bicycling, bird-watching (bald eagles, ospreys, and waterfowl), and sitting around in the hot tub. *Lewiston Inn, Box 688, Lewiston, CA*

96052, tel. 800/286–4441 or 916/778–3385, fax 916/778–0309. Year-round: 5 days, $495 ($560 for 2). Sign up 1 month in advance.

CALIFORNIA Oasis Springs Lodge. If solitude is what you crave, you will like Warren and Linda Quan's fly-fishing resort. It's on a grassy 3,000-acre ranch in northern California, next to the South Fork of Battle Creek, about 30 miles east of Red Bluff—you can see both Lassen Peak and Mount Shasta from some spots. (It's said that long ago the Indians built Mount Shasta so their dying chief might be carried up to see the ocean one last time.) The resort's 6 miles of private water assures that even the most reclusive will find uncrowded fishing here.

The very modern lodge was completed in 1992; the air-conditioned rooms have television, ceiling fans, and some fireplaces. You can stay for as little as 2 days or as long as you like; there's room for 12 people at a time and expansion is planned. Smoking is allowed only outdoors. The meals are served family-style; there's a continental breakfast, a light lunch, and such dinner fare as steak, chicken, salmon, halibut, turkey, and barbecues.

You can fish on your own, or go with a guide ($200 per day for up to 4 people), and beginners can also take 3 hours of private instruction ($65 for up to 3 people). Only catch-and-release fly-fishing is done here; you fish from the bank or wade, and 90% of what you catch is rainbow trout, the rest browns. The ranch has some equipment to lend, but it's best to bring your own gear.

Though there are no amusements or services nearby, there's plenty to do; the resort has a hot tub, a swimming pool, and a tennis court, and you can hike, or go horseback riding at a neighboring ranch ($15 per hour). On one of the hiking trails there grows a huge manzanita tree at least 20 feet tall, and the region has mountain lions and eagles. *Oasis Springs Lodge, Box 454, Payne's Creek, CA 96075, tel. 800/642–4150, fax 510/521–4025. Late Apr.–mid-Nov.: 5 days, $495–$795 per person double occupancy. Sign up 1–2 months in advance.*

CALIFORNIA Trinity Canyon Lodge. This is a good place for those who want to focus strictly on fishing in a backwoods environment. It is in a remote part of northwest California, west of Weaverville and next to the Trinity Alps Wilderness Area. The Trinity River has been designated a Wild and Scenic River, and Highway 299, which parallels it, is an official National Scenic Byway. The Trinity River Canyon is just wide enough for the river and the road, with very few open spots; the Trinity Canyon Lodge occupies one.

The lodge, run by Joe and Diane Mercier, has a rustic appearance and has been here for decades. It can accommodate about 25 people in 7 housekeeping cabins and 3 motel units. The cabins are completely outfitted—you need only groceries—and must be rented for 2 nights or longer. Nearby restaurants and cafés provide meals for those in the motel units.

The Merciers offer half-day ($160 for 2 people) and full-day workshops ($250 for 2, including lunch) on fly-fishing for trout, steelhead, and salmon. More than half the workshops are attended by families (i.e., parent and child, husband and wife). Bring your own equipment; there's a limited supply of loaners.

Guided fishing is also available, but the local guides are not part of the lodge operation. They use drift boats or rafts, and their fees average around $225 per day for 1 or 2 people, including lunch. The majority do strictly fly-fishing, but some of them use other methods also. You can fish in the high alpine lakes of the wilderness area as well as in the river.

In your free time you can visit a ghost town that's close by, go hiking, white-water rafting, or tubing on the river (the lodge provides portage), dunking in private swimming holes, berry picking, or wildlife watching. Or you can drive to Weaverville to see the bright lights of a small town. *Trinity Canyon Lodge, Box 51, Helena, CA 96048, tel. 916/623–6318, fax 916/623–3306. Year-round: 5 days, $300 cabin (1 or 2); $175 motel unit (1 or 2). Price does not include meals; sign up 2 weeks in advance.*

CALIFORNIA Fly-Fishing Outfitters Clinics. These Bay Area clinics are run from the Fly-

Fishing Outfitters shops in Lafayette and San Francisco. Some instruction actually takes place in the city, in locations that run from alleyways to first-rate casting ponds, depending on what's available at the time of the class. For sessions that include actual fishing, however, students provide their own transport (1 to 3 hours inland) to such appropriate waters as Putah Creek, the Yuba River system, and the Stanislaus River.

Fly-fishing gurus Rob and Todd Hakala and Bryan Noguchi offer programs that range from a very basic 2½-hour class that hits on knots, casting, reading water, fly selection, and other fundamentals, to a comprehensive 2-day school that takes place in the Sierra, 100 miles away. These longer schools are intensive, with no more than 4 pupils per instructor. You cover everything from dry-fly fishing and nymph fishing to streamer techniques and other advanced methods. A 2-day parent-child clinic is available, and customized trips of 5 or more days can be arranged.

These clinics have been offered since 1985, a large percentage of repeat students sign up, and classes are filling earlier each year. Lunch and rods and reels are provided. You can stay in nearby motels, but the instructors usually camp, and students are invited to join them (and bring their own food), a good idea if you want to fraternize with the experts.

Free-time activities include all the urban amenities that the Bay Area can offer and the usual outdoor pursuits of the Sierra. *Fly Fishing Outfitters, 3533 Mt. Diablo Blvd., Lafayette, CA 94549, tel. 510/284–3474, fax 510/284–3314; 463 Bush St., San Francisco, CA 94108, tel. 415/781–3474. June–Sept.: 5 days, $500. Sign up 1 month in advance.*

CALIFORNIA Bishop Creek Lodge. At an elevation of 9,000 feet in the scenic Bishop Creek Canyon of the southeastern Sierra is a rustic lodge run by Gary and Suzie Olson. It's about 25 minutes by car northwest of Bishop and about 5 minutes from a trailhead into the High Sierra wilderness. The lodge offers no fishing classes and has no guides; its primary function is to house wilderness hikers and anglers in pursuit of the native golden trout. This rare and beautiful species is found in both the lakes and streams of the High Sierra, the country in which all golden trout originated.

Twelve cabins can accommodate up to 45 in all; kids are welcome. All cabins have bath, kitchen, and bedrooms. A minimum stay of 2 days is required; a free day is allowed for each 7 consecutive paid days, and continental breakfast is included in the price. A restaurant, bar, store, and laundry take care of virtually all your needs. The lodge sells fishing equipment; no rentals are available.

Free-time activities are essentially limited to outdoor pursuits like hiking and horseback riding, unless you want to make the 25-minute drive into Bishop. *Bishop Creek Lodge, Rte. 1, S. Lake Rd., Bishop, CA 93514, tel. 619/873–4484, fax 619/872–1213. Mid-Apr.–late Oct.: 5 days, $275 (cabin for 2)–$675 (cabin for 8). Prices do not include lunch or dinner; sign up 6 months in advance.*

CALIFORNIA California School of Fly-Fishing. When Ralph and Lisa Cutter are not teaching a fly-fishing school in Truckee, they are taking groups of up to 10 on 5-day horseback-fishing trips. Their destination is the Ansel Adams Wilderness, next to Yosemite National Park in the backcountry of the eastern High Sierra, where there are many streams and natural lakes, some as high as 12,000 feet.

Two wilderness camps have been set up for the season by a pack outfitter; the first is about 4 hours' ride from the starting point, and the second about 4 hours' ride from that. From the camps, you walk or ride horses to fishing places within a 1- or 2-hour radius, returning at night to a dinner fixed by the wranglers. The tented camps are remote but comfortable, with pit toilets and solar showers; the food is plentiful and good—salads, vegetables, chicken, and steaks. Everything is provided except sleeping bags and fishing equipment, though the Cutters advise you to bring your own solar shower, since the camp's won't provide enough hot water for all 10 people. The weak point of these trips is the condition of the tents, which get a lot of use; the Cutters bring a spare or two, and if you have one, pack it.

The main activity is catch-and-release fly-fishing for rainbow, brown, and brook trout, as well as the beautiful golden trout. These are not really instructional trips, but Ralph and Lisa are happy to provide brief on-the-spot tips to help you fish these high mountain waters. Many guests just go along for the ride, concentrating on photography, wildflower identification, bird-watching, and other naturalist activities. *California School of Fly-Fishing, Box 8212, Truckee, CA 96162, tel. 916/587–7005, fax 916/587–6686. May–June: 5 days, $895. Sign up 8 months in advance.*

CALIFORNIA **Sierra Bright Dot.** Fred Rowe runs Sierra Bright Dot out of Mammoth Lakes in east-central California. His services vary from half-day fishing trips around Mammoth Lakes to a 5-day guided horseback-fishing trip into the High Sierra. A major focus on these backcountry trips is catching golden trout, native only to this specific area in the ultra-high country, though rainbows, brook, and brown trout are also plentiful. Fred, a good teacher, will instruct you on appropriate techniques for the waters you will be fishing; you wade and fish from the bank of the streams and lakes. Children who are eager to fish and learn are welcome.

Sierra Bright Dot contracts with a packer, who owns the horses and hires the wranglers who do the work, bringing in supplies every couple of days. The base camp is set up on the Clark Lakes, where you spend 2 nights; you then move on to the second camp, at Alger Lakes. These are wilderness camps, with tents and chairs and portable toilets with tarps for privacy. If you want a shower, bring a solar one with you.

Food and all supplies except sleeping bags and fishing gear are provided, though some equipment rentals are available. The food is good; you might have steak, lasagna, or chicken, and fajitas one night for a change of pace. Though golden trout is always catch-and-release, you might have rainbows and brookies for dinner. Vegetables and salads—fruit if you wish—round out the meals; beer, wine, and sodas are included. Dinner is early, so you can fish in the evenings; then you come

back for coffee, hot chocolate, and dessert around the campfire.

Mammoth Lakes is a ski area in the winter, and before you leave on the wilderness trips and after you return, you can find a variety of accommodations, from camping to motels to condo rentals, at off-season prices. The same is true for restaurants.

You can also go sailing, snow-skiing, and waterskiing there. One ski-lift will take you and your mountain bike up to the top for a sweat-free ride back down. *Sierra Bright Dot, Box 9013, Mammoth Lakes, CA 93546, tel. 619/934–5514. May–Oct.: 5 days, $750. Sign up 6 months in advance.*

CALIFORNIA **Bass Fishing Instructional Service.** Gary Harrison runs his business (more a guide service than a school) on the legendary Lake Castaic, perhaps the only body of water on earth where you have a chance of catching a world-record fish every time you dip your line. From January through July of 1993, for example, Harrison's clients landed 82 largemouth bass over 10 pounds. To put that in perspective, the state record for largemouths in Montana is barely 8 pounds. (Harrison's biggest fish is 18 lbs. 2 oz., and the lake record is 22 lbs. 1 oz. The existing world record is 22 lbs. 4 oz.)

Harrison provides all the equipment and bait; anglers need only bring themselves and a lunch. The 2 primary methods of fishing are cast-and-retrieve and trolling, both with live bait. There is not a lot to learn. The main requirement for success is patience and a knowledge of how to land heavy fish. Harrison's style is one of informality with a personal touch, and having fun supersedes all else. His bass boat is a fully equipped 18-foot Ranger that comfortably accommodates his limit of 2 adults, or 2 adults and 1 child (children under 16 free). He prohibits drinking alcohol in his boat and strongly urges catch-and-release.

Lodging can be found at a nearby campground or neighboring motels and hotels; ethnic eateries and family restaurants provide the local dining. *Bass Fishing Instructional Service, 18006 Saratoga Way, No. 510, Canyon Country, CA 91351, tel. 805/251–2277. Year-round: 5 days, $800–$900 ($1,100–$1,300 for 2 people). Sign up 1–2 months in advance.*

ALASKA

SOUTHWEST **Wood River Lodge.** This is a premium (and expensive) fishing camp, about 35 miles north of Dillingham, that's accessible only by air or a long boat trip. The Agulawok River, which runs right by the lodge, reputedly contains more rainbow trout per mile than any other Alaska River, along with other species. Owners John and Linda Ortman, however, don't depend just on the Agulawok; they also fly you to other waters in a float plane, to fish for northern pike, Dolly Varden, arctic char, rainbow trout, lake trout, and all of Alaska's species of salmon.

Fly-fishermen and cast-and-retrieve anglers are both welcome here, but catch-and-release fishing is necessary for all species except spawning salmon (who will soon die anyway). The cost of the camp includes everything you'll need, and although it's usual to bring your own equipment, rentals are available for $5 per day. Fishing excursions for the next day are individually planned between the guests and the head guide each evening. There are never more than 2 or 3 guests per guide, and you fish from boats or wade, depending on where you go and which species you're after.

This is a true wilderness camp, surrounded by forests and mountains, with a plethora of wildlife, including grizzly bears, caribou, moose, waterfowl, and eagles. The camp can accommodate up to 14 guests. You stay in spacious private cabins, and go to the main lodge for social activities and meals. The 5- and 7-course dinners might feature prime rib, steak, ham, or any of several varieties of salmon. Children are welcome. About three-quarters of the guests are return visitors.

The long days on the water and communal feasts don't leave much free time, but people play cards, watch wildlife, take photographs, and exchange fish stories with other guests. *Wood River Lodge, Box 1369, Dillingham, AK 99576, tel. 907/842–5200 or 800/842–5205 (in winter, 406/862–2305), fax 907/842–5200. Mid-June–Sept.: 7 days, $4,000. Sign up 6–12 months ahead.*

SOURCES

ORGANIZATIONS **American Bass Association, Inc.** (886 Trotters Trail, Wetumpka, AL 36092, tel. 205/567–6035) is an advocacy group that works on improving bass fisheries and sponsors fishing tournaments. It publishes *American Bass News.* The **Federation of Fly Fishers** (Box 1595, Bozeman, MT 59771, tel. 406/585–7592) focuses on conservation, education, and restoration and publishes *The Fly Fisher* and *The Quill.* The **National Fresh Water Fishing Hall of Fame** (Box 33 Hall of Fame Dr., Hayward WI 54843, tel. 715/634–4440), an advocacy group, keeps track of record fish and publishes *Official World Fresh Water Angling Records.* **North American Fishing Club** (12301 Whitewater Dr., Minnetonka, MN 55343, tel. 612/936–9333) publishes *North American Fisherman.* The **International Game Fish Association** (1301 E. Atlantic Blvd., Pompano Beach, FL 33060, tel. 305/941–3474), an advocacy group, also maintains a book of fish records and publishes *World Record Game Fishes.* **Trout Unlimited** (800 Follin La., Suite 250, Vienna, VA 22180, tel. 703/281–1100) is "dedicated to conserving, protecting, and restoring wild trout and salmon and their habitat throughout North America." **Walleye International** (21724 Loraine Rd., Fairview Park, OH 44126, tel. 216/333–9494), an information and educational source, publishes *Walleye Magazine* and helps walleye anglers form local chapters.

PERIODICALS How-to magazines include *Bass Fishing* (Rte. 2, Box 74B, Gilbertsville, KY 42044, tel. 502/362–4304) and *Bassin'* and *Crappie* (Natcom, 15115 S. 76th E. Ave., Bixby, OK 74008, tel. 918/366–4441). *California Angler* covers where-to and how-to (all species, all techniques) for California and Baja (1921 E. Carnegie, Suite 3N, Santa Ana, CA 92705, tel. 714/261–9779). *Fishing Holes* (17021 N.E. Woodinville-Duval Rd., Woodinville, WA 98072, tel. 206/489–2919) is about where-to, how-to, and personal experience (all species, all techniques) in the northwestern United States. *Fishing & Hunting News* (511 Eastlake Ave. E, Seattle, WA 98109, tel. 800/488–2827), about where to fish in the West (all species), is published weekly. *Fishing World* (51 Atlantic Ave., Floral Park, NY 11001, tel. 516/352–9700) is a magazine on destinations in the United States, Canada, Mexico, the Bahamas, and the Caribbean. *Fly Fisherman* (Box 8200, Harrisburg, PA 17105–8200, tel. 800/435–9610) is a how-to, where-to (all species), and personal experience magazine. *Fly Rod & Reel* (Box 10141, Des Moines, IA 50340, tel. 800/888–6890) covers how-to and where-to for all species. *In-Fisherman* (2 In-Fisherman Dr., Brainerd, MN 56401, tel. 218/829–1648) is all about freshwater fishing for all species, all techniques. *Salt Water Sportsman* (280 Summer St., Boston, MA 02210, tel. 617/439–9977) is about sport-fishing (all species), including fishing boats and tackle.

BOOKS National or even regional guides to fishing resources are scarce. (Most such guides are done by states, and good sources for them are the state agencies that administer fishing, for example: the California Department of Fish & Game, Vermont Fish & Wildlife Division, Washington Department of Wildlife, and the Virginia Department of Game & Inland Fisheries). However, how-to and where-to guides are not nonexistent. *Angler's Guide to Montana* (Falcon Press Publishing), by Michael Sample, is a brief text locating species and type of water. *Chris Batin's 20 Great Alaska Fishing Adventures* (Alaska Angler Publications), by Christopher Batin, is on glossy paper, with lots of color photographs of the author and friends fishing. *Fly Tying Made Clear and Simple* (Frank Amato Publications), by Skip Morris, is a large-format book with step by step photographs in color. *Joan Wulff's Fly Fishing* (Stackpole Books), by Joan Wulff, is a good book on the fundamentals, with photographs, by the co-owner of the famous Wulff School of Fly-Fishing. *Knee Deep in Montana's Trout Streams* (Pruett Publishing), by John Holt, is a where-to and how-to book with humor. *Scientific Anglers Guidebook to Fly Fishing Mastery* (Scientific Anglers), by Howard West and Mike Dry, is a large-format paperback, with line drawings and photographs in color and black-and-white of people demonstrating techniques.

ALSO SEE If you'd rather make fishing a smaller part of your vacation, you can bring your rod along on a thrilling rafting trip or on a relaxing flatwater canoeing journey. Turn to the River Rafting and Canoeing and Kayaking in Flatwater chapters to find out more.

Golf Schools

by Jonathan Abrahams

ow's your golf game? You hate that question, don't you? It's humbling; *nobody's* golf game is as good as they'd like it to be. You're forced to look squarely in the eye at some of your greatest personal weaknesses: slicing, hooking, shanking. The yips. So your game needs a little work, huh?

You're not alone. Whether you're threatening par or threatening to quit, your game would love some special attention. How about a week at a golf school? Imagine—an entire week devoted solely to you and your game. The game's best teachers, a plush setting, golf during every daylight hour—sounds good, doesn't it? Maybe you could even get rid of that nasty slice.

So what are you in for?

There are a few things you can expect no matter what golf school you choose to attend. Whether the school is part of a large franchise, like John Jacobs', or independently operated, like The Academy of Golf Dynamics, the instruction will almost always be excellent. That's because it's rare to find faculty at a school that isn't made up entirely of Class A PGA Professionals. Almost all schools are located at or near an upscale resort with a quality golf course. Return students and word-of-mouth are essential to a school's business, so they can't afford less than excellent accommodations. The food will be good, and there will be a pool and tennis courts and maybe even a health club. And, of course, golf school is pricey—four days can cost anywhere from $700 to $3,000; chances are your fellow students will be solid, established businessmen and women. More than a few business cards will change hands over lunch during your stay. Above all, you'll spend a lot of time with a golf club in your hand, perhaps more time than you ever have.

Most schools spend 4 to 6 hours a day covering all aspects of the game, from driving to putting. After breakfast, students convene on the driving range to warm up. If the group is more than 10, students most likely are divided into two or more groups, usually based on handicap. Typically, a group of 18 may be divided into three groups. All three groups participate in a warm-up, led by the instructors. After the preliminaries, Group 1 works on full swing fundamentals, Group 2 on chipping and pitching, and Group 3 has their swings videotaped and analyzed. By mid-morning, the groups rotate stations; after lunch, they rotate again. In the late afternoon (usually after 3 PM), students usually are given the option to play. The process starts over on day two, except now the stations are trouble play, sand shots, and your mindset. By the end of the week, students have been immersed in every possible aspect of the game.

Jonathan Abrahams is an associate editor at Golf Magazine *who writes the bulk of the popular instruction articles. A 3-handicap golfer with a scratch swing, Jonathan lives in New York City.*

It's a lot of golf. Expect to get blisters and for those blisters to turn into calluses.

The bottom line is, most schools are credible: good golf, good vacation. But not all schools are the same. There are plenty of distinguishing factors; it just depends on what you're looking for. If you're willing to spend a little more money for higher-end accommodations, try Nicklaus/Flick, which holds schools at the country's most exclusive resorts. If you're concerned with activities geared toward the non-golfer, choose a location where golf is not the focal point. Your family, for instance, will have more options in Vail, Colorado, than in Myrtle Beach, South Carolina. Most schools have a minimum student:teacher ratio of 4:1; more personal attention is available at La Costa (in Carlsbad, CA), where Carl Welty and his partner, Gene Eifrid, teach with a maximum student:teacher ratio of 2:1. For the carefree, Golf Digest includes everything in its package price—transportation to and from the airport, all meals, all golf—so you don't have to worry about money while you're there. Specialization is also becoming popular. Dave Pelz's school is for the short game only. Sports Enhancement Associates' program emphasizes blending the mental and physical aspects of the game.

Now, what *not* to expect: Don't think, no matter which school you attend, that you'll have magically cut 5 strokes off your handicap by the end of the week. Many students look back at their golf experience months later and realize, with disappointment, that their scores are no better than before they attended. There are no quick fixes to your golfing ills. You will pick up a number of fundamentals at golf school that provide clues to some of the game's mysteries, but they will do you no good unless they're applied through consistent practice. The truly dedicated student will consult his local PGA professional before choosing a school, so the experience fits in smoothly with his regular lesson plans. Make your choice carefully. Remember, it's your vacation—your golf game might make you crazy, but the goal is, still, to have fun.

CHOOSING THE RIGHT SCHOOL

Is this school suited to my playing style? Is there a specific swing method taught? If your pro teaches a big-muscle method in the style of Jim McLean, it might be a mistake to go to a school with a small-muscle philosophy like Nicklaus/Flick's. If you've taken any lessons, it's important that you find a school that complements the method that you've been using.

What is the maximum class size? Most people prefer a smaller class because you get more personal attention. A lot of schools will limit the size to 18, but there are a few that don't.

What is the student:teacher ratio? This actually is more important than the class size. You don't want to have a ratio higher than 8:1. The lower the ratio, the more attention you're going to get.

What percentage of instruction time is spent on the golf course? You'll spend most of the day working on the range or practice green until around 3 or 4 in the afternoon, when you can go play for a couple of hours, depending on the sun. As a general rule, the more on-course work, the better.

How extensive is the practice facility? Questions to bear in mind: What is the driving range like? How big is it? Is there a putting green? How big is it? Is there a short-game area? Is there a bunker? All of these facilities will allow you to concentrate on different parts of your game.

Are there indoor facilities in case of rain?

What is the cost and what is included? Prices listed here include lodging, meals, and instruction unless otherwise noted. Also, find out if carts and greens fees are included in the package price. Most schools don't provide transportation between the airport and the hotel. This could mean renting a car or taking the hotel's airport shuttle.

What are the accommodations like? All schools put their guests up in hotels, although the degree of luxury of the rooms and the facilities can vary quite a bit.

What is the food like?

Will laundry service be available? This could save you a suitcase.

Are there non-golf activities available during off-hours? Does the school plan nightly social activities?

Is there a spousal or non-golfing guest rate? What activities are available for non-golfing guests?

How far in advance do I need to book?

How long has the school been in business? If the school is new, be particularly careful to find out about the people in charge and their plans for the program. Make sure that their teaching experience is credible, and that the instruction seems well-conceived and well-organized.

Do you have references from past guests?

MAJOR PLAYERS

GOLF DIGEST INSTRUCTIONAL SCHOOLS

"Hey," some insightful editor at *Golf Digest* must have said long ago, "wouldn't it be terrific if we got all the great teachers that contribute to our magazine together so they could actually teach people face-to-face?" Well, *somebody* liked that idea, and in 1971 the Golf Digest Instructional Schools were formed. Indeed, they served as a showcase for some of the game's great teachers. Guys like Bob Toski, Jim Flick, and Davis Love Jr. worked together for years, feeding off each other's knowledge, learning to specialize their instruction according to the student's needs, and in the process made a big name both for themselves and Golf Digest.

Today, experts such as Scott Davenport, Jack Lumpkin, and DeDe Owens are among the large and highly qualified staff of professionals that teach at the Golf Digest Schools; they can be found at top destinations like Sea Island, Georgia; Cog Hill, Illinois; and Vail, Colorado. The basic philosophy is to identify the student's needs and qualities, and shape a pro-

gram around them. No "swing method" is forced on anyone.

Digest's flexible philosophy is reflected in the variety of schools it offers. In addition to the standard 3- and 5-day schools for all golfers, it offers specialized programs for commuters, low-handicappers, parents and children, women, and those interested in short-game work only. There's also a "VIP School," for those who want to live a little better, get a little more attention, and don't mind paying a little more.

Speaking of attention, Golf Digest distinguishes itself from most other schools in the country with its hospitality. While others might send you directions from the airport in the mail and ask you to take care of at least one meal a day by yourself, Digest takes complete care of you. For the 3- and 5-day programs, they pick you up at the airport, pay for all of your meals, and make sure you get back to your flight on time when the school is over (5520 Park Ave., Box 395, Trumbull, CT 06611–0395, tel. 203/373–7130 or 800/243–6121, fax 203/373–7088).

JOHN JACOBS' PRACTICAL GOLF SCHOOLS

John Jacobs' is huge. A former Tour Player, Ryder Cupper, and Walker Cup captain, Jacobs hooked up with fellow professional Shelby Futch in 1970 to run a golf school. Today, there are 800 John Jacobs' schools, each running 2–5 days, at 30 different locations worldwide.

What makes this man and his schools so popular? The answer lies in his teaching philosophy. It's highly personalized. Instead of forcing a student to adapt to a particular "swing method," Jacobs' instruction is designed to adapt itself to the student and his or her natural game. The goal is not learning how to swing like Fred Couples, but how you can improve your own swing. It's less intimidating for the student, and gives him or her the feeling that improvement is most certainly within reach.

One thing to expect at a John Jacobs' school is large classes. But Jacobs has a large number of PGA Class A Professionals on staff at each site, so the student:teacher ratio never gets out of hand. Just don't expect to get to know all your fellow students. At Marriott's Seaview Resort in New Jersey, for example, a class will get as many as 50 students. But with 10 instructors, everyone gets their fair share of attention. Five hours per day are spent on instruction, including video analysis; all aspects of the game are covered. On-course work comes afterwards. And as a parting gift, students get a copy of the *John Jacobs' Instruction Manual* to take home with them.

Specialization is also a big thing at John Jacobs'. Just a golf school? No. How about a golf school for women in business, or a school devoted only to the short game? What do you need? Jacobs will take care of it (7825 E. Redfield Rd., Scottsdale, AZ 85260–6977, tel. 602/991–8587 or 800/472–5007, fax 602/991–8243).

NICKLAUS/FLICK GOLF SCHOOLS Does Jack actually teach here? No, but the guy who *teaches* Jack teaches here. And that's only a sliver of his résumé. Jim Flick may be a slight man—he'll be sure to tell you after he belts a 270-yard drive—but his accomplishments as a teacher of golf are on a scale larger than that of just about anybody in the business. The college roommate of Arnold Palmer at Wake Forest, he moved on to help guide the then-fledgling Golf Digest Schools to prominence in 1972. In 1990, when he began to work with Nicklaus on his game, the Golden Bear found Flick's ideas so much like his own that they formed the Nicklaus/Flick Golf Schools. To this day, Flick has personally taught more than 900 classes—more than anyone else alive.

Flick's teaching philosophy has endured— and will continue to do so—for a few reasons. It focuses on the golf club and its motion, rather than various positions the body should or shouldn't be in. Flick's method does not espouse absolutes dictating the correct golf swing, but rather allows the student to concentrate on quality of contact and ball flight. It's a "user-friendly" system that pays as much attention to the student's mind and emotional state as his shoulder turn. "Students must be prepared emotionally before I can prepare

them physically," says Dean Reinmuth, coach to Phil Mickelson and a member of Flick's top-notch staff. These people really know how to teach.

The instruction program is broken up into 4 sessions: Master Golf I, II, III, and IV. The sessions get shorter and more advanced as they progress, with the focus becoming on-course play. The student's entire golfing life is examined: short game, long game, state-of-mind, equipment evaluation, and fitness. Each student receives a videotape and the *Master Golf Workbook,* a manual written by Nicklaus, Flick, and Ken Bowden. There are never more than 18 students and the student:teacher ratio is never more than 6:1.

Nicklaus/Flick schools are also distinguished by their locations; they're absolutely top-shelf. Pebble Beach, Kauai Lagoons, PGA National, Boyne Highlands (MI) Resort, The Scottsdale Princess, Las Campanas Resort in Santa Fe— all are at the top of their class in terms of golf, accommodations, and dining. You will live well at Nicklaus/Flick (11780 U.S. Hwy. One, N. Palm Beach, FL 33408–9809, tel. 407/626–3900 or 800/642–5528, fax 904/322–2567).

FAVORITE SCHOOLS

THE MID ATLANTIC

NEW JERSEY **John Jacobs' Practical Golf Schools.** The Seaview Resort is officially a Marriott, but don't expect the standard 10-story hotel with lots of lights and a red roof. Years ago, Seaview was a very exclusive private club with guest quarters for members who came in from Philadelphia and New York for the weekend. Although, the Seaview lost a little of its old private club charm when Marriott acquired the property and expanded the existing accommodations to 300 rooms.

Students enjoy a large buffet breakfast before they hit the plush 22-acre practice facility at 9 AM. Each practice session is personalized, focusing on the individual's needs, with lots of video analysis. There can be as many as 50 students, but the student:teacher ratio is never greater than 5:1. Lunch—also included in the package price—breaks up the daily 5-hour instruction, then it's back to work until 3 PM, when students are allowed to go play. Seaview has a couple of fine golf courses: The Bay, a Donald Ross classic from 1915, and The Pines, a newer, tougher track built in 1942.

Wagers on the course should be kept to a minimum, because only 10 minutes away lies Atlantic City and all its trappings. For less costly fun, the hotel itself has swimming pools, tennis courts, game and exercise rooms, and a health club. Several malls dot the area, but antiques aficionados will want to head to the small town of Smithville, just a few minutes away, where they can shop in a more intimate setting. Wrap the day up with dinner at Marriott's main dining room, featuring a Friday seafood buffet that's the best in the area. *John Jacobs' Practical Golf Schools, 7825 E. Redfield Rd., Scottsdale, AZ 85260– 6977, tel. 602/991–8587 or 800/472–5007, fax 602/991–8243. May–Sept.: 4 days, $1,095–$1,470; 2 days, $695–$845. Price does not include dinner. Non-golfing companion rate (includes 2 meals): 2 days, $175; 4 days, $595.*

THE SOUTH

FLORIDA **Ben Sutton Golf Academy.** Twenty-five years ago, a retired Hoover engineer decided to get a bunch of buddies together and go on a golf vacation. The group didn't just want an ordinary golfing trip; they wanted their games to improve at the same time. So they took along a few pros, and the first golf school was born. The engineer's name was Ben Sutton, and he is the pioneer of the modern golf school.

Today, the Ben Sutton Golf Academy continues to operate in the same progressive spirit. Unlike most schools, which spend the majority of instruction time teaching the student how to swing the club, Ben Sutton's program is specifically designed around playing the game. Other schools have "player's" programs, usually for those with handicaps of 15

or less, that include extra playing time. But Ben Sutton goes beyond that. In its 5-day program (there's also a 3-day and 8-day) the majority of time, regardless of the student's ability, is spent on the 9-hole teaching course. Working on long irons on the range is one thing; hitting long iron shots to an elevated green with a lake on the left is something completely different. By working on shots under playing conditions, students eliminate the need to bridge the gap between practice tee and course.

That's not to say there's no time spent on the range. Ben Sutton's range is a 360° grass practice tee that's totally exclusive to the school. There's the requisite putting green and short-game area, as well, but most of the work is done on the practice course.

After 6 hours of instruction, students are free to play Sun City Center's 27-hole private golf course, a challenging layout that is relatively hilly for Florida. Carts and greens fees are taken care of by the school. Students stay at the Sun City Center Hotel, a typical resort residence with swimming pools, tennis courts, and a solid (if unspectacular) restaurant. Breakfast and dinner are eaten at the hotel and included in the package; lunch is at the country club and is extra. Students may bring guests, provided they pay the double occupancy rate, and they are welcome to everything the students are—golf, meals, all but instruction.

One drawback: Ben Sutton's schools are so popular that they occasionally get crowded. There can be as many as 150 students at one school, and although they have 32 Class A PGA Professionals on staff, the student:teacher ratio can get as high as 7:1. *Ben Sutton Golf School, Box 9199, Canton, OH 44711, tel. 216/453–4350 or 800/225–6923, fax 216/453–8450. Year-round: 3 days, $600–$675; 5 days, $1,020–$1,125; 8 days, $1,600–$1,800. Non-golfing companion rate (includes meals and golf): 3 days, $285; 5 days, $525; 8 days, $750.*

FLORIDA **Dave Pelz Short Game School.** "How can I cut strokes off my scores?" Despite all the swing theories and golf gurus running around, there's only one real answer to this question, no matter who you are: Work on your short game. Improve your chipping, pitching, sand play, and putting (especially putting), and your scores will go down. Why? The golf swing itself is not the easiest motion for the average Joe. The short game swings, on the other hand, are simple. Anybody can make a putting stroke. Hit it all over the park with a grotesque swing but putt well, and you'll be a good player. Hit everything down the middle but putt lousy, and you're just another also-ran. P.S.: The secret to good putting is hitting your chips, pitches, and sand shots close to the hole.

It doesn't take a rocket scientist to figure that out, but one did anyway; as a result, the Dave Pelz Short Game School was born. Pelz spent 14 years as a research scientist for NASA; 16 years ago he decided to devote his life completely to golf—specifically, the short game. As you might imagine, Pelz's teaching philosophy is pretty cutting edge. Unlike other golf schools that merely include the short game, Pelz's school covers the short game *only* and uses a method that's uniquely his own. He espouses one swing motion for all wedge shots, systematically broken down into different lengths, according to the length of shot. He recommends carrying at least three wedges of different lofts in your bag: Some of his disciples on Tour (and he's got a few) carry as many as four. He's got two authentic robots, Perfy (a putting specialist) and Wedgy (a wedge wizard), to demonstrate his theories.

Pelz's schools are 3 days long, with about 8 hours of instruction daily, divided between indoor learning sessions and outdoor execution sessions. Players of all abilities are represented at a school—there's sometimes even a Tour pro or two—because Pelz's fundamentals are applicable to any player. He's a big believer that improvement is closely linked with knowledge of proper execution, so there's a good deal of time spent in the classroom. Maximum enrollment is 16, and the student:teacher ratio is never greater than 4:1.

Pelz offers three types of sessions: The Executive, headed by Pelz himself, which includes three nights of lodging at the Boca Raton Resort and Club. Pelz doesn't show for the lower-priced Premiere Session, but his partner, former PGA Tour player Tom Jenkins, does, and he teaches all the same stuff. The Alumni session stretches to 4 days and focuses more on on-course situations. It's expensive, but the Boca resort is very impressive. It's got just about everything you might want in Florida: Two great golf courses, tennis courts, a beach club with private beach, a marina, three fitness centers—this place is stocked. *Dave Pelz Short Game School, The Boca Raton Resort & Club, Box 5025, Boca Raton, FL 33431-0825, tel. 407/395–3000, ext. 3753 or 800/833–7370, fax 512/261–5391. Year-round: 3 days, $1,975–$2,550; 4 days, $1,795 (alumni only). Price does not include meals. Non-golfing companions stay at no extra charge to single occupancy rate.*

FLORIDA **Doral Golf Learning Center with Jim McLean.** If you're looking for someone on the cutting edge of golf instruction, you've found him in Jim McLean. A former college teammate of Bruce Lietzke and John Mahaffey at University of Houston, and a teaching editor at *Golf Magazine,* McLean has gone on to become one of the most successful teachers in the industry. His philosophy focuses on controlling the swing with the big muscles of the hips, back, and shoulders. He works regularly with a number of PGA Tour players, most notably Tom Kite, who worked with him over several months prior to his 1992 U.S. Open victory.

Doral offers several programs for various levels of players, but the best of the best is McLean's 5-day Players' School. Here, instructors work with golfers with a handicap of 15 or better on actually playing the game. Classes are limited to 12 students, and the student: teacher ratio is 3:1. Five rounds on a number of Doral's 99 holes is included. McLean helps each student establish a personal goal for the week, then charts his or her progress as the session continues. He and his very capable teaching staff rely heavily on video analysis and a wide range of teaching aids. At the end of the week, the student receives a videotape that includes footage of their swing, plus some personalized instruction from McLean.

There's a whole lot of technology going on at Doral, which is indicative of McLean's attitude toward teaching. He's always trying to learn something new.

One of the week's highlights is the opportunity to play the Blue Monster, the best and toughest of the courses on the complex, and the site of the annual Doral Ryder Open. In fact, the entire spread at Doral is fairly plush. Rooms are spacious, but lodging is not included in the package price, so reserve early. Breakfast and lunch, served at the Champions Club each day, is a bit more adventurous than your standard club food. Dinner is up to the students, although one night during the week, McLean and a few staff members have been known to take the group out for stone crabs. That meal is on McLean, and you should take your freebies when you can. Doral is expensive, and although there are other hotels in the vicinity, life is much easier if you're staying on-site.

Non-golfers, paying standard resort prices, can play tennis, make arrangements to indulge in the luxury of the Doral-Saturnia spa, or hit Miami proper. The ocean is right nearby, and South Beach, the newest, trendiest strip on the east coast, is a few minutes' drive. *Doral Golf Learning Center with Jim McLean, 4400 N.W. 87th Ave., Miami, FL 33178, tel. 305/591–6409 or 800/72–DORAL, fax 305/599–2890. Year-round: 5 days, $2,250. Price does not include lodging or dinners.*

NORTH CAROLINA **Pinehurst Golf Advantage Schools.** Pine trees, water sports, tennis, constant activity—brings you back, doesn't it? Camp Menohapatanga? At The Pinehurst Golf Advantage Schools, there's a definite summer-camp feel. Set in the self-proclaimed "golf capital of the world" at Pinehurst, North Carolina, the Advantage Schools put their students up in a grand old hotel built in 1901 and provide them with 3 meals a day. The breakfasts are buffets and the dinners are 5-course gourmet meals (probably better than what you got at Menohapatanga).

Pinehurst is a sprawling complex. In addition to the 7 golf courses and 24 tennis courts, there's a marina, high-end croquet courts, and a gun club (for those of you who really get frustrated with your game). There's never a shortage of things to do for the golfer or the non-golfer. The World Golf Hall of Fame is at Pinehurst, as well.

Headed by former PGA president Don Padgett, the instruction program covers all areas of the student's game, and adds a bonus: club-fitting. Including this was a smart move by Padgett. Few people, pros included, give club-fitting the attention it deserves. Fact is, without properly fitted clubs—and it's a very precise process—you're not going to play your best golf. There's also video analysis, unlimited range balls, and a daily clinic, in addition to 3 hours of daily work on your game. Maximum class size is 20 and the student:teacher ratio is never higher than 5:1.

Three hours is less time on the practice tee and putting green than most other schools provide, but there's a good reason for it. Students head to the golf course at 2:30 PM to apply what they've learned during the morning hours. Carts and greens fees are included in the package, which brings us to perhaps the best part of the Advantage Schools. Among the facility's 7 courses is Pinehurst No. 2, widely regarded as one of the finest courses in the world. Designed by Donald Ross near the turn of the century, this course is a timeless classic that can be enjoyed by all levels of golfer. It hosted the Tour Championship from 1991-92 and in 1995 will be the site of the U.S. Open. It'll cost a bit extra to play, but the experience is well worth it. *The Pinehurst Golf Advantage Schools, Box 4000, Pinehurst, NC 28374, tel. 919/295–8128, fax 919/295–8110. Mar.–Oct.: 4 days, $1,210–$1,490; 6 days, $1,655–$2,100. Price does not include premiums for playing on courses No. 2 and No. 7. Non-golfing companion rate: 4 days, $575; 6 days, $895.*

SOUTH CAROLINA **The Phil Ritson Golf School.** "Less is more" might be the best description of this school's philosophy. Unlike other schools that boast of their ability to administer a golf overdose during the course of a week, Ritson believes that no golfer should have to endure more than 3 1/2 hours of instruction a day. The 5-day school, set on Pawley's Island, a half hour from Myrtle Beach, is typically made up of 3 half-day sessions at the practice facility, covering everything from driving to putting, and two 9-hole playing lessons. Classes are small—4 students, 1 teacher—so students aren't trying to connect to a number of different teachers.

Phil Ritson has been around for a very long time. Not only has he taught a lot of PGA Tour pros, he's taught a few of the guys who teach the Tour pros. He produced a very successful videotape called "Golf Your Way," a good indication of his teaching philosophy: Take whatever skills and swing the student has, and build upon them. With a sprawling practice facility, including a covered hitting area and an indoor teaching center, Pawley's Plantation provides an ideal arena to showcase his talents.

The only thing is, it's not his talents. It's his partner, Mel Sole, who does the teaching. They met in their native South Africa almost 30 years ago, and have been working together since 1969. Ritson and Sole are completely on the same page when it comes to the golf swing, and Sole is a highly qualified professional, so expect the instruction to be top-notch.

Students have the option to play golf on the Jack Nicklaus signature course during the free half of the day. But golf is not free. According to Sole, students are so worn out after half a day of instruction that they tend to cancel any tee times they've made in favor of lounging by the pool. As a result, golf is not included in the package rate. Maybe you buy that, maybe you don't. In any case, you buy the tee times if you want to play extra golf.

The highlight of this school is the accommodations. Students are put up in luxury villas that overlook the ninth fairway. Two and three bedrooms, two full baths with Jacuzzis, a full working kitchen—these are the kind of digs one could get used to. For non-golfers, the school provides a list of activities and sights to see and experience. Water sports, Civil War memorabilia, and country music: It's the best of the coastal South. *The Phil Ritson Golf School, Pawley's Plantation Golf*

& Country Club, Hwy. 17, Box 2580, Pawley's Island, SC 29585, tel. 803/237–4993 or 800/624–4653, fax 803/237–8397. Year-round: 5 days, $970–$1,170. Price does not include lunches, dinners, or golf. Non-golfing companion rate fluctuates according to group size.

THE MIDWEST

MICHIGAN **Rick Smith Golf Academy.** "Myrtle Beach of the North" is what people are calling Northern Michigan, the country's newest hotbed of golf activity. Courses are popping up everywhere, good courses designed by people like Fazio, Dye, Trent Jones, and Nicklaus. There's a lot of desirable real estate and the cool climes are ideal for growing bent grass, which makes for wonderfully fast, well-manicured greens. One of the centerpieces in this new golf mecca is the Treetops Sylvan Resort in Gaylord, home of the Rick Smith Golf Academy. Here's the scoop on the 3—count 'em—18-hole courses: The Treetops original, designed by Robert Trent Jones, is ranked 27th among the country's resort courses by *Golf Digest*. In 1992, they added another 18, designed by Tom Fazio, who never, *ever* makes a weak design; and in July of 1993, a new course, designed by Rick Smith himself, opened. Insiders say it's the best of the three. Add a 9-hole par-3 course, designed by Smith, and you're in Golf Land. The best part: Students have free access to it all.

This guy Smith may have an average name, but he's one of the hottest young teachers in golf today. Besides being a top-notch architect, he's making quite a dent on the PGA Tour, teaching players like Billy Andrade and the 1993 U.S. Open winner, Lee Janzen. Rumor has it he's also been working with that other guy, Nicklaus.

Great courses, great teacher—sounds too good to be true. So, here's the catch. While it's Rick Smith's Academy, he doesn't teach the 3-day program. That is the job of Henry Young, a PGA pro of 20 years, who doesn't teach on tour and doesn't design big-name golf courses. But he has been working with Smith since

Smith was a teenager, so it's safe to say that Young was instrumental in shaping Smith's teaching philosophy.

Class starts at 4 PM on Friday. Four students, no more, and Henry gets things started by doing some full-swing work and video analysis. Henry Young, like Smith, is the kind of teacher who isn't married to a particular method, but who shapes his lesson around the student's individual needs and qualities. Saturday and Sunday mornings are split between short game and putting from 8:30 to 10:30 and full swing from 10:30 to 12:30. An hour for lunch, then the students are set free to experience any one of the resort's golf courses. This is a very straightforward, fundamental approach: Practice in the morning, play in the afternoon. There's not a lot of attention paid to on-course work or mental training. But in the span of 2½ days, Rick Smith (and Henry Young) offer about the right amount of instruction. And with only 4 students, there's more individual attention here than just about anywhere else.

Unlike some other schools, breakfast and dinner are included in the package, while lunch is extra. Typically, Treetop, aside from their better-than-average rooms, offers swimming, tennis, guides to local sightseeing, and so on. Unlike many resorts, they offer daycare. Children sightsee and shop on nearby scenic Mackinac Island or Traverse City while their parents golf in peace. *Rick Smith Golf Academy, 3962 Wilkinson Rd., Gaylord MI 49735, tel. 517/732–6711 or 800/444–6711, fax 517/732–6595. May–Sept.: 3 days, $691. Price does not include lunches.*

THE SOUTHWEST

ARIZONA **Sports Enhancement Associates.** Not your typical name for a golf school, but not your typical golf school, either. S.E.A. is the baby of Chuck Hogan, an unusual golf professional who has dedicated himself to teaching golf based not just on perfecting the swing, but on increasing the level of human performance—which is to say, using your body and your mind together for an optimal per-formance. The idea is to help the student practice more effectively, overcome jitters, and manage inconsistency, as well as master technique. Rather than learning to work hard, Hogan believes the student should learn to play hard. It's a marriage of the mental and physical aspects of the game, and since 1984, it has produced a golf school program unlike any other.

Instruction is provided by three profession-als—Lynn Marriott, LPGA Professional of the year for 1992; TJ Tomasi, Class A Professional and former editor at *Golf Illustrated;* and Hogan himself. No one else teaches. When Hogan is there (he does about half the schools), classes have a limit of 18 students. When Hogan's not teaching, Tomasi and Marriott work the schools themselves, with a maximum of 12 students. The student:teacher ratio is never more than 6:1, and all levels of ability are represented.

Hogan's a studious guy, and his school reflects it. Forty percent of the student's time is spent in the classroom, discussing concepts, determining the student's needs, and developing a strategy to address them. That takes most of the morning. After lunch, the group heads out to the practice tee, where the teachers implement the strategies they formulated in the classroom. Over the 5 days, students will play 27 holes of supervised golf, in addition to any golf they choose to play in the late afternoon. Greens fees and carts are included.

The setting for the 4½-day school is Sedona, Arizona, a tourist-oriented arts-and-crafts center surrounded by some of the most picture-perfect, red rock landscapes in the Southwest. The Sedona Golf Resort features an 18-hole championship course designed by Gary Panks and David Graham. Accommodations are not included in the package price. Students have the option of booking rooms at the upscale Los Ebrigedos Hotel ($165 per night, discounted), or the more modest Bell Rock Inn ($80 per night, discounted). Either way, students take care of their own breakfasts and 3 dinners. Lunch is provided by the school, and there are 2 gourmet dinners preceded by cocktail receptions at Los Ebrigedos. Non-golfers can experience Sedona as well: Do a little shopping, go horseback riding, hike the scenic trails. *Sports Enhancement Associates, Box 2788, Sedona, AZ 86336, tel. 602/284–9000 or 800/345–4245, fax 602/284–1948. Spring and Fall: 4¹/₂ days, $1,695. Price does not include lodging or some meals.*

TEXAS **The Academy of Golf Dynamics.** Austin, Texas, is home to a few of golf's greatest names. Ben Crenshaw, Tom Kite, and Harvey Penick all get their mail here. Nicklaus has a house here, but he's got a house just about everywhere. In any case, with this illustrious roster of residents, it seems only right that there be a first-rate golf facility.

The Academy of Golf Dynamics, at the Hills of Lakeway development, is just that. With a 500-yard range, sprawling putting green, practice bunkers, and 3 practice holes in addition to one of Jack Nicklaus's most charming courses, the Academy has a facility for learning that outdistances most of the competition.

The Academy's director, PGA pro Bill Moretti, teaches with a progressive philosophy. Like many others, he's not married to any swing "method," but he also believes in letting a student's personality help shape the individual lesson plan. Everybody is videotaped, but some students will connect with technology more than others. As a result, some students will spend a good deal of time with teaching and training aids, while others will learn more through plain old personal advice, and the good old beating of balls.

The big advantage here are the 3 practice holes, which allow the teachers to work on-course with the students daily. Fundamentals are covered, of course, but there is a much greater emphasis on actually playing the game than at most schools. Moretti is a big believer in creating the perfect learning environment. As a result, he guarantees a teacher:student ratio of no more than 3:1, lower than most. After experimenting with different session lengths, Moretti decided to make all his schools 3 days, a length of time he found most conducive to learning. Students spend the mornings working on fundamentals and the afternoons working on on-course situations. At 3 PM, you

are free to go play (price included); if you choose not to, teachers are available for further instruction. It's an extremely complete program. The Academy also offers a parent and child session, as well as corporate and private packages.

The base price for the Academy does not include lodging. There are different choices for accommodations, from The Lakeway Inn, an unassuming hotel set above Lake Travis, to course-side villas. The school will fill you in on the details. Breakfast and lunch are included—standard country-club fare at the Hills Club—but not dinner. Most of the non-golf action takes place on Lake Travis. If you're not into water sports, you're going to be hard-pressed to find something to keep you busy. Austin is a city first, a tourist attraction (a distant) second. *The Academy of Golf Dynamics, 45 Club Estates Pkwy., Austin, TX 78738, tel. 512/261–3300 or 800/879–2008, fax 512/261–8168. March–Oct.: 3 days, $695 midweek, $795 weekend. Price does not include lodging or dinner.*

THE ROCKIES

COLORADO **Golf Digest Instruction School at Vail.** You're guaranteed to add at least 10 yards to your drive at Golf Digest's Vail school. The catch is, you won't take that distance home with you. The Vail Valley lies high in the Rocky Mountains, more than 8,000 feet above sea level. The air is thinner, so resistance is lower and the ball flies farther. But the thin air won't cure your slice. That's the job of the pros from Golf Digest. Maximum class size is 21, and the student:teacher ratio is never greater than 7:1.

But the setting of the Vail school is so breathtaking that you probably won't care what happens to your game. First of all, you're surrounded by mountains. Then there's the Aspen trees and wildflowers that blanket the mountainsides. Throw in the winding creeks and rivers and you might just want to put your clubs down, grab a comfortable chair, and soak it all in.

You might—if you weren't practicing and playing golf at Singletree Golf Club. Singletree was designed by Jay Morrish in the early 1980s, when Morrish was Jack Nicklaus's top design man. (Morrish has since joined forces with Tom Weiskopf). Morrish didn't get a lot of credit for his work on the course, and Singletree doesn't get much attention compared to Country Club of the Rockies, Nicklaus's creation across the street. Don't be fooled: It's one of the best courses in Colorado. It carves its way in and out of the foothills of the town of Edwards, and features dramatic changes in elevation, great views of the Vail Valley, and superbly manicured greens. With 4 sets of tees, it's a fair but challenging test for all levels of golfer.

Singletree is about 15 minutes down the road from the Vail Village and the Sonnenalp Inn, where students stay. There's a Bavarian motif at Sonnenalp, and it is reflected in each of their 3 restaurants. Golf Digest's all-inclusive policy means that meals are included. There's a spa and luxury boutique at Sonnenalp for the non-golfer (neither, of course, are free), but there's so much more to do outside the hotel. Go hiking, fishing, whitewater rafting, horseback riding, take a chair lift up one of the mountains. There's endless ways to have a fabulous vacation in Vail. Just take it slow at first—the thin air takes a few days to get used to. *Golf Digest Instruction Schools, 5520 Park Ave., Box 395, Trumbull, CT 06611–0395, tel. 203/373–7130 or 800/243–6121, fax 203/373–7088. June–July: 3 days, $2,350–$2,670. July–Aug.: 3 days, $2,150–$2,470. Non-golfing companion rate (includes all meals): $725.*

WYOMING **John Jacobs' Practical Golf Schools at Jackson Hole.** If Jesse James was looking to cut a few strokes off his handicap, he'd probably come to John Jacobs' school at Jackson Hole. First, being an ornery, independent kind of guy, he'd like Jacobs' flexible, unrestrictive teaching philosophy. Second, he'd like the Wort Hotel, where he could hang out with other cowboys in the loud, rustic Western bar. 'Course, if his game didn't improve, there's no telling what would happen.

Sure, sure, it's the 1990s, but Jackson Hole, Wyoming, still retains most of its old Western charm. It's a beautiful town, perched high in the Grand Tetons, and though Jesse James probably won't show up, you'll still find your share of cowboys. Students stay 5 nights at the Wort Hotel, the biggest hotel in this small town. Five breakfasts and 2 dinners of local cuisine with an elegant touch are provided at the hotel, and 4 lunches are served between sessions at the Jackson Hole Golf and Tennis Club.

The club is 15 minutes away, and each morning students are transported there after breakfast. Four 5-hour days of instruction cover all aspects of the game. Class size never gets larger than 20, and maximum student:teacher ratio is 4:1. At 3 PM, the students are free to play on the golf course, redesigned by Robert Trent Jones and ranked in the top 25 of the nation's public courses by *Golf Digest*. Greens fees and carts are included.

During the 19th-century silver rush, Jackson was a destination point for opportunity-hungry cowboys. As a result, there's a lot of history here for the non-golfer to experience. It's also laid-back and relatively unaffected for a resort town, so it attracts a lot of artists and craftspeople. Beautiful, original jewelry and art can be found by the shopper with a nose for quality. It's also a great place to just sit back, breathe the fresh air, and look at the mountains. *John Jacobs' Practical Golf Schools, 7825 E. Redfield Rd., Scottsdale, AZ 85260–6977, tel. 602/991–8587 or 800/472–5007, fax 602/991–8243. Aug.: 4 days, $1,095–$1,470. Price does not include some dinners. Non-golfing companion rate (includes most meals): $595.*

THE WEST COAST

CALIFORNIA **La Costa Golf School.** Over the years, golf schools have tended to develop into something more commercial and less personalized. Not at La Costa. Here, you choose who you want to take the school with (no more than 4 students), when to take it, and for how long. It's extremely private. You can come for a single day, or as many as 8. PGA professionals Carl Welty and Gene Eifrid are the only instructors. The worst student: teacher ratio is 2:1. But it could be as good as 1:2, because even if you're alone, Welty and Eifrid will give you their undivided attention.

These guys might be the video mavens of golf instruction: You're on camera from the moment you get there. The first thing every student does is play 9 holes under video surveillance. The tape is then analyzed to determine the student's strengths and weaknesses and to design a lesson plan around them. After that, it's 6–8 hours of instruction daily, broken down into equal thirds of on-course work (videotaped), practice drills and lessons (videotaped), and time in the classroom (video analysis). It almost never rains at La Costa, but Welty favors indoor instruction at times. When students can't see where the ball goes, they concentrate more on form and technique and less on result.

Unlike most schools, La Costa does not let you pay in package form. You've got to do the breakdown yourself, which means paying Welty and Eifrid between $35, $40, $50, or $85 per hour for their services, depending upon the number of golfers in your group (fewer golfers, more money). Rooms at La Costa are $215 a night. Do some quick arithmetic and the cost of a 3-day school for 2 comes out to about $2,700. Meals are not included. (Did we say this one was a bit less commercial?)

Yes, it's pricey. But it's perhaps the most personalized school around, offering the most individual attention, and furthermore, La Costa is not just another resort. The golf course is great: 18 of its 36 holes host the PGA Tour's Tournament of Champions each year. There are men's and women's spas, a fitness center, as well as the usual tennis court and swimming pool facilities. You're free to choose your meals during your stay, and 5 on-site restaurants offer plenty of dining options. (You'd better have a fat wallet.) And if you're a traditionalist, La Costa is the place for you, as well: They run their school the way they used to in the good old days. *The LaCosta Golf School, Costa del Mar Rd., Carlsbad, CA 92009, tel. 619/438–9111, ext. 4258, or 800/653–7888, fax 619/438–3758. Year-round custom-length sessions: $140 per hour for 4 students, $120 for 3 students, $100 for 2, $85 for 1. Price does not include meals or lodging. Rooms at the resort start at $215 double occupancy.*

CALIFORNIA Nicklaus/Flick at Pebble Beach. It's important to remember that Pebble Beach is not only a golf course, but a town as well, because this Nicklaus/Flick school is not at Pebble Beach the golf course. It's at the Inn at Spanish Bay, in Pebble Beach the town, only a few minutes from Pebble Beach Golf Course. All of which, it must be said, is set on the fabulous Monterey Peninsula.

Two different 3-day sessions are held from May to September. Master Golf I features a full day of instruction at Spyglass Hill plus 9 holes of golf daily at 1 of the 3 area courses (Spyglass, Pebble Beach, or Spanish Bay). Master Golf III limits practice sessions to a single half-day. Three 18-hole rounds are included. Students stay at the Inn at Spanish Bay, and again, it's not Pebble Beach—but it's just as good, if not better. The rooms are huge, with fireplaces and beautiful views of the ocean and the Links at Spanish Bay. There are also tennis courts and a health spa. Here, the living is very, very plush.

Breakfast is at the Inn each morning at 7 AM. The students are brought to Spyglass Hill Golf Club, considered the toughest of the Peninsula courses, where they take advantage of the club's extensive practice facility. There's never more than 18 students per school, and they are broken up into 3 groups according to handicap. Maximum student:teacher ratio is 6:1—higher than some schools, but Jim Flick's in-your-face teaching style narrows the gap considerably. A lunch of the usual sandwiches and salads is at Spyglass, while dinner is left up to the student. Good thing, because the Peninsula is filled with restaurants as spectacular as the ocean views. It would be a shame to stay in the hotel the entire trip. *Nicklaus/Flick Golf School, 11780 U.S. Highway One, North Palm Beach, FL 33408-9809, tel. 407/626–3900 or 800/642–*

5528, fax 407/626–4104. May–Sept.: 3 days, $2,950–$3,575 (Master Golf I) or $2,595–$3,220 (Master Golf III). Price does not include dinners or extra rounds of golf. Non-golfing companion rate (includes meals): $725 for Master Golf I, $750 for Master Golf III.

SOURCES

ORGANIZATIONS The **National Golf Foundation** (tel. 407/744–6006) isn't golf's governing body, but it is golf's largest research resource, and it has its collective finger on the pulse of just about everything that's happening in the game. It also happens to publish a list of the country's golf schools.

Before you commit to any golf school, be sure that those teaching the golf swing are members of the **Professional Golf Association of America** (tel. 407/624–8400). Class A certification by the PGA of America indicates that the teacher knows what he's doing. This is important not only in choosing a golf school, but when taking individual lessons, as well.

Your local PGA chapter has a list of certified pros in your area.

PERIODICALS The leading golf magazines rarely run school listings anymore, but they do showcase the instruction of many of the teachers at the major schools. To catch a glimpse of some of the material you may learn at school, take a look at *Golf Magazine* (2 Park Ave., New York, NY 10016, tel. 800/876–7726); *Golf Digest* (Box 395, Trumbull, CT 06611–0395, tel. 800/PAR–GOLF); and *Golf Tips Magazine* (12121 Wilshire Blvd., Suite 1220, Los Angeles, CA 90025–1175, tel. 310/820–1500).

BOOKS For a complete listing of just about all the golf schools in this country and others, try *The Guide to Golf Schools & Camps,* published by ShawGuides Inc., or *Golf Schools—The Complete Guide,* by First Person Press. Both list all the basic information for the golf-school shopper. For a more personalized look, author Robin McMillan reviews several major schools in his book, *The Golfer's Home Companion,* published by Simon and Schuster.

Hang Gliding

by Erik Fair

ang gliding is the flyingist flying there is. Hang glider pilots eschew the confines of cockpit or cabin and hang out in the breeze. They feel airspeed with their skin and hear its whisper in their ears. The silent, swooping sensations hang glider pilots feel recall the flight of mythological Icarus, whose wax wings carried him toward the sun.

Hang gliders, which weigh 50 to 75 pounds, are the only fabric-and-frame aircraft light enough to be foot-launched by a human being. The size of the hang glider (often called a wing) varies according to the pilot's weight. Solo pilots fly wings with 130 to 175 square feet of sail area; tandem pilots require 180 to 220 square feet of sail to support the weight of two people.

One common misconception is that a hang glider is powered by fickle wind. The wings are actually powered by gravity, which causes them to fly downward through whatever air mass they are in. A hang glider can climb away from the ground only if the air mass is rising faster than the glider is flying downward through it. Hang gliders can stay aloft in the wide band of air that is deflected upward when wind strikes the face of a cliff. They also climb away from the ground in masses of hot air (thermals) that rise faster than 200 feet per minute.

Wind direction, velocity, and degree of turbulence affect safety during launch and landing. Most pilots don't fly in winds greater than 25 mph, and experience teaches them how to use weather conditions to predict and avoid turbulence. A beginner's inexperience at judging wind conditions is one of two main reasons why professional instruction is a must. The other is that trial-and-error learning is especially stupid in any form of aviation.

There are a variety of safe, enjoyable ways for you to try hang gliding for the first time. One option is bunny-slope training, which typically costs from $50 to $100 for a half- or full-day lesson. You spend the first few hours running around on flat ground, learning how to control the glider as it floats overhead. After you develop a feel for the friendly way the glider tugs up at your pants, you try a take-off on a gentle slope. Gravity and lift work their magic and suddenly you're moon-walking, then *really flying,* just a few feet off the ground. Several heartbeats later, you gape at your feet, knowing—though not quite believing—they actually left the ground. You need at least average strength, aerobic capacity, and flexibility to enjoy slope training. Avoid it if you have leg or back problems that keep you from running.

If the bunny slope sounds a little tame, you may opt for a tandem flight. For $100 to $150

Adventurer and writer Erik Fair is the author of California Thrill Sports *and winner of the 1991 Max Karant Award for Excellence in Aviation Journalism. He's taught hundreds of folks how to fly a hang glider and wrote a book for them called* Right Stuff for New Hang Glider Pilots.

you will spend half an hour in ground school practicing launch procedures, then, safely under the wing of your instructor, trot off a mountain top or cliff for a high-altitude dance with blue space. A tandem flight gives you ground clearances of several hundred to several thousand feet, plus 10 to 60 minutes of air time on your first excursion. Experienced tandem pilots turn the glider over to you following launch. With your pilot in the "driver's ed." instructional position, you are suddenly in command. If you live in the flatlands, modern towing techniques will allow you and your instructor to safely launch, via tow-rope and winch, from the back of a boat or truck. Tandem is great for those who weigh less than 200 lbs. Some pilots will fly 200- to 225-pound passengers in strong wind conditions.

Vicarious thrill-seekers can have fun just watching others carve circles in the sky. Observation is free. Call the nearest hang gliding school, ask where and when the flying is, get directions to the LZ (landing zone), and show up an hour early. If it's a cliff site, just start asking questions and watch. If it's a mountain site, offer to serve as a driver and notice how popular you become. Hang glider pilots gladly befriend anyone willing to ride with them to the launch site and drive their car back to the LZ. You'll get a great taste of hang gliding and make a new friend, too.

No matter how you start out, you'll learn that relaxation is the heart and soul of hang gliding. That's because a hang glider literally follows your spine. With your body hanging in a hammocklike harness attached to the glider's center of gravity, you pull your weight forward to fly faster and push it backward to slow down. Nudge yourself to the right or left and the glider will follow your lead. When you relax your grip and just hang there, the glider flies straight and level, just above the minimum speed required to sustain flight.

If you want to become capable of soloing, you'll need to train a few days a week for several weeks. You might learn the *skills* necessary to fly by yourself during a two-week vacation, but you won't develop the judgment needed to fly safely without professional supervision.

To earn a United States Hang Gliding Association (USHGA) Hang I (beginner) rating, you must demonstrate the ability to perform 3 consecutive smooth launches, followed by 3 landings on your feet into the wind. You will also have to perform controlled "S" and 45-degree turns and land within 100 feet of a designated target. Some folks can do this in a single half-day lesson, but most require 2 to 4 lessons. A Hang I rating simply means you can launch and land on a bunny slope under professional supervision. To earn a Hang II (novice) rating—which allows you to fly under your own supervision in mild conditions—you also have to perform precise, linked 90- and 180-degree turns and land within 75 feet of a target. Naturals have been known to accomplish these feats in 3 lessons, but most people require between 4 and 12.

Fortunately, it is very easy to incorporate 2 or 3 days of hang gliding into a week-long vacation. California, particularly Southern California and the Bay Area, offers the best year-round conditions and training areas. But there are a number of good seasonal places in New England, the Southeast, the Southwest, and the Rocky Mountains. And developments in towing technology (launch via truck, boat, or ultralight air-tug) have opened up the vast flatlands of the Midwest to hang gliding.

Because many hang-gliding sites are threatened by development or liability considerations, secure locations are the sport's most treasured commodity. A secure site is one where the landowner formally acknowledges and permits hang gliding. These sites usually have bathrooms, launch ramps, picnic areas, and other conveniences.

Most schools will have you sign a liability-release form, which says that you are willing to assume the risks associated with leaving the ground under your own power. A good school will make sure you read and clearly understand this document before you sign it.

CHOOSING THE RIGHT SCHOOL

You should choose a hang gliding school primarily on its adherence to the regulations that govern the sport. The certification of a school's hang gliders by the Hang Glider Manufacturers Association (HGMA) insures that they are strong, sophisticated aircraft, thoroughly tested for structural strength and aerodynamic stability. Certification of a school's instructors by the United States Hang Gliding Association (USHGA) guarantees that they are experienced hang glider pilots who have taught at least 10 days on a training hill under the supervision of a certified instructor, attended a 2- to 3-day training-and-certification seminar, and passed a written test. Ask these questions before you pay money or sign a liability release form:

Are your instructors certified by the USHGA? The only acceptable answer is yes. All schools listed below employ only certified instructors.

Will I be flying a glider that is certified by the HGMA? Don't take no for an answer, unless the glider has been specially modified for use on a bunny slope. HGMA-certified gliders are about five times stronger than they need to be to withstand normal flight loads in normal weather conditions. Since instructors of first- and second-day students teach only in very mild conditions, they will sometimes install lighter frame parts in a training glider. Even then, the glider is twice as strong as it needs to be and will save you 5 to 10 pounds of extra baggage on the hill.

Is this a secure site? Avoid schools who use "bandit" sites, where there's a good chance that a badge-toting "smokey" will run you off mid-lesson.

What kind of instruction do you offer? Whether you are interested in tandem flights or slope training (or some combination of the two), make sure the school you choose offers what you want. All schools listed below offer tandem flights as well as bunny-slope training.

How long has your company been in business, and how long have you been teaching? Experience means a lot. It's the only way you learn to read the wind.

What is the best time of year to hang glide here? With the exception of California—where blue skies, sunshine, predictable windflows, and varied terrain make for some of the world's best year-round hang gliding—most areas have definite gliding seasons.

What other attractions are in the area? This is especially important if you're traveling with non-pilots.

How far in advance do I need to book? Although some schools accept walk-in students when not fully booked, it's best to make reservations at least two weeks in advance. In these listings, chamber of commerce telephone numbers are given for assistance in finding accommodations near the schools.

Do you have references from former students?

FAVORITE SCHOOLS

THE NORTHEAST

NEW HAMPSHIRE **Morningside Flight Park.** Morningside is the finest hang gliding training area in the Northeast. Its centerpiece is a 250-foot gently sloping hill, wide enough to accommodate 20 gliders side by side. The hill is manicured and drained, like a golf course, and a big bull's-eye is painted in the landing area for students practicing spot landings. One amenity beloved by novices and veterans alike is the fleet of all-terrain vehicles (ATVs) that owner Jeff Nicolay has rigged to shuttle pilots and gliders from bottom to top between flights.

First-day bunny-slope students can expect quite a few 10- to 20-second flights from 15 to 40 feet up the slope—as many flights as will fit in the 4-hour lesson. Morningside also offers the least expensive ($50) and the shortest (less than 5 minutes) commercial tandem flights in the country. That's good news for those who just want to say "I did it!" and bad news for folks who want to savor soaring for as long as possible. An excellent observation opportunity is found 10 miles away at Mt. Ascutney, one of the most popular mountain-soaring sites in the East.

Morningside Flight Park has been going strong since 1975, when owner Phil Haynes's love of hang gliding led him to lease his dairy farm to veteran pilot Jeff Nicolay. The school is in Western New Hampshire, about 2 hours from Boston. The lilac blossoms of spring and the vibrant colors of a New England fall make May, September, and October the best times of year to visit. The school closes when the ground freezes (usually after Thanksgiving), and reopens after the spring thaw in early April.

Morningside has a spring-fed pond for swimming, and a petting zoo with ducks, geese, horses, and Tennessee Fainting Goats. (Though these goats pass out when they're startled, they have grown accustomed to hang gliders—so you can, too!) There are also tent camping facilities and bathrooms with hot showers. The retail store stocks local maple syrup as well as hang gliding T-shirts and gear. *Morningside Flight Park, RFD 2, Claremont, NH 03743, tel. 603/542–4416. Claremont Chamber of Commerce, tel. 603/ 543–1296. Apr.–Nov. (lessons by appointment only): 4-hour bunny-slope lesson, $85; tandem flight (from 430 ft. hill), $50.*

THE SOUTH

GEORGIA **Lookout Mountain Flight Park.** This is the school to choose if you want to become a solo pilot. Owner Matt Taber and head instructor Buzz Chalmers discourage the "looky loo" crowd from taking single-day, bunny-slope lessons at their 65-foot training hill in Lookout Valley. These trainers favor a method that is not aimed at providing flights after one lesson. If you decide to take slope lessons at this school, you'll probably be talked into a 2- or 3-day lesson package, and there will be earnest talk of turning you into a hang glider pilot. If that's not on your agenda, by all means take a tandem flight with these guys; Chalmers and his instructors give 200 to 300 a year.

Lookout Mountain is one of the highest points on a 21-mile "soarable" ridge above Lookout Valley. This northwestern corner of Georgia is covered by hardwood trees that make the fall foliage season a beautiful time to hang glide here. Come for the crisp mountain air and the "wonder winds"—gentle upward drafts caused by warm air rising from the valley—that increase during the fall and spring seasons. The top of Lookout Mountain is directly accessible by Georgia Highway 189, and it's a convenient place to watch hang glider pilots as they perform exciting high-wind launches or get wafted up 1,000 feet by the evening wonder winds. (Don't worry: Wonder winds don't suck people off the training hills!)

Another great observation opportunity is The Great Race, held here each spring. It's a pedal-to-the-metal contest that runs from the end of the ridge and back—a total of more than 40 miles. The best pilots from all over the country tune-up their high-performance gliders and show up for the party.

A pro-shop next to the launch ramp sells film, T-shirts, postcards, and snacks, and is a good place to watch some of the best hang glider pilots in the country begin their flights. For the rest of the family, Chattanooga, Tennessee, and vicinity (about 20 minutes away) features an excellent fresh-water aquarium and Ruby Falls, an underground cavern with a waterfall. Whitewater rafting is an hour away on the Ocoee River, site of the 1996 Olympic Kayak Run. *Lookout Mountain Flight Park, Rte. 2, Box 215H, Rising Fawn, GA 30738, tel. 706/398–3433. Closest accommodations at the Lookout Inn, tel. 706/820–2000, or call the Chattanooga Chamber of Commerce, tel. 615/756–2121. Closed Wed. Year-round (lessons by appointment only): 2-day bunny-slope weekend package, $199; tandem flight (from 2,000-ft. mountain), $89.*

NORTH CAROLINA **Kitty Hawk Kites.** This is, without question, the world's foremost hang gliding school, giving 10,000 to 15,000 bunny-slope lessons a year. Kitty Hawk employs up to 30 certified instructors during the peak months of June, July, August, and September, so it can maintain a 5:1 student:instructor ratio. Even during slower months, there are 15 instructors here to handle the load. Lighter crowds, combined with the cooler northeasterly winds that are more comfortable for pilots, make the spring and fall prime times to visit Kitty Hawk. You can buy a lesson here any day of the year (except New Years Day), weather permitting.

The school is located at Jockey's Ridge State Park, part of North Carolina's Outer Banks, and lessons center around the East Coast's highest (110 feet) natural sand dune. You spend half an hour in ground school, then move on to a 3-hour lesson; here you're guaranteed to take 5 flights off the dune.

Although the emphasis at Kitty Hawk is on bunny-slope lessons, the instructors also offer tandem flights using modern truck- and boat-towing techniques. (Both locations are about 45 minutes from the training dunes.) Truck-tows, which can lift you and your wing up to 1,000 feet, take place either at a beach or an airstrip. Boat-tows (up to 1,500 feet) are provided on nearby Albamarle Sound. The Novice-Pilot package includes unlimited sand dune lessons, 20 tandem tows, and a graduation flight from an inland mountain.

Mother's Day Weekend has been special at Kitty Hawk since 1972, the first year of the annual Hang Gliding Spectacular. This gathering of eagles includes sand-skimming races and duration contests that last for hours (the longest flight wins). The spot-landing contest harks back 50 years, to when hang gliders performed so badly that only half of those competing made their target landings. Pilots often bring examples of these antique gliders to the contest. At the end of the weekend, Francis Rogallo—the man who designed the first flexible wing (which was later used to create the hang glider) for NASA in the 1940s—joins Kitty Hawk owner John Harris in giving out awards to the winners.

Kitty Hawk's retail store, across the street from the training dunes, is an attraction in itself. In addition to hang gliding and flying souvenirs and apparel, the store provides an area with toys for the kids to play with, a playground with tube slides and ball pits, an indoor rock wall for climbing, and roller-blade lessons and rentals. *Kitty Hawk Kites, Box 1839, Nags Head, NC 27959, tel. 919/441–4124 or 800/334–4777. Outer Banks Chamber of Commerce, tel. 919/441–8144. Closed New Year's Day. Year-round (lessons by appointment only): 3-hour*

bunny-slope lesson (5 flights), $69; tandem truck-tow flight (to 1,000 ft.), $75; tandem boat-tow flight (to 1,500 ft.), $99.

THE MIDWEST

WISCONSIN **Raven Hang Gliding.** Who says the Midwest is too flat to have a first-class hang gliding school? Not Raven Hang Gliding owner Brad Kushner, a man who has parlayed unique local terrain and modern towing technology into a little bit of hang gliding heaven in Whitewater, Wisconsin. The center of the school is a private airport where Kushner houses his Dragonfly, a motorized, ultra-light aircraft that's a cross between a hang glider and an airplane. It's specially designed for towing hang gliders to altitude, just as airplanes tow sailplanes. Kushner and crew will use one of two runways to tandem air-tow you to 2,500 feet for a smooth flight down.

Kushner has been flying for 20 years and teaching for 17. His methods include special instruction for people with disabilities, including paraplegics, using equipment that permits rolling takeoffs and landings. Kushner has also helped develop thriving hang gliding clubs in Chicago, Milwaukee, Madison, and at the University of Wisconsin at Whitewater.

Whitewater is surrounded by dozens of grassy little 30- to 80-foot bunny slopes that face all different wind directions. Kushner selects a training hill based on weather conditions, and then meets students there in his Isuzu Trooper II, which tows a custom-designed Hang Trailer containing training equipment as well as a supply of hang gliding books, T-shirts, and souvenirs.

The town of Whitewater stands at the center of a densely populated triangle, an hour from Milwaukee and Madison, Wisconsin, and 2 hours from Chicago, Illinois. You can enjoy swimming, fishing, and boating at Lake Koshkonong 20 miles away, or at Lake Geneva, a playground for Chicago's well-to-do that is famous for its bed-and-breakfast accommodations. *Raven Hang Gliding, Box*

101, Whitewater, WI 53910, tel. 414/473–2003. Whitewater Chamber of Commerce, tel. 414/473–4005. Mar.–Nov. (lessons by appointment only): 1-day bunny-slope lesson, $85; 5-day package, $350; tandem flight (aero-tow to 2,500 ft.), $90; 5-day novice training package (with 10 tandem flights), $995.

THE SOUTHWEST

UTAH **Wasatch Wings.** You can learn to hang glide twice as fast at Wasatch Wings. It's one of the few places in the country where you can earn a Hang I (beginner) rating in a single week, or a Hang II (novice) rating in 2 weeks. The wind conditions at Point of the Mountain, Utah—which sits astride the narrowest portion of Salt Lake Valley—make this possible. The morning wind funnels straight up its 400-foot south-facing slope, and the afternoon wind funnels straight up its 1,000-foot north-facing slope, enabling owner Gordon Pollack to give his students 2 lessons a day. At most schools you can only take 2 to 4 lessons a week. These fantastic weather conditions, combined with a great training hill, are the key to the enduring success of Wasatch Wings.

Pollack reports that student pilots from all over the country come to Point of the Mountain to refine their skills. Many are accompanied by certified instructors from out of state who want to take advantage of the intense training the conditions allow.

The area is especially breathtaking in the fall, when the red-and-orange scrub oak and yellow sage of the Salt Lake Valley stand out against the green pines of the Wasatch Mountains. You can enjoy the views on tandem flights that Pollack gives from 4,600-foot Frances Peak and 3,000-foot Camel Pass. Mountain biking, hiking, and swimming are available throughout the area, most notably at Deer Creek Lake. Salt Lake City is 30 miles away. Wasatch Wings, 2534 Murray Holiday Rd., Holladay, UT 84117, tel. 801/277–1042. Mountain Shadows Campground, tel. 801/571–4024. Salt Lake City Chamber of Commerce, tel. 801/364–3631. Closed Sun. Open

mid-Apr.–mid-Nov. (lessons by appointment only): 3- to 4-hour bunny-slope lesson (8–10 flights), $75; tandem flight (from 3,000–4,600 ft.), $125.

THE ROCKIES

COLORADO **Golden Wings.** This is the only full-service hang gliding center in the Rockies. Because of a relatively short gliding season (early April through early October), and summer winds that can change from weak to wicked in a matter of minutes, the eastern foothills of the Rockies isn't the ideal location for a hang gliding school. Golden Wings makes it work, using a mobile training unit that gives instructors total control over training conditions for first- and second-day students.

Co-owners Ludwig Goppenhammer, Terry Hackbart, and Vicki Damaskopolou have built a remarkable hang gliding flight simulator on the back of a flatbed truck. You hook into a glider tethered to the truckbed by lines that allow you to fly a few feet in the air before running out of slack. One instructor stands in front of you and issues commands that help you float up, up, and away to where you can practice basic controls to your heart's content. The other instructor drives the truck down the road fast enough for the wind to lift you and the glider into the air. If you have any problems, the instructor uses the tethers to pull you back into correct form.

After a few sessions on the truck simulator, you proceed to North Boulder, a 350-foot training hill about 20 miles from the shop. Or, you can take a tandem flight via a truck-tow system that reels you and your instructor out to 1,500 feet before cutting you loose for a free-flight down. The best times to hang glide in this area are early spring and early fall, when the temperatures are milder and the winds are smoother.

Beer fans will be happy to note that Golden Wings is within walking distance of the Coors Brewery. The town of Golden has a definite Old West flavor, complete with an old-fashioned Main Street. It's just a few minutes from downtown Denver and within striking distance of some of the best hiking, mountain biking, and whitewater rafting in the United States. This is the only hang gliding school in the country that has an accommodation package, combining nights at a local inn with days of lessons. *Golden Wings, 1103 Washington, Golden, CO 80401, tel. 303/278–7181 or 800/677–4449. Accommodation packages through the Table Mountain Inn, tel. 303/ 277–9898. Early Apr.–early Oct.: 3 days of lessons and 5 nights at the inn, $425 per person double occupancy; 5 days of lessons and 7 nights at the inn, $620 per person double occupancy; half-day flatbed simulator lesson, $85; slope lesson (350-ft. hill), $85; tandem truck-tow flight (1,000–1,500 ft.), $85.*

THE WEST COAST

CALIFORNIA **Air Time of San Francisco.** This is the only full-service hang gliding shop near southern San Francisco's Fort Funston cliff, one of California's most popular soaring sites. This 200-foot-high coastal cliff is a playground for hundreds of local pilots year-round. Whether you're flying or just watching from the observation deck, you'll get a beautiful view of blue-green waves breaking on the beach below.

Jeff Greenbaum fell in love with hang gliding in 1984 and bought Air Time in 1988. He and his instructors give bunny-slope lessons at The Bowl, a training dune below the cliff. As a first-day student you can watch with envy as the local pros swoop silently overhead, then dazzle yourself by afternoon's end, when you fly 5 feet above the training dune. You can also take a tandem flight from the cliff or one of several local mountains. The best time to visit is between March and October, when the wind conditions are most reliable.

Air Time of San Francisco is two blocks from the entrance to the San Francisco Zoo and a mile from world-famous Golden Gate Park. Ocean Beach, a popular stunt-kite flying site, is just a few minutes away. *Airtime of San Francisco, 3620 Wawona St., San Francisco,*

CA 94116, tel. 415/759–1177. San Francisco Chamber of Commerce, tel. 415/392–4511. Sundays reserved for students. Year-round (lessons by appointment only): 6-hour bunny-slope lesson at The Bowl, $129; tandem flight (at Fort Funston or nearby mountain site), $175.

CALIFORNIA **Torrey Pines Flight Park.** This is some of the most active airspace in the country. The 340-foot-high, 4-mile long cliff overlooking Black's Beach in La Jolla is the only legal coastal-ridge soaring site in Southern California, and it's a great place to watch hang gliders, radio-controlled model sailplanes, and full-size sailplanes, all soaring together. Torrey Pines has been a hang gliding mecca since the early 1970s, so popular that in 1993 the Glider Port was designated a historical landmark.

The City of San Diego issues an annual lease for the operation, which includes a retail store, a spectator area, and a snack bar dubbed The Cliff Hangar Café. The current leaseholder is UP International, a hang glider and apparel manufacturer. The many pilots who fly here have a time- and space-sharing system that works very well, but the traffic can still be intimidating for beginners. First-timers here stick to observation or one of the 30-minute tandem flights offered by the park's instructors.

The Flight Park is just 15 minutes from Balboa Park, home of the internationally renowned San Diego Zoo. And it's 20 minutes from Sea World. *Torrey Pines Flight Park, 2800 Torrey Pines Scenic Dr., La Jolla, CA 92037, tel. 619/452–3203. San Diego Chamber of Commerce, tel. 619/456–4092. Year-round (lessons by appointment only): half-hour tandem flight (from Torrey Pines cliff), $100.*

CALIFORNIA **Windsports Hang Gliding School.** You may have already seen Windsports owner Joe Greblo fly a hang glider—in car commercials, California Tourism spots, and on Rescue 911 episodes, to name just a few. He is one-half of Stunt Kites, the TV-and-film industry's most frequently employed hang gliding stunt team. He is also a USHGA regional director and one of the developers of the USHGA's Tandem Rating Program.

Greblo has been running Windsports, one of the oldest continuously operated hang gliding schools in the United States (and perhaps the world), since it opened in 1974. The school has three components: a 1,200-square-foot Pro Shop in Van Nuys, a bunny slope in the San Fernando Valley, and a more advanced launch site 3,500 feet above Joe's vacation home at the base of Los Angeles's Kagel Mountain.

You start with an hour of ground school at the shop, then spend an afternoon working with a team of instructors on the 150-foot slope called Simi Valley. The slope is so gentle that your instructor can run right alongside you while you skim for hundreds of feet, just 3 to 5 feet above the ground. Joe supervises the more advanced lessons at Kagel Mountain, where the landing site is maintained by the City of Van Nuys. Greblo helped develop the Flight Park here, which includes a parking area, picnic tables, horseshoe- and barbecue-pits, and portable toilets. Tandem flights are offered at Windsports only to those who spend an afternoon on the bunny slope.

If you come fly with Windsports, Joe will have you picked up at the airport, provide you with a written syllabus of your course, and even rent you a room in his own house. Universal Studios is just 10 minutes away and Magic Mountain Amusement Park is 20 minutes from Greblo's home. *Windsports, International, 16145 Victory Blvd., Van Nuys, CA 91406, tel. 310/474–3502. Van Nuys Chamber of Commerce, tel. 818/989–0300. Closed Mon. Year-round (lessons by appointment only): bunny-slope (training hill) lesson, $99; tandem flight, $125; complete Hang Gliding Introduction (ground school, day on bunny slope, tandem flight), $199; 7-day package with lodging at Joe Greblo's house, 4 slope lessons, and one tandem flight, $625 per person.*

SOURCES

ORGANIZATIONS United States Hang Gliding Association (Box 8300, Colorado Springs, CO 80933, tel. 719/632–8300) provides general information on ratings, services, certification, and membership. Its official monthly publication, *Hang Gliding Magazine*, features an annual New Pilot Edition for beginners.

PERIODICALS *Hang Gliding Magazine* (6950 Aragon Cr., Suite 6, Buena Park, CA 90620, tel. 714/994–3050) has articles and photographs of interest to hang glider pilots of all skill levels.

BOOKS *Right Stuff for New Hang Glider Pilots* (Publitec Editions), by Erik Fair, is primarily aimed at people already enrolled in hang gliding lessons, but it also gives outsiders an inside look at some of the zanier aspects of hang gliding's offbeat culture. Peter Cheney's *Hang Gliding for Beginning Pilots* is thorough and well-illustrated, the best written resource available to the novice hang glider pilot. Both can be ordered through the United States Hang Gliding Association (*see* Organizations, *above*).

ALSO SEE People who like to fly may like to jump and fly. The Skydiving chapter tells you how to get started.

Hiking and Backpacking

by Peter Oliver

If horse racing is the sport of royalty (as is its claim), hiking is the sport of the populace—the sport for everyone and anyone. So elementary and plodding is hiking that even considering it a sport might be doing injustice to the whole premise of sport as athletic exercise and expression. No special skills are required, nor is extraordinary physical condition. No snazzy sporting gear or apparel is needed either.

Hiking isn't defined by rules or much restricted by any specific parameters, other than the fact that you need reasonably solid ground to walk on. Perhaps it is because hiking involves the most rudimentary of human motor skills that it can be recast under so many different headings: trekking, walking, backpacking, tramping (the British term), scrambling, rambling, and so on. Such semantic excess. Let's just call a hike a hike.

Although hiking is something you can easily do under your own guidance, and most hikers do just that, organized trips also make sense: While selecting a route, planning an itinerary, getting the right gear and maps, planning meals, and making other necessary preparations have some hikers toiling with expeditionary zeal, signing up with a trip organizer returns trip preparations to the basics. All you need to do is decide where to go and how strenuous you want the trip to be, then choose a trip to match.

Your choices are virtually limitless. On the one hand, there is backpacking—the pervading image of hiking as a sport, trekking into the wilderness bearing your housing and food on your back. This is hiking at its most demanding, where you earn your reward, say, the chance to experience the blissful solitude of sunset in some remote wilderness. Then again, the weather can be miserable or the bugs unrelenting; your equipment could fail or your feet might blister; and the food is seldom anything to write home about: It has to be light in weight and therefore involves quantities of dried ingredients like rice, as well as nuts, dried fruits, and freeze-dried coffee and prepared foods. Backpacking is a quest for exhilaration that isn't for everyone.

But for anyone unwilling to accept the possibility that things can and do go wrong, there are alternatives—for instance, naturalist-led day hikes covering relatively flat terrain, with nights in comfortable beds in country inns and meals in cozy or elegant dining rooms where the fare tends toward the elegant—for instance, apple-pecan pancakes at breakfast, spinach quiche or hearty sandwiches on homemade bread at lunch, beef bourguignon, salmon doused with beurre blanc or sorrel sauce, or grilled boneless chicken breasts with a Dijon mustard sauce. Such trips are often organized with elderly hikers in mind (though not exclusively) and often come with a naturalist bent—bird-watching, flora identifica-

---

New York City–based outdoors writer Peter Oliver has hiked all over the United States. His favorite destinations are New Hampshire's White Mountains and grizzly country in Montana.

tion, and so on. The only gear you need is a camera and sun block, and often opportunity is provided, for those who want it, to cut a day's hike short and return to the inn porch to fall asleep reading a book.

Another option is llama trekking, wherein beasts of burden carry most camping equipment and food, allowing hikers to cover more terrain than if carrying their own gear, and making for campsite meals that by backpacker standards would be considered decadent—with fresh meats, poultry, fruits, and vegetables, at least at the beginning of the trip, and even wine to wash it down. Pack animals other than llamas, which are particularly well suited to travel in mountainous terrain, are sometimes used.

Some organizers combine hiking with biking, river rafting, horseback riding, antiquing, or fishing. About the only ancillary activities that can be ruled out are those rooted in a mechanized, televised, electronically digitized rat race from which any hike is at its essence an escape.

Such a wide range of options not surprisingly engenders a wide range of prices. There's a direct correlation between comfort and cost on the trail; a straightforward, simple, carry-all-your-own gear 6-day trip with the Sierra Club, say, runs as little as $330, while an inn-to-inn jaunt, complete with van transport to the trailhead and sumptuous meals, is easily thrice the price.

No matter what the trip you'll need appropriate footwear: Sometimes walking or running shoes will do, but more probably a sturdy pair of hiking boots will be required, especially in the mountains and particularly if off-trail scrambling is involved.

CHOOSING THE RIGHT TRIP

Your primary concern ought to be safety, especially for longer, more rigorous trips. Guides should be equipped with the proper technical and first-aid gear and well-trained in such emergency procedures as CPR as well as safety procedures—for instance, what to do when

above tree line in a lightning storm. This may be difficult to determine, because no governing body certifies trail guides or rates guided hiking tour operators, and the value of the regional groups' efforts to do so is debatable. In some areas, specifically national parks, the number of outfitters may be restricted, and in such cases there is at least some assurance that an outfitter is a responsible one. The larger trip organizers (*see* Major Players, *below*) do make some attempt to separate the wheat from the chaff.

So ask questions—lots of them—to be sure the outfitter is reputable and the particular trip is right for your abilities, interests, schedule, and budget. Start with these:

How long has the company been in business? Chances are that a company that has been around for a few years has ironed out all the kinks and has already answered the questions and met the challenges that you throw at them.

What are your guide's qualifications? The better the guide, the better the trip, simple as that. Find out how long the guides have been hiking in the area and how long they have been guiding groups, and ask about any other abilities or fields of expertise. Knowledge of local plants, animals, and geological phenomena is a decided plus. Make sure at least one guide with your group is certified in first aid and can administer CPR.

What size is the group, and who are its constituents? Most trips set out with 5 to 10 hikers; if the group is larger, you lose the sense of remoteness and isolation that is one of the sport's great rewards. Group members' age, physical fitness, and hiking experience determine what a group can and can't do. Some trips are organized with families, women, men, or teens in mind—and if you don't fit in, you might not have a good time.

With smaller groups, there's the flexibility to change the itinerary if you want to. In some cases, outfitters encourage suggestions and participation by group members in the trip planning.

How long is each day's hike, and how strenuous? A 10-mile hike through flat or rolling countryside may be easier than 3 miles in the mountains. Most trip organizers rate their trips, but unlike river rafting or rock climbing, hiking has no standard rating scale to determine a hike's relative difficulty. A trip that one organization considers moderate may be strenuous according to another. Be sure to question the outfitter carefully so that you know what you're getting into.

What are accommodations like? Make sure you know what to expect. If you're staying at inns or resorts, find out what the rooms are like and ask about the availability of a fitness center, swimming pool, or any other facilities you may want to use. If you're camping, ask what the campsites are like and what kind of shower and latrine arrangements are usual. Before you sign up to use the outfitter's tents or sleeping bags, make sure they are suited to the location.

What's the food like? Don't expect anything spectacular, except on llama-trekking journeys or inn-to-inn trips. But some outfitters set more store by good food than others, and some are more virtuosic with dried and freeze-dried foods than others.

What's the cost and what's included? Typically (and for the trips described below unless otherwise noted), your trip fee includes guide service, all meals, any transfers after the group has assembled, and accommodations during inn- or lodge-based trips, but not tents, sleeping bags and pads, backpacks, and other camping gear for backpacking trips; sometimes the outfitter can rent you what you need. Most trip organizers provide lists of necessary gear. Meals and motel lodging before the trip heads off down the trail and after the walk's conclusion may be included—or they may not.

Ditto for transportation from the nearest airport, which is important only if you're not driving to the assembly point; if transfers are not included (as is usually the case), you may need to rent a car. Airfare into the area is always extra.

Do you have references from past guests? To answer qualitative questions about the outfitter's operation, there's no substitute for polling past guests; if most seem satisfied, you probably will be, too. Ask for references even if you have no questions: A company's willingness to give them to you is an indication that the feedback you get will be positive.

How far in advance do I need to book? Usually you'll also need to make your plans at least 3 months in advance, primarily so that outfitters can be sure there are enough participants before making the complex preparations involved in setting up a trip (some trips may be canceled if not enough people sign up).

MAJOR PLAYERS

AMERICAN WILDERNESS EXPERIENCE

This company, founded in 1971, is a trip wholesaler representing numerous smaller outfitters. As a result its trip offerings are all over the block. Hiking is just one of several activities in the AWE fold, and the relative difficulty, luxury, and cost of any trip varies from one outfitter to the next. There are llama trekking trips, backpacks, hikes with pack stock, lodge-based trips, and more. AWE is a good starting point for anyone interested in what's possible under the broad banner of "adventure travel" (Box 1486, Boulder, CO 80306, tel. 303/444–2622 or 800/444–0099, fax 303/444–3999). *Also see* Horse Packing and Trail Riding.

HIKING HOLIDAYS This outfitter focuses its attention primarily on the eastern United States, although trips to Europe and New Zealand are also offered. For the most part, the hiking is at a relaxed pace over easy to moderate terrain, with options usually provided for those who prefer to bypass more arduous parts of a hike, such as a climb to a mountain summit. Hiking Holidays is thus a good choice for senior hikers or anyone more interested in a little exercise and a lot of fresh air rather than the physical exertion of backpacking. Lodging is in country inns of a fairly high order, and meals in some cases can be quite spectacular. Given the relative level of luxury, trip costs tend toward the higher end (Box 750, Bristol, VT 05443, tel. 802/453–4814, fax 802/453–4806).

HOSTELLING INTERNATIONAL/AMERICAN YOUTH HOSTELS

This organization is probably better known for its cycling program. However, the venerable AYH, founded in 1934 and now renamed, also conducts several hiking tours in the western United States, as well as in Canada and Europe. Hiking trips usually rely on vans to shuttle hikers from hostels to trailheads. Accommodations and meals in hostels, whose amenities and character vary, help to keep trip costs reasonable. Most HI/AYH hiking trips are moderately difficult and run from 9 days to 2 weeks. Many trips are for adults and seniors (733 15th St. NW, Suite 840, Washington, DC 20005, tel. 202/783–6161, fax 202/783–6171).

MOUNTAIN TRAVEL-SOBEK

The merging of Mountain Travel and Sobek in 1991 brought together two of the pathfinding organizations in adventure travel. River-running was the claim to fame of Sobek, established in 1973; wildlife-watching, trekking, and mountaineering were the strengths of Mountain Travel, founded 4 years earlier. These activities continue as the primary offerings of the merged company.

Primarily an international adventure-travel operator, the organization focuses its attention on exotic locales such as African rivers and Patagonia. However, it does offer some North American trips, mainly in Alaska and the Southwest. The emphasis in most is on a combination of adventure and cultural experience, although the balance of that equation differs, and trips range from fairly relaxed affairs to serious expeditions. Prices are in the mid- to high range; accommodations vary. A number of trips of 2 weeks and longer are available (6420 Fairmount Ave., El Cerrito, CA 94530, tel. 510/527–8100 or 800/227–2384, fax 510/525–7710).

REI ADVENTURES

Affiliated with the outdoor gear and clothing chain, REI Adventures spans the adventure-travel spectrum: hiking, biking, kayaking, mountaineering, and the like, with trip difficulty ranging from moderate to expeditionary. REI's scope is international, but the company does have some trips in the Pacific Northwest and Alaska (Box 1938, Sumner, WA 98390, tel. 212/891–2631 or 800/622–2236, fax 206/891–2523).

ROADS LESS TRAVELED

While bicycle touring is the primary focus of Roads Less Traveled, this Rockies specialist has added more hiking as well as some hiking-and-biking trips to its roster in recent years. Difficulty varies, though it tends to fall in the moderate range, covering 6 to 10 miles in a day and never more than 1,000 feet of elevation gained. You're free to walk at your own pace. Lodging is in inns, B&Bs, guest ranches, and the occasional mountain hut, and these supply your breakfasts and dinners; trail lunches consist of pasta with pesto sauce, spinach quiche, and other not-so-basic picnic fare. Prices are moderate to high (Box 8187, Longmont, CO 80501, tel. 303/678–8750, fax 303/678–5568).

SIERRA CLUB OUTINGS DEPARTMENT

Its well-known political activities aside, the Sierra Club also has perhaps the most extensive adventure-trip list of any organization anywhere, including around 100 hiking and backpacking trips. This means trips of widely ranging character, reflecting the wide-ranging interests of the trip leaders, who are all Sierra Club members and volunteers. Precise offerings vary from year to year; destinations change, leaders may change, trips with the same leader to the same destination use different routes, or trips with a special focus are replaced by trips with a different focus to the same area or by trips with the same focus into a different area. As might be expected from a leader of the environmental movement, the preponderance of trips involve roughing it. However, not all is strenuous backpacking; some trips involve tent camping at a base just a short walk from the nearest trailhead, and several trips are designed specifically with families, small children, and senior hikers in mind. Groups usually hit the trail with about 15 hikers. Tent camping and campsite dining help to keep most trip costs low to moderate, and meals and guiding are always included but not backpacks, tents, sleeping bags and pads, and other camping equipment. In addition to regular backpacking and hiking trips, the Club also oversees a service program, in which hikers can do their thing with a purpose, from archaeology to trail maintenance. Enrollment for most trips begins in January; sign up as soon as possible after that (730 Polk St., San Francisco, CA 94109, tel. 415/923–5630, fax 415/776–4868).

TIMBERLINE BICYCLE TOURS   This bike-tour specialist, founded in 1982, also offers hiking tours and several hiking-biking combos, primarily in the West. Lodging is in inns and mountain lodges, tending toward upscale, with meals of comparable quality. As a result, costs are generally moderate to high (7975 E. Harvard, #J, Denver, CO 80231, tel. 303/759–3804).

FAVORITE TRIPS

THE NORTHEAST

MAINE   **Acadia National Park with Toddlers.** For the most part, hiking is an activity for which small children—or parents with small children—need not apply. That's what makes this 7-day Toddler Tromp from Sierra Club Outings noteworthy: It is designed specifically with kids in mind. Rather than long, demanding hikes from one destination to another, it consists of shell-collecting, blueberry picking, and campfire sing-alongs near the base camp. The most strenuous activity is the easy hike to the summit of 1,530-foot Mt. Cadillac.

Acadia National Park epitomizes all that is Maine: mountains and islands, a rocky, jagged coastline, small, yacht-filled harbors, and lobstermen. July and August are the height of the tourist season, and the park can be fairly crowded, so this trip is hardly a wilderness escape. But July and August are also the months when the weather is most agreeable, another factor to consider for young and inexperienced campers. This is a good trip—so it's unfortunate that by the time you're ready

to step out, Sierra Club leaders may have replaced it. *Sierra Club Outings, 730 Polk St., San Francisco, CA 94109, tel. 415/923–5630, fax 415/776–4868. Late July–early Aug.: 7 days, $570 adults, $380 children. Sign up 6–7 months in advance.*

MAINE   **The Coast.** Walking the World organizes trips exclusively for people 50 and older. That is to say, *active* people 50 and older: While this 8-day trip is certainly less strenuous than many in this chapter, it is hardly one that has been condescendingly toned down to attract the life-long armchair set.

The easy-to-moderate itinerary does not run along a continuous trail; Maine's ruggedly indented coast would hardly permit it. Instead, you take short boat and van rides to trailheads for the coastal and island hikes, which average from 6 to 9 miles. The most extended are in Acadia National Park, where mountainous islands meet the sea. For the most part, this is not a wilderness escape: One of the attractions of the area is its Down East culture of clapboard homes, lobster boats, and leatherneck seamen; in late September, there's also the changing foliage. Accommodations are in comfortable bed-and-breakfasts. Group size is 12 to 18. *Walking the World, Box 1186, Fort Collins, CO 80522, tel. 303/225–0500, fax 303/225–0538. Late Sept.: 8 days, $1,395. Price does not include 5 dinners; sign up 6–8 months in advance.*

NEW HAMPSHIRE   **Day-tripping in the White Mountains.** Hiking in the White Mountains doesn't have to be rugged. Below tree line, the White Mountains can be positively tame, with their mixed forests, waterfalls, deep gorges, and occasional stunning views. Representative of the more leisurely opportunities in the area is this 5-day trip offered by Stonehurst Manor, a very stylish, turn-of-the-century 25-room inn outside North Conway. From here you make 4- to 14-mile group day hikes both below and above timberline in the Mt. Washington area, with daily itineraries varying according to the weather and the group's fitness level and interests. Your non-hiking traveling companions can relax back at the manor, read books, swim, and the like, or explore North Conway's shops. A feeling of intimacy is maintained by restricting the group size to fewer than 8. The trip cost varies depending on whether you go for a standard room or opt for a deluxe version, with a fireplace. *Stonehurst Manor, Box 1937, Rte. 16, North Conway, NH 03860, tel. 603/356–3271 or 800/525–9100, fax 603/356–3217. Apr.– Nov.: 5 days, $557. Sign up 2–3 months in advance.*

NEW HAMPSHIRE **Hut-to-hut in the White Mountains' Presidential Range.** The Presidential Range of these mountains, capped by 6,288-foot Mt. Washington, is the most uncompromising stand of peaks in the Northeast; the highest wind speed ever (231 mph) was recorded at the Mt. Washington summit's weather station, and it's brutally cold in winter and only occasionally warm in summer. But it's also a place of austere beauty unlike anything else in the Northeast: a weather-scoured succession of peaks, mostly above tree line and presenting panoramas that sweep more than 100 miles in any direction on good days.

This 4-day Appalachian Mountain Club trip makes the traverse of the Presidential Range and neighboring peaks, which is one of the truly classic hikes in the East—or in the United States, for that matter. Daily hiking may include gains of more than 4,000 vertical feet, covering 5 to 8 miles. Overnight lodging is along the route in spare but comfortable huts, where bunks are furnished with scratchy wool camp blankets and pillows but not linen; you may want to bring sheets, if not your own sleeping bag. Meals are served family-style, but with 4 courses are a bit more elaborate than you might expect. If you have less time or energy, go for a 3-day option, which takes in fewer peaks. *Appalachian Mountain Club, Box 298, Gorham, NH 03581, tel. 603/466–2727, fax 603/466–2720. June– Aug.: 10 days, $790 ($740 for AMC members). Price does not include bed linens; sign up at least 2 months in advance.*

NEW YORK **High Peaks Traverse in the Adirondacks.** It was in these mountains of upstate New York that the early apostles of America's environmental conscience, including Ralph Waldo Emerson, searched for intimacy with the wilderness. Theodore Roosevelt and other later adventurers also made frequent visits. (In fact, it was in the Adirondacks that Roosevelt, on a backcountry outing, was hastily sworn in as president after the assassination of William McKinley.) The High Peaks, crowned by 5,543-foot Mt. Marcy, are the focal point for many hikers' efforts here.

This 5-day program from the Adirondack Mountain Club focuses on trails in the checkerboard of public and private land known as Adirondack Park, the largest park in the country outside Alaska. The main base camp is the Adirondak Loj, a bunkroom-style log retreat, named by an early proponent of phonetic spelling, near Lake Placid. From here, groups go out on day hikes according to participants' fitness and inclination. With groups numbering from 4 to 8, this is a good choice for families with children or other hikers who might not be up to the challenge of strenuous summit hikes but still appreciate being surrounded by the great outdoors. Meals and bunkroom accommodations are nothing fancy, but neither is the tab. The Loj sleeps up to 46. *Adirondack Mountain Club, Box 867, Lake Placid, NY 12946, tel. 518/523–3441, fax 418/523–3518. July–Aug.: 3 days, $175–$220 adults, $115 children under 12; 5 days, $270–$320 adults, $210 children. Sign up 3–4 months in advance.*

VERMONT **The Long Trail.** This 200-mile footpath completely traverses the state from north to south and crosses all of the state's high peaks. But it is often not especially good for backpackers (although many backpackers do take it on) because campsites are in short supply and water is hard to find along the ridgetop in summer. However, because it leads with regularity from mountain summits to settled valleys and back, it is ideally suited for inn-to-inn hikers who enjoy demanding hikes by day and comfortable country inns by night.

Like almost all trips along the Long Trail, this one bites off only a small segment—in this case in central Vermont—and includes 8- to 10-mile day hikes through both rugged and not-so-rugged terrain. Accommodations and meals are in country inns tending more toward the casual end of the elegance scale. There are never more than 10 hikers. Fall trips, the most popular, are also the most expensive. Late May and early June, when spring is still in blooming evidence at higher elevations, is a good alternative. *Country Inns along the Trail, RR#3, Box 3115, Brandon, VT 05733, tel. 802/247–3300, fax 802/247–6851. May–Oct.: 5 days, $629–$749. Sign up 3–4 months in advance.*

VERMONT **The South.** Southern Vermont, the most settled part of the state, can't escape the influence of tourism, especially around such population centers as Manchester. But there are still plenty of forested hills as well as relics of pre-Revolutionary settlements that are harder to find farther north.

Fall foliage weeks and spring, when wildflowers and apple blossoms are in bloom, are probably the best times to visit, and country inns and tour operators do a brisk and competitive business then. Thus choosing when to go to Vermont is less difficult than choosing whom to go with. The particular appeal of this 5-day trip from the National Audubon Society is its naturalist orientation, to allow plenty of time to learn about the region's tree, plant, and bird life. The pace is leisurely, just 4 to 8 miles a day on mostly easy trails and back roads. Lodging and dining is in rather deluxe country inns. Group size is limited to 20. *National Audubon Society, 700 Broadway, New York, NY 10003, tel. 212/979–3066, fax 212/353–0190. May, Oct.: 5 days, $799. Sign up 2 months in advance.*

VERMONT **The Lake Country.** You hear a lot of old-time Vermonters claim that the state has become overly gentrified—that it is now less rural than suburban. That certainly isn't true of Vermont's far north, a world of exceedingly small towns and hundreds of small lakes and ponds, where dirt roads are more common than paved ones. Words like "resort" and "condominium" are used relatively infrequently.

This Hiking Holidays trip through the area begins, ironically, in Stowe, a town driven by tourism in general and skiing in particular, and at the Green Mountain Inn, a model of gentrified, country-inn luxury. But from there the trip leads along back roads into Vermont's backwoods. The going is fairly easy, with mileages of from 4 to 6 a day, although there are a couple of climbs to summits overlooking fjordlike Lake Willoughby. All nights are in country inns, not necessarily in digs as posh as the Green Mountain Inn, but comfortable enough with excellent food, including vegetarian lasagna and a Mexican buffet. Late September and early October are probably the best times to go—for the foliage—and as a result these trips are likely to fill up early. *Hiking Holidays, Box 750, Bristol, VT 05443, tel. 802/453–4816, fax 802/453–4806. June–early Oct.: 6 days, $799. Sign up 2 months in advance, 4 months for fall trips.*

THE MID ATLANTIC

VIRGINIA **Shenandoah Mountains.** While Shenandoah is one of the United States' most visited national parks, the overwhelming majority of the visiting horde remains carbound, and this most crowded of parks isn't particularly crowded with hikers, especially given the fact that there are more than 100 trail miles.

This 5-day trip from Hiking Holidays is in May, when the spring bloom of dogwoods and azaleas is the main feature, and in October, when the highlight is the fall foliage. The Shenandoah Mountains run as a long ridge rising above the Virginia flatlands to the east, and summit views tend to be of the sweeping, panoramic variety. The hiking is not especially strenuous, usually 4 to 7 miles per day; the few, optional ascents to summits above 4,000 feet can be bypassed by those who choose to, although are well worth the effort for the views. Nights are in country inns with private baths, putting this trip fairly high on the luxury level, showing off the civilized, old-world gentility of rural Virginia. Group size ranges from 10 to 18. *Hiking Holidays,*

Box 750, Bristol, VT 05443, tel. 802/453–4816, fax 802/453–4806. May, Oct.: 5 days, $899. Sign up 3 months in advance.

WEST VIRGINIA **Monongahela National Forest.** There is something anciently mysterious and brooding about West Virginia, something bred deeply in a conspiracy of geology and human history. You don't need to know much about the geology of the Appalachians to get a sense that here, in West Virginia, the mountains have eroded and compressed upon themselves through aeons of time.

This Sierra Club trip heads through some of West Virginia's wilder country, the Otter Creek and Dolly Sods wilderness areas of the Monongahela National Forest. Although this is a backpacking trip—and one in the mountains, for that matter—the pace is leisurely, with 2 rest days, and there is relatively little climbing. The aim here is to enjoy the forests, creeks, and waterfalls in their transition from summer into fall. Despite the relatively easy going, however, you still must carry your own pack, up to 10 miles a day, and thus should be in reasonably decent physical shape. Like all Sierra Club Outings trips, this one may not be available when you want to go—but you should be able to find something similar that interests you. *Sierra Club Outings, 730 Polk St., San Francisco, CA 94109, tel. 415/923–5630, fax 415/776–4868. Late Sept.: 6 days, $395. Sign up 6–7 months in advance.*

THE SOUTH

FLORIDA **Florida Trail.** A hiking trip in February? A hiking trip in Florida? Incongruities, perhaps, but a rare opportunity to experience a wilderness Florida that contrasts strikingly with the Florida of golfing communities and Cadillacs. This 6-day Sierra Club trip is in this wilderness, specifically in the Ocala National Forest, the southernmost national forest in the United States, on the 1,100-mile Florida Trail, which crosses forest land en route from the Panhandle in the north to Big Cypress National Preserve in the

south. The trail is one of the country's least publicized long trails, partly because some sections remain to be fully developed, although the section through the national forest is well maintained.

Daily hiking distances are under 10 miles, the terrain is flat, and food is stored along the route, to somewhat lighten your backpack (but only somewhat; this trip does call for carrying a pack of some size and camping out at night). Insects, intolerable in summer, are minimal at this time of year. After 4 days of backpacking, you pick up canoes for 2 days of canoeing at crystal-clear Juniper Springs. This much is guaranteed: you *will* see herons and alligators. Group size is 12. Like all Sierra Club Outings trips, this one may not be available when you want to go—but you should be able to find something similar of interest in the area. *Sierra Club Outings, 730 Polk St., San Francisco, CA 94109, tel. 415/923–5630, fax 415/776–4868. Mid-Feb.: 6 days, $330. Sign up 6–7 months in advance.*

NORTH CAROLINA **Blue Ridge Mountains.** At 6,684 feet, Mt. Mitchell is the highest mountain in the United States east of the Mississippi. Yet its distinction comes with almost total anonymity. No doubt, the reasons for this are the fame of New Hampshire's Mt. Washington and its notorious weather, and the immense popularity of Great Smoky Mountains National Park just to the west of Mt. Mitchell and ticky-tacky Gatlinburg, Tennessee, nearby. In this context, people tend to overlook the rugged and commanding upthrust of the Blue Ridge Mountains, of which Mt. Mitchell is king.

On this 5-day trip from Hiking Holidays, day tramps of 4 to 7 miles through deep, wild Linville Gorge and up Grandfather Mountain combine to provide a moderate amount of physical exertion. But since nights are spent at local inns, there is no need to transport heavy packs. A predominant feature of mountains at this latitude is the rhododendron cover, and the spring bloom makes April the preferable time to hike here; in fall, foliage is obviously the main attraction, although similar color shows can be enjoyed in almost any mountainous region of the East and may actually be more spectacular farther north. *Hiking Holidays, Box 750, Bristol, VT 05443, tel. 802/453–4816, fax 802/453–4806. Apr., Oct.: 5 days, $799. Sign up 2 months in advance.*

THE MIDWEST

MICHIGAN **Lake Superior Shoreline.** Michigan's upper peninsula is a kind of land between, framed by a trio of Great Lakes (Superior, Huron, and Michigan) and suspended between the rest of the United States and Canada. The Lake Superior shoreline is the peninsula at its most scenic, with long, relatively deserted beaches and the cliff formations of Pictured Rocks National Lakeshore.

This Sierra Club Outings jaunt is in fall, when the colors of the peninsula's mixed forests are changing—and mid-summer's voracious insects are much less prevalent. The going here is fairly easy—5 to 6 miles a day over flat terrain; this is more a trip for foliage fanciers and photographers than hard-core hikers, although backpacking and camping are involved. Group size is around 15. Note that, like all Sierra Club Outings trips, this one may be replaced by slightly different programs when you want to go. *Sierra Club Outings, 730 Polk St., San Francisco, CA 94109, tel. 415/923– 5630, fax 415/776–4868. Mid-Sept.: 6 days, $385. Sign up 6–7 months in advance.*

THE SOUTHWEST

ARIZONA **Grand Canyon's South Rim.** About 90% of the nearly 4 million people who visit the Grand Canyon each year approach the national park from the south. The vast majority drive up, look out over the inspiring vista, take a few photos, and depart. Relatively few actually venture down into the canyon, to the banks of the Colorado River more than 4,000 feet below—despite the fact that doing this is the best way to understand the Canyon's geological history, complexity, and dimension.

This 5-day Timberline Bicycle Tours trip is one of those rare outings where going downhill may be more demanding that going up. The South Kaibab Trail from the rim to the river is extremely steep, covering 4,400 vertical feet in 6 miles, and its route which follows ledges along the canyon walls is an acrophobe's nightmare. The program also includes hiking in Havasu Canyon, whose waterfalls make it the Grand Canyon's most spectacular tributary canyon. On this trip, you overnight at Phantom Ranch, the only lodging within the canyon, and at Supai Lodge on the Havasupai Indian Reservation. Be prepared for encounters with mule-pack groups descending and climbing the canyon-wall trails. *Timberline Bicycle Tours, 7975 E. Harvard, #J, Denver, CO 80231, tel. 303/ 759–3804, fax 303/368–1651. May, Oct.: 5 days, $795. Sign up 6–8 months in advance.*

ARIZONA **Grand Canyon's North Rim.** The Canyon's North Rim is the adventurous way to experience this natural wonder. On average about 1,000 feet higher than the South Rim, the North Rim endures harsher weather. It's harder to get to, over rougher roads with fewer amenities for travelers. Fewer people visit.

This 7-day Sierra Club Outings trip explores the many faces of the canyon—its forests, its vistas, its desert-like qualities—and shows clearly how much more the canyon is than a deep gouge in the earth defined by the Colorado River. The walking is in the moderate range, with excursions up and down canyon-wall trails accounting for the most rigorous stretches. May is ideal, when the spring bloom is in full flush and daily temperatures still low. You do some backpacking, but also some car camping—that is, day hikes from sites accessible by car. In other words, it's nothing fancy—just straightforward, unpampered hiking and camping. Group size is about 15. Note that by the time you get ready to sign up, the Sierra Club may well have replaced this trip with something entirely different in the area, perhaps a strenuous backpacking trip with long mileages. *Sierra Club Outings, 730 Polk St., San Fran-*

cisco, CA 94109, tel. 415/923–5630, fax 415/ 776–4868. *Mid-May: 7 days, $450. Sign up 4–5 months in advance.*

ARIZONA **Land of the Navajo.** Not all camping trips involve arduous treks with heavy packs, or even long, daily hauls from one camp to the next. On this 7-day Earth Treks trip in the northeast part of the state, there is walking and camping, but it's not particularly demanding, with only a mile or two a day, since the primary focus here is cultural. It is a chance to experience first-hand the current and historical cultures of tribes of the Southwest, not only the Navajo but also the Anasazi, Hopi, and Zuni. Among the highlights of the trip is a hike in Canyon de Chelly, a 700-foot-deep sandstone gorge that contains Anasazi ruins, which has developed a cult following in recent years. Still, the gorges, deserts, and mesas are just a backdrop here. Group size is no more than 9. *Earth Treks, RFD 2, Box 785, Thorndike, ME 04986, tel. 207/589–4311. Late June: 7 days, $650. Sign up a month in advance.*

NEW MEXICO **Carson National Forest's Pecos Wilderness.** The Pecos Wilderness of the Carson National Forest sprawls for 225,000 acres across the Sangre de Cristo range, the southern terminus of the Rocky Mountains. With mountain bases at around 9,000 feet, this high area remains relatively cool in summer despite its southern latitude. The high-alpine lakes seem more characteristic of mountains farther north.

This 5-day Farmer Llama Treks trip makes the going easier (you leave the packing to the animals); trails are easy to moderate, with daily elevation gains averaging about 1,000 feet and daily distances from 4 to 6 miles. Designed with families in mind, it offers the experience of tent camping and wilderness hiking without the rigors of backpacking. A bonus for adults as well as kids: To identify wildlife and wildflowers, a naturalist accompanies each group, which numbers from 6 to 8. Try to add a couple of extra days to your trip to visit Santa Fe and get a taste of southwestern culture. *Farmer Llama Treks, Box 1254, Pampa, TX 79065, tel. 800/451–0583. June–Aug.: 5 days, $645. Sign up 1 month in advance.*

UTAH **Bryce and Zion National Parks.** These parks, about 80 miles apart in the southern part of the state, are great examples of the different ways in which erosion and geology can shape the landscape. Bryce is known for its hoodoos, rock spires sculpted by erosion with a delicate artistry. Zion is rockier, with cliffs rising as much as 3,000 feet above the various forks of the Virgin River.

This 6-day trip from American Wilderness Experience is lodge-based and van-supported—that is, nights are spent in relatively small but comfortable lodges near the parks and the 10 to 16 hikers in each group are shuttled by van to and from trail heads. On any given day, you may have several different hiking options, from short and easy to long and more difficult; the group splits up and you choose where you want to go. Rather than pushing from one point to the next, the objective here is to explore, to appreciate the mazelike and intricate beauty of canyons and side canyons, and to understand the forces of nature that created them. This weather, insufferably hot in summer, offers warm days and crisply cool nights in spring and fall. *American Wilderness Experience, Box 1486, Boulder, CO 80306, tel. 303/444–2622 or 800/444–0099, fax 303/ 444–3999. Apr., Sept.–Oct.: 6 days, $930– $1,055. Sign up 6 months in advance.*

UTAH **Capitol Reef National Park.** Capitol Reef seems forever the odd man out among southern Utah's national parks: Most people head for the better known Arches, Bryce Canyon, Canyonlands, and Zion. Capitol Reef's main feature is the so-called Waterpocket Fold, where one tectonic plate rose up and folded over another, creating a reeflike wall, where erosion has subsequently created deep canyons; natural arches; needlelike, erosion-sculpted rock hoodoos; and other colorful rock formations.

This 7-day Sierra Club Outings trip explores the complex, mazelike layout created by water, erosion, and geology, and involves considerable hiking with a substantial pack, as well as some tent camping. Staging time is spring, by far the best time to visit, since summer in this desert climate can be brutally hot and side-canyon streams reduced to a trickle. By the time you read this, the Sierra Club may well have changed the program, substituting a base camp trip for the backpacking—but then, maybe not. *Sierra Club Outings, 730 Polk St., San Francisco, CA 94109, tel. 415/923–5630, fax 415/776–4868. Mid-Apr.: 7 days, $445. Sign up 3–4 months in advance.*

UTAH **Rainbow Bridge.** Called a rainbow of stone by the Navajo, Rainbow Bridge is the world's largest natural stone arch and a highlight of this 8-day Earth Treks trip in southernmost Utah, where canyons, deserts, rivers, and mountains converge. The itinerary also skirts the southern periphery of Lake Powell, the most dominant physical feature in the area, formed by the damming of the Colorado River. Exploring side canyons through the ancient bedrock and cresting the plateau for mountain and canyon views are the elements that give this trip its character. And unlike the canyons in the national parks to the north, these canyons see relatively few visitors. Backpacking and camping are involved, but the going is fairly easy, with daily mileages averaging 3 to 6 miles and only moderate changes in elevation—less than 1,500 feet. April is ideal, with warm days, cool evenings, and wildflowers and cacti in bloom. Group size is 5 to 7 hikers. *Earth Treks, RFD 2, Box 785, Thorndike, ME 04986, tel. 207/589–4311. Early Apr.–May: 8 days, $550. Sign up 2–5 months in advance.*

THE ROCKIES

COLORADO **San Isabel National Forest's Holy Cross Wilderness.** All right—so this isn't purely a hiking trip, but it does provide an idea of what's possible when hiking is combined with other activities—in this case mountain biking. This 5-day trip from Roads Less Traveled starts in one of Colorado's most famous and overdeveloped mountain resorts, Vail, where mountain huts provide a base

camp for 2 days of hiking. The area's predominant feature is Mt. Elbert, at 14,433 feet the highest mountain in the Colorado Rockies. In fact, with several peaks topping 14,000 feet, this entire range of mountains represents the Rockies at their loftiest. The hiking portion of the trip, which traverses a stretch of the 470-mile Colorado Trail, is followed by 2 days of mountain biking southward from Leadville along the Continental Divide, with lodging and dining in country inns along the way.

In many ways, this is a good trip for someone wanting to test the adventure-travel waters without making a full commitment. For one thing, it is relatively short. It also includes a sampling not only of different modes of travel but of different lodging styles, from reasonably fancy digs at Vail to backcountry mountain huts. Some travelers might prefer the slower, quieter pace of hiking; others might be more appreciative of the greater amount of terrain that can be covered by bike. An average active adult can handle the challenges. *Roads Less Traveled, Box 8187, Longmont, CO 80501, tel. 303/678–8750, fax 303/678–5568. July–Aug.: 5 days, $775. Sign up 3–4 months in advance.*

COLORADO **San Juan Mountains for Seniors.** The San Juans are a striking swath at the edge of the mesas and deserts to the south and west. Many people consider them the jewels of the Colorado Rockies because of their impressive, rocky upthrust and deep, aspen-gladed valleys. That's a matter of opinion; what is indisputable is that they are high, with several peaks above 14,000 feet. Even valleys tend to be around 9,000 feet.

But they are not the exclusive domain of young, well-conditioned backpackers. Still, this 7-day trip for 12 to 18 active people over 50, offered by Walking the World, an organization catering exclusively to active people over 50, is far from easy, though the use of llamas to schlepp the load moderates the steepness and elevation that make the San Juans such a visual spectacle. Daily mileages range from 6 to 8, with elevation gains moderate, up to 1,000 feet. Among the highlights are excellent fishing and abundant wildflowers at higher elevations. *Walking the World, Box 1186, Fort Collins, CO 80522, tel. 303/225–0500, fax 303/225–0538. July.: 7 days, $1,295. Sign up 3–5 months in advance.*

COLORADO **Vail and Aspen Wilderness.** Putting "wilderness" in the same phrase with "Vail" and "Aspen" might strike some outdoor enthusiasts as treason, or at least a contradiction in terms. These famed resort towns, after all, are perhaps *the* major hubs of Rocky Mountain resort development. However, surrounding and between them in several national forests is a quartet of large, officially designated wilderness areas—the Flat Tops Wilderness, Gore Range Wilderness, Hunter Frying Pan Wilderness, and Holy Cross Wilderness—and it can be relatively quick and easy to get away from the resort scene into high-alpine country. Mostly you're above 9,000 feet, but the tree line in this part of the Rockies is at 11,000 feet. The result is that evergreen forests account for much of the terrain you might expect to be above the tree line, although open meadows and tundra occupy a large percentage as well.

Paragon Guides offers custom 3- to 5-day llama-trekking trips in the area, with nights spent at backcountry tent sites. Because llamas bear most of the load, this is a good choice for parents interested in introducing children to the joys and challenges of backcountry travel. Before signing up with your kids, however, contact the outfitter to make sure they will be up to the task—usually 3 to 8 miles of hiking and 600 to 2,800 feet of altitude changes, depending on the route. *Paragon Guides, Box 130, Vail, CO 81658, tel. 303/ 926–5299, fax 303/926–5298. July–Sept.: 3–5 days, $530–$880. Sign up 1 month in advance.*

COLORADO AND WYOMING Mountain **Parks of the West.** Using a van to travel among three national parks—Rocky Mountain, Grand Teton, and Yellowstone—this 15-day Hostelling International/American Youth Hostel trip is great for first-time visitors to the Rockies or hikers who simply can't make up their minds about a destination. As a national park sampler, it can also provide lessons in the subtle and obvious differences among mountain

ecosystems—from a geological and ecological standpoint, all mountains are not created equal.

A ranger-led interpretive program introduces each park. Thereafter the program consists of 5- to 10-mile day hikes over hilly terrain—though the walking is always tailored to suit participants, who may even be involved in itinerary planning. Nights are spent in dormitories in simple but comfortable hostels. Meals are comparably simple, and vans are used to shuttle hikers to and from trail heads as well as between parks. And despite the organizational title, these are adult-oriented trips; one departure is for those 50 and older. Groups usually include about 9 participants, and the trip begins and ends in Estes Park, Colorado. *Hostelling International/American Youth Hostels, 733 15th St. NW, Suite 840, Washington, DC 20005, tel. 202/783–6161, fax 202/783–6171. July (exclusively for hikers 50 and over), Aug.: 15 days, $1,150. Price does not include sleeping bag or sheet sleep sack, necessary in hostels; sign up at least 1 month in advance.*

IDAHO **Sawtooth National Forest's Sawtooth Wilderness.** The Sawtooth Mountains, appropriately named for the jagged profile they etch against the sky, constitute just part of the extraordinary expanse of protected wilderness in central Idaho near the border with Montana; the area is also known for its numerous small lakes and relatively few people. That it was not made a national park comes with pluses and minuses. The absence of that designation preserves its relative anonymity; on the minus side, trail- and land-use restrictions that might guarantee its preservation are missing.

The unique aspect of this 7-day Sierra Club trip into the area is that it is for artists, those skilled at or interested in learning the art of landscape painting. As a result, considerable layover time is worked into the itinerary at Sawtooth and Baron Lakes and at Tenlakes Basin. And despite being in the mountains, the hiking does not call for an extraordinary amount of climbing, nor does it aspire to elevations much above 9,000 feet. Still, this is a backpacking trip, and participants must be in decent physical shape and able to carry their own packs. Artistic skills aren't a prerequisite, and those who prefer doing their artwork with cameras rather than paints are invited to participate. Note that this trip, like all Sierra Club Outings, may have been replaced by others in the area, with a different focus, by the time you want to go. *Sierra Club Outings, 730 Polk St., San Francisco, CA 94109, tel. 415/923–5630, fax 415/776–4868. Early Aug.: 7 days, $435. Sign up 6–7 months in advance.*

IDAHO AND MONTANA **River of No Return Wilderness.** The largest expanse of designated wilderness area in the continental United States, this vast forestland sprawling through 7 national forests takes in classic Rocky Mountain country: high mountains, deep valleys, lakes, meadows, and streams. Although summits typically average about 2,000 feet lower than Colorado summits, the mountains are big, wild, and as spectacular as anyplace in the Rockies.

One of the interesting aspects of this 8-day adventure in the area with Wild Horizons Expeditions is its nod to ecological education, in the form of a day-long seminar on the ecology of the northern Rockies. The 7 days that follow hold particular appeal for those who appreciate solitude and remoteness, not easily come by elsewhere in the Rockies in the middle of the summer. Those are privileges that must be earned, however, by carrying a sizable backpack distances of 8 to 10 miles, with up to 1,500 feet of elevation changes in any given day. However, there are 2 layover days. Camping is at beautiful high-mountain lakes and occasionally you are lucky enough to glimpse elk, bighorn, mountain goat, and other native species; moose are frequently sighted. Group size is never more than 8. *Wild Horizons Expeditions, 5663 West Fork Rd., Darby, MT 59829, Dept. F, tel. 406/821–3747. Mid-July: $850. Tents, backpacks, and sleeping bags and pads provided; sign up 6 months in advance.*

MONTANA **Glacier National Park.** The preserve's celebrated backcountry chalets, now closed until 1995 to improve sewage and other systems, provided not only fairly comfortable overnight lodging, but also safe haven from grizzly bears, who could rightfully be considered the park's dominant species. Anyone traveling in the Glacier backcountry always had to be particularly wary of bear encounters; now, without the chalets, overnight travelers must redouble their caution.

This is perhaps the best reason to sign on with an experienced guide service such as Glacier Wilderness Guides, which offers 6-day backpacking trips in summer. Itineraries vary according to current trail conditions and the desires and physical fitness of a particular group, but daily distances typically range between 6 and 8 miles, with moderate elevation gains, and daily itineraries provide a sampling of the glacially sculpted rock walls and parapets that are Glacier's glory—as they are the glory of Waterton National Park, Glacier's adjoining sister park across the Canadian border. Other highlights are tramps through high alpine basins, past waterfalls and ice caves, and berry picking. And yes, glaciers—not enormous, but still rare within the continental United States.

If you're disinclined to lug a 35-pound pack, you have the option of hiring a sherpa to do the job (at an additional cost of $90 per day). Trips that include horse packing or rafting in addition to backpacking are also available. *Glacier Wilderness Guides, Box 535F, West Glacier, MT 59936, tel. 406/888–5466 or 800/521–7238, fax 406/862–5333 (summer) or 406/862–4802 (winter). May–Sept.: 6 days, $450. Sign up 4–5 months in advance.*

WYOMING **The Shoshone National Forest's Absaroka Wilderness.** The Absarokas aren't exactly a forgotten land, but with Yellowstone National Park to the north and west, these mountains in the Shoshone National Forest are often bypassed by visitors seeking the twin spectacles of geology and nature. In a way, the national park acts as a kind of decoy for the Absarokas, diverting visitor interest. Yet they are one of the highest and wildest ranges in the northern Rockies, including 12,000-foot peaks and some of the biggest expanses of alpine tundra south of Canada. And they contain literally hundreds of lakes and thousands of waterfalls.

This 6-day Wild Horizons Expeditions trip is a good way to experience the wild nature of the region during the height of the tourist season, when the park itself tends to be heavily populated. A couple of caveats, however. It's not for people who aren't in good shape: Although there are 2 layover days, you normally cover 6 to 7 miles a day with a backpack, with up to 2,000 feet in elevation changes, and about half of the hiking is through high open country off-trail. Nor is this trip for those who have problems at higher altitudes, or for those who worry about bears, since the wildlife roster of the region includes grizzlies (though the chances of a bear encounter are remote, especially when traveling with an experienced guide). You do, however, usually see elk, moose, and bighorn sheep. Groups usually set out with 6 to 8 hikers. *Wild Horizons Expeditions, 5663 West Fork Rd., Dept. F, Darby, MT 59829, tel. 406/821–3747. Aug.: 6 days, $650. Price includes sleeping bags and pads, backpacks, and tents; sign up 2–3 months in advance.*

WYOMING **The Tetons' Western Slope.** The Tetons are not the tallest mountains in the West; it is just their extraordinary, rocky forcefulness that makes them seem so. It is probably a fair guess to assume they are the most photographed mountains in America, as an embodiment of the lore of Western wilderness. They have served as the backdrop for hundreds of commercials; if you want to make a statement about how rough-and-tough your product is, having the Tetons in the background amplifying your cause with a chorus of Rocky Mountain ruggedness is a can't-miss gimmick.

Most Teton visitors approach the mountains from the east, through Jackson, Wyoming, and Grand Teton National Park. In mid-summer, that can mean crowds—minimal, perhaps, once you're a half-mile or so from any trailhead, but enough to intrude upon your sense of backcountry solitude. Approach from the west, however, and the mountains are still there in all of their glory but without nearly as many people. The western slope, which receives more snow and rainfall, is a world of rushing streams and wildflowers in mid-summer, capped by that famous Teton rock.

On this 7-day Sierra Club trip, pack animals lug the equipment from one site to the next, and the itinerary includes 3 layover days to allow plenty of time for fishing, photography, or more hikes. Unfortunately, like all Sierra Club Outings trips, this one may well be unavailable when you get ready to sign up. *Sierra Club Outings, 730 Polk St., San Francisco, CA 94109, tel. 415/923–5630, fax 415/776–4868. July: 7 days, $975. Sign up 6–7 months in advance.*

WYOMING **The Wind River Range.** While the Tetons are Wyoming's most famous mountains, outdoor enthusiasts in the Jackson area prefer the Wind Rivers, to the east, when they want a more private backcountry experience. Unlike trails in Grand Teton National Park, those in the Wind Rivers get relatively little traffic, at least in their interior reaches. Part of the reason is that the going can be fairly rugged for those determined to reach the range's highest summits, including 13,804-foot Gannett Peak, the highest mountain in Wyoming. Daily distance averages 8 to 9 miles.

This strenuous 7-day Wild Horizons Expeditions trip is a full-bore mountain country backpack, with all the demands and rewards of such a journey. The route includes steep climbs and rugged off-trail exploring. Such effort, however, yields the best of the Wild River backcountry: high alpine lakes and basins, craggy mountainous features, and glaciers that are a rarity in most other ranges of the lower 48 states. There is also some terrific fishing for those so inclined, wilderness solitude, and a sense of physical accomplishment. The group size is limited to 8. *Wild Horizons Expeditions, 5663 West Fork Rd., Dept. F., Darby, MT 59829, tel. 406/821–3747. Aug.: 7 days, $750. Price includes sleeping* *bags and pads, backpacks, and tents; sign up a month in advance.*

WYOMING **Yellowstone National Park.** Yellowstone is the oldest and perhaps most famous park of the national-park system, yet what do most people really know about it? That Old Faithful spouts punctually every hour and that bison roam freely. That's not much, and that's because most visitors stick to the roads and familiar tourist attractions. Despite the fact that 3 million people visit Yellowstone each year, most of the park's 2 million plus acres see little or no human traffic. Yellowstone presents a far greater opportunity to explore and experience true wilderness than you'd ever expect in a place so popular.

September is an ideal time to visit. Most tourists are gone, the mosquitoes are in retreat, and elk are engaged in their fall rut. Trees and meadow grasses are beginning to take on the hues of autumn. This 7-day Wild Horizons Expeditions trip explores the lakes, geysers, meadows, and forests of the Yellowstone high country. You might not be far from the park's most famous attractions as the crow flies, but the Yellowstone backcountry feels far removed from their bustle. There is little strenuous climbing involved here, but this is an extended backpacking trip, and you'll be required to transport a sizable pack. Among the highlights of the trip is visiting forest sections ravaged by the fires of 1988. These forests are now in their early stages of rebirth—a fascinating lesson in ecological life cycles. Groups number no more than 8. *Wild Horizons Expeditions, 5663 W. Fork Rd., Dept. F, Darby, MT 59829, tel. 406/821–3747. Sept.: 7 days, $750. Price includes sleeping bags and pads, backpacks, and tents; sign up a month in advance.*

THE WEST COAST

CALIFORNIA **Lake Circuit, Yosemite National Park.** Yosemite is the place where a family in an air-conditioned motor home waits for hours in traffic for 5 minutes of Instamatic picture-taking; its towering granite cliffs are a testing ground for dedicated climbers.

But Yosemite is much larger than most people think—3 times the size of Rocky Mountain National Park. And you don't have to scale a 3,000-foot cliff to escape the traffic jams and madding crowds and find the park's secluded, pristine reaches. This 10-day Sierra Club Outings trip is specifically for photographers, following in the footsteps of Ansel Adams, whose black-and-whites helped make Yosemite so famous. Overnight campsites are chosen with photogenic values in mind; time along the trail is ample to take full advantage of photographic possibilities. In other words, the hiking is fairly easy, though backpacking and tenting are parts of the deal. *Sierra Club Outings, 730 Polk St., San Francisco, CA 94109, tel. 415/ 923–5630, fax 415/776–4868. Mid-July: 10 days, $480. Sign up 5–6 months in advance.*

CALIFORNIA **Stanislaus National Forest's Emigrant Wilderness.** Lying on the northern periphery of Yosemite National Park, this 118,000-acre wilderness area features much of the granite ruggedness that is the underpinning of the Yosemite Valley's templelike quality as well as, sequestered within the granite peaks, high-alpine lakes and meadows, and lots of history: During the Gold Rush in the mid-19th century, this was center of frenetic prospecting.

This 9-day trip from Sierra Adventures stands out in its effort to mix hiking with other activities: a day of rafting on the Stanislaus River, exploration by motorcoach of abandoned Gold Rush towns, and wine tasting at local wineries. The hiking is in the easy to moderate range; the most difficult days are the 8-mile hikes to and from the base camp, though you must carry only a day pack containing lunch and a jacket, since camp mules bring in your personal gear and camp equipment. This base-camp approach allows the 12 hikers in the group to spend their time in the wilderness on day hikes that most match their interests and abilities. *Sierra Adventures, Box 3656, Sonora, CA 95370, tel. 209/532–0152 or 800/ 351–5041, fax 209/532–1979.*

Late May–Aug.: 9 days, $1,190. Sign up 2 months in advance.

CALIFORNIA **The Northern Coast.** Despite areas of heavy development, the coastline of this part of the state remains Mother Nature's world. The forests of Point Reyes National Seashore reach to the dunes and the sea, a place that speaks a mood of splendid desolation when the chilling fog rolls in. Muir Woods, closer to San Francisco, while not as desolately beautiful nor as unpopulated, also has plenty going for it.

Backroads' 12-person trip spends 6 days exploring the dunes, the forests, the deep canyons, the wind-raked promontories. Nights are in local inns—fairly elegant ones, with dinners (this being on the periphery of California wine country) accompanied by quality cabernet or chardonnay. In summer, variations in temperature can also be wild. Temperatures exceeding 90°F inland can make the fog-cooled 50s by the sea seem refreshing or frigid, depending on your state of mind and dress. Go ahead—this is not a rugged trip for backcountry purists but for those who want only to appreciate surprisingly wild country so near to civilization. *Backroads, 1516 5th St., Berkeley, CA 94710, tel. 510/527–1444 or 800/462–2848, fax 510/527–1444. May–Oct.: 6 days, $1,295. Sign up 2 months in advance.*

WASHINGTON **Backpacking in the Northern Cascades.** The Northern Cascades, among the more rugged mountain ranges in the United States, is perhaps best known for the volcanic domes that rise high above all the other peaks, notably Mt. Rainier and Mt. St. Helens (or what's left of it). The fact that most of the Northern Cascades top off fully 7,000 feet short of Mt. Rainier hardly means they are small fry. Here is a profusion of spiked peaks, above-timber-line basins, glacial remnants, and, in areas protected from logging, dense evergreen forests. North Cascades weather can also be rough: Rain and fog are not uncommon, at least on the western slope, although it is also not uncommon to break through a fog in high-alpine country, to find mountain summits rising above a sea of clouds.

This particular Outdoor Discoveries trip is only for serious backpackers. The going is tough, covering 6 to 12 miles a day with considerable elevation changes. Because it's also as much a wilderness course as a backpacking adventure, you learn some basic rock climbing and rappelling, route-finding and compass navigation, low-impact camping, and backcountry safety practices, among other wilderness skills. Since the group is limited to 10, with 2 instructors, learning opportunities are considerable. Custom trips are available. *Outdoor Discoveries, Box 7687, Tacoma, WA 98407, tel. 206/759–6555. July–Aug.: 7 days, $650; 14 days, $1,200–$1,300. Price does not include food (available at an additional $8 per person per day); sign up 2–3 months in advance.*

WASHINGTON **Backpacking in the Olympic Peninsula.** Nowhere in the United States outside Alaska do mountains meet ocean with such dramatic force. Within the peninsula's relatively small confines are glaciated peaks, rain forests, broad beaches, some of the oldest trees in North America—and some of the most expansive logging clear cuts.

This REI Adventures backpacking trip takes full advantage of the peninsula's unusual variety of terrain: thick forests, deep river valleys, high alpine areas. Traveling in a group of 8 to 10, you cover 8 miles or less per day, but because this world reaches from sea level to summits above 7,000 feet, the ups and downs can be as considerable as the moods of the weather. Guides are excellent sources of information about minimum-impact camping, wilderness safety, and navigation. *REI Adventures, Box 1938, Sumner, WA 98390, tel. 206/891–2631 or 800/622–2236, fax 206/891–2523. July–Aug.: 7 days, $675–$750. Price includes tents; sign up 6–7 months in advance.*

WASHINGTON **A Lodge-based Trip in the Olympic Peninsula.** While Olympic National Park's mountainous interior, capped by 7,995-foot Mt. Olympus, is pretty much the domain of backpackers, a lot of spectacular terrain can be reached on relative easy day hikes from the nearby towns of Lake Crescent, Forks, and

Quinault. And there is certainly something to be said for having the roof of a comfortable lodge over your head when damp weather rolls in, as can happen on this 6-day trip from Backroads.

Not *all* of the peninsula is particularly rainy, though. One of the highlight hikes of this trip is along the relatively rain-free Hurricane Ridge near the northern coast. This is mountainous hiking made relatively easy. A road leads to the ridge, and from there the hiking is mainly flat and even downhill. On clear days, Hurricane Ridge affords a terrific view of the peninsula's glaciated interior. The rain forests near Lake Quinault show the other side of the peninsula's character: huge trees, a dense canopy of green upon green upon green.

The hiking is at a fairly relaxed pace, ranging from 3 to 12 miles a day. Nights are in lodges that tend to be in the mode of rustic elegance. Meals can be quite fancy—even by the standards of this region, which is renowned for its seafood. Group size is up to 20. *Backroads, 1516 5th St., Berkeley, CA 94710, tel. 510/527–1555 or 800/462–2848, fax 510/527–1444. July–Aug.: 6 days, $1,195. Sign up 3–4 months in advance.*

ALASKA

SOUTHEAST **Chitistone Canyon, Wrangell-St. Elias National Park.** If you already knew that Wrangell-St. Elias is the largest national park in the United States, go to the head of the class; you probably deserve a seat in the front row if you've even heard of this vast wilderness of glaciers, rivers, and high mountains, fully 6 times the size of Yellowstone. Wildlife ranging from Dall sheep to grizzlies make the park their home, and it is a world dominated by other species and natural forces, the sort of place where man instinctively feels like a visitor.

It's also the sort of backcountry where you need considerable outdoor experience, a first-rate guide, or both. This 11-day Sierra Club Outings trip follows a route known as the Goat Trail; favored by mountain goats, it certainly taxes the abilities of humans, and the terrain can be as rugged and unforgiving as it is beautiful. You must be experienced and in good condition. Group size is usually about 15. *Sierra Club Outings, 730 Polk St., San Francisco, CA 94109, tel. 415/923–5630, fax 415/776–4868. Late July–early Aug.: 11 days, $995. Sign up 5–6 months in advance.*

CENTRAL **Wildlife Safari.** The prospect of taking on the Alaskan wilderness can seem daunting to those without experience in wilderness travel. The sheer size of the terrain and the possible hazards (getting lost, encountering inhospitable wildlife) seem to insist upon special backcountry awareness and skills. This 11-day Mountain Travel-Sobek trip to Denali National Park and the Kenai Peninsula, on the coast south of Anchorage, is proof that that needn't be so.

Denali National Park, of course, is home of Mt. McKinley, at 20,320 feet the highest mountain in North America. But such big, glaciated mountains are only part of what southern Alaska is all about. This trip also explores vast tundral meadows and glacially cut fjords that lead to the Gulf of Alaska, and as a safari of sorts, focuses equally on seeking out wildlife and photographing them—caribou, grizzly bears, Dall sheep, sea mammals, and eagles. Overnights are in cabins, and walks are on the easy to moderate side, with an average of 5 miles of hiking each day with minimal elevation changes. A short raft trip on the Kenai River and a sailing excursion to Kenai Fjords National Park are also part of the itinerary. Groups are limited to 16. *Mountain Travel-Sobek, 6420 Fairmount Ave., El Cerrito, CA 94530, tel. 510/527–8100 or 800/227–2384, fax 510/525–7710. July–Aug.: 11 days, $2,850. Sign up 3–6 months in advance.*

HAWAII

KAUAI, MAUI, AND THE BIG ISLAND

Island-hopping in Paradise. Hawaii's landscape amazes both for its sheer beauty and for its variety. Far from the broad sand beaches and bikinis, in the islands' mountainous interior, dense jungle, active volcanoes, peaks rising above 10,000 feet, and waterfalls dropping more than 400 feet astonish and enchant those adventurous enough to penetrate it.

This 13-day island-hopping trip from American wilderness Experience starts on Kauai, along the Na Pali Coast and Waimea Canyon. This is one of the world's rainiest places—a fact that might do little for anyone seeking a deep, dark Hawaiian tan but one that adds considerably to the dense jungle and floral spectacle of this dramatically mountainous shoreline. From here, the trip leads to the island of Maui and on to Hawaii, to explore volcanic landscapes and to learn about traditional Hawaiian life. Hikes are generally short and relatively easy; in addition to hiking, days are filled with sea kayaking, swimming, and other activities. Accommodations vary, from oceanfront campsites to rustic cabins to modern hotels. Wherever you bed down for the night, expect to eat well—Hawaii's climate is ideal for growing fresh fruits and vegetables—and you finish off the trip with a celebratory luau. Group size ranges from 4 to 16. *American Wilderness Experience, Box 1486, Boulder, CO 80306, tel. 303/444–2622 or 800/444–0099, fax 303/444–3999. May–Dec.: 13 days, $1,875–$2,100. Price does not include two meals; sign up 3–4 months in advance.*

SOURCES

ORGANIZATIONS American Hiking Society (Box 20160, Washington, DC 20041, tel. 703/255–9304, fax 703/255–9308) is an advocacy group promoting proper trail management throughout the United States and is also a general clearinghouse on hiking information. **Appalachian Mountain Club** (5 Joy St., Boston, MA 02108, tel. 617/523–0636, fax 617/523–0722) is the leading hiking organization in the Northeast. The club maintains backcountry huts and lodges in New Hampshire's White Mountains as well as the Catskills of New York and the Berkshires of Massachusetts. The club is also active in maintaining trails in these areas and offers an extensive program of outings, seminars, and workshops. **National Audubon Society** (700 Broadway, New York, NY 10003, tel. 212/979–3066, fax 212/353–0377) is primarily a naturalist organization, which is to say, it focuses mostly on birdlife and wildlife rather than outdoor recreation or broader environmental issues. Short outings, typically for bird-watching, are organized through local society chapters; longer trips and international outings are organized through the national organization. The Society is an active book publisher; its magazine, *Audubon,* issued as part of club membership, does an excellent job of covering wildlife-related issues. **Sierra Club** (730 Polk St., San Francisco, CA 94109, tel. 415/923–5630, fax 415/776–4868) is one of the preeminent advocacy groups in the United States promoting responsible environmental and wilderness management. It also offers perhaps the most extensive trip schedule of any organization in the country, although technically the club doesn't organize trips itself; trips are organized by individuals and outfitters under the club's auspices. The club magazine, *Sierra,* issued as a part of club membership, is first-rate in covering environmental issues.

PERIODICALS The publication of the American Hiking Society, *American Hiker* (Box 20160, Washington, DC 20041, tel. 703/385–3252) reports on hiking-related issues and hiking destinations. The monthly magazine *Backpacker* (Rodale Press, 33 Minor St., Emmaus, PA 18098, tel. 215/967–5171) is the leading magazine in the United States devoted specifically to hiking and backpacking. It is an excellent source of information on trips and equipment, including boots, clothing, and camping gear. Also included is a classified-ad section with organized-trip listings. The foremost magazine in the country on outdoor and adventure recreation, hiking, and backpacking is *Outside* (1165 N. Clark St., Chicago, IL 60610, tel. 303/447–9330). The basic editorial line-up is comprised of articles on environmental issues, personal narratives, capsule reports on recommended trips, and product reviews. The classified-ad section includes extensive listings of trip organizers. It's published monthly.

BOOKS The *Backpacker's Sourcebook*, by Noelle Liebrenz, is helpful. *The Complete Walker III*, by Colin Fletcher, gives the last word on the pleasures and techniques of the sport. *Hiking*, by Cindy Ross, concentrates on recounting the pleasures.

The Appalachian Mountain Club (*see* Organizations, *above*), publishes, among other books, trail guides for many parts of the Northeast. Backcountry Publications (The Countryman Press, Box 175, Woodstock, VT 05091, tel. 802/457–1049, fax 802/457–3250) publishes guides to hiking, cycling, and skiing in the eastern United States. Among its best offerings for hikers is the series "50 Hikes in," with the areas covered ranging from Maine to West Virginia. Guidebooks from the Mountaineers (306 2nd Ave. W, Seattle, WA 98119, tel. 206/284–6310, fax 206/284–4977) cover the Northwest, including the Northern Rockies, California, and British Columbia. Books and trail guides from the Sierra Club (*see* Organizations, *above*) focus primarily though not exclusively on areas in the West. Wilderness Press (2440 Bancroft Way, Berkeley, CA 94709, tel. 510/843–8080, fax 510/548–1355), which publishes guides covering California and other parts of the West, stands out for its guides covering the Pacific Crest Trail.

ALSO SEE If you like to feel the trail under your feet and enjoy mountain vistas from on high, see Climbing and Mountaineering. Wilderness and Survival Schools covers still other ways to push yourself to the limit on the trail.

Horse Packing and Trail Riding

by Scott S. Warren

orse pack and trail riding trips are a great way to see America's wilderness lands. Because the horses watch the trail, you don't have to; you can concentrate on the scenery rather than on your feet, as backpacking backcountry travelers must do. Then there are the pleasures: the smell of leather in the fresh mountain air, the feel of the reins in your hand, the steady cadence of a horse beneath you. At the end of the day, a horseback rider has energy to spare, even though you've covered more mileage in a day than your backpacking brethren. Because horses demand a fair amount of care both before and after their day's work, there's more downtime for riders than on rafting, mountain biking, backpacking, and other wilderness trips—time you can spend exploring the area on foot, angling, taking photographs, sketching, or looking at wildflowers.

Nor do you have to leave creature comforts back in civilization. On *horse pack trips*, the animals carry equipment and supplies from campsite to campsite, and you can enjoy luxuries that you might expect to leave behind when venturing into the woods; on *trail riding trips*, which involve making day rides out of a base camp, the comfort quotient is even greater. In either case, guides handle the particulars of setting up camp and meal preparation. Almost without exception, lodging is in tents, either lightweight backpacking tents or roomier wall tents, though a few inn-based trips do exist.

On trips into the wilderness, the food is generally straightforward, cooked over a campfire or cookstove: steak, chili, biscuits, fresh-caught fish, and beans. Usually vegetables and other perishables are more in evidence earlier in the trip. Outfits that truck food into a base camp are often better supplied with fresh vegetables, but a cook who's a whiz with a Dutch oven can make you forget you ever missed something. While a cook goes along on some trips, guides often pull double duty in the kitchen on others. A little help from group members is always appreciated.

Cost is about $100 to $125 per person per day, more for inn-to-inn trips, depending on the accommodations.

Most horse pack outfitters operate in the West, whose vast wilderness lands make for superb riding. But parts of New York, Vermont, Pennsylvania, West Virginia, and North Carolina can also be explored by overnight horse trips.

Different pack trips entail different levels of difficulty. On any trip, horses walk or move at an easy trot for most of the 6 hours you spend on the trail during the day. Unless otherwise noted, the following trips are suitable for begin-

---

Writer-photographer Scott Warren covers the great outdoors for National Geographic World, Outside, *and other magazines. He has lived in five western states, but now makes his home in Durango, Colorado, not far from where he took his first horse pack trip.*

ning riders. This does not mean that you will miss the spectacular scenery. Rather, it means that you will likely cover fewer miles in a day and you will follow better-established trails. Trips for more experienced riders entail more riding time, rougher terrain, and a faster pace. A key determinant in the pace of any trip is the number of so-called layover days, where you spend an additional night or two in the same campsite. Because there's considerable work involved in moving from one place to another—that is, for the outfitter—a trip with more layover days feels more leisurely. In addition, it allows you to spend more time getting to know a small area relatively well.

Regardless of your riding ability, you should be in reasonably good physical condition before signing up—partly because many trips in the West visit elevations above 10,000 feet and partly for the simple reason that you'll end up extremely saddle sore if you're not, from the exertion it takes to stay in the saddle for 4 to 6 hours each day.

CHOOSING THE RIGHT TRIP

All outfitters who operate on federal lands (and that includes most of the outfitters of the trips listed below) are required to have a permit. If you strike out on your own, make sure that the outfitter you ride with does. Also ask the following:

How large is the group and how many guides are there? To lessen groups' impact on the environment, most are limited to 12 riders or fewer. Some go down to just 3 or 4. Most outfits post at least 2 wranglers per dozen guests; some bring along another person to act as cook and assistant wrangler.

What about the horses and saddles? If you have a preference for riding English or western, make sure the outfitter can accommodate you. Stock should be well tempered, comfortable with greenhorns, and steady with adverse trail and weather conditions. You'll be trusting the horse to pick his or her way along the path while you watch the scenery, so you want a horse you can trust.

How much time is spent in the saddle each day and how difficult is the riding? Six hours is a long day in the saddle; usually, it's much less—about 4 hours. Most trips move at a walk; there may be opportunities to trot and lope (western-speak for canter) on day rides from base camp. There's usually little in the way of formal instruction but eager riders can learn a lot by asking questions.

How many layover days are there? Some trips include a longish ride every day. However, most trips build in time to explore an area at your leisure—hiking, climbing, fishing, or just relaxing. Find out what participants do when out of the saddle, and whether the wranglers plan other activities for down time.

What are the wranglers' qualifications? Guides should be experienced backcountry travelers; at least one member of the group should have first-aid training, if not wilderness first-aid training. Knowledge of area flora and fauna, as well as its history, geology, and ecology, is a big plus.

How many years has the outfitter been in the business? Experience counts. Also find out how long the outfitter has been packing in the area you will be exploring. He should know the weather conditions, where to find the best fishing and swimming holes and the best spots for wildlife viewing and photography as well as shelter when storms blow up (as they do with predictable suddenness in the mountains). Many outfitters are third-generation ranchers and know all the local lore.

What are the meals like? Cowboy cooking is the norm, but menus vary. If you care, ask to see what's planned.

What are accommodations like? Don't allow yourself to be surprised. If you're staying at inns or resorts, either at the beginning or end of the trip or en route, find out what the rooms are like and ask about the availability of any facilities you may want to use. If the trip involves camping, find out about the campsites and about shower and latrine arrangements. If you plan to use the outfitter's tents or sleeping bags, make sure they are suited to the location.

What's the cost and what's included? The price for most trips, and for all those below unless otherwise noted, includes all meals while you're on the trail, the guiding, your horse, and your tent but not a sleeping bag and pad.

You must always bring your own personal gear and clothes, but some outfitters provide ponchos.

Trips generally start at a ranch or inn or, in California, a pack station, from which you are then trucked to the trailhead; be sure to find out whether the outfitter will pick you up at the nearest airport and transport you to the starting point or whether you'll have to arrange and pay for your own transportation. Note that it is standard policy to tip the head wrangler to divide among the staff, usually from 3% to 5% of the cost of your trip if it has been a good one, up to 10% if it has been outstanding—but it's a very personal matter.

How far in advance is it necessary to book? Most outfitters prefer to book their trips at least 3 months in advance. However, some trips are so popular that it's wise to reserve 6 months ahead. Of course, last-minute cancellations always crop up—large organizations like American Wilderness Experience can almost always slot you in somewhere—but the itinerary may not be your first choice.

MAJOR PLAYERS

By their very nature, pack outfitters are an independent lot. They typically offer rides in one particular region or area established by the U.S. Forest Service, Bureau of Land Management, or other government agency that issues outfitting permits. However, two large organizations are worth investigating.

AMERICAN WILDERNESS EXPERIENCE

AWE, founded in 1971, represents numerous smaller outfitters all over the country. Because it is particular about which outfitters it works with, you can be sure that a trip you book through AWE is top-notch. Most of the dozen-odd trips involve day-riding out of wilderness base camps (Box 1486, Boulder, CO

80306, tel. 303/444-2622 or 800/444-0099, fax 303/444-3999). *Also see* Hiking and Backpacking.

EQUITOUR Although most of its trips are overseas, this enterprise, founded in the early 1980s, conducts some 15 trips in the United States as well, generally contracted through local outfitters. About half involve horse-packing, and the rest make day trips out of ranches, small inns, and wilderness base camps. Equitour trips are aimed at an upscale crowd, and use pleasant country inns as overnight accommodation when available (Box 807, Dubois, WY 82513, tel. 307/455-3363 or 800/545-0019, fax 307/455-2354).

FAVORITE TRIPS

THE NORTHEAST

NEW YORK **Adirondack Mountains.** Sprawling over 6 million acres, this mountain range in upstate New York represents one of the largest tracts of wilderness in the East; it includes forested valleys, secluded lakes, quiet streams, and 5,244-foot Mt. Marcy, the highest point in New York State. An exploration of the Cold River area, this 4-day trail ride is conducted by the Cold River Ranch, an updated turn-of-the-century lodge accommodating 9 guests 20 miles west of Lake Placid. Each night is spent in semi-permanent camps that include roomy cook tents and rustic lean-tos, part of the Adirondack Mountain Club hut system. Each day's ride brings excellent vistas of the surrounding mountains and forest, plus the chance to spot such wildlife as beaver, white-tailed deer, and black bear. Horses are gentle, well-broken, and sure-footed. Food runs toward the hearty and simple: eggs and pancakes for breakfast, sandwiches made with tuna or canned chicken with mayo for lunch, steak or fried chicken cooked over the fire for dinner. Groups set out with 6 or 7 participants and 2 or 3 wranglers with several years of guiding experience and CPR and basic first-aid training. The ranch has been offering trips since 1971. *Cold River Ranch, Coreys, Tupper*

Lake, NY 12986, tel. 518/359–7559. Mid-Sept.–late Oct.: 4 days, $600. Sign up 1 month in advance.

VERMONT **Green Mountain Inn-to-Inn Ride.** Undulating between valleys and ridge tops, Vermont's Green Mountains constitute a wonderful place for trail riding. What makes an equestrian excursion here even more alluring is the luxury of a hot shower and soft bed that cozy country inns can provide after a day in the saddle. You spend the first night at the Kedron Valley Inn, founded in 1820 and located just outside of Woodstock in south central Vermont. The next day kicks off 4 full days of riding with a trip to the colonial Echo Lake Inn, overlooking tiny Echo Lake, and then on to the Inn at Weathersfield, in the town of Chester, through countryside crisscrossed by old stone fences and punctuated by abandoned cellar holes. The final night, you're back at Kedron Valley.

There are 10 to 30 riders on the trip, accompanied by a single wrangler; you ride for 4 or 5 hours each day, and cover an average of 20 miles. You ride English saddle horses, including thoroughbreds, registered Morgans, and half-Arabians, using German-made Stubben saddles and Australian-made Winpec saddles. Lunches are ham, turkey, or bologna sandwiches along with vegetable, tomato, or beef soup and perhaps a hunk of Vermont cheddar cheese; you're on your own for breakfast and dinner. Dinners at the Kedron Valley Inn are vaguely French but incorporate local ingredients. *Kedron Valley Stables, Box 368, South Woodstock, VT 05071, tel. 802/457–1480 or 800/225–6301, fax 802/457–3029. Mid-May–mid-Sept.: 6 days, $1,255. Sign up 2 months in advance.*

VERMONT **Sugarbush Tolt Trek.** A tolt is a gait, somewhere between a trot and a canter but particularly smooth. It's specific to the Icelandic horses that are used on this 6-day inn-to-inn trip sponsored by the Vermont Icelandic Horse Farm, located in the Mad River Valley in the northern part of the state. Here, too, the inns are charming and upscale and the meals lavish, particularly the breakfasts. This is a trip for true horse-lovers—and

experienced riders at that. You spend 6 hours a day in the saddle, covering distances of about 10 miles as you take in the local scenery—overlooks that show off the foliage in fall, and paths alongside the Mad River in summer. Usually there are 10 or 12 riders per group, accompanied by a couple of wranglers. Booking well in advance is critical for the popular fall departures. *Vermont Icelandic Horse Farm, RR 376-1, Waitsfield, VT 05673, tel. 802/496–7141, fax 802/496–5124. May–Oct.: 6 days, $1,045. Sign up 6 months in advance.*

THE MID ATLANTIC

PENNSYLVANIA **Grand Canyon Country.** Carved by Pine Creek, Pennsylvania's 800-foot-deep Grand Canyon winds among the more pristine tracts of forest land in the mid-Atlantic region. The Mountain Trail Horse Center, founded in the 1970s and under its current ownership since 1982, does custom trail riding trips out of backcountry camps; each day you set out in the company of a pair of guides on different trails or logging roads or go bushwhacking through different parts of surrounding state forest lands. Rides can be as short or as long as you wish—you can even try a moonlight excursion. Keep an eye peeled for wildlife: deer, black bears, eagles, or even coyotes, which you'll doubtless hear before seeing. The camp is usually moved at least once. There are usually a dozen riders at the base camp at any given time. Guides have training in mountaineering as well as first aid. Horses are varied enough to accommodate participants' different tastes and riding experience.

You can opt for economy, basic, or deluxe packages. If you sign up for the economy package, you provide the gear and the food. Basic packages include both, but the fare is simple—like hot dogs and baked beans. If you go with deluxe packages, wranglers set up camp before you arrive, and hors d'oeuvres and cold beer are served before dinners that include steaks and fish, grilled over an open fire, as well as homemade pies and desserts. Don't fail to reserve well ahead for trips in fall, which is particularly colorful in the area, and for departures in June, when blossoming mountain laurels transform the hills into a sea of pink. *Mountain Trail Horse Center, Inc., RD 2, Box 53, Wellsboro, PA 16901, tel. 717/376–5561, fax 717/376–2453. Apr.–Nov.: 5 days, $330 economy, $466 basic, $517 deluxe (less if you sign up with more than 6). Price does not include food or gear on basic trips; sign up 6 months in advance.*

THE SOUTH

NORTH CAROLINA **Great Smoky Mountains National Park.** This 7-day trip from American Wilderness Experience is all about a North Carolina mountain spring. You begin with a 2-night stay at the rustic Cataloochee Ranch, with dinner and an orientation. After a day of riding through the hills ablaze with Carolina rhododendron and wild azalea blossoms, you set out for 3 nights of camping in the park, for more mountain scenery and visits to the historic Steve Wood and Little Cataloochee homesteads within the park. Because each day's ride is fast-paced, covering 12 to 18 miles at trots, canters, and gallops, this trip is designed for intermediate and advanced riders. *American Wilderness Experience, Box 1486, Boulder, CO 80306, tel. 303/444–2622 or 800/444–0099, fax 303/444–3999. June: 7 days, $900. Sign up 4–6 months in advance.*

THE MIDWEST

SOUTH DAKOTA **Badlands National Park.** This vast, stunning wilderness in western South Dakota, filming location for parts of *Dances with Wolves*, is a haunting place, with its high grassy prairies, strangely eroded cliffs, and surprisingly plentiful wildlife (especially pronghorn antelope). On this 4-day trip run by Dakota Badlands Outfitters and bookable through American Wilderness Experience, guides can tell the area's tall tales—of General Custer, pioneer wagon trains, and Sioux war-

riors, for whom the land was sacred. Partly to make the trips seem more authentic, a horse-drawn chuckwagon accompanies riders on the fall departures. These involve day rides out of a base camp. Spring departures involve horse packing. Each day you journey 8 to 12 miles; at day's end, a comfortable camp awaits, complete with a campfire and cowboy coffee. Taking the ride in the spring reveals some spectacular wildflowers; autumn brings on delightfully warm afternoons and cool, starry nights. Group size is usually between 6 and 8. *American Wilderness Experience, Box 1486, Boulder, CO 80306, tel. 303/444–2622 or 800/444–0099, fax 303/444–3999. May–mid-June and Sept.–Oct.: 4 days, $600. Sign up 4–6 months in advance.*

THE SOUTHWEST

ARIZONA **Monument Valley.** The towering mesas, buttes, and thin, knobby spires of this area, part of the Navajo Nation, have served as the backdrop for many John Ford westerns, and to the Navajo it is a land of legend and lore, as you'll learn on this 8-day American Wilderness Experience trip from your guide, who is Navajo.

After being picked up at the airport and overnighting in Gallup, New Mexico, you stop at the historic Hubbell's Trading Post en route to the your trailhead, in Monument Valley. From there, you travel around the North Window, where a pair of buttes frame a spectacular view of the distant desert, and to the foot of Thunderbird Mesa, where there's a base camp equipped with safari-style tents and hot showers. From here, rides each day, averaging 8 to 15 miles, take in such landmarks as the Totem Pole, Rooster Rock, Hunt's Mesa, and Ford's Point, as well as unnamed natural arches, prehistoric cliff dwellings, and petroglyphs. Meals are wholesome and hearty, and include dinners of barbecued brisket or turkey with all the fixings. Because Monument Valley is part of the Navajo Nation, alcoholic beverages are not permitted. Group size is usually 25 to 30. *American Wilderness Experience, Box 1486, Boulder, CO 80306, tel. 303/444–2622 or*

800/444–0099, fax 303/444–3999. May–June and Sept.–Oct.: 8 days, $1,400. Sign up 3–6 months in advance.

ARIZONA **Superstition Wilderness.** This area of the Tonto National Forest, just east of Phoenix, is one of the country's best back-country destinations in winter or early spring. This 6-day AWE trip begins at the Peralta trail-head, at the edge of the wilderness, and heads through stands of giant saguaro cactus en route to the first night's camp at JF Ranch, a privately owned cattle spread. The next day you trail over Tortilla Pass and into beautiful Angel Basin, a stream-crossed meadow at the inter-section of two canyons, and explore a nearby prehistoric cliff dwelling. The next night's camp is at Reavis Ranch, the homestead of an eccentric hermit around the turn of the cen-tury and now abandoned. The Southwestern terrain ranges from cactus-studded deserts and rugged canyons to fragrant pine forests and breezy mountain ridges, which you cover at about 8 to 12 miles per day; there are 2 layover days. Camps are comfortable but in primitive settings, and meals are cowboy-campfire cui-sine, ranging from salads and fruit to steaks and stews. Group size is 8 to 10. *American Wilderness Experience, Box 1486, Boulder, CO 80306, tel. 303/444–2622 or 800/444–0099, fax 303/444–3999. Feb.–Apr.: 6 days, $850. Sign up 3–6 months in advance.*

ARIZONA **White Mountains.** This high country in the eastern part of the state, Arizona's second highest mountain range, includes a wonderful mix of forests, mead-ows, streams, lakes, and rivers. This 7-day excursion from Equitour, which starts with a drive in vans from Gallup, New Mexico, final-ly saddles up at Hannegan Meadow, near Alpine, for the ride to the first night's camp at Lake Sierra Blanca. The next day you ride along the Black River, a beautiful little stream being considered for Wild and Scenic River status. Following its west fork, you climb to jewellike Big Lake, surrounded by broad, grassy meadows and known for its fishing. Of the trails you ride on succeeding days, most travel through gigantic pine forests; you also follow the Mogollan Rim, a geological fault

that extends from central Arizona to north-western New Mexico, with fine views over the Apache reservation. You're almost always at an elevation of 6,000 to 8,000 feet, and you are apt to spot deer and, if you're lucky, elk. On a typical day, you spend 5 or 6 hours astride the outfitter's quarter horses, cover-ing around 20 miles; there are 2 layover days. Group size ranges from 15 to 30, with 4 staffers. The food is hearty, long on meat and potatoes—burgers, pork chops, chicken, and the like, all cooked over an open fire. *Equitour, Box 807, Dubois, WY 82513, tel. 307/455–3363 or 800/545–0019, fax 307/455–2354. July–Aug.: 7 days, $1,000. Sign up 3 months in advance.*

NEW MEXICO **Gila Wilderness.** This half-million acres in southwest New Mexico's Gila National Forest, a spectacular land of deep canyons and forested mountain ridges, was the first area in the United States to be des-ignated a wilderness area. Today it serves as a magnificent setting for this 8-day horse pack trip from AWE.

The trip begins in Glenwood, New Mexico, where you overnight in a basic motel. The next day, you saddle up and head off into the high country east of town. Over the next 6 days you ride from semi-arid hills covered in piñon pine into forests of ponderosa pine and aspen surrounding the 10,600-foot high Mogollon Baldy Lookout, an abandoned fire lookout tower atop the region's highest peak; typi-cally, you spend 5 to 6 hours in the saddle and cover 8 to 10 miles. The fishing is superb in many of the streams, and you may spot deer, elk, antelope, mountain lion, and black bear, as well as the occasional eagle soaring on the air currents high above the mountains. Two layover days, one each at your first and sec-ond camp, give you time to explore at your own speed. Meals involve lots of Dutch oven cooking. Usually there are about 8 to 12 peo-ple in each group. Your final night is spent back at Glenwood. *American Wilderness Experience, Box 1486, Boulder, CO 80306, tel. 303/444–2622 or 800/444–0099, fax 303/444–3999. June–Aug.: 8 days, $955. Price does not include transportation to and from El Paso ($100) but does include the first and last night's* *motel accommodation; sign up 3–6 months in advance.*

NEW MEXICO **Taos Photo Hunt.** On this 5-day trip sponsored by the Taos Indian Horse Ranch in northern New Mexico's Sangre de Cristo range, you stalk wildlife with a camera. You look for mule deer, elk, bighorn sheep, black bears, and mountain lions using traditional Indian hunting techniques. The area, held sacred by the Pueblo Indians, ranges from rolling tundra to forests of Douglas fir, oak, cedar, and pines. Some hiking is involved, but you also ride from 10 to 30 miles a day, spending an average of 10 hours in the saddle and sleeping in lean-tos along the trail. You're asked to travel light and bring no more than 10 pounds of gear. Horses are Arabians, quarter horses, Morgans, and Appaloosas. Meals are steaks and chops, unless you've requested vegetarian fare, along with food you've harvested yourself, such as wild mushrooms and asparagus. There are 6 or 7 participants and 2 or 3 staff members in most groups. The ranch has been around since 1969. *Taos Indian Ranch, Box 3019, Taos, NM 87571-3019, tel. 505/758–3212 or 800/659–3210, fax 505/758–3212. May–June and Sept.–Oct.: 5 days, $2,500. Sign up 6 months in advance.*

NEW MEXICO **Woman's Rite of Passage.** This 5-day pack trip, designed specifically for women over 37 and offered by the Taos Indian Horse Ranch, includes instruction in horsemanship, camp living, tracking, wilderness survival, and other aspects of Plains Indian culture that relate specifically to women; dream interpretation is also part of the curriculum and self-examination is emphasized. Group size is limited to 7, and the warm camaraderie that develops during the course of the trip stands out. Riding consists of about 10 hours in the saddle a day, typically traveling 10 to 30 miles. Steaks and chops are on the menu, along with vegetarian fare and wild mushrooms and asparagus that you've picked. Overnights are in lean-tos. A recent doctor's statement of good health is required of each participant, as well as a short essay explaining your reasons for want-ing to sign up. *Taos Indian Ranch, Box 3019, Taos, NM 87571-3019, tel. 505/758–3212 or 800/659–3210, fax 505/758–3212. Sept.: 5 days, $2,500. Sign up 6 months in advance.*

UTAH **Capitol Reef National Park.** While the RV crowd is taking the mechanical horse-powered route to better-known Bryce and Zion National Parks, Hondoo Rivers and Trail Outfitters hoofs it on 5-day trips to the south-central portion of the state into the stunning Capitol Reef National Park, smack in the middle of Utah's colorful canyon country. Each day, you're in the saddle an average of 6 hours, covering 10 to 12 miles through dramatic deserts ringed by rock formations that reminded early settlers of the nation's capitol. Hidden canyons offer wonderful exploring. Cryptic petroglyphs carved by the prehistoric Fremont Indians adorn the brilliant orange sandstone walls. Evenings are highlighted by spectacular sunsets, and the weather is almost always inviting—dry and warm during the day, cool at night. Meals are cooked over the campfire—everything from prime rib to jailhouse chili. Group size is 8. *American Wilderness Experience, Box 1486, Boulder, CO 80306, tel. 303/444–2622 or 800/444–0099, fax 303/444–3999. May–Sept.: 5 days, $640. Price includes first night's hotel; sign up 4–6 months in advance.*

UTAH **High Uinta Mountains.** Stretching across northeastern Utah, the Uintas Mountains, the only major range of the Rockies that runs from east to west, include Utah's highest summits, among them 13,526-foot Kings Peak. Piute Creek Outfitters operates custom trips in the western portion of the range, primarily in the 80,000-acre lake region—which means good fishing for small rainbow trout and opportunities for stunning photographs. Itineraries vary, but many trails pass through lush spruce and fir forests and across verdant meadows with terrific mountain vistas and, especially in July, an explosion of wildflowers; deer, elk, and other species of wildlife abound. Meals make virtuosic use of the Dutch oven: One night, there may be meat loaf, and another you chow down on runaway horse, an everything-but-the-kitchen-sink concoction based on ground beef and macaroni; there's always a steak dinner with corn-on-the-cob and homemade sourdough bread. Your mounts are all quarter horses, raised by the Arnolds, who run Piute Creek Outfitters and have been leading trips in the area since 1974; the foals go out on trips with their mothers even when they are very young, so they are accustomed to following the leader. Trips are all custom; the Arnolds take out as few as 4 or as many as 8. If you can't assemble a party of at least 4 or want to go out with another group, they try to match you up with someone else who wants to travel at roughly the same time and for the same number of days. Usually there are 3 or 4 wranglers on each trip. Fees vary depending on how long you stay out; if you make a commitment to help the Arnolds with the grooming and other heavy chores, you get a 20% discount. *Piute Creek Outfitters, 3000 North 900 East, Kamas, UT 84036-9509, tel. 801/783–2769 or 800/ 225–0218. July–Aug.: 5–9 days, $750–$1,188. Price includes sleeping bag and pad; sign up 6 months in advance.*

UTAH Wasatch Plateau. Although the name Wasatch conjures up visions of the popular ski mountains that are Salt Lake City's steep and rugged backdrop, the Wasatch uplift actually extends deep into the southern portion of Utah, where it rises as a high plateau rich with spectacular vistas, lush forests, and good trails. One of the best is the Hole Trail to the upper reaches of the Wasatch Plateau—and that's the trail you follow for much of this 5-day AWE trip. Views to the east take in Castle Valley, an expansive land of barren desert and strangely eroded buttes, or castles (as they're sometimes called in these parts). As you climb to the 11,230-foot summit of the aptly named Big Mountain, you explore a range of terrain, from thick forests of spruce and fir to sub-alpine meadows filled with colorful wildflowers. Typically you ride about 6 hours a day, covering 10 to 12 miles. There are 1 or 2 layover days. Food is traditional cowboy fare—steak and potatoes, barbecued chicken, and such. Group size is usually 8. *American Wilderness Experience, Box 1486, Boulder, CO 80306, tel.*

303/444–2622 or 800/444–0099, fax 303/444– 3999. June: 6 days, $640. Price includes first night's lodging; sign up 3–6 months in advance.

THE ROCKIES

COLORADO The Great Colorado-to-Wyoming Trail Ride. Northern Colorado's Zirkel Range, in the heart of the Rockies, provides some truly pleasurable riding, thanks to beautiful scenery and well-maintained trails. This 6-day ride through the area is staged by Steamboat Lake Outfitters, a company founded in 1983. It starts at Steamboat Lake, 25 miles north of the ski resort town of Steamboat Springs, and follows the north fork of the Elk River before entering the Mount Zirkel Wilderness in the Routt National Forest. With your Appaloosa or quarter horse doing the huffing and puffing, you cross the Continental Divide and then drop down to the Encampment River. From a 2-night camp on the Wyoming state line, you take a day ride to West Fork Lake. Then it's off through the Medicine Bow National Forest's Encampment Wilderness, an unspoiled area guaranteed to expand your wildlife-spotting experience. Usually you spend from 4 to 6 hours in the saddle; the mileage varies depending on the group and the weather. The last night is at the secluded Water Valley Ranch, where comfortable suites and western meals of steak and prime rib top off your wilderness excursion. Meals on the trail are similar western fare, starring steaks and chicken, with cowboy entertainment in the form of western songs and a lesson in rope-throwing after dessert. Group size usually ranges from 10 to 20, with 5 to 10 staffers as necessary. *Steamboat Lake Outfitters, Box 749, Clark, CO 80428, tel. 303/879–4404, fax 303/879–5590. July– Aug.: 6 days, $1,250. Sign up 3 months in advance.*

COLORADO Maroon Bells–Snowmass Wilderness. In the Maroon Bells–Snowmass Wilderness in the White River National Forest, near jet-setting Aspen, 13,000- and 14,000-foot snow-capped peaks frame aspen-covered valleys. This is the setting for an 8-day trip from A. J. Brink Outfitters, a firm that has built a good solid reputation in the area since it was founded in 1975 and that boasts sizable numbers of repeat customers and referrals.

The riding begins by following East Maroon Creek to a camp just below 12,450-foot Triangle Pass, where you spend 2 nights; on your second day out, you ride over to Copper Lake and then over another high pass before returning to camp. The next day sees you stopping in the old mining town of Gothic en route to a camp in Rustlers Gulch, where you spend 2 more nights; the second layover day gives you time to visit the old mines in the area. Then it's on to the Crystal River Valley, beautiful Snowmass Lake, and picture-perfect Crater Lake. Given the quality of the outfitting and the stunning scenery, this is one classy trip. You cover from 8 to 12 miles a day on average, and typically spend between 4 and 6 hours in the saddle, astride quarter horses. Group size ranges from 10 to 15. Meals are fresh and homemade—with bacon and eggs, eggs Benedict, or french toast and sausage for breakfast, make-your-own sandwiches at lunch, and, for dinner, ham and sweet potatoes, Chinese stir-fries, pork chops with stuffing, and even roast beef along with the usual fried chicken and steaks. *A.J. Brink Outfitters, Glendevey Route Colorado, Jelm, WY 80263, tel. 303/435–5707. July–Aug.: 8 days, $840. Sign up 8 months in advance.*

COLORADO **Roosevelt National Forest's Rawah Wilderness.** This 7-day AWE trip begins and ends in the beautiful Laramie River Valley across from the northwest corner of Rocky Mountain National Park at the historic Glendevey Lodge, which, in its day, has served as a stage stop, a hunting lodge, and an inn used by lumberjacks who were in the area to cut ties for the nation's railroads; today, it's simple but cozy. On the third day out, you trade the comfort of the lodge for a rather posh base camp, where tents come equipped with cots and stoves for heating. For the next 3 days, you make day rides out of camp to explore forested canyons, linger alongside

lakes and streams teeming with trout, and poke around the foothills of some breathtaking peaks; usually you spend 5 to 6 hours in the saddle, covering distances of 10 to 12 miles. Meals are hearty and western style, with dishes such as fried chicken and Dutch apple pie served in the lodge, and stews and steaks and potatoes whipped up by the wranglers on the trail. Group size is usually 6 to 8. *American Wilderness Experience, Box 1486, Boulder, CO 80306, tel. 303/444–2622 or 800/444–0099, fax 303/444–3999. July–Sept.: 7 days, $985. Sign up 3–6 months in advance.*

COLORADO **Sangre de Cristo Mountains.** A formidable citadel of 13,000- to 14,000-foot peaks, this range runs from northern New Mexico into central Colorado, where you find both incredible vistas and some truly rugged terrain. This 5-day AWE trip, best handled by experienced riders, shows off some of its most viewful corners. Passing up main trails, you bushwhack through hidden valleys and over isolated passes, cresting the mountains several times—and seldom passing another backcountry explorer. On average, you spend 6 to 7 hours in the saddle each day, covering 10 to 15 miles; there is 1 layover day. Meals are gourmet camp fare. Most groups number under 8. *American Wilderness Experience, Box 1486, Boulder, CO 80306, tel. 303/444–2622 or 800/444–0099, fax 303/444–3999. July–Sept., 5 days, $600. Sign up 4–6 months in advance.*

COLORADO **San Juan Mountains–Continental Divide.** Take a deep breath before leaving for this trip from San Juan Outfitting, a firm founded in 1975: You won't enjoy this much oxygen again for the next 8 days. The views are as good as they get, since you're constantly above timberline among 13,000-foot peaks; the San Juans are the newest range of the Rockies, and the most rugged, as a result. The start of the trip, at the top of 10,850-foot Wolf Creek Pass, and its end point in Silverton, the famous mining town, are both on the 2,700-mile Continental Divide Trail; the route between them takes in alpine lakes, glacial cirques, stretches of tundra that drop off into deep, forested canyons, the half-million acre Weminuche Wilderness in the San Juan National Forest, and two landmarks used by the Spaniards when they mined for gold in the area: the Rio Grande Pyramid, a triangular rock formation, and the Window, a notch in the rocks that perfectly resembles its namesake. No wonder there's a 2-year waiting list for the trip.

Daily riding distances range from 11 to 23 miles, requiring an average 4 to 8 hours in the saddle, but with 2 layover days. Your mounts represent all breeds, including Arabians, Morgans, and quarter horses. Meals feature stuffed Cornish game hen, Navajo tacos, breaded pork chops, shrimp stir-fries, New York strip steaks, and the occasional homemade apple pie. No more than 6 riders saddle up for each departure, accompanied by 3 or 4 wranglers. *San Juan Outfitting, 186 County Road 228, Durango, CO 81301, tel. 303/259–6259. Aug.: 8 days, $1,650. Sign up 2 years in advance.*

COLORADO **Ute Mountain Ute Tribal Park.** Located just south of Mesa Verde National Park in southwestern Colorado, the 150,000-acre Ute Mountain Ute Tribal Park is rich in archaeological treasures and Native American history, as quickly becomes evident on this trip from Rapp Guides and Packers, founded in 1980. You begin at Weber Canyon Ranch, then follow Weber Canyon for 13 miles along the Mancos River to a base camp at the mouth of Morefield Canyon. Then, over the next several days, you go out on day trips led by a Ute guide—to unexcavated Anasazi cliff dwellings and ruins built some 700 years ago. Rock art abounds, as do a variety of artifacts, including pottery shards and skeletal remains, tools and arrowheads, and bits of yucca fibers the Indians used for sandals. The Utes, who now own this land, are not related to the ancient ruin dwellers, but have their own culture and traditions, which your guide may share with you, with a little coaxing. Most days see you spending from 4 to 6 hours in the saddle, covering from 3 to 13 miles. Dinners feature T-bone steaks with corn on the cob and green chilis on the side, grilled swordfish, and Navajo tacos and beans; desserts are fresh out of the Dutch oven. Overnights are in wall tents in a grove of elder trees. The typical group numbers between 8 and 12. *Rapp Guides and Packers, 47 Electra Lake, Durango, CO 81301, tel. 303/247–8923, fax 303/259–2953. Apr.–May and Sept.–Oct.: 4–7 days, $150 per day. Sign up 6 months in advance.*

COLORADO **Weminuche Wilderness.** At a half-million acres, the Weminuche Wilderness, named for one of the seven bands of the Ute Indians, encompasses a good portion of the San Juan Mountains, whose 10,000-foot average elevation makes them the highest mountain range in all of North America. Be glad you're not hiking, as this 6-day ride from Rapp Guides and Packers climbs quickly to the Continental Divide and trails along the crest to a base camp at the head of Starvation Gulch, a beautiful high meadow named for the unfortunate experience of a group of explorers who died here in the 1800s, where you spend 3 nights and the intervening days exploring the alpine terrain of the surrounding Rio Grande and San Juan national forests; you may want to wet a line and go for rainbows, brookies, or cut-throat trout at a number of superb fishing spots. On the fourth day camp is moved into the area alongside terrifyingly steep-banked Elk Creek, where you spend the trip's last 2 nights; if you opt to pay extra, you can return to Durango or Silverton and civilization aboard the coal-fired Durango & Silverton Narrow Gauge Railroad, known for its spectacular route carved into the mountainsides. Most days have you in the saddle for about 4 hours, covering 10 miles. Meals rely heavily on fresh ingredients—steaks, fish, vegetables, and the like. Group size usually ranges from 4 to 7, and a staff of 2 or 3 wranglers goes along. *Rapp Guides and Packers, 47 Electra Lake Rd., Durango, CO 81301, tel. 303/247–8923, fax 303/259–2953. Aug.: 6 days, $840. Sign up 6 months in advance.*

COLORADO **Gunnison National Forest's West Elk Wilderness.** Chalk up points if you've even heard of the jagged West Elk Mountains, equidistant, about 65 miles, between Grand Junction and Gunnison and 240 miles southwest of Denver. This 6-day trip sponsored by Dell and Linda Ferrier's Bar Diamond Ranch, which has been around since 1935, takes in some of the best of the area. It begins with a night at the ranch, followed by a 5-hour ride to a base camp deep in the wilderness at 10,000 feet, where you spend the next 5 nights. On day rides from here, sightings of deer, elk, eagles, beavers, and even bighorn sheep are common, and the views are spectacular—from 13,000-foot West Elk Peak, you can see 100 miles in every direction. A typical day's ride has you in the saddle for 4 hours, covering between 10 and 12 miles. For this reason, and because the stock is extra-gentle, this trip is suitable for riders as young as 6. Meals are ranch-style, featuring eggs, pancakes, french toast, or hot cereal for breakfast, and steaks, pork chops, ham, chicken, burgers, and trout with potatoes for dinner. Most groups number between 4 and 8, and go out with a staff of 3. *Bar Diamond Ranch, Box 688, Hotchkiss, CO 81419, tel. 303/527–3010, fax 303/872–3861. July–Sept. 6 days, $600. Sign up 2 months in advance.*

IDAHO **Edna Lake and the Sawtooth National Forest's Sawtooth Wilderness.** Idaho's Sawtooth Mountains, in the central Rockies, rake the horizon like the blade of a two-man crosscut saw for which they were named. The folks at the Mystic Saddle Ranch, which has been doing pack trips since 1969, can provide you with gentle, easygoing horses—and a comfortable introduction to the area from a base camp at jewellike Edna Lake, located at the headwaters of the South Fork of the Payette River, in the heart of the Sawtooth Wilderness. From the camp, you can visit neighboring lakes, climb nearby peaks, cast flies into the area's blue-ribbon trout streams, photograph wildflowers, or simply stretch out on a boulder and catch a few rays. Most trips are guided, though there is one drop-off trip that has travelers exploring on their own. Day trips are in the 10-mile range, usually with about 4 hours in the saddle. Breakfasts star homemade cinnamon rolls along with the usual eggs and hotcakes; at dinner, you might be served salmon, smoked pork chops, pork tenderloin, chicken Kiev or chicken teriyaki, or the like. Group size is usually between 8 and 12, with a staff of 2 or 3. Longer custom trips are also available. *Mystic Saddle Ranch, Stanley, ID 83278, tel. 208/774–3591. July–Sept.: 5 days, $650. Sign up 6–9 months in advance.*

IDAHO **Selway-Bitterroot Wilderness in the Clearwater and Nez Perce National Forests.** Outfitter Jim Renshaw is one of the best guides to the rugged, vast, and unspoiled Bitterroot Mountains, another range of the Rockies. His family started taking dudes out on trips in the 1920s, and Renshaw himself has been guiding since 1953. This 7-day outing, which uses good, gentle mountain horses—Morgans and quarter horses, among others—takes you to alpine lakes and streams where the fishing is good and the scenery is better, with a good chance of spotting deer, elk, moose, beavers, or mountain goats. Typically, you ride for 4 hours a day, from 12 to 16 miles, and move only a couple of times to allow plenty of leisure to explore the area surrounding each camp. The menu offers steaks, pork chops, trout, and such. Groups number 4, with a staff of 2 or 3. *Renshaw Outfitting, Box 1165, Kamiah, ID 83536, tel. 208/926–4520 or 800/452–2567, fax 208/935–0726. July–Aug.: 7 days, $900. Sign up 2 months in advance.*

MONTANA **Bob Marshall Wilderness–Dearborn River.** Extending south from Glacier National Park in northern Montana, the Bob Marshall Wilderness, in the Flathead and Lewis & Clark national forests, is a real jewel in the nation's wilderness system. It not only encompasses some amazing mountain terrain, but it is also rich in wildlife, including grizzly bear. This 5-day ride run by outfitters Lass and Ron Mills up the Dearborn River is both a good introduction to the area and to trail riding. The Mills have been doing pack trips in the area since 1968.

The trip begins with a 10-mile ride through Devil's Glen along the Dearborn River, where you set up base camp for the entire trip. Here, you can go fishing, take riding lessons, or saddle up for guided group trips to higher country for spectacular vistas of the Dearborn drainage and beyond—usually with about 4 to 5 hours in the saddle and mileages of 6 to

8. In addition, special short outings are offered for youngsters. Groups usually number 6 to 8. *American Wilderness Experience, Box 1486, Boulder, CO 80306, tel. 303/444–2622 or 800/444–0099, fax 303/444–3999. June: 5 days, $875. Sign up 6–8 months in advance.*

MONTANA **Bob Marshall Wilderness–The Chinese Wall.** Stretching for many miles along the crest of the mountains, the Chinese Wall is the flagship landmark for the Bob Marshall Wilderness. It's a natural granite escarpment rising precipitously out of the forest floor. The area is characterized by lodgepole pine forests and rocky outcroppings, and rugged buttes that you can ride or clamber up for great views. As is typical of trips run by Lass and Ron Mills, the itinerary combines riding with layover days. Typically, you cover 8 to 12 miles in about 6 hours in the saddle on day rides, and there are usually about 8 riders. *American Wilderness Experience, Box 1486, Boulder, CO 80306, tel. 303/444–2622 or 800/444–0099, fax 303/444–3999. July–Aug.: 8 days, $1,400. Sign up 6–8 months in advance.*

MONTANA **Yellowstone National Park.** Yellowstone is everything you've heard—an expansive wonderland of forests, meadows, mountains, geysers, and wildlife. The traffic along the infamous loop road is also just as awe-inspiring. Few visitors ever do get out of their vehicles to do more than snap a few pictures, however, so it's easy to find true wilderness—as on this 7-day trip from the knowledgeable veteran packer, the personable R. K. Miller, who has been doing pack trips in the area since 1973.

Within the first hour of riding you leave civilization behind, traveling past geothermal features such as hot springs, geysers, mud pots, and such. And the abundance of wildlife—everything from deer and elk to moose, bison, and bear—is unsurpassed. Daily distances range from 8 to 14 miles, with an average of between 4 and 7 hours in the saddle. There are usually 2 or 3 layover days. For breakfast, you might have crêpes or blintzes as well as hotcakes; at dinner, typical offerings include shish kebabs, fresh fish caught on the trip, salads, and fresh vegetables, along with homemade strawberry shortcakes or fresh pies and cookies. Most groups include between 4 and 6 riders, accompanied by from 2 to 4 staffers, and the animals are all quarter horses, mountain-trained and well-behaved. *R.K. Miller's Wilderness Pack Trips, Box 467, Livingston, MT 59047, tel. 406/222–7809, fax 406/222–7809. July–Sept.: 7 days, $1,550. Sign up 4 months in advance.*

WYOMING **The Outlaw Trail.** A ride with some real flavor, this 8-day trip offers the opportunity to relive a bit of the Old West. This part of northern Wyoming was the lair of many outlaws, including the Wild Bunch, Civil War deserters, and bands of Sioux, Arapahoe, and Cheyenne Indians. In addition to enjoying the area's rich history, experienced riders have a chance to cut loose and gallop across the wide open plains. The adventure begins in Riverton, Wyoming; you spend the first night at a motel in Lander. The next day you're transported by van to Buffalo Creek Canyon, which serves as base camp for 2 nights. From here, you ride into the foothills of the Bighorn Mountains into the canyons south of camp and to the venerable Sheparson Ranch, and a 50-mile-long rock formation known as the Red Wall, the Hole-in-the-Wall Gang's wall. During your stay on the ranch land, you break camp 3 times. Daily mileages are about 20 miles, and 5 or 6 hours on horseback is typical; you ride mixed breed horses, with various temperaments. The hearty meat-and-potatoes fare includes burgers, chicken, and pork chops, and groups usually have about 15 riders, who are accompanied by 4 staffers. *Equitour, Box 807, Dubois, WY 82513, tel. 307/455–3363 or 800/545–0019, fax 307/455–2354. May–June and Aug.–Sept.: 8 days, $1,145. Sign up 3–4 months in advance.*

WYOMING **Pony Express Ride.** The 1,900-mile Pony Express route originally stretched from St. Joseph, Missouri, to Sacramento, California. This 6-day Equitour trip covers a fraction of the distance at a much slower pace, around 15 to 20 miles a day, with from 4 to 6 hours in the saddle—and you won't encounter such distractions as Indian and outlaw ambushes.

The ride starts at Sweetwater Station, a one-time Pony Express stop south of Riverton, Wyoming. From here you travel west toward the unspoiled Wind River Mountains, arriving at a camp that serves as your base for the next 6 days. Rides on subsequent days take you along other stretches of the winding Sweetwater Creek, through Sweetwater Canyon, Alkoli Creek, and Rock Creek, to Radium Springs (another former Pony Express station), and to South Pass on the Continental Divide. Besides ushering Pony Express riders over the crest of the Rockies, this pass was also on the Oregon Trail, used by settlers, and the ruts of their wagons are still evident today. The trip ends with a visit to historic South Pass City, one of the few towns that grew up along the Oregon Trail; it's preserved as something of a living museum, so that you can see how settlers lived, worked, and prepared their meals. Appropriately enough, it's chuck-wagon cooking at mealtimes: roasts, stews, fried chicken, and such. No group has more than 16 riders, with local ranch-bred quarter horses and between 6 and 8 staffers riding shotgun. *Equitour, Box 807, Dubois, WY 82513, tel. 307/455–3363 or 800/545–0019, fax 307/455–2354. June–July: 8 days, $1,095. Sign up 2 months in advance.*

WYOMING **Wind River Mountains.** Because most tourists head for the better-known Tetons nearby, the Wind Rivers—some of the grandest mountains in the West—are also some of region's least explored. You have ample opportunity to try your luck with rod and reel in some of the high-country lakes and to explore hidden streams. You can also rub elbows with a number of granite summits along the Continental Divide on this 7-day trip from the Skinner Brothers—Wyoming-raised Monte, Bob, and Courtney, old hands here (having been outfitting trips since 1956), with a real love of sharing the area with others. You ride through rolling valleys, alpine meadows, and fields of wildflowers; there are a thousand lakes in the area and stunning high mountain peaks. Usually you cover around 10 miles a day, and spend between 4 and 5 hours in the saddle; there are 3 layover days. The menu is basic western fare—hotcakes,

eggs, and sausage for breakfast, sandwiches at lunch, and steaks, roasts, fish, and chicken at dinner, followed up with pie or some canned fruit. Most trips saddle up with 10 riders and 4 staffers. *Skinner Brothers, Box 859, Pinedale, WY 82941, tel. 307/367–2270 or 800/237–9138, fax 307/367–4757. Aug.: 7 days, $630. Sign up 1 month in advance.*

WYOMING **Gros Ventre Mountains.** Most visitors who land in Jackson, Wyoming, head straight to either Grand Teton or Yellowstone National Park. But a third area nearby is often overlooked: the Gros Ventre Mountains, which rise east of town in the Bridger-Teton National Forest, practically in Yellowstone's backyard. This 5-day trip, bookable through AWE, uses 2 different base camps to take in some high mountain vistas, explore the Flat and Granite creek drainages (the fishing is terrific), and visit Turquoise Lake and Sleeping Indian Mountain. Wildlife abounds, and you might spot elk and moose. Most day-rides are 8 to 10 miles, with about 6 to 7 hours in the saddle. Meals are cooked on camp stoves or over the open fire—steaks perfumed with mesquite, stews, and Dutch oven biscuits and cobblers. The typical group saddling up includes 8 riders. *American Wilderness Experience, Box 1486, Boulder, CO 80306, tel. 303/444–2622 or 800/444–0099, fax 303/444–3999. July–Sept.: 5 days, $780. Sign up 3–6 months in advance.*

THE WEST COAST

CALIFORNIA **Mendocino Coast.** The northern California coast—a long string of hidden coves, steep headlands, and crashing surf—offers breathtaking scenery each day and comfortable bed-and-breakfasts each night. This 7-day ride out of the Ricochet Ridge Ranch near Fort Bragg, skirts bluffs high above the Pacific, ventures into dark and misty redwood forests, and allows time for galloping through the surf. While riders with only average skills can be accommodated, this trip is designed for more experienced riders. You spend an average of 5 hours in the saddle each day, covering around 20 miles.

Lunches, served on the trail, are build-your-own sandwiches, with your choice of 3 cheeses, 3 mustards, and 3 breads; and breakfasts include fresh berries and homemade breads and muffins in addition to eggs. With the exception of a salmon barbecue, which is served outdoors, you eat dinner in restaurants; appetizers, entrées, and wine are included in the trip price, along with 3 evenings' entertainment by a classical guitarist, a classical pianist, and a local Mendocino music group. Most groups have between 14 and 16 riders and 3 staffers. The ranch, in business since 1972, has been offering these inn-to-inn rides since 1985. *Ricochet Ridge Ranch, 24201 North Highway 1, Fort Bragg, CA 95437, tel. 707/964–7669, fax 707/964–9669. June–Oct.: 7 days, $1,580. Sign up 3–6 months in advance.*

CALIFORNIA **High Sierra Opener.** Having been in business since 1915, the folks at Mammoth Lakes Pack Outfit are almost intimately familiar with the rugged stretch of the Sierra Nevada range in which they operate. This season-opener sees their area at its most pristine. Upon climbing 10,750-foot high Duck Pass, you enter the Inyo National Forest's John Muir Wilderness, full of high lakes and streams that are still full of snowmelt, even this late in the year. Once you've established base camp, you go out for day rides covering between 8 and 12 miles, taking in exposed granite peaks, pine forests, and grassy meadows; typically you spend from 4 to 6 hours in the saddle. Horses, matched to riders' abilities, are trail-wise and dependable. Breakfast stars strawberry pancakes and fresh trout or scrambled eggs, and you're served sandwiches for lunch, trailside, and steak, barbecued chicken, potatoes, and fresh vegetables for dinner, perhaps topped off with strawberry shortcake. Most departures set out with between 6 and 12 riders and 3 staff members. *Mammoth Lakes Pack Outfit, Box 61, Mammoth Lakes, CA 93546, tel. 619/934–2434, fax 619/934–3975. July: 5 days, $650. Price does not include tents; sign up 3–4 months in advance.*

CALIFORNIA **Hilton Lakes Angler Trail Ride.** This 5-day trip from Rock Creek Pack Station into the John Muir Wilderness was designed with fishing in mind. The quarry: rainbow, brook, brown, and golden trout. And no catch and release here: When you catch it, you can eat it. The route explores Tamarack Basin, and it climbs through Little Lakes Valley, sprinkled by 10 small lakes, to reach such fishing hot spots as Davis Lake and Dorothy Lake. Daily rides cover about 5 miles, with around 3 hours in the saddle; that, plus the 2 layover days, leaves plenty of time for casting. Meals include not only plenty of fresh trout, but also basic eggs, bacon, and hotcakes at breakfast, and T-bone steaks, roasts, and spaghetti at dinner. Groups are small, usually about 10 anglers and a staff of 3. The outfitter has been in business and running trips in the area since 1947. *Rock Creek Pack Station, Box 248, Bishop, CA 93515, tel. 619/872–8331 (winter) or 619/935–4493 (summer), fax 619/873–3950. June: 5 days, $450. Sign up 6 months in advance.*

CALIFORNIA **Pacific Crest Trail Ride.** Running from Mexico to Canada along the backbone of the West Coast, the Pacific Crest Trail is one of this nation's great backcountry pathways. One of its most alluring sections runs along the higher reaches of the Sierra Nevada Mountains, and that's the stretch covered by this 100-mile ride from Rock Creek Pack Station. The route crosses Mono Pass and heads into the Inyo National Forest's John Muir Wilderness; there, it passes Mammoth Divide and the Minarets, well-known Sierra landmarks, and climbs Donohue Pass, gateway to Yosemite National Park, where the trip explores some rather scenic areas before coming to an end in Tuolomne Meadows, in the park. Daily distances range from 12 to 15 miles, with an average of 6 hours in the saddle and 3 layover days. Bring both your fishing tackle and wildflower identification book; the waters are jumping with golden, rainbow, and brook trout, and the meadows are ablaze with wildflowers. Rock Creek Pack Station, in operation since 1919, stands out; guides are knowledgeable about both the natural and human history of the area. Meals are western-style, with scrambled eggs and hotcakes with bacon or sausage for breakfast, and fresh trout and T-bone steaks and roasts at dinner. Group size is typically around 10, with 3 staffers. *Rock Creek Pack Station, Box 248, Bishop, CA 93515, tel. 619/872–8331 (winter) or 619/935–4493 (summer), fax 619/873–3950. July–Aug.: 12 days, $1,225. Sign up 2 months in advance.*

CALIFORNIA **Kings Canyon National Park.** Like better-known Yosemite, Kings Canyon encompasses an astounding range of high Sierra terrain, including jagged summits, deep canyons, glacial cirques, tumbling waterfalls, and thick forests. Yet it's far less known than Yosemite. Following the Pacific Crest Trail, this 10-day Pine Creek Pack Trains trip between Pine Creek and the Taboose Pass trailhead takes in such scenic places as Evolution Valley, Le Conte Canyon, and the South Fork of the Kings River, and crosses a number of high passes, including 12,000-foot Muir Pass. You spend between 4 and 6 hours a day on your gentle, well-mannered mountain horse, and cover from 8 to 10 miles; there are 3 layover days. The western-style fare here stands out: For breakfast, the hotcakes are sourdough-based, the eggs served rancheros style with chili, and the french toast topped with blueberries or raspberries, and biscuits and gravy sometimes put in an appearance; for dinner, you might have enchiladas, lasagna, and sourdough or garlic bread, followed by chocolate mousse or just-baked carrot cake or apple pie. Most groups have between 4 and 11 riders, with 4 wranglers. *Pine Creek Pack Trains, Box 968, Bishop, CA 93515, tel. 619/387–2797. Sept.: 10 days, $1,100. Sign up 4–6 months in advance.*

WASHINGTON **Pasayten Wilderness.** North Cascade Safaris' owner Claude Miller grew up in these mountains and knows their summits, valleys, and hidden lakes inside and out. Beginning at the Billy Goat Corral, this 5-day ride heads directly to Hidden Lakes, where you set up in a base camp. Here, you can try your luck among numerous fishing holes, go for guided day hikes, or saddle up your gentle, good-natured horse for a morning on the trail with the guide, to look for elk and mountain goat or visit flower-filled meadows such as those in the Tatoosh Buttes area. There are 2 or 3 layover days. Rides cover anywhere from 10 to 12 miles a day, with around 5 hours in the saddle. Meals are western-style with Basque touches: The scrambled eggs are made with peppers, for instance, and there's beef stroganoff and chicken cacciatore for dinner. Most groups number between 4 and 9, with 2 staffers. Miller has been in business since 1970. *North Cascade Safaris, c/o Claude Miller Pack Trips, Box 250, Winthrop, WA 98862, tel. 509/996–2350. June–Sept.: 5 days, $625. Sign up 2 months in advance.*

WASHINGTON **Pacific Crest Trail.** The northern Washington section of this famed backcountry route, 35 miles extending from Manning Park at the Canadian border in the north to Harts Pass in the south, cuts through some of the more pristine alpine terrain of the North Cascades. This 10-day trip run by Claude Miller follows 14 miles of the trail, beginning at 6,197-foot Harts Pass. From there, the route crosses Frosty Pass, a meadow at 7,200 feet, and eventually returning to Harts Pass by way of the middle fork of the Pasayten River. Most days you ride between 10 and 12 miles, with about 5 hours in the saddle; there are 3 layover days—one near Frosty Pass and the others along the Pasayten, both sites good for fishing and just relaxing. The food is much like that served on Miller's Pasayten Wilderness trip (*see above*). Groups usually consist of from 4 to 9 riders, with 2 wranglers. *North Cascade Safaris, c/o Claude Miller Pack Trips, Box 250, Winthrop, WA 98862, tel. 509/996–2350. July–Sept.: 10 days, $1,250. Sign up 2 months in advance.*

ALASKA

SOUTHEAST **Kenai Peninsula.** This 5-day trip, which begins near Homer, follows the eastern shore of Kachemak Bay. Along the way, there's nonstop scenery, and wildlife abounds—bear, caribou, and otter, as well as bald eagles and sea birds. You ride about 10 miles daily and spend about 4 hours in the saddle; groups usually include between 8 and 10 riders and 2 wranglers. Nights are at the Swift Creek Cabin, a rustic log cabin that accommodates 8. Water is drawn from streams, the old-fashioned way, and meals are cooked on a wood stove. The company was founded in 1983. *Alaska Horseback Vacations, Seaside Farm, 58335 East End Rd., Homer, AK 99603, tel. 907/235–7850. June–Sept.: 5 days, $625. Sign up 4–6 months in advance.*

SOURCES

ORGANIZATIONS There is no national association of horse-packing outfitters, but region-al organizations provide information on outfitters in their respective states. Try **Colorado Outfitters Association** (Box 440021, Aurora, CO 80044-0021, tel. 303/368–4731), **Idaho Outfitters and Guides Association** (Box 95, Boise, ID 83701, tel. 208/342–1438, fax 208/338–7830), **Montana Outfitter and Guide Association** (Box 9070, Helena, MT 59604, tel. 406/449–3578), **Washington Outfitters & Guide Association** (22845 N.E. 8, Suite 331, Redmond, WA 98053, tel. 206/392–0111), and **Wyoming Outfitters Association** (Box 2284, Cody, WY 82414, tel. 307/527–7453).

ALSO SEE There are plenty of other ways to explore America's forests. If you'd like to do it under your own steam, see Hiking and Backpacking. If not, look into River Rafting.

Mountain Biking

by Bill Strickland

Mountain bikes are time machines. Ride one and you become a kid again. Splash through mud, ride through grass, jump a rock, color outside of the lines. It's improvisation and freedom, jazz instead of classical.

And boy can it take you places. I've watched black bears scamper up the sides of hills. I've lain on mountaintops while lightning storms raged seemingly only inches from my head. I've gotten lucky and looked out from the top of Washington's Capitol Peak on a clear day that revealed all the state's volcanic ranges in one sweeping view.

But guess what? I'm not even that good a mountain biker. I've only been riding off-road for about a year. That's the other incredible thing about mountain biking. Although its image is that of the gnarly muddy dude thrashing a way-wicked trail and slinging lingo unintelligible to humans not on an adrenaline spike, its reality is me and you. Regular people who discover how easy it is to move among forests, over deserts, up hills, into canyons, through creeks.

Sure, you need real skill to hack the most technical stuff. Make a mistake in certain sections of the rides we list and you could die. Easily. But there are plenty of simple and safe rides for absolute beginners, too.

One reason that anyone can mountain bike is that the bikes themselves may be the most user-friendly two-wheelers ever made. They have more gears for easier pedaling, simple shifting, flat handlebars (for an upright sitting position and more stability), and fat knobby tires (for a cushy and super-grippy ride). On the other end of the spectrum are the daredevil machines. If you're fit and you know what you're doing, you can take yourself to the edge of control in settings where your natural instinct is to be as careful as possible. You can shoot the rim of a hundred-foot drop-off, bomb down a rock-strewn trail at insane speeds, catch big air.

The number of operators offering mountain biking trips is increasing with the popularity of the sport. As with road tours, mountain bike touring companies provide all sorts of support and expertise. But the biggest benefit to biking with an outfitter may be their knowledge of the terrain. Getting lost on the road can be an inconvenience. Getting lost in the wilderness is plain dangerous. Take a tour and you don't have to worry about your lousy sense of direction or how to read the trail network map.

You also don't have to worry about ancillary concerns: Do I have enough food and water to ride through that patch of desert?

Managing editor of Bicycling *magazine Bill Strickland hates cars and gas consumption, so he pedals his way to work. In more than ten years of riding he's toured every corner of the United States. Strickland also writes a mountain biking skills column for* Mountain Bike *magazine.*

Will the trail empty out near an inn? How much equipment should I carry? All these problems are taken care of. You don't even need to own a mountain bike, since most companies rent good models.

The format of off-road touring resembles that of road touring. Most vacations are 2- to 10-day trips along preplanned routes. Trails include major points of interest and unique geographic features, as well as a variety of descents and ascents, and a few different types of terrain—from red rock to alpine meadows.

At least 2 accomplished outdoorsy guides lead each trip. One rides with you while the other drives a support van along the route. In some areas, such as stretches of narrow singletrack, the support vehicle can't follow you. In these instances, it will parallel your route on the closest road or drive ahead to wait for you. The vans carry your gear, supply water and snacks, usually house mini bike shops for trailside repairs, and can even haul a few tired adventurers.

The going can be as tough or easy as you like. There are day-long treks over highly "technical" (difficult to ride because of obstacles in the trail) terrain on which it's not uncommon to walk your bike up and down slopes and over obstacles. And then there are casual jaunts on flat dirt roads that wind through forests or pretty backcountry. Easier trips usually spend a lot of time off the trail at attractions that include everything from museums to lakes.

This diversity means that there's a tour for anyone. What's more, there's variety even within a single tour. Most companies customize their routes slightly to allow you to ride more or less mileage, or to take different routes—so you can stay on the dirt road if you're unsure about that rocky trail.

There's a lot of diversity in the price of the trips, too. For example, a 5-day trip can range from $575 to $1,025. Prices can vary due to several factors: accommodations, food, amount of equipment provided, extra off-bike activities, demand for the trip.

More than road touring, mountain bike trips seem to create a sense of comradeship. The challenges are usually greater, or at least more obvious. Riders coach each other through the toughest parts, share advice, and swap war stories.

However, sometimes the group experience seems to work against the lure of the outdoors. Some people find it disconcerting to pick their way through an isolated forest with 10 other people. There are the practical inconveniences, too. Your schedule is tied to the group's. You wake when they do, begin riding when they do, and eat when (and probably what) they do. And when rain turns the trail to soup, don't think you can delay your trip for a day. Put on your foul-weather duds, pal, the group is heading out.

Still, most cyclists say the advantages of commercial off-road touring outweigh the disadvantages. The exception being getting stuck on an inappropriate trip.

I've talked to beginners who signed up for harsh, technical rides and spent most of their time dragging their bikes behind them or sightseeing from the seat of a van. Not exactly a peak outdoors experience. Neither is the trip where a true gnarly dude is confined to tame dirt roads. The trick is to match your physical ability and off-road experience to the right trip. It's okay to challenge yourself with a tour slightly over your head, or to take it easy on a relative snoozer. Just be realistic and honest with yourself about your ability.

Trip descriptions should give an accurate picture of how tough the riding will be, but don't get fooled by the mileage listings. Off-road miles are tougher than road miles. So don't think that 15 trail miles a day will be a snap compared to that 30-mile-per-day road trip you did once. A general rule for figuring your endurance is that one mountain bike mile equals at least 3 road miles. On tough singletrack and technical slickrock, or in steep territory, it can be even harder.

Pay attention to other factors, too. The number of off-bike activities is a measurement of the difficulty of the tour (the more off-trail activities the less strenuous the tour). Weather can cook you or help you, and also affects the scenery. Spending a fall weekend on a New England mountainside is more beautiful and more comfortable than a summertime jaunt in the same area.

Right now, the best commercial rides are found in the Southwest and Rockies, and on the West Coast, where high-altitude ascents lead to overlooks of mind-boggling vistas. Any territory near canyons or mountain peaks is also guaranteed good riding. The east, especially New England, is loaded with trails, but commercial touring has yet to thoroughly invade the region. West Virginia and North Carolina are also ready to explode as hot spots. Once the touring companies expand into these areas you'll be able to find organized off-road thrills almost anywhere.

Don't kid yourself about your level of comfort when you're choosing a trip. The riding is tough, so don't feel foolish if you want to interrupt your days in the wilderness with nights of pampered comfort. Unlike a road tour, you're likely to get dirty and all-over tired. Tents and cold showers don't do much to alleviate this condition.

Mountain bike touring isn't for everyone. This is because at its worst it can be jarring, difficult, and dirty. But at its best it can be jarring, difficult, and dirty. Know what I mean? If you do, I'll see you out there.

CHOOSING THE RIGHT TRIP

Everything associated with mountain biking—manufacturers, event organizers, and touring companies—has just begun the transition from niche sport to big-time popularity. There are some growing pains, which we try to help you avoid. To be included in these listings, each touring company has to meet these minimum criteria: offer trips along preplanned, established routes; offer at least 2 mileage options each day; offer some type of support (such as motorized route patrols, sag service for tired or injured riders, and luggage transport); provide or assist in arranging

lodging and provide at least some meals, including snacks for munching while guests cycle; require the use of helmets (you never appreciate a skid lid until you need it).

But don't stop with the listings. Make a few phone calls to learn more about the companies you're considering. Don't be shy about asking these questions. You're about to spend a decent chunk of money. Think of it this way: For the cost of a 7-day tour, you could buy a trick new bike.

How tough is the trip? We offer as many details as we can, but the listings are just a guide to set you on your way. Tell the guides how much (or if) you've ridden off-road. Describe your road-riding experience and your physical condition. Ask if the riding is technical or buff (smooth), on trails or dirt roads. You may be surprised to find that some of the riding occurs on pavement. This is sometimes necessary to link the off-road routes. It erodes the atmosphere, but provides a break from the rigors of the wilderness.

How much can the mileage be increased (or decreased)? The distances probably won't vary widely—off-road companies don't have as much leeway as road operations—but you'll get an idea if you can shorten a ride and stay on your bike, or if you'll be stuck in the van when you're tired.

What are the trail options? Can you find singletrack spurs off the dirt road? Will you be stuck on the technical trail, or is there an easy parallel path for a break?

What are the accommodations like? Some trips are able to offer plush rooms even on truly wild excursions. This is because ski lodges and hunting inns are located near many trails. However most offer more rugged accommodations. If you'll be camping (as is common), check such details as the availability of hot showers and rest-room arrangements.

What are the meals like? Some campfire cooks are fit for the finest restaurants. Some serve up basic grub. Also, most companies skip at least one lunch or dinner. We list these deletions, but changes may occur.

What's the cost and what's included? Prices in these listings are per person, double occupancy, and include gratuities, entrance fees to parks and attractions, and camping fees. Airfare and the cost of renting bikes or camping equipment isn't included in prices we quote, unless we note otherwise. Renting camping equipment (tent and sleeping bag) usually costs between $30 and $55 per trip. Sometimes there are extras. We tell you about as many as we could find, but always ask if there are others: $50 for the optional mule ride down the canyon or $30 for the massage.

What's the weather like when I'll be touring?

Will laundry service be available? It's usually not on off-road tours, but if so, it could save you a suitcase.

What extras are included? Many companies offer T-shirts, sweatshirts, water bottles, or other freebies.

What is the makeup of my touring group? You can find out ages, gender, marital status, home state, and sometimes even off-road cycling experience. This helps you predict the atmosphere of your entire trip. You should also ask about group size.

Is this same tour available for singles (seniors, women, whatever)? We note as many of these as we can, but schedules may change. Some companies offer reduced rates for kids and families.

How extensive is the support? This could be the difference between walking out of the forest with a broken-down bike, or having it repaired on the spot. Some companies may make only one or two runs along a route. Others constantly patrol. Find out how many guides work each trip. The more the better.

What is the rental equipment like? Find out what brand of bike is offered, how many sizes are available, and how old the fleet is. A few companies offer you your choice of suspension or rigid bikes. If you're going on a camping trip, check the quality of the rental equipment. Gear is never more important than on a long mountain biking trip.

Do you offer free helmet use?

Who are the leaders, how old are they, and how are they trained? It may sound nosy, but in the wilderness you need guides who are not only expert cyclists but also expert outdoors types.

How long has the company been in business? This is especially important in such a newly popular field. You won't necessarily have a problem with an outfitter new to the sport, but an outfitter who's been running off-road trips for several years is probably more prepared to meet challenges and answer questions.

Can the leaders handle minor mechanical repairs (and is there a charge)? No type of cycling is tougher on equipment than mountain biking. You can count on at least one flat and something else that will need fiddling with. If it's just a quick brake adjustment, I'd expect a freebie. But be reasonable: If you do a biff and pretzel your wheel, cough up a tip for the guide who rebuilds it.

How far in advance do I need to book? Some trips are more popular than others and can fill up as much as a year in advance. So although 2 to 3 months is usually far enough in advance to book a trip, you should probably reserve as early as possible. If you find you've waited too long, don't hesitate to put your name on a waiting list, since cancellations may mean you get a spot on a trip even if you call only days in advance.

Do you have references from past guests? To be honest, I never call the telephone numbers I get. But if a company ever refused to give me some names, it would make me wonder why.

MAJOR PLAYERS

There are no gargantuans in this field. The sport is still young and small local companies match the free spirit of off-road cycling. The logistics are harder to handle than those of road tours, and the big outfitters aren't completely set up yet to develop a network of mountain bike tours. Give them a few years.

Thankfully, small scope doesn't mean poor quality. Here are 7 off-road touring companies that offer consistent high quality, good variety, and an extra something special. The service at all 7 is exceptional. If you can't find exactly what you're looking for in our listings, give these touring experts a call and ask about their other offerings.

BACKCOUNTRY This company is known for its environmentally conscious touring programs and exploration of new trails in the Southwest, Rockies, and on the West Coast. Founded in 1986, one of its owners, Doug McSpadden, is a former U.S. Forest Service employee and guide for The National Outdoor Leadership School. There always seems to be a bit of singletrack on a Backcountry tour. No dirt-road-only trips.

Backcountry destinations include Montana, Utah, New Mexico, Colorado, Oregon, Washington, Wyoming, and Canada. A dozen trips are offered, each run up to 10 times a year. The company has 125 Trek 950 mountain bikes in its rental fleet, and a customized trailer provides trail support.

Accommodations are usually in historic inns or lodges, although there are some camping options. The company also offers hiking, whitewater rafting, and horseback riding (Box 4029, Bozeman, MT 59772–4029, tel. 406/586–3556, fax 406/586–4288).

BACKROADS This is the biggest touring company in the world. In business since 1979, it offers more than 90 different road trips each year. Although it's one of the best all-around bicycling outfitters, in the mountain biking world it's just about average. At press time 5 domestic mountain bike trips were scheduled each year to destinations including California, Oregon, Utah, and Arizona. Foreign off-road trips are also offered in China, Mexico, Costa Rica, Thailand, Bali, and Australia.

Backroads doesn't offer new or unique trails—you'll get the classics and well-known routes on these trips—but it maintains the quality and first-rate service that made it such a powerhouse in road touring. The campfire menu, prepared by the guides using Backroads' fleet of custom-designed trailers, reads more like the bill of fare at a fancy big-city gourmet eatery: smoked salmon, homemade pasta with pesto, and fresh fruit pies are only a few examples. I've never eaten better than on a Backroads trip. The accommodations are often inns on the National Register of Historic Places, or comfortable lodges with regional flavor.

Backroads rents its own line of mountain bikes, made by Chimayo. The company has its own travel agency, and also offers skiing, walking, hiking, and custom-designed tours for groups (1516 5th St., Suite B122, Berkeley, CA 94710–1740, tel. 510/527–1555 or 800/462–2848, fax 510/527–1444).

ELK RIVER TOURING CENTER This is one of my favorites. The center is a former sheep farm in an area of Pocahontas County, West Virginia, that could become the next mountain biking mecca—at least for us East Coasters. It's mountain singletrack without altitude problems, technical challenges as good as any of the rocky trails farther north in the east, and incredible valley vistas. Pocahontas was named by *Outside* magazine as one of the country's 100 best counties for experiencing the outdoors. The trail network needs development and grooming, but this will happen as the flow of grateful mountain bikers increases.

The company offers 6 tours, and runs about 39 trips per year. It also hosts the annual West Virginia Fat Tire Festival in June, a week of tours, races, riding clinics, blue grass music, and all-around fun. The owners, Gil and Mary Willis, are dedicated to providing instructional programs, such as mountain biking lessons for beginners. This is another idea waiting to blossom into a standard practice.

The food is delicious, and the high-carbohydrate, low-fat meals are perfect for the fitness minded. Specialties include whole-wheat French bread and trout from the Elk River. Vegetarian meals are always available. Accommodations are a comfortable mix of bed-and-breakfast rooms and cabins (Hwy. 219, Slatyfork, WV 26291, tel. 304/572–3771).

KAIBAB MOUNTAIN BIKE TOURS I like this outfitter for the feeling of confidence and competence inspired by every one of its guides. The company was established in 1987 to provide trips in southern Utah and the Colorado Plateau. It offers a good mix of classic trips—the White Rim Trail, the Maze District, Kokopelli's Trail—with extras such as half- or full-day treks into canyons, and hiking trips using pack llamas.

Eight tours are offered, and about 43 trips are run each year. Support is provided by 3 custom-designed 4-wheel-drive trucks. The company started its own bike shop in 1990.

The tours are mainly dirt-road or rocky-surface trips, but some singletrack options can be found. A high-carbohydrate menu emphasizes fish, chicken, pasta, fruits, and vegetables. It's a camping-only company (Box 339, Moab, UT 84532, tel. 801/259–7423 or 800/451–1133, fax 801/259–6135).

RIM TOURS This was the first mountain bike touring company in Moab, Utah. They're a fixture in the industry, and have a well-deserved reputation for doing the classic rides—Telluride to Moab, White Rim Trail, Colorado Trail, Tour of the San Juans, and the Maze—and doing them exceptionally well. Just saying that you took your tour with Rim or browsed in Rim Cyclery, the affiliated bike shop, will lend a certain hipness to your vacation tales.

The company offers more than 20 different trips, each of which is run at least twice per year. The food and lodging usually consists of camping and cooking out; the support van carries all the necessary equipment. A few trips have bed-and-breakfast accommodations (94 W. 1st North, Moab, UT 84532, tel. 801/259–5223 or 800/626–7335).

ROADS LESS TRAVELED Nobody does better Colorado trips than Roads Less Traveled. Today, most organizers operating in Colorado share the same trails, but since 1988, this company has searched out virgin (commercially virgin, at least) singletrack in the Rocky Mountain state. They also put together a better-than-average package including riding, off-bike adventures such as hiking and rafting, accommodations that range from plush mountain lodges to tents, and exceptional food. Even on camping trips the menu includes such dishes as grilled salmon and Thai curry chicken, and vegetarian meals are always available.

Thirteen tours are offered in Colorado, New Mexico, and Utah. About 40 trips are run each year. My budget likes this company, too. The prices are often slightly cheaper than those of other major operators, and trip quality doesn't suffer (Box 8187, Longmont, CO 80501, tel. 303/678–8750 or 800/488–8483, fax 303/678–5568).

WESTERN SPIRIT This is another one of my favorites, mainly because of the personnel. These people—from owner Lu Warner on down—have a knack for finding rarely used singletrack and interesting new routes in the same old territory. The guides call this "unpublished" riding. They're also good at customizing their tours for special groups—so good that Ibis and other mountain bike–industry types go to Western Spirit for yearly company outings.

Established in 1989, Western Spirit offers 10 tours in Utah, Colorado, and Idaho. About 50 trips are run each year. The camping trips are done with style (one of the company's mottoes is "Civilized tours in uncivilized terrain"), and the food is delicious and abundant.

This is also one of the most environmentally conscious touring companies. All tours are low impact, and each trip purchase includes membership in the International Mountain Bicycling Association, a group dedicated to promoting responsible land use and achieving fair land access policies for mountain bikes.

The company is also a pioneer in instructional programs for novices and intermediates—the equivalent of taking a tennis or golf lesson from a pro (Western Spirit Cycling, Box 411, Moab, UT 84532, tel. 800/845–2453, fax 801/259–2736).

FAVORITE TRIPS

THE NORTHEAST

MAINE **Mud in Your Eye.** You can't ride all there is to ride here. There's just too much.

Back Country Excursions is run from a lodge outside the town of Limerick, in the middle of 12 acres of heavy forest and hills. Doesn't sound so big? This 12 acres is surrounded by 10,000 acres of a semi-wilderness preserve. And just across the New Hampshire border, close enough to cast a shadow on the trails, are the White Hills.

Each day you'll cover 20 to 35 miles of singletrack and dirt roads that wind their way up to the ridges of the foothills (no murderous climbs here), around lakes, through bogs, rocky terrain, and forest so thick you can't get your bike off the trail. There are great gradual descents and a few screamers. You can ride along the tops of several ridges without doing a lot of climbing. A fit beginner will learn a lot about mountain biking on these varied trails, while more advanced riders can bang away.

I like this area because it feels so out of the way, yet is only 2½ hours from Boston, and 6 from New York City. The lodge is comfortable but rustic. Accommodations here are your sleeping bag in one of the lodge's large common rooms, in bunks in one of two dormitory-style rooms, or in a tent (yours or a rental) at one of the abundant tent sites. Most cyclists opt to camp somewhere on the property, returning for meals, showers, a visit to the hot tub or sauna, and to meet their guide each day.

This trip is run 12 to 15 times a year. Trips ranging from a weekend to a week can also be arranged. *Back Country Excursions, Box 365, Limerick, ME 04048, tel. 207/625–8189. Mid-May–mid-Oct.: 2 days, $65. Price does not include lunch or dinner. Mountain bike rental, $30 per day.*

VERMONT **Craftsbury Mountain Biking Center.** I like the concept of this trip. You show up, tell the veteran (and native) mountain biking guides what kind of riding you'd like to do, and they direct you to the perfect trail. Thorough maps are provided, but you go it alone on the trail. You get the best of commercial touring—someone else handles all the logistics—with the excitement of on-your-own exploration.

The center is sort of a sports resort. In winter it's got skiing. In summer there's hiking, horseback riding, and cycling, among other activities. It's on the shoreline of a lake, so you can swim, canoe, or sail when the your ride ends. Within a 10- to 15-mile radius of the center are more than 200 miles of dirt roads and a uncounted number of trails.

You'll bike 15 to 30 miles a day through typical northern Vermont terrain: hilly, technical, and rugged, with lots of potential resting spots for swimming, shopping, and chowing. There are dairy farms snuggled at the feet of the hills, and quintessential white-house New England towns on top.

You need at least 4 people to set up a stay at Craftsbury—unless you get lucky and can piggyback with other stragglers. Lodging options include bed-and-breakfast rooms, suites with private baths, and cottages with kitchenettes. The food—the group decides how many meals a day are provided—is all homemade. The baked goods and home-grown vegetable dishes are so popular that Craftsbury just published its own cookbook. *Craftsbury Mountain Bike Center, Box 31, Craftsbury Common, VT 05827, tel. 802/586–7767 or 800/729–7751, fax 802/586–7768. May–Oct.: $96 a night for 2 people. Prices vary with dining and lodging selections. Price does not include guide ($60 per day). Mountain bike rental, $25 per day or $35 for 2 days.*

THE MID ATLANTIC

PENNSYLVANIA **Pocono Whitewater Gorge.** I cut my teeth—and a few other body parts—on these trails. This rich mountain biking region centered in the town of Jim Thorpe (he's buried there) has expert, near-vertical, singletrack; flat novice cruising territory, with gorgeous river scenery; and everything in between.

Pocono Whitewater, primarily a rafting company, runs guided tours through the area. They know the trails. Want to catch a quick trip to the top of the mountain? Take a jaunt through the tiny tourist town? Follow the Lehigh River for 30 flat miles? Shake your bones on classic eastern rock-track? No problem.

The town is a tourist hot spot: good food, lots of shops, vintage buildings, and excellent inns. Combined with the closeness of the trail network (almost all are directly accessible from town), this makes the area perfect for family getaways. You'll also get to see some wildlife, including eagles and hawks in migration season, lots of deer, and maybe even a small black bear.

The company doesn't offer lodging, but arranges package deals with inns in Jim Thorpe. You can be out of your car and biking some of the East's sweetest singletrack within 2 hours of leaving either New York City or Philadelphia. Many of the tours are day trips, such as the popular 25-mile ride through Lehigh Gorge.

The average daily distance covered is 25 miles. About 1,500 trips are run each year, ranging from a weekend to a week. *Pocono Whitewater Mountain Bike Tours, HC-2, Box 2245, Jim Thorpe, PA 18229, tel. 717/325–3656 or 800/944–8392. Apr.–Oct.: $35 per day. Price does not include meals or lodging (lodging typically $65–$125 a night). Mountain bike rental, $25 per day.*

WEST VIRGINIA **Cranberry to Canaan.** This state makes me glad I'm an Eastern mountain biker. It has it all: smooth and technical singletrack, long climbs, heart-beater descents, grand views from atop mountains, extended ridge rides, and valley cruises. And Pocahontas County contains more than 302,000 acres of national forest. Everything is greener than the West, and not quite as high, so altitude sissies like myself can climb, climb, climb, and never suck air.

This 5-day trip into the Monongahela National Forest crosses a few passes before flattening out into a nice valley ride. If you tire, catch the shuttle back to the touring center, which is surrounded by a network of mapped and marked trails. Beginners will fall in love with the sport; advanced mountain bikers new to this area will wonder why they waited so long.

On one of your 15- to 25-mile daily rides, be sure to check out Prop's Run, a 6-mile technical downhill that ranks high on my list of favorite trails. The good old boys down there tell me that there's even better riding over the ridge.

Two nights are spent at Elk River Center, one at a bed-and-breakfast inn, one at a cabin in the forest, and one at a ski chalet. This trip is run about 6 times per year. *Elk River Touring Center, Hwy. 219, Slatyfork, WV 26291, tel. 304/572–3771. Late May–early Oct.: 5 days, $579. Mountain bike rental, $25 per day.*

WEST VIRGINIA **Twin Peaks.** West Virginia is almost heaven for hard-core riders. I've ridden the toughest trails this state has to offer. These singletracks are wet, soupy, muddy, treacherous launching pads that also happen to be more fun than any others in the East.

This 4-day trip is full of those trails, beginning from the Elk River Touring Center and heading into the vast Monongahela National Forest. The days are long, and since the shuttle van can't drive where you ride, much of the ride can't be supported. This means you have to carry some gear at times, but if you're the right kind of rider, this just adds to the fun.

You'll cover 20 to 40 miles a day, about 95% of it on singletrack—this is definitely one for the overdrive crowd. But the accommodations appeal to the lamb in all of us: lodges and bed-and-breakfast inns.

This trip is run about 5 times per year. If you need to rent a bike, ask for one of the special Ibis rental bikes with front suspension. You'll need it on these bumpy trails. *Elk River Touring Center, Hwy. 219, Slatyfork, WV 26291, tel. 304/572–3771. Late June–mid Oct.: 4 days, $459. Mountain bike rental, $25 per day.*

THE MIDWEST

MICHIGAN **Lake Superior Wilderness Trek.** Michigan's upper peninsula may be the wildest and most undeveloped area in the Midwest. There aren't the incredible vistas, challenging climbs, and thrilling descents of the country's peak mountain biking areas; but off-roaders in this part of the nation can still find plenty of fun.

This 5-day tour is based in Big Bay, at an operating lighthouse that doubles as a bed-and-breakfast. From here, you'll explore doubletrack and singletrack that twists through thick woods or winds down to Lake Superior. You'll also climb what locals call the Huron Mountains (which are more like big hills), on technical logging trails. The area has nearly 100 waterfalls, miles of shoreline, and thousands of small lakes. It's covered by second-growth forest, and is sparsely populated. It's a die-hard dirthead's dream.

Daily distances range from 10 to 25 miles. An experienced cyclist who's never ridden off-road will have a blast, but a true beginner could spend a lot of time befuddled. For those who need a break from the bike, there's a canoe trip, kayaking, and a nature hike. A chef on the premises cooks up a health-conscious mix of fresh vegetables and local game to keep guests' energy up. This trip is run 3 times per year. *Michigan Bicycle Touring, 3512 Red School Rd., Kingsley, MI 49649, tel. 616/263–5885. July–Aug.: 5 days, $809. Sept.: 5 days, $759. Shuttle from Marquette, $25. Mountain bike rental, $95.*

THE SOUTHWEST

ARIZONA **North Rim of Grand Canyon.** The south rim is the tourist-in-cars-looking-for-McDonald's magnet. This is the rim with the pine forest, awesome singletrack, and dirt roads that border the big rip. It's the rim you can have practically to yourself.

This 4-day trip begins in the huge Kaibab National Forest, then follows the rim via a network of crisscrossing dirt roads and the singletrack of the well-known (among mountain bikers, at least) Arizona Trail. After covering 20 to 25 miles each day, the guides set up a camp for the night. The food is gourmet campfire, with Dutch-oven specialties such as poached fish and pesto pasta. You'll sleep just 10 to 20 feet from the drop, sheltered and comfortable on a carpet of pine needles.

The singletrack can be technical and tough, but because it parallels the dirt road, the less hardy can cruise the smooth surface for a while. There's some climbing, of course—and some descending. You'll be spending a lot of time at 8,000 feet, which can be hard if you're not used to altitude. You'll also spend a day hiking down into the Grand Canyon. The trip is run about 6 times per year. Rent a bike if you go—they're Trek 950s with front suspension. Cool. *Kaibab Touring Center, Box 339, Moab, UT 84532, tel. 801/259–7423 or 800/451–1133, fax 801/259–6135. June to Aug.: 4 days, $480. Shuttle from St. George, $50. Mountain bike rental, $18 per day.*

ARIZONA **Sedona's Red Rock Country.** My fat-tire friends in the West rave about Sedona. "It's unspoiled and undiscovered," they tell me, "and it has the great scenery and singletrack of Utah."

You won't find much singletrack on this dirt-road trip, but you can't deny the beauty of this region. The 6-day tour begins in Flagstaff, atop the Colorado Plateau, and winds through the largest ponderosa pine forest in the world. Then it's on to Sedona and red rock heaven. Mesas, buttes, and cliffs surround the city. As you leave town, you'll pedal along the base of cliffs that hide ancient Indian dwellings (but you'll have to rent a jeep to get to them).

The accommodations include lodges and historic inns. Most meals are eaten at the inn restaurants, with picnic lunches packed for on the trail. There are loads of shops and galleries at every stop. Daily rides range from 16 to 61 miles, but some of them are on pavement. Beginners may opt for the shuttle on some of the longer climbs—but it's all ridable. There are no real technical challenges. This trip is usually run 9 times a year. Special dates are available for singles tours. *Backroads, Suite Q333, 1516 5th St., Berkeley, CA 94710–1740, tel. 510/527–1555 or 800/245–3874, fax 510/527–1444. May–Oct.: 6 days, $998. Mountain bike rental, $119.*

NEW MEXICO **Off-Road Enchantment.** The general mountain biking public is just beginning to discover this trail-wealthy state, and this 5-day trip gives you a sample of some of the area's best riding.

The singletrack and dirt roads of New Mexico rival the much-acclaimed routes of Utah, and the accommodations and off-bike activities are more plentiful here. For instance, at the end of a day of mondo trail climbing you can take your helmet off in a luxurious inn in Taos instead of bunking down in the dirt. The quirky, arty culture of the Taos area seems well-suited to the mountain biking mind-set, too.

This trip is offered 3 times a year for hardcore pedallers, and 5 times a year for beginners. The mileage is reduced for beginners, who bike from 20 to 25 miles a day as opposed to the 30 to 35 biked by advanced riders; and time spent on the trail is tempered with other activities such as a day of whitewater rafting. A highlight of either trip is the dirt road ascent of 13,161-foot Mt. Wheeler, the highest peak in New Mexico. This is the biggest climb of the trip, but not the only one. Ascension is a way of life in this region. *Roads Less Traveled, Box 8187, Longmont, CO 80501, tel. 303/678–8750 or 800/488–8483, fax 303/678–5568. June, Sept., and Oct.: 5 days, $845 for advanced, $920 for novice. Mountain bike rental, $95.*

NEW MEXICO **Taos to Sante Fe.** This trip is aimed at mountain biking beginners and riders who don't mind spending as much time off the bike as on. The 7-day tour of the region includes a healthy schedule of attractions such as museums, galleries, churches, shops, and nature reserves. There's still plenty of riding though, including a couple of tough ascents and one spectacular 4,000-foot descent along the back roads of the Sangre de Cristo Mountains. Although you don't have to be an expert on fat tires to take this trip, you do need to be fit.

The trip is run 4 times a year, and features accommodations in bed-and-breakfast inns, historic homes, and inns with the particular flavor of the region. You'll also find Southwestern flavor in the food, from huevos rancheros for breakfast to lots of chilies in every other meal. Daily mileage ranges from

15 to 60 miles, with some days spent almost entirely on pavement. You do need a mountain bike, although you might want to take a hybrid for the time spent on roads. *Butterfield and Robinson, 70 Bond St., Toronto, Ontario, Canada M5B 1X3, tel. 416/864–1354 or 800/678–1147, fax 416/864–0541. June, Sept., and Oct.: 7 days, $1,885. Price includes mountain bike rental but does not include 2 dinners and 1 lunch.*

UTAH **Bryce and Zion National Parks.** Your first day on this trail you take a 2,000-foot descent. Enough said? Advanced riders will enjoy the trip the most, but novices can manage a shortened and shuttled version. The difficulty here is not the singletrack, which isn't technically challenging, but the high level of fitness required to ride the entire trip.

You'll cover from 20 to 35 miles a day on this 5-day beauty, beginning at the Brian Head ski area and descending into Bryce on dirt roads. From the bottom of Bryce Canyon, you can either hike into the red-rock canyons or explore the singletrack of the surrounding forests. Most first timers opt for the look at the natural amphitheater of the canyon.

There's climbing, too. Advanced riders can take a longer option and grunt up the mountains and through the alpine setting. Others continue their descent toward Zion, where you find yourself at the base of a sheer canyon. It's the opposite of Bryce, where you stood on top.

Accommodations are in rustic lodges, so don't expect the plush resort-style comforts common in Colorado or New Mexico. The food, however, is up to Roads Less Traveled's usual high standards. The trip is run about 6 times per year. *Roads Less Traveled, Box 8187, Longmont, CO 80501, tel. 303/678–8750 or 800/488–8483, fax 303/678–5568. May–June and Sept.–Oct.: 5 days, $795. Shuttle from Las Vegas, $40. Mountain bike rental, $95.*

UTAH **The Maze and Cataract Canyon.** You'd probably never bike the Maze on your own. This red-rock district, one of 3 in Canyonlands National Park, can be a logistical nightmare. But with the support van hauling your supplies, it's possible to explore its winding routes.

While you're pedaling among the rock pillars, looking for petroglyphs on the walls, you can test your skills on some of the technical slickrock and sandstone rides. There are a lot of ledge drops (natural stone steps) as well as easy cruising. Daily distances average about 27 miles, and veterans tell me the riding is rougher than the famous White Rim Trail, which doesn't have as many ledges or loose-rock sections.

The 5-day ride ends with a hike into Cataract Canyon. When you get to the Colorado River, you'll whitewater raft out. The cost of the trip includes a round-trip flight from Moab to Lake Powell, where the trip begins. You can bring your own camping equipment or rent it from Kaibab. *Kaibab Touring Center, Box 339, Moab, UT 84532, tel. 801/259-7423 or 800/ 451-1133, fax 801/259-6135. May and Sept.: 5 days, $825. Mountain bike rental, $18 per day.*

UTAH **Trail of the Ancients.** Follow the dirt roads and singletrack of southern Utah into the Abajo Mountains, and you'll find the ruins of the ancient Anasazi Indians. It's not an easy trip—physically or logistically—but what's inaccessible to cars and hikers is within reach of mountain bikes. And this 5-day ride is sweet proof of that.

The journey begins about 50 miles south of Moab at the Natural Bridges National Monument with a 1,200-foot climb. Eventually you leave the red-rock canyons and enter alpine country, where you can look down on the desert and canyonlands. The ride ends in Monticello, just east of the 11,360-foot Abajo Peak.

Most of the riding is on dirt roads, and the company has the coolest rental bikes in the country—Ibis Mojo mountain bikes with Manitou front suspension forks. These rentals are better than most people's personal mounts.

The average daily distance is 20 miles. An intermediate rider should have no problem. Beginners may suffer a little, but they'll survive. This is a camping trip and is run about 7 times per year. *Western Spirit Cycling, Box 411, Moab, UT 84532, tel. 800/845-2453, fax 801/259-2736. May, June, and Sept.: 5 days, $595. Mountain bike rental, $125.*

UTAH **The White Rim.** This is a Canyonlands classic, run by one of the first (probably the original—but all kinds of companies are laying claim to the title now that mountain biking has taken off) off-road touring companies in the country.

The views from this 100-mile, 4-wheel-drive road are spectacular. It follows the Green and Colorado rivers from high atop Canyonlands National Park. The riding is rolling, with a lot of ledges and loose rock to test your technical ability. There are some short, way-steep hills and scary descents; but the trail can be mastered by beginners, who will find these small challenges a good introduction to the big-time drop-offs and descents found elsewhere on slickrock.

Why is this a classic? Many trails offer bits of the same scenery you'll catch here. But on a run of the White Rim, each day's vista seems to connect with the previous day's to make bigger and bigger—and more and more breathtaking—panoramas. It's like having a mural unrolled before you. The route's legend also stems from its whiteness. You cycle on a layer of white sandstone that seems to stretch endlessly along the ridge into the distance.

There are side hikes into the canyons on this 4-day camping trip, but you can expect to ride about 20 or 30 miles a day. About 17 trips are run each year. The company's road bike stable includes thoroughbred Kleins and Mountain Goats with front suspension. *Rim Tours, 94 W. 1st North, Moab, UT 84532, tel. 801/259-5223 or 800/626-7335. Late Mar., Apr., May, Sept., early Oct.: 4 days, $465. Mountain bike rental, $88; with front suspension, $104.*

THE ROCKIES

COLORADO **Crested Butte.** This is one of those must-ride regions for anyone aspiring to true mountain bikerhood. Crested Butte is surrounded on 3 sides by mountains (13,000-footers!), and these are filled with singletrack and dirt roads that provide some of the sweetest riding in the country.

It's all here: the tech stuff, the buff stuff, screaming descents, big-altitude gaspers. And the views. Many towns in this state are stuck in box canyons, surrounded by mountain faces. But the Butte is more open. Long valleys stretch away with the big peaks in the distance.

The food and drink in Crested Butte's restaurants are mountain biking legends. Try to get to Donita's Cantina, owned by longtime fat-tire priestess Kay Peterson.

Because so many riding options are available, this 4-day tour can cater to a mixed group of the rawest novice to the most die-hard dirthead. Accommodations are in one of the inns in the center of town. Expect to average 20 to 30 miles per day. And expect to suck big wind if you're a flatlander. The altitude will get you by the third day. This trip is run about 2 times each year. *Rim Tours, 94 W. 1st North, Moab, UT 84532, tel. 801/259-5223 or 800/626-7335. July–Aug.: 4 days, $590. Price does not include 2 dinners. Mountain bike rental, $88; with front suspension, $104.*

COLORADO **Kokopelli's Trail.** This is the real thing—an isolated, 5-day trip on singletrack and dirt roads that would be almost impossible to do on your own. You won't see anyone here but fellow adventurers.

The 150-mile trip travels along an established trail from Grand Junction, Colorado, to Moab, Utah. You start in big desert, spend a few days on the Colorado plateau with canyon scenery, and then move up into the mountains for some alpine riding. Finally, you drop back into Moab and civilization. This ride, with its climbs, long distances, and technical terrain, is tough—probably too tough for a lot of riders. But it's a mountain biking experience that can't be duplicated anywhere else in the country.

This is a camping trip, with one night's accommodation in a Moab hotel. You'll average 30

miles per day. The trip is run about 4 times per year. *Roads Less Traveled, Box 8187, Longmont, CO 80501, tel. 303/678-8750 or 800/488-8483, fax 303/678-5568. May, Sept., and Oct.: 5 days, $575. Mountain bike rental, $95.*

COLORADO **Leadville Hot Springer.** My Colorado cycling buddies call this one "vistas for the lazy." *Lazy* is a relative term for those hammerheads, but it's true that this 5-day trip puts you amid incredible alpine scenery without requiring you to conquer the terrain. Beginners will never want to go home. If this trip doesn't make you into a mountain biker, nothing will.

You ride through the Arkansas River valley, paralleling the Continental Divide. Although you pass by 14,000-foot peaks every day, you'll be losing altitude—descending about 2,000 feet over the course of the trip. The riding is forest doubletrack, with one day of sweet singletrack, and you'll average 25 miles a day. There's also a whitewater raft trip on the Arkansas, and a visit to the hot springs on the last night. Accommodations are in cabins and bed-and-breakfast inns. The trip is run about 4 times per year. *Roads Less Traveled, Box 8187, Longmont, CO 80501, tel. 303/678-8750 or 800/488-8483, fax 303/678-5568. June–Aug.: 5 days, $845. Shuttle from Denver, $30. Mountain bike rental, $95.*

COLORADO **San Juan Hut Systems.** This is a great guided-but-guideless trip. The 207-mile dirt road route between Telluride, Colorado, and Moab, Utah, is well-marked; and 7 huts stocked with food, water, and sleeping equipment are scattered along the trail at 15- to 30-mile intervals. You just follow the map to each hut, bed down for the night, then head out for the next outpost in the morning. You get a feeling of self-sufficiency that makes your vacation a true adventure, without worrying about details and logistics.

A fit beginner could handle the route, but since you're on your own it's a good idea to have an experienced cyclist along. About 30 miles are covered each day, including a fair amount of climbing, but nothing too technical or steep. You'll ride past the San Juan mountains, John Brown Canyon, and several towers, pinnacles, and plateaus. You have to carry some gear—about 3 liters of water per rider, plus rain and cold-weather wear—and it's a good idea to bring repair and first-aid kits, just in case.

The food on the trip is surprisingly varied considering the limited cooking facilities. Standard fare includes spaghetti, stir-fry, a variety of Mexican entrées, soups, and pancakes. The huts sleep a maximum of 8, but there's no minimum to schedule a trip. *San Juan Hut Systems, Box 1663, No. 4, 117 N. Willow St., Telluride, CO 81435, tel. 303/728–6935, fax 303/728–7144. June–Sept.: 8 days, $375. Mountain bike rental, $140.*

IDAHO **Backcountry Hot Springs.** This is Western Spirit's most popular Idaho ride, because the wide-open scenery and riding are followed by a hot springs soak every night. While the guides make camp (and great spinach lasagna and black bean enchiladas) you soak away your trail aches. The 5-day ride begins in Ketchum and follows Warm Springs Road. Here fissures in the shore of Warm Springs River spill near-boiling water into the stream. You can control the temperature by using rocks to divert the water.

Daily rides average 12 miles, most of which is on dirt road. There is some singletrack and some significant climbing, notably an 8-mile grind on the third day, but an athletic beginner should have no trouble, especially with the soothing therapy of the hot springs. Nearly 90% of Idaho is controlled by the Bureau of Land Management or the Forest Service, so maintained trails are everywhere. The area is so rural that, on the last day, you have to help chase deer from the airplane runway so your plane back to Ketchum can land!

If you go, rent a bike. The rentals are Ibis Mojo mountain bikes with Manitou front suspension forks. This trip is run about 8 times per year. *Western Spirit Cycling, Box 411, Moab, UT 84532, tel. 800/845–2453, fax 801/259–2736. July–Aug.: 5 days, $625. Mountain bike rental, $125.*

IDAHO **Idaho Singletrack.** Here's a rare gem. This 5-day trip is one of the few predominantly singletrack mountain bike tours in the country. You begin at Elephant's Perch in Ketchum (literary pedal turners should be sure to ride a few loops around Hemingway's grave), then head into the wilderness. Because it's a camping trip, the leaders are free to alter the itinerary to find the best singletrack. So they can steer you away from rain, overly dry areas, and other potential downers. The group can also decide whether to tackle tougher trails or take an easy spin.

Whatever the course, one almost-mandatory stop is at Galena Lodge, the site of the 1988 National Off-Road Bicycle Association national race course. Trail surfaces are usually coarse soil packed with pine needles, or clay; and there are some tricky sections, some long grunts, and some easy climbs. Idaho is big country, and big fun on a bike.

This company rents Ibis Mojo mountain bikes with Manitou front suspension forks that are better than most people's personal mounts. Daily distances range from 15 to 30 miles, although a killer group might go up to 40. The trip is run about 3 times per year. *Western Spirit Cycling, Box 411, Moab, UT 84532, tel. 800/845–2453, fax 801/259–2736. July to Aug.: 5 days, $575. Mountain bike rental, $125.*

MONTANA **Beartooth Bike.** This 6-day trek near the Montana–Wyoming border begins and ends in Bozeman, Montana, and covers portions of Yellowstone Park, and the Beartooth and Absaroka mountain ranges. You're cycling in the middle of about 900,000 acres of wilderness, which means the riding never gets boring. You'll spend time at 11,000 feet, in the bottom of canyons, and soaking in natural hot springs.

The distance covered each day averages from 45 to 50 miles. That's a lot on a mountain bike. The riding can get somewhat technical, with climbs up to 5 miles long, ridge rides, and wicked descents, spicing up what is otherwise an easy spin on dirt roads. Beginners may struggle because of the fitness- and skill-levels required for this trip. There's a one-day layover in Cook City, just outside Yellowstone, which you can use to rest (or to keep on riding as you explore the area).

The accommodations are in resorts and inns. The trip is run about 3 times per year. *Backcountry, Box 4029, Bozeman, MT 59772–4029, tel. 406/586–3556, fax 406/586–4288. July–late Aug.: 6 days, $999. Mountain bike rental, $99.*

MONTANA **Montana Off-Road.** This is what the hullabaloo is all about: true singletrack mountain biking. The riding—everything from ridge running to crossing mountain passes and circling alpine lakes—is physically challenging, technically tough, and a fat-tire rider's dream. The singletrack ranges from needle-carpeted buff to loose-rock slopes where almost everyone has to get off and walk. You'll only be able to cover about 15 miles per day on this 5-day trip: That's how demanding this one is.

Starting in Bozeman, this trip runs south into the Gallatin and Madison mountain ranges. Many times there is no van support (it can't drive where you're riding), but it will be there with your luggage at the end of the day. The accommodations are in resorts, lodges, and a guest ranch. The trip is run twice per year, and is for advanced riders only. *Backcountry, Box 4029, Bozeman, MT 59772–4029, tel. 406/586–3556, fax 406/586–4288. July–Aug.: 5 days, $899. Mountain bike rental, $129.*

THE WEST COAST

CALIFORNIA **Haute Route.** This ride isn't for everyone, but if it appeals to you, it could be one of the best mountain biking excursions you'll ever make.

The trip is run on 2 separate weekends. The first begins at Big Bear Lake and descends to the Deep Creek Hot Springs, where you make camp, cook out (steak-and-potatoes fare), and soak away the trail. The terrain is tough—not yet extreme, but only for the hardy. There are a lot of up-and-down stretches, and a lot of technical challenges.

Water can be scarce as you ride through remote sections of the national forests and desertlike areas east of Los Angeles. The scenery changes as you move through pine forests into stretches of Joshua trees, then skirt the Mojave River and enter the desert, finally ending up amid patches of scrub oak. You may not have known there was this much wilderness left in the area.

The second weekend is harder. You'll climb back up to the Blue Ridge, then creep up and over 9,000-foot Mt. Baden-Powell (named for the man who founded the Boy Scouts). Once you conquer this peak, though, it's all screamer downhill back to Los Angeles. But even this section is technical, with some loose, rocky sections.

Expect to average 30 to 35 miles per day. This is a camping trip, run only one time per year. You can also sign up for a single weekend. *Victor Vincente of America, 1582 Pride St., Simi Valley, CA 93065, tel. 805/527–1991. Apr. and May: 4 days, $220; 2 days, $110.*

CALIFORNIA **Otter Bar Lodge.** This resort is filled with water seekers during the peak kayak season, but in the late summer and fall, Otter Bar becomes mountain biking territory.

Klamath National Forest, where most of the guided rides take place, contains about 3,000 miles of dirt roads and 300 miles of trails. Only the Pacific Crest National Scenic Trail is closed to mountain bikes. The lodge is remote (more than 2 hours from Eureka), and the surrounding fir trees and wildlife make it feel even farther from civilization.

Using Otter Bar Lodge as your base, you'll spend 7 days exploring the Trinity Alps and Marble Mountain wilderness areas. Jammers can make the climb from 1,200 to 6,000 feet, while a shuttle takes beginners up steep ascents. The riding runs from quick buff descents to bone-jarring technical roller coasters. Most trails are old logging roads, but the guides know where to find singletrack.

Along with biking 15 to 40 miles a day, you'll spend time rafting on the Klamath River. Accommodations at the inn are pretty plush: the hot tub and sauna get high marks, as does the gourmet California cuisine. One night is spent in an old lookout cabin set on a 6,000-foot ridge, with a 360° view of the surrounding mountains. About 8 to 10 weeks are open to bikers. *Otter Bar Lodge, Box 210, Forks of Salmon, CA 96031, tel. 916/462–4772. Aug.– early Oct.: 7 days, $1,150. Price includes mountain bike rental.*

OREGON **Oregon Cascades.** If I had to pick one West Coast mountain biking trip for beginners, this 5-day excursion on the east side of the Cascades might be it. The riding is challenging yet possible, and the scenery is first-rate.

The trip begins in Deschutes National Forest, near Eugene, then traverses the Newberry National Volcanic Monument (50,000 acres of lava flows and blow-your-mind geologic features) before entering thickly forested areas rich with waterfalls and lakes.

There's some climbing, but no killer ascents. Most of the riding is on dirt roads, but sampler sections of singletrack will show the novices what the sport is all about. Advanced riders won't be bored—there are many longer trails that snake through the forest. You can expect to ride anywhere from 25 to 55 miles a day. Food and lodging are provided by 2 resorts: Black Butte Ranch and Sun River Resort. The trip is run about 6 times per year. *Backcountry, Box 4029, Bozeman, MT 59772– 4029, tel. 406/586–3556, fax 406/586–4288. Late June–early July and Sept.: 5 days, $1,029. Price includes shuttle from Eugene. Mountain bike rental, $129.*

WASHINGTON **Mount St. Helens.** My pedaling friends in the Pacific Northwest tell me that a trip here will be the closest you can get to mountain biking on the moon until anti-gravity treads are invented.

Much of the land surrounding the volcano is still ashed over, although growth has returned to some patches of land. This 6-day trip on the dirt roads and singletrack of the nation-

al forest surrounding Mount St. Helens explores both types of terrain.

The riding can be tough. You'll cycle completely around the mountain, do plenty of climbing, and catch some speedy singletrack descents. You'll also cruise through some of the evergreen forests Washington is famous for. You'll average about 28 miles a day.

There's one night of camping near the base of the volcano (all the gear is supplied). Other accommodations are in lodges and inns. Since you're in Washington, expect salmon for dinner at least once. This Sunday-to-Friday trip is run about 4 times per year. *Bicycle Adventures, Box 7875, Olympia, WA 98507, tel. 206/786–0989 or 800/443–6060, fax 206/786– 9661. June–Sept.: 6 days, $1,032. Shuttle from Portland, $68. Mountain bike rental, $142.*

WASHINGTON **North Cascades.** This is a completely different Washington. The scrappy grass and rock terrain found on this 6-day trip reminds me more of the Midwest than the West Coast, but there are still plenty of evergreens to cool your wheels under.

You're riding on the east side of the Cascade Mountains, which means you're likely to be in a very un-Washington-like climate: dry and sunny. The trails here, near the town of Winthrop, are some of the finest I've ever ridden. The Methow Valley singletrack is buff, twisty, and well-groomed by the large cross-country skiing and mountain biking population of the area. There are some gnarly technical courses, too. The climbs can be killer, but because you're not into big-time elevation, fit flatlanders will feel comfortable.

You'll average about 25 miles per day. There's a rafting trip down the Methow River, which is included in the cost. The trip is run only twice each year. Go before too many people find out about the Methow Valley and spoil it. It's a mountain biking boom area waiting to happen. *Bicycle Adventures, Box 7875, Olympia, WA 98507, tel. 206/786–0989 or 800/443–6060, fax 206/786–9661. May and Oct.: 6 days, $1,020. Shuttle from Wenatchee airport, $68. Mountain bike rental, $136.*

SOURCES

ORGANIZATIONS **American Youth Hostels** (Box 37613, Washington, DC 20013, tel. 202/783–4943) runs off-road tours and provides inexpensive accommodations. **Bikecentennial** (Box 8308, Missoula, MT 59807, tel. 406/721–1776) sells cycling maps and provides information about off-road touring. It publishes *The Cyclists' Yellow Pages* (including a special mountain biking supplement) and *Bike-Report.*

The **International Mountain Bicycling Association** (Box 412043, Los Angeles, CA 90041, tel. 818/792–8830) advocates responsible trail use, and helps resolve land access issues. It publishes *IMBA Trail News.* The **League of American Wheelmen** (Suite 120, 190 W. Ostend St., Baltimore, MD 21230, tel. 410/539–3399), a cycling enthusiast organization, runs events and provides touring information. It also publishes *Bicycle USA.* Although it's not heavily off-road oriented, it may be of some help. The **New England Mountain Biking Association** (69 Spring St., Cambridge, MA 02141, tel. 617/497–6891) advocates responsible trail use and helps resolve land access issues. **Rails to Trails Conservancy** (Suite 300, 1400 16th St. NW, Washington, DC 20036, tel. 202/797–5400) promotes conversion of abandoned railroad land to cycling trails and provides touring information.

PERIODICALS *Bicycle USA,* the magazine of the League of American Wheelmen (*see above*), is published 8 times per year and is distributed to members. Every issue contains at least one touring feature and lots of information on rides and events. *Bicycling* is a how-to magazine, with mountain bike touring articles throughout the year and a special touring issue. It's published 11 times per year (Rodale Press, 33 E. Minor St., Emmaus, PA 18098, tel. 215/967–5171). *Bike Midwest* lists off-road rides and events in this region. It's published 7 times per year (Suite C, 2099 W. 5th Ave., Columbus, OH 43212, tel. 614/481–7723). *The Cyclists' Yellow Pages,*

an annual publication distributed to Bikecentennial members (*see above*), lists sources of off-road touring information and maps. *Dirt Rag* lists off-road rides and events in New England, the East Coast, the Midwest, and the Southeast. It's published 7 times per year (5732 3rd St., Verona, PA 15147, tel. 412/795–7495). *Mountain Bike,* the sister magazine of *Bicycling,* has a special off-road touring issue each year and mountain bike-touring articles throughout the year. It's published 11 times per year (Rodale Press, 33 E. Minor St., Emmaus, PA 18098, tel. 215/967–5171). *Northern California Cyclist,* published 11 times per year, lists off-road rides and events in this region (Suite 304, 490 2nd St., San Francisco, CA 94107, tel. 415/546–7291). *Southern California Cyclist,* also published 11 times per year, lists off-road rides and events in this region (Box 3571, Manhattan Beach, CA 90266, tel. 213/546–7181). *Sports Etc/Northwest Cyclist* lists off-road rides and events in the Pacific Northwest. It's published 10 times per year (Box 9272, Seattle, WA 98109, tel. 206/286–8566). *Texas Bicyclist,* published 9 times per year, lists off-road rides and events in this state (Suite 1604, 3600 Jeanetta, Houston, TX 77063, tel. 713/782–1661).

BOOKS Pick up a copy of *500 Great Rail Trails* (Living Planet Press) to discover the U.S. rail-trail system, a series of abandoned rail lines that have been converted to bike trails. The 162-page guide tells you where the trails are and how long they run; it also gives highlights along the route and tells you where to get a map. Some of the best touring books available are those in the *Bicycling the Back Roads Series: Northwest Oregon, Northwest Washington, Pacific Coast, Southwest Washington* (The Mountaineers Books). Each book has more than 200 pages compiled by local experts, with detailed route directions, sightseeing tips, and lodging and food recommendations for the area covered. Some other excellent series include the *America by Mountain Bike Series: Arizona, Central Appalachia, New Mexico, Northern California/Nevada, Northern New England, Smoky Mountain Country* (Menasha

Ridge Press), which offers 230-page volumes of well-mapped and detailed off-road rides throughout the United States written by local experts; and *Mountain Bike Adventures Series: Four Corners Region, Northern Rockies, Washington's North Cascades and Olympics, Washington's South Cascades/Puget Sound* (The Mountaineers Books), whose 228-page volumes include many mapped routes along with good introductory material on mountain biking.

ALSO SEE If you enjoy the off-road bike tour experience, you may like seeing the country on road tours, too. See the Bicycling chapter for more information.

Race Car Driving Schools

by Michael B. McPhee

ere's a way to experience speed without first writing a will. Race car driving schools are becoming enormously popular, as growing numbers of men and women are strapping themselves into powerful racing cars on wide-open tracks and safely driving well beyond speed limits that are legal on highways and country roads.

Elaina Litvak, a 40-year-old junior high school art teacher, finally agreed to try racing her boyfriend's souped-up Audi. "We had a short classroom session, then got in our cars and followed the instructor around several laps," she said. "The last laps we got up over 100 miles per hour.

"When you've never done this before," she continued, "the whole thing is overwhelming. But you settle down real quick. Soon, I tried catching a Corvette. I did everything I was told not to do, going for speed only. It really scared me. In the afternoon, I did a lot better."

Cindy Parmenter, a 39-year-old financial analyst, took up vintage-car racing with her husband. "It's a great feeling of power, the whining of the engine, the shifting, the tremendous exhilaration.

"Coming out of a corner into a straight, it takes guts not to take your foot off the gas or blip the brakes. But you do it, and God, it's great. When I spun out for the first time last weekend, I was filled with adrenaline, but I wasn't as scared as I thought I would be."

Both women say that, whether or not they ever race again, they now feel much more confident driving on the street—knowing the limits of braking, how to handle a corner better, how to avoid accidents.

Race car driving schools cover a lot of driving techniques in a lot of different vehicles, including drag racing, go-cart, stock car, and ice driving. But the main focus in this chapter is on schools that offer road racing, Grand Prix racing, and street courses.

Road racing and Grand Prix racing schools use the same squiggly, circular track, usually less than 2 miles long with 12 to 18 turns. Road racing is done in a car with fenders, like a sports car, and you can bump the other cars without doing too much damage. These cars reach speeds of up to 120 miles per hour.

Grand Prix racing schools use cars with open wheels, which stick out from the auto body, and no fenders, such as those used at the Indianapolis Motor Speedway. These cars are much more powerful, traveling at speeds up to 140 to 160 miles per hour.

The street schools use regular street sedans, like Volvos, BMWs, and Toyotas. Some schools let you bring your own car. These schools offer defensive driving courses, which teach you skills that help you handle situations that could

Outdoor writer Michael B. McPhee has contributed to The New York Times, The Washington Post, *and* The Boston Globe. *He believes firmly that speed is an almost universal aphrodisiac.*

arise on any local street—skills like cornering, braking, skid control, or evasive driving to avoid a ball or a child. Street schools also offer high-performance courses, which concentrate on highway driving—how to handle a car at highway speeds, how to avoid sliding, how to pass and handle curves.

Skids and slides are the bane of all driving because they bring you close to losing control of the car. Consequently, all schools concentrate on avoiding slides, or getting out of them once they start. All schools approach the problem differently, but they all have their own slide or skid cars equipped either with outriggers that prevent you from rolling over in a high-speed slide, or cars with special suspensions that slide easily at low speeds. All schools also have their own skid pads—specially prepared sections of asphalt greased or oiled to cause cars to slide.

All driving schools are set up to teach you quickly. All have half-day introductory courses that give you 10 or 12 laps of driving. Most courses are 2 days long; the more thorough ones last for 3 days. Some schools have 5-day courses for the serious wannabe racer. All the schools have surprisingly good safety records.

A typical day begins with a classroom session, where you learn the best line through a curve (in other words, the most efficient path around a curve), how to exit a turn with the greatest speed and acceleration, and how to avoid or cope with sliding. Then it's out onto the track, either on foot or in a van or another car. A few schools have cars with twin seats that allow the instructor to sit beside you as you take laps.

Lunch may be catered by the school, but you are usually on your own. Afternoons are spent in the cars, applying what you've learned in class and practicing car control. You fend for yourself for dinner, but usually you get together with other students to talk about life in the fast lane. Nights are low-key as a rule, as the exhausted students hit the hay early for another day of driving.

Be prepared to spend $1,000 to $1,500 for a weekend and up to $2,500 for a course that's 3 to 5 days long.

CHOOSING THE RIGHT SCHOOL

In picking the right school, ask yourself why you're doing this. Do you want the sensation of driving an open-wheel Grand Prix at 150 miles per hour? Then sign up for a Grand Prix course for 1 or 2 days. Do you want to learn how to race? Then pick a 5-day racing course with certification at the end. Do you want to learn how to drive your car defensively in town? Choose a street-driving course. Or do you want to go as fast as you possibly can? Then pick a drag racing or go-cart school.

Here are some other questions to ask to help you decide which school is right for you:

How long has the school been in business and what is its safety record? A school that has been around for a while has a safety record you can evaluate. Also important, it should have ironed out any problems in its curriculum and instructional routines.

What's the cost and what's included? Always ask if the school supplies the car or if you must drive your own. Courses in which you use the school's vehicles generally cost more. Only one school listed here provides accommodations and meals; the others generally leave you on your own, although a few do serve you lunch. Since there's no standard, we tell you what's included in the prices we list within the italicized service information at the end of each review. If you have any doubts, always ask for clarification.

Driving schools don't usually put you up, but they often know about the best deals in town. Sometimes a school works out a special rate for its students at a nearby hotel. Find out what the guest quarters are like, and what facilities the property offers, before you book.

Am I liable if I crash a car? Policies vary dramatically from school to school. At some schools, you are responsible for all damages to the cars you use; others sell insurance policies that limit your liability to a few thousand dollars, with or without a deductible; others never hold you responsible. (If you plan to use your own car, make sure that your regular insurance covers any damages incurred while in a race-car driving school.)

How many students are in the school and how many students per teacher? The total number of students means less than the number of students in a class, and the number of students in a class means less than the number of students per teacher. A 4:1 student-to-teacher ratio is average for most courses.

How much driving time will I have? This depends on the philosophy of the school. Some split the time 50-50, in part because they don't have enough cars. Others provide plenty of time on the track—also known as seat time—on the principle that you learn by doing.

How fast can I go? Some schools limit your RPMs (and fine you if you rev the engine too high) or require you to stay together and wait for the slowest student; others let you push the car as hard as you want on so-called hot laps.

Who teaches at the school? Are there any famous racers currently teaching? For the beginner, names don't matter much, unless you want to meet your racing hero. Most schools share instructors. Celebrity drivers tied to schools don't mean anything unless they actually teach you, as they do, say, in Bobby Rahal's school in Ohio or in Buck Baker's stock-car school. Just because so-and-so went there 10 years ago doesn't mean anything. It's more important to find teachers actively involved in racing (not just in teaching)—in other words, teachers who are currently competitive.

Do you have references from past students? It's often more helpful to get a former student's description of his or her experience than it is to get one from a professional driver working at the school.

How far in advance do I need to sign up?

What accreditation does the school have? Of the six groups that sanction automobile racing, only two are involved in racing schools: the Sports Car Club of America (SCCA) and the International Motor Sport Association

(IMSA). Most of the schools described below are sanctioned by one or the other. The school curriculums are developed by the schools themselves, who then apply to one of the two sanctioning groups. The instruction varies from school to school. However, whether a school is accredited by the SCCA or IMSA really matters only if you want to be licensed in order to race. You can't participate in an organization's races without being licensed by it.

The SCCA, the larger of the two, focuses primarily on road racing in a variety of cars, from full-bodied GT (Grand Tour) passenger cars to Formula cars with open cockpits, and sanctions club racing, solo racing around pylons, and road rallies. It's very social, oriented toward beginners and amateurs. To be SCCA-licensed you must complete a 3-day program at one of the 17 SCCA-accredited schools and take a 1- or 2-day course at one of the SCCA regionals, listed in SCCA's monthly *Sports Car Magazine*. It costs $45 for a novice permit plus $55 for membership.

The IMSA is much smaller, and its members are mostly self-styled professionals who also belong to the SCCA. IMSA licenses are awarded by all IMSA-accredited schools on completion of a 3-day course, a passing grade on an exam, and payment of a $225 fee. Keep in mind that the majority of races offer a minimal amount of money, and few pros ever break even.

MAJOR PLAYER

SKIP BARBER RACING SCHOOL The Skip Barber Racing School, accredited by both the SCCA and IMSA, is the largest racing school in the world. After almost two decades of teaching, it also has the most celebrated alumni; in fact, 11 of the 33 starting drivers in the 1993 Indianapolis 500 were Skip Barber graduates!

Courses are available at 17 to 23 different tracks throughout the United States, and the school is known for offering the same curriculum, with the same quality cars and the same level of teaching, at each of its tracks. Programs run year-round on the West Coast, from April through October in the Northeast and Midwest, and from October through April in Florida and Georgia.

There are a variety of programs, roughly divided into race car driving–competition and advanced defensive driving for street drivers. Class sizes range from 14 students with 4 instructors to 28 students with 7 instructors.

On the racing side, a 3-hour introductory course ($295) gives you 90 minutes of classroom theory on car control and safety. The other 90 minutes is behind the wheel of a Formula Ford (a smaller version of an Indy car) reaching speeds of 100 mph, while an instructor follows behind in another car.

Twenty percent of the 3-day intensive racing course ($1,995) is spent in the classroom, where you learn cornering techniques, shifting, accelerating, and braking. The remainder of your time is spent in cars on the track, reaching speeds of 120 mph. A 2-day amateur racing program for graduates costs $1,350.

The 1- and 2-day advanced defensive driving programs ($475 and $925 respectively) teach such skills as how to control skidding, decrease braking distances, and avoid accidents. Students drive BMW 325i's, since the school is sponsored by BMW. The street-driving courses are given only in Wisconsin, Connecticut, Florida, and California.

Students are not liable for damage to cars. The school provides names of local hotels that offer students special rates (Rte. 7, New Canaan, CT 06018, tel. 203/824–0762, fax 203/824– 0760; and, on the West Coast, Sears Point International Raceway, 29355 Arnold Dr., Sonoma, CA 95476, tel. 707/939–8007, fax 707/939– 8055).

FAVORITE SCHOOLS

THE NORTHEAST

NEW HAMPSHIRE Motion Dynamics/David **Loring Drivers School.** This small, SCCA-accredited school in the town of Loudon, about 30 minutes from Concord, was started only in 1991 and offers just one course on selected Thursdays. The one-day arrive-and-drive course includes use of an SCCA spec racer, a road-racing sports car specifically designed to be used in SCCA-sanctioned road-racing competitions. These small sports cars are capable of racing up to 120 miles per hour. Because of their design, they are considered the ideal learning car—easy to handle and not too powerful.

Three hours of classroom instruction are followed by speed laps on the New Hampshire International Speedway. This class gives a maximum of 6 students one full day of driving experience. The level is determined by the students themselves. Students leave a $2,000 damage deposit on cars. No insurance is offered. *Motion Dynamics/David Loring Drivers School, Box 2245, Rte. 16, Conway, NH 03818, tel. 603/447–3543, fax 603/447– 1920. Apr.–Oct.: 1-day course, $1,300.*

THE MID ATLANTIC

NEW JERSEY **Bertil Roos Driving School.** With almost two decades of experience, this is one of the older schools. It offers both racing and street-driving courses and an unusual guarantee: You can get your money back if you're not satisfied. It is accredited by both the IMSA and SCCA.

The Roos school, held at the Pocono International Raceway in Long Pond, New Jersey (about 30 minutes from Wilkes-Barre or Allentown, Pennsylvania), is more wide open than most driving schools. In other words, unlike the many schools that restrict the speeds at which you can drive and prohibit you from actually racing, the Roos school has no speed or rev limits, and allows its instructors to encourage students to actually race and pass each other, so students here end up driving faster (nearly 140 mph) than students at most other schools.

For street driving, the school has specially engineered slide cars with pivoting rear wheels that are constantly sliding, creating ice- and snow-driving conditions more closely (the school claims) than do slide cars with outriggers.

The racing classes cover basic car handling techniques, as well as racing in traffic, passing, and drafting (or tailgating to reduce wind resistance). Some are Grand Prix courses.

The Roos school is unique in that it stresses eye technique, or ocular driving technique, in which the student is taught to always look at the correct place on the course relative to the car, the track, and other cars. This is a help not only in racing but in ordinary highway driving. The school also emphasizes the line-recovery technique—keeping the car on the correct line through the track.

The defensive driving courses are taught in Volvo 850 GLTs, which is no surprise, since the school is sponsored by Volvo. Slide cars are Volvos as well. Racing classes can take up to 18 students, but the student-to-teacher ratio usually stays around 3:1. There's no liability for basic courses; in advanced courses you could pay up to $2,500 in damages. *Bertil Roos Driving School, Box 221, Blakeslee, PA 18610, tel. 800/RACE–NOW or 717/646–7227, fax 717/646–4794. Apr.–Oct.: half-day racing course, $395; full-day, $795; 3-day Grand Prix racing program, $2,250; 6-race program with Bertil Roos, $5,100; 1-day defensive driving course, $470; 2 days, $975.*

PENNSYLVANIA **Frank Hawley's Drag Racing School.** This operation based in Gainesville, Florida, runs a gas dragster program in July at Maple Grove Raceway in Reading (*see* The South, *below*).

THE SOUTH

FLORIDA **Frank Hawley's Drag Racing School.** Drag racing is a sprint between 2 cars, designed to see which one can accelerate faster. The vehicles are placed side-by-side, looking down a 1/4-mile stretch of pavement. A series of flashing lights signal the drivers to start racing, and the first to cross the finish line wins. It sounds simple, but drag racers have taken this form of competition to a level

that just a decade ago seemed inconceivable. Some cars use 4 engines, some burn especially flammable mixtures of alcohol, some even use jet engines. All are modified so severely that they may not be driven legally on the street.

The basic course gives you 2 days on the Gainesville (Florida) Raceway, in a gas or supergas dragster (the latter looks like a production model but runs with a high-performance engine and modified design).

The school provides everything—dragster, driving suit, helmet. The first day includes classroom instruction and equipment inspection. Then you're strapped into the car for warm-up exercises—practice with car control and burnouts (spinning the tires prior to racing). The second day has some more classroom work, then 6 runs, beginning with 4 short ones and working up to 2 down the length of the 1/4-mile track. Students frequently reach speeds of 150 mph.

Driving alcohol-powered dragsters and funny cars (a drag-race vehicle with a fiberglass body) is taught in a 3-day course. This is basically the same course given for the gas and supergas dragsters, except that these cars are much more powerful and require the driver to use a clutch, so more instruction is necessary.

Pro-stock motorcycle racing is taught in a 2-day course, using a 4-valve Suzuki motorcycle with 225 horsepower. This course has become very popular among Europeans. Students can reach speeds of 180 mph.

Classes are limited to 8 students for the gas dragster programs, 6 for the alcohol-powered dragster courses, and 4 for the motorcycle programs. Each class usually has one main instructor and a helper. Students are liable for up to $2,500 in damages if they crash or cause engine damage through over-revving. The gas dragster program is offered in September at Bakersfield Raceway in Bakersfield, California, 90 minutes northeast of Los Angeles, and in July at Maple Grove Raceway in Reading, Pennsylvania. *Frank Hawley's Drag Racing School, Box 140369, Gainesville, FL 32614, tel. 904/373–7223, fax 904/338–*

1813. *Year-round: gas and supergas 2-day course, $1,150; alcohol and funny-car course, $1,500; 1-day personal training clinic with your own car, $1,500 (additional days, $1,000 each).*

FLORIDA **Southard's Racing School.** This is another fired-up, hell-bent stock car school, the only one in the country that teaches on either dirt or asphalt. The asphalt's on the New Smyrna Speedway in Smyrna Beach, Florida, about 60 miles northeast of Orlando. The dirt's on the Ocala Speedway about 40 miles due north of Orlando.

There are three variations on the 5-day course: You can take 4 days of classroom instruction and a single day of studying the chassis of the race car; no driving is included. Or you can bring your own car and on the fifth day, the only driving day, drive the school's car in the morning with an instructor and your own car in the afternoon. The third option is the same as the second, except that the school provides the car. Classes are limited to 8 students and 2 or 3 instructors. Students are not liable for damages—unless, of course, it's your own car. *Southard's Racing School, Box 1810, New Smyrna Beach, FL 32170, tel. 904/428–3307 or 800/422–9449. Year-round: 4-day course, $650; 5-day course with no driving, $600; driving with your own car, $900; driving with the school's car, $1,700.*

FLORIDA **Right On Track.** Programs of this newish school, based in Illinois, are offered at Morso Motor Sport Park near West Palm Beach in winter (*see* The Midwest, *below*).

GEORGIA **Road Atlanta Driver Training Center.** Located about 45 minutes from the city, Road Atlanta offers both a racing program and a street-driving program. Both the 2- and 3-day programs are accredited by the IMSA and SCCA.

Courses are taught on a long, 2½-mile track in 300 ZX Nissans and 240 SXs (yes, the school is sponsored by Nissan) with instructors in the cars. You reach speeds of 80 to 120 mph. Because the racing is done in sedans, most of the techniques you learn can also be applied to street driving. Class sizes increase to meet the need, but the student-to-teacher ratio remains about 4:1 or 5:1.

The track was paved in 1993, enabling courses to be taught year-round on a smooth surface. However, students are liable for any damages to cars up to $5,500 unless they take out the $75 insurance policy that cuts the liability to $2,250. *Road Atlanta Driver Training Center, Rte. 1, Braselton, GA 30517, tel. 404/967–6143. Year-round: 1-day road racing course, $495; 2 days, $1,195; 3-day competition road racing, $1,500; 1-day performance handling class or defensive-driving program, $325; 2 days, $550.*

GEORGIA AND NORTH CAROLINA **Buck Baker Racing School.** Stock-car racers are a breed of their own—the rough-and-tumble Saturday night boys who drive modified American sedans with very large engines around an oval track at frightful speeds. This is the school for those of you who want to hit the fast lane. Within 2 days, students with no racing experience average 165 mph around the Atlanta Motor Speedway (the third fastest track on the Winston Cup circuit) with other cars on the track. "We're into training here," they tell you, "not talking." And they back up this boast: After 13 years of teaching like this, students are still not liable for damages.

Two-day courses, given on Friday and Saturday, are taught at the 1½-mile Atlanta track, and 3-day programs at the 1-mile North Carolina Motor Speedway in Rockingham, about 90 minutes east of Charlotte. Of the 2 tracks, the Speedway is a bit slower (students average 140 mph) but more challenging.

Both courses are taught using powerful V-8 Winston Cup cars. You spend the first day in classrooms, learning driving techniques and rules and studying the chassis; then you're outside, inspecting the track, looking for the best line to steer into and out of the corners. The next day or 2 you're in the cars. An instructor rides with you as needed. There can be 4 or 5 cars on the track at any time. Expect 12 to 15 students per class, with 5 instructors.

Graduates who want an advanced course sign up for a one-on-one session with Buck's brother Buddy, an equally accomplished stock-car racer, who goes out on the track in another car and pulls maneuvers on you. The school also offers a graduate refresher course for those with "the need for speed"—those who want to run laps as fast as they want, with no instruction. *Buck Baker Racing School, 50000 Currituck Dr., Charlotte, NC 28210, tel. 704/527–2763 or 704/596–8930, fax 704/596–8931. Year-round: 2 or 3 days, $1,800; graduate refresher course, $500 per day.*

THE MIDWEST

ILLINOIS **Right On Track.** This relative newcomer, founded in 1989 and accredited by the SCCA, is a mobile school based at Black Hawk Farms Raceway (just north of Rockford) that moves with the weather. There are classes year-round at tracks in various locations, including Indianapolis Raceway Park and nearby Putnam Park. In winter, they're usually at Morso Motor Sport Park near West Palm Beach, Florida, or at Phoenix (Arizona) International Raceway.

The school provides more seat time and hot laps than many other schools, in an effort to produce better drivers. The 3-hour introduction to racing includes a brief classroom course and nearly 2 hours of driving. A 2-day competition program has students learning in an SCCA spec racer—an open-cockpit, rear-engine race car. Every student rides in a special two-seat race car with an instructor before driving solo on the track. Classes can hold up to 16. You are liable for any damages to the cars. Catered lunches are included in the price.

The school's high-performance defensive driving program uses 5.0 Mustangs, BMW 325s, and Chevrolet Camaros. You can opt for a one-day course, which teaches skid control, emergency lane changes, and braking, as well as steering through a series of pylons. Or go for the 2-day course, which offers more of the same, but with more actual driving time. Instructors accompany you most of the time.

Right On Track, 80 Bond St., Elk Grove Village, IL 60007, tel. 708/956–4755, fax 708/956–8214. Year-round: 3-hour introduction to racing, $300; 2-day competition course, $2,400; 1-day high-performance driving school, $495; 2 days, $800.

INDIANA **Fast Company Racing School.** This relatively new mobile school, founded in 1992, teaches only race car driving, and mostly to corporate clients. The school is based at the Indianapolis Raceway Park but moves to the Las Vegas Raceway Park in winter. The program is the same in both locations.

The school takes an aggressive approach to training and driving, and you have no speed limits, even in the introductory courses. You are, however, liable for full damages (unless you pay an additional $150 to cap your liability at $3,000).

The half-day introduction to racing puts you into a SCCA spec racer. There's 1 hour in the classroom and 2 hours of driving. The 3-day competition course tries to get you up to top speed as quickly as possible, and includes running starts and practice races with other cars on the track. Introductory courses may have up to 60 students with 4 instructors. The 3- and 5-day programs have a maximum of 14 students and 3 instructors.

The 5-day SCCA-licensing program course is taught in conjunction with the SCCA 3-day course and culminates in a full-blown race. *Fast Company Racing School, Box 151, Greencastle, IN 46135, tel. 317/653–2532 or 800/444–3278, fax 317/653–3046. Jan.–Mar. in Las Vegas, Apr.–Oct. in Indianapolis: half-day introductory course, $250; 3-day competition course, $1,595; 5-day licensing course, $2,750.*

OHIO **The Mid-Ohio School.** This new school, founded in 1993, is owned and operated by '86 Indy winner Bobby Rahal. It's based at the Mid-Ohio Sports Car Course, in Lexington, Ohio, an hour north of Columbus and an hour south of Cleveland.

For serious Indianapolis wannabes, Mid-Ohio has a 5-day fantasy driving camp taught by

Rahal, 3-time Indy winner Johnny Rutherford, and Derek Bell, a two-time World Sports Car Champion. It takes place in August in conjunction with the Indy car race in Lexington, Ohio. The first part of the program includes a demanding 3-day race, with an opportunity to socialize with the pros and talk with them about driving and racing techniques.

Then, on race weekend, you accompany Rahal and Rutherford to the track, where you tour the pits and paddocks (garages), talk with the crews and some drivers, then watch the race from a trackside hospitality suite.

Another school offering, a one-day, high-performance, street-driving course, gives you classroom instruction, car control, and lapping. The 2-day course gives you the chance to master what you learned on day one. The courses are accredited by the SCCA.

A one-day defensive-driving course teaches safe and responsible driving, car control, and greater confidence in emergency situations. A course for teens is also available.

Classes are limited to 25 with a student-to-teacher ratio that never exceeds 4:1. Students are liable for all damage to cars. Rental cars are Hondas. *The Mid-Ohio School, 94 N. High St., Suite 50, Dublin, OH 43017, tel. 614/793–4609, fax 614/793–4621. Mar.–Oct.: 1-day defensive driving, $450; 1-day high performance, $500; 2-day high performance, $900; 1-day teen course, $300. Price does not include car rentals, $150 per day extra. Aug.: 5-day fantasy camp, $4,000. Price includes car, lodging, meals, and ground transportation.*

OKLAHOMA Stephens Racing. Founded in 1986 and accredited by the SCCA, this road-racing-only school in Tulsa, Oklahoma, is growing rapidly and now has its own facility, with 17 cars and a 1.8-mile track. It's headquartered at the Hallett Motor Racing Circuit, in Hallet, Oklahoma, about 40 minutes west of Tulsa.

The half-day introductory course focuses on braking and is followed by 2 hours of driving. The one-day program gives the same instruction with more driving sessions, and ends with a practice race. The 2-day program

offers more of the same, except that students drive in the opposite direction on the second day. Classes are limited to 18 students, with 4 instructors.

Students are liable for all damages, including over-revving the engine and not shifting properly. A $100 insurance policy limits liability to $1,000. *Stephens Racing, 2232 S. Nogales, Tulsa, OK 74107, tel. 918/583–1134, fax 918/583–1135. Year-round: half-day introductory course, $350; 1-day course, $600; 2 days, $1,100; 3 days, $1,600; 4 days, $2,100; 5 days, $2,600. Prices include lunch.*

THE SOUTHWEST

ARIZONA Bob Bondurant School of High Performance Driving. From a base in Phoenix, this IMSA- and SCCA-accredited school offers a complete schedule of courses in Grand Prix road racing, advanced road racing, high-performance defensive driving, and advanced highway driving. Classes are taught year-round on the Firebird International Raceway, as well as on a special adjacent track designed by Bondurant strictly for driver training.

The racing classes use Mustang GTs and Formula Fords. The student-to-instructor ratio is 3:1.

The most popular program is the 4-day Grand Prix road racing course. Days are split between classroom sessions and driving. The first 2½ days are spent in Mustang GTs with the instructor in your car. The last day and a half, you're in a single-seat Formula Ford. A 3-day course, with fewer hours of instruction and slightly less driving time, is also available.

High performance courses, which you can take for either 1, 2, or 3 days, include classroom discussions, driving at high speed, and driving the Bondurant skid cars. Even the one-day course will teach you accident evasion techniques and skid control.

An advanced teenage driving course teaches young drivers basically the same techniques as the high performance course, but without the high speed track time. Students are liable for damages but can pay an additional $50 for insurance protection, with a $750 deductible. Advanced courses are available for graduates of each course or for drivers already certified by the SCCA or IMSA. *Bob Bondurant School of High Performance Driving, Box 51980, Phoenix, AZ 85076-1980, tel. 602/796–1111, fax 602/796–0660. Year-round: 1-day high-performance course, $450 with your own car, $600 with a Bondurant car; 2 days, $895 or $1,195; 3 days, $1,325 or $1,775; 2-day teenage course, $895 or $1,195; 3-day Grand Prix competition course, $1,895; 4 days, $2,495.*

ARIZONA **Right On Track.** Established in 1989, this Illinois-based program is a good bet if you want plenty of seat time and hot laps in winter. Venue then is the Phoenix International Raceway (*see* The Midwest, *above*).

NEVADA **Fast Company Racing School.** This mobile school founded in 1992, which teaches race car driving only, is based at the Indianapolis Raceway Park but moves to the Las Vegas Raceway Park in the winter months (*see* The Midwest, *above*).

THE ROCKIES

COLORADO **Danny Collins Racing School.** Danny Collins has operated this IMSA- and SCCA-accredited, Denver-based, mobile racing school since 1964. He trains drivers year-round, weather permitting, using 5 area tracks; most courses are taught at Second Creek Raceway, about 15 minutes from Denver.

Many of the students are vintage-car racers, as well as SCCA racers. Collins will teach you in whatever car you bring. Insurance is included in the fee.

A one-day introductory course provides one-on-one instruction in an SCCA spec racer or a Formula Continental. The 2-day course teaches the standard racing techniques with emphasis on Collins's safe-passing techniques, which he developed in 1991 with Indy racer Janet Guthrie. *Danny Collins Racing*

School, 1626 Albion St., Denver, CO 80220, tel. 303/388–3875. Year-round: 1 day, $250 in your own car, $600 in the school's car; 2 days, $500 or $1,200. Prices include lunch.

COLORADO **Go 4 It Services.** This school is run by the SCCA Rookie of the Year for 1991, Mike Pettiford. It's a mobile operation that sees most of its action at Second Creek Raceway, 15 minutes outside of Denver, and Mountain View Motor Sports Park in Mead.

Pettiford focuses on driving rather than classroom study, and tailors his program to the needs of each student. He offers all the standard racing courses as well as driving courses for motorcycles, all-terrain vehicles (ATV), and 18-wheelers. The high-performance courses are accredited by the SCCA. Students are liable for damages.

In the racing program, the one-day course concentrates on rules, braking, and turns. The 2-day course uses a skid pad and emphasizes car control. The 3-day program concentrates on racing, passing, lapping, and race strategy. The school rents a Chevrolet IROC-Z, a Camaro, and Mazda RX7s. Classes are restricted to 4 people with one instructor.

The street driving program can run from 10 hours to 4 days. A winter program is also available, with instruction in defensive driving on ice, correct braking on ice and snow, recovering from skids, and methods of getting stuck cars out of snow. *Go 4 It Services, 713 Grant Ave., Louisville, CO 80027, tel. 303/666–4113, fax 303/665–1303. Year-round, but Dec.–Jan. primarily for winter driving courses: 1 day, $300; 2 days, $550; 3 days, $800; street driving, $40 per hour. Price does not include car rentals, which cost $700 extra per day.*

COLORADO **Jean Paul Luc Winter Driving School.** This Steamboat Springs school will make you more confident when the road glazes over. Formerly the Ford Michelin Ice Driving School, founded in 1983 by 1980 World Champion Rally racer Jean Paul Luc, it helps develop good reflexes and teaches you how to enjoy driving on snow- and ice-covered roads and how to avoid panic situations. You'll also have fun sliding and spinning.

A half-day course gives you classroom theory and 2 hours on an ice track. The one-day course offers more driving and a video session. The 1½-day program is a Grand Prix, rally-racing course with ice driving.

Classes average 8 students, with 2 instructors. The program is sponsored by Jeep Eagle, so cars include Eagle Visions, Grand Cherokees, and Eagle Talons. Liability is covered in the price of the course. *Jean Paul Luc Winter Driving School, Box 774167, Steamboat Springs, CO 80477, tel. 303/879–6104, fax 303/879–6105. Dec.–early Mar.: half-day introductory course, $90; 1-day course, $190; 1½-day course, $340.*

THE WEST COAST

CALIFORNIA **Frank Hawley's Drag Racing School.** This Florida-based school has a gas dragster program in September at Bakersfield Raceway in Bakersfield, California, 90 minutes northeast of Los Angeles (*see* The South, *above*).

CALIFORNIA **Jim Hall Kart Racing School.** Go-carts are deceptive in appearance. They are usually about 3 feet wide and 5 feet long, with wheels no bigger than 12 inches in diameter. The chassis usually sits 3 or 4 inches off the ground. The driver is squeezed in, with his or her knees sticking up about wheel level. The carts look like they would putter around a track at 15 miles per hour. In reality, they are as hornets are to ladybugs—they can scream around a track at speeds approaching 130 miles per hour.

Many drivers, including some Indy winners, learned to race first in go-carts, primarily because of the relatively low cost, but also because the vehicle dynamics are exactly the same as in a full-sized race car.

Here in Ventura, there are two tracks: One is 0.3 miles long with 9 turns; the other is 0.4 miles long with 11 turns. Instructors stand out in the infield of the race course and watch every corner.

Courses are offered in half-day modules, numbered 1 to 10 (a half day to 5 days). The first half-day module teaches vehicle dynamics, the best path to drive through each turn, and safety. It also includes 3 sessions on the track of 12 laps each. Each class builds on the last one, with more instruction and more driving, culminating in out-and-out racing.

The school is open year-round and has graduated more than 13,500 drivers since it opened in 1982. *Jim Hall Kart Racing School, 1555-G Morse Ave., Ventura, CA 93003, tel. 805/654–1329, fax 805/654–0227. Year-round: first half-day module, $125; additional modules, about $200 each; 2-day package, $600; 3-day package, $900.*

CALIFORNIA **The Russell Racing School.** Jim Russell opened the first racing school in England in 1957; this American branch—headquartered at the Laguna Seca Raceway in Monterey, California—opened in 1980. It's accredited by both the SCCA and IMSA.

A 3½-hour Russell "test drive" gives you 90 minutes of classroom instruction followed by 2 hours of driving an open-wheel Formula Ford.

Most courses, however, last 3 days. In the comprehensive 3-day race driving course, only half a day is spent in the classroom. The rest of the time you're on the track, lapping and passing, and in timed sessions.

In the 3-day advanced racing course, students drive a Formula Russell car, which is a step up from a Formula Ford, with slick tires, wings, and 5-speed transmission. The emphasis is on advanced car handling and passing, and there are drills on breaking out of a pack of cars at the start.

The Russell street course, taught in Mitsubishi Diamantes, emphasizes defensive rather than high performance driving.

All courses are limited to 15 students, with 5 instructors. In the 3½-hour and 3-day programs students have no liability for the first accident; for the second, they are liable for up to $1,000 in damages. In a Russell car, students are responsible for up to $2,500 in damages. *The Russell Racing School, 1023 Monterey Hwy., Salinas, CA 93908, tel. 408/372–7223, fax 408/372–0458. Year-round:*

3 1/2-hour program, $299; 3-day comprehensive race driving course, $1,895; 3-day advanced course, $2,495; 5-hour street course, $349. 3-day programs include lunch.

OREGON **Pitaressi Motor Sports Racing School.** Along with Roos, this popular Portland school, accredited by the SCCA and IMSA, offers probably the best hands-on racing program. Expect to make plenty of mistakes and learn from them. The school is heavy on car control, and students are made to skid crash through traffic cones up to 20 times before they get up to speed on the race track. The school is so into skid control that it certifies skid-car instructors for law enforcement agencies in North America and supplies other driving schools with skid cars that it imports from Europe.

The school uses the Portland International Raceway, 10 minutes from downtown Portland. Sponsored by Toyota, the program uses MR2s for its driving cars as well as skid cars, which every student learns to handle. All cars have roll cages, harnesses, and dual controls so instructors can ride along. Classes are given every other weekend year-round. December and January classes concentrate on skidding and ice driving.

Students are responsible for damage to cars. *Pitaressi Motor Sports Racing School, 1940 N. Victory Blvd., Portland, OR 97217, tel. 503/285–4449, fax 503/285–0363. Year-round: half-day driver safety course with use of skid car, $175; full-day, $295; 2-day high-performance defensive-driving course, $1,300; 3-day racing course, $1,800. Prices include lunch.*

SOURCES

ORGANIZATIONS The two organizations that award accreditation to racing schools are the **Sports Car Club of America** (9033 E. Easter Pl., Englewood, CO 80112, tel. 303/694–7222, fax 303/694–7391) and the **International Motor Sports Association Inc.** (Box 10709, Tampa, FL 33679-0709, tel. 813/877–IMSA, fax 813/876–4604). Write to them for lists of other approved programs.

PERIODICALS *Racer* (Racer Communications Inc., 1371 E. Warner Ave., Suite E, Tustin, CA 92680, tel. 714/533–4083), a monthly magazine with color photos and high-quality graphics, includes articles on current racing issues and profiles of the sport's daring participants. Published twice a month, *On Track* (OT Publishing, Inc., Box 8509, Fountain Valley, CA 92728, tel. 714/966–1131, fax 714/556–9776) gives in-depth coverage of the international racing scene. *Super Stock and Drag Illustrated* (1655 Broadway, New York, NY 10023, tel. 800/333–3007 or 515/247–7631) is a monthly magazine for drag racing buffs—both those who do it and those who prefer to read about it.

BOOKS Among the best how-to books on racing are *Competition Driving,* by Alain Prost; *Jackie Stewart's Principles of Performance Driving,* by Jackie Stewart, and *Bob Bondurant on High Performance Driving,* by Bob Bondurant. All are available from Classic Motorbooks (Box 1, Osciola, WI 54020, tel. 800/826–6600, fax 715/294–4448).

River Rafting

by Lee R. Schreiber

If the river is the highway into the wilderness, then the raft is the ideal mode of transportation. Rafts can take you places that roads, trails, and footpaths cannot. Then there are the whitewater thrills: Spray that soaks your clothes and stings your face, the roar of rushing water that drowns out your screams, the rolls and drops that leave your heart somewhere back *there*. Unlike canoes, rafts are stable in these high or rough waters, and unlike kayaks, they can carry many passengers and their gear, not to mention the vegetables, fruits, and other ingredients that make for delicious open-air meals.

The United States has some of the most diverse and scenic river highways in the world, from mild to wild, particularly in the mountains of the West. Many people think the Colorado is the finest rafting river in North America, but there are many that are almost its equal. While some rivers are not dammed and raftable only during spring runoff, there are others, particularly in the Northeast, whose flow is maintained at runnable levels from spring through fall by regular water releases from the dams.

Many reputable outfitters can show you America's rivers on guided trips, which make even the rowdiest of this whitewater accessible to the inexperienced. On these trips, the greatest risks are banged shins, sprained ankles, and nasty sunburns. Today's rafts are designed to smack against waves or rocks and bend almost in two without breaking or flipping over, and only occasionally get "wrapped" (around a rock) or "Maytagged" (tossed and turned, as if in a spin cycle). Far from being the high-risk sport that it is often perceived to be, the odds of being seriously injured while whitewater rafting on a commercial trip are about 25,000 to 1, and there is barely one death per million river runners.

Your rafting experience depends first of all on the river. Most provide serenity and the opportunity to catch wildlife unawares, to reach areas deep in the wilderness that would otherwise be accessible only by long hikes.

Other rivers stand out for their whitewater. River rats classify whitewater as *Class I* (mild, with slow current and small riffles), *Class II* (beginner, with moderate waves and rapids, few obstructions, and easy maneuvering), *Class III* (intermediate, with swift current and more obstructions), *Class IV* (advanced, with powerful waves and numerous obstacles; previous experience recommended), *Class V* (expert, with complex and difficult rapids with very strong current and many obstructions). *Class VI* waters are considered unrunnable, entailing probable serious injury. In general, the steeper the river's drop in altitude, the faster the water and the wilder the ride. (When you encounter water too rough

---

Outdoors writer Lee Schreiber, the founding managing editor of Golf Illustrated *and* Backpacking Journal *and the author of six books, has traveled the world in search of a place to enjoy, simultaneously, his three passions: whitewater rafting, poker, and a good cigar.*

to tackle safely, outfitters either portage around the rapid or resort to "lining"—that is, they empty each boat of all but cargo, then attach it to one or more ropes held by several crew members, who walk along the shore guiding the craft through the whitewater while you go around the rapid on foot.)

Outfitters run some terrific Class IV–V water in the East, including West Virginia's New, Gauley, and Cheat rivers, but almost all the runs are day trips. In the West, trips may last a week or two because western rivers themselves are longer, with longer rapids, longer stretches of flatwater, and more and bigger wilderness areas than those found in the East.

The craft you ride varies from outfitter to outfitter and even from trip to trip; sometimes you can bounce around from one kind of boat to another on the same trip. Some outfitters use *motorized rafts,* which allow you to cover more miles of river in less time. The downside is the intrusion of noise and modern technology into the wilderness. You may raft in a so-called *oar boat,* on which a professional guide takes the oars and does the work; no previous rafting experience is required, even on rivers with some serious whitewater. Or you can run the river in a *paddle boat,* where you and the other passengers wield the oars under the guidance of an experienced paddle captain; here you may need experience and a certain level of fitness, depending on the water you'll be covering. Some outfitters also give you the option of traveling in *inflatable kayaks* (called duckies or orange torpedoes); these usually accommodate a single person and require some skill and strenuous paddling. Still other outfitters use *dories*—flat-bottomed, splay-sided wooden row boats with upturned ends, which can usually accommodate 4 passengers plus a guide, and may come equipped with back rests and cushioned seats. Major John Wesley Powell used them to explore the Grand Canyon in 1869—but you can be sure that his craft didn't have padding.

Beyond that, every outfitter has its own style. Some take care of all the camp chores and discourage guest participation, while others invite it. Every trip has its own pace, though usually you spend 4 or 5 hours a day on the river and the rest of the time—during a stop for lunch and at day's end—swimming in placid pools, picnicking, or hiking through the countryside that borders the river. Food on raft trips is invariably tasty (though the freshest foods, like Cornish hens or rack of lamb, come early on, and the vegetable lasagnas show up toward the end; but some outfitters have more interesting menus than others. On multiday trips, particularly down the great western rivers, expect to pay between $100 and $150 per day—sometimes as much as $200.

CHOOSING THE RIGHT TRIP

Outfitting your own trip is recommended only for experienced rafters. Most of us must choose a trip offered by a commercial outfitter. To do this, first pick the river you want to run, then ask several outfitters who run it the following questions:

Are you affiliated with any regional or national organizations? Most companies are; it lends a certain legitimacy and provides a higher authority in case a problem arises.

Are you licensed by the state? Licensing requirements vary from state to state, but, in general, they keep outfitters and guides alert to safety and environmental rules.

What is your safety record, and what are your safety procedures? All rafters should wear life preservers, and commercial outfitters require them (and provide them to all their guests). Helmets are a good idea on Class V and sometimes Class IV water; if you'll be rafting waters with those ratings, ask whether helmets will be provided.

How long has the company been in business? A company that has been in business for a few years is apt to have systematized its operations so that trips go smoothly.

What's the cost and what's included? Ask specifically about ground transportation, camping and personal gear, meals, and drinks, since policies vary widely from one outfitter to the next.

In general, outfitters provide all meals during the trip, as is true on all trips below unless otherwise noted. However, if the itinerary has you overnighting in a town before your river journey begins or after it ends, you may be on your own for meals then. Once the journey has begun, most outfitters serve unlimited water, juice, lemonade, or punch both on and off the river; soda, beer, or wine is usually available at least off the river and sometimes on, and there may or may not be a charge.

As for camping gear, many companies provide a tent but charge extra to rent you a sleeping bag and pad (or ask you to make your own arrangements); unless otherwise noted, that's the case on all the trips described below. Personal gear is another matter. You may need a wetsuit, and it may or may not be included.

Usually included, but not always, is shuttle service to and from the put-in point—known more informally among river runners as, simply, put-in; when it is, it's usually from some central point and not from the airport. However, some firms shuttle you to put-in but not from take-out. Don't forget about your car and your luggage; some outfitters transport your luggage from put-in to take-out at no extra cost, but charge extra to bring your vehicle.

All prices quoted below are adult fares, per person; discounts are usually available for youngsters on trips appropriate for them.

What are your guides' qualifications? Ask how long they have been working with the outfitter and how many years of rafting experience they have. Make sure that they have first-aid certification, if not specialized wilderness first-aid and swift-water rescue training. Knowledge of the history, flora, fauna, and geology of the area is a decided plus.

What's the passenger-to-guide ratio? There is usually one staffer for every 3 to 6 passengers.

How many people will there be in your rafting party? The norm is between 20 and 25. If there are too many in your group, you lose

a sense of wilderness that is one of the pleasures of river rafting.

How much whitewater will there be on the trip? If you are looking for rowdy whitewater, you don't want to end up on a sedate float trip—or vice versa. If you want to ride in an oar boat or an inflatable kayak, find out how much paddling experience is required. Most outfitters want paddling guests to be in good physical condition, and some give a Class V paddler's test, with exercises to evaluate heart, grip, lungs, and even mental adaptability; some even give a prerun oral and written whitewater-safety exam.

What kind of boats do you use? Find out whether the outfitter uses oar boats, paddle boats, motor-powered rafts, or another craft. Ask about the maximum boat capacity, and find out how many people will be riding in each boat (some outfitters routinely don't fill boats to capacity). Find out whether the outfitter's boats are self-bailing. Most top companies have gradually replaced their fleets with self-bailing rafts, which are harder to flip than rafts that aren't; a boat full of water is unstable and hard to keep level. If you'd like to paddle part or all of the distance in an inflatable kayak, and you have the experience to do so, ask whether they're available.

What's the food like? Some outfitters stick to home-cooking, while others aim for Continental flair and ethnic accents; Dutch-oven cooking—that is, baking in a closed pot over an open fire—is fairly commonplace.

What kind of service do you provide? Some outfitters pamper guests and won't allow them to lift a finger; others let them help with camp chores and still others insist on it. Decide what type of service you want and then find the outfitter that provides it.

What are your days like? Find out how much time you spend on the river, and what passengers do the rest of the time. Ask whether people on this trip usually see wildlife, and what kind; and find out, if you're interested, whether there's fishing, what people catch, and whether rods are provided.

What conditions should I expect? Ask about the weather—and find out whether it'll be buggy. You don't want to find out only after put-in that it's the height of black fly or mosquito season.

Do you have a list of previous clients whom I can contact? Reputable outfitters are happy to share the names of previous guests. Talks with them may reveal things about the trip that'll make you decide for or against it.

How far in advance do I need to book? In most cases, it's between 2 and 6 months, but sometimes you must commit yourself even farther ahead, as much as a year in advance. If you have your heart set on going on a specific trip, always call at the last minute if that's possible. Cancellations do occur.

MAJOR PLAYERS

AMERICAN RIVER TOURING ASSOCIATION

Known as ARTA, this nonprofit corporation, in business since 1963, offers about 20 different trips in 5 western states from April through October. Most runs have at least Class III water, appropriate for families and first-timers, while several trips have Class V stretches that challenge the expert paddler. ARTA boats include both 14-foot paddle boats that carry up to 6 guests and a guide, and 18-foot oar boats that accommodate 2 to 4 plus a guide; about half its guests ride in oar boats on longer trips (while most ride in paddle rafts on 1- to 3-day trips). You can opt to share an inflatable kayak on about half of ARTA trips; an equal proportion of the fleet is self-bailing—a little under half of the oar rafts, nearly three-quarters of paddle rafts, and all of the inflatables. Food is first-rate if not fancy, and guides are personable and well-educated, usually ecology-oriented or knowledgeable about local history, with an average 6 years' rafting experience. There is usually one guide trained in either swift-water rescue or wilderness first aid on every trip, and the ratio of guests to staff ranges from 3:1 to 6:1 (the lower ratio applies to difficult trips where there are no paddle rafts

and lighter boats are required). An ARTA trip is informal, and guides make a point of eating with guests. If you want to help in the kitchen, fine; if you want to read a book, that's okay, too. The staff, however, won't set up your tents (they show you how) or wash your dishes (that's up to you). Prices are $100 to $125 per day (24000 Casa Loma Rd., Groveland, CA 95321, tel. 209/962–7873 or 800/323–2782, fax 209/962–4819).

DVOŘÁK'S KAYAK AND RAFTING EXPEDITIONS

Bill and Jaci Dvořák, whose family-owned outfit, founded in 1969, is one of the finest in the country, operate on 10 western rivers through 29 canyons from March through October. They use 12-foot paddle rafts, that accommodate up to 4 passengers and a guide as well as 16-foot oar boats that accommodate up to 7 passengers and a guide; most of the fleet is self-bailing. Both inflatable and hard-shell kayaks are available. Guides have CPR, first-aid, and swift-water rescue training, and an average 3 years' rafting experience; on most rafting trips, there's a guide for every 5 passengers. The Dvořáks will take care of all the camp chores, but you're free to pitch in if you want. You'll find lots of fresh fruit and vegetables on the menu, along with western omelets at breakfast and chicken enchiladas and fajitas at dinner. Prices on the Green River, which are representative, average about $130 a day (17921 U.S. 285, Suite F, Nathrop, CO 81236, tel. 719/539–6851 or 800/824–3795, fax 719/539–3378). *See also* Canoeing and Kayaking in Flatwater and Canoeing and Kayaking in Whitewater.

ECHO: THE WILDERNESS COMPANY

One of the best among several strong California-based outfitters, this firm has been in business since 1971 and runs photo-workshop trips, wine-tasting trips, fly-fishing trips, and classical- and bluegrass-music trips on some of the wildest, most scenic rivers in California, Oregon, Idaho, and Arizona from April through September. On every trip, you can opt for either an oar boat, which accommodates 2 to 4, or a paddle boat, which accommodates 4 to 6; single and double inflatable kayaks are available on the Middle Fork, Main Salmon, and Rogue, but not the American or Tuolumne. The outfitter has a reputation for hiring adaptable, experienced guides with strong personalities; all those on the Rogue, Middle Fork, Main Salmon, and Tuolumne are certified in advanced first aid and swift-water rescue, while many are emergency medical technicians and several are paramedics. They have an average 8 years' experience on the Main Salmon, 4 years' on the Rogue. There is a guide for every 4 guests on the Middle Fork and Tuolumne—which require precision boat handling—and a guide for every 4½ guests on more forgiving rivers. Marinated leg of lamb, baked salmon, and vegetarian lasagna are signature dishes. Trip costs range from $135 to $145 a day (6529 Telegraph Ave., Oakland, CA 94609–1113, tel. 510/652–1600 or 800/652–3246, fax 510/652–3987).

FAR FLUNG ADVENTURES This outfitter, founded in 1975, operates year-round, mostly on well-traveled rivers such as the Salt in Arizona and the Rio Grande in northern New Mexico. But it is really known for its trips in Texas, in and around Big Bend National Park. Guides are friendly professionals with an average of 600 days' river-rafting experience; all are trained in emergency medicine and swift-water rescue. There's one for every 3 to 6 guests. You ride in 14- to 16-foot oar or paddle boats accommodating 4 to 6 passengers plus a guide, and all craft used in white-water are self-bailing. Meals are hearty, not gourmet: breakfasts with bacon or sausage, dinners with steak and potatoes, and make-your-own-sandwich lunches. Average cost of a 7-day trip is $95 per day (Box 377, Terlingua, TX 79852, tel. 915/371–2489 or 800/359–2627, fax 915/371–2325).

GRAND CANYON EXPEDITIONS COMPANY Though most customers fly into and out of Las Vegas, there's no glitz in Mike Denoyer's relatively small operation. Yet this outfitter has been called the Rolls-Royce of Colorado River companies: Every detail of every trip is just a little bit better than on most other out-

fitters' excursions. You can opt for motorized raft runs that take 8 days, paddle expeditions that take 15, or 8-day specialty trips for students of astronomy, geology, photography and the like. Though the capacity of all rafts is 20, there are never more than 14 people in a boat. The 8-day trips run around $200 per day (Box 0, Kanab, UT 84741, tel. 801/644–2691 or 800/544–2691, fax 801/644–2699).

HOLIDAY RIVER EXPEDITIONS This operation, founded in 1966, runs 12 different sections of 8 rivers in 3 western states from May through September; the only constant is the high quality of the equipment, guides, and food. The outfitter uses oar or paddle boats, depending on the stretch of water they're running and the interests of the guests on the trip. Oar-powered boats carry from 4 to 6, paddle boats from 6 to 8; boats are 16 feet to 17½ feet long, and all are self-bailing. Inflatable kayaks are available on most trips. Guides are a diverse lot, but have an average 4½ years of rafting experience and are trained in river rescue, first aid, and CPR, some at advanced levels. They set up camp and cook the meals, but guests are responsible for setting up their own tents; if you want to help with the cooking, you're welcome to pitch in. The passenger-to-guide ratio averages 5:1. Most trips are geared for novice or intermediate paddlers and average $135 per day (544 E. 3900 S, Salt Lake City, UT 84107, tel. 801/266–2087 or 800/624–6323, fax 801/266–1448).

HUGHES RIVER EXPEDITIONS With nearly 30 years experience as a professional guide, Jerry Hughes runs a very tight ship at this family-owned operation, founded in 1976. He offers relatively few trips, most on Idaho and eastern Oregon rivers from May into September; the bulk of trips are on the Middle Fork of the Salmon and the Snake through Hells Canyon. On Hughes trips, the staff attends to virtually every detail, right down to hors d'oeuvres and dinner (roast Cornish hens and the like); by the time you reach camp at the end of each day, the Hughes crew has already pitched the tents, unloaded the gear, and organized the kitchen. Most guides are 35 to 45 years old with an average 12 years of rafting experience; everyone has first-aid and CPR training, and many have emergency medicine, advanced first-aid, or swift-water rescue training (and Hughes has a program of financial incentives to encourage all its guides to acquire the more advanced skills). Water conditions permitting, you can opt for paddle boats or inflatable kayaks as well as oar boats; small, more difficult streams like the Middle Owyhee require smaller and lighter craft, while larger streams are safe for larger oar rafts. All guest boats are self-bailing. The food includes steaks, lobster tail, halibut, baked Cornish hens with wild rice and chutney, and thick-cut pork chops, along with an array of fresh fruit and vegetables; baking-powder biscuits, whole-wheat cornbreads, muffins, coffee cakes, and layer cakes keep the Dutch ovens busy. The superb service comes at a price; most trips cost around $200 a day (Box 217, Cambridge, ID 83610, tel. 208/257–3477, fax 208/257–3476).

OARS This operation, whose name is an acronym for Outdoor Adventure River Specialists, has been taking dudes down a variety of western rivers since 1968. Operating from April into October, it runs several trips in affiliation with other top companies, such as Holiday River, ARTA, and Mountain Travel-Sobek. You can opt for oar or paddle boats and, on some trips, reserve inflatable kayaks. Some 60% of the fleet is self-bailing. Meals always include fresh fruit and vegetables; the staff cooks whip up hearty hot breakfasts, bring out sandwiches and salads at lunch, and bake lasagna or grill salmon steaks for dinner; one night, there's even a Mexican feast. Guides have first-aid and CPR training and an average of 7 years rafting experience. Passengers aren't routinely asked to help with camp chores, but it's always an option; about half the people on any given trip pitch in. There's usually one guide for every 4 passengers on oar trips, one for every 6 passengers on paddle trips. The 6-day run on the Main Salmon costs about $165 per day (Box 67, Angels Camp, CA 95222, tel. 209/736–2924, 209/736–4677, or 800/346–6277, fax 209/736–2902).

MAINE On the Penobscot and the Kennebec. Unicorn Expeditions has been running trips on the wild rivers of New York and Maine since 1979, and unlike most area operators—whose excursions last no longer than a weekend—it has a rafting package that keeps you on the water for 5 days, combining river runs and camping on the Kennebec and the Penobscot with a night in cabins around a lakefront lodge. The Kennebec, about 5 hours by car from Boston and home to some of New England's most popular whitewater rafting, snakes through the spectacular, steep-walled Kennebec Gorge, through Class III and IV rapids. The West Branch of the Penob, as it's known among river rats, is one of the most scenic runs in the East, full of moose, osprey, eagles, and other wildlife. It's also one of the most challenging and dramatic runs in the region, thanks to such natural wonders as the awesome 2-mile-long Ripogenus Gorge—your starting point—where the river descends a stomach-dropping 70 feet per mile over Class V rapids with names like the Exterminator and through the whitewater maze called the Cribworks. The water then smooths out beneath Mt. Katahdin, Maine's tallest peak, before challenging Nesowadnehunk Falls and the finale, Pockwockamus Falls. Except for one 5-mile stretch on the upper Penobscot, which is not suitable for kids (they get shuttled around it), this is good for families. You ride in 14-foot, self-bailing paddle rafts with a guide in each; though each boat can handle up to 10, it usually carries only 8 passengers. The outfitter provides hearty meals, not gourmet fare; barbecued steak is the standard lunch, and lobster puts in appearances at dinner. Campsites are alongside pools where you can often swim—a possibility despite the latitude, since Maine's rivers drain from shallow lakes and run warmer than those in some other parts of the country. You're free to help with camp chores, or you can just kick back if you want. Expect mosquitoes at night, temperatures in the mid-70s to mid-80s, and water temperatures about 60°F. *Unicorn Expeditions, Box T, Brunswick, ME 04011, tel. 207/ 725–2255 or 800/864–2676. Mid-June–early Sept.: 5 days, $524. Sign up 3–6 months in advance.*

THE SOUTHWEST

ARIZONA **After John Wesley Powell on Motorized Rafts.** Grand Canyon Expeditions covers in 8 days much of the same 300 river miles that it took Major John Wesley Powell a month to explore, a stretch of the Colorado that is probably unsurpassed in the world for its combination of whitewater challenges, scenic virtues, and opportunities for off-river exploration. The grandest canyon of them all—from 4 to 18 miles wide and averaging a mile in depth—is no less incredible when you see it from water level instead of the rim. On its walls, nearly 2 billion years of the earth's past is visible, along with every color in the rainbow. In the desert that borders the river on both sides, cactus and wildflowers proliferate, while lush ferns blanket the glens into which magnificent waterfalls cascade. You are likely to see bighorn sheep, mule deer, coyote, and ringtailed cats along the river as well as in the tributary canyons. Each day, you may spot hawks, golden eagles, falcons, great blue herons, or egrets. Deep within the "grand, gloomy depths" that Powell described, there is glorious whitewater—about 200 negotiable rapids in all (including the major ones like Soap Creek, Hermit, Sockdolager, and Lava Falls)—not to mention dozens of hikes to side canyons such as Havasu, the ancestral home of the Havasupai Indians. Here, the red cliffs, green vegetation, and turquoise water are truly spectacular. Some rafters are reluctant to ride a river in a motorized craft. But Grand Canyon Expeditions' 37-foot, self-bailing rafts are spacious, seaworthy, and nonintrusive, allowing you to see the canyon in its entirety in a relatively short time. From put-in at Lees Ferry in Grand Canyon National Park to take-out at Pearce Ferry on Lake Mead, the outfitter's attention to its guests is unflagging. The guides' Dutch-oven cooking is simple but superb. Campsites are diverse and scenic—from sugary sand beaches to a site of ancient Indian ruins. Unusual among river trips, the price of this Grand Canyon run includes round-trip transportation to and from the nearest airport, at Las Vegas. June is the most popular month. *Grand Canyon Expeditions Company, Box O, Kanab, UT 84741, tel. 801/644–2691 or 800/544–2691, fax 801/644–2699. Mid-Apr.–mid-Sept.: 8 days, $1,595. Sign up 10 months in advance.*

ARIZONA **Grand Canyon by Dory.** The gorgeous, flat-keeled wooden dories used by Grand Canyon Dories are akin to those that Major John Wesley Powell took on one of the first expeditions through the canyon in 1869. They offer a totally different experience from conventional or motorized rafts. From the oarsman's perspective, they are more responsive than rafts while demanding better knowledge of the intricacies of the current and the placement of the rocks. For passengers, the ride through riffles is friskier yet the pace of the trip is more leisurely: While motorized craft run the canyon in about 8 days and oar boats in 14, Grand Canyon Dories' trip takes 19 days in early spring and fall, 16 days from spring through late summer.

This company, founded in 1971, has a 2:1 guest-to-crew ratio—probably the lowest on the river—and the guides are among the most experienced in the canyon; their average age is around 38, and nearly a third are women. The food is basic American: hot breakfasts, sandwiches and salads for lunch, and lasagna, salmon, steak, or chicken for dinner. Campsites are on riverside beaches. *Grand Canyon Dories, Box 216, Altaville, CA 95221, tel. 209/736–0805, fax 209/736–2902. Late Apr.– late Sept.: 16 days, $2,791. Apr. and Oct.: 19 days, $2,850. Sign up 12 months in advance.*

ARIZONA **Oar Boats Down the Grand Canyon.** Dick McCallum, the founder and owner of Expeditions, Inc., a small family outfit, has been running rivers throughout the world since 1957. But for him the Grand Canyon will always be a special place. Expeditions' trips down the Colorado are mainly on 18-

foot oar-powered boats, though there is a paddle boat option for those who are willing to make that commitment and even a kayak for experienced paddlers; some people paddle every day and some just want to pit their skills against the Colorado. McCallum and company don't use motors, so the main sound is that of the river rushing through the canyon.

The 14-day trip covers the 226 river miles from Lees Ferry to Diamond Creek, a stretch offering varied experiences away from the river. Campsites might be on wide beaches or on cozy inlets. The guest-to-crew ratio is never more than 5:1, and the guides are all experienced hands who take pride in their knowledge of river lore and love to share it. Expeditions also takes pride in its cuisine, which includes fresh fruit and produce throughout the trip. (Dinners may be full-scale Mexican feasts, or include sautéed boneless chicken breasts or pizza prepared in the Dutch oven; breakfasts are hot or cold, as lavish as you want; lunches are usually cold cuts, tuna, and egg salad.)

Active people who like to hike take these runs, because there's plenty of time to explore off the river, and though McCallum encourages guests' participation in all aspects of the trip, he respects a preference to take it easy. *Expeditions, Inc., R.R. 4, Box 755, Flagstaff, AZ 86001, tel. 602/774–8176, fax 602/774–4001. Apr. and Oct.: 14 days, $1,900. May–Sept.: 12 days, $1,875. Price includes sleeping gear but not tent; sign up 12 months in advance.*

ARIZONA **On the Salt River through the Sonoran Desert.** Winding deep in the White Mountains of Arizona, the Salt cuts through a series of rugged granite gorges in the Sonoran Desert wilderness. In early spring, when the snow at the headwaters melts and bright wildflowers dot the desert floor, Far Flung Adventures' rafting season comes into bloom.

Far Flung's 5-day, 52-mile trip down the Salt from the Highway 60 bridge to the headwaters of the Roosevelt Reservoir near the Highway 288 bridge is chock full of whitewater challenges and hiking opportunities in and around the side canyons, which reveal the many facets of the desert ecosystem. A portion of the trip passes through the White Mountain Apache Indian Reservation. Guides row you past woodlands of juniper, oak, and piñon into areas of arid desert vegetation; on your fourth day out, you can see an eagle's nest from your raft. Most campsites are on wooded beaches and sandbars. If you have rafting experience, you can opt to paddle.

The Salt's water quality is clear, though occasionally silty. Most of the whitewater is rated Class II–III, but there are at least a half-dozen tricky Class IV drops, not to mention the often unrunnable Class V Quartzite Falls. When water levels are low, you may run Quartzite; more often you'll portage or line around it.

Temperatures on the Upper Sonoran desert can range from 70°F to 100°F during the day and drop as low as 40°F at night. March and April are considered optimal months for weather and whitewater conditions. *Far Flung Adventures, Box 377, Terlingua, TX 79852, tel. 915/371–2489 or 800/359–2627, fax 915/371–2325; or Box 2804, Globe, AZ 85502, tel. 602/425–7272. Early Feb.–mid-June: 5 days, $650. Sign up 2–3 months in advance.*

TEXAS **Floating the Rio Grande's Lower Canyons.** Far Flung's 7-day trip through an 85-mile stretch in the Chihuahuan Desert, in 14- to 16-foot paddle or oar boats that accommodate 4 to 6 passengers and a guide, is not a run you make for unadulterated whitewater thrills. Generally, the whitewater you encounter on the first 4 or 5 days is relatively mild, including Big Canyon (Class II–III), Palmas Canyon (Class III), and Rodeo (Class II–III); the sixth day brings the best run of whitewater on the trip, Burro Bluff rapid (Class III–IV). The attractions here are scenery and wildlife. Throughout the run, the river is lined with limestone cliffs with names like Las Vegas de las Ladrones (Outlaw Flat) and Complejo del Caballo (Horse Highlands); beyond them are spectacularly sculpted side canyons. Stay alert and you may catch a glimpse of a peregrine falcon, bighorn sheep, cougar, or even a bear; more than 400 different species of birds have been catalogued in the canyons, and close to 100 species may be sighted during spring and fall migrations. In the early spring, wildflowers abound, and in late summer you can gather prickly pear and pitaya—the fruit is ripe then and delicious. Autumn, with its cooler temperatures and higher water levels, is the peak time to explore the many tributary canyons, where you usually make camp. Group size ranges from a minimum of 4 to a maximum of 16. *Far Flung Adventures, Box 377, Terlingua, TX 79852, tel. 915/371–2489 or 800/359–4138, fax 915/371– 2325. Monthly, year-round, coinciding with the full moon: 7 days, $650. Sign up 1 month in advance.*

TEXAS **Floating the Remotest Rio Grande.** This 65-mile, 7-day run through two magnificent limestone canyons, in the eastern part of Big Bend National Park along the Mexican border, is easily the most remote in Texas: Put-in at Talley is a 2-hour drive from Rio Grande Village along the eastern side of the Chisos Mountains, past the ruins of the Mariscal Mine. The scenery is the reward. After about 3 miles on the river, the expedition enters Mariscal Canyon within the Chihuahuan Desert and continues southeasterly between 1,600-foot cliffs to the Tight Squeeze, the only really challenging rapid on the entire trip: Here, the entire river flows through a narrow channel no wider than a raft. Subsequent miles bring you to the unusual Cactus Garden, across the border in Mexico, where you might find more than one of a half-dozen cactus varieties blooming simultaneously—not to mention many arroyos and canyons, 105°F hot springs you can soak in, and such picturesque Mexican villages as San Vicente and Boquillas. Among the most notable campsites is the broad, grassy stretch at Cross Canyons, where ancient Indian petroglyphs are displayed on a huge boulder. The Mexican-style egg dishes prepared at breakfast go right along with the scenery.

Conditions are usually best in spring and fall: Peak seasons are March and April, and October and November, when temperatures are 80°F to 90°F by day and 50°F to 60°F at night (down from summer highs that can reach a brutal 110°F). Water temperatures are generally at least 65°F in spring, more than

80°F in summer. Water levels are usually highest from August to October because of late-summer thundershowers. Far Flung uses 14- to 16-foot oar boats accommodating 3 to 6 passengers and a guide, but if there are at least 5 willing paddlers, you can opt for a paddle boat—and no experience is required. *Far Flung Adventures, Box 377, Terlingua, TX 79852, tel. 915/371–2489 or 800/359–4138, fax 915/371–2325. Year-round: 7 days, $600. Sign up 1 month in advance.*

UTAH **The Colorado River through Cataract Canyon.** Sheri Griffith Expeditions' 5-day run, named for the 36-mile-long canyon that is its major feature, actually covers 96 river miles in southern Utah's spectacular Canyonlands National Park. Anasazi and Fremont Indians lived here 700 to 1,500 years ago, and you can still see evidence of their existence along the river, along with about 300 million years of geological history. Because of the canyon's diverse environments, many species of plants and wildlife thrive, including both water-storing cacti and fragile wildflowers; if you look carefully, you might spot mule deer, bobcats, coyotes, muskrats, owls, and eagles; the herd of desert bighorn sheep here is the largest in the West. The river is also home to the endangered Colorado squawfish and humpback chub.

July, when the water level drops and the rapids become more moderate, is the best time for first-time river runners and youngsters, though the trip is never really suitable for children under 10. In May and June, you can experience some of the region's most challenging whitewater. In any season, the biggest thrills come on your third day out, when the Colorado flows into the Green, doubles in size, and drops precipitously over at least 24 rapids in 17 miles, including a Class V stretch that includes Big Drops, Little Niagara, Satan's Gut, and Mile-Long, a series of sheer drops and powerful whitewater. You spend the last day floating into Lake Powell, where you climb aboard a chartered aircraft for a 30-minute trip back to Moab, the trip's starting point and the site of the lot where guests' cars are parked. The trip is in 18-foot, 6-passenger oar-powered rafts; paddle boats are available by advance arrangement at some water levels (sometimes at additional cost). Campsites are on sandy beaches, and meals are western-style—grilled steaks with fried potatoes, southwestern barbecued chicken and steamed vegetables, fajitas and a Mexican casserole, with Dutch-oven cakes and crisps for dessert. All guides are trained in first aid, CPR, wilderness medicine, and river rescue. Griffith also offers luxury trips, with a fancier menu; staffers break and set up camp each day, so that all you have to do is sit back and relax. *Sheri Griffith Expeditions, Box 1324, Moab, UT 84532, tel. 801/259–8229 or 800/332–2439, fax 801/259–2226. May–mid-Sept.: 5 days, $748. Price does not include tent but does include flight and ground transportation from take-out to Moab; sign up 3–6 months in advance.*

UTAH **Floating the Green River through Dinosaur National Monument.** "Bus" Hatch, who built his first wooden boat in 1929, was one of the pioneers of the river-running industry. Now, 65 years later, his heirs are still providing first-rate service on this 47-mile stretch of the Green River in Dinosaur National Monument—a relatively easy trip with mostly Class II–III whitewater.

Beginning near Maybelle, Colorado, at the northern border of the Monument, Don and Meg Hatch River Expeditions' 5-day run of the Green passes through Lodore, Whirlpool, and Split Mountain canyons—all serpentine, high-walled chasms, but each distinct: In Lodore, the bright green box elder trees contrast starkly with the vermillion-tinted cliffs; both Whirlpool and Split canyons have bone-white sandstone walls. En route, you're likely to see bighorn sheep, deer, beaver, and otter. Releases from the dam at Flaming Gorge Reservoir sustain the river at runnable levels throughout the season. Mostly, the Hatches use 18-foot, self-bailing oar boats with 5 passengers, but paddle options are available as well. Of the campsites, Rippling Brook, usually reached on the second or third day, is a favorite. In addition to a sandy beach and a scenic little swimming hole, it has a couple of good hiking areas nearby. Blueberry pancakes always appear during the trip at break-

fast, and the afternoon watermelon breaks are popular; rainbow trout and orange or teriyaki chicken are among the selections served at dinner. The passenger-to-guide ratio is usually 5:1 or less, and guests are usually required only to set up their own camp area, though they're welcome to help the guides with chores. *Hatch River Expeditions, Box 1150, Vernal, UT 84078, tel. 801/789–4316 or 800/342–8243. Mid-May–mid-Sept.: 5 days, $530. Price does not include tent; sign up 2–3 months in advance.*

UTAH **Petroglyphs and Pottery Shards: Floating the San Juan.** The San Juan River—which runs through the San Juan Canyon, cutting and winding through the San Juan Goosenecks—is probably the least traveled of the forks that flow from the Grand Canyon on the Colorado River. That's the destination of a 5-day OARS trip, which uses oar rafts that accommodate 4 passengers and a guide. The waters are calm and usually warm in the canyon, and the surrounding area holds more archeological and geological interest than most of the Colorado River tributary trips: You see signs of the ancient Anasazi Indian culture and stunning rock formations and petroglyphs, and you may find pottery shards and ceremonial medicine sticks. The campsites are on broad, sandy beaches surrounded by tall, red-rock walls and cliffs. From put-in near Bluff, Utah, past Mexican Hat and on to take-out at Clay Hills Crossing, the 84 river miles move quickly but easily; the waters are fast-moving, but with no rapids above Class II. For that reason, this trip is excellent for novices and families with young children. *OARS, Box 67, Angels Camp, CA 95222, tel. 209/736–4677 or 800/346–6277, fax 209/736–2902. Late Mar.–Aug.: 5 days, $656. Price does not include tent; sign up 6–9 months in advance.*

UTAH AND COLORADO **Running the Green: Whitewater through Butch Cassidy Country.** Modern-day adventurers can follow in the path of such legendary figures as outlaw Butch Cassidy and explorer John Wesley Powell, who called the canyon wilderness covered by this 6-day, 86-mile Dvořák trip on the

Green River "a region of wildest desolation"; it remains one of the most primitive desert wilderness areas in the United States, scattered with Indian petroglyphs, abandoned homesteads, and caves. On the river, there are more than 60 rapids, progressing from unnamed Class I riffles to Class III+ raft-rattlers such as Three Fords, Steer Ridge, and Coal Creek, which will give you a taste of whitewater but won't get you too wet. Though the river is navigable from April to October, Dvořák runs scheduled trips only from May into September (but will do custom trips before or after then if conditions permit). The experience is most exciting in late May and June, when the water is highest, while July and August runs provide hot weather, warm water, and good swimming; fall pairs the same warm water with crisp, clear air. You make the run in 14- to 16-foot paddle or oar rafts, most of which are self-bailing; inflatable kayaks are almost always available. Campsites along the Green are numerous and spacious. Most areas adjoin side canyons with good hiking; some are near streams and springs. Dvořák does a lot of baking, and whole-grain breads, brownies, and upside-down cakes make regular appearances, along with pancakes, French toast, and western omelets in the morning. One additional highlight to this run is worth mentioning: the flight to put-in. The air charter, which usually takes off at 8 AM on the departure day (and is included in the trip price), gives each passenger a 45-minute bird's-eye view of the entire stretch of raftable river. *Dvořák's Kayak and Rafting Expeditions, 17921 U.S. 285, Suite F, Nathrop, CO 81236, tel. 719/539–6851 or 800/824–3795, fax 719/539–3378. Apr.–Oct.: 6 days, $825. Price does not include tent; sign up 3–6 months in advance.*

UTAH AND COLORADO **Floating the Yampa through Dinosaur National Monument.** The Yampa is the last major undammed river in the Colorado River system, and Holiday River Expeditions' 4- and 5-day trips on 46 miles of it are extraordinary, taking you through the rugged Dinosaur National Monument wilderness, and along 25 miles of the scenic Green River, notable for the exciting green waters of Whirlpool Canyon and Split Mountain Gorge. In May and June, the only months that waters are high enough for this trip, the Yampa reveals not only its several miles of Class I–III waters but also the daunting Class IV Warm Springs. En route, sheer, white tiger-striped sandstone cliffs rise to 2,000 feet and dizzying overhangs stand sentry over the fast-moving waters; you may glimpse bighorn sheep, deer, otters, beavers, golden eagles, and other birds of prey. The trip, usually made in 17½-foot self-bailing rafts that accommodate 4–6, is ordinarily an oar-powered affair because the water is so cold at this time of year, but paddle trips are available to those who have the right gear (wetsuits) and the right attitude (energetic). Both the 4- and 5-day trips allow plenty of time for hiking in and around side canyons ribboned with waterfalls or displaying ancient art on rocks and in cool caves. The campsites are well-used but well-maintained. Dinners include chicken fajitas, grilled salmon, and filet mignon plus potatoes and rice. Don't pass up the Big Drop Omelet for breakfast. *Holiday River Expeditions, 544 E. 3900 S, Salt Lake City, UT 84107, tel. 801/266–2087 or 800/624–6323, fax 801/266–1448. May–June: 4–5 days, $552–$622. Price does not include tent; sign up 3 months in advance.*

THE ROCKIES

COLORADO **Classical Music River Journey on the Dolores.** Each June, musicians from the Los Angeles Philharmonic and the Santa Fe Symphony load their instruments onto one of Dvořák's rafts for an 8-day, 100-mile trip on the river the Spanish originally dubbed El Rio de Nuestra Señarret de Dolores (the River of Our Lady of Sorrows), through southwestern Colorado's remote Four Corners wilderness area. You ride in 14-foot paddle and oar rafts accommodating 5–7 people, over the Class III–IV torrent at Ponderosa Gorge and the Class II–III waters of Arret Canyon downstream. En route, you and up to 16 other passengers are treated to 4 after-dinner fireside chamber concerts of Bach, Handel, Mozart, Ravel, Hindemith, and Dvořák (fifth cousin to outfitter Bill Dvořák) amid the tall sandstone cliffs and towering Ponderosa pines of huge natural amphitheaters. Great blue heron have been known to flock around these sessions, and Dvořák's symphonic journey has become something of a classic since it was first offered in 1984. Meals are appropriately highbrow, and include shrimp scampi and blackened salmon. Some say the trout fishing on the river is Colorado's best; off-river, you can explore 800- to 1,200-year-old Anasazi Indian ruins. *Dvořák's Kayak and Rafting Expeditions, 17921 U.S. 285, Suite F, Nathrop, CO 81236, tel. 719/539–6851 or 800/824–3795, fax 719/539–3378. June: 8 days, $1,450. Price does not include tent; sign up 9–12 months in advance.*

IDAHO **Running the River of No Return: the Main Salmon.** This majestic stream, which flows through the 2.3-million-acre Frank Church River of No Return Wilderness Area—the largest designated wilderness area in North America outside Alaska—stands out for its mix of big whitewater and unspoiled wilderness. Everything about the Salmon is big. The river as a whole is the longest undammed river in the Lower 48, and during an average spring run-off, its whitewater is so fearsome that explorers Lewis and Clark decided to take another route when they saw it in 1805. (The same awesome whitewater prompted a 1935 National Geographic expedition to dub it "The River of No Return.") The Class III–IV Bailey Falls, Devil's Toe, Ludwig, Dried Meat, and Vinegar are the most challenging rapids as well as some of the most colorfully named, and there are also several Class IV–V rapids, including Salmon Falls, Elkhorn, and the awe-inspiring Big Mallard.

ECHO's 6-day, 81-mile run, in paddle rafts, oar rafts, and inflatable kayaks, captures a big part of the Salmon's flavor, leading you from put-in at Corn Creek (a 2½-hour drive from the town of Salmon via a remote stretch of rather bad road) through a huge canyon with steep, sparsely forested walls and wide-open country of sagebrush and grass. Each day presents its bit of whitewater followed by stretches of calm water. Wildlife sightings are a con-

stant, especially around the river's hot springs. Bighorn sheep wander to the river's edge, eagles swoop overhead, and an occasional moose stands in silent stateliness. On rare occasions, one of the estimated 5,000 extant mountain lions will show its face. Here and there is the evidence of human habitation: on cave walls, the handiwork of the Native Americans who called this canyon home for many centuries; as well as homesteaders' and miners' empty cabins, some of which are now museums. Among these is the former home of Jim Moore of Sylvan Hart—also known as Buckskin Bill, the last of the Mountain Men.

Campsites are among the finest on any river: wide, sandy beaches near clear side streams and hot springs. For dinner, there's vegetarian lasagna, grilled lamb, chicken fajitas, or other hearty fare, with chocolate or lemon cake for dessert. *ECHO: The Wilderness Company, 6529 Telegraph Ave., Oakland, CA 94609, tel. 510/652–1600 or 800/652–3246, fax 510/652–3987. June–Sept.: 6 days, $865. Price includes sleeping bag; sign up 1–6 months in advance.*

IDAHO **Whitewater and Rocky Mountain Kettle Cuisine: the Salmon's Middle Fork.** The primitive, awesome Middle Fork of the Salmon, one of the original 8 rivers to be designated Wild and Scenic by Congress in 1980, is still untamed and, for the most part, untouched; like the Main Salmon, it meanders through the Frank Church River of No Return Wilderness Area. Its whitewater is rated up to Class V in May and June, Class IV in July and August. It's an extraordinary stream, and the outfitters that run it are all topnotch. Even in that company, the 6-day, 105-mile trip run by Rocky Mountain River Tours (founded in 1978) stands out. Owners Dave and Sheila Mills use 2 paddleboats (accommodating 6), 4 oar boats (accommodating 4), and 4 inflatable single-passenger kayaks. There's one guide for every 4 guests.

In 1992, the Idaho Governor's Conference on Recreation and Tourism cited the Mills for their efforts to provide a quality whitewater rafting experience while preserving Idaho's environment. Sheila Mills's Dutch-oven cooking is an essential part of the experience, and after each trip many participants buy copies of her cookbook, *Rocky Mountain Kettle Cuisine II,* so that they can re-create, at home, her unusually interesting fare: sweet potato pancakes, fondue, or squash bread at breakfast; and for dinner, lemon-broccoli risotto with grilled catfish, Thai shrimp and Caribbean beans with papaya salsa, or crab-stuffed chicken breasts. Guides, most around 40 years old with a decade or more on the Middle Fork, are among the state's most experienced. Virtually every camp is spectacular, with a white sand beach, hot springs, and a stand of towering conifers. The Mills make camp early each day; you can help with camp chores if you wish, and there's ample opportunity to hike, fish for trout, swim, or just watch the deer, elk, mountain sheep, goats, otter, birds, and other wildlife. You can also explore caves with ancient pictographs and other Tukedeka Indian sites, old mines, homesteads, and hot springs—many accessible only by river. *Rocky Mountain River Tours, Box 2552, Boise, ID 83701, tel. 208/345-2400, 208/756-4808 June–Aug., fax 203/939-9370. May–Sept.: 6 days, $795–$1,370 (special rates in May). Prices include sleeping bags and pads; sign up 6 months in advance.*

IDAHO **Running the Snake River through Hells Canyon.** The Snake is one of America's Wild and Scenic Rivers, and Hughes River Expeditions' 83-mile trip down it runs through the rugged heart of the extraordinary Wallowa-Whitman National Forest straight into Hells Canyon, the country's deepest chasm (at one point, it's an incredible 8,032 feet from rim to river); the only people you're likely to see are other rafting parties, jet-boaters, and the occasional hiker, tramping the trail that skirts the river. The Snake runs high and fast between grass-covered slopes or stark basalt cliffs and beneath a scattering of ponderosa pines, producing some of the best Class III–IV whitewater in the Rockies. Water conditions permitting, rafts (all self-bailing) are normally 16- and 17½-foot oar boats accommodating 4 guests and a guide; 13- to 16-foot paddle rafts accom-

modating 4 to 6 guests and a guide; and, in less challenging waters, one-man inflatable kayaks. In between rapids, Hughes allows ample opportunity to explore abandoned homesteads and Native American petroglyphs, rock shelters, and house pits, and to look for mule deer, black bear, bighorn sheep, mountain goats, cougar, elk, golden eagles, and chukar partridge. Smallmouth bass, rainbow trout, white sturgeon, channel catfish, and steelhead proliferate in these waters, and fishing is excellent. However, since the river has been dammed, there are few beaches, so campsites are in scenic grassy clearings several yards off the water. Hughes's luxurious menu includes Cornish game hens and Dutch-oven desserts. *Hughes River Expeditions, Box 217, Cambridge, ID 83610, tel. 208/257-3477, fax 208/257-3476. Late May–Sept.: 5 days, $960. Price includes sleeping bags and pads; sign up 2–6 months in advance.*

IDAHO **A Wilderness Experience on the Wildest Selway.** This river is one of the remotest in the Lower 48, and the surrounding 1.24-million-acre Selway–Bitterroot National Forest is among the most beautiful anywhere. To help preserve the Selway's unspoiled canyon, the Forest Service allows no more than one trip to launch each day. So ARTA's 5-day run down the Selway—which you make, depending on the water level, in 4 18-foot oar rafts or 3 18-foot paddle rafts accompanied by a 14-foot paddle raft (all self-bailing)—is among the very best wilderness experiences in the United States.

The Selway drops an average of 28 feet per mile (steep for navigable whitewater—the Colorado drops 8 feet per mile through the Grand Canyon), and during the river's rather short season (mid-June to mid-July), the Class IV+ whitewater flows up to an amazing 10,000 cubic feet per second; in one 5-mile stretch, the river falls 300 feet. In addition to such whitewater challenges, the entire 47-mile trip provides top-notch catch-and-release fishing, superb campsites, scattered remnants of the great culture of the Nez Perce Indians, and extraordinary wildlife—eagles, hawks, grouse, deer, elk, bighorn sheep, mountain goats, moose, and black bear.

Campsites are small, sandy beaches edged with moss and ferns. Evergreens dominate the landscape; footpaths such as the Selway River Trail, which parallels the river, lead through the lush groves of fir and pine you can see from the river, and cedars 5 feet in diameter rise to 100 feet in the clear mountain air. *ARTA, 24000 Casa Loma Rd., Groveland, CA 95321, tel. 209/962–7873 or 800/323–2782, fax 209/962–4819. Mid-June–mid-July: 5 days, $990. Price does not include tent; sign up at least a year in advance.*

WYOMING **The Grand Teton Float Trip on the Snake River.** On OARS's 5-day Snake River float trips from just south of Yellowstone, the scenery is some of the most dramatic in the United States: The ragged 10,000-foot saw-toothed granite peaks of the Grand Tetons loom above you like sentries. But the trips are perfect for kids and first-timers. Rapids are never above Class I, and for 3 days you're based at wilderness camps alongside Jackson Lake, a short float downstream and a 16-mile motor-powered ride from put-in at Flagg Ranch. En route, there are hidden estuaries and wildflower-carpeted meadows to explore, inevitably revealing moose, antelope, elk, killdeer, pelicans, bald eagles, osprey, great blue heron, beaver, sandhill cranes, or even, with luck, shaggy bison. A series of glacier-fed waterfalls is accessible by a vigorous hike; cutthroat trout are native to the waters; and the sunsets are amazing. The last 2 days are on the Snake with the motors turned off, gliding in front of the awesome Teton range. *OARS, Box 67, Angels Camp, CA 95222, tel. 209/736–2924, 209/736–4677, or 800/346–6277, fax 209/736–2902. Late May–early Sept.: 5 days, $770. Sign up 2–3 months in advance.*

THE WEST COAST

OREGON **Floating the Free-Flowing Lower Owyhee.** The 220-mile Owyhee (pronounced *oh-WHY-hee*), undammed in its entirety, is one of the longest wilderness rivers in the Lower 48, and probably one of the most obscure. That's because it winds through remote parts of northern Nevada, southwestern Idaho, and southeastern Oregon, and because it has such a short season: mid-April through May. However, it has great scenery—rugged canyons of basalt and reddish-purple rhyolite, with cliff walls rising 1,000 feet up to meet sagebrush plateaus. Since it is undammed, the Lower Owyhee, in southeastern Oregon, is only runnable when the high-mountain snows are melting and even then offers nothing more challenging than Class III waters. The 6-day, 63-mile trip from Rivers Odyssey West (ROW) shows off this wild, free-flowing stream at its best. You can opt for oar or paddle boats, or inflatable kayaks.

Enthusiastic, experienced river runners, cooks, naturalists, and entertainers all, ROW guides hold seminars on the area's natural history and varied wildlife daily. The passenger-to-guide ratio is 4:1. They happily do all the work, but encourage you to paddle, gather firewood, or help out around the campfire as the staff prepares dishes such as apple-pecan pancakes or eggs Benedict for breakfast, Thai tuna salad and guacamole in addition to the more usual cold cuts and peanut butter-and-jelly sandwiches at lunch, and, in the evening, hors d'oeuvres followed by platters of baked salmon, stuffed Cornish hens, or spinach lasagna, with double fudge brownies, pineapple upside-down cake, and other sweets for dessert. You don't have to help prepare this spread; you go off for a soothing soak in one of the nearby hot springs instead, where only the occasional bighorn sheep and antelope will watch you. ROW is committed to what it calls "responsible stewardship" of the rivers on which it operates, and carries out everything that comes in, even campfire ashes. *Rivers Odyssey West, Box 579, Coeur d'Alene, ID 83816, tel. 208/765–0841 or 800/451–6034, fax 208/667–6506. Mid-Apr.–May: 6 days, $990. Price includes transportation to and from Boise; sign up 2–4 months in advance.*

OREGON **Whitewater on the Middle Owyhee.** The Middle Owyhee has some of the Northwest's best runnable whitewater, as well as some of its most dauntingly unrunnable. You can see it on a 7-day, 95-mile run with Hughes River Expeditions in 16-foot oar rafts with 2 guests and a guide in each boat, or—water conditions permitting—in 13- or 15-foot paddle rafts accommodating between 4 and 6 guests and a guide, or in inflatable kayaks. There are usually 10 guests and 5 guides on Hughes's Middle Owyhee trips.

After a few hours of flatwater and gentle curves, you hit the rapids: a ¼-mile-long, Class IV+ S-turn, littered with boulders; about a half mile beyond, the Class V+ Cable, which you must line through or portage around; the notorious Class IV Ledge, a narrow gap punctuated with apartment-size boulders; and the grand finale, winding Class IV+ Half Mile and the ferocious Class VI Widowmaker, which you line—its scattered boulders are house-size. In between are seemingly endless miles of snappy little rapids punctuated by silent stretches, where you're floating between steep basalt and rhyolite cliffs and grassy slopes and past steep trails to magnificent overlooks, petroglyphs, and hot springs. Throughout the trip, you can expect to see lots of wildlife: Canada geese, mule deer, bighorn sheep, coyote, antelope, bobcats, cougar, prairie falcons, chukar, otter, and golden eagles.

The first night's camp—on a natural terrace surrounded by junipers—is typical of those on the Middle Owyhee. Here you get your first taste of the outfitter's hors d'oeuvres and excellent meals. *Hughes River Expeditions, Box 217, Cambridge, ID 83610, tel. 208/257-3477, fax 208/257-3476. Apr.–May: 7 days, $1,550. Price includes sleeping bags and pads; sign up 2–6 months in advance.*

OREGON **A Whitewater Expedition on the Upper Owyhee.** ROW's 7-day, 120-mile trip travels a section of this river so remote that only 200 rafters run it each year; it's one of the most remote rivers in the United States outside Alaska. The area is home to the Lower 48's largest breeding population of bighorn sheep and antelope and it's on the Pacific Flyway, which means that golden eagles, falcons, hawks, and waterfowl abound, and many nest in the area. In early spring, the only time the Upper Owyhee can be run, the desert canyon is bursting with bloom, and otter and beaver are hard at work. In keeping with the remote quality of the area, ROW's trips are more expedition-style than its trips on the Lower Owyhee. Camp comforts are at a minimum; you won't find little tables and chairs at mealtimes, as on other trips, for instance. Oar rafts predominate on these trips on the stream, which is rated up to Class IV.

Day hikes up the canyon take in Native American rock carvings and frontier settlers' abandoned stone cabins, many complete with cookstoves and whiskey bottles. The campsites are on white-sand beaches among twisted juniper trees and sagebrush. Food is about the same as on Lower Owyhee trips, but a bit simpler. *Rivers Odyssey West, Box 579, Coeur d'Alene, ID 83816, tel. 208/765-0841 or 800/451-6034, fax 208/667-6506. Mid-Apr.–May: 7 days, $1,180. Sign up 2–4 months in advance.*

OREGON **Running the Rowdy Rogue.** Named for a renegade band of Native Americans in the Siskiyou Mountains, the Rogue begins its run in central Oregon's Cascade Mountains and heads south and then west before emptying into the Pacific several miles north of the California border. Big, full, and fast, it is one of the most beautiful rivers in the Northwest, maybe in the entire country. ECHO's 4- or 5-day, 45-mile trip, using 15- to 17-foot oar rafts that accommodate 2 to 4, 14-foot paddle rafts that accommodate 4 to 6, and inflatable single and double kayaks, covers by far the wildest and most exciting section of the Rogue—a stretch so special that Congress designated it Wild and Scenic. It is especially satisfying for wildlife lovers, since you often sight deer, otter, osprey, great blue heron, raccoons, spawning salmon, and even black bear at night, and occasionally hear a coyote howl. But the waters challenge whitewater enthusiasts; daily dam releases assure mostly Class III–III+ levels, with at least 3 challenging Class IV rapids at Rainey Falls, Mule Creek Canyon, and Blossom Bar. For an even wilder ride, you can opt for a kayak for part or all of the run.

ECHO's campsites on the Rogue are sandy, heavily forested, and isolated—perfect complements to a sunset drink and a hearty, well-prepared dinner of barbecued steak or chicken fajitas. The season runs from June through September, but July and August are probably optimal considering weather and water temperatures. *ECHO: The Wilderness Company, 6529 Telegraph Ave., Oakland, CA 94609, tel. 510/652–1600 or 800/652–3246, fax 510/652–3987. June–Sept.: 4–5 days, $570–$650. Price does not include tent; sign up 1–6 months in advance.*

WASHINGTON AND OREGON **The Grande Ronde by Dory.** For solitude, wildlife, and lovely scenery coupled with the gentlest of thrills, an excellent choice is this 5-day, 75-mile trip in the Blue and Wallowa mountains by Northwest Dories, an affiliate of Grand Canyon Dories. As on the latter's trips, this one is in dories. Though the Grande Ronde moves swiftly, frequent stops for fishing and hiking keep the pace leisurely. Bird-watching is the order of the day, and you may spot nesting bald eagles and osprey, as well as deer, elk, beaver, geese, and bear. The canyon walls stair-step upward on either side, with small terraces where grass, flowers, and trees grow; occasionally you see bizarre basalt spires known as hoodoos.

The waters of the Grande Ronde rise to Class II at Red Rock, Vincent Falls, and Sheep Creek. Northwest Dories, unusual among area outfitters, tackles the rumbling Class III Narrows just above the confluence with Joseph Creek. Campsites are in wild wooded areas by the river, dinners often star fresh trout, and the guides tend to be older and more experienced than most on this river (with 30% of them women). There is normally one guide per 4 guests on this trip; you help load and unload the boats, but the guides do all the other camp chores, except washing your dishes. *Northwest Dories, Box 216, Altaville, CA 95221, tel. 800/877–3679, fax 209/736–2902. June: 5 days, $619. Sign up 2 months in advance.*

ALASKA

SOUTHEAST **Floating the Alsek River.** The people at Mountain Travel-Sobek have been known to call the Alsek the "most spectacular wild and scenic river in the world," and few who have made this 12-day, 180-mile run argue with that assessment. Fed by numerous side streams and glaciers, the river gathers force as it races toward the coast with exhilarating Class III–IV whitewater in the shadow of huge, stark peaks and ominous glaciers, between barren rock canyons, through sweeping forests, and across vast alluvial plains. Sometimes you can even glimpse a grizzly from the boats, and day hikes into the mountains offer splendid river views and long looks at moose, mountain goat, and red fox.

Midway through the run, which you make in 18-foot oar rafts, ultra-stable to avoid flipping into the icy waters, comes the encounter with 5-mile-long, 30-foot-wide Turnback Canyon. The huge rapids and low water temperatures here make it too dangerous even to line; instead, you ride over the rocky chasm via helicopter. On the other side, the terrain is palpably greener. Bald eagles perch along the mossy cliffs. Flowing down from the Fairweather Range are at least a dozen glaciers, a congregation of mammoth, fantastically shaped ice floes, whose huge chunks break off and fall into the clear water. One of these glaciers, the Walker, is a popular destination of hikers.

Each campsite is more ruggedly beautiful than the last. You might dine on shrimp-stuffed avocado or freshly caught salmon, and spend evenings around the campfire watching the Northern Lights. In summer, temperatures range from the 50°F to 75°F by day down to the 40s at night; rain is common. *Mountain Travel-Sobek, 6420 Fairmont Ave., El Cerrito, CA 94530, tel. 510/527–8100 or 800/227–2384, fax 510/525–7710. Early July–mid-Aug.: 12 days, $2,195. Price does not include several meals; sign up 6–9 months ahead.*

SOUTHEAST **Rafting the Tatshenshini River.** Alaska Discovery, which has plied these northern waters since 1972, offers an unmatched 10-day, 160-mile adventure on the legendary Tat, through some of the wildest and remotest river country in North America. Alaska Discovery runs the river in 18-foot oar rafts that accommodate 4 guests and a guide; up to 4 passengers can wield paddles on request.

The wildest rapids come soon after launch, plunging each raft into the whirling Class III waters of the Tatshenshini Gorge. The rest of the run includes mostly Class II whitewater. The real draw is the scenery, and sometimes you spend 2 nights in a single campsite because there is so much to explore. Near the river, hikes reveal moose, bear, mountain goat, lots of bald eagles, and, occasionally, wolves. At the confluence of the Tatshenshini and the Alsek, the outfitter's campsite offers a wonderful view of both river valleys bookended by glacier-encrusted peaks. The next site is near a glacier that, atypically, is good for hiking.

As you enter the rugged country where the Alesk divides the Fairweather and St. Elias ranges, you raft in view of dozens of other majestic glaciers, and in Alsek Bay, your view is filled by 7-mile-wide Alsek Glacier and behind it, 15,000-foot Mt. Fairweather.

From take-out at Dry Bay, a bush flight along the Gulf of Alaska conveys you to the town of Yakutat, where you catch a jet to Juneau. In summer, temperatures range from 50° to 75° by day, dropping to 45° to 55° at night.

Alaska Discovery invites all guests to help with camp chores, and for every 3 to 5 passengers there is one guide; some are specialists in natural history, fishing, or edible plants. You dine on salmon, halibut, or steak. Though the trip price is on the high side, it does include air charter to Haines and the one-way jet airfare from Yakutat to Juneau. Since put-in is in Yukon Territory, Canada, all guests need identification, such as a birth certificate or a passport. *Alaska Discovery, 5449-4 Shaune Dr., Juneau, AK 99801, tel. 907/780–6226, fax 907/780–4220. Early July–early Sept.: 10 days, $2,250. Price does not include 2 dinners; sign up 3–6 months in advance.*

SOURCES

ORGANIZATIONS **America Outdoors** (Box 1348, Knoxville, TN 37901, tel. 615/524–4814) is an advocacy group of outfitters. **American Rivers** (801 Pennsylvania Ave. SE, Suite 303, Washington, DC 20003, tel. 202/547–6900) is one of the country's leading river conservation organizations. **Friends of the River** (128 J St., 2nd Floor, Sacramento, CA 95814, tel. 916/442–3155, and Fort Mason Ctr., Bldg. C, San Francisco, CA 94123, tel. 800/374–8377) concerns itself with the environment and, among other activities, works on commission with outfitters to arrange rafting trips. The **Idaho Outfitters and Guides Association** (Box 95, Boise, ID 83701, tel. 208/342–1919) and the **Oregon Guides and Packers** (Box 10841, Eugene, OR 97440, tel. 503/683–9552) can provide information on outfitters in their areas. The **National Association of Canoe Liveries and Outfitters** (Box 248, Butler, KY 41006, tel. 606/472–2205 or 800/736–2256), which lobbies on behalf of outfitters, can send you lists of outfitters nationwide.

PERIODICALS The magazines *Men's Journal* (Box 54729, Boulder, CO 80322, tel. 800/678–2231) and *Outside* (1165 N. Clark St., Chicago, IL 60610, tel. 303/447–9330) regularly cover rafting.

BOOKS *The Big Drops: Ten Legendary Rapids,* by Robert O. Collins and Roderick Nash, gives a feel for whitewater. For ideas about other outfitters, consult *The Complete Guide to Whitewater Rafting Tours,* by Rena K. Margulis, or, perhaps better, the annually updated *Paddle America,* by Nick Shears (Starfish Press, 6525 32nd St. NW, Box 42467, Washington, DC 20015), which lists every outfitter in the country. Also providing good descriptions of the great river runs in the country are *Running the Rivers of North America,* by Peter Wood; *Whitewater Adventure: Running the Great Wild Rivers of America,* by Richard Bangs, one of the country's best-known adventure-travel writers; *Whitewater Rafting in Eastern North America* and *Whitewater Rafting in Western*

North America, by Lloyd D. Armstead; *The Whitewater Source Book*, by Richard Penny; *Wild Rivers of North America*, by Michael Jenkinson; and *Wildwater: Exploring Wilderness Waterways*, by Buddy Mays.

ALSO SEE If you want to get an up-close-and-personal look at whitewater, try a kayaking trip on an American stream (*see* Canoeing and Kayaking in Whitewater). Our chapter on Wilderness and Survival Schools also covers a couple of programs that will put plenty of spray in your face.

Sailing Schools

by Michael B. McPhee

ailing is wonderfully demo-
cratic. You don't need to
have exceptional strength,
endurance, or wealth to enjoy it, or even to
become quite good at it. Sailing, in fact, is one
of the few sports you get better at as you get
older.

There are an estimated 4.5 million sailors in
the United States today, a number that's
increasing from 5% to 8% each year. One reason for this growth is that boats are smaller,
lighter, and faster than they were a decade
ago. They're also easier to sail and more main-
tenance-free. But the main reason is that boats
cost less, so people of modest income can own
them without throwing themselves into debt.
Today, a family can buy a small boat and
everything needed to use it, from a trailer to
life jackets, for as little as $2,500. For many,
that's no more than the cost of a family vacation.

Sailors are also realizing that you don't have
to own a yacht any more to sail in some of the
more exotic waters of the world: You can easily fly to Tortola or Fiji and charter a boat,
with or without crew, and if you bring friends
along to split the expense, the trip could end
up costing less per person than if you stayed
at a hotel.

The catch, of course, is that you can't just sail
off alone, with no training; sailing requires

both knowledge and experience. The good
news is that sailing schools are proliferating
around the country, and there's a whole range
to choose from, catering both to day sailors
who want to learn how to sail small boats
around a lake or bay to more ambitious sailors
who want to learn navigation, with the expec-
tation of chartering a large boat without
crew—called bareboat chartering—somewhere in the world.

Regardless of your goal, sailing is relatively easy
to learn. It has a strange vocabulary, and some
of the concepts take some getting used to, but
within a week, with good instruction, you can
make sense of it all and be on your way.

Most sailing school courses range from 1 to
10 days. Plan on 3 or 4 days of schooling and
sailing to become confident about getting yourself back to the dock. People with mechanical aptitude learn faster, but nearly everyone
can pick up the basic skills in less than a week.

If your goal is to learn sailing well enough
to charter a boat, it's best to get some sailing
experience after beginners' school. You should
become very comfortable with boat handling,
strong winds (over 15 knots), and emergency
procedures, then take another 5 days of advanced instruction and sailing. It's one thing
to make a sailboat go where you want it to go.
It's another thing entirely to learn how to deal

Outdoor writer Michael B. McPhee has contributed to The New York Times, The Washington
Post, *and* The Boston Globe. *The author of* Fodor's Sailing: A Celebration of the Sport and the
World's Best Places to Enjoy It, *he has logged more than 10,000 miles of offshore passages
and has owned boats ranging from a Hobie Cat to a wooden Norwegian 8-meter sloop.*

with storms, navigation, currents, and shipping lanes.

Some schools claim they can take beginners and prepare them for chartering in 3 to 5 days, but that's a tremendous amount to learn in such a short time. Furthermore, sailing is as much experience as it is knowledge, maybe more so, and I believe you can't expect anybody to learn how to sail in only 5 days and then go out where the weather can get seriously rough. Besides, sailing is meant to be relaxing—you're only going to go 6 miles or so an hour—so the journey should be as enjoyable as the destination. If you're constantly worried about the unknown because you don't have enough experience, you won't enjoy yourself.

Normally, schools for beginners are offered in 3 different formats—a week-long course, a 2-weekend course, or a course lasting one day or night each week for 4 or 5 weeks. Most of those programs last about 20 hours, with a combination of 3- or 4-hour sessions on midweek mornings or afternoons, and 6- or 8-hour programs on Saturdays or Sundays.

Training is on anything from small 14-foot skiffs to 30-foot cruising boats equipped with bunks. Some go inland—on lakes and rivers—others sail on open bodies of water, where tidal currents become a factor. Some stick close to shore, others take you out into the Great Lakes or open ocean, where learning navigation is a must.

Regardless of the format, you spend the first few hours of a basic course in a classroom or on a boat tied to the dock learning the nomenclature, safety procedures, and such elementary concepts as how a boat moves against the wind. During the remaining time, you're sailing—putting all that knowledge into practice. If you're learning on a smaller craft, you can usually expect 2 students to a boat, with an instructor following alongside in a powerboat, shouting up to you as he pulls alongside, or addressing the entire fleet of boats with a bullhorn. Larger boats, of, say, 20 feet or longer, usually carry up to 4 students and an instructor.

With few exceptions, the day-sailing schools—the ones that teach the basics—offer no food or lodging. When classes end, you're on your own.

More advanced students learning how to cruise usually sleep on the boats for up to a week in extremely tight quarters. Some of these boats stay under sail all night; others anchor in a bay or tie up at docks. Some return to the same port, others sail to a different one each night. Not all your time is spent sailing. There's often time for fishing, sunbathing, and swimming; in the evenings, the student crew sometimes takes dinghies ashore or sits around drinking and telling stories.

Friendships and animosities develop quickly in such close quarters, but learning how to cope with them is part of the training for bareboat chartering. In general, sailing schools are a great way to make new friends, since you're all thrown together in a challenging, confusing situation where everyone's making mistakes. Sometimes you show your vulnerabilities, but you all learn from each other's mistakes as well as from your own.

Most schools realize that it takes time to remember that port is left and starboard is right, that you pull the tiller to windward in order to fall off to leeward, or that you need to harden the jib sheet before you can point higher. Don't worry if you get confused. The names and concepts take time to digest. Very soon, you'll be gliding out across the water agreeing with Rat in *The Wind in the Willows* that "there is nothing, absolutely nothing, half so much worth doing as messin' about in boats."

CHOOSING THE RIGHT SCHOOL

Pay a visit to a school you're considering, if it's nearby, and look at its boats. They should be clean and well maintained. If you see lots of patches on the boats and sails, if the ropes on the sails are frayed and worn, or if there is water sloshing around in the boats, the school probably doesn't take much pride in its fleet or in its program.

Once you've narrowed down the choices, ask each school:

Who are your competitors and what are their weak points? The answer to this may give you some insight into the strengths of the program you're considering. If you're also looking at one of the competing schools, you can ask them to respond to the criticism.

What type of boat does the school use? It makes sense to learn on a boat that's similar to one you hope to buy or rent someday, but ultimately the type of boat you learn on is much less important than the quality of the program. If you're taught well, you'll be able to apply the same principles to virtually any boat (except for catamarans and other multihulled craft).

If you're planning to sail small boats, you want to learn on one with a centerboard that can, and should, tip over. (Capsizing should be an important part of any day-sailing program, because you want to learn how to recover and continue on your way.)

If you're learning on a larger, heavier boat, you want one that's responsive, like a J-24, so you can feel every change as the boat responds to the wind, and learn how to react quickly and decisively.

Can I continue to take classes until I've mastered the course? Some schools offer extra lessons without cost or let you repeat a portion of the course. Others give a full or partial refund if you're unhappy with the results.

How many hours are spent not just in the boat but underway, with the sails up? A certain amount of classroom time is necessary so you can learn terminology, safety, and general principles. But you want as much time underway as possible—perhaps 70% of the program; that's when you're learning. The better schools get you in the boats right away, give you basic instruction, and shove you off under close supervision. Remember that some schools consider lunchtime or sleeping time as time spent in the boat.

If you're planning to go bareboat chartering, you want a learning experience as close to the real thing as possible, so try to sleep on a boat that remains under sail at least a few of the nights. You may have a more fun, relaxed time if you're tied up at a dock every night, but you won't learn as much.

How many students are in each boat, and how much time does each get to steer and work the sails? Expect 2 students on smaller boats and up to 4 students with an instructor on boats 20 feet or longer. Divide the hours sailing by the number in your boat to figure out how much time you get to steer or work the sails. Sailing is mostly experience, so make sure the school keeps you busy all the time.

Can I be certified on completion of the course? You'll frequently hear the word *certified,* as in, "This course will enable you to become certified." But the truth is, right now there is no single set of standards by which to judge the competency of a sailor.

However, various organizations are rushing to set those standards, including the United States Sailing Association (U.S. Sailing) and the American Sailing Association (ASA).

The private, profit-making ASA, based in California, has established a series of courses, exams, and 7 levels of certification for sailing students, ranging from beginning sailing through advanced coastal navigation. Successful completion of each course and a related exam certifies you at that level. ASA schools are concerned with providing a high-quality education, but they are not the final word in sailing schools. In fact, several of the best schools in the country, although very concerned with establishing standards and working hard toward that end, are not members of ASA. Be wary when ASA schools tell you that charter boat operators do not let you bareboat charter their vessels without an ASA certification. This is generally not true. U.S. Sailing is a nonprofit, nongovernmental body that for years set the standards for sailboat racing in the United States, under the authority of the International Yacht Racing Union (IYRU). U.S. Sailing is expanding beyond racing and moving into recreational sailing, but as of yet has not developed proficiency standards for sailing students. Most of its focus is on day sailing of smaller boats.

What are the instructors' qualifications? Some of the small-boat sailing schools use college kids as teachers. There's nothing inherently wrong with this—but it does say something about the seriousness of the program, and you may want to ask if there are older instructors as well.

Some instructors claim a racing background. Don't settle for that as an explanation of experience; responsibilities on a racing boat can be very specialized. The more teaching experience a person has the better. Someone with, say, 10 years of teaching would be great, since poor teachers don't last. It's also a good idea to find someone with significant offshore experience, since offshore sailing requires everyone to handle nearly every job.

As for certification, the most universally accepted qualification is a Coast Guard license, which is common among instructors only in chartering courses. At that level, you should demand it. The ASA also has certification criteria for instructors as does U.S. Sailing.

What is the school's safety record? Most have stellar records. But don't be afraid to ask. Find out about the last 3 injuries, and their outcomes. If you're day sailing, ask how they plan to retrieve you when your boat tips. Do they have a support boat with an engine on it? The good schools always have a supervisor in a powerboat right in the sailing fleet, ready for anything.

Don't let any school tell you nobody tips over. The good schools test everyone's ability to swim in a life jacket. Then they go out and tip all the day-sailing boats over. You spend the rest of the day drying out. It's a great icebreaker.

What's the cost and what's included? Most day-sailing classes provide nothing but instruction; you're on your own for meals and accommodations. Some day-sailing schools, however, let you sleep on boats at no additional charge, or offer packages that include room and board. Manuals, notebooks, and certification exams and certificates are usually extra, but not always.

Most live-aboard sailing courses include provisioning (meals and drinks), but not all. Some even ask you to pay for the instructor's meals! All day-sailing programs described below do not include food or lodging, unless otherwise noted. For live-aboard programs we tell you whether or not provisioning is included.

FAVORITE SCHOOLS

THE NORTHEAST

REGION-WIDE **Offshore Sailing School.** This huge Florida-based operation offers courses in the New York City area from April through early October—one in Jersey City, New Jersey; a second in Port Washington, New York; and a third in Greenwich, Connecticut. Classes are taught in Newport, Rhode Island, from May through September; a 7-day live-aboard chartering course, a special offering of this branch, costs $1,395 (*see* The South, *below*).

REGION-WIDE **Women's Sailing Adventures.** Women's Sailing Adventures was founded in 1989 by Sherry Jagerson, an energetic woman who experienced her share of problems on male-dominated boats before striking out on her own. She's a veteran of 3 1978 Bermuda Races ("I was hired as a cook, although I'd never even cooked on a boat before, and I wasn't even a good cook") and the disastrous 1979 Fastnet Race, where two dozen boats were lost in a storm. She has had myriad crew jobs, owned her own sail loft, and made on-board computers for race boats. Jagerson has been teaching women how to sail since 1980.

The school offers 4-hour beginner courses in Westport, Connecticut, usually on J-24s. All instruction is on board, and the boats are under sail about 75% of the time, usually with 3 students and an instructor.

The mainstay of the school are the 2-, 3-, and 7-day courses that run out of Westport; Falmouth, Massachusetts; Tenants Harbor, Maine; and Stonington, Rhode Island. The student-to-instructor ratio is an impressive 4 or 5 to 2. Sailing is in 37- to 44-foot boats. Students live on board and anchor off different harbors and islands each night.

During the warm months, there are also 7-day sailing trips through the San Juan Islands out of Bellingham, Washington, near the Canadian border, and along the California coast starting in Long Beach. Jagerson or her business partner, Carol Hayward, come along on virtually every trip.

From January through May the school also offers beginner and intermediate courses in the Caribbean. *Women's Sailing Adventures, 39 Woodside Ave., Westport, CT 06880, tel. 203/227–7413 or 800/328–8053. May–Sept.: 4-hr. beginner course, $40; 2-day course, $300; 3-day course, $450; 7-day course, $1,095. Price includes all provisioning except lunch on 2-, 3-, and 7-day courses.*

CONNECTICUT **Coastline Sailing School.** This school offers a wide variety of courses on Long Island Sound, some of the best sailing ground in the country. Based in Noank (near Mystic), it's primarily a big-boat school for sailors who have chartering in mind.

Founded in the mid-'80s, Coastline today has 15 boats, primarily 30-foot Ericssons, and teaches roughly 100 students a year. There are 4 instructors, all of whom are ASA certified and have Coast Guard licenses.

The Weekender course for beginners runs from 10 to 4 on a Saturday and Sunday. The first 2 hours are spent on the boat tied to the dock, learning terminology and safety procedures. The next 4 hours, you sail in the delightful Fisher's Island Sound. Each boat carries a maximum of 4 students and an instructor. The school can fill 5 boats on some weekends, and on some days you sail together in a small fleet.

Coastline also teaches 4 ASA certifying courses with overnights on board, as well as 4 advanced courses. The ASA courses are:

An expensive 2-day coastal cruising course, designed for sailors who want to become competent to skipper a sailing vessel over 30 feet, introduces novice sailors to such boats. A maximum of 6 students leave on a 38-foot Ericsson Saturday morning and return on Sunday night. However, for most students, even the very gifted, this is not enough time to learn that skill. (Some schools take 5 to 7 days for this course.)

A 3-day coastal cruising course offers the same instruction on similar boats.

The 5-day course on either the Ericsson or a Gulfstar 50 is for students with some experience who want to earn their bareboat chartering certification. The emphasis is on crew safety and emergency procedures. There is a maximum of 6 students per boat, and you may sail as far as Martha's Vineyard or even Nantucket.

Finally, the school offers a 7-day sailing vacation to Martha's Vineyard, which with good weather can be one of the best sailing trips in the country. The vacation course is exactly the same as the 5-day bareboat course except it's 2 days longer and includes the ports of Edgartown and Vineyard Haven. *Coastline Sailing School, Eldridge Yard, Marsh Rd., Noank, CT 06340, tel. 203/536–2689 or 800/ 749–7245, fax 203/572–0778. Mid-Apr.–mid- Oct.: Weekender course, $265 ($25 extra to stay on board Saturday night); 2-day coastal cruising course, $425, including meals (3 days, $595); 5-day bareboat chartering course with provisioning, $765; 7-day vacation course, $1,095.*

CONNECTICUT **Longshore Sailing School.** Based in Westport and founded in 1960, Longshore is one of the best organized day-sailing schools in the country. It uses boats under 16 feet long, so you don't get any chartering instruction, but you do receive a thorough education in how to sail. Its youth sailing program is one of the largest in the country.

Longshore has 7 staff members and 18 instructors, all U.S. Sailing certified, who teach nearly 1,400 students a year in more than 70 boats. You sail at the mouth of the Saugatuck River, at Westport, which gives you experience with salt water, tidal currents, and ocean buoys while affording a fair amount of protection from storms.

Longshore is unique in that it requires its students to swim 50 yards and tread water for 2 minutes. And that's the first thing you do—take a swim. Everyone then goes into the classroom with wet hair, and no pretensions.

For adults, there are 4 levels of instruction: basic boating, which satisfies the State of Connecticut's requirement for skipper licenses for any boat either 20 feet or longer, with sail or engine; basic sailing; intermediate sailing; and advanced sailing. All courses have the same format: 12 hours of instruction in 4 sessions over 2 consecutive weekends. If you can't make one of these 3-hour periods, you must make it up in private instruction at $30 per hour.

Students begin the basic programs learning terminology in a classroom, then gather on the dock for a rigging demonstration. Then they break into pairs and rig the boats themselves.

On the second day they learn how to stop a sailboat and how to dock or beach it. They then shove off, 2 students per boat, and sail a figure-eight course over and over for the rest of the day. One instructor is at the dock with a bullhorn and others are in support boats on the course. The third day focuses on sailing upwind and downwind, then out on the figure-eight course aligned into the wind. The fourth day is spent sailing a triangular course, practicing sail trim, reaching, and jibbing.

The intermediate course follows a similar format, concentrating more on why a boat sails, and adding additional sailing time. The advanced course offers more of the same at a higher level. Students sail solo on Lasers, which are very small, high-performance boats.

The school does not provide accommodations, but the nearby Inn at Longshore has attractive rooms as well as a restaurant and lounge. There's also a snack bar near the school for burgers and fries. This is a very popular program, so sign up at least one month in advance. *Longshore Sailing School, Longshore Club Park, 260 S. Compo Rd.,* *Westport, CT 06880, tel. 203/226–4646, fax 203/454–4120. Early May–late Sept.: 12-hour basic boating for adults, $85; all other adult courses, $130.*

CONNECTICUT Sea Sense. Founded in 1989, New London–based Sea Sense is designed primarily for women. Founded by Patti Moyer and Carol Cuddyer, two professional sailors with more than 50 years combined experience, the school has 10 licensed female captains and 5 student instructors who are working toward their captain's license. Moyer and Cuddyer teach as well. The women founders have spent much time and effort developing teaching methods to suit women, who usually have less upper-body strength than men. Scheduled courses are for women only. The school handles about 200 sailing students each year, as well as about 50 power-boat students.

Chartering is the primary goal here, with very little effort spent on day sailing, except on a student's own boat (instructors can be hired out for the day to drive to your marina and teach you privately on your boat). None of the courses follows a strict curriculum; instructors teach to meet the participants' needs in a noncompetitive, nonthreatening environment. The emphasis is on hands-on learning, but all students are given a thorough orientation, with a strong emphasis on safety. There are usually 2 instructors on board, with no more than 6 students.

Courses of 3, 5, and 7 days are given for all levels—beginner, intermediate, and expert. You live on board the 35- to 45-foot boats, and sail to different ports each night, where you tie up, anchor, or pick up a mooring. Couples and men can request customized classes. The school also operates out of Wisconsin and Florida. *Sea Sense, 25 Thames St., New London, CT 06320, tel. 203/444–1404 or 800/332–1404. May–Sept.: 3-day course, $485; 5 days, $750; 7 days, $995; private lessons on your boat, $250 a day, plus transportation. Prices include provisioning.*

MAINE Bay Island Sailing School. Founded in 1981, Bay Island runs a number of courses from beginning sailing through bareboat certification from its base at Journey's End Marina in Rockland, Maine. During these, you sail in some of the country's most scenic waters, with lighthouses and seals and ruggedly beautiful spruce-covered islands.

A Rhodes 19-footer and a Cal 27-footer are used for the beginner classes, one of which is a 5-day course for 4 hours a day (the other runs a weekend). Both have a 4:1 student-to-teacher ratio and use the boats and the bay as the classroom. The intermediate coastal cruising course, which uses exclusively Cal-27s, has the same student-to-teacher ratio and schedule.

The bareboat charter certification class is taught on 36- to 40-foot boats. There are 2 programs: Bareboat I, Monday to Friday, with a sleep-aboard on Thursday and a student-to-teacher ratio of 6:1; and Bareboat II, a Monday-to-Saturday program (5:1 student-to-teacher ratio), where you live on board and anchor in different harbors.

Keep in mind that learning to bareboat requires living on a boat, not returning to the home dock each night. You need to experience anchor drift, high winds, and rain during the night. Bareboat I, therefore, cannot adequately prepare a bareboat skipper. Bareboat II seems to be a better option, at a reasonable price. *Bay Island Sailing School, 21 Elm St., Camden, ME 04843, tel. 800/421–2492 or 207/236–2776, fax 207/236–2776. June–mid-Sept.: 5-day beginner class, $335; 2-day beginner class, $395; 5-day bareboat course with 1 overnight, $585; 6-day bareboat live-aboard course, $1,235; 5-day or weekend coastal cruising course, $395, with no provisioning.*

MAINE **WoodenBoat Sailing School.** This offshoot of the very successful *WoodenBoat* magazine offers one of the best and most thorough ways of learning to sail—using traditional methods, on board traditional wooden craft—while sailing the marvelous coast of Maine.

The school, founded in 1981, teaches some 700 students each year between June and mid-October. Beginners, intermediates, and advanced sailors are taught, on everything from 12-foot Beetle Cats to 170-foot topsail schooners. Most courses operate out of Brooklin, a 3-hour drive north of Portland and an hour from Bar Harbor. Some winter courses are given in the Caribbean.

Here you are taught theories of hull and rig balance, reefing, storm sailing, jury-rigging, knots, and sailing in fog. The school's focus is on instilling "sea sense"—the ability to tune in to the boat, the weather, and the crew, and apply good judgment so that they all work together harmoniously. The program does not cover everything you need to know to pass an ASA exam, but it does cover the skills needed to skipper a boat confidently, even in adverse conditions.

Beginners and intermediates take the Elements of Seamanship course, which is about 30% classroom, 70% under sail in anything from 12- to 14-foot day sailers to 28-foot Friendship sloops. Classes are limited to 10, with no more than 3 students per boat. The 5-day program runs from Sunday night to Friday night. For an additional fee, the school can provide room and board on its "campus," which includes a campground and an inn.

Those with some experience on the water who want to learn about larger boats can take the 6-day Craft of Sail course, either on a 36-foot ketch or a 32-foot Friendship sloop. The 6-day Advanced Craft of Sail course is usually offered in September, when winds are higher. Craft of Sail for Women, also 6 days, is designed for, and taught by, women.

The only live-aboard program is the 6-day Coastal Cruising Seamanship course taught on board *Christmas,* a 45-foot cutter that's arguably one of the finest wooden yachts in North America. Students—no more than 5—sail from Sunday night to Saturday, anchoring at different islands each night. Knowing the boat, the backgrounds of the instructors, and the coast of Maine, I would say this is the ultimate week-long school in terms of knowledge gained, uniqueness of craft, location, and sheer pleasure. And it's probably the best value, too. *WoodenBoat, Box 78, Naskeag Rd.,*

Brooklin, ME 01616, tel. 207/359–4651, fax 207/359–8920. June–mid-Oct.: 5-day Elements of Seamanship or 6-day Craft of Sail courses, $450 (room and board costs $295, camping site with meals, $165); 6-day Coastal Cruising Seamanship course, $925 with provisioning.

MASSACHUSETTS **Community Boating.** This is the largest and oldest public sailing establishment in the United States, located on the beautiful tidal pool of the Charles River in Boston. Its staff teaches more than 2,000 people a year how to sail, many of them kids 10 to 17 who participate for $1 for the entire summer.

The program, run April through October, is too good to be true. For a basic membership fee you can sail on your own as often as you want or take as many lessons as you want on the school's fleet of 150 boats, which includes 25-foot Cape Cod Mercurys, Lasers, 470s, 23-foot Sonar keelboats, and 22-foot Typhoons. Most of the instructors are graduates of the school who volunteer their time. Classes, covering everything from rigging to advanced racing, meet for 1 to 2½ hours, usually on weekday evenings and weekends. If you want a private sailing lesson, just show up; there's usually an instructor ready to go off sailing with you. The school is open weekdays from 1 PM to sunset, and weekends from 9 AM to sunset. Membership includes unlimited sailing lessons, unlimited boat usage and classroom instruction, and free guest privileges. *Community Boating, 21 Embankment Rd., Boston, MA 02114, tel. 617/523–1038, fax 617/523–7699. Apr.–Oct.: 2-day membership, $50; 7 days, $70; 30 days, $80; 75 days, $175; season, $215.*

MASSACHUSETTS AND RHODE ISLAND

Womanship. Womanship, one of the largest of the women's schools, definitely has the most diverse course offerings. It's based in Annapolis, Maryland, but offers courses out of Boston and Newport from mid-May to mid-October (*see* The Mid Atlantic, *below*).

NEW YORK **Oyster Bay Sailing School.** This relatively small school is designed primarily for local residents and those vacationing nearby. It offers 3 courses based exactly on the requirements for the 3 levels of ASA certification, covering everything from introductory boating to advanced coastal cruising.

The 3-day basic sailing course is taught on Long Island Sound on 23-foot Sonars, which are day sailors with no cabins. Each boat carries just 3 students and one instructor. On the first day, you're in the classroom learning knots, rules, safety, and other basic skills, and on the boats familiarizing yourself with the equipment. The second day is spent sailing. The third day you take the boats out and follow a chase boat, then sail a course. Lodging can be arranged at the nearby East Norwich Inn. Graduates are given 4 free hours in one of the Sonars.

The coastal cruising course is taught over 2 full days on either a C&C 32 or a Pearson 34, both capable boats. Students can sleep on the boats, tied up at the dock, at no additional cost. No classroom instruction is given—the program starts right on board. Instruction includes maneuvering under power, engine maintenance, steering with a wheel, docking, and crew dynamics. Class is limited to 4 students.

The 3-day bareboat course is usually taught on weekends on a 35-foot Choy Lee or a 38-foot Beneteau. Instruction includes charts, navigation, weather, fog, night sailing, and meal planning. There's a limit of 4 students for this course. *Oyster Bay Sailing School, West End Ave., Oyster Bay, Long Island, NY 11771, tel. 516/624–7900 or 800/323–2207, fax 516/922–4502. Apr.–mid-Oct.: 3-day basic sailing course, $375 weekdays, $425 weekends; 2-day coastal cruising course, $365 without provisioning, but no extra charge for sleeping on board; 3-day bareboat course, $450 including provisioning.*

RHODE ISLAND **J World.** Founded in 1981, J World has grown nearly as fast as the design of boat the school is named for and which it uses in its courses (primarily J-24s, J-22s, and J-80s). The school has 4 domestic locations: Newport, Rhode Island, where its headquarters are; Annapolis, Maryland; Key West, Florida; and San Diego, California. The 4 schools offer the same programs and prices.

Courses in Newport and Key West are taught on J-24s. By summer 1994, all locations will offer courses on the new J-80s.

Some 15 full-time instructors teach about 1,500 students each year. Student-to-instructor ratios are no more than 4:1.

There are 2 levels of recreational sailing courses—beginner and intermediate—and 3 levels of racing courses.

The beginner course (Introduction to Sailing) is taught from 9 to 4 over 5 consecutive weekdays. After a one-hour lecture each morning, you're on the boats for the rest of the day. To qualify for the 5-day Intermediate Sailing course you need to complete the beginner program or be able to tack and steer a boat comfortably. This course teaches students how to dock and anchor, read charts, identify buoys, plot a course, and so on, with the goal of preparing for bareboat chartering tests administered by chartering companies. J World, although not a member of any certifying organization such as ASA, does issue diplomas with a course description that can be shown to charter companies.

For students with less time, there are also 2 weekend sailing programs, one for beginners and another for intermediates. There are no lectures; both have you out on the water 8 hours a day.

Three racing courses are offered Monday through Friday: R-1 (Introduction to Racing) and R-2 (Advanced Racing) include 2 days of boat handling, a third day practicing starts, and 2 days of short course racing. The 2-day R-3 (Championship Racing) course, for the near-professional, covers strategy and tactics.

A weekend racing course (W-3) is for competitors who need to perfect their skills. There's no actual boat work, as in the 5-day racing programs, but you do learn the skills you need to get a boat around a course faster.

At press time, J World was planning to expand beyond day-sailing courses and offer 3- and 5-day live-aboard cruising for bareboat chartering, probably out of Newport and Key West. *J World, Box 1509, Newport, RI 02840, tel. 401/849–5492 or 800/343–2255, fax 401/849–*

8168. Mid-May–Sept.: 5-day courses, $695; weekend courses, $295.

THE MID ATLANTIC

MARYLAND **Annapolis Sailing School.** With some 3,500 students, 50 instructors, and 62 boats, this school, founded in 1959, is one of the oldest and largest private sailing schools in the country. Its base is Annapolis, but it has branch schools in St. Petersburg and Marathon, Florida; and St. Croix in the U.S. Virgin Islands.

The school is unique in that it uses Rainbows, 24-foot keelboat day sailors that were designed specifically for the school so that they won't capsize. Cruising classes are taught on live-aboard Annapolis 26s, Newport 30s, O'Day 37s, or Morgan 44s.

There are 3 formats for the beginner course: an extremely popular 2-day weekend course; a 3-day, Wednesday through Friday course; and a more relaxed 5-day weekday course. The program for days one and two are the same for all 3 courses; the additional days are for supervised sailing, with an instructor in a support boat nearby. Students in the 3- and 5-day classes often sail across Chesapeake Bay to restaurants for lunch, or join together at anchor for a floating picnic.

The 2-day advanced beginner course uses boats 30 feet and longer to prepare students for bareboat chartering.

There are two types of live-aboard cruising courses, both of them either 2 or 5 days long. The first type is a flotilla cruise for which couples or groups each have their own boat and cruise in a fleet, with an instructor following in a powerboat or sailboat. The other is a cruising course in which a group of students sail together on one boat with an instructor. On the flotilla course, at least one student must have skippering experience. Both courses are on 37- to 44-foot boats. *Annapolis Sailing School, Box 3334, Annapolis, MD 21403, tel. 800/638–9192 or tel. and fax 410/267–7205. Apr.–Oct.: 2-day beginner course, $185; 3 days, $285; 5 days,*

$375; 2-day advanced beginner course, $280; 2-day flotilla cruising course, $350 per boat without provisioning; 5 days, $1,390 without provisioning; 2-day cruising course without provisioning, $380; 5 days, $870 with provisioning.

MARYLAND **Havre de Grace Sailing Services.** Located on the upper Chesapeake Bay, 30 miles north of Baltimore and 65 miles south of Philadelphia, family-owned Havre offers courses on the Chesapeake Bay and in the Florida Keys from bases in Miami and Key West. Havre de Grace has a standing policy of guaranteeing you'll learn to sail. If you don't get enough out of a course, you may attend as long as you need, at the school's expense, until you learn what you signed up for.

The 4-day, basic day-sailing course uses a 19-foot Flying Scot. The 3-day Learn to Charter course, for students who have a basic understanding of sailing and want to go on to bigger boats, uses 32- to 37-foot Hunters. Instruction covers all mechanical and electrical components of a boat, diesel maintenance, sail trim, reefing, man overboard procedures, anchoring, and navigation. You can take the course from Monday through Thursday, or do the work on two consecutive weekends.

Since you pay per boat, the cost is relatively low if you can gather a group of 4 persons or if you are willing to be paired with others. The boat docks each night and students generally eat in town and sleep on board. This is a limitation, because, as we've said before, you can't become totally proficient at bareboat chartering when you return to the same dock each evening. All instructors have Coast Guard captain's licenses and are ASA-certified to teach basic sailing. Some captains, but not all, are ASA-certified to teach bareboat chartering.

A 3-day Learn to Charter course is taught on Hunter 33.5s. The class is limited to 4 students.

On the 5-day Ocean Cruising course, from Miami or Key West, students also leave Monday and return Friday. A few nights are spent sailing—which is as it should be—and

at anchor. *Havre de Grace Sailing Services, Tidewater Marina Bldg., Box 441, Havre de Grace, MD 21078, tel. 410/939–2869 or 800/526–1528, fax 410/939–2519. Apr.–Oct.: basic 4-day course, $290–$360; 3-day Learn to Charter course, $350–$450; 5-day Ocean Cruising course, $950.*

MARYLAND **J World.** This school has grown nearly as fast as the design of boat for which it's named and which it uses in its courses—primarily J-24s, J-22s, and J-80s. The school is based in Newport, Rhode Island, but offers classes in Annapolis from April through October on J-22s (*see* The Northeast, *above*).

MARYLAND **Womanship.** Founded in 1985 in Annapolis, Womanship definitely has the most diverse course offerings of the women's schools. With its motto, "Nobody Yells," Womanship steers clear of any feminist leanings while making it clear that it doesn't take a man to teach sailing or learn.

The school's strength is in the quality of its staff: experienced female instructors, most on the far side of 30 and some in their 40s and 50s. Womanship also emphasizes that teamwork and confidence are as important as the skills learned, and its instructors try to teach using support and encouragement. The school has less of an emphasis on qualifying for ASA certification than it does on teaching sailing and skippering, and students of any level of experience may join.

Womanship offers courses on the Chesapeake Bay from a base in Annapolis; out of various New England harbors, primarily Newport and Boston; in Washington's San Juan Islands, from Friday Harbor; along Florida's Gulf Coast and Biscayne Bay; and in the Virgin Islands. It also offers special courses in flotilla sailing throughout the world and passages between points of varying distances.

There are also a slew of customized courses, such as mother-daughter courses and courses for couples, families, and groups. The scheduled courses are for women only; men may join in the customized or couples courses. All classes are taught on Westerly, Beneteau, and Jeanneau boats ranging from 39 to 45 feet long.

Womanship averages about 1,000 students each year.

The Chesapeake program includes 2- and 3-day beginner day-sailing courses. Most 3-, 5-, and 7-day programs, in Annapolis and elsewhere, are live-aboard, with changing anchorages at night. Beginners, intermediates, and advanced students are usually grouped together on the same boats. *Womanship, The Boat House, 410 Severn Ave., Annapolis, MD 21403, tel. 410/269–0784 or 800/342–9295, fax 410/263–2036. Apr.–Oct.: 2-day day-sailing course, $248; 3-day day-sailing course, $358; 3-day live-aboard course, $464–$488 with provisions; 5 days, $726–$784 with provisions; 7 days, $984–$1,254 with provisions.*

MARYLAND **Women for Sail.** Based in Arlington, Virginia, this is the only large-boat sailing school exclusively for women. It is owned by two women, run by women, and teaches only women. And it's doing well. Since 1985, it has averaged about 1,200 students a year. During the summer, the school expands to 30 staff and instructors, including Tania Aebi, who at 16 was the youngest woman ever to sail alone around the world.

"We are noncompetitive and teach in a non-threatening manner," says founder Jill London. The school has 5 boats, which it owns. This is often a good sign, because it usually means that the boats are well maintained and that the school can offer lower prices than schools that charter boats. Women for Sail emphasizes hands-on training right from the start, with little classroom time.

Courses (the same at each location) are taught in Key West, Florida (year-round); Annapolis, Maryland (May through September); and San Diego (March through May).

In the 2-day day-sailing course, taught on 24-foot C&Cs and offered in Annapolis, the boat ties up each night, but students can sleep on board at no additional cost. In the 3-, 5-, and 7-day live-aboard courses, taught on 43-foot Irwins and offered in Key West and San Diego, boats anchor or tie up at a different port each night.

All North American courses, with 6 students and 2 instructors, are geared toward bareboat certification. At least one of the instructors is a U.S. Coast Guard licensed captain. *Women for Sail, 3467 S. Wakefield St., Arlington, VA 22206, tel. 703/998–5002 or 800/346–6404, fax 703/931–0718. May–Sept.: 2-day day-sailing course, $195; 3 days, $395 with provisioning; 5 days, $625 with provisioning; 7 days, $825 with provisioning.*

THE SOUTH

FLORIDA **Annapolis Sailing School.** With some 3,500 students, 50 instructors, and 62 boats, this is one of the oldest and largest private sailing schools in the country. Its primary location is, of course, Annapolis, Maryland, but it also offers a year-round program in Marathon and St. Petersburg (*see* The Mid Atlantic, *above*).

FLORIDA **Blue Water Sailing School.** This no-nonsense sailing school gets you out on the water and gives you a solid lesson. All courses, from basic sailing to bareboat chartering, are from Saturday afternoon to Friday afternoon. The boats sail from Fort Lauderdale on Sunday morning and anchor each night at different harbors in the Florida Keys. Exams and certifications are given on Friday afternoon. A maximum of 4 students are sent out with a Coast Guard licensed captain on 30- to 45-foot boats.

The basic sailing course is for students with no experience. The intermediate and chartering courses are for students with basic training. The advanced course offers coastal navigation and certification for chartering and includes a passage to the Bahamas.

This program is set up the way a sailing program should be—it gives students plenty of time to learn the intricacies of living on a boat; plenty of time to encounter storms, ships, and other unexpected hazards; and enough experience to gain a modicum of confidence. The school even tells prospective students with no experience that it's impossible to learn to charter in a week, except possibly for pilots or mechanics or persons with some of the knowledge required of a skipper. *Blue Water Sailing School, 1414 S. Andrews Ave., Ft. Lauderdale, FL 33316, tel. 305/768–0846 or 800/522–2992, fax 305/768–0695. Year-round: all 6-day courses, $899–$999 with provisioning.*

FLORIDA **Chapman School of Seamanship.** This school is referred to merely as Chapman's and is best known for publishing the bible of all coastal piloting. The guide explains nearly every skill a skipper needs to safely cruise between ports. Most boats other than day sailors carry a copy.

The school, like the book, has a military, no-nonsense feel to it, which isn't bad and might be exactly what some skippers are looking for.

From May through December, Chapman offers standard 2-, 3-, and 5-day ASA certification classes on inland waters—mostly on the Intercoastal Waterway near St. Lucie Inlet. These are day-sailing programs, with no provisioning.

Chapman also offers a live-aboard offshore sailing course with up to 5 students and one instructor taking 22- to 38-foot boats to the Bahamas. The course is relatively unique in that all levels of students go out on the same boats for 6 days and 5 nights. You elect which level of certification you want to work toward, and the licensed captain will work with you toward that end. Students may elect any of the ASA courses, from basic sailing through chartering, coastal navigation, and advanced coastal cruising. Prior to returning, the captain reviews all material with all students, then hands out the tests. You know whether you passed or not before you step back on the dock. This non-profit organization has a tremendous reputation for its integrity and thoroughness. *Chapman School of Seamanship, 4343 S.E. St. Lucie Blvd., Stuart, FL 34997, tel. 407/ 283–8130 or 800/225–2841, fax 407/283–2019. May–Dec.: 2-day certification course, $225; 3-day bareboat chartering course, $425 without provisioning; 6-day offshore sailing course, $940 with provisioning.*

FLORIDA **Florida Sailing and Cruising School.** This school operates year-round along the barrier islands off the southwest Florida coast, from a base in Fort Myers. The program is designed exactly to the ASA requirements, so you can expect to learn exactly what the ASA specifies and probably not much more.

The 2-day basic day-sailing course is taught on 24-foot keelboats in the Charlotte Harbor area. The 3- and 4-day courses, on 30- to 35-foot boats, combine basic sailing and coastal cruising, with 2 to 4 students on board.

The 5- and 6-day courses teach a combination of basic sailing, coastal cruising, and bareboat chartering. Boats usually spend at least one night at anchor, but tie up other nights. Students can sleep on boats or in area hotels. This is bad news, as sleeping on a boat tied to a dock is no preparation for chartering. *Florida Sailing and Cruising School, 3444 Marinatown Land NW, North Ft. Myers, FL 33903, tel. 813/656–1339 or 800/262–7939, fax 813/656–2628. Year-round: 2-day basic sailing course, $245; 3-day basic sailing and coastal cruising course, $495; 4-day basic sailing and coastal cruising, $695; 5-day bareboat chartering course, $695; 6-day bareboat chartering course, $895; 10 days, $1,695. Prices do not include provisioning.*

FLORIDA **Havre de Grace Sailing Services.** This program guarantees you'll learn to sail. Based in Maryland, it offers programs in the Florida Keys out of Miami and Key West from January through March (*see* The Mid Atlantic, *above*).

FLORIDA **J World.** This fast-growing school based in Newport, Rhode Island, offers courses in Key West from January through April. You sail the craft for which the place is named (*see* The Northeast, *above*).

FLORIDA **Offshore Sailing School.** This is one of the largest sailing schools in the country, and perhaps the best known, with more than 3,000 students attending each year. Founded in 1964 by Steve Colgate, a formidable ocean racer, the school has developed into a year-round program of classes, cruises, vacations, charters, and parties. It has taught more than 75,000 students.

The school is affiliated with U.S. Sailing and offers its own certification for bareboat chartering. All instructors have U.S. Sailing certification, and instructors on boats with engines have Coast Guard licenses. Classes are taught at Captiva Island, Florida; at Newport, Rhode Island; and at 3 schools in the New York City area.

Day-sailing courses are taught on 27-foot Solings, an Olympic-class boat. There may be as many as 20 students, but boats carry no more than 4 students and an instructor.

Day-sailing classes last from 3 to 7 days, generally with 2 hours of classroom in the morning or evening and 3 hours of sailing in the afternoon (or vice versa depending on winds and tides). In a 7-day course, students arrive on Sunday for an evening classroom session, sail Monday through Thursday with instructors, and Friday and Saturday without instructors. The goal of the day-sailing classes is to get people comfortable handling a boat by themselves, with a crew standing by. In all but the 7-day bareboat chartering course from Newport, students sleep on shore each night.

The bareboat chartering courses are numerous; in Florida, 4- and 7-day courses are available. *Offshore Sailing School, 16731 McGregor Blvd., Ft. Myers, FL 33905, tel. 813/454–1700 or 800/221–4326, fax 813/454–1191. Year-round: 3-day day-sailing courses, $450 without accommodations, $795 and up with accommodations; 3-day bareboat course, $450; 7-day bareboat charter course, $1,095 with accommodations ashore.*

FLORIDA **Sea Safari Sailing School.** Operating every week of the year out of St. Petersburg, Sea Safari teaches only on multihull catamarans—large sailboats with twin hulls with a cabin stretched on deck between them. Berths and heads are usually placed in the hulls.

Catamarans are wonderful boats—fast, stable, easy to handle. They don't heel (tilt) more than 10 degrees, and they're roomy and dry to sail. However, they sail much differently from mono-hull boats, so if you're not plan-

ning to buy or charter a multihull, it makes little sense to learn on one.

Sea Safari, run since 1990 by Captain Laurel Winans and her son Chip, offers 2-, 3-, 5-, and 7-day courses. The 5- and 7-day programs are for ASA certification.

Much of the school's emphasis is on comfort and relaxation, unlike, say, the no-nonsense programs offered by Chapman or Blue Water. The brochure highlights all the sights that will be seen—the sandy beaches, the snorkeling, and so on—and even boasts that students will have their choice of great restaurants at night. This is fine for beginners or intermediates, but experts might want to think twice.

Up to 6 students can enroll in each live-aboard class, although the boats have only 3 berths, albeit queen-size. *Sea Safari Sailing, 12060 Carver Ave., New Port Richey, FL 34654, tel. 813/856–0157 or 800/497–2508, fax 813/856–0157. Year-round: 2-day course, $395; 3 days, $495; 5 days, $695; 7 days, $895. Prices do not include provisioning.*

FLORIDA **Sea Sense.** This school based in New London, Connecticut—designed primarily for women to learn sailing and power-boating—also runs courses out of St. Petersburg and Miami from September through May (*see* The Northeast, *above*).

FLORIDA **Womanship.** This Annapolis-based school, whose motto is "Nobody Yells," has courses along Florida's Gulf Coast and Biscayne Bay (*see* The Mid Atlantic, *above*).

FLORIDA **Women for Sail.** Key West is a venue for these noncompetitive live-aboard courses (*see* The Mid Atlantic, *above*).

NORTH CAROLINA **Water Ways.** Founded in the late 1980s, Water Ways teaches some 200 students from April through November from its base in Wrightsville Beach. In addition to ASA-certified courses, it also teaches a waterway cruising course on the section of the Atlantic Intracoastal Waterway that runs from Norfolk, Virgina, to Miami, Florida. Many boaters prefer to use the waterway in transit north or south rather than sail in the open ocean despite the fact that the trip can be quite confusing and demanding when traffic is heavy, as you follow a series of fixed buoys with land on both sides. The course is 2 days and 1 night on board a 35-footer, learning chart and buoy reading, and understanding sound and light signals, VHF radio, traffic, and other skills you need to sail here. Classes are limited to 3 students.

ASA courses come in several configurations. There's a 2-day basic sailing course, a 2-day basic coastal cruising course, and a 4-day bareboat chartering course. The school uses 4 22- to 35-foot boats and has 3 ASA-certified instructors. Mornings are spent in classrooms and afternoons, sailing.

Water Ways also offers a crash 6-day course designed to take a beginner through to bareboat certification. Mornings are spent in the classroom, afternoons sailing, and evenings ashore enjoying Wrightsville Beach's active nightlife. You're on board one night.

Hard as it is to believe, the same crash course is given in 3 days, with 2 nights spent on board the boat. Both courses have the same tuition, but on the 6-day program you're on your own for food and lodging. However, it's hard to comprehend how a school can take beginners and certify them to charter in just 6 days without having them live on board, let alone in 3 days. *Water Ways Inc., Box 872, Wrightsville Beach, NC 28480, tel. 910/256–4282 or 800/562–SAIL, fax 910/256–5898. Apr.–Nov.: 2-day waterway course, $300 with provisioning; 2-day basic sailing course, $200; 2-day basic coastal cruising, $250; 4-day bareboat chartering course, $450 with provisioning; 3-day (with provisioning) or 6-day (without provisioning) crash bareboat chartering course, $800.*

THE MIDWEST

REGION-WIDE **Sailboats, Inc.** This well-established school offers a variety of facilities along the shores of Lakes Superior and Michigan from July through September. Although it's not affiliated with ASA, it's a member of the National Association of Sailing Instructors and Sailing Schools (NASISS) and offers its own bareboat certification, which it requires for chartering one of its own hundred-odd charter boats on the 2 lakes.

The basic program (Course I) takes beginners or novices with no open-water experience and teaches them the rudiments of charter sailing in 8 hours of classroom work and 16 hours on the water. Course II consists of classroom sessions the first 2 mornings, and sailing the first 2 afternoons and the entire third day. Course III, a variation of Course II, provides you with 8 hours of cassette and workbook lessons to be done at home, then 2 days of sailing. Classes meet once weekly for 3 weeks.

Classroom sessions are held in Minneapolis, Milwaukee, Superior, Madison, Chicago, and Indianapolis. Sailing sessions, using 25- to 40-foot boats, head out to the Apostle Islands on Lake Superior from Bayfield and Superior, Wisconsin, and on Lake Michigan from Chicago; Manitowoc, Wisconsin; and Hammond, Indiana.

The school also offers an advanced, 4-day, live-aboard course called Blue Water Cruising to graduates of the basic chartering courses. The boat sails at night. *Sailboats, Inc., 250 Marina Dr., Superior, WI 54880, tel. 715/392–7131 or 800/826–7010, fax 715/392–7133. July–Sept.: Course I, $450–$495; Course II, $495; Course III, $450; 4-day Blue Water Cruising course, $895, including provisioning.*

ILLINOIS **Chicago Park District's Rainbow Fleet/Judd Goldman Adaptive Sailing Programs.** Since 1934, these programs have offered city dwellers, particularly beginners, a great way to learn to sail. The programs are particularly well equipped for sailors with various disabilities.

The 34 instructors, many of whom are college students and about half of whom are certified by U.S. Sailing, teach up to 500 students a year on Lake Michigan. Among the 50-odd boats in the school fleet are Hobie 16s catamarans, Barnett 14s dinghys, and Freedom 20s (keelboats for sailors with disabilities).

The vast majority of classes are private, on a one-on-one basis. The private beginner course consists of 5 hour-long classes. Adult groups meet in 2-hour classes, usually on 5 evenings, spread out over 2½ weeks, or over 5 weekends. The first half hour of the course is spent in a classroom and the rest in the boats. Classes are taught at 3 lakeside locations, all within Chicago: North Shore Beach, Burnham Harbor, and South Shore Beach.

The program for people with disabilities is taught with 2 students and one instructor in each boat. The 6 2-hour lessons are on Freedom 20s, which have special seats that slide from port to starboard so that students can easily change sides after tacking. About 50 students with disabilities take lessons each year, but over 500 use the school's facilities. *Chicago Park District's Rainbow Fleet/Judd Goldman Adaptive Sailing Programs, 425 E. McFetridge Dr., Chicago, IL 60605, tel. 312/294–2270, fax 312/362–1005. Memorial Day–Labor Day: all programs, $85.*

WISCONSIN **Milwaukee Community Sailing Center.** Since 1979, this private, nonprofit operation has been offering lessons to the public along the shores of Lake Michigan on property leased from the City of Milwaukee. The school has a strong interest in teaching people with disabilities.

The goal of the adult beginner course is to teach students to safely skipper a boat in up to 10 knots of wind. Beginning sailors have a choice of three formats. The daytime course meets for 3 hours, either mornings or afternoons, every weekday for 2 weeks. The evening course meets on 8 weeknights for 2 consecutive weeks. The intensive weekend course meets Friday evening, then all day Saturday and Sunday. Fees include unlimited use of boats for one calendar year.

Regardless of the meeting schedule, the first lesson is on dry land, where you learn terminology, rigging, and other basics. Subsequent lessons are all in the boats, 2 or 3 students in each, with a volunteer instructor. A staff instructor follows the fleet in a safety boat. All students must be able to swim 75 yards in a life jacket. Training includes cap-

size and man-overboard drills. Eventually students sail alone, again with the staff instructor following.

Programs run from May through October and teach about 200 adults and 500 youths 17 and younger. Boats include Designers' Choices, Capri 14s, and Ensigns (22-foot keelboats). There are also a few Solings and J-24s. There are 14 instructors, most of them high school and college students, all with their Level 1 U.S. Sailing certification.

An Introduction to Racing course meets for 5 consecutive weekdays or weeknights, and teaches basic racing rules and spinnaker sailing. There are a variety of other advanced courses as well as a full complement of youth courses, including a program for children 8 to 12 in which kids learn to sail using tiny dinghys, one student to a boat, in some of the lagoons around the city. You must be a member in order to take any course; it costs $75 to join if you live out of town and are using the center only to take a course. *Milwaukee Community Sailing Center, 1450 N. Lincoln Memorial Dr., Milwaukee, WI 53202, tel. 414/277–9094, fax 414/277–9124. May–Oct.: membership fee, $185 adults; intensive weekend beginner course, $150; all other adult courses, $60–$65. Youth lessons: beginners, $75; intermediates, $50; advanced, $25.*

WISCONSIN **Sea Sense.** This Connecticut-based program for women, whose primary goal is to prepare students for chartering, offers courses in Sturgeon Bay and Milwaukee from May through September (*see* The Northeast, *above*).

THE SOUTHWEST

TEXAS **Texas Sailing Academy.** Founded in the early 1960s, Texas Sailing offers a thorough training program with everything from day sailing to bareboat chartering on 65-mile-long Lake Travis on the edge of Austin, in a conference and vacation area. It has a variety of well-equipped boats from 21- to 42-feet long. The 5 instructors, all Coast Guard Master rated, teach about 100 students a year. The school, affiliated with U.S. Sailing, recommends that every student take its 8-hour boating safety class, taught completely in a classroom, before signing up for any of the sailing courses.

The 13-hour beginner sailing course is taught on Beneteau 23s, with 2 students and an instructor per boat. Three sessions lasting 4 hours each are given on the water, and there's one hour in the classroom. An exam and sailing test are given at the end, and you are expected to tack, dock, and sail a short course proficiently.

The intermediate sailing course aims to have students comfortably handle a cruising sailboat under sail or power. It is taught on boats 26- to 35-feet long, and requires 8 hours in a classroom and 20 hours of sailing. Each boat has a maximum of 4 students and one instructor. All instruction is conducted during daylight hours, although students overnight on the boats.

Bareboat chartering is taught on 45-footers and takes 8 hours. Many students take it back-to-back with the coastal cruising-oriented intermediate course, for a Friday-through-Sunday package. Coastal navigation and other advanced courses are available. Students may stay on the boats at night for free. *Texas Sailing Academy, 103-B Lakeway Dr., Austin, TX 78734, tel. 512/261–6193 or 800/864–7245, fax 512/261–8351. Year-round: beginner sailing, $275; intermediate sailing, $425; bareboat chartering and intermediate package, $850. Prices do not include provisioning.*

THE WEST COAST

CALIFORNIA **Crabtree Maritime Services.** This establishment is based about 4 hours by boat up San Francisco Bay from the Golden Gate Bridge. It's a one-man operation run by Sam Crabtree, a Coast Guard–licensed captain and owner of a well-equipped Cal 39-foot sloop, on which the courses are taught.

The thorough courses include lots of mileage at sea, some of which is at night under sail. Crabtree takes sailors right out into the commercial fishing grounds, through the shipping lanes, into difficult harbors and anchorages. If I were shelling out good money for a sailing course, I'd want to be in a course like Crabtree's, learning navigational lights and radar rather than partying in some restaurant near the home dock.

Three-day courses for beginning sailors emphasize boat handling and coastal piloting en route to Drakes Bay or Half Moon Bay. Five-day courses travel to Monterey Bay, with students standing watch on one all-night sail. These require some sailing experience. The 8-day courses travel from San Francisco to Noyo (Fort Bragg), tacking at times up to 100 miles offshore. Instruction includes everything needed to skipper a passage, such as radar, LORAN, traditional navigation with sextant, and sailing through fog.

Crabtree also offers a variety of 1- and 2-day sailing trips within San Francisco Bay. Of particular interest is his overnight course on piloting and seamanship in the Delta, an area thick with navigational hazards, buoys, currents, and other challenges. *Crabtree Maritime Services, 710 Shady Glen, Martinez, CA 94553, tel. 510/372–0144 or 800/491–TRIP. Year-round: 3-day course, $295; 5 days, $475; 8 days, $750; overnight courses, $195–$225 with provisioning.*

CALIFORNIA **J World.** This school, founded in 1981, is headquartered in Newport, Rhode Island, but offers courses out of San Diego from January through November (*see* The Northeast, *above*).

CALIFORNIA **Santa Barbara Sailing Center.** This small school founded in 1967 concentrates on day sailing, with only one overnight course. The student-instructor ratio is 4:1.

The 16-hour, 4-day basic course uses 21- and 24-foot keelboats. You can sleep aboard at no extra charge. Graduates can move on to the 2½-day, live-aboard, basic coastal cruising course, taught on a 30-foot boat that ties up at the dock at night.

The 2½-day bareboat chartering course is taught entirely on Catalina 30- or 36-footers. The boats sail 23 miles out to the Santa Cruz

Islands, where they anchor for the night. Dinner and breakfast are cooked on board. Students must provide provisions for themselves and the instructor. *Santa Barbara Sailing Center, The Breakwater, Santa Barbara, CA 93109, tel. 805/962–2826 or 800/350–9090, fax 805/966–7435. Year-round: basic 4-day course, $259; 2 1/2-day basic coastal cruising, $379 without provisioning; 2 1/2-day bareboat course, $389 without provisioning.*

CALIFORNIA **Club Nautique.** Founded in the early '60s and affiliated with both U.S. Sailing and the ASA, Club Nautique operates out of Alameda and Sausalito on San Francisco Bay. Because sailing conditions are usually pretty strong on the bay, the school focuses on large-boat sailing and is considered one of the top schools in the country for teaching advanced, offshore sailing. However, it has a strong program for beginners as well. Roughly 1,000 students sign up for classes each year. Its fleet includes some 45 boats ranging in size up to 45 feet, and there are some 30 instructors (all of whom have Coast Guard licenses).

The school offers all the ASA courses and certifications. Beginning sailing is taught either on weekends or together with coastal cruising on weekdays. Each class has 20 hours of instruction, nearly all on the boat on the water. You can take either course on 2 consecutive weekends, or take both courses back to back from Monday to Friday. If you don't understand the lessons, you can take either class as many times as you need to learn the material. Each boat carries a maximum of 4 students and an instructor. All students are welcome to overnight on the boats for free.

Bareboat chartering is taught in 4 straight days, usually Friday through Monday, with the last 2 days spent on an overnight cruise in the bay. Students cook all meals. Some of the advanced classes sail all the way from Hawaii or Mexico back to San Francisco. *Club Nautique, 1150 Ballena Blvd., Suite 161, Alameda, CA 94501, tel. 510/865–4700 or 800/343–SAIL, fax 510/865–3851. Year-round: beginning courses, $395 without provisioning; basic coastal cruising, $495 without provisioning; both courses together,*

$495–$695, depending on the season; 4-day bareboat chartering course, $895 without provisioning.

CALIFORNIA **Women for Sail.** The only large-boat sailing school exclusively for women, this operation offers courses out of San Diego from March through May (*see* The Mid Atlantic, *above*).

CALIFORNIA AND WASHINGTON **Women's Sailing Adventures.** This Connecticut-based establishment, founded in 1989 by the energetic Sherry Jagerson, offers courses along the California coast from Long Beach and out of Bellingham, Washington (*see* The Northeast, *above*).

WASHINGTON **San Juan Sailing.** Based in Bellingham, a 90-minute drive north of Seattle, this well-organized, family-owned sailing center offers good experience to novices.

There are 5 levels of weekend courses and a 6-day Learn-n-Cruise course. The 2-day weekend courses run from beginning sailing, for those who have never set foot on a boat before, to advanced sailing, including navigation and anchoring. All but the beginning course are live-aboards. The school lists 32 hours of instruction for each course, but counts all time spent on the boat in the figure—even the time you're asleep. Certification tests are given for an additional fee.

The 6-day course is an ideal way to learn to sail because it provides sufficient time and varying experiences for you to become relatively competent. The boats sail through the San Juan Islands with no set itinerary, going with the weather and currents. Aside from one dinner ashore, all meals are prepared and eaten on board, an important learning experience for a future charterer. The boats are either Pearson 38s or Nordic 40s, with up to 6 students and one instructor.

San Juan also offers a variety of advanced courses that follow ASA guidelines, as well as offshore passages to Hawaii and the Marquesas. *San Juan Sailing, 1 Squalicum Harbor Esplanade, Bellingham, WA 98225,* *tel. 206/671–4300, fax 206/671–4301. Apr.–Oct.: 2-day weekend courses, $149–$199 without provisioning, $199–$249 with provisioning; 6-day course, $695 with provisioning.*

WASHINGTON **Womanship.** This diverse school for women, based in Annapolis, offers courses through the San Juan Islands, out of Friday Harbor, from July through October (*see* The Mid Atlantic, *above*).

SOURCES

ORGANIZATIONS **United States Sailing Association** (Box 209, Newport, RI 02840-0209, tel. 401/849–5200, fax 401/849–5208), commonly referred to as U.S. Sailing, and the **American Sailing Association** (13922 Marquesas Way, Marina del Rey, CA 90292, tel. 310/822–7171, fax 310/822–4741) are the country's major sailing organizations. ASA's free 2-page member list is available on request.

A recent trend has been for parks and recreation departments of larger cities to establish urban sailing programs, or at least to make city land available to private sailing schools at a nominal cost. (The largest and oldest of these schools is Community Boating, Inc., in Boston; *see* Favorite Schools, *above*.) So if you live in a city and need to stay close to home, check with your city's parks and recreation department.

PERIODICALS There are numerous sailing periodicals, virtually all of which are worth reading. The biggest difference among them is their target audiences—some are very technical, others are for cruising, and still others are purely for racing.

The monthly *Sail* magazine (Charlestown Navy Yard, 100 1st Ave., Charlestown, MA 02129, tel. 617/241–9500) is good on all aspects of sailing, from day sailing to ocean voyages. There's very little for the beginner sailor, but lots of sound, practical how-to arti-cles, firsthand tales by fellow sailors, and boat want ads in the back for fantasizing. *Cruising World* (Cruising World Publications, Inc., 5 John Clarke Rd., Newport, RI 02840, tel. 401/847–1588) is a monthly magazine written for sailors who cruise on their sailboats, but highly readable for anyone with just an elementary understanding of sailing. Lots of stories written from the decks of cruising boats all over the world, lots of repair articles, recipes, and humor. *WoodenBoat Magazine* (WoodenBoat Publications, Inc., Box 78, Brooklin, ME 04616, tel. 207/359–4651) is a very high quality, bimonthly magazine written specifically for wooden boat owners and lovers. Because of its quality, *WoodenBoat* has become enormously successful in a short time, especially considering its small target audience.

BOOKS In addition to the schools described above, there are hundreds of other reputable programs around the country, particularly for day sailing. The free *Community Sailing Directory (1994),* published by the nonprofit United States Sailing Association (Box 209, Newport, RI 02840-0209, tel. 401/849–5200), lists nearly 900 programs across the country.

Your telephone directory (see "Boat Dealers" and "Marinas") can give you other options. These folks want you to start boating, so they're likely to know about local schools.

For how-to, try *The Craft of Sail* (Walker), by Jan Adkins. This is a well-written book for beginners, describing not only how a boat works but why as well, with lots of beautiful drawings. For good reading, try *Men At Sea* (Random House), by Brandt Aymar, a collection of the best sea stories of all time. *The Big Book of Sailing* (Barron's Educational Service), by Grubb and Richter, is an attractive book with great stories and chilling biographies of seafarers, richly illustrated in a large, coffee-table format.

ALSO SEE If you enjoy sailing boats, you may like sailing surfboards. The Windsurfing chapter tells you where you can learn.

Scuba Diving

by Lisa Skriloff

ome divers like to see fish; they like to be surrounded by fish. For them, it's the marine life that makes scuba diving thrilling. Some divers like warm water, while others say warm-water diving is as adventurous as diving in your bathtub. They prefer the more rugged and challenging deep dives, where the water temperature is in the fifties. Or ice diving, or exploring underwater caves. Still others like the look at history that wreck diving affords, and go off in search of portholes, bottles, ammunition, or gold.

There are dive courses available in almost every state in the country, as well as places to go diving on one-day or weekend excursions. But if you've got a whole week and want to learn to dive, the warm water destinations of Florida, the U.S. Virgin Islands, and Hawaii are the ones that offer courses on trips of at least 5 days. In the Florida Keys you'll find warm water, schools of yellowtail snappers, sunken Spanish galleons, and a coral reef that extends north to Fort Lauderdale. In volcanic Hawaii there are caverns, underwater lava tubes, sea turtles, and octopus. Under Frederiksted Pier in St. Croix, U.S. Virgin Islands, you'll see seahorses and try night diving. And on the north side of St. Croix, where the reef drops off and descends vertically for hundreds of feet, there's wall diving.

Jacques-Yves Cousteau and Emil Gagnan started this sport when in 1943 they invented the Aqua-lung, the first self-contained underwater breathing apparatus (SCUBA). Since then, scuba diving has grown enormously—with 650,000 new divers in 1992 alone joining the estimated 3 million to 4 million already certified. Couples are even getting married underwater! If you're over the age of 12 you can become a certified diver, no matter your level of physical ability, although you must be able to swim. The vast majority of divers are college-educated, fairly affluent, and work in professional or management positions.

Although scuba diving is open to all and is, statistically speaking, a safe sport, there are obvious dangers to being underwater, dependent on only your equipment and your knowledge. Before you can dive (or even rent a tank of compressed air), you must have basic scuba certification (your C-card), which you earn in a course consisting of classroom work, pool instruction, and 4 or 5 checkout dives in open water (ocean, river, lake, quarry, etc.).

The courses are usually provided by dive shops and by YM- and YWCAs at night or on weekends over a period of a few weeks. At these local courses you meet like-minded people from your area—future dive buddies. After you have completed your class and pool work, the dive shop or Y arranges for you to take your checkout dives nearby. You can also take your class and pool work near home, then request a referral letter and go to a resort for

---

Lisa Skriloff, who lives in New York, has been a scuba diver since 1984. She holds a PADI Advanced Open Water certification card and has logged over 100 dives in Hawaii, New York, Pennsylvania, Florida, the Bahamas, Panama, and throughout the Caribbean.

your checkout dives, after which you can spend the rest of your vacation diving.

On the other hand, you might want to take all your diving instruction at a resort and complete every aspect of certification while on vacation. Solo travelers are paired with a buddy for the (usually) 4-day course.

Another option is a resort course, an abbreviated version of a certification course (completed in about a day, as opposed to 4). This allows you to dive at the resort offering the course, but only that resort, for the remainder of your stay. A resort course does not certify you.

There are several major agencies that grant recreational scuba certification, and all dive shops are affiliated with one or more of them: the Professional Association of Dive Instructors (PADI), the National Association of Underwater Instructors (NAUI), Scuba Schools International (SSI), the YMCA National Scuba Program, and the National Association of Scuba Diving Schools (NASDS). About 70% of divers hold PADI cards, most of the rest have NAUI certification, and the balance is divided among the other agencies. Sanction by an agency means that the affiliated dive center conforms to that agency's education methods and uses its diver manual. When you complete your course, your C-card is mailed to you by the national dive agency under whose auspices it was given.

There's not much difference among the training programs of the various agencies—all courses cover the same material—but they may differ in the manner of presentation. Once you are certified, you can dive at any resort in the world, even if its agency affiliation is different from that on your C-card. How do you choose one over the other? If you're planning to take the course near home and then complete the checkout dives at a resort on vacation, it's best to choose a local dive ship affiliated with the same agency as the resort. You might choose a dive shop for its facilities (an on-site pool, perhaps), its programs (such as weekend getaways with cheap group airfare), the convenience of its schedule, its amenities (a repair shop), and its members' activities (meetings, parties, even a newsletter). If you will be learning to dive while on vacation, choose your destination first, based on the region and the characteristics of its dive sites; its agency affiliation makes little practical difference.

During the classroom sessions, the instructor gives lectures and teaches the material in the diver manual, which is required reading. Slides and videos are often used, and quizzes follow each chapter of the text, to help you prepare for the final, a multiple-choice written test. (It's really difficult to fail; after the final, any wrong answer is reviewed by the instructor until you know it.) The course material covers diving equipment, the effects of pressure on your body, and the dive tables— charts that tell you how long it's safe to stay submerged at various depths, and how long you must stay on the surface between dives on a single day. It also covers safety rules, such as not flying for 24 hours after a dive, and the buddy system. Much of this information is designed to prevent you from getting the bends, a serious condition that can occur if your body is subjected too quickly to changes of pressure.

The pool instruction usually starts with a brief test of your swimming ability. Then you learn to manage your equipment and master such skills as clearing your mask underwater (in case it fills with water or fogs up), communicating underwater with a companion, and using a compass. You also learn to snorkel. You can learn at your own rate and practice until you become comfortable underwater. You then move to open water, where you demonstrate these skills for your instructor's approval during your checkout dives.

The use of most necessary gear is normally included in the price of a scuba diving course, so you shouldn't buy it until afterward. You are lent a tank of compressed air; a buoyancy compensator (or dive vest), known as a BC; a regulator (through which you breathe the air in your tank); gauges that indicate your depth and the air remaining in your tank; a weight belt to help adjust your buoyancy; and a dive watch. A wetsuit is provided if water temperature demands it. You also need a mask, a snorkel, and fins, which most courses don't supply. You should buy (or rent) these beforehand, to ensure proper fit. Expect to pay $45–$100 for a mask, $12–$42 for a snorkel, and $55–$135 for a pair of fins. Prescription masks can be made to order, but many people wear contact lenses. Some shops have rental/purchase plans, so if you decide to rent a few times before taking the plunge, your rental fees can be charged against the purchase price.

CHOOSING THE RIGHT COURSE

Following are some questions to ask about scuba diving courses. Some pertain to all certification courses, others only to courses taken at a resort.

How long have you been in business?

How many students are there in each class? How many instructors per student? In general, classes are limited to 8 people, sometimes fewer, and there is at least one instructor per class. There are usually 2—an instructor and a divemaster (instructor-in-training)—for the open-water certification dives. A low student:instructor ratio is preferable, but the course may be more expensive.

What is the schedule of classroom sessions and pool sessions? Most courses take from 24 to 32 hours, divided between classroom study and pool work, plus 4 checkout dives (and sometimes an open-water snorkel dive). The 4- or 5-day courses given at resorts generally cover classroom and pool work in 20 hours, plus checkout dives, but some let you study the manual in advance and cover pool work, checkout dives, and tests in 3 days.

What's the cost and what's included? Cost can range from about $300 to $900. The prices given here are for basic certification courses and include the diver manual and other course materials, rental gear used during class and pool sessions, checkout dives, and transportation to dive sites. They do not include mask, fins, snorkel, or the use of dive gear dur-

ing checkout dives, unless noted. If you take your course at a resort, packages may be available that include lodging.

What kind of dive sites are used for the open water checkout dives? What will the diving conditions be like? New divers may feel more comfortable in shallower waters. And learning about the expected water temperature and visibility at different resorts at different times of year will help you choose where to go.

How demanding is the course? Do I need to be in good condition? It's best to be in good aerobic condition for diving, but you needn't be an overall athlete. For your swim test, you'll probably be asked to swim no more than 200 yards and float or tread water for 10 minutes. Although dive equipment is heavy, it's weightless underwater. For that matter, so is a neutrally buoyant diver, which means that an extra 10 pounds is not the hindrance it is, say, on a runner.

What is there to do in free time? At some resorts, there's nothing much to do but dive, while others have lots of activities or are located in or near lively towns. This is especially important if you're traveling with nondivers; you'll be fully occupied during the day and tired after a day's study and training.

What are the accommodations like? Is the hotel close to the course location? Weigh the advantages and disadvantages of luxury versus laid-back lodging; crossing an elegant lobby with wet dive gear can be intimidating (and frowned upon). Also consider the distance you must drag your gear bag, dripping wet, from the dock to your room if there are no lockers.

Is laundry service available?

How far in advance do I need to sign up? People usually book 4 to 6 weeks in advance, but most schools can fit you in even if you decide to go on the spur of the moment.

Do you have references from past students? It's a good idea to ask the opinion of someone who knows from experience just how a school operates.

THE NORTHEAST

NEW YORK **Hamptons Learn-to-Dive.** In the sometimes fast-food world of scuba instruction, Annie Libby's Bespoke Scuba is like a catered meal served on fine china. Bespoke means "custom-made," and this school offers just that: Top-of-the-line, learn-to-dive packages that may include a stay at local inns like the charming Maidstone Arms. Instruction is given at a local pool, and the checkout dives are done at nearby Fort Pond Bay, off Montauk, or at an exotic location on a Bespoke trip.

Among the students here you'll find family groups, corporate executives and their clients, denizens of the Hamptons, and a variety of vacationers. If you have a group of 4 to 10 persons, Bespoke will also bring scuba gear and instructors to *your* pool. You must live within a 100-mile radius of the Hamptons, but the course price is the same. The student-to-instructor ratio is never greater than 8:1, and Libby is usually there, too. *Bespoke Scuba, 125 E. 63rd St., New York, NY 10021, tel. 800/537–2328 or tel. and fax 516/267–2169. May–Sept.: 4-day course, $885. Price covers use of equipment on open-water dives, including wet suit. Package accommodations average $200 per night.*

THE SOUTH

FLORIDA **Fort Lauderdale Reef and Wreck Diving.** If you have any nervousness about learning to dive, it will soon be dispelled at Pro Dive. You get an immediate sense of the professionalism of the staff and instructors here, where novices are trained and where experienced divers learn to become instructors and dive-resort operators. You also get a sense of the fun you'll have when you see the photos of former student groups. Class size is 6 people maximum. Checkout dives are at offshore coral reefs and wrecks, including the *Mercedes I.*

Many divers stay right at the 16-story Bahia Mar resort (which has a special rate for divers), where the retail shop, classroom, pool, dive boat, and your hotel room are all within steps of each other. Rooms reserved for divers are on the marina side, which means you don't have to lug your gear too far, and the hotel has a convenience store as well as 4 dining rooms. Nearby, on the Intracoastal Waterway, is Bahia Cabana, a small establishment with the casual air that divers like. Fort Lauderdale's wonderful beach is right across the street, easily accessible by an overpass. *Pro Dive, Bahia Mar Yachting Center, 801 Seabreeze Blvd., Fort Lauderdale, FL 33316, tel. 305/761–3413 or 800/772–3483, fax 305/761–8915. Year-round: 4-day course, $295. Price includes equipment for checkout dives.*

FLORIDA **Key Largo Reef and Wreck Diving.** If you like diving in shallow, warm waters among schools of approachable fish, try Key Largo, in Florida's Middle Keys. Because the Florida Keys National Marine Sanctuary and the adjacent John Pennekamp Coral Reef State Park have been protected from spearfishing and coral collection for more than 30 years, divers will be surrounded by friendly fish. One dive site is Molasses Reef, home to yellowtail snappers, schools of barracuda, and giant rays. Another popular site is French Reef, notable for its swim-through caves.

The famous Christ of the Abyss, a nine-foot bronze statue standing in about 25 feet of water, is visible from the surface, so that both snorkelers and divers can see it. In fact, most dive sites in the Middle Keys are suitable for both, which means that snorkelers traveling with divers can go out on the same boat.

Stay at the Marina del Mar Oceanside (or the slightly less expensive Marina del Mar Bayside) while you learn to dive with Ocean Divers, and you'll be immersed in scuba camaraderie—there are many avid and novice divers among the guests. Classes are held in the dive shop, and the hotel's pool is used. *Ocean Divers, 522 Caribbean Dr., Key Largo, FL 33037, tel. 305/451–1113 or 800/451–1113,* *fax 305/451–5765. Year-round: 4-day course, $395.*

FLORIDA **Key West Reef Diving.** Southpoint Divers, at the Hyatt Key West Resort, teaches a course you can complete in just 3 days, which allows more time for diving during your stay. The textbook is sent to your home, so you can do some reading in advance, and most classes have fewer than 4 students, so instruction goes fast. Not that the learning is unpleasant—classes usually take place at sunset at a table on the Hyatt dock. The checkout dives are done at shallow reefs, like Western Dry Rocks or Rock Key, where you see turtles, nurse sharks, spiny lobster, green eels, parrot fish, yellow jack, and rays.

Besides the reef dives, deep dives, and wreck dives around Key West, there's a museum exhibiting gold, silver, and artifacts from the wreck of the Spanish galleon *Atocha*. Key West makes a nice compromise destination if your traveling companion doesn't plan to scuba dive, since there's so much else to do in the famous town. Dress is always casual; shorts and T-shirts go everywhere.

The hotel, too, has the laid-back atmosphere divers want, with rooms overlooking the pool or the ocean, a poolside café, and a more formal indoor-outdoor dining room. Southpoint Divers also has dive packages with lodging provided at reasonably priced guest houses nearby. *Southpoint Divers, 601 Front St., Key West, FL 33040, tel. 305/292–9778 or 800/824–6811. Year-round: 3-day course, $310; 6-day Hyatt dive package, $1,400, including 3-day course, mask, fins, snorkel, lodging, breakfasts, and sunset cruise.*

FLORIDA **Live-Aboard Cruise to Dry Tortugas.** Lost Reef Adventures, an independent dive shop in Key West, and the Yankee Fleet's dive boat have teamed up to create a package that combines a 4-day certification course with a cruise to the Dry Tortugas for 2 days of live-aboard diving. Lost Reef, which also rents and repairs equipment, gives its course under either PADI or NAUI guidelines and takes you out for your checkout dives in its own boat. Divers usually stay at the Days Inn (whose pool is used for classes) or at Island City House, a nearby Victorian bed-and-breakfast with tropical gardens and a pool. Both have doubles and housekeeping suites that sleep up to six, and you can explore the interesting town of Key West as you learn.

You spend the last part of your vacation doing nothing but diving in the Dry Tortugas, a pristine cluster of coral reefs 70 miles west and part of the Fort Jefferson National Monument. Here, in warm water with frequent 100-foot visibility, divers swim along the reefs and explore 16th-century shipwrecks. Some stops are made at virgin sites, where the fish are unafraid and curious, and you're given a tour of the old brick Fort Jefferson before dinner.

The 100-foot-long, air-conditioned diesel cruiser *Yankee Freedom* takes only 28 divers on each trip. The cost of the cruise segment includes an optional third night aboard ship when docked back at Key West. *Lost Reef Adventures, 261 Margaret St., Key West, FL 33040, tel. 305/296–9737 or 800/952–2749. Yankee Fleet, Box 5903, Key West, FL 33041, tel. 305/294–6963 or 800/634–0939 (July–Aug. 508/283–0313). Sept.–June: 4-day course, $300; 2 days, 3 nights aboard* Yankee Freedom, *$350, including meals, air, and weight belts, but not dive gear.*

HAWAII

THE BIG ISLAND **Waikoloa Reef Diving.** When you take this course with Red Sail Sports at the Hyatt Regency Waikoloa, you're at a great diving location—a volcanic site where divers can see underwater lava flows and tunnels formed when the lava hit the sea. You might go to the Pentagon on one of your checkout dives, where lava formations make an interesting cave with five openings, and there's a resident white-tip reef shark. Or perhaps you'll go to the Mauni Lani caves, home of Hawaii's famous green sea turtles.

At the Hyatt Regency Waikoloa, you get a luxury vacation, and you might even win a chance to buy a ticket to swim with dolphins in a pool (the dolphins can't handle all the people who want to do this, so numbers are restricted). The 1,241-room hotel sits on 62 acres, with interconnected canals, waterfalls, and swimming pools, seven restaurants, plenty of other water sports, and a program just for kids. You might also stay at the Royal Waikoloan on the same property, or at the Ritz-Carlton or Mauni Lani, 3 miles away.

The 4-day course (PADI or NAUI) can start any day of the week, and the ratio of students to instructors is held to 4:1. *Red Sail Sports, Hyatt Regency Waikoloa, 1 Wai Beach Resort, Waikoloa, HI 96743, tel. 808/885–2876 or 800/255–6425, fax 808/885–4169. Year-round: 4-day course, $395. Price includes mask, snorkel, and flippers and all equipment on checkout dives, including wet suit.*

MAUI **Lahaina Divers Reef Diving.** Whaler's Village, on the island of Maui, is a quaint place right on the water. Beneath the surface, though, things are positively fascinating; there you see tropical fish, rays, octopus, eels, and white-tip reef sharks against a volcanic terrain. Even in the shallow water off the coast of Lanai, on the checkout dives (which are usually conducted in an area chosen more for calm water than for visual interest), there are lava tubes and pinnacles.

The town has little gift shops, open-air cafés, and the casual feel of a beach town. Lahaina Divers puts up its clients at local condominiums and inns. Classes start twice a week for the 3-day PADI certification course, with instruction in English or Japanese. You're expected to pick up the textbook before the course starts and complete a required reading and study assignment. This gives you a jump-start on the training and allows maximum time for diving.

Lahaina Divers takes certified divers to Molokini Crater sites, where marine life and volcanic formations are plentiful, and where the water is shallow enough for snorkelers to enjoy. On these trips, both snorkelers and divers can spend the day together on the same boat. *Lahaina Divers, Box 1547, Lahaina, Maui, HI 96767, tel. 800/998–3483. Year-round: 3-day course, $232.*

U.S. VIRGIN ISLANDS

ST. CROIX **Cruzan Divers' Reef Diving.** Cruzan Divers is in Frederiksted, on the quiet side of St. Croix, where the pace is more laid-back than it is on the more touristy Christiansted side. Cruzan puts little emphasis on luxury, but your fellow vacationers here are likely to be scuba divers, with whom you can swap fish tales about the one you saw swim by. The diving is good year-round, with water temperature a warm 79°F to 80°F in winter, 82°F to 83°F in summer.

Classes are held in the dive shop, and pool work takes place in the shallow water of the harbor. For your open-water checkout, you might dive around and under the Frederiksted Pier, an easy shallow-water dive where you'll encounter sea horses; or go by boat to Rainbow Reef, Butler Bay wrecks, or King Reef.

Once you get certified, come back to the pier on a night dive, when the lobsters emerge from their hiding places, soft corals come out to feed, and you can touch the sleeping parrot fish. Cruzan Divers also takes boat trips to the north side of the island for wall diving. You slowly ascend from your maximum depth, examining, as you go, the sponges, frogfish, and elkhorn coral living along the wall. You might also spot parrot fish, angelfish, grouper, trunkfish, spotted drum, and eagle rays.

You can stay at the Frederiksted Hotel or at other local digs. In your off-hours, you'll find the nearby beaches are beautiful and clean, and there's horseback riding in the rain forest. And if the bright lights call you, you can always drive or take a taxi-bus to Christiansted. *Cruzan Divers, 12 Strand St., Frederiksted, St. Croix, USVI 00840, tel. 809/772–3701 or 800/352–0107. Year-round: 5-day course, $600. Price includes equipment for checkout dives.*

SOURCES

ORGANIZATIONS Contact the following certifying agencies for the address of an affiliated dive shop in your area and for dive-travel package information: **National Association of Scuba Diving Schools** (1012 S. Yates St., Memphis, TN 38119, tel. 901/767–7265); **National Association of Underwater Instructors** (Box 14650, Montclair, CA 91763, tel. 909/621–5801); **Professional Association of Dive Instructors** (1251 E. Dyer Rd., No. 100, Santa Ana, CA 92705, tel. 714/540–7234), which awards its 5-star rating to shops that have repair centers and are qualified to train divers to become instructors; **Scuba Schools International** (2619 Canton Ct., Fort Collins, CO 80525-4498, tel. 303/482–0883); and **YMCA National Scuba Program** (6083-A Oakbrook Pkwy., Norcross, GA 30092, tel. 404/662–5172).

Divers Alert Network (Box 3823, Duke University Medical Center, Durham, NC 27710, tel. 919/684–2948) is an international non-profit agency that promotes diving safety and sells low-cost diving insurance. The $25 annual membership fee provides an emergency hotline, medical-question line, emergency evacuation (if you're over 100 miles from home), a first-aid manual, and a subscription to *Alert Diver* magazine. **Handicapped Scuba Association** (116 W. El Portal, Suite 104, San Clemente, CA 92672 or 7172 W. Stanford Ave., Littleton, CO 80123, tel. 303/933–4864) certifies dive shops for teaching people with disabilities and provides a list of accessible resorts.

PERIODICALS *Rodale's Scuba Diving* (Box 7589, Red Oak, IA 51591-0589, tel. 800/666–0016), published 8 times a year, covers the practice of diving, dive-travel, the marine environment, health, safety, and dive equipment. *Skin Diver* (Box 52595, Boulder, CO 80322-2595, tel. 800/800–3487) is a monthly with heavy advertising that covers the most popular dive destinations and lists dive shops by state. It's best for new divers. *Scuba Times* (Box 40702, Nashville, TN 37204-9905, tel. 800/950–7282), published bimonthly, has articles on destinations, diving news, and products. *Underwater USA* (Box 705, Bloomsburg, PA 17815, tel. 800/228–3483) is a monthly tabloid newspaper that covers dive sites in the United States, travel, diving news, and equipment; the same company publishes the specialty newsletters "Reef Explorer" and "Wreck Explorer." "Undercurrent" (Box 175, Great Neck Rd., Suite 307, Great Neck, NY 11021, tel. 800/237–8400, ext. 555) is a monthly newsletter (no advertising) that offers objective reviews of resorts, liveaboards, and equipment.

BOOKS Pisces Diving and Snorkeling Guides, a series of 24 guidebooks sold in dive shops, provide dive sites, history, and tourist information for a particular region. The series includes *The Hawaiian Islands, The Florida Keys, The U.S. Virgin Islands,* and *Northern California and the Monterey Peninsula. A Handguide to the Coral Reef Fishes of the Caribbean,* by Joseph Stokes, is a good fish identification book.

Sea Kayaking

by Rena Zurofsky

he first time I tried sea kayaking was in Currituck Sound, behind the Outer Banks of North Carolina. It was early morning, and before shoving off I'd received a life jacket and basic instruction on how to hold the paddle. The water was smooth as glass; it reflected the sky so particularly that when I dipped my paddle I was startled to see clouds waver apart. And as I glided forward, a fish leaped over the bow of my orange plastic boat and disappeared down the other side. I was the one who was hooked.

One of the country's fastest-growing sports, sea kayaking can be as thrilling or as peaceful as you make it. More stable than a whitewater kayak, more comfortable than a canoe, a sea kayak—even one loaded with a week's worth of gear—is maneuverable enough to poke into hidden crevices, explore side bays, and beach on deserted spits of sand. Designed by Inuit peoples for hunting, transportation, and swift travel through icy Arctic waters, kayaks are used today in open oceans, sounds, and large bays, as well as on lakes and slow rivers.

Anyone who doesn't mind getting a little wet and has an average degree of fitness can be a sea kayaker. The basic stroke is a surprisingly easy push-me-pull-you done with a double-bladed paddle; most people pick it up with a minimal amount of instruction. And you don't need that much in the way of basic gear to go sea kayaking, although you do need a kayak. These are made from many materials, including but not limited to seal skin (the original kayaks), wood, canvas, Kevlar, fiberglass, and plastic. Some designs are wide and very stable; others are narrow, fast-moving, and often quite tippy. Then there are collapsible, or folding, kayaks, which can be dismantled and packed into a large duffel bag. Most common are single and double kayaks, although there are custom multiples as well.

Kayaks generally have a fairly roomy cockpit; you sit with your legs comfortably stretched in front of you and your feet braced on adjustable pedals, which work the rudder of your boat. A spray skirt draped around your waist stretches to the rim of the cockpit. Although it can seem a touch claustrophobic, its function is to keep water out of your cockpit, not to keep you locked in. If you should happen to be knocked over by a wave, either the skirt will automatically come free or you can yank the escape cord and slide right out for a swim.

Don't assume that 10 minutes without tipping has adequately prepared you to circumnavigate Baffin Island. There's a lot to learn, and until you know your way around tides, currents, and nautical charts, you should go with an experienced guide who also knows what and how to pack and where to pitch a tent. A reputable outfitter can supply such a guide.

Freelance writer Rena Zurofsky has kayaked the waters of Maine, Mexico, and the northwest coast. In her other life, she is a museum administrator.

Sea kayaking trips with an outfitter generally follow the same basic routine: You and 5 to 11 other paddlers meet 1 or 2 guides either at the put-in or at some other point from which you are shuttled to the put-in. On the first day you work on kayaking technique. You usually learn both the wet exit (how to fall out) and self-rescue (how to get back in). On succeeding days, paddling is interspersed with time to hike, play in the surf, improve your kayaking skills, or just lie around eating the M&Ms and peanuts that seem to be a staple of every mess kit. Itineraries are flexible; how far you paddle each day depends on the ability and stamina of the group as a whole. Although many intrepid sea kayakers do major open-water crossings, it is more common to make modest island crossings of up to, perhaps, 10 miles.

Different outfitters prefer different approaches to guiding, but most station one guide near the front of the group and another near the back to act as "sweep" to make sure the slowest paddlers don't fall behind. Kayaking guides are often trained biologists, botanists, or geologists; those who are not are usually extremely knowledgeable about the locations to which they escort you. Before you leave, you will be provided with reading lists: Use them to enhance your experience.

Most kayak outings are camping trips. You'll be surprised by how much gear can be wedged—with much planning and effort— through the waterproof hatches located in the front and rear of each kayak: clothes, tent, sleeping gear, cooking gear, food, fresh water, first-aid kit, cooking equipment, and more. Still, even fully loaded, a kayak rarely draws more than a few inches of water, and because of its low center of gravity, a packed boat is in fact a more stable craft.

The food on sea kayaking trips varies in quality. On a true expedition, you are expected to carry your share of the provisions in your boat. To keep weight and volume down, pasta, rice, and beans are usually a significant part of your diet, but some outfitters use miniature freezer packs to carry meats, and many fish along the way. All of the outfitters listed below make a point of including as many fresh vegetables and fruits as possible; some stick to strictly vegetarian meals. Keep in mind that on longer trips, if there is no resupply point, you are eventually reduced to dried fruits and few vegetables.

Breakfasts usually consist of granolas, pancakes, oatmeal, or hot multigrain cereal, sometimes eggs and bacon. Lunches are often peanut butter, cheeses, salami, local jams, and homemade breads. Dinners are where an inventive guide can really go to town. Of course, there are the oh-so-familiar "Italian" or "Mexican" menus that are still tasty thanks to an appetite sharpened by a day's paddle. But you might also be served fish chowders, Thai chicken stews, and curried lentils that would be equally savory on shore. There's often wine, and always coffee, tea, and cocoa.

Food is usually prepared over a campfire or a camp stove. You sit where you can and use basic utensils. In our listings, guides tend to do the work unless chore sharing is specifically stated or unless you offer to help. Most people do.

Compared with bicycling or golf-school vacations, sea kayaking is inexpensive. Prices range from less than $100 to $200 per person per day, depending on whether the trip includes special transportation, such as an air charter, or hotel stays. Costs are kept low because camping is the norm and food supplies can be bought in bulk.

This is far from a complete listing of sea kayaking trips and outfitters. Furthermore, if you would rather design your own trip, most operators will customize a tour for you.

CHOOSING THE RIGHT TRIP

In choosing an outfitter, your primary concern should be safety. An outfitter should be equipped with both the proper technical and first-aid gear, and should know what to do with them. Question every outfitter carefully so that you know what you're getting into.

How long has the company been in business?
A couple of years of experience gives an out-

fitter time to work out problems with its operation and itineraries. All of the outfitters listed here have been in business a minimum of three years, although many have been leading trips for five or more.

How long have the guides been leading trips and how long have they been leading in the area where I want to go? The outfitters we list all use guides that have at least five years of kayaking experience, although not necessarily in a particular location. Sometimes it's best to have a guide who knows an area really well, but a guide's first visit can also be exciting. You decide.

What kind of training do the guides have? Look for outfitters whose guides have successfully completed a guiding course, such as those offered by Outward Bound, National Outdoor Leadership School, and Maine Island Kayak Company, or have been certified by either the American Canoe Association or the British Canoe Association.

Because organized sea kayaking is still very much in its infancy, no certification is usually needed to become an outfitter of guided tours. (The state of Maine requires that all outfitters be Registered Maine Guides, a license that involves considerable wilderness training, as well as the ability to make fish chowder.)

What is the participant-to-guide ratio? 5:1 is a recommended maximum, although some reputable outfits push to 6:1 or even 8:1 on calm waters.

How difficult, challenging, and scary is the trip? We've tried to give you an idea of how much skill and stamina you'll need to complete each of the following trips, but you should always ask for more information before you sign up. Keep in mind that if you're interested in a trip but are concerned that it is too advanced for you, most outfitters will happily give you extra instruction (at a price) before you set out. You should also be sure to figure out your own fear levels. Again, be honest with yourself. Knowing how to handle surf is not the same as wanting to learn. At best, a novice among experts curtails every-

one else's enjoyment; at worst, he can put himself in danger. I try to break through the next level with each trip, so I evaluate carefully how much I can handle at once—big waves *and* big mammals?

Is seasickness an issue? If you get seasickness, some trips just won't be any fun. Watch for Hawaii's giant swells.

What will the weather be? It is important for you to evaluate honestly your own tolerance for heat and cold. Nothing can ruin a trip faster than pervasive discomfort.

What are the accommodations like? Most of the time you sleep in tents, but sometimes there are huts or lean-tos and sometimes you sleep under the open skies. If tents are provided, ask how many people sleep in each one.

What's the food like? Some guides are terrific cooks; others just don't care about food. Ask for a menu, and, if you can, talk to someone who has taken the trip.

What kind of boats will you be using and is there a variety of boats to choose from? You'll often hear guides talking about "wearing the boat." That means that the kayak becomes an extension of its paddler, a state that makes the paddling experience not only more comfortable but also much more fun. Ask whether the outfitter stocks a variety of boats, so you can experiment until you find the kayak that best fits your weight, strength, ability, and paddling style.

What's the cost and what's included? The trips we list start at the point of put-in and include transportation back to that point. Transportation from and to the local airport is not included, although some outfitters provide it at a nominal fee. The trip fee also covers meals from lunch the first day to lunch the last. Unless otherwise stated, outfitters on these trips provide all kayaking gear (boats, spray skirts, personal flotation devices, wet suits, neoprene booties if necessary, and paddles), plus tents, cookware, and first-aid equipment, but *not* sleeping bags and pads.

How far in advance do you need to sign up? As you might expect, outfitters want you to sign up as far in advance as possible for a simple reason: If they don't get enough customers, it's not financially worth it to run the trip. For trips offered regularly, 30 days in advance might do. For trips offered infrequently or in faraway places, signing up anywhere from six months to a year in advance is not outrageous. There are, however, always last-minute cancellations, so if you want to go on a trip a week from next Thursday, give the outfitter a call; a spot may have opened up.

Can you supply names of people who have taken this trip? This is one sure way to find out whether a good, safe time is usually had by all.

MAJOR PLAYERS

Sea kayaking is only lately becoming widely popular, so no organizations run trips throughout the nation. The following, however, do offer a host of trips in limited areas.

SIERRA CLUB OUTINGS DEPARTMENT

This organization has a huge roster of expeditions and other trips, all run by leaders who are both members and volunteers. But unlike its selection of backpacking and hiking trips, which number in the hundreds, there may be only half a dozen sea kayaking trips. From year to year, destinations change, leaders change, trips to a particular area or with a particular leader may follow a different itinerary. Still, there are almost always a couple of trips to Alaska and off the coast of Georgia; Baja trips are offered fairly frequently; and trips in the Midwest, to destinations such as Wisconsin's Apostle Islands, put in an occasional appearance. Camping out and group participation in camp chores are the operative protocols, and costs are low to moderate (730 Polk St., San Francisco, CA 94109, tel. 415/923–5522, fax 415/776–4868).

ALASKA DISCOVERY
This company holds the exclusive concession for sea kayaking trips in Glacier Bay National Park. In other words, these guys know what they're doing

(5449-4 Shaune Dr., Juneau, AK 99801, tel. 907/780–6226, fax 907/780–4220).

BLUE MOON EXPLORATIONS
Blue Moon's Kathleen Grimbly combined her interest in cultural anthropology and nature studies with kayaking. As a result, you are as likely to dine on traditional Pacific Northwest Indian planked salmon on her trips as you are to paddle with migrating orca whales. Blue Moon specializes in customized tours, including corporate retreats and women's workshops (Box 2568, Bellingham, WA 98227, tel. and fax 206/966–8805).

MAINE ISLAND KAYAK COMPANY
With more than 10 years of experience, MIKCO offers instructional seminars and island-camping trips all along the Maine Island Trail, as well as in Nova Scotia. Although the back office can be a little confused at times (sometimes they change put-in sites with little warning), MIKCO trips are professional and enjoyable, with camp food that's a revelation (70 Luther St., Peaks Island, ME 04108, tel. 207/766–2373, fax 207/773–8601).

OUTWARD BOUND
If you don't mind the constant emphasis on team-building and community, Outward Bound programs offer some of the best paddling-skills workshops and trips in the country. Be aware, however, that having fun is often second on the agenda, and food is even lower still. Outward Bound runs sea kayaking programs in Maine, North Carolina, Minnesota, and Oregon (Rte. 9D, R2, Box 280, Garrison, NY 10524–9757, tel. 914/424–4000 or 800/243–8520, fax 914/424–4280). For more about Outward Bound, *see* Wilderness and Survival Schools.

SOUTHWIND SPORTS RESOURCES
This extremely professional operation places a strong emphasis on training and skills, for both beginner and advanced paddlers. It has a full complement of kayaks, so you're sure to find a model that suits you best (1088 Irvine Blvd., Suite 212, Tustin, CA 92680, tel. 714/261–0200).

FAVORITE TRIPS

THE NORTHEAST

MAINE **Prospect Harbor via Jonesport to Machias.** Fog makes this trip an exercise in trust: Trust that the guide can read his or her compass; trust that he or she hears the big boats out there; trust that the shadow the guide is asking you to strain to see is in fact a granite-and-pine island where you can legally rest.

This trip is the quintessential tour of the Maine Island Trail, a 325-mile-long waterway in northern Maine that stretches from Casco Bay to Machias. You travel along the northern edge of the trail, which has the most demanding water, the most varied terrain, the most striking vistas, and the fewest signs of civilization.

You meet at 8 AM in the Prospect Harbor area, where you spend the entire first day developing your kayaking skills. Wet suits are distributed so that you can practice wet exits and self-rescues. Although the Maine coast has its calm moments, wind, rain, and waves are a real possibility; big-boat traffic and fog are virtual certainties—especially around the Petit Manan bar, an underwater ridge whose volcanic spires stretch 3 miles out into the sea. The spires force the cold Labrador current to the surface of the water, causing this area to have the reputation of second foggiest spot on the East Coast.

The island and mainland landscapes you paddle past are striking in their variety. Although much of the underlying rock is granite, you see everything from mile-long white sand beaches to imposing cliffs climbing out of the surf. At the southern end of the trip the vegetation is deciduous, but soon you see conifers, then subarctic jack pines. Many of these islands are owned by the Nature Conservancy and are home to eagles, puffins, and other seabirds. On those that are not privately owned, you hike along cobble beaches and over grassy slopes. You may even attempt a stop on the island called Ladle Ledges, if Bojangles, the foul-tempered territorial black ram, allows it. You might also see seals, harbor porpoise, and minks.

As on most kayaking trips, the distances you cover are dictated by a combination of group strength and weather conditions. Assume you'll paddle anywhere between 8 and 15 miles per day, unless you are totally weathered in. Every few nights the group may opt to remain at a campsite for more hiking or kayaking instruction. Campsites are strictly wilderness, and you are expected to pack out everything you've brought in.

Food on this trip consists of fresh vegetables, home baked breads, grains, even pizza. Fish may be caught and lobster may be bought. Depending on the time of year, you may dig for mussels or forage for berries. On or about the fifth day, you stop in Jonesport, where fresh provisions are picked up and you might get a shower.

A maximum of 6 people are accompanied by 2 guides on this trip. Single kayaks are used. You should be in good physical shape with some previous paddling experience. *Maine Island Kayak Company, 70 Luther St., Peaks Island, ME 04108, tel. 207/766-2373. June and July: 7 days, $795; 8 days, $900; 9 days, $975.*

THE SOUTH

FLORIDA **The Everglades and the 10,000 Islands.** Alligators, mosquitoes, and gnats—all are abundant in these swampy waters. But although every kayaker is sure to be bit by the latter two, as far as I know no kayaker has actually been eaten by an alligator. That's not to say that you won't be tense when one or more suddenly emerges from the quiet waters.

On this outing you just day-trip into the mangrove swamps of the Everglades, and reemerge to camp on the breezy, sandy beaches on the Gulf of Mexico. Some days you may not even venture into the mysterious mangroves. The group dynamic and the weather (if it blows out of the west) put you inland onto the 100-mile-long Wilderness Waterway (a marked water trail that runs from Flamingo to Everglades City) or keep you on the Gulf, where you can kayak from key to key, or back and forth between the mainland and the islands.

Beginning in Everglades City, the group heads south, camping in places with names like Pavilion Key and Turkey Key. These are sandy spots that are less atmospheric but more comfortable than the wooden stilt "chickees" and shell mounds available in the mangrove swamps themselves. Actually, sleeping on a sandy beach with the Gulf waters lapping the shores is not exactly lacking atmosphere, is it?

You paddle 5 to 6 hours a day. If the waters are clear you might see black-tips or nurse sharks. You're almost certain to spot dolphins. There are eagles, ospreys, swallow-tailed kites, the occasional flamingo, and alligators (only in the swamps). Some motorboat and sailing traffic is sure to be about, especially at Everglades City and Flamingo, but most beaches are absolutely pristine, framed by beach grasses and coastal palms.

The guide prepares your meals, but you are welcome to bring gear and fish for the group's dinners. Since you have to carry your whole week's worth of water in your boats, much of the food is freeze-dried, and pastas and beans are a significant part of your menu.

The maximum group size is 8, accompanied by one guide, in rigid single and double boats. This trip is suitable for all levels of paddlers. The best time to go is winter, and even then the days will be quite warm and moist, though cooler in the evenings. *Florida Bay Outfitters, 104 Overseas Hwy., Key Largo, FL 33037, tel. 305/451–3018. Mid-Nov.–mid-Apr.: 7 days, $650. Price includes sleeping bags and foam pads.*

NORTH CAROLINA **The Outer Banks.** For those of you who have avoided Outward Bound because you don't *want* to lose your fear of rappelling, this sea kayaking venture is a way in. Okay, in order to build group spirit you and your 10 fellow paddlers have to discuss every move you make, but that isn't

really a bad idea. And you spend one day doing some type of public service—working with wild ponies, studying dune formation, or hanging out with retired fishermen—but that isn't so bad either.

The North Carolina Outward Bound School offers 9 days of cruising the Outer Banks with 2 guides that have wilderness-survival expertise and are trained in basic communications and group facilitations. Their job is to "facilitate" good group interaction and to teach you skills like compass-reading and navigation. And to get you in shape for your solo camping experience—an Outward Bound must.

The trip starts at New Bern airport, and put-in is nearby, on the Neuse River. You paddle along the river and around the waters near Cape Lookout National Seashore, south of the Wright Brothers national monument. Happily, this area is well-removed from the heavily built-up beach towns of more northern Outer Banks. If conditions are calm, you may try ocean kayaking; otherwise, there is room enough and interest enough to stay on the inland side. It's pretty easy paddling, in and out of marshlands and tidal flats. You are challenged physically when you learn wet exits and self-rescues, but few crossings are more than a mile.

At night, you camp in the wilderness on remote beaches, with no facilities. You rise at dawn and spend the day in motion, paddling as many as 25 miles if conditions are excellent. But there are also days when you pass the time exploring dunes, acquiring map and compass skills, or engaging in service activities. At the end of the trip, you are left alone for 24 hours, an experience that is usually so peaceful that you wish it lasted longer.

The maximum group size is 10, accompanied by 2 guides, in single and double kayaks. The minimum age is 18. This trip is suitable for all levels of paddlers. *North Carolina Outward Bound School, 121 North Sterling St., Morganton, NC 28655-3443, tel. 704/437–6112 or 800/554–5375. May, Sept., Oct.: 9 days, $1,095 ($100 discount if you sign up 90 days in advance).*

THE MIDWEST

MINNESOTA AND ONTARIO Lake Superior: Sibley Peninsula and Pukaskwa Park. Kayaking around these two island-dotted landscapes is like taking a trip into a fabulous canvas: Everywhere are bold strokes of bold colors, deep greens and blues, cut by the sharp gray of granite cliffs and boulders. The world's largest freshwater lake, Superior provides a kayaking experience that is just as varied as that offered by an ocean: still waters, wind and waves, fog and rain.

This trip begins at the University of Minnesota in Duluth, where you catch a van to a small inland lake, Marie Louise, on Ontario's Sibley Peninsula. You spend 2 nights camping here, with the first day devoted to improving your paddling skills while kayaking on Marie Louise, and then trying them out on an afternoon excursion on Lake Superior. There, the steep-banked, pebbly beached, rugged islands have quartz veins running through them, and if conditions are right, you can look down into the water where the quartz gleams through.

On the third morning you're driven to Canada's Pukaskwa National Park, on the northeast corner of the lake, for an afternoon put-in that begins 5 full days of paddling.

There's a lot to learn on this trip: You make open-water crossings, explore the interesting coast and rock outcrops, and tackle potentially wild river entries, made difficult to cross because of the runoff from upriver waterfalls. Caribou sightings are a definite possibility, and you may also see moose, white-tailed deer, black bears, river otters, osprey, and eagles.

Although this trip can be rough at times, it is an excellent introduction to different conditions and good for beginners: Open-water crossings are minimal (less than 1 mile) and paddling distances are just 8 to 10 miles per day. Kayakers with more advanced skills enjoy the landscape and are challenged by the often-changing weather.

Just because the trip is school-sponsored doesn't mean that you travel with a young and rowdy crowd. The group tends to be mixed, with some teenagers and some middle-aged folks. Often a professor comes along. Sometimes no one in the entire group is affiliated with the university. Chores are assigned. The maximum size of the group is 8 paddlers, accompanied by 2 guides, in rigid single or double kayaks. *Kayak and Canoe Institute, University of Minnesota Outdoor Program, 121 Sports and Health Center, 10 University Dr., Duluth, MN 55812-2496, tel. 218/726–6533, fax 218/726–6539. Late July–early Aug.: 9 days, $521, $331 for UMD students. Price includes van transportation from Duluth.*

THE SOUTHWEST

UTAH Lake Powell. If you wanted to kayak much of the Colorado River, you'd need a whitewater craft and a great deal of skill and nerve. But the imposition of the Glen Canyon Dam has rendered one part of that mighty river into a 186-mile-long lake that even a beginning kayaker can handle. And the desert Chinook winds make for an occasionally wavy good time.

Starting off from Hall's Crossing in the southeast corner of the lake, you paddle a mere 3 to 10 miles a day, maybe 15 if the group is really cooking. You must like heat and sun, because temperatures average in the low 80s and shade is hard to find. Under these conditions, falling out of your kayak is a welcome cold relief.

When you're not on the water, you have the opportunity to take hikes in the side canyons. Some hikes lead to Anasazi ruins; others just lead you to discover gleaming, sinuous slickrocks, and desert flora and fauna—cacti and turkey vultures and rattlesnakes.

The downside of this trip is that the lake gets 3 million visitors annually, and most of them believe in motor boats and jet skis. And then there are the houseboats, which are moored in every scenic cove. Luckily, your kayak takes you into the shallow, narrow, out-of-the-way places the houseboats can't go. And Glen

Canyon Dam's seasonal releases reveal or conceal caves, coves, and beaches along the lake's 1,960 miles of shoreline, which means there is plenty of quiet and solitude, if you know where to find it.

You camp in private red-rock canyons, or surrounded by gleaming white slick-rocks or sand, with the vivid blue of the water creating a landscape of stark contrasts in color and light. Although nights dip into the 30s, camping in this environment is an aesthetic tour de force, since the colors flattened by the light of day are often heightened by moonlight. The food is vegetarian, with a lot of pastas, soups, and chilies.

This company specializes in creating trips that can be joined by people with disabilities, who make up about half of most groups and participate in every activity. The guides are well trained to work with them.

The maximum size of the group is 8 paddlers, accompanied by 2 guides. Only triple kayaks are used. This trip is suitable for all levels. *Wilderness Inquiry, Inc., 1313 Fifth St. SE, Box 84, Minneapolis, MN 55414-1546, tel. 612/379–3858 or 800/728–0719, fax 612/379–5972. Mar.–Apr.: 8 days, $695. Price does not include $175 for round-trip van from Minneapolis (1 1/2 days each way; be prepared to be driven through the night).*

THE WEST COAST

WASHINGTON **San Juan Islands, Orca Waters.** The name of this trip says it all and should set your mood for 5 days with orcas, also known as killer whales (although their black-and-white markings always make me think of them as water pandas). Despite their name and their size (adults generally reach about 25 feet in length), they have never been known to so much as dump a kayaker. Actually, the pods that revisit these waters tend to feast on salmon, herring, and other local fish.

The trip sets out from Friday Harbor, a San Juan port that can be reached by a 4-hour ferry ride from Seattle. The San Juans are in the rain shadow of the Olympic and Cascade mountains, so they enjoy a mild, sunny climate, which means you just might stay dry while you're kayaking.

You launch from the west side of the island and head northwest. The trips vary in itinerary because the goal is to follow the whales, but you often cross into Canadian waters. An average day's paddling is 5 or 6 hours, depending on the winds, tides, and currents among the countless islands that make up the San Juan archipelago. As with most trips, wildlife sightings aren't guaranteed, but certain pods of orcas have returned again and again to these waters, and outfitters such as Sea Quest, which is run by a marine biologist, have long made it their business to know the best spots to spot whales. In addition to the orcas, you may luck into the occasional loner minke whale, or some gregarious seals and sea lions. Birds in the area include bald eagles and the adorable, piping, orange-trimmed oyster catcher.

A maximum of 12 are taken in rigid double kayaks by 2 guides. Paddling instruction takes place on land, and you won't learn a wet exit and self-rescue, so it's comforting to be in the bigger double boats when whales surround you. It is also good to be in the bigger boats when some of the local motor boat traffic attempts to rush the whales. *Sea Quest Expeditions, Zoetic Research, Box 2424, Friday Harbor, WA 98250, tel. 206/378–5767. June–Sept.: 5 days, $399.*

ALASKA

SOUTHEAST **Glacier Bay Grand Sea Kayak.** It's a rare sea kayaker who hasn't gone or doesn't yearn to go to Alaska. Forget the cold. It isn't that cold in summer: 50°F to 80°F, although it gets colder at night. Instead, picture deep icy bays in perfect blue stillness, interrupted by the great cracking sound of a glacier calving and huge chunks of ice thundering into the water. Imagine the sounding of whales, their breath almost welcomed for its heat (although, really, it is very fishy). Although law dictates that you don't get too close to the whales, and the guides will do their best to have you all maintain respectful distances, the whales have been known to make their own approaches and surface as little as 20 feet away!

For this 7-day Alaska Discovery trip you begin in Gustavus and are flown into Glacier Bay National Park. You paddle the entire length of the east arm of the bay, a route that totals 60 miles of rigorous paddling.

There's the chance—the risk—that grizzly bears and wolves will share your sunlit nights. The guides choose your campsites for availability of water, protection from the weather, and accessibility to hiking trails. They lead beach and meadow walks, carrying bear mace for your protection. The food is not strictly vegetarian, but vegetarians are accommodated. Anglers can fish for salmon and halibut (bring your own gear). You move camp daily, and you're expected to share the chores.

You get basic paddle training, but no training for wet exits, because, frankly, you don't want to fall out in this water. Alaska hands may grouse that you won't see the variety of marine life that you might on a trip in nearby Icy Strait, but odds are you'll spot Stellar's sea lions, sea otters, harbor seals, and harbor porpoises.

The old rain forest at the entrance to Glacier Bay is 200 years older than the back of the bay, where the glacier is still retreating. As you head north, the vegetation alters, moving from conifers to cottonwood, finally to scrub brush and lichen before turning to barren rock. Birds abound, including bald eagles, an assortment of gulls, loons, horned and tufted puffins, cormorants, hawks, ptarmigans, owls, kingfishers, and herons. Be aware, however, that as you travel north, the land and climate support life in less abundance. To see wildlife, you must be patient. The weather is likely to be wet, with rain falling at some point in the day, either in a heavy mist or a downpour, and skies often overcast. Consider in your planning that June gets 18 hours of light, but August gets the Northern Lights.

The maximum group size is 10 paddlers in double kayaks, accompanied by 2 guides.

Energetic beginners will do okay, but you need to be fit because on some days you must work hard on the water to reach the desirable campsites. Note: Trips alternate paddling south-to-north and north-to-south, but all end in Gustavus. *Alaska Discovery, 5449-4 Shaune Dr., Juneau, AK 99801, tel. 907/780–6226, fax 907/780–4220. June–Aug.: 7 days, $1,800. Price includes round-trip air charter between Gustavus and Glacier Bay as well as rain and sleeping gear.*

HAWAII

KAUAI **Na Pali Coast.** There are real reasons why the Hawaiian islands are called paradise: the ocean breezes, the wavering palms, the fast hard rains that cool you for the few minutes it takes to dry off. There are private pools and waterfalls, fragrant naupaka, beach morning glories, and dense vegetation from coconut palms to the multibranched, broad-leafed milo tree. But paradise comes at a price for paddlers, and the cost, in this case, is surf.

Hawaii is the surf capital of the world, and on this 5-day Na Pali Coast trip you may have to steer straight into a 6-foot wave that's just about to crash or, if you're lucky, ride it in. If the idea of eating sand fills you with fear, this is probably not the trip for you. But if you're daring and you don't get seasick, these ocean swells will float you to semiremote gleaming white sand beaches, such as the gorgeous crescent of Milolii.

Actually, you camp on only two beaches, Kalalau and Milolii, taking day trips out from each. So if you're rejected by the ocean, you can hike to deep pools and great sand dunes, or follow trails to waterfalls. And the sea conditions can't be too bad, anyway, since the outfitter regularly gets ice floated in (to Kalalau, at least). There aren't too many outfitters, except those in the Arctic, who can accomplish ice!

The trip puts in at Haena Beach Park early in the day, before the winds come up. Your days of kayaking—short hops of only about 6 miles—may take you exploring into sea caves that open into vaults of light or contain secret waterfalls. Although paddling instruction is strictly basic, fit beginners will do just fine. The primary concern is seasickness. You will probably learn a wet exit by doing one in the surf zone. On at least 2 days—if the group wants to—you paddle to good snorkeling spots. Free time is a Hawaiian specialty, and the guides give you as much as you want.

The beaches that are your base are equipped with open-air showers and very basic toilet facilities, but you still sleep in a tent or right out under the stars. Wild passion fruit, guavas, papayas, and bananas are on the menu, as are fresh ahi (yellowfin tuna), fresh vegetables, local Portuguese breads, and wine. There's poi if you want it, too. Chores are shared.

Unfortunately, others know about this little bit of paradise, so you'll be buzzed occasionally by pleasure boaters and helicopter tours. The maximum group size is 12 paddlers accompanied by 2 guides in double kayaks. *Kayak Kauai Outfitters, Box 508, Hanalei, Kauai, Hawaii 96714, tel. 808/826–9844 or 808/822–9179, fax 808/822–0577. May–Aug.: 5 days, $900. Price includes transport by van from Hanalei or Princeville Airport.*

SOURCES

ORGANIZATIONS There are many regional kayaking clubs, and most of them actively schedule trips throughout the United States. The best way to find out about clubs near you or about clubs that operate in the areas you wish to visit, is to contact the **Trade Association of Sea Kayakers** (Box 84144, Seattle, WA 98124, tel. 206/621–1018). TASK can also refer you to member outfitters. You can also call *Canoe* magazine's Club Hotline (tel. 800/MY CANOE), or refer to the back pages of *Sea Kayaker* magazine.

PERIODICALS A monthly magazine, *Canoe* (Box 316, Kirkland, WA 98083-3146, tel. 206/827–6363 or 800/678–5432) includes articles on canoeing and kayaking techniques, destinations, and resources. *Paddler* (Box 775450, Steamboat Springs, CO 80477, tel. 303/879–1450) covers canoeing, kayaking, and rafting; it contains a calendar of events and equipment reviews. The quarterly *Sea Kayaker* (6327 Seaview Ave. NW, Seattle, WA 98107-2664, tel. 206/789–9536) discusses equipment, technique, and journeys in-depth.

BOOKS *Sea Kayaking: A Manual for Long-Distance Touring,* by John Dowd, is a reference covering equipment, techniques, survival skills, and expedition planning. Fully illustrated, *The Essential Sea Kayaker,* by David Seidman, covers basic and advanced sea kayaking techniques, and tells you what to wear, how to travel to your put-ins, and more. You'll learn about safety and how to read charts and recognize sea conditions when you read *The Coastal Kayaker's Manual,* by Randel Washburne. This book also gives you information on what to wear and how to pack. Maps and descriptions of trips along the Northeast Seaboard can be found in *Sea Kayaking along the New England Coast,* by Tamsin Venn. Its Hawaiian counterpart is *Paddling Hawaii,* by Audrey Sutherland, and for information on the West Coast, try Joel Rogers's *The Hidden Coast—Kayak Explorations From Alaska to Mexico.*

ALSO SEE There are lots of other trips that you can take in a kayak. Canoeing and Kayaking in Flatwater tells you about the calm ones, and Canoeing and Kayaking in Whitewater puts you on the rapids.

Ski Schools

by Rosemary Freskos

hether you're an expert parallel skier or a beginner with a sense of adventure, a ski school vacation can be life-enhancing. It's not the same as simply going to a resort and taking one or two hour-long lessons. What we're talking about here is *intensive* skiing—skiing every day for up to 6 hours with an instructor watching you and drilling you and pushing you ahead. Not only do you learn how to ski better, you also learn that if you try harder, you can always do better, on and off the slopes.

Just about every ski resort in the United States has a ski school, but they are not all the same. Some small operations at small resorts offer only short group lessons and private lessons; others have 1,000 instructors teaching programs for every level.

The better (and usually bigger) ski schools demand and get the most professional teachers, usually those that are certified by the Professional Ski Instructors of America, or PSIA. To get certified, a skier must first take a ski school instructor-training course and become an instructor. Then he or she can take a PSIA exam. Instructors commonly pass PSIA Levels I and II within two years; passing Level III is a rare achievement that takes from 5 to 8 years. (Most instructors teach for only 4 years before moving on to other professions.)

There are different methods of teaching peo-ple how to ski, but PSIA-certified instructors learn to teach using the organization's American Teaching System (ATS), which aims to make learning to ski as easy as possible. Following the ATS manual, instructors teach both novices and experts by breaking down the act of skiing into basic components: pressure control movements, edging movements, rotary movements, and balancing movements. The ATS allows an instructor to adapt his or her lessons to the particular terrain and to the ability of the skiers being taught.

Although the ATS is most popular in the United States, it is certainly not the only way to go. The Austrian, French, and Swiss teaching methods are also used. With these methods you still need to learn the basic wedge turn, but you learn a different style of skiing. For example, the Austrian style is more rigid than the American; it emphasizes a stable upper body and strong counter rotation, with legs held together. On the other hand, the French style is to rotate the body and lean into the turns. Some resorts have their own teaching methods, usually variations on the ATS, and some are now using the Perfect Turn method, which was developed by Maine's Sunday River resort.

No matter what method is used, the quality of teaching at any school is greatly affected by the ski school director, who motivates

Rosemary Frekos, a regular contributor to Fodor's guides, has been writing about snow sports for some two decades. She took her first ski lessons on Ohio's modest slopes and has since skied at most of the world's major ski resorts. She now lives and skis in the Lake Tahoe region.

instructors and adapts the teaching system to best suit the area's terrain and clientele.

Once you're with an instructor what can you expect? In the first hour you learn to balance, walk around and climb by side-stepping. Then you learn to slide down a very gentle incline, turn, and, hopefully, stop. The most important lesson is the one on how to fall and how to get up. By the second lesson you should feel secure enough to get that "whee" thrill of sliding while in control. You'll be making linked wedge turns and steering around obstacles. Those are the basics. Some skiers stay there for years; others get their skis together and make decent parallel turns in 3 or 4 days. It's up to you.

Once you've felt the power of mastering the "white bread" slopes—smooth and flat—the urge to go higher, longer, and steeper will drive you to learn to ski the crusty "sourdough," where skiers hoot and holler with excitement.

Age is no excuse to avoid skiing, but physical condition is. It's best to have all your parts working up to optimum level before tackling the slopes; this lessens the chance of pulled muscles and broken limbs. But even if you're in good shape, don't overdo it. Four to six hours of skiing is only for those in top condition; 2 to 3 hours of steady skiing is usually enough for the average person. If possible, avoid beginning your lessons on a weekend, since midweek classes are usually smaller and the slopes, less crowded. It's also less expensive to ski during the week.

Safety is a primary concern of ski areas as well as most skiers. The National Ski Patrol, a well-trained organization of volunteers and paid members is an important part of every ski area's staff. They help skiers in trouble and try to prevent accidents and promote safe skiing.

CHOOSING THE RIGHT SCHOOL

Many people plan their vacation and then ask about the ski school, but if you really want to *go to ski school* you must concentrate on asking questions about the ski school programs rather than about the resort. Start with these:

How long has the ski school been in business? The more experience the school has, the more smoothly your lessons are likely to go.

Who are the instructors and what are their qualifications? Instruction costs the same no matter how well qualified or inexperienced the instructor. Although it's good to have an instructor who is PSIA certified, there are instructors who are not certified who are just as good.

If I'm not improving or communicating with my instructor can I request another one and another class at no extra charge? Sometimes you just don't feel comfortable with a particular instructor. Make sure you have the option of switching.

How large are the classes and if I'm the only one signed up for a group lesson will I still get the group rate? The maximum number of skiers for a good class is 10, but it's better to have just 6. At most schools you still pay the group rate if you're the only one who has signed up for a group class.

Do you use video for student analysis? Progressive schools film you while you're skiing and use the tape to show you what you're doing wrong (or right). Some even give you the tape at the end of the course.

What's the cost and what's included? Pricing for ski school programs varies in a big way. Some schools supply only lessons; others include lodging, meals, lift tickets, and rentals. Unless otherwise stated, prices given here are for the particular program that is described and include your lessons only. When lodging is included, prices are per person, double occupancy, unless otherwise stated.

What are the accommodations like? Ski areas have hotels, apartments, and, sometimes, bed-and-breakfasts. If you're buying a package, ask for specifics about your room. If you need to book your own accommodations, make sure you know all your options.

What is the food like? Find out what kind of restaurants are on the mountain and if there is a grocery store nearby.

Do you have references from past guests? It's a good idea to talk with someone who has taken the course and can tell you more specifics about how it is run. Be sure to ask who the best instructors are.

How far in advance do I need to book? Special programs fill up quickly, so you may need to reserve a spot a few months in advance; other programs will take you on arrival at the resort.

FAVORITE SCHOOLS

THE NORTHEAST

MAINE **Sunday River.** Janet Spangler's 6-day Women's Ski Experience focuses on self-empowerment: Women come together for a holistic approach to skiing—including lessons on nutrition, stress reduction, and massage—and they learn lessons applicable to life on the way.

Spangler, who designed the program, has been teaching at ski areas in the East since the mid-80s. Every member of her 15-woman staff is PSIA certified. Sunday River is where the Perfect Turn Skier Development Program began and all Women's Ski Experience professionals (as the ski instructors are called here) use this method.

The program starts off on Sunday afternoon, when the group of about 40 women gathers at a reception to check in and watch an "If You Ski Like This" video. Each woman picks her skiing level with the assistance of a pro, and then identifies her personal learning style (i.e., experiential, analytical), and groups of 5 or 6 are formed.

A group headquarters is set up in a banquet room at the resort's Summit Hotel. This is where you eat your breakfast (a hot and cold buffet spread that changes daily), stretch, and change into ski clothes. Afternoon refreshments are served here, and this is where you come to see yourself skiing on video.

The 5-hour daily coaching sessions focus on group progress in the morning. You have lunch together every day at a different restaurant at the resort. The afternoons are more specialized—you may work on bumps, gates, or steep terrain. You will be filmed at some point in the week, and later you watch and critique yourself. The video is yours to keep. In the late afternoon you can attend seminars covering ski tuning, conditioning, and nutrition, or relax on your own.

The program ends after the Friday session, but there's a festive dinner on Thursday night at the Summit. Everyone gets some kind of award to wrap up the week.

In recent years a new peak and trails were added at Sunday River, bringing the total number of trails to 90 on the 5 peaks (tallest has a vertical drop of 2,011 feet) that comprise the ski terrain. The area has a base elevation of 782 feet and is served by 12 lifts. Although much of the skiing could be classed as intermediate, there are a number of expert runs at the summits, including White Heat, billed as the longest, steepest, and widest trail in the East accessible by a lift.

Women can request a roommate to share hotel costs (not included) or bring a male guest who can make his own skiing arrangements. *Sunday River Resort, Box 450 Bethel, ME 04217, tel. 207/824–3000 or 800/543–2754, fax 207/824–2111. Dec.–Mar.: 6 days, $559. Price includes breakfasts, lunches, 1 dinner, and lift tickets.*

NEW HAMPSHIRE **Waterville Valley.** This resort is renowned for its European style, classic ski week, in which skiers ski and participate in après-ski activities with the same group and instructor all week. Josef Jung—former technical director of the St. Moritz, Switzerland, ski school—directs and trains an international staff of 150 instructors trained in the American Teaching System (ATS).

Beginners, experts, and everyone in between can take advantage of the resort's Ultimate New England Ski Weeks, which include 5 days of lessons and lift passes with 5 nights in an all-suite lodge. Ski week activities begin on Monday mornings, but if you arrive on Sunday afternoon you can ski the half-day free. There's a welcome party on Monday after lessons. You spend 4 hours a day with an instructor—2 in the morning and 2 in the afternoon. There are never more than 10 skiers in one group. Video analysis is done once during the week, and instructors will give you race training if you want to enter the Thursday Fun Race.

Waterville Valley has 53 runs, 60% of which are intermediate, 20% beginner, and 20% advanced. Base elevation is 1,984 feet, and the vertical drop is 2,020 feet. There are 13 lifts, including a base-to-summit high-speed detachable quad.

This is a family-oriented resort—an ice-skating party, hot chocolate by a bonfire, horse-drawn sleigh rides, and a magic show are all part of the ski week festivities. At the end of the week everyone attends the farewell awards dinner.

There are 8 other ski resorts clustered in these White Mountains, most within a 20-minute drive of one another. The clapboard structures of Waterville Valley's charming New England–style Town Square village sit on the valley floor, surrounded by 4,000-foot mountains that form a stunning backdrop. Town Square houses several shops, restaurants, and a country store. When you're not skiing downhill, you can try going cross-country skiing or snowshoeing on over 100 km of trails at the resort, including 7 km of groomed and tracked trails. Or you can work out at the multimillion-dollar indoor sports center. Teens have their own night club on weekends and holidays, and there are day and evening child-care facilities for younger kids. *Waterville Valley Resort, Town Square, Waterville Valley, NH 03215, tel. 603/236–8311 or 800/ 468–2553, fax 603-236–4174. Mid-Dec.–early Apr.: 5 days, $860–$1,075 for 2 people. Price includes lodging, 1 dinner, and lift tickets.*

VERMONT **Killington.** Killington, like California's Mammoth, deserves superlatives: It's the largest ski resort in the East and one of the best. Its 6 different peaks, covered by 155 trails, would take a week to explore. It has a total of 19 lifts, including a 3½-mile gondola and 2 high-speed quads. Because Killington makes snow—more than any other area in the world—it has the East's longest ski season, running from mid-October to June.

A leader and innovator since its inception in 1958, the Killington Ski School is headed by John Okolovich, who has a staff of 235 full- and part-time instructors. Most are selected from the top graduates of Killington's Instructors' Training Program given each year in late November. The Killington Ski School uses the Accelerated Learning Method (ALM), and it has 99% of beginners skiing from Killington Peak by the third day.

If you've never skied before or you've only skied the so-called bunny hill, sign up for the Introduction to Skiing Program. It's a 1- to 7-day class that aims to get people comfortable enough on skis to enjoy and appreciate skiing. This program begins with a half-hour film about the ALM, and then you are shuttled to Snowshed, where the elevation is 2,500 feet, and the slope is an open 300 feet wide with specially contoured terrain for teaching different techniques. It's separate from other parts of the mountain but open to all skiers (quite a few take advantage of the run, which is serviced by 4 lifts). Here you are introduced to exercises—stopping, wedge turns, side stepping, and getting on and off a lift—at learning stations. Each skier progresses through the stations at his or her own pace. When you are able to control your speed and direction, you are assigned to a compatible group, and the group continues as a whole through more advanced stations.

Students learn about chair lifts on an instructor-pushed model prior to their first ride. The 2-hour lesson is followed by coaching and skiing tips. A lift pass for Snowshed and Rams Head areas is included, as is equipment.

This instructional program is available in 1- to 7-day formats to allow for different learning speeds. You could, for example, go through the stations for a few days, or you could work in a group with an instructor and skiers at your level after doing the stations just once.

Killington does not own lodging, but you can find out about a variety of packages from the Killington Lodging Bureau and Travel Service. *Killington Ski School, c/o Killington Lodging*

Bureau and Travel Service, Killington Rd., Killington, VT 05751, tel. 802/422–3333 or 800/621–MTNS, fax 802/422–4391. Oct.–June: $45 per day. Price includes limited lift pass and rentals.

VERMONT **Okemo.** For several years Okemo has been making improvements that have placed it in the major resort category and attracted a lot of vacationing families. High-speed lifts, snowmaking on 95% of the runs, meticulous snow-grooming, mostly gentle intermediate slopes (along with steeper gladed trails), and modernized day lodges are some of the draws. In addition, all facilities at the bottom of the mountain are easily accessed.

Okemo has developed a number of instruction programs, but one of the perennial favorites is the Women's Ski Spree, under the direction of Jennifer Speck and completely designed and run by women. Jennifer's philosophy is to let women advance at their own pace and have the best ski experience possible. The 5-day package includes lifts; 3 hours of instruction (by women) each morning; afternoon on-snow clinics with options on gates, bumps, fears, and more; indoor clinics on equipment; free ski tuning; and fitness conditioning. There's a bountiful breakfast and lunch daily, and a welcome party and farewell dinner. Programs start on Monday mornings, but Sunday arrivals can ski free.

Okemo has 72 trails serviced by 10 lifts, including 6 quads. The base elevation here is 1,150 feet, and the vertical drop is 2,150 feet.

Lodging packages are available at the slopeside hotel and condos or at country inns in the nearby village of Ludlow. *Okemo Mountain Resort, RFD 1, Ludlow, VT 05149, tel. 802/228–4041, fax 802/228–4558. Jan.–March: 5 days, $495. Price includes lift tickets, breakfasts, lunches, and 1 dinner.*

VERMONT **Stowe.** Stowe ski school was founded in 1936 by one of the great Austrian ski teachers, Sepp Ruschp. It is now comprised of 3 ski schools, all under the direction of Ruschp's son Peter, assisted by David Merriam, the only member of the 10-person

PSIA Demonstration Team that is now working in the East.

About 60% of the 135 instructors here have some level of PSIA certification. The schools use the ATS but make an effort to customize the method to students' individual goals and learning styles. Classes are skill-taught, meaning that instead of being taught how to turn, you learn the skills involved in making a turn, enabling you to make the actual turn with your own knowledge. Class size is limited to 8.

Stowe's Mt. Mansfield Ski School offers the Mountain Experience Week, designed to acquaint intermediate skiers with the different terrain and conditions on Mt. Mansfield and then teach them how to master it. You're in the same group and with the same coach all week, for a 2-hour daily lesson in the morning or in the afternoon.

The mountain's base is at 2,000 feet, and the vertical drop is 2,360 feet. There are 10 lifts, including a high-speed gondola, serving 45 trails, 59% of which are intermediate.

The 200-year-old town of Stowe is a picturesque New England village, with clapboard and saltbox houses and churches tucked into the mountains. Stowe Mountain Resort, the only slopeside lodging, has 5-day packages with lift tickets; some packages also include meals. *Stowe Mountain Resort, 5781 Mountain Rd., Stowe, VT, 05672, tel. 802/253–3000, fax 802/253–8756. Jan.–Apr.: 5 days, $104.*

VERMONT **Stratton.** Skiers at this sophisticated resort have been signing up for the Tyrolean Ski Week, a program of instruction that can accommodate skiers of all levels, since the early 70s. The goal in this informal program is a close instructor-student relationship. In addition to helping to improve your skiing ability, your instructor acts as a host and guide for the week, giving you tips about what to do on and off the mountain.

The program was named when the ski school was staffed mostly by Europeans and followed a European style of teaching, but now it uses the ATS. The staff of 150 is directed by Austrian-born Alois Lechner, who has been at Stratton for more than 20 years. The ski school staff doubles as the Stratton Mountain Boys, who entertain at ski week parties as well as at other resorts and ski shows.

You arrive Sunday in time for a half-day of skiing, but the champagne welcome party isn't until Monday. Monday through Thursday there is instructor-escorted skiing from 9:30 AM until noon, when everyone breaks for a hearty, complimentary lunch with the instructors, and then more skiing until 4 PM. Daily activities are determined by the group, but usually there aren't many drills. Instead, you may learn more about how to find good trails or snow. Thursday night is the Tyrolean dinner and awards party, and Friday is a free skiing day. Equipment rental is included as is continental breakfast (weekdays), a group photo, and video analysis.

The village at the base of the mountain has covered parking for 700 cars, a condo-hotel, restaurants, and a minimall with about 25 shops. The lower mountain is accessible to beginners and intermediates from the 8 lifts at the base lodge. A high-speed gondola serves the upper, more difficult and expert runs, and there are 4 quad chair lifts as well. Stratton has 92 runs, base elevation is 1,900 feet, and the vertical drop is 2,000 feet.

There's plenty to do in the town of Manchester, a factory outlet haven that bustles year-round. The Mountain Villa is a convenient place to book a room, but the resort has many other options. *The Stratton Corp., Stratton Mountain, VT 05155, tel. 802/ 297–2200, 800/THE MTNS, or 802/297–4000, fax 802/297–2939. Dec.–March: 5¹/₂ days, $295. Price includes breakfasts, lunches, one Tyrolean dinner, lift tickets, and rentals.*

VERMONT **Sugarbush.** More than 15 years ago Denise McCluggage and Sigi Grottendorfer set out to change the way people thought about moving downhill and developed the Centered Skiing method. Using Eastern philosophy with Western psychology, as well as visualization techniques, the 5-day Centered Ski Week aims to help primarily intermediate and advanced skiers who

have reached a plateau and are frustrated by their inability to ski more challenging terrain.

Each day begins with a round-table breakfast with informal ski-talk. This is followed by a 2-hour workshop led by Paul McKinnie, the "Zen ski master." Using books, music, and illustrations, he tries to teach you GRACE— that is how to be Grounded, Relaxed, Aware, Centered, and Energized. You go through stretching and aerobic movements from yoga and aikido, and you participate in games that promote trust and confidence.

Once on the slopes, you join a group of no more than 5 skiers per instructor. The instructors follow the Centered Skiing program, which involves a bit of New Age thinking. They might tell you to surround yourself in a white light to protect yourself from collisions with other skiers, or have you and other group members concentrate your psychic energy to pull someone gracefully down the mountain. Most of the time it works, but sometimes it doesn't. Equipment such as Big Foot skis, which are short (only 63 centimeters) and extra wide, are used to learn balance and centering.

The 5-day program begins on Monday (you ski free on Sunday afternoon) and includes daily lift tickets, 7 hours of instruction and workshops each day, breakfast, lunch, and video analysis and review.

Sugarbush is comprised of Sugarbush South and Sugarbush North. The base elevation is 1,535 feet at Sugarbush North, 1,575 feet at Sugarbush South; the vertical drops are 2,600 feet and 2,400 feet, respectively. There are 16 lifts serving 110 trails, of which 30% are expert and 47% intermediate, with diverse terrain.

The luxurious Sugarbush Inn is most convenient to the slopes. A car is helpful even though free shuttles circulate the area. *Sugarbush Resort, R.R. 1, Box 350, Warren, VT 05674, tel. 802/583–6341, 802/583–2381, or 800/537–8427, fax 802/583–3209. Jan.–Mar.: 5 days, $499; 3 days, $339. Price includes lift tickets, breakfasts, and lunches.*

THE MIDWEST

MICHIGAN **Boyne USA Resorts.** The venerable Boyne Ski School, founded in 1947, has taught more than 600,000 people how to ski. Midwesterners, especially those from Chicago and Detroit, consider it the best place to ski within the region.

The resort's all-inclusive old-fashioned Ski Weeks are based on the premise that you have come for a week's skiing vacation and that everything should be taken care of—lodging, lifts, lessons, full breakfast, lunch, and dinner, as well as evening entertainment.

Many of the ski school's 85 instructors are Austrian-born, as is director Toni Sendlhofer. He requires that all instructors attain American certification, and the school uses the Austrian-American Teaching Method, established in 1948. Instructors teach 4 hours daily and stay with the same class throughout the week. During lessons, instructors introduce and demonstrate a new drill or skill, after which skiers try it themselves. There's also time for questions and answers as well as free skiing. Skiers can opt for a specialty seminar that may focus on moguls, snowboarding, or racing technique. A goal for repeat visitors is improving racetime at the Thursday fun race, which takes place on a modified giant slalom course.

A welcome reception and dinner on Sunday night begin the week. Evening activities include seminars on equipment and safety, the latest Warren Miller ski film, and dancing to live music at the Zoo bar. Thursday everyone wins prizes at the awards banquet, where ski instructors in Austrian garb entertain. The official week ends after lunch on Friday, but you can ski the rest of the day on your own. You are videotaped throughout the week and receive a customized video souvenir at the end of the program.

What Boyne Mountain's runs lack in length and vertical drop (500 feet), they make up for in sheer numbers: There are 17 runs, and the longest is over 5,200 feet. With 10 lifts, including one of America's first 6-place, high-speed chair lifts, challenges to skiers of all levels are easily accessed. Boyne Highlands, with 33 runs, 8 lifts—including Michigan's only high-speed super chair—and one rope tow, is 25 miles away. *Boyne Mountain, Boyne Falls, MI 49713, tel. 616/549–6000. Boyne Highlands, Harbor Springs, MI 49740, tel. 616/526–3000 or 800/GO–BOYNE. Dec.–Feb.: 5 days, $580–$800. Price includes lodging, breakfasts, lunches, dinners, and lift tickets.*

MICHIGAN **Shanty Creek–Schuss Mountain.** These two neighboring resorts joined forces to become one of Michigan's larger complexes, with 400 feet of vertical on 29 runs, some lighted for night skiing. The base is at 675 feet, and there are 9 lifts. The skiing is typical midwestern: Expert runs tend to be less intimidating than those at the bigger mountains, making it possible for a beginner to learn to ski all the terrain in a short time. The wide, groomed cruising slopes are especially suited to families with children.

The ski school is run by Michigan native Karen Brozek, who was formerly at Boyne Resorts. She has been teaching for 21 years and holds a Level III certification from PSIA. Karen and her staff of 18 instructors use the ATS. Since this is a small ski area, you won't feel the peer pressure or fear factor that you might get at the major mountain resorts. The 5-day Midweek Ski Getaway includes 5 nights lodging, 5 days lifts, 5 clinics, and daily breakfast and dinner.

There are more than 600 accommodations with a variety of lodging options near the slopes. Two large restaurants, cocktail lounges with entertainment, and cafeterias are located at the ski area. *Shanty Creek–Schuss Mountain, Bellaire, MI 49615, tel. 616/533–8621 or 800/678–4111, fax 616/533–7001. Jan.–Feb.: 5 days, $339. Nov.–Dec. and Mar.–season end: 5 days, $324. Price includes lodging, lift tickets, breakfasts, and dinners.*

THE SOUTHWEST

NEW MEXICO **Taos Ski Valley.** Advanced skiers come to Taos not only because more than 51% of the runs are for experts but also because they can learn how to ski those runs at the renowned Ernie Blake Ski School, ranked number one in North America by *SnowCountry's* skier poll in 1992–93. The school, which has been under the direction of Jean Mayer since 1957, is constantly changing its teaching methods to keep up with advances in technology and technique.

One of the best packages available here is the Super Ski Week, designed by Alain Veth, a former French National Ski Team member and technical representative on the U.S. Ski Team. The focus of this program is to make strong intermediate skiers better by going back to the basics. You go through drills and exercises that teach you how to maneuver, using gates, and you take seminars that cover various technical topics such as avalanche awareness and ski technique (historic skiers and their techniques).

On the first day you break into groups of up to 7 skiers and free ski on the easier, groomed slopes paying attention to balance, flexibility, stance, and the basic turn. Day 2 is a challenge: Advanced skiers are asked to slow down to a beginner's wedge in the fall line, and this helps them to feel the turn and appreciate it as a new skier would. The third and fourth days see more advanced drills on moguls and a slalom course. A race is held and a test is given on day 6, but competition is underplayed. The course ends with the class free skiing with the coach and a guest coach, usually a celebrity instructor. There is much camaraderie in this intensive course.

With groomed beginner and intermediate runs on 49% of Taos's slopes, and expert mogul slopes making a total 72 runs, served by 11 lifts, Taos has something for everyone, and it sees itself as a family place. Take note of the elevation here: The base of the ski area is at 9,207 feet, and it's 11,819 feet at the top. The weather is usually sunny (same latitude as Atlanta), and the dry powder snow averages 321 inches annually.

Lodging and dining options are numerous. If you stay in one of the 5 lodges or 7 condo complexes at the Ski Valley, you won't have to travel far to the slopes and you can enjoy the superb continental cuisine served by the lodge restaurants. But lodging at the nearby town of Taos is cheaper, and the town has historical sites and many galleries of resident artists. *Taos Ski Valley, Box 90, Taos Ski Valley, NM 87525, tel. 505/776–2291, fax 505/776–8596. Dec.–Mar.: 6 days, $422–$482. Price includes lift tickets.*

UTAH **Park City Ski Area.** Home to the U.S. Ski Team, Park City is one of the most accessible large ski resorts, just a 40-minute drive from Salt Lake International Airport. Because Pacific storms have lost much of their moisture by the time they reach Utah's high Wasatch Mountains, the snow here is powder—light and dry.

You don't have to want to be an instructor and you don't have to be an expert to join the 6-day Ski Instructors Training Program: This is an opportunity for solid intermediate and advanced skiers to get better without paying for private lessons.

You ski in a group of 10 with one instructor for about 6 hours most every day, less on the two days when there's video analysis. You rotate among three instructors if you're taking the program to be hired; otherwise you stay with the same instructor the whole time. This is a back-to-basics approach with an emphasis on balance and stance.

The mountain has 86 runs and 15 lifts, including a 4-passenger gondola. The terrain is varied, including 5 bowls and one 3½-mile green run. The base is at 6,900 feet, and the vertical drop is 3,100 feet.

The resort town is filled with interesting shops, restaurants, and hotels, many within easy walking distance of the ski lifts. Nearby are Deer Valley and Park West, and Snowbird and Alta are about one hour away. Because the program runs in the early season, you pay less for lodging. *Park City Ski Area Ski School, Box 39, Park City, UT 84060, tel. 801/649–8111 or 800/227–2754, fax 801/649–5964. For lodging, Park City Ski Holidays, tel. 800/222–7275. Early Dec.: 6 days, $185. Price includes lift tickets.*

THE ROCKIES

COLORADO **Aspen.** Thomas Crum, Aspen Ski School instructor and author of *The Magic of Conflict,* uses aikido to teach skiing. His week-long program, the Magic of Skiing, is open to skiers of all levels. An expert in aikido, Crum applies the philosophy and principles of that sport to helping you develop a better mind-body relationship.

There are usually between 20 and 40 participants in each session. Check-in is in the late afternoon, on either Saturday or Sunday depending on the session. Participants meet each other, set goals for the week, do exercises, and see an aikido demonstration.

You eat breakfast at your hotel, then meet the group for stretching, warm-up, and breathing exercises. Groups of 5 or 6 students of similar ability are formed. You can switch groups if your needs change during the week. Each day your group decides where to ski. You hit the slopes before 10 and ski until the lifts close at 3. Crum decides a theme for the day's lessons, such as balance or steering, but instructors also ask you what you want to accomplish and proceed from there. Your group stays together for breaks and through lunch (not included), which you have at one of the on-slope restaurants. Video feedback is used at different times; you watch the instant replay on the mountain and again off the slopes if you'd like. Every afternoon there is a meeting for review and questions. You have a day off from lessons in the middle of the week. (Price includes 5 days of lessons and a lift ticket that's good for 6 of the 7 days.)

The 4 mountains at Aspen have a total of 270 trails and 42 lifts. Aspen Mountain is the most challenging, with no beginner trails. Its base is at 7,945 feet, and its vertical drop is 3,267 feet. Tiehack, with a base at 7,870 feet and a vertical drop of 2,030 feet, is preferred for beginners. You can also ski Snowmass (base 8,223 feet, vertical drop 4,087 feet), known for its powder and variety of terrain, and Aspen Highlands (base 8,000 feet, vertical drop 3,800 feet).

If you sign up for the early January program, you will stay at the Little Nell Hotel, a grand hotel with fireplaces and oversized feather quilts in every room. At other times, you'll be housed at Aspen Meadows, a historic hotel on 40 acres of mountain meadows. Both are in Aspen and convenient to its après-ski and nighttime activities. *The Magic of Skiing, Aiki Works, Inc., Box 7845, Aspen, CO 81612, tel. 303/925–7099 or 716/924–7302, fax 303/925–4532. Jan.: 7 days, $1,945; Feb.: 7 days, $1,695. Price includes lodging, breakfasts, and lift tickets.*

COLORADO **Copper Mountain Resort.** You can learn to ski the French way by booking a 7-day Club Med vacation at this Colorado resort, which has 98 trails covering 1,360 acres (vertical drop is 2,780 feet) and served by 20 lifts. Rated among the best in Colorado, Copper Mountain Resort is known for its super steeps, bowls, and great cruising runs. Base elevation is 9,712 feet and summit elevation is 12,313 feet.

The Club Med Ski School, which is not affiliated with the Copper Mountain Ski School, is comprised of an international English-speaking staff. The 40 instructors rotate weekly among groups of different levels and ages, but all are certified by the French Ski School and are trained to teach the French method. This is similar to the ATS, but the folks at Club Med say they pay more attention to the finer details of turning techniques.

Instructors lead groups of skiers through 2-hour morning sessions and then 2 more hours in the afternoon. Each group has 8 to 11 people of approximately the same level, determined by a ski-off. Mornings are heavier on drill work, and in the afternoons you do more skiing with the instructor. The same instructor stays with the group for the week. Video analysis is done once early in the week and then again later in the week so that the instructor and skier can evaluate progress.

When you sign up for a Club Med ski vacation, you become a "member" of the club, and you stay at the Club Med Village, a complex of 4 towers with room for 470 skiers. All lodging and meals are included in the cost, as are your lift tickets and ski lessons. Rooms are typical of all Club Meds—rather spartan, with twin beds and no locks; valuables are left in a safe, and beads are used for purchases.

Meals at Club Med are tremendous: The breakfast buffet includes everything from eggs and bacon to cereal, fruit, and yogurt, and there's enough food at lunch to fill you for the rest of the day—grilled meats, seafood, salads, soups, desserts, and free beer and wine. Hot chocolate awaits in the locker room when you're done skiing for the day. Supper is the lightest meal, and you can either eat at the buffet, which has a different theme every evening but always beer and wine, or at the Kiva Restaurant in the same building. In the evenings you can dance till the wee hours, or if you have the energy, join aerobics classes.

The Club Med Village is at the west end of Copper Mountain Village and close to several ski lifts; there's a free shuttle system to take skiers to lifts that are farther away. Club Med members are an eclectic mix of singles, couples, and families from all over the world. Group participation is encouraged in all après-ski activities by the staff, who mingle with and act like guests. *Club Med, 40 W. 57th St., New York, NY 10019, tel. 800/CLUB MED, 303/968–2161, or 303/969–2165. Dec.–Apr.: 7 days, $900–$1,390. Price includes lodging, meals, and lift tickets.*

COLORADO **Crested Butte.** If you've never skied before or you aren't sure you want to ski again, consider Crested Butte's early-season Learn to Ski Free Program. From mid-November to mid-December, beginning beginners get free instruction and free lift tickets as well as discounted lodging packages.

Under the direction of Jean Pavillard, the Crested Butte Ski School uses learning stations scattered over the lower mountain to teach first-timers the basics. You start off inside at Station 1 watching a video that gives safety tips and explains how to put on boots and snap into bindings. When you're ready, head for Station 2, where you side-step up a slight incline and learn to snowplow down. At this point the group breaks up: Those that are ready head for the next learning station; those that

aren't continue side-stepping and snow-plowing. At every station there's a ski school instructor who teaches you a different technique. You proceed through the stations at your own pace, repeating each one until you are skilled enough to move on to the next. After 2 days you should be riding the Keystone Lift and skiing down the easy slopes, though theoretically, you could continue with the stations for the entire month at no charge. Companions with more skiing experience also ski free during this time period.

Crested Butte is a laid-back resort on the other side of a mountain it shares with Aspen. Base elevation here is 9,375 feet. The resort has 85 runs with a vertical drop of 2,775 feet (3,062 feet if you hike to the peak) and is served by 13 lifts, including one high-speed quad. Known for its double black diamond extreme skiing, Crested Butte also has plenty of gentle terrain for beginners and moderate steeps for intermediates. Don't come here for glamour and glitz; this is a resort where the shuttle bus to downtown plays Grateful Dead tunes and hot shot telemarkers wear torn jeans and old wool sweaters. *Crested Butte Mountain Resort, Box A, Mt. Crested Butte, CO 81225, tel. 303/349–2252, 800/754–3733, or 800/544–8448, fax 303/349–2397. Mid-Nov.–mid-Dec.: unlimited days, free. Lodging, from $85 per person for 3 nights.*

COLORADO **Keystone.** Phil and Steve Mahre, Olympic medalists and professional racing champions, have been hosting the Mahre Training Center at Keystone since it began in 1984. At these instructional camps, beginners to experts learn through a 5-step system of progression developed by the Mahres.

The technical progression is based on balance, weight transfer, and fluid vertical motion. Learning these skills gives you a foundation upon which to build. The goal is to develop better control and more efficient skiing by practicing a variety of drills. Gate drills and video feedback are part of the program.

The staff for these camps are Keystone Ski School instructors who have been working with the Mahres since the program's first year. Each session takes 25 to 90 skiers, who are then broken into groups of up to 8 skiers according to ability. Classes run from 9 AM until noon, break for lunch, and then from 1 PM until 2:30 or 3:30.

The 5-day camp begins with an orientation and welcome party held at the Keystone Lodge the day before skiing begins. Indoor evening sessions include a question-and-answer period with either Phil or Steve and seminars on ski technique and ski equipment. During the day, one of the Mahres is available for hands-on demonstration and pointers. The camp ends with a fun race and an evening awards party.

Keystone is a family-oriented resort, with 89 runs on 3 mountains. Keystone is the gentlest, North Peak is steeper with more moguls, and the Outback has mostly gladed trails. Base elevation is 9,300 feet, and vertical drop is 2,340 feet. There are 19 lifts, including 2 gondolas and 3 high-speed quads.

The Keystone Lodge, with restaurants, lounge, and indoor-outdoor pool, is the most convenient place to stay, but there are plenty of other options at the resort. A group lodging rate is available to students of the camp, and the resort has packages that include lodging, lift tickets, and airfare from major cities. *Keystone Resort, Box 38, Keystone, CO 80435, tel. 303/468–2316 or 800/222–0188, fax 303/ 468–4007. Mahre Training Center, tel. 800/ 255–3715. Nov.–Mar.: 5 days, $595. Price includes lift tickets.*

COLORADO **Steamboat.** Intermediate and advanced skiers can skip the regular ski school here and sign up for one of the programs offered by the Billy Kidd Center for Performance Skiing, headed by former World Champion and Olympic medalist Billy Kidd.

The center offers racing camps, the Nelson Carmichael Bump Camps, and a program called Billy Kidd Challenge, in which groups of skiers with similar abilities set out with a coach looking for the biggest challenges the group can handle, whether it be mogul fields, black diamond terrain, or race courses.

All Billy Kidd programs are taught using Kidd's own teaching method, one that relies heavily on video. Every coach carriers a portable video camera and playback equipment so that you can see how you did immediately following a run. Classes of no more than 6 skiers are taught by one coach, who stays with the group throughout the program. You meet early on the first day to discuss the program before heading for the slopes, where you meet the other days. Up to 7 hours are spent on snow, with a lot of instant replay, and you watch videos in a classroom at the end of the afternoon. You work on the skills required for racing, bumps, and powder skiing. Lunch is with your coach, but breakfast and dinner are up to you. At night there are ski-related seminars, such as a ski and boot analysis, held at the round-up room in Gondola Square.

At the end of the program you get a copy of your group's video, which you can use in the future to monitor your advancement. You also get a 30-page profile of your skiing, telling you what you do well, what you need to work on, and how your equipment fares. The report also includes a fitness program, photo, and diploma. If you don't see an improvement in your skiing, you get your money back.

The coaching staff roster here is impressive: Jace Romick, former U.S. Ski Team member and number one downhiller in 1982; Jon Smalley, former U.S. Ski Team freestyle coach; Jarle Halsnes, 3-time World Pro Racing Champion; and 15 other skiers with similar credentials.

The 108 trails at Steamboat are served by 20 lifts, including the 8-person Silver Bullet gondola. Base elevation is 6,900 feet with a 3,668-foot vertical drop. Steamboat is known for its gladed areas, and there are also many open runs, some of which are steep and bumpy. *Billy Kidd Center for Performance Skiing, Steamboat Ski School, 2305 Mt. Werner Circle, Steamboat Springs, CO 80487, tel. 303/879–6111, ext. 543, fax 303/879–7844. Early Dec.–early Apr.: 3 days, $450; 2 days, $300. Price includes lunch.*

COLORADO **Winter Park.** Colorado's oldest major ski area, Winter Park, is unusual in that it is owned by the city and county of Denver and operated by volunteer trustees.

Under this successful partnership, it has evolved from its beginnings in 1940 as a small day area to a top resort with more than a million skier visits annually.

The Winter Park Ski School, headed up by former PSIA president Jerry Muth, has 200 instructors, 95% of whom are certified by PSIA at various levels. The school has programs for all skiers, but one of the most flexible for beginners is the Discover Skiing Package, which includes 4 nights lodging, 3 days of rentals and lift tickets, and a couple of 4½-hour lessons.

As a beginner skier, you are first taught the basics, using the ATS, at the resort's new learning area, Discovery Park. This area consists of 30 acres of varied terrain designed specifically for teaching. It is best to take your first lesson on the day you arrive, but you can take your second lesson on either day 2 or day 3. Whether or not you move out of Discovery Park on your second lesson depends on the ability of your group as a whole.

Winter Park has 113 trails served by 20 lifts, including 5 high-speed express quads. The base elevation is 9,000 feet, and it has a vertical drop of 3,060 feet. Accommodations range from motels to condominiums to mountain inns where breakfast and dinner are included in the cost. Central Reservations can help you with lodging. *Winter Park Resort, Box 36, Winter Park, CO 80482, tel. 303/725–5514, fax 303/892–5823. Central Reservations, tel. 800/453–2525 or 303/447–0588. Nov.–Apr.: 3 days, $295–$435. Price includes lodging, lift tickets, and rentals.*

COLORADO **Vail.** One of the best reasons to start skiing early in the season is Pepi's Wedel Weeks for intermediate to advanced skiers. Four sessions of this 7-day ski program are given from November to early January. The program is designed to get skiers warmed up and focused for the season and to build skiing friendships that might continue throughout the year.

The word *wedel* (pronounced *vay-del*) refers to the short stylized ski turn made famous by

the Austrians, but this turn is only one of the techniques you learn during the week. You get the personal attention of Pepi Gramshammer, a former member of the Austrian Ski Team and the Professional Ski Racers Association, and his partner, John Horan-Kates, owner of East West Outdoors, an outfitter that specializes in sports vacations; they ski with every group at least once during the week.

Wedel Week starts with a Sunday reception and buffet and ends with a farewell dinner and awards ceremony. Vail's top instructors teach groups of 7 skiers, divided by ability into 9 different levels, in morning and afternoon sessions, covering wedel turns, carved turns, slalom and giant slalom as well as moguls and sometimes powder skiing. They use the ATS. Instructors stay with the same group the whole week.

Vail has the largest ski school in the world, with more than 1,200 instructors, but Wedel Weeks are limited to 100 skiers, 75% of whom are repeat participants. The mountain's base is at 8,200 feet, and the vertical drop is 3,250 feet. There are 121 runs served by 25 lifts, including one gondola and 8 high-speed quads.

Lodging choices for the program are first-class: the Gasthof Gramshammer, Lodge at Vail, Sonnenalp Resort, and Christiania—all in the center of the village. There's a raclette party and fashion show on Wednesday and a farewell dinner on Saturday, but other evenings are free. The ski groups eat breakfast together. *Pepi's Wedel Weeks, 231 E. Gore Creek Dr., Vail, CO 81658, tel. 303/476–5626 or 800/323–4386. Nov.–Jan.: 7 days, $1,550. Price includes lodging, breakfasts, 2 lunches, 2 dinners, and lift tickets.*

WYOMING AND IDAHO **Grand Targhee.** The spirited energy of the WomenSki the Tetons program comes from its one-woman staff: Patricia Karnik, who personally guides each workshop. A free-style competitor in the 1970s, she has been teaching people to ski for more than 20 years. Using visualization, discussion, video, and "kinesthetic awakening" (exercises that help you isolate individual body parts to become aware of their movements), women in Patricia's classes not only learn to turn their skis properly, they also learn to stretch their limits.

Patricia accepts no more than 7 women at a time in any of three group levels—WomenSki I, novice; WomenSki II, terminal intermediates stuck in a stem christy; and WomenSki III, advanced skiers who want to cover more difficult terrain.

The skiing day begins with breakfast at 7:30, after which you participate in an hour-long session of kinesthetic awakening exercises, such as writing your name with your big toe or balancing on one foot and slowly turning parts of your leg, which aim to train your muscles into skiing action. By 9:30 you're on the slopes. Competence, confidence, power, and versatility are covered over the 4 days. At the end of each day, you may watch a video and discuss what you've learned. You are filmed the first and last day for comparative analysis, and you also watch a video of "perfect skiing" done by others.

Even though lunch and dinner are not included in the cost of a workshop, you usually eat with the group, and lots of friendships are formed. There aren't many distractions at this small resort, just three lodges, five places to eat, and a self-contained village at the base. Driggs, a tiny town 12 miles away, provides additional nightlife.

Groups II and III go to the town of Jackson and Jackson Hole Resort for a change of pace. Group III includes a day of skiing Targhee's 1,500 acres of untracked slopes reached by Sno-Cat.

One of the best powder skiing resorts in the world, Targhee has uncrowded slopes, views of three states from its summit, and a small base village only 50 yards from the lifts. On the sunny side of the Tetons, it is usually warmer than neighboring Jackson Hole and has lots of open, intermediate terrain without the terrifying pitches of Jackson's slopes. Base elevation is 8,000 feet. There are 45 trails with a vertical drop of 2,600 feet, served by 4 lifts. *Patricia Karnik, Box 25011, Jackson, WY 83001, tel. 208/354–8586 or 800/TAR-GHEE, fax 307/353–8148. Dec.–April: 5 nights/4 days, $1,150–$1,450. Price includes*

lodging, breakfasts, lift tickets, and airport shuttle.

THE WEST COAST

CALIFORNIA **Squaw Valley, Lake Tahoe.** Another program for intermediate and advanced skiers aiming to ski tougher terrain, the Squaw Valley Ski School's 5-day Advanced Skiing Clinc (ASC) has been dubbed Marine Corps Boot Camp Revisited by former students. The resort's best instructors lead small, well-matched groups through 5½ to 6½ hours of intensive skiing daily.

French champion Emil Allais started the Squaw Valley Ski School in 1949, but the French method of teaching has given way to the ATS. The ASC program gets an equal mix of men and women, with husbands and wives, fathers and sons, and daughters and mothers, but you must be over 18 years old. ASC started as an instructor training course; it was the first of any ski week to focus on the intermediate skier, and one of the first to use on-hill video feedback.

The program begins Sunday evening with an orientation, and by 8:30 Monday morning, before the lifts officially open, you are on the hill being evaluated for placement in smaller groups of up to 5 skiers. Your skiing is videotaped every day, and the tape is viewed during lunch, which is included in the cost of the clinic. Afternoons are spent skiing with the instructor until the lifts close. The same instructor stays with the group all day. You spend one evening at a local ski shop learning the art of fine-tuning your equipment, and one evening at a workshop tuning your skis to match the snow type. You learn about waxing, filing, and more. On Thursday you concentrate on racing and gate training, getting ready for the big Friday morning race. There's a banquet on Thursday evening, and after the race on Friday, awards are given, you watch the week's video, and your instructor gives you a written evaluation of your progress.

Squaw Valley consists of 6 peaks with over 4,000 acres of open bowl skiing. Base elevation is 6,200 feet, and there's a vertical drop of 2,850 feet. The 32 lifts include one gondola and one cable car.

Lodging is not included in the cost of the ASC; most students stay at the Resort at Squaw Creek, but the village at Squaw Valley has a variety of condos and hotels. *Squaw Valley Ski School, Squaw Valley, CA 96146, tel. 916/583–0119 or 800/545–4350. Early Dec.– Mar.: 5 days, $675. Price includes lunches and lift tickets.*

CALIFORNIA **Mammoth Mountain.** For the past 40 years, owner, founder, and true mountain man Dave McCoy has shaped Mammoth into a world-class skiing area. At 79, he continues to be a dominant and creative force in all facets of the community, so it is no surprise that the 5-day Senior Ski Camp here is superb.

You must be an intermediate or advanced skier over 50 years old to join a senior camp, where you work on your basic technique without the pressure of competing with young daredevils. The ski school staff, under the direction of Jack Copland, tries to identify the goals of each student and work with that student on creating a program to attain those goals. You spend 6 hours daily with your instructor in groups of no more than 6 skiers. The ATS is used. In the morning you warm up with exercises and visualization before you start skiing. There's a lunch break, and you are videotaped every afternoon. Viewing is indoors.

Senior Ski Camp includes instruction and one social evening in a bar. If you're interested in racing, there is one chance to race toward the end of the week.

Even though Los Angeles is 300 miles to the south, Mammoth Mountain is where Angelenos and other Southern Californians come to ski. It has 3,500 skiable acres (200 with snowmaking), with 150 runs served by 30 lifts capable of moving 43,000 skiers per hour. The base is at 7,953 feet, and the vertical drop is 3,100 feet. It also has big, comfortable day lodges with well-stocked restaurants and bars and an assortment of lodging options. The Mammoth Mountain Inn, with both condominiums and hotel rooms, is the only lodging located at the base of the lifts, so it is generally used for optional lodging packages with instructional programs. Despite its convenient location, however, some skiers prefer to stay in town, where there are more than 50 restaurants, lots of shops, and lodging to fit all budgets. A free shuttle bus makes the 4-mile trip every 15 minutes. *Mammoth Mountain, Box 24, Mammoth Lakes, CA 93546, tel. 619/934– 2571, fax 619/934–0603. Dec.–Apr.: 5 days, $210 for just lessons, $390 for lessons and lift under 65, $300 over 65.*

OREGON **Timberline.** Lots of the skiers at the Timberline Summer Ski Race Camp are under 18, but everyone over 11 is welcome. The program, begun in 1956, is designed to increase your confidence, perfect your skills, and teach you slalom and giant slalom racing techniques and tactics. Training takes place at 8,500 feet on the Palmer Snowfield, which is reached by two chair lifts, including a high-speed detachable quad.

The 12-day camps are co-ed and designed for parallel skiers and above, including recreational, high school, college, and United States Ski Association level racers. Although adults can attend all sessions, those who want to ski just with other adults should sign up for the shorter, 6-day Masters Camps for 21 and over only.

You and 15 to 35 other skiers eat breakfast together at 6:30 AM then hit the snowfield by 7:15 and ski until 1 PM. The area where you ski is an open 160 acres. The base is at 6,000 feet, and the vertical drop is 2,500 feet. After lunch, camp instructors lead the group through various exercises and games, including off-slope slalom drills, weight training, hiking, soccer, swimming, and volleyball. Adults may play golf or tennis. In the evening there are informative seminars covering tuning, boot fitting, and race strategy. There's also video review and other movies. Rossignol sponsors the camp and provides free demo skis for participants.

All camps include dormitory-style lodging at the magnificent Timberline Lodge, a National

Historic Landmark built in the 1930s; adults can upgrade to a private room by paying a supplement. Breakfast and lunch are served in the ski area day lodge, and dinner is in the Cascade Dining Room. Lifts, coaching, lodging, meals, and Portland Airport shuttle are included in the cost. *Timberline Summer Ski Race Camp, Timberline Lodge, OR 97028, tel. 503/231–7979 or 503/231–5402, fax 503/272–3710. June–Aug. 12-day camp, $1,540; 5-day camp, $760. Early June and Aug.: 6-day Adult Masters Camp, $975. Price includes lodging, meals, and lift tickets.*

SOURCES

ORGANIZATIONS Most large cities have local ski clubs and councils that sponsor trips and outings; check the telephone directory or the bulletin boards at local ski shops. State and regional associations publish brochures promoting ski tourism. Among the biggest of these groups are the **California Ski Industry Association** (340 Townsend St., San Francisco, CA 94107, tel. 415/543–7036, fax 415/777–0383), **Colorado Ski Country/USA** (1560 Broadway, Suite 1440, Denver, CO 80202, tel. 303/837–0793, fax 303/837–1627), **Ski New England** (Box B800, Campton, NH 03223, tel. 603/236–8832, fax 603/236–4542), **Ski New Mexico, Inc.** (Box 1104, Santa Fe, NM 87504, tel. 505/982–5300, fax 505/984–1184), and **Vermont Ski Areas Association** (26 State St., Montpelier, VT 05601, tel. 802/223–2439, fax 802/229–6917).

Skiers that are 50 and over might consider joining the **Over the Hill Gang** (3310 Cedar Heights Dr., Colorado Springs, CO 89090, tel. 719/685–4656), a national organization with local chapters that sponsor ski trips and other year-round outdoor activities for members.

A member of Professional Ski Instructors of America (PSIA), **Amateur Ski Instructors Association, Inc.** (28 Park Dr., Woodstock, NY 12498, tel. 914/679–4609) is a nonprofit group open to anyone interested in skiing, although most of its members are from the East. Its objective is to train and certify those who are interested in teaching beginning skiers, thereby encouraging the safety and quality of skiing for everyone.

PERIODICALS News, views, and recommendations on skiing can be found in the "Insiders' Ski Letter," a newsletter with no ads and no photos (Editor/Publisher, I. Wm. Berry, 115 Lily Pond La., Katonah, NY 10536, tel. 914/232–5094). *SKI Magazine,* which has articles on all aspects of the sport, is published 8 times yearly (Box 55533, Boulder, CO 80322, tel. 800/678–0817). *Skiing* (Box 54189, Boulder, CO 80322, tel. 800/825–5552), published 9 months annually, also has articles focusing on all aspects of the sport. *SnowCountry* (Box 2072, Harlan, IA 51593, tel. 800/333–2299), published 8 times a year, includes stories on mountain people and lifestyles; it also has technical and instructional articles for all winter sports.

BOOKS *Handbook of Skiing* (Borzoi/Alfred A. Knopf), by British writer Karl Gamma, is a well-illustrated volume covering all aspects of learning to ski. It is especially good for beginners. *Inner Skiing* (Bantam), by Timothy Gallwey and Bob Kriegel, focuses on the psychological aspects of the sport. *SKI Magazine's Managing the Mountain* (Fireside/Simon & Schuster), by Seth Masia, covers terrain-specific problems and tactics for skiers of all levels. *Ski Taos Style* (Market Relations Press), by Jerome Gladysz and Taos's instructors, explains the Taos ski school teaching methods, aiming to improve the skills of intermediate and expert skiers.

ALSO SEE Once you've mastered the downhill, it's time to test your stamina. Turn to Cross-Country Skiing to see how it's done.

Skydiving

by Erik Fair

Just take one step—out of a perfectly good airplane—and you instantly become a member of an ultra-exclusive club. Considerably less than one-tenth of 1% of the earth's population skydives.

Within a few seconds of exiting the airplane, you will find yourself immersed in the flap and roar of terminal velocity—plummeting, at 120 miles an hour, toward the hard earth 10,000 feet below. Sound terrifying? The simple truth is that the psychological requirements of skydiving are harder to meet than the physical requirements. Tandem jumps have been enjoyed by all kinds of people, including the elderly and people with developmental, physical, hearing, and visual impairments. If you weigh over 250 lbs. or have significant back or joint problems, you may want to pass. Otherwise, all you really need is an attitude.

Thirty seconds into your 50- to 60-second free-fall you will remember the skydiving instructor and *two* parachutes buckled to your back. Your brain will flash: "Salvation!" and you will open your mouth to shriek, "This is great!" But your cheeks won't work because they'll be plastered against your cheekbones.

After you lose your staring contest with the ground and get a brief look at the breathtaking scenery all around you, you will suddenly feel you've been jerked blindfolded up a 300-foot chimney. A split-second later you'll be floating along in a soft and noiseless world, dangling beneath a beautiful canopy, headed for the landing zone (the LZ). Just about 5 minutes later, you'll be on the ground grinning and reveling in the knowledge that you have just experienced raw speed—the purest rush that thrill-sports have to offer.

It is the speed reversals that will stand out in your memory. When you exit an airplane you go from zero to 120 mph in just seconds. The acceleration simply takes your breath away, mainly because you think you're about to die. But once you stabilize in free-fall it's as if speed slows down. You say to yourself: "Wow, I've never gone so fast this slowly before!"

When it's time to throw your parachute, you feel like you've been catapulted upward. The sensation reverses, and you say to yourself: "Wow, I've never slowed down this fast before!" The next thing you know you're floating through space like a bubble. It all happens in less than a minute, and you're left dangling under a canopy wondering, "How many time zones did we go through? Is this the same planet?"

That's why they call skydiving "the granddaddy of all thrill-sports."

Adventurer and writer Erik Fair is the author of California Thrill Sports *and winner of the 1991 Max Karant Award for Excellence in Aviation Journalism. Fair's awe of skydiving is the result of one tandem jump, one Accelerated Free Fall jump, and a life-long love affair with blue space.*

Many people have fears about skydiving based on horror stories that are the legacy of outdated equipment and training techniques—"Both chutes failed. He landed on power lines. He broke both legs when he hit the ground." Yes, original skydiving equipment was much less advanced than today's. Old-style round parachutes had a descent rate of 17 to 23 feet per second and almost zero forward speed—about what you'd reach if you jumped off the top of a parked van. This gave the parachutist little control over landings, so they truly did "hope to hit the LZ" and buckle their knees to keep from breaking their ankles. The vertical descent rate of modern squares or parafoils is 0 to 18 feet per second, with a forward speed of 0 to 25 miles per hour. You can control these rates enough to land on a dime—gently, like a bird.

The style of jumping is changing, too. When you employ the original static-line jump, you dive alone from 3,000 to 4,000 feet, and your chute is immediately jerked open by a steel cable attached to the airplane. Using a one-way radio your instructor coaches you through canopy-check, approach, and landing. Many schools still offer static-line jumps for those who treasure the solo experience above all else, or who fear 50 to 60 seconds of 120 mph free-fall. But these jumps are being replaced by tandem and Accelerated Free Fall (AFF) jumps, both of which enable you to experience the thrill and angst of free-fall, from up to 13,000 feet, on your very first jump.

A tandem jump, which typically costs about $150, is the hair-raising experience described at the beginning of this chapter. You can expect 30 to 60 minutes of ground school before your jump. This will include a briefing on jump procedures, familiarization with equipment (especially the location and grasping of the rip cords), a walk-through of the exit sequence, and practice of free-fall body positioning. Pay attention! Ground school is where you learn how to remain calm and do something besides pass out if the certified tandem instructor buckled to your back dies of a heart attack the instant you leap out of the airplane. If that happens, *don't worry:* You

don't need the instructor nearly as much as you need the two parachutes buckled onto his or her back.

You see, the rip cords for both the main parachute and the emergency reserve parachute are strategically mounted on the front of your harness, where they can easily be reached by either you or your instructor. Structural failure of both parachutes is practically unheard of in skydiving, but one fact remains: When you're headed toward the earth at 120 mph, *somebody* has to pull the rip cord before the ground arrives! Ergo, the bottom-line rules of tandem skydiving: (1) If you think you're going to pass out, first make sure your instructor hasn't died of a heart attack, and (2) If your instructor is unconscious, or looks the slightest bit woozy, don't pass out!

There are two key differences between the Accelerated Free Fall and the tandem jump. First, an AFF jump is twice as expensive, about $300, because you jump with two instructors. Second, you're not buckled to either of them, so you have considerably more responsibility.

The two instructors grab onto your hip straps and dive right alongside you when you leap solo from 9,000 to 13,000 feet, give you hands-on help stabilizing your body during free-fall, and don't let go until a split-second after you deploy your main parachute. Through radio contact, the first jump-master will coach you through a sequence of checks to confirm that you are dangling safely underneath a flyable (and "landable") canopy. He or she also coaches you through maneuvers necessary for a safe approach and landing.

One other difference between an AFF jump and a tandem jump is the length of time you spend in ground school: 4 to 7 hours as opposed to 30 to 60 minutes. This preparation includes more extensive familiarization with equipment, including the automatic deployment device; memorization of jump procedures; and repeated practice of the exit sequence, free-fall body positioning, and deployment techniques, including cut-away of a failed main parachute and deployment of the reserve chute. You'll practice everything until it's second nature, so you'll know what to do instantly if both your instructors get struck by lightning.

If skydiving sounds a little overwhelming, you may want to look before you leap (literally) by attending a Boogie. This is a day or weekend when skydiving addicts flock together to fall through the sky. Many schools listed below have regular Boogies that are great opportunities to sop up some of the skydiver's hari-kari culture without actually jumping out of an airplane.

On the other hand, if skydiving sounds like the sport for you, you should know that it takes 25 jumps to earn an A License in skydiving, the minimum license you need to hurl yourself through space under your own supervision. Because it takes 1 or 2 months and $1,500 to $2,000 to do 25 jumps, you're not likely to earn a license over your vacation. Go for a single tandem or AFF jump. If it really turns you on, call the United States Parachute Association (USPA) for a list of their members near you. All of the schools listed here offer full instructional programs. If you commit to becoming a skydiver, you will have student status for your first 8 tandem or AFF jumps, then you'll jump alone as a supervised novice, until you've logged 25 jumps.

CHOOSING THE RIGHT SCHOOL

Selecting a skydiving school worthy of your trust is a relatively straightforward proposition, because skydiving is well regulated. The United States Parachute Association (USPA) develops training techniques and standards, and certifies instructors, schools, and drop zones. The Federal Aviation Administration (FAA) works cooperatively with the USPA and the Parachute Industry Association to regulate the testing of skydiving harnesses and reserve parachutes for strength, reliability, and rate of descent under maximum load. The FAA also regulates the packing and periodic repacking of reserve parachutes and governs the operations of the pilots and airplanes that transport skydivers. When choosing a trip, be sure to ask the following questions:

Are you a member of the USPA? Make sure the school and its instructors are certified. All of the schools described here have USPA certification.

How long has the school been in business, and how long have the instructors been teaching? A good track record is a good sign that a school is doing something right.

What types of jumps do you offer? If you are interested in a particular jump experience— for example, the solo sensation of a static-line jump—make sure that the school you choose offers it. The schools listed here offer tandem, AFF, and static-line jumps unless otherwise noted.

What facilities are available at your drop zone? A drop zone is any area that the FAA has declared legal for skydiving, and many are nothing more than obscure runways or big patches of dirt. Many schools in this chapter offer unusually well-equipped drop zones, with extras such as classrooms, snack bars, observation areas, swimming pools, and camping sites.

What kind of planes do you use? Remember this rule of thumb: Bigger, faster airplanes (especially twin-engine or turbine airplanes) can carry more people to higher altitudes faster than conventional single-engine airplanes. That usually translates into higher jumps, longer free-falls, lower costs per jump, and less time to sweat bullets on the way to your "moment of truth." Cessna 182s, which seat 4 to 5 people, are usually the smallest plane used for skydiving.

When is the best time of year to jump? Interesting scenery and a comfortable climate are important to consider when choosing a school, and both can vary seasonally. For example, Minnesota may be particularly beautiful in the fall foliage season but is probably too cold for comfort in the winter months.

What other attractions are in the area? This is especially important if you're bringing non-divers on your trip—give them something to keep their minds off of how crazy they think you are!

How far in advance do I need to book? Although some schools will accept walk-in jumpers when not fully booked, it's best to make reservations for your jump two weeks in advance. In these listings, chamber of commerce telephone numbers are given for assistance in finding accommodations near the schools.

Do you have references from past students? It helps to talk with someone who has already made the jump.

FAVORITE SCHOOLS

THE NORTHEAST

MASSACHUSETTS **Pepperell Skydiving Center.** As you slice through the air over Sports Center Airport (about 50 minutes northwest of Boston), you can take in excellent views of the Atlantic Ocean, downtown Boston, and the mountains of southern New Hampshire, including Mt. Monadnock. And all of these places can be reached in less than two hours by those who choose to remain on the ground. Tony Carbone, the director of Pepperell as well as the Northeast Conference of the USPA, has been skydiving since 1976 and instructing since 1980. The center uses 4 airplanes, including a 23-passenger DeHavilland Twin Otter with a special seat for an observer. It costs $17 to come along for the ride and watch up to 22 jumpers exiting the airplane. Drop-zone facilities include a swimming pool, snack bar, and electrical hook-ups for RVs. Nearby Nashua, New Hampshire ("If we screw up, we land there," jokes Carbone), has numerous hotels and restaurants. *Pepperell Skydiving Center, Rte. 111, Pepperell, MA 01463, tel. 508/433–9222 or 800/759–5867. Nashua Chamber of Commerce, tel. 603/881–8333. Year-round (weekends only Feb.–Mar): tandem (from 12,500 ft.), $185; AFF (from 12,500 ft.), $300; static-line (from 3,500 ft.), $225.*

THE MID ATLANTIC

WASHINGTON, D.C. **The Skydiving Center of Greater Washington, D.C.** This D.C. center has a microclimate perfect for skydiving. Storm fronts that roll through D.C. seem to run out of rain before they get to this rural airport 55 minutes from the Beltway, and it's cooler here in the summer and warmer in the winter. Though they've only been in business since 1990, co-owners Kevin and Cindy Gibson have 25 years of drop-zone experience between them. Kevin is former editor of *Parachutist Magazine* and one of the first USPA-certified tandem jump-masters. He spent many years teaching tandem-jump techniques to other instructors all over the United States. Cindy gives instruction for accelerated free-fall and static-line jumping. Her forte is teaching women body-positioning techniques that take advantage of their lower center of gravity and encouraging them to rely more on technique than force in steering an open canopy. The school has a Cessna 182 and a Twin Otter that lets you jump from 13,500 feet instead of 9,000 feet. The Otter has 22 seats, so for an extra $28 nonparticipants can come along to watch you jump. The views of the Patuxent River, Chesapeake Bay, and Maryland's eastern shore include sandy shorelines, rocky cliffs, lush tide marshes, and several bird estuaries. The drop-zone facilities are modest—indoor and outdoor observation areas, picnic facilities, and a snack bar—but that doesn't stop the school from gathering a crowd of young thrill-seekers. It is, as Kevin admits, "A real yuppie hangout, with polo shirts and everything."

In addition to the traditional tourist sights of D.C., you can visit Solomon's Island, a well-preserved old seafarer's town with cozy bed-and-breakfasts, several nightclubs, and fishermen who still go out to sea each morning. St. Mary's City, one of the oldest settlements on the coast; the Maritime Museum; and the Patuxent Naval Air Station and Museum are also nearby. *Skydiving Center of Greater Washington, D.C., St. Mary's County Airport, 315 Airport Dr., Suite 600, California, MD 20619, tel. 301/870–3686. St. Mary's County Chamber of Commerce, tel. 301/884–5555. Year-round (winter jumping only as weather permits): tandem (from 9,000 ft.), $195 for first jump, $155 per additional jump; AFF (from 9,000 ft.), $295 for first jump, $145–$175 per additional jump; static-line (from 3,000 ft.), $180 for first jump, $50 per additional jump.*

THE SOUTH

FLORIDA **Air Adventures Florida.** You'll feel like an astronaut re-entering the atmosphere when you leap out at 12,500 feet and see both coasts of Florida and Lake Okeechobee below. Nonjumpers will also appreciate the ideal location of this school in South Central Florida near Lake Okeechobee, two hours from Miami and Naples, and an hour and 45 minutes from Palm Beach. Judging from the high volume of students here, 30 to 40 new jumpers a week, the scenery isn't the only thing Air Adventure has going for it. Owner Marty Jones has been skydiving for 30 years (since he was 13) and instructing for more than 25 years. He employs up to 10 instructors at a time, depending on the demand. Winter is the busiest season for the school, since that's when most tourists hit the area. The excellent array of aircraft—two Cessna 195s, a Turbine Pilatus Porter, and a DC-3—translates into inexpensive high-altitude jumps for first-timers. The school has also gone out of its way to design a drop zone to attract families and vicarious-thrill seekers. There's a restaurant and snack bar, electrical hook-ups for RVs, a comfortable waiting room with lots of entertaining videos, and a game room designed especially for kids.

Nearby Clewiston offers classic Florida airboat rides (for those who like their sports a little closer to the ground) and Roland Martin's Marina, which hosts numerous bass-fishing tournaments. *Air Adventures Florida, Airglades Airport, Hwy. 27, Clewiston, FL 33440, tel. 813/983–6151. Clewiston Chamber of Commerce, tel. 813/983–7979. Year-round: tandem (from 12,500 ft.), $150; AFF (from 12,500 ft., 1 tandem jump prerequisite), $250. No static-line jumps.*

FLORIDA **Skydive DeLand.** It's not surprising that skydiving has flourished in DeLand: The school's hangar is surrounded by leading manufacturers of skydiving equipment, including Bill Booth's Relative Workshop, one of two companies that pioneered the development of tandem parachutes and training techniques. The close proximity of the manufacturers attracts some of skydiving's most innovative instructors, such as Rob Laidlow, author of the instructional book *Skydive University*. This school hosted the 1993 Skydiving National Championships and is the home drop zone of the national skydiving team, Vertical Express. Tom Cruise did his first jumps here while filming *Days of Thunder* in Daytona Beach, and Ronald Reagan, Jr., has jumped here, too. It's like a little skydiving community, and local skydivers even open their homes (for a fee) to out-of-town students.

You can afford to do high-altitude jumps here, because the aircraft (two Twin Otters) can seat up to 44 jumpers and there are often enough students to fill them. Ground facilities are also first-rate. There's a restaurant, a souvenir shop with T-shirts to advertise your experience, bathrooms, showers, classrooms, an equipment shop, tent sites, and a few electrical hook-ups for RVs. About the only thing that's less than superlative here is the free-fall view of the airport and several small lakes. The best time to dive is from late October through May, because, as the local saying goes, the best summer you'll ever have is winter in Florida.

DeLand is only 45 minutes from Walt Disney World and 30 minutes from Daytona Beach. The legendary Fountain of Youth, at nearby Ponce De Leon Springs State Park, is a great place to take loved ones who have worried themselves gray over your skydiving escapades. *Skydive DeLand, DeLand Municipal Airport, Box 307, DeLand, FL 32723, tel. 904/738–3539. In-house Skyland Travel agency (tel. 904/734–1004, fax 904/734–1047) handles accommodations; ask about accommodations with local skydivers. Year-round: tandem (from 13,500 ft.), $150; AFF (from 13,500 ft.), $275. No static-line jumps.*

GEORGIA **Atlanta Skydiving Center.** Owner Bill Rhodes captures the spirit of this school with his motto: "Any excuse for a Boogie is fine by me." In addition to his regular program, he guarantees at least 3 Boogies a year by renting a DC-3 for Thanksgiving, Labor Day, and Christmas. The group jumps are fun for the experienced divers who participate and the beginning jumpers who watch. The center's private skydiving-only airport is the oldest of seven drop zones in Georgia and is only 35 miles from Atlanta. In between Boogies, you'll be transported by one of two Cessna 182s or a D-18 Twin Beech to exit points high above granite-capped Stone Mountain and the Atlanta skyline and countryside. You can watch a lap at the Atlanta International Raceway while you're racing toward the earth! Two large trailers house classrooms, a lounge, an equipment room, bathrooms, and showers. On-site camping and picnic areas are also available, as are a variety of other accommodations within a 5-mile radius.

The Six Flags Over Georgia amusement park and Stone Mountain State Park are less than an hour away. High Falls State Park's natural-rock water slide is just 15 minutes away, and nearby Jackson Lake Marina offers boating and fishing. *Atlanta Skydiving Center, Rte. 1, County Line Rd., Jenkinsburg, GA 30234, tel. 404/775–9150. Accommodation referrals available. Mar.–Nov., Wed.–Sun.; Dec.–Feb., weekends as weather permits: tandem (from 10,500–13,500 ft.), $150; AFF (from 10,500–13,500 ft.), $250; static-line (from 3,000 ft.), $150.*

THE MIDWEST

MISSOURI **Missouri River Valley Skydivers.** This drop zone was one of the biggest and busiest in the Midwest until the great floods of 1993. It's 2 miles north of the Missouri River, and owner Tom Dolphin is rebuilding his entire facility. At press time the school was slated to be up and running by spring 1994. Three powerful, high-capacity Cessna 182s, an E-50 Twin Bonanza, and a Pilatus Porter Turbine were flown to safety before the flood reached them.

When you jump here you can see the Kansas City skyline, the Missouri River running north to Iowa and south to St. Louis, and a bucolic patchwork of farm fields, small towns, and flood plains. The drop zone is 3 miles from Lexington, Missouri, home of a Civil War

Museum and battleground, and 30 miles from Liberty, site of Jesse James's first bank robbery. Nearby Kansas City has a great zoo and the Worlds of Fun amusement park. *Missouri River Valley Skydivers, Rte. 1, Box 46, Henrietta, MO 64036, tel. 816/494–5315 or 800/776–5315. Lexington Chamber of Commerce, tel. 816/259–3082. Mar.–Oct.: tandem (from 9,500 ft.), $145; AFF (from 10,000 ft.), $285; static-line (from 3,200 ft.), $125.*

WISCONSIN **St. Croix Valley Skydiving Club.** This classic skydiving club has been going strong for 33 years and has hosted the North Central Conference Memorial Day Boogie for three years in a row. It runs on its members' enthusiasm and love of the sport, with all profits from student jumps put toward expanding the facilities, which so far include a clubhouse, student classrooms, and electrical hook-ups for RVs. Gino Broom owns the whole drop zone, including the airport, which is in the heart of the St. Croix River Valley. And since the airport is used only for skydiving, there's no competing air traffic. The school has two Cessna 182s as well as a Beech Queen Air that takes large groups to 13,500 feet. From heights like that, you really get the full impact of the beauty of the surrounding countryside. The river bluffs of St. Croix Valley National Park, the Minneapolis skyline, Cedar Lake, and lush Wisconsin farmland are breathtaking. The fall foliage is particularly stunning. Instructor Kerry McCauley admits "it gets cold around here—we usually stop student jumps in November because we can't trust 'em to pull the right handles with ski gloves on." The size of the Beech Queen Air means that, for $15, a favorite fan can come along for moral support. For those who stay on the ground, there's a clubhouse with a VCR and lots of skydiving videos.

Nearby, there's inner-tubing on the Apple River, canoeing on the St. Croix, miniature golf, and a water theme-park. *St. Croix Valley Skydiving Club, St. Croix Valley Airport, Box 92, Osceola, WI 54020, tel. 715/294–4262. Somersett Chamber of Commerce, tel. 715/247–3366. Apr.–Oct., Wed.–Sun.: tandem (from 10,000 ft.), $150; AFF (from 12,500 ft.), $250; static-line (from 3,500 ft.), $145.*

THE SOUTHWEST

ARIZONA **Skydive Arizona.** This may be the best place in the country to observe gangs of skydivers at their zaniest. Skydive Arizona hosted the 10th World Championships of Formation Skydiving in 1993, and Boogies take place on most major holidays (Easter, Halloween, Thanksgiving, Christmas, and New Year's Day). Former *Parachutist Magazine* editor Kevin Gibson says the Arizona weather and superb equipment here make this "the best skydiving facility in the country." And judging from the crowds at the Boogies, a lot of people agree with him.

In business since 1979, the school moved to its new drop zone, adjacent to the Eloy Municipal Airport, in 1991. Extras at the new site include a swimming pool, shaded observation area with picnic tables, and several freelance "videographers" on hand to record your free-fall for posterity. The impressive array of aircraft—a Twin Otter, Super Otter, King Air, and DC-3—enables the school to take a large number of students up for high-altitude jumps.

The clear desert skies here offer visibility of up to 60 miles year-round, but the views are best at certain times of the year. In March, the land is cool and green from the winter rainy season; April brings yellow, white, and purple desert flowers; and in May, the cacti add their bright yellow blooms. Summers—June through August—can be scorchers!

Eloy is an hour from both Phoenix and Tucson. Casa Grande Ruins National Monument is on the road to Phoenix, and the Arizona-Sonora Desert Museum is just outside Tucson. *Skydive Arizona, Eloy Municipal Airport, 4900 N. Taylor Rd., Eloy, AZ 85231, tel. 602/466–3753. Eloy Chamber of Commerce, tel. 602/466–3411. Year-round (closed Tues. and Wed. June–Aug.): tandem (from 12,500 ft.), $125; AFF (from 12,500 ft.), $250; static-line (from 3,500 ft.), $105.*

TEXAS **Skydive Dallas/Aerodrome Skydiving.** Stop screaming and smile for the camera! A unique feature at this ultramodern facility, founded in 1991, is the video that's included in the price of a tandem or static-line jump. An instructor wearing a helmet camera does the filming, and you can choose background music from a library of 50 songs, including such apropos titles as Tom Petty's "Free Falling." The school was opened by two local entrepreneurs, Dr. Lee Schlichtemeier and his wife, Carol, who fell in love with skydiving after a couple of tandem jumps. Now they own Tri-County Airport, about an hour northeast of Dallas, and a 15,000-square-foot hangar that holds student classrooms, a pro shop, a restaurant, and a lounge. Kids can romp in indoor and outdoor play areas with slides, swings, and games.

Manager Alphonse Trone will be the first to say that this is already one of the premier skydiving facilities in the United States. And he'll back up his claim by showing you the star of the hanger—a million-dollar Cessna 208 Caravan single-engine turbine. The plane can unload 15 jumpers at 13,000 feet two or three times an hour! Whether you leap from the Caravan or from one of two Cessna 182s, you'll find yourself flying over the Red River, Lake Texoma, and the brown-and-green geometric patterns of plowed farm fields. On clear days you also get a view of the Dallas skyline. *Skydive Dallas/Aerodrome Skydiving, Rte. 2, Box 15, Whiteright, TX 75491, tel. 903/364–5103. Accommodation referrals on request. Year-round: tandem (from 13,000 ft.), $165; AFF (from 13,000 ft.), $250; static-line (from 3,500 ft.), $150.*

THE ROCKIES

MONTANA **Skydive Lost Prairie.** The views here start on the ground and only get better when you take to the sky in one of the school's two Cessna 182s. This get-away-from-it-all drop zone in northwest Montana is in a secluded valley that was first homesteaded less than 100 years ago. It's accessible only via a gravel road that winds through a pine forest for 4 miles before the trees part to reveal Lost Prairie, tucked in the foothills of the Rockies. Aerial views here include the Rocky

Mountains, McGregor Lake, and (on a clear day) glaciers at Waterton/Glacier National Park. Each fall, the larch trees claim the distinction of being the only pines to turn yellow as they drop their needles. It's a spectacular scene.

The Skydive Lost Prairie Jump Meet, held each year in the last week of July or first week of August, is the largest gathering of divers in the northwestern states. Many of the divers fly their own planes to this meet and make up some of the cost by giving great air tours of the Canadian Rockies. During the rest of the year, the school's isolation and low number of jumpers make it a peaceful retreat. Instructor Todd Kleem teaches here spring through fall and at Skydive Arizona in the winter, because as Lost Prairie's owner Fred Sand will tell you, winter diving in Montana is for "addicts only."

The school is about 35 miles west of Kalispell. It has its own bar, café, and great places to camp. Cabin accommodations and plenty of fishing and hiking are available at McGregor Lake Resort, just 10 minutes away. Glacier National Park is a 2-hour drive. *Skydive Lost Prairie, 3151 Lower Lost Prairie Rd., Marion, MT 59925, tel. 406/858–2493. McGregor Lake Resort, tel. 406/858–2253. Apr.–Oct.: tandem (from 9,000 ft.), $134; AFF (from 10,500 ft.), $259; static-line (from 3,500 ft.), $134.*

THE WEST COAST

CALIFORNIA **Perris Valley Skydiving School.** The lake town of Perris, California, along with neighboring Elsinore, is part of skydiving history. These were two of the first places in the country where people made non-military jumps—where jumping suddenly became recreation. Perris Valley Skydiving School is one of the biggest schools in the nation. Current owner Jeff Jones is the son of Bill Jones, who was instrumental in the development of Accelerated Free Fall teaching techniques for the USPA. And although Perris Valley has only been around since 1986, the Joneses have operated various drop zones around the country for 30 years.

The school has a very popular instruction program, issuing more than 200 A licenses a year. It also has excellent aircraft: a King Air, two Twin Otters, and a DC-3. During jumps on clear days you can see north to Los Angeles and south to San Diego. Even the everyday scenery is far from mundane, with snow-capped mountains (San Gregonio and San Jacinto) to the east, and the Ortega Mountains, Pacific Ocean, and Catalina Island to the west. Perris and Elsinore Lakes also stretch out below. Those who like their air adventures a little tamer can enjoy the scenery from a hot-air balloon, another popular activity in Perris.

There's a trailer where free-fall videos are produced and another large trailer housing classrooms and offices. There's also a swimming pool, a snack bar, and a bar where you can get beer and wine (after your jump!). Perris's Orange Empire Railway Museum features rides on antique trains pulled by real steam engines. *Perris Valley Skydiving School, 2091 Goetz Rd., Perris, CA 92570, tel. 909/657–1664 or 800/832–8818. Perris Chamber of Commerce, tel. 909/ 657–3555. Year-round: tandem (from 12,500 ft.), $160; AFF (from 12,500 ft.), $307. No static-line jumps.*

CALIFORNIA **Sky Dance Skydiving.** This was the first school in California to offer tandem jumps, but it's the instruction that makes it the premier school in the Bay Area. Co-owner Dan O'Brien is an accomplished competitive skydiver; and his partner, Ray Farrell, is a master parachute rigger and one of the few instructors in the country qualified by the USPA to train other tandem instructors. A host of other experienced instructors pitch in to carry the heavy student load.

Sky Dance hosted the 1992 National Skydiving Championships, and with Boogies on Memorial Day, July 4th, and Labor Day, it's another great place to watch experienced skydivers hurl themselves through space in clusters. The school has standard ground facilities with a few extras, such as the observation lawn with picnic tables and a snack bar open on weekends. Dan and Ray take their students up in a Cessna 182, a Beechcraft King Air, and a Twin Otter. The thrill of the jump will have to suffice here, because the scenery is on the average side—farm fields, barns, and the town of Davis. Summer and winter temperatures here are extreme, so spring and fall are your best bets.

Sky Dance is an hour-and-a-half from San Francisco, 25 minutes from Wooz Amusement Park in Vacaville, and just 20 minutes from historic (if touristy) Old Towne Sacramento. For more thrills, drive an hour to run the whitewater of the south fork of the American River, from Chile Bar to Coloma, in a raft. *Sky Dance Skydiving, 24390 Aviation Ave., Yolo County Airport, Davis, CA 95616, tel. 916/753-2651. Davis Chamber of Commerce, tel. 916/756-5160. Year-round, Wed.–Sun.: tandem (from 9,000 ft.), $125 or (from 13,500 ft.), $155; AFF (from 10,500–13,500 ft.), $278; static-line (from 3,000 ft.), $188.*

OREGON **Skydive Oregon.** This is the home of the highest altitude jumps in the country. Joe Webber, Skydive Oregon's owner and operator, uses his Beechcraft Westwind Twin Turbine to drop you off at 14,500 feet! In fact, the plane can carry 14 jumpers to this height three times an hour. You appreciate the extra seconds of soaring through space when you see the views: Mt. St. Helen, Mt. Rainer, Mt. Hood, the Columbia and Willamette River gorges, the Portland skyline, and the Pacific Ocean. Although the area is lovely all year, in April and May the flowering of local orchards turns the ground pink, white, and lavender.

Weber, who has been skydiving since 1972, declares, "I built this airport and drop zone because I wanted the best place to skydive— and I got it." Indoor facilities include three classrooms, bunkrooms for 30, and a video lounge with a wood-burning stove. Outside, you can sit on the porch and gaze at the Cascade Mountains, beyond the picnic tables and barbecue. Portland is only 45 minutes away, and Mt. Hood National Forest, with camping, hiking, and fishing, is right next door. *Skydive Oregon, Skydive Oregon Airport, 12150 S. Hwy. 211, Molalla, OR 97038, tel. 503/829-3483 or 800/934-5867. Molalla Chamber of Commerce, tel. 503/829-6941. Nov.–Jan. (by appointment only): tandem (from 10,000 ft.–14,500 ft.), $129; AFF (from 10,000 ft.–14,500 ft.), $225; static-line (from 4,000 ft.), $119.*

SOURCES

ORGANIZATIONS **United States Parachute Association** (1440-P Duke St., Alexandria, VA 22314, tel. 703/836–3495) will supply you with a complete list of all USPA Group Members (schools, programs, clubs, and drop zones) in the United States and general information on ratings and certifications. Membership includes a subscription to its monthly publication *Parachutist Magazine.*

PERIODICALS *Parachutist Magazine,* the official publication of the United States Parachutist Association (*see* Organizations, *above*), has equipment reviews, "there I was" stories, competition reports, and inspirational pictures of people plummeting through space. *Skydiving Magazine* (Box 1520, DeLand, FL 32721, tel. 904/736–4793) is similar, but it's more tailored to the leading-edge or advanced sky diver.

BOOKS *Parachuting, The Skydiver's Handbook,* by Dan Poynter, is the most definitive text on skydiving for basic- to intermediate-level enthusiasts. It's detailed, accurate, and entertaining. *Skydiving, a Dictionary,* by Bill Fitzsimons, is full of humorous skydiving terminology. *Parachuting's Unforgettable Jumps III,* by Howard Gregory, gives a historical view of both military and sport jumping. *Skies Call,* by Andy Keech, is three volumes of outstanding color photos by a gifted parachuting photographer. *Parachuting Manual with Log,* by Dan Poynter, is a pocket-sized, first-jump-course logbook that's full of excellent illustrations and essential information. It's the least expensive way to learn lots about skydiving. A *Parachuting Manual With Log for Accelerated Free Fall* is also available.

ALSO SEE If you like hanging out in the skies with a giant tarp over your head, you may like gliding through them with your own wings. Check out the Hang Gliding chapter for more information.

Snowmobiling

by Rosemary Freskos

he secret is finally out: Snowmobiling is one of the most exciting and comfortable ways to experience America's backcountry in winter. Driving one of today's light, nimble snowmobiles is a cross between riding a motorcycle, driving a car, and steering a sled with handlebars, except that you control the speed at all times. An extensive network of marked and often groomed trails throughout the United States and Canada means that the average rider can explore hundreds of thousands of acres of spectacular territory too remote to be easily reached by any other means. You can snowmobile wherever snow and terrain permit, and there are trails for every ability, from packed and groomed tracks that soothe nervous beginners and rolling terrain where intermediates can practice slaloms to thrilling steeps and deep powder, the rider's equivalent of skiing off-piste. No wonder snowmobiling is such a fast-growing sport in North America's snowbelt—Maine and Quebec, Minnesota and Wisconsin, the mountain states and Alaska.

Once you're hooked, a day trip doesn't offer nearly enough time to explore the wilderness, swoop through the evergreens, blast over hilltops, and carve rooster tails in meadows of fresh powder. That's where snowmobile tours come in. A number are available, ranging in length from a weekend to a week and longer; the outfitters take care of all the arrangements.

These trips can involve camping or bedding down in a comfortable inn, hearty campfire cooking or elegant feasts. They might run at a relaxed pace of about 100 miles a day hitting top speeds of 30 to 40 miles per hour, with time for photography and exploration, or they could be hauls of up to 200 miles a day with speeds topping 50 miles per hour. Snowmobile tours are definitely the best way to get into the sport, and prices generally run a reasonable $100 to $200 per person per day, including lodging, meals, clothing rental, and a guide.

Some of the best areas for riding don't have organized tours. To visit them, contact snowmobile associations, state tourism boards, local chambers of commerce, and regional and local national park and forest offices for lists of lodges with rental equipment and areas with extensive snowmobile trails. Some rental services offer only detailed trail maps, but others can fix you up with a guide for around $100 to $150 per day per group. Depending on the area and the amount of competition there, the average snowmobile rental fee ranges from $65 to $100 for single riders, from $80 to $125 for doubles, as sleds that can hold a pair of riders are called. If you have a choice of machine, opt for more power at higher altitudes, because the engine's performance is hampered by the thinner air of the mountains. A deposit of $70 to $200 is usually required.

Rosemary Freskos, a regular contributor to Fodor's guides, has been writing about snow sports for some two decades.

When you plan your trip, try for February and March rather than December and January: The days are longer, so you'll get more time on the trail. Perhaps more to the point, the weather is warmer. Even die-hard winter lovers appreciate a few extra degrees.

CHOOSING THE RIGHT TRIP

You're better off asking lots of questions before signing up than being surprised at what you've gotten yourself into.

How long has the operator been in business? Longer is better, especially if you're new to snowmobiling. An outfitter who has been in business for a while has experience resolving a range of questions and problems that come up—precisely the ones that will be new to you.

What are the guides' qualifications? They should not only know the area but also know how to fix mechanical breakdowns on the trail. If you will be far from civilization, they should also have first-aid training, including CPR, if not more advanced training in emergency and wilderness medicine.

What is the ratio of customers to guides? The standard is generally one guide for every 5 customers.

How many people are on each tour? Many outfitters sign up a large number of people and then break the crowd into smaller groups. Others—especially outfitters who run customized trips only—limit the number of guests. The optimal size is 5 to 10 riders of similar abilities.

How much riding will be done each day and what is the average speed? What kind of terrain will be covered? As in any sport, snowmobiling has its experts and its novices and a wide range of intermediates. It's important to choose your comfort zone, whether it involves easy riding on groomed trails or long-distance bushwhacking in the backcountry. Novices might shoot for 100 miles a day, with speeds hovering in the 30 to 40 miles per hour range, while aggressive riders can cover twice the distance in a day, and handle 50 miles per hour.

What's the cost and what's included? Some operators' prices include lodging and meals, snowsuits, gloves, boots, helmets, snowmobiles, gas, and oil, as is true on all the trips described below unless otherwise noted; our prices are per person based on double occupancy except when otherwise specified. Question operators carefully to determine their specific policies. Also find out who pays for any necessary repairs during the trip and for trailering sleds to the starting point, whether you're bringing your own sled or using the operator's. If trail fees are required where you'll be riding, make sure they're included as well. Always inquire whether you are eligible for a refund if there's no snow. If gas and oil are not included, get an estimate of the cost for the trip.

Similarly, if you are not driving to the group assembly point, ask whether transfers from the airport are included—and find out how much they will cost you if they're not. Airfare is almost always extra.

What are the accommodations like? Most operators use comfortable, moderately priced lodging. Make sure you know what to expect.

What are meals like? Don't look for fancy cooking. Plain fare is the rule—meat and potatoes, chicken and salads—except in more luxurious packages.

What kind of equipment does the outfitter supply? Whether a snowmobile is provided or you rent one, get its make, model, and year; make sure that the sled is light and easy to maneuver and find out whether it comes with heated hand grips, an electric starter, automatic oil injection, or other conveniences. If the sled in question has an electric starter, make sure that it is also equipped with a backup manual starter you can use if the battery is weak. If you don't like what's being provided, ask whether upgrades are available, at additional cost. If the outfitter is providing the snowmobile, either as part of the package or as a rental at extra cost, ask what damages you are liable for in the event of an accident. If your own homeowner's policy does not cover such damages, you may want to acquire a snowmobile accident policy, offered by many operators as an option, particularly on trips that involve riding off established trails; such a policy costs between $10 and $15 a day and covers damage to your snowmobile and to the one in front of you should you run into it, above a set deductible, normally around $250 to $300.

What kind of clothing is provided? The right clothing is absolutely essential. You'll need an insulated snowsuit, a full helmet, special gloves, and waterproof, insulated boots; if you don't already have your own, they can represent a sizable outlay of money. Typically, outfitters do not provide silk or polypropylene long johns, thermal boot inserts, and other essential underpinnings.

Will a support vehicle accompany the tour? Lodge-to-lodge and other long-distance trips are typically accompanied by a van or truck, which tows a trailer that can be loaded with two or more snowmobiles and which carries luggage, parts, and food and other supplies—as well as snowmobilers who decide not to ride on any given day.

Do you have references from past guests? They may be able to articulate strengths and weaknesses of a given operator that would be hard to find out about on your own.

How far in advance do I need to book? If your destination is a popular one or you visit during a holiday, reserve a visit a couple of months ahead—or longer.

MAJOR PLAYERS

DECKER'S SNO-VENTURE TOURS Richard and Audrey Decker founded this operation in 1980 and still lead most of the tours. They are known for their attention to the kind of details that make their tours among the most deluxe in the business and were voted the favorite of *Snowmobile Magazine* readers not long ago. Their all-inclusive tours go to Oregon, Wisconsin, Minnesota, Michigan, and Wyoming (particularly Jackson Hole and nearby Yellowstone National Park), as well as Alaska. A well-stocked trailer goes as a support vehicle on all trips, and for every 10 riders there's one guide, who cooks family-style

meals. All have 20 years' snowmobiling experience (but no rescue and emergency medical training). Prices, $95 to $100 per day, do not include boots, suits, helmets, gloves, or snowmobiles, but they do cover accommodations in lodge-style establishments or fully-equipped motels (Box 1447, Eagle River, WI 54521, tel. 715/479–2764, fax 715/479–9711).

INTERNATIONAL SNOWMOBILE TOURS This company was formed in 1980 by Dick Squiers who, with his tour coordinators, Don Bole and Max Buell, claim some three quarters of a century of combined snowmobiling experience. IST runs 10 to 12 tours per season, primarily in Minnesota, Michigan's Upper Peninsula, Wisconsin, and Ontario, including several for aggressive riders with high skill levels who can maintain speeds of 50 miles per hour and go 200 miles a day. No clothing or snowmobile rentals are included in the prices but new Polaris liquid-cooled snowmobiles may be rented for $100 per day. Group size is usually about 20, and IST guides are all experienced deep-snow riders, with outgoing personalities, at least 20 years' experience and training in first aid, wilderness and emergency medicine, and CPR. A support vehicle is present only on tours that involve motel transfers. Generous meals are included, as is lodging, primarily in Best Westerns, Holiday Inns, and similar hostelries. Prices range from $95 to $110 per day (427 Sycamore St., Chesterfield, IN 46017, tel. 317/378–5074).

SENIOR SNO-WORLD TOURS Owner-operator Roger Matthews has been active in the industry since 1967, much of the time promoting the sport in his home state, Michigan. However, his most popular tours are to Jackson Hole, Yellowstone National Park, Alaska, and Ontario. Tours are geared mainly to beginners and intermediates who don't want to spend all their time sledding, most at the upper end of the age spectrum; seniors-only groups are a specialty. There is one guide with at least 20 years' experience per 15 snowmobilers (with no more than 30 riders per tour); each guide has rescue and emergency medical training. Snowmobiles, meals of basic fare (steaks, plain seafood, roast beef, or the like) and motel-style accommodation are all included in the prices, but not personal gear except on the special seniors trips (3701 Buttrick Rd. SE, Ada, MI 49301, tel. 616/676–5885, fax 616/676–5898).

YELLOWSTONE ADVENTURES One of the top choices if you want to visit the national park is Yellowstone Adventures, just outside the park gates in busy West Yellowstone. Founded in 1973, Yellowstone Adventures is the town's exclusive Ski-Doo dealer and its rental fleet of 110 sleds is replaced every year. It also puts together custom packages that include lodging, snowmobile rental, clothing, discounts, and complimentary gifts, but not meals. Lodging is in modern, fairly fancy motels with hot tubs and the occasional indoor swimming pool. Guides tend to be personable, outgoing, and knowledgeable about the area, with 8 to 10 years of experience and emergency medical training. There's usually one for every dozen riders, and there are usually 5 to 12 sledders per trip. Packages cost an average $65 to $100 per day, on the average (131 Dunraven St., Box 669, West Yellowstone, MT 59758, tel. 406/646–7735 or 800/231–5991, fax 406/646–9608).

YELLOWSTONE TOUR & TRAVEL This operator, one of the largest in Yellowstone National Park, does not have tours. Instead, the specialty is 2- to 7-night all-inclusive packages, which include everything, even discount airfares. Accommodations tend to be comfortable but not deluxe, meals are usually plain but tasty, and the 200-sled rental fleet includes some 8 different models of Arctic Cats, Yamahas, and Polaris snowmobiles equipped with hand and thumb warmers and, usually, with luggage racks. YT&T also conducts tours via snowcoach, jumbo over-snow vehicles that look like tanks with windows; the visibility isn't quite as good, but they let you cover the miles without getting wind in your face. Average daily cost of packages is approximately $120 per day (Box 369, West Yellowstone, MT 59758, tel. 406/646–9310 or 800/221–1151, fax 406/646–9490).

FAVORITE TRIPS

THE NORTHEAST

MAINE **Aroostook County.** Known as the Crown of Maine, the northeastern tip of Maine, where dawn first breaks each morning in the United States, is a vast land of small communities set among forests, lakes, streams, and farms. Local snowmobile clubs maintain over 1,500 miles of groomed trails, all marked for gas, food, lodging, mileage, and directions. Towns are just far enough apart along the trails to make it easy to escape civilization without leaving the comforts of a gas station too far behind.

Kent and Kathy Forbes's operation specializes in custom trips in this area; you decide the number of nights and the type of lodging and dining as well as how many miles of riding, and the Forbeses set it up. Kent Forbes accompanies small groups and has a staff of guides to help him out with groups of larger than 5. Favorite routes explore the Fish River chain of waterways, known for its great ice fishing for salmon and trout; the historic town of Fort Kent, on the banks of the St. John River, known for its role in the Aroostook War of 1839 between the United States and British Canada; and tiny Eagle Lake, a former logging hub now catering to snowmobilers, where you might spot moose, deer, coyote, and fox. Presque Isle, a half-day ride from Caribou, has great facilities for shopping and dining. Yamaha snowmobiles are used. Prices vary according to the lodging you choose and the number of people in your party. *Crystal Snowmobile Tours, Box 1448, Caribou, ME 04736, tel. 207/498–3220 or 207/492–7471. Dec.–Mar.: about $350 per day per couple, not including meals, clothing, gas, and oil; sign up 1–2 months in advance.*

THE MIDWEST

MICHIGAN AND WISCONSIN **Lake Superior Shore Tour.** This 7-day International Snowmobile Tours program out of Newberry, Michigan, takes you across Michigan's Upper

Peninsula to Boulder Junction, Wisconsin, on some of the best groomed trails in the area. Overnight stops are at Gwinn, Baraga, White Pine, Boulder Junction, and Iron River—all areas noted for their snowfall. A support vehicle brings your luggage, so all you have to do is enjoy the drive, the hearty meals, and the socializing. You need moderate skills to handle the trip: You should be able to maintain speeds of 35 miles an hour for prolonged periods, usually 135 miles a day and about 8 hours out. Breakfast is a buffet of pancakes, french toast, and cereal; dinner is prime rib, steak, or seafood. Accommodations for the 20 tour participants and the guide who accompanies them are basic two-story motels like Best Western properties or the equivalent. *International Snowmobile Tours, 427 Sycamore, Chesterfield, IN 46017, tel. 317/378– 5074 or 800/378–8687. Feb.: 7 days, $650. Price does not include snowmobiles, gas, oil, or lunch; sign up 6 months in advance.*

MICHIGAN AND WISCONSIN **Winter Wonderland.** This 6-day tour from Decker's Sno-Ventures starts in Eagle River, Wisconsin, and loops to Copper Harbor, Michigan, and back—600 miles at between 75 and 110 miles a day at an average speed of 20 to 40 miles per hour. The terrain and scenery change as you go: The first day, you ride through forests sprinkled with lakes to the foothills of the Porcupine Mountains (a.k.a. the Porkies) and into White Pine, Michigan, to rustic Konteka Lodge. The next day's highlights include a ride to the magnificent Lake of the Clouds overlook and across a 300-foot-high trestle bridge. Pushing on, you follow the bend of the Keweenaw Peninsula, a historic mining area; stop en route to admire copper craft work; and picnic trailside on wine and meat-filled turnovers known as pasties, traditional miner's fare. Your destination is the Lake Fanny Hooe resort in Copper Harbor, a sparkling town when seen from above, outlined by Lake Superior's bright blue waters. The tour continues through other historic towns, such as Calumet, then back through Houghton to Bruce's Crossing and a farewell banquet. The group size is anywhere from 6 to 30, with a guide for every 10 riders. *Decker's Sno-Venture Tours, Box 1447, Eagle River, WI 54521, tel. 715/479–2764, fax 715/479– 9711. Feb.: 6 days, $595. Price does not include clothing, snowmobiles, gas, and oil; sign up 2 months in advance.*

MINNESOTA **North Coast Grand Tour.** Every year since they opened in 1983, Scott Borland has driven the North Shore and Gunflint Snowmobile Trails, following the forested ridge line of the rugged hills overlooking Lake Superior. He's the leader of this trip out of Duluth. He's also an expert snowmobiler with some 30 years' experience.

Lowland meadows, swamps, thick forests, cascading rivers, and waterfalls plummeting into the lake make for stunning scenery. There are no towns along your main route, but shelters with firewood and outhouses are located every 10 miles, and gas, food, and lodging are accessible via groomed side trails. Traveling with a guide in a group of up to 8 riders, you cover 75 to 100 miles a day of these trails. Snowmobiles are new Ski-doo Safari 377s.

Every day, Scott prepares a hot lunch of grilled trout or steak, and accommodations range from a remote but modern cabin inaccessible by road at Little Ollie to the rustic rooms at the Trestle Pine Inn, a favorite gathering place of sledders, to the luxurious condos at Blue Finn Bay, where you can swim in a pool, soak in a hot tub, and have a hearty dinner of lake trout or herring. Most days allow time out for hiking from your sled, and there are many special events, including a Mongolian firepot dinner, a sort of meat-and-vegetable fondue, served in the traditional Mongolian tent known as a yurt; other dinners range from basic burgers to fresh lake trout, elegantly presented. Keep an eye peeled for a glimpse of the Northern Lights. *Boundary Country Trekking, 590 Gunflint Trail, Grand Marais, MN 55604, tel. 218/388–9424 or 800/322–8327, fax 218/388–4487. Feb.: 4 days, $1,200. Price does not include gas and oil; sign up 3 months in advance.*

THE ROCKIES

COLORADO **The Sunlight-to-Powderhorn Trail and Beyond.** Some of the country's best snowmobiling terrain is in Colorado, but multiday tours are hard to find. This 5-day tour from American Wilderness Experience stands out. The three-story, 11-room Electric Mountain Lodge where it's based, voted one of the Northern Hemisphere's 10 best snowmobile lodges by *SnowGoer Magazine* in 1993, is an exceptionally cozy home-away-from-home with its huge stone fireplace and spacious hot tub—just the place to unwind after a day out on the trail. The lodge is about midway along the 125-mile-long Sunlight-to-Powderhorn Trail, 14 miles from the nearest road (and accessible only by over-snow vehicle after the snow falls); in addition, there are some 200 miles of groomed trails in the area, with great powder riding, panoramic views over Colorado's Uncompahgre Plateau, Grand Junction, and the mountains of Utah. Several day trips, covering between 40 and 100 miles per day both on and off trail, take you exploring through the area; there's also an overnight trip to the town of 80-mile-distant Glenwood Springs, notable for its huge outdoor hot-spring pools, steaming with therapeutic, sulfurous vapors. You go out in groups of up to 8, accompanied by one of the lodge guides, all of whom have at least 5 years of experience plus training in CPR, advanced first aid, and emergency medicine. Snowmobiles are new 440cc Arctic Cat Panther long-track vehicles with handwarmers. Food is hearty, all-American, and high in carbohydrates, with beef stew, steak, barbecued chicken, pasta, salad, homemade bread, and goodies like chocolate-chip cookies or brownies for dessert. *American Wilderness Experience, Box 1486, Boulder, CO 80306, tel. 303/444–2622 or 800/444–0099, fax 303/444–3999. Jan.–Mar.: 5 days, $1,065. Sign up 6 months in advance.*

MONTANA **Yellowstone National Park out of West Yellowstone.** Having catered to snowmobilers ever since the sport emerged on the scene in the late 1960s, this town is widely known in the field as the Snowmobile Capital of the World. Every year in winter, the place bustles with the sledding crowd, especially on weekends. You can ride snowmobiles around town, rent them in any number of places, lodge in more than a dozen motels, and chow down in over half a dozen restaurants. Nearly a dozen feet of snow fall every year. Four miles from town, in the national park, there are 440 miles of groomed trails; moose and elk abound, a bison may decide to share your trail, and Old Faithful spouts off, the best-known of some 10,000 thermal features that let off huge clouds of steam when the weather's cold. In the nearby Targhee National Forest, in Idaho, and the Gallatin National Forest, in Montana, there are thousands of acres of powder fields and mountain riding—snowmobile playgrounds par excellence.

One of the best resort motels in the area, the Stage Coach Inn, has complete 5- and 6-day packages. Guides are not available—you go out with a trail map. The inn is modern, with custom touches like the sweeping staircase in the lobby and antler lamps and willowlike chairs in the guest rooms. *Stage Coach Inn, 209 Madison Ave., West Yellowstone, MT 59758, tel. 406/646–7381 or 800/842–2882, fax 406/646–9575. Dec.–Mar.: 5–6 days, $715–$840. Prices do not include meals or gas after the first tank; sign up 6 months in advance (or call for a cancellation exactly 30 days in advance).*

WYOMING **Togwotee Mountain, the Continental Divide, and Yellowstone.** Northern Wyoming's high mountain valley, which starts at 6,200 feet and rises to 13,000 feet, contains some of the country's finest deep powder, some 500 inches a year, and some of its steepest mountains; these dare hard-core riders, while the well-groomed trails of the national park welcome novices. Senior Sno-World's basic tour of this area, designed for under-the-hill riders as well as the older clientele that this outfitter seeks to attract, begins in Jackson Hole; a 50-mile van trip puts you at Togwotee Mountain Lodge, nestled in the jack pines at 8,500 feet on the Continental

Divide Trail, which encompasses some 330 miles of groomed, interconnected trails from Pinedale north. The rest of the package involves guided day-tripping out of the lodge in late-model Arctic Cat Jags. Some days, you cover 100 to 125 miles on groomed trails and cross-country; other days, there's time to play in the powder, with only 40 to 60 miles on the itinerary. The challenges are the pleasures: high peaks, deep valleys, and flat trails, where you can jump, side-hill, or simply cruise past mountain sheep, moose, elk, and coyote. Speeds range from the 35 to 40 miles per hour for slower groups to 70 miles per hour for faster ones. Six 5- and 6-day tours for seniors only include a lesson the first day, as well as a sleigh ride in the National Elk Refuge, home to 10,000 elk. Accommodations are in comfortable motels, and meals are buffet-style—breakfasts of eggs, bacon, pancakes, and cereal, and dinners of a seafood or roast beef. *Senior Sno-World Tours, 3701 Buttrick Rd. SE, Ada, MI 49301, tel. 616/675–5885, fax 616/676–5898. Dec.–Mar.: 8 days, $1,129–$1,219; 5 days, for seniors only, $869–$939. Prices do not include some lunches, 2 days' snowmobile rental, and, except on seniors' tours, clothing; sign up 6 months in advance.*

WYOMING Yellowstone from the East. Pahaska Tepee, a rustic resort at the eastern entrance to Yellowstone, makes a totally different base from the motels in busy West Yellowstone, at the park's western gate, 85 miles to the west. Because the town is so far away, you tend to go there only once, and spend your time, instead, playing in the powder closer to the lodge—following the Gibbon River, where coyotes sometimes fish for trout; heading off to Norris Junction, with its own spate of geysers and thermal features, a bit smaller than those around 69-mile-distant Old Faithful; and to Artists' Point, for a view of 200-foot Yellowstone Falls, a cascade of ice in winter. Carry cross-country skis on your sled, and you can enjoy silent, remote trails off-limits to snowmobiles. Guides are not provided, since the routes are well-marked.

The 50-unit resort started out in 1905, when Buffalo Bill Cody, called Pahaska by the Indians, built a hewn-log lodge near the banks of the Shoshone River. Now a National Historic Landmark, it is the most distinctive structure on the property. Current guest quarters are scattered around the grounds in small, basic A-frame cabins with private baths but no phones or TVs. The resort's hillside Reunion Lodge, a 7-bedroom, 8-bath log home decorated with original southwestern art and anchored by a massive 36-foot-tall fireplace, is also available. On the lodge's package, you stay at Pahaska for 3 nights and spend another 2 or 3 nights at any one of several West Yellowstone motels. Menus offer such hearty fare as mountain man skillet at breakfast (home fries topped with fried onions, ham, mushrooms, tomatoes, cheese, and eggs); chili, soup, and burgers and other sandwiches at lunch; and, at dinner, steak and seafood. *Pahaska Tepee Resort, 183-R Yellowstone Hwy., Cody, WY 82414, tel. 307/527–7701 or 800/628–7791, fax 307/527–4019. Dec.–Mar.: 5 days, $750. Price does not include lunch, gas, or oil; sign up 6–12 months in advance.*

THE WEST COAST

CALIFORNIA Tahoe National Forest. The 175 miles of uncrowded trails that Eagle Ridge Snowmobile Outfitters owner Brad Ehrhorn uses on his tours are some of the best groomed in California: They wind past Jackson Meadows reservoir and frozen Weber Lake, and through deep-powder Pirazza Meadows and pristine forests with the majestic Sierra as a backdrop. Because this is also '49er country, overnight stops are in old mining towns, including Sierra City, the northernmost of the Gold Rush towns, and Bassett's Station, a boom-day stagecoach stop and now a peaceful hamlet with a B&B, motel, general store, and a total population of 8. There are 650 square miles of riding here, so the specific terrain you visit is selected for its interest and challenge—you might indulge in a relaxing trail ride at 5,000 feet in the Plumas National Forest, or, if you're expert, hill-climb up to 8,500 feet in the Sierra. Groups include from 2 to 6 snowmobilers, and each group is accompanied by an experienced guide. Snowmobiles are new every year; high performance vehicles are available for experienced riders. Lodging at Bassett's Station is in an elegant B&B complete with jacuzzi and hot tub. Meals are in restaurants, where you can order basic burgers and sandwiches; your B&B breakfast, which is included, is fancier. *Eagle Ridge Snowmobile Outfitters, Box 4581, Incline Village, NV 89450, tel. 702/831–7600, fax 702/832–7430. Nov.–Mar.: 2 days, $350. Sign up 1 week in advance.*

OREGON **Crater Lake Caper.** This 6-day package in the Cascade Mountains from Decker's Sno-Venture Tours is a great bargain. The Diamond Lake Resort in Diamond Lake, your lodging place for the duration, is on the doorstep of an area of giant trees and Crater Lake National Park. Every day there's a different guided trip. One day you power up to the 8,363-foot summit of Mount Bailey for an awe-inspiring view of 10 mountain peaks and majestic Mount Thielsen; on another you wind your way up over 2,000 vertical feet to cross the eerie Pumice Desert and end up on the rim of Crater Lake, one of the 8 natural wonders of the world. The over 400 miles of trails are by turns wide and well groomed, and tight and wooded, with some climbing and hilly routes. Daily distances covered range from 75 to 110 miles, usually at an average 20 to 40 miles per hour. *Decker's Sno-Venture Tours, Box 1447, Eagle River, WI 54521, tel. 715/479–2764, fax 715/479–9711. Mar.: 5 days, $545. Price does not include snowmobiles, gas, oil, or clothing; sign up 2 months in advance.*

ALASKA

CENTRAL **The Denali Frontier.** You won't find the usual tourist crowd at the wilderness lodge that Andy and Debbie Eversole have built in the middle of Denali National Park. Some people come from Anchorage, 130 miles to the south, but Michigan, Minnesota, Wisconsin, and Montana are also represented. Since the place is small, accommodating only 25 guests in the main lodge and in a trio of cabins, it's easy to get to know people, and no more than 5 riders go out with the

guides on the day trips that are included in packages here. If you're just beginning, you'll probably stick to the park's scenic 40 miles of groomed trails. If you're an expert, you'll beat a path through untracked snow, racing over the foothills and flying off moguls. If you can handle untracked terrain—a skill that can be learned in a couple of days—the possibilities for exploring are limited only by the gas in your tank. You can cover as few as 10 or 15 miles a day, or as many as 70, depending on how fast you want to ride, though most people average between 20 and 40 miles per hour. Keep an eye peeled for moose, fox, and other Alaskan critters, which are commonly sighted, and admire the terrain: hills, valleys, and flat swamps, at elevations ranging from 1,300 to 3,500 feet.

Evenings are spent socializing by the fire and enjoying home-cooked meals of such hearty fare as roast beef, fried chicken, and ham, all with homemade mashed potatoes, served by candlelight. *McKinley Snowmobile Adventures, Box 13363, Trapper Creek, AK 99683, tel. 907/733–1310. Nov.–Apr.: 3–7 days, $775–$1,750. Sign up 2 months in advance.*

SOUTHEAST **Eureka Lodge and the Iditarod Dog Sled Race.** Much more than just snowmobiling, this week-long trip combines a look at the most famous dogsled race in the world and the chance to explore untamed backcountry.

The week kicks off in Anchorage with a visit to the Iditarod mushers in their motels and follows them for the next 2 days on the trails. Then you and the dogs part ways as you make the run to Eureka Lodge, your base in this wide-open region for the next 5 days. Here, you run cross-country toward the Horse Pasture area, notable for its scenery; sled on scenic rivers like the Caribou, Alfred, Squaw, and Nelchina; and explore deserted gold-mining camps. About 100 miles of groomed trails in the immediate area of the lodge give you access to open meadows, challenging mountains, and rolling valleys—the sheer size of the area is enough to take your breath away. Typically you average 75 to 125 miles a day, at speeds of between 40 and 70 miles per hour, depending on the group. On an optional 105-mile trip to Valdez for experienced drivers with extensive mountain and sidehill experience, you cross the Nelchina, Stephens, and Valdez Glaciers; traverse the 6,000-foot-high Scott Ice Field; overnight in Valdez; and return the next day.

This is a true frontier adventure through untracked wilderness that few snowmobilers ever see. The group size is 10, with 2 guides. *Senior Sno-World Tours, 3701 Buttrick Rd. SE, Ada, MI 49301, tel. 616/676–5885, fax 616/676–5898. Mar.: 9 days, $1,695. Price does not include snowsuits, helmets, and boots; sign up 6 months in advance.*

CANADA

ONTARIO **Via the Snow Train to the North.** In the 10,000-square-mile Nordaski region of northern Ontario, hundreds of miles of groomed trails link Hearst, the area's principal town, with other communities distinctive for their mix of French-, Ojibway-, and Cree-speaking residents. Because downtown Hearst is open to snowmobile traffic, you can ride directly from your lodging to the trails. Here, and on the numerous old logging roads into the bush, you experience true deep snow country, where up to 4 feet of powder is present all winter.

Dick Squiers developed his tour of the area in the 1970s and has been running it 2 to 3 times a year since then. Groups of 30 converge in Sault Ste. Marie, Canada, over the bridge from Sault Ste. Marie, Michigan, where you board the Algoma Central Railway's Snow Train for a day-long, 297-mile ride north over rivers, across high trestles, past Bridal Veil and Black Beaver falls, then through beautiful Agawa Canyon. In Hearst, where you're based for the duration of the trip, you break up into smaller groups of riders of similar abilities, and spend the rest of the week day tripping around the area with your guides. The challenge here is riding in deep snow—daily mileages surpass 100 miles over rolling terrain, at an average speed of between 30 to 50 miles per hour, depending on the group.

The Christmas–New Year's week trip is especially popular. *International Snowmobile Tours, Inc., 427 Sycamore, Chesterfield, IN 46017, tel. 317/378–5074 or 800/378–8687. Dec.–Mar.: 6 days, $650. Price includes train fare but not snowmobiles, clothing, gas, oil, and some lunches and dinners; sign up 6 months in advance.*

ONTARIO **Via the Snow Train to Wawa.** Embarking at Sault Ste. Marie, Michigan, Senior Sno-World Tours also makes use of the Algoma Central Railway but after 5 hours jumps off in the town of Wawa. There are usually 10 to 15 people per group, and each group is accompanied by a guide.

The snowmobiling around Wawa is as good as it is farther north, with plenty of groomed trails with good snow cover and scenery of frozen lakes and rolling meadows interspersed with thick forest. The sheer size of the area is enough to overwhelm even experienced sledders. Daily mileages range from 75 to 125 miles, depending on the speed of the group. Although high speeds are not encouraged, a faster group will average 60 to 70 miles per hour, and a slower one only 35 to 40. Lodging is in single-story motels, with facilities such as hot tubs, saunas, and swimming pools. You also have the option of traveling an extra 210 miles north to Hearst—the trip is included in the price. *Senior Sno-World Tours, 3701 Buttrick Rd. SE, Ada, MI 49301, tel. 616/676–5885, fax 616/676–5898. Feb.: 8 days, $659. Price does not include snowmobiles, clothing, gas, oil, and some meals; sign up 6–8 months in advance.*

QUEBEC **Loop Lac St-Jean.** This 7-day North American Sno-Tours loop tour out of Quebec City covers more than 950 miles of scenic territory, usually about 150 miles a day at speeds of about 35 miles an hour; even though the trail network is excellent and the trail well groomed, you need a fairly high level of proficiency. The loop follows rivers, ferries across lakes, traverses dams, and flashes in and out of forests and glades. Lunches are at comfortable, well-stocked snowmobile clubhouses along the trails, locally known as Club Relais, and lodging is at wayside inns and some more deluxe hotels. Most partici-pants bring their own sleds, but rentals are available (for an additional $100 a day). Each tour is accompanied by a support vehicle and by experienced guides, some bilingual and all with some medical emergency training. (If your skills are not up to the demands of this program, look into the special departures for seniors and couples, whose pace is more relaxed.) *North American Sno-Tours, Box 1016, Meredith, NH 03253, tel. 603/279–3985. Jan.: 7 days, $750. Price includes lodging but not gas, oil, snowmobiles, clothing, or any meals except breakfast; sign up 3 months in advance.*

SOURCES

ORGANIZATIONS The **International Snow-mobile Industry Association** (ISIA, 3975 University Dr., Suite 310, Fairfax, VA 22030, tel. 703/273–9606) is a central source for gen-eral information. The ISIA publishes a trail map directory to 20 states and 8 Canadian provinces, a guide to publications about snow-mobiling, and a safety handbook. In the Northeast, the **Vermont Association of Snow Travelers** (Box 839, Montpelier, VT 05602, tel. 802/229–0005), a nonprofit group of vol-unteers, operates a trail system and publish-es a newsletter and vacation information. The **Western Maine Mountains International Snowmobile Network** (Western Maine Mountains Chamber of Commerce, Box 934, Wilton, ME 04294, tel. 207/864–3932) can tell you about its 260-mile marked and groomed loop, partly in Quebec, and put you in touch with 5 area chambers of commerce that can help you plan a tour with overnight stops in each of their towns. In the Rockies, the **Utah Travel Council** (Council Hall/Capitol Hill, Salt Lake City, UT 84114, tel. 801/538–1030) publishes a free brochure and trail maps on snowmobiling throughout the state. The **California/Nevada Snowmobile Association** (Ken Nelson, Bucks Lake Lodge, Box 236, Quincy, CA 95971, tel. 916/283–2262) can also be helpful.

PERIODICALS The quarterly *Snowmobile Magazine,* which concentrates on product evaluation and destinations, and *SnowGoer Magazine,* which focuses on snowmobile technology, are both published by Ehlert Publishing Group (319 Barry Ave. S, Wayzata, MN 55391, tel. 612/476–2200); *SnowGoer*'s December issue is a comprehensive annual vacation guide that details every snowmobile area in the East, Midwest, and Canada but covers the West only sketchily. *Snowest Magazine* (Harris Publishing Co., 520 Park Ave., Idaho Falls, ID 83402, tel. 800/638–0135) discusses snowmobiling in the West; an annual subscription includes the *Western Guide to Snowmobiling,* a state-by-state guide to hot spots and guide services in 12 western states and British Columbia.

VIDEOS Two practical guides include the International Association of Snowmobile Administrators' *Snowmobiling Safety and You: Snowmobile Operations and Tracks of Winter: Guide to Responsible Snowmobiling* (Outdoor Empire Publishing, 511 Eastlake Ave. E, Seattle, WA 98109, tel. 206/624–3845). *Snowmotion: The Art of Sledding* (Petersen Production, Inc., 314 West Pender St., Vancouver, B.C. Canada V6B 1T3, tel. 604/669–8890) captures powder bashing, grabbing air, racing, and incredible mountain scenery—in a jazzy, adventure-flick format.

ALSO SEE If you like a blue-and-white color scheme in the wilderness and the feel of icy wind on your cheeks, see the Cross-Country Skiing and Ski Schools chapters.

Surfing Schools

by Erik Fair

xperienced surfers call beginning surfers Kooks. The plight of the Kook is summed up by the East Coast editor of *Surfer Magazine,* Amy Van Sant, who says: "Anyone who has surfed for over a year instantly hates anyone who has surfed for less than a year." Van Sant and her West Coast counterpart Ben Marcus laugh at the "hate statement." Although they admit that it's at least partially true, they insist that the rewards of surfing far outweigh all the kookiness you'll endure as you evolve into a special kind of being—one who can compete for the most magical and natural commodity on earth: a ridable breaking wave. "The first time you stand up on a breaking wave," says Marcus, "you'll feel like a supreme being who has conquered a whole ocean. You'll think you're moving much faster than you really are, and the sound of the water peeling off the rails (sides) of your board is unbelievably crisp." But the biggest thrill for any beginning surfer, says Marcus, is "the personal satisfaction of mastering something that is very difficult and very frustrating."

For the raw beginner, just balancing on a surfboard while lying down is awkward. The idea of reading waves seems as unfathomable as the ocean itself; and the chances of simultaneously catching a breaking wave and standing up are slim and none. Throw in the indignity of starting at the absolute bottom of a rigid pecking order, and it's easy to understand why 90% of all surfers seem to be confident young men with thick skin.

In reality, surfing can be enjoyed by anyone of any age—as long as he or she realizes that surfing's learning curve is as personally defined as it is limitless. If you have average strength, stamina, and flexibility coupled with above-average patience, tenacity, and humility, you can learn to surf. Naturally, the more fit and philosophical you are, the faster you'll negotiate the metamorphosis from Kook to Surf God.

First things first: Before you can catch a wave, you need to understand it. The formation of a wave begins when breezes blowing hundreds or even thousands of miles away from shore sweep unobstructed across the ocean. Their force is absorbed by the surface of the ocean and translated into an ocean swell. Eventually the long bands of swell encounter shallower waters and, ultimately, the shoreline where you eagerly await your first surfing lesson. As each band nears the shore, friction from the rising ocean bottom slows down the lower part of the swell. The upper part of the swell keeps moving at the swell's original speed, and water piles up until something has to give. When it does, the wave breaks. The steepness and composition of the ocean bottom combine with the size, shape, direction, and speed of the swell to determine just where and how that happens. Other variables include tides, changes in the contour of the ocean floor caused by the force of breaking waves, and local breezes, which can knock a perfectly surfable swell into a useless chop.

Adventurer and writer Erik Fair is the author of California Thrill Sports. *He has been marinating in southern California's surfer-dude culture for most of his adult life.*

From a beginner's perspective there are 3 types of breaking waves: (1) waves you can have fun with, (2) waves that will scare the bejabbers out of you, and (3) waves that will eat you for breakfast. What an instructor is looking for is a gradually sloped sandy ocean bottom and relatively slow-moving 1- to 3-foot waves with a soft (sometimes called crumbly) break. He or she will also look for waves that break as far as possible from the shoreline, in water shallow enough for you to stand up in. Stay away from big, fast, steep waves that break with a cool-looking curl and a bone-rattling "WHOMP!"

Once you understand the natural forces you're dealing with, it's time to get familiar with the equipment involved in surfing: the board. A board is a magical planing device that allows you to scoot, perfectly balanced, along the face of a breaking wave and carve elegant turns by subtly shifting your weight.

As a beginner you need a relatively big board that has plenty of flotation and is stable enough to withstand your clunky initial attempts at weight-shift control. You'll probably want a board that is at least a foot taller than you are, about 3 inches thick, and 19 to 22 inches wide in the middle. Avoid the short, thin, cool-looking Tri-Fins or Thrusters that most experienced surfers use. Some schools use soft surfboards, made out of plastic foam, that float well and won't hurt if they hit you. Other schools use traditional hard boards carved out of polyurethane foam blocks and coated with fiberglass. These can definitely hurt you if they hit you, but this won't be a problem as long as you observe normal safety procedures. Most schools use a "leash" as a safety measure. This device attaches a hard board to your ankle to prevent it from shooting out of a wave like a missile aimed at someone's head.

Once you have a good beginner's board, an experienced instructor, and suitable surf conditions, it's time to learn a few skills. First, you learn how to lie down on the board and stay balanced, in both side-to-side and front-to-aft positions. Next, you learn how to rotate your arms in a smooth paddling motion and stay balanced while being pitched up and down and side to side on your way to the spot where waves are breaking.

Once you're in the water, you'll need to be able to read the waves, so you can match the wave's speed and catch it at the exact moment it breaks. Unfortunately, your biggest problem at this point is still staying balanced while being pitched up and down by a rolling sea. During your first few lessons count on your instructor to read waves for you, pushing you into position to actually have a chance of catching a few waves. To catch a wave you have to shift your weight slightly to the rear, so the nose of your board doesn't "pearl" (dive into the wave and flip you over like a piece of driftwood). This is relatively easy to do the first few times because, hey, no one's asking you to stand up yet. That will come after you develop a feel for all the above techniques.

The motion you'll use to stand up is called a pop-up, which is a sudden, smooth motion from a face-down, lying-down position to a side-straddle crouched position with one foot in front of the other. Practicing a pop-up on dry land is one thing. Doing it while catching a wave and balancing on a speeding surfboard is quite another. With good instruction you can expect gradual progress from your belly to your knees to a nervous crouch to a full Bronze Surf-God stand up. It takes most beginners from 1 to 4 lessons (2 to 10 hours) to stand up in the water. It all depends on the surf spot, surf conditions, your ability, and your instructor's ability.

Private or group lessons given by the hour or half-day are the most popular type of surfing school option for adults. Costs typically range from $25 to $70 an hour for private lessons and from $15 to $30 an hour for group lessons. These lessons are usually tailored to the age and level of the students.

Most 3- to 7-day surf camps are designed for and run by a younger crowd, with most participants between the ages of 10 and 16. However, some schools, such as those listed here, reserve one session for adults. A week will give you the chance to progress from just balancing efficiently to learning to catch better waves more quickly and to angle across the face of a wave rather than taking it straight into shore. Virtually all camps take place between June and August, and most involve camping out in tents, telling tall tales around a campfire, and surfing your brains out during the day. Costs range from $200 to $800 per camp, depending on number of days and type of accommodations, if any, offered.

CHOOSING THE RIGHT SCHOOL

Lots of folks learn how to surf by trial and error, or from buddies or freelance instructors loosely affiliated with a local surf shop. The risks and rewards of trial and error are obvious. And who knows how competent your buddy is? Be wary of informal referrals from surf shops; sales people may confuse your best interest with their own. Ask these questions before choosing an instructor:

How long have you been teaching, and what certifications do you have? There is no official instructor certification in the world of surfing, so you should look for an instructor who has a lot of experience and other certifications, such as CPR and first aid, for proof that he or she is worthy of your trust. Beyond that, find an instructor whose personal style you feel comfortable with.

What's the cost and what's included? Prices for camps in these listings are per person and include food, lodging, and surfboards. Prices for lessons also include use of a board. Find out what kind of board is offered (soft or hard), because you might want to bring your own. Also ask if you need to bring your own leash or water wear (such as a wet suit).

What are the accommodations like? Accommodations at most surf camps are camping or dorm style, so make sure you know what you're getting into. In these listings, chamber of commerce telephone numbers are given to assist you in finding lodging near surf schools that offer only daily lessons.

What is the food like? Food is provided at the camps listed here, but it is basic camping fare. If you're not prepared to dine on the likes of hot dogs and simple Mexican dishes, surfing school may not be your ideal vacation.

Do you have references from past students? This is one way to get the scoop on how well a surfer teaches.

How far in advance do I need to book? You may need to sign up 2 months in advance for surfing camps and 2 weeks in advance for private lessons.

FAVORITE SCHOOLS

THE MID ATLANTIC

DELAWARE **Surf Sessions.** Bret Buchler is a true surfing addict—just ask his children, Baptiste and Abi, who were surfing by the time they were 3. Bret started at 22 when he caught his first wave in Ocean City, Maryland, in the summer of 1976. By that fall the charm of the waves had lured him to California. Three months later, still not satisfied, he took a 6-month surfing safari to Hawaii. From there it was a stint as a crew member on a ship making a round-the-world voyage, during which he surfed in France and Israel. He finally returned to Fenwick Island, Delaware (half a mile from Ocean City, Maryland), where he founded Surf Sessions in 1989. Buchler combines his passion for the sport with his skill as a teacher (he teaches geography in a junior high school) to come up with a great program.

Surf Sessions, one of only 2 established surfing schools on the East Coast, offers weeklong overnight camps from June through August, and day lessons from May through October. Although most of the camps are for kids (ages 12–18), the last one each summer is for adults (usually between 21 and 40).

Your week starts on Sunday evening with a 30-minute orientation session on water safety, followed by 30 minutes of stretching exercises and pop-up practice on the beach. Sunday evening Buchler and his 2 assistants take you into the water, guide you to the right spot, and push you into a few small waves. Bret teaches on 2- to 3-foot waves that are ideal for beginners and can almost always be found between Indian River Inlet, Delaware, and Assateague Island, Maryland.

For the first day or so, until you no longer need pushing, you ride straight into shore in whitewater. Then the instructors give verbal cues—"paddle hard," "keep paddling," "watch the wave," "go left," "go right"—to help you catch some waves on your own. By the third day you can leave the little whitewater behind and get into the line where slightly larger waves are breaking. Here you learn to read the waves and how to angle across the face of a wave rather than riding it straight into shore. The days are intense: You stay in the water as long as waves are breaking and your energy level holds up.

Each night you return to camp headquarters in a house 50 feet from the beach. Two bedrooms with bunk beds house 10 campers. They may not be the most luxurious accommodations, but you'll be too tired to care. Meals are catered, and there's a fireplace where sleepy surfers gather to swap stories about the day. *Surf Sessions, Rte. 3, Box 275 B, Fenwick Island, DE 19944, tel. 302/539–2126. June–Aug.: 7-day camp, $400. May–Oct.: 2-hour lesson, $20 for first lesson and $15 for subsequent lessons. Sign up 1 day in advance for lessons, 2 months in advance for camps.*

THE SOUTH

FLORIDA **Cocoa Beach Surfing School.** Craig Carroll has been surfing for 27 of his 35 years, and in 1993 he started the only surf school in Cocoa Beach. The warm water temperatures (we don't need no stinking wet suits) and gradually sloping, sand-bottom beaches make this the most comfortable spot on the East Coast for beginning surfers. Cocoa Beach is also a top vacation spot for non-surfers; it's only an hour east of the Orlando area (Walt Disney World) and half an hour north of the Kennedy Space Center.

Although he teaches surfing to all ages—he started his son Corey at 6 months—Carroll's week-long day camps in July and August are usually attended only by children (ages 7–15). He gives adults 1-hour private lessons and 2-hour group lessons year-round. Carroll has had great success with his adult pupils, and says he hasn't had one yet who couldn't stand up at least once by the end of his or her first lesson. The 2- to 3-foot waves characteristic of the summer make it the best season to make your first attempts. Carroll provides only soft boards and leashes, so if you want to learn on a fiberglass board you'll have to bring your own. *Cocoa Beach Surfing School, 955 Sandalwood La., Rockledge, FL 32955, tel. 407/639–4076. Rockledge Chamber of Commerce, tel. 407/459–2200. July–Aug.: 5-day kids' day camp, $120. Year-round: 1-hour private lesson, $25; 2-hour group lesson, $20 per person (4-person minimum). Sign up 2 weeks in advance.*

THE SOUTHWEST

TEXAS **Riding a Wave Machine.** You definitely need an ocean to learn how to read wave conditions, but you no longer need one to catch a breaking wave. Not since Thomas Lochtefeld invented a million-dollar machine called a Flow Rider that can pump out a perfectly ridable simulation of a 5-foot wave—one with a true shoulder that breaks continuously, as long as the machine is turned on. This effect is created by shooting a 3- to 4-inch sheet of water up the machine's foam-coated, wave-shaped concrete structure. The water's 10 to 14 mile-per-hour upward flow can support a surfer. Even pro surfers rave about how realistic the Flow Rider feels and how useful it is for practicing difficult maneuvers.

The Texas incarnation of Lochtefeld's invention is at a wave pool dubbed the Boogie Bahn. It's the first man-made wave pool in the country to offer waves big enough and well-shaped enough to allow you to catch a breaking wave, drop into it, and do turns back and forth across its face. You can practice the physical skills and timing of catching a wave without having to deal with the mysteries and inconsistencies of an ocean.

The safe environment created by the machine gives you the freedom to experiment away, without much risk of hurting yourself. You are not allowed to stand up or use hard surfboards, because the water park owners are not ready to assume the risk of beginners falling into 3 or 4 inches of water from a standing position or sending hard surfboards flying around the relatively small area. Instead, you ride the wave lying down or kneeling on a soft body board—not exactly Surf God position, but still a blast. You also get a chance to watch exhibitions by experienced surfers who *are* allowed to stand up and show off their skills.

There are no instructors here, so most people come with a friend who knows at least a little about how to ride a wave. Bring your own body board, or rent one. *Schlitterbahn at the Rapids, The Boogie Bahn, 370 W. Lincoln, New Braunfels, TX 78130, tel. 210/625–5510, ext. 525. For an updated list of other Flow Riders write or call Thomas J. Lochtfeld, 5508 Pacifica Dr., La Jolla, CA 92037, tel. 619/273–0307. New Braunfels Chamber of Commerce, tel. 210/625–2385. Year-round: 1-day pass at Boogie Bahn, $25. Price does not include board rental.*

THE WEST COAST

CALIFORNIA **Paradise Surfing Lessons.** Malibu Point is one of the finest and most consistent point breaks in the world. And—blame it on the Frankie and Annette *Beach Blanket Bingo* surfing movies of the fifties and sixties—it's also the best known surfing spot in the continental United States. Throw in the glitter of nearby Hollywood, and it's easy to understand why Ted Silverberg hit a gold mine in 1983 when he decided to start a surf school here.

Silverberg, now 34, has been surfing since he was 13. He worked his way through law school by renting surfing equipment to Hollywood movie studios and teaching stars and stuntmen how to surf well enough to perform their roles without drowning. His school offers private instruction to people of all ages and abilities, ranging from custom-tailored lessons for adults to an annual special outing for students with visual impairments from the Braille Institute. Silverberg says some of his most rewarding moments have come while taking a child with such an impairment for an exhilarating tandem ride.

Although he no longer teaches, Ted supervises a staff of 4 to 5 instructors who give around 25 private lessons a week. All equipment is provided, and, because Silverberg keeps 65 surfboards and 125 wet suits in stock to accommodate the whims of Hollywood Studios, you are virtually assured of a perfect fit. Most of Paradise Surfing's private lessons take place at Pointe Dume, the private beach where Silverberg makes his home—along with Barbara Streisand, Johnny Carson, Julie Andrews, and Sylvester Stallone. *Paradise Surfing Lessons, 28128 Pacific Coast Hwy., Malibu, CA 90265, tel. 310/457–9829. Malibu Chamber of Commerce, tel. 310/456–9025. Year-round: 2-hour private lesson, $50. Sign up 2 weeks in advance.*

CALIFORNIA **Paskowitz Surfing Camps.** This school has a family history. Director Moses Paskowitz is one of 9 children in an 11-member surfing family. As a teenager, he learned to surf at his father's school in Tel Aviv, Israel, and since 1977 he has headed up his family's surf camp in their new home in San Onofre, California. The Paskowitz's camp is the longest-running and largest surf camp in Southern California. Between the 10 summer surf camps and year-round private lessons, Moses and his 7 brothers, archetypal surfer dudes, introduce more than 200 people per year to the sport.

Taking one of Paskowitz's surf camps is like spending a week or 2 with your favorite cousins. The brothers teach while matriarch Juliette and sister Navah run the camp headquarters. Although luxury accommodations are available at hotels nearby, the vast majority of the Paskowitz's students prefer sleeping bags under the stars or the 2-person tents the school sets up at San Clemente's San Mateo campground.

The family works hard to minimize Kook talk and instead preaches the Aloha spirit, which Moses defines as "Hey, do unto others as you would like them to do unto you." In addition to delivering top-flight one-on-one instruction during 2 daily surf sessions, Moses and the boys dispense philosophical tidbits ranging from "Hey, no one owns the waves" to "Hey, the ocean always forces you to go forward" and "If Elvis surfed, he'd be alive today."

Each of the week-long summer surf camps run between June and August draws between 15 and 25 campers from all over the world. The number of adults at the camps has grown annually, and currently about 25% of the campers are 18 or older. The rest of the crowd is between 12 and 17. Your fee includes tent; chow (prepared by Juliette and Navah); all surfing equipment, including traditional fiberglass boards, wet suits, and leashes; and video teaching sessions (you're filmed by one of the brothers). During the week most students progress from a beginning site called Blue Lagoon to Old Man's, a popular intermediate site adjacent to Lower Trestles, an advanced site dominated by highly territorial local surfers. *Paskowitz Productions, Box 522, San Clemente, CA 92674, tel. 714/240–7698. June–Aug.: 7-day camp, $795. Sept.–May: 1-hour private lesson, $50. Sign up 2 months in advance for camps, 2 weeks in advance for lessons.*

CALIFORNIA Richard Schmidt Surf Camp. This Santa Cruz camp is one of only a few in Northern California. Cold water and a shoreline exposed to winds make most of the area a tough place to surf. A notable exception is the Monterey Bay coastline near Santa Cruz. This extraordinarily beautiful and pristine area (also known as the Monterey Bay National Marine Sanctuary) is protected from oil drilling and other sources of pollution. The bay protects the beaches from swell-busting wind, thus offering a wide variety of beaches that are open to swells from almost any direction.

Richard Schmidt's school is a cut above many others for a number of reasons. First, he has been surfing for more than 25 years, teaching surfing for upwards of 15 years, and running surf camps for a third of that time. Second, as a lifelong resident of Santa Cruz and a professional lifeguard for the city, he is intimately

familiar with the area's beaches and ocean conditions. Third, he teaches nearly as many adults as teenagers. Finally, he has developed a unique teaching technique that allows him to guarantee stand-up surfing by the end of the first lesson.

Schmidt doesn't just get you into position to catch a wave and shove you in the right direction at the right time like most instructors. He actually catches the wave right alongside you. "That way I'm right there when the wave breaks," says Schmidt, "and I can stabilize your board with one hand, while yanking you to a standing position with the other." He has even developed a harness with a handle on the back to facilitate these yank-ups.

Schmidt runs 4 one-week camps between July and August. Approximately 5 of the 15 participants each week are adults, many of whom take lessons with their kids. Tents are provided at a local KOA campground with a grocery store, hot showers, batting cage, Jacuzzi, and in-ground swimming pool. The cost of the camp includes food (prepared by Richard's wife, Marisa); camping fees; transportation to and from surf sites; all equipment, including wet suits, leashes, and soft boards; plus special "yank-up" instruction from Schmidt and 2 other instructors. A video of you surfing is also included in the price. *Richard Schmidt Surf Camp, Dufour St., Santa Cruz, CA 94060, tel. 408/423–0928. July–Aug.: 7-day camp, $650. Year-round: 1-hour private lesson, $50; 2-hour group lesson (minimum of 4 students), $70. Sign up 2 months in advance for camps, 2 weeks in advance for lessons.*

HAWAII

OAHU Oahu Hawaii Beach Boys Association. According to surfing industry insiders, the beaches of Waikiki may be the best place in the United States to learn how to surf. Minimum tidal currents coupled with wave-breaking areas several hundred yards offshore means two things. First, Waikiki waves are among the safest for beginners to learn on. Second, they provide the longest rides possible. Waikiki is also one of the most reliable surfing areas in the world because there are very few days when there are no ridable waves. That's because Waikiki Beach develops surfable waves from swells approaching from a number of directions: South and southwest swells come in from the South Pacific, and northeast and easterly tradewind swells wrap around Koko Head Point to become surfable waves.

The Beach Boys Association is a loose association of the area's top surfing instructors who get their customers from the numerous hotels on the beach. Rabbit Kekai, Blackout Whalex, Clyde Aikau, and Captain Bob are 4 of the association's most colorful and experienced instructors. Rabbit Kekai, for instance, has been surfing and teaching for most of his adult life. Now in his 70s, he is still going strong. The epitome of surfing spirit and informality, the Beach Boys Association headquarters is nothing more than a desk under a beach umbrella behind the statue of Hawaiian surfing legend Duke Kahanamoku. Just go to the Hyatt Hotel on Kuhio Beach in Waikiki and ask for directions to the "Duke" statue. *Hawaii Beach Boys Association, Inc., Clyde Aikau, President, 41-703 Mekia, Waimanalo, Hawaii; or call George Downing, tel. 808/732–4563. Year-round: 1-hour private lesson, $50–$75 (depending on instructor); 1-hour group lesson (minimum 3 students), $25. Half-, full-, and multi-day lesson fees are negotiable.*

SOURCES

ORGANIZATIONS The **United States Surfing Federation** (7104 Island Village Dr., Long Beach, CA 90803, tel. 310/596–7785) and the **Surf Industry Manufacturer's Association** (3334 E. Coast Hwy., #416, Corona Del Mar, CA 92625, tel. 714/760–0784) can provide the latest information on the sport and its equipment.

PERIODICALS *Surfer Magazine* (Surfer Publications, Inc., Box 1028, Dana Point, CA 92629, tel. 714/496–5922) and *Surfing Magazine* (Western Empire Publications, Inc., San Clemente, CA 92672, tel. 714/492–7873) are the two major surfing magazines in the United States. Both feature hot surfers and surfing spots, new maneuvers, contest results, surfing political issues, and surfing heritage. They celebrate the sport with top-flight graphics and photography.

BOOKS *Surfer's Start-Up: A Beginner's Guide to Surfing* (Pathfinder Publishing), by Doug Werner, is an easy-to-read book that arms the beginning surfer with solid knowledge about equipment and technique. Werner's book also captures the spirit of surfing and gives a bunch of inside tips on how to survive localism (surfing's rigid pecking order) during the first year. The black-and-white illustrations are excellent. *How to Surf*, compiled by *Surfing Magazine* editor Nick Carroll, is actually part of a special collector's series published by the magazine. It provides excellent information on the natural elements of surfing. Successive short articles read like chapters and take you from selecting your first surfboard to learning various turns.

ALSO SEE There are other ways to ride the surf: How about putting a sail on your board? Turn to Windsurfing for schools that will show you how it's done.

Tennis Camps

by Susan Farewell

hether you've just taken up the sport or you're a top seed at your club, a week at a tennis camp can do wonders for your game. (Just imagine spending several hours each day with someone whose job is to help you play better.) There are dozens of places where you can do this around the country—so many, in such a wide range of styles, that you can afford to be choosy.

Some tennis camps colonize college campuses or ski resorts in summer, others are held at posh resorts in glamorous locations, and a few were designed and built exclusively for teaching tennis. A handful are under the auspices of some tennis great, while others are run by pros who have built their reputation by teaching.

Some camps will give you a week-long, 6-hour-a-day tennis-a-thon, while others offer a vacation with tennis as the primary—but not the only—activity.

Most camps aim to refine and improve your existing style of play. Others—they're rare—have you re-learn the game *their* way. There is a host of teaching styles, and each camp has its own repertoire of drills.

No matter where you go, you should be beyond beginner level, and you need to be in good condition. After all, you're just cheating yourself if you can't keep up with the drills.

Five- to 7-day tennis camp programs usually involve working over all aspects of the game, from serves, strokes, and net shots to strategy for both singles and doubles play. Nearly all begin by evaluating your ability and grouping you with others at your level. Depending upon the camp, you either move from pro to pro during the day or stay with one pro for the duration. At some point during your stay, the staff videotapes you and analyzes your game during the playback. (Sometimes you get to keep the tape.) Most tennis camps have ball machines; sometimes you use them under the instructor's eye and sometimes they're for extracurricular practice. Instructors might be former pros, new-to-the-tour pros, someone who's developed some particular method, or, occasionally, a superstar teacher—someone who achieved fame and fortune for his or her teaching abilities and methods alone. You will sometimes see it mentioned that a camp's instructors are members of the USPTA, and while this does signal their status as professional tennis players, it isn't an endorsement of them as teachers.

A big selling point at many schools is the number of hours you're on the courts each day and the ratio of students to instructors. Generally speaking, the more hours on the court and the fewer students per instructor, the better. But 5 hours on the court at a program with a 6:1 ratio may be no more rewarding than 3 hours in a program with twice the number of instructors.

Susan Farewell is a Connecticut-based travel and fitness writer. Her eclectic style of play comes from a dozen years of visiting tennis camps and resorts the world over.

Off court, most tennis camps fall somewhere on the comfort spectrum between courtside boot camps and exclusive private clubs. Accommodations vary dramatically—sometimes even within the same camp. At tennis camps on college campuses, you usually sleep in no-frills dormitories, where you share a room with at least one fellow camper and use a bathroom that's down the hall. When the camp is held at a resort, you may wind up in anything from your standard hotel room with two double beds to a luxurious suite with a fireplace, patio, and amenities galore. Most resort camps offer a tuition-and-lodging package; if you don't like the basic quarters it includes, you can usually pay extra for an upgrade. When the camp is on a college campus, you eat institutional cafeteria fare; when you're at a fancy resort, menus are fancy, too. Resort programs usually include access to other recreational facilities as part of the package.

Although tennis camps can cost anywhere from less than $500 to more than $2,000 for 5 to 7 days, most run between $700 and $1,200.

CHOOSING THE RIGHT CAMP

Asking a few key questions will help you find the best camp for you.

What are the accommodations like? They could be anything from Spartan dorm to posh resort hotel. Know what you're getting into.

What is the food like? A camp's cuisine takes its cue from the setting: you eat institutional fare on college campuses and feast on more ambitious dishes at luxury resorts. Whatever the case, also find out what your options are if you feel like a change of pace.

What's the cost and what's included? Unless otherwise noted, prices given in the reviews below are per person and include lodging, based on double occupancy, and meals.

What are the teachers' credentials? Even at a camp run by a well-known player or teacher, you spend lots of time with other instructors; find out who they are, and what their playing and teaching experience is.

What's the ratio of students to instructors? And how many hours each day do you spend on the court with your instructors?

How long has the camp been run? If the program is new, be particularly careful to find out about the people in charge and their plans for the camp. Make sure that their teaching experience is credible, and that the instruction program seems well-conceived and well-organized.

What's the ratio of students to courts? Even with a good student-to-instructor ratio, too few courts means lots of time spent waiting around for your turn. The ideal ratio would be 2 players to each court, but don't count on seeing that too often; 4:1 should be fine, since not every student will be on the courts at all times.

How physically demanding is it? Find out what drills are involved, and how many hours a day you spend in strenuous physical activity. Then decide whether you want to commit yourself to the level of work.

Are courts covered in case of rain? You don't want to risk losing tennis time to inclement weather.

What are the court surfaces? Trying out all the different surfaces is important, but you may want to hone your skills on the surface you play on at home.

Is there unlimited access to tennis facilities during free time? You want to be able to try out your new moves while the lessons are fresh.

Are courts lighted for night play? This extends the amount of time available for extracurricular play. You'll also appreciate lighted courts if you're there when the weather is hot.

What's the clientele? Some camps attract mostly singles, others are more popular with couples and groups of friends traveling together, or people of a similar age. The more expensive the program, the older the crowd. Unless otherwise noted, all of the camps listed here attract a varied group from 20s to 60s.

How social is the program? Some programs have a lot of planned, off-court socializing, and some don't. If you want to play all day and party into the night, don't choose a program whose campers regularly turn in early.

How far in advance do I need to sign up for camp? Few camps have a strict deadline, but all recommend reserving as early as possible. This is especially true for traditional holiday or vacation times and for camps held only seasonally. Still, if they've got the room, they'll sign you up at the last minute.

Is laundry service available? The answer to this determines how many complete tennis outfits you need to pack.

Do you have references from past students? To clarify your ideas about instruction, accommodations, and food, there's no substitute for a talk with someone who has done the drills, slept in the beds, and eaten the meals.

FAVORITE CAMPS

THE NORTHEAST

MASSACHUSETTS **Amherst Tennis Camp.** The most impressive statistic about this operation at Amherst College in western Massachusetts is not its number of tennis courts (36) but the percentage of students who come back for more (40%). This probably has a lot to do with the good value you get from your tennis camp dollar: your room, 3 meals a day, at least 5 hours of instruction daily, a 4:1 student-to-instructor ratio, and 3 half-hour private lessons during the week. There are also dozens of instructors, a mix of USPTA players, college tennis instructors, and foreign pros.

Amherst offers advanced clinics, designed for those wanting to refine their game; doubles clinics, which pay special attention to ball placement, strategy, and team communication; clinics for single people, which include fun tournaments, softball and volleyball games, and other social activities; and open sessions, which address both the basics and more advanced techniques.

In all the clinics, you work on strokes and strategy for both singles and doubles play.

After 35 or 40 minutes with one instructor, another instructor arrives to go over a different aspect of the game. You're videotaped a couple of times so that you can see your progress, and you can take home the tape, along with your private instructor's written assessment of your game, with suggestions for ways you can improve your game at home.

Off court, this is a sociable program, popular among professional men and women in their 30s and 40s. Lodging is in single dormitory rooms; you make your own bed and share baths and rec rooms. You can opt for less Spartan accommodations off-campus, but then you'd miss out on the camaraderie that develops among campers. Meals are buffet-style in the school's cafeteria; one night you may get spareribs, and another spaghetti, but there are usually calorie-wise and vegetarian options. You have access to the college's indoor swimming pool, cushioned outdoor running track, and other facilities. *Amherst Tennis Camp, Box 2271, Amherst College, Amherst, MA 01002, tel. 413/542–8100, fax 413/542–5789. Mid-June–mid- or late Aug.: 7 days, $790. Sign up at least 1 month in advance.*

MASSACHUSETTS **Total Tennis.** Held on the campus of Williston-Northampton prep school in the heart of the Pioneer Valley, just 20 minutes from Amherst, Total Tennis is close to Tanglewood, the summer home of the Boston Symphony Orchestra, and Jacob's Pillow Dance Festival. It's easy to reach from New York and Boston, and draws heavily from both cities.

One of the distinguishing features of Total Tennis is that you work with a single pro throughout the program; each is assigned to a quartet of students for the duration in the interest of fostering group spirit and allowing an instructor to get to know each student's game. The goal is ultimately to make you comfortable with the fundamentals before you work on other aspects of the game. Although there are instructional guidelines and goals, all Total Tennis pros have considerable latitude to use the methods they think will work with their group.

You have at least 5 hours a day on the court plus 2 half-hour private lessons. There are 10 red-clay courts and another 5 with all-weather hard surfaces. If it rains, you use the indoor courts at the Ludlow Tennis Club, about 20 miles away. In free time, you can work with the ball machine, play round-robin matches, or practice with other campers. There's also a pool, a fitness center, a gym where you can play volleyball or basketball, and a ¼-mile track.

Unlike many college dorms in the Northeast, those used by Total Tennis are air-conditioned and have daily maid service. Most single campers share a double room, but single rooms are available ($25 per night surcharge). Meals, served in the school's cafeteria, consist of standard cafeteria fare—hearty, healthful, and American. On Wednesday and Saturday evenings, predinner cocktails are served on the lawn.

Usually, about half of Total Tennis's campers are traveling solo, and off-court hours mean cocktail parties, mixed-doubles round-robins, volleyball games, and dancing at local nightclubs on nights when the camp hasn't scheduled instructional films or lectures on topics ranging from rackets and strings to sports psychology. *Total Tennis, Box 1106, Wall Street Station, New York, NY 10268, tel. 718/636–6141 or 800/221–6496. Early June–Labor Day: 6 days, $750; 7 days, $800. Sign up 2–3 months in advance.*

VERMONT **Bolton Valley Resort/International Tennis School.** With its location in the mountains of northern Vermont, Bolton Valley Resort's tennis school is a good choice if you prefer playing tennis where the weather is fresh and cool. It also is a good bet for families; there's day care for children 3 months and older, and an all-day children's tennis camp for kids 3 to 12 years old.

The program, which admits absolute beginners as well as more advanced players, is run by Anthony Boulle, a native of South Africa and former nationally ranked touring pro in the United States who has worked with such tennis luminaries as Fred Stolle, Harry Hopman, and Vitas Gerulaitis. Boulle's style

is relaxed and easygoing, and you take home solid, uncomplicated advice that's easy to remember and put into effect back on your home court.

Each day there are 3 hours of instruction; each lesson is videotaped and analyzed. The program spends about half of the lesson time every day on one specific point—ground strokes, net play, serving and returning serves, overheads, drop shots, lobs, strategy—and the other half going over the other fundamentals and playing matches. There's a 5:1 student-to-pro ratio, and there are 10 courts (2 indoors). Outside class, you get unlimited court time and use of a ball machine.

Breakfast and dinner are served at Lindsay's, a small restaurant on the resort's grounds. Dinners include pasta, seafood, and vegetarian dishes, cooked with a continental flair. You stay at the Swiss chalet–style Bolton Valley Lodge just up a hill from the courts or, for an extra charge, you can opt for one of the resort's condos. Off-court, you can explore the resort's 6,000 acres of mountains and woods on foot, or work out in the sports center, which has 2 pools (1 indoor, 1 outdoor), saunas, a Jacuzzi, and an exercise room. *Bolton Valley Resort/International Tennis School, Bolton Valley, VT 05477, tel. 802/434–2131 or 800/451–3220. July and Aug.: 5 days, $423. Price does not include lunch; sign up any time.*

VERMONT **Killington School for Tennis.** The Accelerated Tennis Method, developed at this big ski-and-summer resort, is a step-by-step approach that starts you at the net, working on volleys, and gradually moves you back toward the baseline, expanding your repertoire of moves and strokes as you work with more of the court.

Upon arrival your game is analyzed, and you are given drills specifically chosen for your game and then paired off with others of similar ability. The program here is highly structured and organized. You get 5 hours of instruction daily, and the 4:1 student-to-teacher ratio allows for considerable personal attention. Practice sessions are videotaped and replayed in slow motion for detailed analysis. Each session focuses intently on one aspect or skill of the game.

Killington emphasizes achieving ball control—direction, pace, and spin, including top spin. Once you've worked over the various strokes, you move on to singles and doubles strategies. Pros make themselves available for optional hitting sessions for an hour or so in the evening, and there are round-robin and mixed doubles tournaments throughout the week. At the end of your stay, you get a personal critique of your game and an Accelerated Tennis Method manual. Tennis facilities include 8 clay and cushion courts, 5 of them lighted for night play, and 8 enclosed ball lanes with ball machines.

Accommodations are courtside at the resort's Villager Motor Inn, which has terrific views of the surrounding mountains. Three meals a day are included in the package, and the menu offers varied choices and always plenty of healthful options. Tuesday dinner is an outdoor barbecue.

Off-court diversions include an 18-hole golf course, hiking, and mountain biking, and the towns of Woodstock and Manchester are a short drive away. *Killington School for Tennis, Killington, VT 05751, tel. 802/422–3101 or 800/343–0762, fax 802/422–3283. Late May–late Sept.: 5 days, $890. Sign up at least 2 weeks in advance.*

VERMONT **Stratton Tennis School.** Stratton is an especially good choice if you're vacationing with someone who doesn't play tennis. There's golf, mountain biking, hiking, and horseback riding in the cool Green Mountains, and the galleries, antiques shops, theaters, concerts, and restaurants of Manchester are a 20-minute drive away.

Not that the tennis at Stratton isn't serious. Rated one of the top 50 tennis resorts by *Tennis Magazine,* Stratton was the site of the 1993 Acura U.S. Women's Hardcourt Championships. There are 15 outdoor and 4 indoor courts. Tennis director Kelly Gunterman started his teaching career working for John Newcombe. Gunterman and his staff build on your skills and help you overcome your game's weaknesses. The 5-day program includes a 3-hour clinic each morning, each focusing on a different aspect of the game: volleys and overheads, ground strokes, serve and returns of serve. On the fourth day you review what you've learned and play doubles with the pros, and on the last day you get individualized attention and more doubles with the pros. There are video critiques of your game throughout the program, and you get unlimited access to the outdoor courts after classes. Additional 2-hour afternoon clinics are available at an extra charge, and you are given an instructional video to take home with you.

Breakfast and lunch are served at the resort's Sage Hill restaurant, and there's no shortage of dinner options nearby. You lodge in the chalet-style Stratton Mountain Inn, a 125-room hotel just a short walk from the tennis courts. Other recreational facilities include a fitness center with racquetball, a 75-foot lap pool, whirlpool, steam rooms, aerobics classes, and massage, and trails for hiking, mountain biking, and horseback riding. *Stratton Tennis School, Box 710, Stratton Mountain, VT 05155, tel. 802/297–4230 or 800/843–6867. Late May–early July and early Sept.–early Oct.: 5 days, $345–$385. Price does not include dinners; sign up any time.*

VERMONT **Sugarbush Tennis School.** One of the main draws here is tennis director Nigel O'Rourke's innovative PowerDrill, a practice exercise that condenses into a half-hour-long routine many of the training principles and practice moves used by touring pros.

Ranked as one of the country's top 50 tennis resorts by *Tennis Magazine,* Sugarbush's tennis program attracts both beginners and highly competitive advanced players who come for the resort's plush accommodations and pristine mountain setting as well as its full-throttle tennis instruction. A former Canadian Davis Cupper and ATP player, O'Rourke aims to maximize your speed, strength, and endurance by getting you to hustle all over the court—finishing points and running down even balls that seem impossible—while working to improve your game's strengths.

You can sign up for 2 to 5 days of half-day group lessons (2½ hours) or full-day lessons (4½ hours), usually with a 4:1 student-to-pro ratio. All packages include the PowerDrill and round-robin tournaments, and, during your free time, use of the 5 clay and 6 Har-Tru courts, ball machines, and the resort's swimming pools, fitness rooms, racquetball courts, steam baths, and saunas. Sugarbush staffers will fix you up with other campers for extracurricular matches.

Lodging is in the tony Sugarbush Inn or in 1-, 2-, or 3-bedroom condos with fireplace or wood stove, private sun deck, and kitchen. A Modified American Plan option includes a breakfast and dinner daily at one of the resort's three restaurants. *Sugarbush Tennis School & Club, R.R. 1, Box 350, Warren, VT 05674, tel. 802/583–2381 or 800/537–8427, fax 802/ 583–3209. Mid-June–mid-Sept.: full-day program, $145 per day; half-day program, $125 per day. Price does not include lunch or dinner; sign up at least 6 weeks in advance.*

THE MID ATLANTIC

PENNSYLVANIA **Tennis Camps Ltd. at Swarthmore College.** The programs held on the 325 manicured acres of this 125-year-old college, 12 miles from Philadelphia, are especially popular with singles wanting to meet other singles while improving their tennis. But this isn't the Love Boat, and the meeting and mixing happens off the court.

The 6-day clinics include 5 hours of instruction daily (with a 4:1 student-to-instructor ratio) and 3 half-hour private lessons. After your game is evaluated and you've been grouped with others at the same level of play, the instruction focuses on game-sharpening drills and strategy, with the emphasis on improving consistency and increasing power. You're videotaped and your strokes are analyzed, and there are supervised matches between campers as well as exhibition matches between instructors.

Accommodations are on campus in single or double rooms in the Wharton Dormitory or—

costlier and less readily available—quarters in the more luxurious Ashton House, a beautiful Victorian stone mansion on campus. Meals are hearty, well-balanced, and planned by the college dietician. You have access to the school swimming pool, Nautilus equipment, outdoor track, and (by appointment) its masseuse. *Tennis Camps Ltd. at Swarthmore College, 444 E. 82nd St., Suite 31D, New York, NY 10028, tel. 212/879–0225 or 800/ 223–2442, fax 212/879–0226. Mid-June–mid-Aug.: 6 days, $750 ($790, but excluding dinners, if you opt to stay at Ashton House). Sign up 2–4 months in advance.*

THE SOUTH

FLORIDA **Harry Hopman/Saddlebrook International Tennis.** The late Harry Hopman was the most successful captain and coach in Davis Cup history, winning 16 times over 21 years. The Australian teams he led included Ken Rosewell, Rod Laver, Fred Stolle, John Newcombe, and Tony Roche. Hopman was known as a strict disciplinarian who demanded the best of his players, and usually got it.

Hopman's tough ways prevail at Saddlebrook, a 480-acre resort north of Tampa, whose tennis program he started. Now run by Tommy Thompson and Howard Moore, this camp is best for intermediate or advanced players looking to tune up their game, and of those, only players who are willing to really push themselves. The instructors expect you to know your strokes before you get here. Don't waste your money by coming here without being in good shape.

Your group stays with the same pro for the week, and there are never more than 4 players to an instructor. You do 5 hours of imaginative, fast-paced, hard-hitting drills a day, all created by Hopman and all meant to make you react instinctively to the ball. By mid-session, you play a match with one of the pros—who then explains why you lost.

In addition to the on-court training, you do fitness and agility exercises and study the mental aspects of the game in a classroom.

The equipment used for the video and computer analysis of your game and techniques is state of the art.

Not surprisingly, Saddlebrook's tennis facilities are top-of-the-line. The 45 courts represent every Grand Slam surface—clay, Har-Tru, even grass—and 9 of them are lighted for night play. Players of all ages come to Saddlebrook from around the globe, from all walks of life. Because it is one of the United States Tennis Association's National Training Centers, players on the way up occasionally train here. (When you see them, take note: They're doing the same drills you are.)

You can lodge in standard hotel rooms or 1- and 2-bedroom suites; meals are available in several restaurants at the resort and nearby. You have use of the resort's enormous swimming pool and its two Arnold Palmer–designed golf courses, elaborate fitness center, and jogging and bicycle trails—in case you have energy left over after the tennis. Rates are highest from late December through April, and January, February, and March are the busiest months. *Harry Hopman/Saddlebrook International Tennis, 5700 Saddlebrook Way, Wesley Chapel, FL 33543-4499, tel. 813/973–1111, ext. 4211 or 800/729–8383, fax 813/973–2936. Year-round: 5 days, $810–$1,050. Price does not include meals; sign up at least 1 month in advance.*

FLORIDA Nick Bollettieri Tennis Academy. This is the world headquarters of the tennis school that produced Andre Agassi, Monica Seles, and Jim Courier. It's also the largest tennis training operation in the world, and even at its Adult Tennis Camps, aimed at the recreational player, you get the benefits of coach Nick Bollettieri's years of coaching both pros and young players who went on to be pros.

Each day starts with a half hour of stretching, strength, and aerobics exercises, then moves on to intensive drills that cover all your strokes. Every session highlights a specific stroke, and there are 2 sessions a day. You spend between 4½ and 5 hours a day on the court, and another 30 to 45 minutes a day viewing tennis videos, listening to lectures, or watching demonstrations on strokes, strategies, strength, conditioning, and the mental aspects of the game. By the end of the week, there are some competitive drills and some supervised match play. The program includes extensive use of videotaping as well. The student-to-pro ratio ranges from 3:1 to 5:1, and Bollettieri keeps your group moving from court to court, changing pros every half hour. There are 53 courts in all—35 hard courts, 14 clay, and 4 indoors.

Campers stay in 2-bedroom town houses around the courts. Each has a living room, TV, and kitchen. Meals are basic and served cafeteria-style. There's also a small pool and whirlpool, and a fitness center with Nautilus equipment, free weights, rowing machines, stationary bicycles, treadmills, and the like.

From September to May, Bollettieri offers Specialty Weeks that focus on a particular theme, such as singles play, doubles strategy, or mental toughness. Adult sessions are also held in satellite schools in the United States, Canada, and Europe. *Nick Bollettieri Tennis Academy, 5500 34th St. W, Bradenton, FL 34210, tel. 813/755–1000 or 800/872–6425, fax 813/758–0198. Year-round: 7 days, $1,095. Sign up 1 month in advance.*

FLORIDA Welby Van Horn Tennis Camp at the Boca Raton Resort & Club. Praised by *World Tennis Magazine* as "one of the top four outstanding tennis coaches in the world," Welby Van Horn brings his tennis camp to this posh 356-acre beachfront resort each summer. Camps include 5½ hours of tennis a day, with a 3:1 student-to-pro ratio. Van Horn is present at all clinics, along with his team of USPTA instructors. There are 34 outdoor clay-based courts, 9 lighted for night play.

Tennis packages include accommodations in the Spanish-Mediterranean-style Cloister; you can pay extra to stay in the Tower or the Boca Beach Club, which have Intra Coastal Waterway or ocean views. There are several restaurants at the resort, where you can grab a salad or linger over northern Italian cuisine by candlelight. Off court, the resort offers 2 championship golf courses, 3 swimming pools, 2 state-of-the-art fitness centers, and a half-mile stretch of Atlantic beach, marina, and water sports. *Welby Van Horn Tennis & Golf Camps, Box 259, Gracie Station, New York, NY 10028, tel. 212/734–1037 or 800/424–4550. Mid-June–mid-Aug.: 7 days, $695. Price does not include meals; sign up any time.*

SOUTH CAROLINA **Van der Meer Tennis-University.** Although he was a top-rated player in his native South Africa, Dennis Van der Meer is best known as "the pro who teaches the pros." He coached Margaret Court and Billie Jean King and has taught hundreds of tennis teachers and thousands of players, from 3-year-olds to senior citizens, from beginners to touring pros.

Of the 6 Van der Meer TennisUniversity facilities worldwide, the main location is the Tennis Center on Hilton Head Island. Most sessions of the 5-day adult program are for intermediate and advanced players, though beginners can be accommodated. The 6:1 ratio of players to pros may sound high, but with 6 hours of instruction each day, you get your share of coaching and hitting. In addition to providing video analysis and an evaluation of your strokes and tactics, Van der Meer's method works on your consistency, agility, and footwork, and teaches you how to concentrate, overcome tension, and keep from choking.

Van der Meer is completely involved in his program. He is personally on hand several weeks a year and leads clinics when he's around (the center will provide a list of dates on request). He's as amusing as he is well-informed, and his enthusiasm for helping players makes it clear why he is so successful as a teacher and why people return to this camp. The Tennis Center has 28 courts—25 hard and 3 clay—of which 8 are lighted, and 4 of those are covered. The nearby Shipyard Racquet Club, which Van der Meer recently took over, has 14 clay and 6 hard courts.

Packages include lodging at the Players Club Resort, next to the Tennis Center, which has a Nautilus equipment center, pool, Jacuzzi, sauna, and restaurant, and is within walking distance of the beach. There are also many other hotels, resorts, and restaurants nearby. *Van der Meer Tennis Center, Box 5902,*

Hilton Head Island, SC 29938, tel. 803/785–8388 or 800/845–6138, fax 803/785–7032. Year-round: 5 days, $315–$425 depending on the season ($100 more for clinics personally led by Dennis Van der Meer). Price does not include meals; sign up 3–6 months in advance; 6 months for Van der Meer-led clinics.

THE SOUTHWEST

ARIZONA **John Gardiner's Tennis Ranch on Camelback.** John Gardiner invented the concept of tennis clinics; his Carmel Valley resort in California (*see below*) was the very first, and this Tennis Ranch, just outside Scottsdale, Arizona, may just be the ultimate, providing comprehensive tennis instruction in luxurious, resortlike surroundings on 53 landscaped desert acres.

The Tennis Clinic Week includes 21 hours of clinic instruction, 4 hours of optional round-robin play, complementary court time, and 2 half-hour-long massages.

Gardiner's emphasizes doubles play, especially for intermediate players. There are more campers here in the 45-to-60 age range than there are at many camps. About 35 people usually participate in each session, more during holiday periods and in February and March.

There are 24 tennis courts and 30 instructors. Two of the courts have computerized ball machines, which can be programmed to fire off a random sequence of lobs, serves, and shots of varying spins.

You stay in standard rooms; 2-bedroom, 2-bath suites; or casitas, adobe-colored brick structures with arched windows and doorways. There are also 2- to 5-bedroom homes. Each room has a private patio or enclosed sun room, with a spectacular view of the valley. Each of the larger houses has a private swimming pool, and many have private tennis courts and spas.

A carafe of freshly squeezed orange juice and the *Arizona Republic* are delivered to your doorstep every morning, and there are coffeemakers in each room. Breakfast and lunch are buffet-style (lunch can also be à la carte) and quite lavish; dinner is served in a room with views of Paradise Valley below. The menu changes daily, but always features New American cuisine—local fare with a continental or Pacific Rim influence. Men are required to wear jackets (but not ties) after 7 PM.

The ranch has a large pool at the clubhouse, and several smaller pools throughout the grounds, along with whirlpools and saunas. There is also a fitness room with top-of-the-line workout equipment, and hiking and jogging trails. *John Gardiner's Tennis Ranch on Camelback, 5700 E. McDonald Dr., Scottsdale, AZ 85253-5268, tel. 602/948–2100 or 800/245–2051, fax 602/483–7314. Mid-Apr.–mid-Dec.: 7 days, $2,080. Mid-Dec.–mid-Apr.: 7 days, $2,385. Sign up 6 weeks in advance.*

TEXAS   **The John Newcombe Tennis Ranch.** The one thing you learn here—if nothing else—is that although tennis should be played well and taken seriously, it's a game, and it should be fun.

John Newcombe (a.k.a. "Newk"), a U.S. Open and Wimbledon champion and Australian Davis Cupper, along with Trinity University tennis coach Clarence Mabry, converted this onetime dude ranch into a tennis school, and the two still run the place, with the help of several other tennis greats.

The program here begins with a preview of the stroke of the day and a video with tips by the various pros. Then you get 2½ hours of drill work on the courts. You're videotaped in action and critiqued just before lunch. You go back to the court in the afternoon for more drills, strategy sessions, and supervised match play. Clinics use the station-to-station method, whereby participants move as a group from court to court, and from pro to pro. Spring and fall (when the weather's not too hot) are the most popular seasons, and clinics during this period can fill up with as many as 80 participants, but the student-to-pro ratio rarely exceeds 4:1, and is often less.

Packages include accommodations in apartment units with fireplaces, kitchens, and patios or balconies, all with court views. There's an Old West feel to this place, and it still looks very much like the dude ranch it once was. Meals are a big part of the fun here. Breakfast, lunch, and dinner are lavish buffet spreads with plenty of nutritionally balanced choices, but the kitchen staff takes special pride in its Western-style dinners, such as mesquite-grilled rib-eye steaks, roast prime rib, and smoked barbecued meats. Other cuisines—including French, Italian, Oriental, and Mexican—are also offered. The socializing doesn't end after mealtime. There are parties, dancing, and live entertainment in the evening—anything from a movie to "blooper" videos of campers on the court to a stage show or comedy routine put on by the staff. The gregarious staff create an infectiously collegial atmosphere. The week ends with a doubles tournament and an awards banquet.

There are 28 hard outdoor courts, 8 of them lighted and 4 covered. There are also a swimming pool and whirlpool on the premises, and nearby are horseback riding, golf, river rafting, and bungee jumping, as well as such regional attractions as the Alamo and Sea World. *The John Newcombe Tennis Ranch, Box 310469, New Braunfels, TX 78131, tel. 210/ 625–9105 or 800/444–6204, fax 210/625–2004. Year-round: 5 days, $755–$875. Sign up 1 month in advance.*

THE WEST COAST

CALIFORNIA   John   Gardiner's   Tennis Ranch. This 25-acre Carmel Valley ranch was the first American tennis camp, started in 1957 by John Gardiner, a local tennis teacher who was convinced that people would take a vacation where the main activity was playing tennis.

He was right, and even three decades later this is still one of the most sought-after—and exclusive—tennis camps around. It is also the only one with one court per guest room—14 of each.

The basic clinic runs 4 hours a day, supplemented by optional sessions and as much recreational tennis as you can play (the watchwords around here are "Repetition is the law of learning" and "Never have so many tennis balls been hit by so few"). The student-to-instructor ratio is 4:1, so you get plenty of individual attention, and you can pretty much set your own pace.

During the session there are also mixed doubles tournaments and various social events. At the end of the week, there is a "graduation" ceremony with champagne, prizes, and diplomas.

Guest rooms are in cottages of varying sizes in a woody setting just steps away from the courts. All have private patios and fireplaces. They fill up quickly, especially with repeat guests, often celebrities, politicians, and corporate executives. The ranch tends to attract very well-to-do couples, generally over the age of 50. This is a very traditional, almost old-fashioned, sort of place, where guests are requested to wear predominately whites on the courts (not that everyone does).

The food at John Gardiner's is a big part of the experience. The elaborate breakfast buffet is served on the glass-walled sun porch, and lunch is a selection of hot and cold entrées served poolside. Dinner is formal; it begins with drinks and hors d'oeuvres in the elegant clubhouse, then moves to the dining room. Gardiner's specialties are lamb dishes and soufflés. There are also lots of local fruits and vegetables as well as fresh Pacific seafood.

The ranch has 2 heated swimming pools, an outdoor whirlpool, and saunas. Golf is nearby. *John Gardiner's Tennis Ranch, Box 228, Carmel Valley, CA 93924, tel. 408/659–2207 or 800/453–6225, fax 408/659–2492. Late Mar.–late Nov.: 5 days, $1,800–$1,900. Sign up 1–2 months in advance.*

CALIFORNIA Reed Anderson Tennis School. "We teach individuals, not systems," says Reed Anderson, who's been teaching individuals how to improve their tennis game for nearly two decades, first for a Billie Jean King/Dennis Van der Meer tennis instruction program and now at his own school.

Anderson has a very personalized approach:

Your instructor starts by analyzing your strokes and your game, and videotaping your moves. You then spend the rest of your 3-hour morning sessions (afternoons are free time) working on strokes, court positioning, specialty shots, game situation drills, singles and doubles strategy, and mental toughness, with extensive use of video. The student-to-pro ratio never exceeds 5:1 and is often less than that. All tennis packages include unlimited court time, use of a ball machine, use of a fitness center, and match play service.

Although Anderson's school migrates between its winter quarters in Palm Springs and its summer home in Ojai, east of Santa Barbara, the program is identical at both.

Winter sessions are held at the Autry Resort Hotel and Racquet Club, a 14-acre resort property on the southeast edge of Palm Springs, with 6 outdoor courts, 2 lighted for night play. The hotel has 3 outdoor swimming pools, as well as 2 whirlpools. The place looks appropriately like a desert oasis; tall, swaying palm trees tower over low-slung white stucco buildings. Packages that include lodging are available, but prices vary dramatically depending upon the season, the size of the room, and its view.

The Spanish Colonial–style Ojai Valley Inn & Country Club is home to Reed Anderson's summer sessions. There are 8 cushioned outdoor courts here, 4 lighted for night play. The resort is set on 220 landscaped acres, ringed by mountains in the always-sunny Ojai Valley. The buildings are adobe-style stucco topped with red-tile roofs, surrounded with fountains and flower beds. Packages including lodging are also available here in a range of prices and room sizes.

Participants tend to be couples aged 35–55, although there are also plenty of singles, and older and younger people, as well. The tennis packages don't include meals, but the hotels in both locations have restaurants, and in Palm Springs you have many others nearby. There aren't as many options in Ojai, but Santa Barbara is a 40-minute drive away. *Reed Anderson Tennis School, Box 9572, Palm*

Springs, CA 92263, tel. 619/328–1171 or 800/288–1171, fax 619/324–6104. Oct.–May in Palm Springs and June–Sept. in Ojai: 5 days, $325. Price does not include lodging or meals; sign up 2 weeks–1 month in advance.

CALIFORNIA **Vic Braden Tennis College.** Winning isn't everything to Vic Braden. "Remember," he says, "fifty percent of all tennis players who played today lost." Still, he's also the first to point out that playing well and winning cheers people up. Braden became famous through his "Tennis for the Future" TV series, his 5 tennis instruction books, and 40 years of teaching everyone from pros to beginners.

Braden's teaching method mixes upbeat humor and high-tech gadgets, such as a digitized analysis of your game that helps you spot imperfections. Probably the toughest thing about this school is that you're forced to change your bad habits, even if they're your best shots. Braden insists that each shot be hit in a particular way ("Tennis is an engineering problem," he says), which can mean that much of your game will have to be overhauled.

Braden's Tennis College facilities are among the most extensive and sophisticated anywhere. In the classroom, Braden—in person or on video—presents a daily lecture, and courtside viewing rooms allow for instant-replay videotape analysis. There are 17 hitting lanes with ball machines, and 17 hard courts, 14 with lights. The surfaces of the main 3 teaching courts have been painted with targets, Xs, and dotted lines, so you can work through the school's different drills even without an instructor. Although the student-to-pro ratio can reach 6:1, you're on the courts with your pro for a minimum of 6 hours a day.

In addition to being a tennis instructor, Braden is a psychologist, and he puts a lot of emphasis on getting you over the mental hurdles of the game and becoming more comfortable on the court.

Guest rooms are in modern wood-frame structures and come in a variety of sizes and con-figurations (and prices), from basic hotel room to suites with kitchens and patios. All are adjacent to the tennis courts and within walking distance of the 2 swimming pools and whirlpool. The on-site restaurant offers burgers, pizzas, and pasta dishes; other dining options are a short drive away. *Vic Braden Tennis College, 23335 Avenida La Caza, Coto de Caza, CA 92679, tel. 714/581–2990, 800/225–5842 in CA, or 800/422–6878 outside CA. Year-round: 5 days, $650. Price does not include lodging or meals; sign up 2–3 weeks in advance.*

SOURCES

ORGANIZATIONS **United States Tennis Association** (Membership Department, Box 673, White Plains, NY 10602-0672, tel. 914/696–7000) is a volunteer, nonprofit organization established in 1881. Membership benefits include USTA league and tournament programs; discounts on apparel, publications, videos, and travel packages; and annual subscriptions to the monthly newsletter "Tennis USTA" and *Tennis Magazine.*

PERIODICALS *Tennis* (5520 Park Ave., Box 395, Trumbull, CT 06611-0395, tel. 203/373–7000) is a monthly magazine with how-to tips, features on professional players, tennis resort information, fitness tips, and more. *Tennis Week* (124 E. 40th St., Suite 1101, New York, NY 10016, tel. 212/808–4750) is a fortnightly magazine covering professional tennis news, racquet roundups, book reviews, how-to information, and more. *Tennis Magazine* (available through the USTA, address above) prints a comprehensive list of tennis camps and clinics every year in its February issue.

BOOKS There are many tennis instructional books available. A current favorite is *Winning Ugly,* by Brad Gilbert (with Steve Jamison), which details Gilbert's technique for outsmarting an otherwise superior opponent. A great read is W. Timothy Gallwey's *The Inner Game of Tennis* (Bantam Books).

Van and 4-Wheel-Drive Tours

by Sandra Widener

ould you like to take off into the wilderness on a cross-country off-road camping trip? How about a month-long van trip through an entire region, stopping in cities and camping along the way? Outfitters have trips to fit anyone's desires, most in two categories: van tours and 4-wheel-drive tours (aka Jeep tours). Let's consider both kinds.

A Jeep tour can be as a painless jaunt through spectacular country, punctuated by the witty insights of a knowledgeable guide, with nights spent in relative luxury in charming bed-and-breakfast. Or it can be a rugged vacation where you cover a lot of breathtaking ground by day on death-defying trails a horse would blink at, and camp by night, cooking over a fire.

In the Rockies, the western national parks, the Southwest, Alaska, and Hawaii, 4-wheel-drive trips are common, and often take travelers into backcountry locations dedicated hikers could reach only with days of effort. Four-wheel-drives go down trails and up rocky riverbeds that are normally inaccessible; they make it easy to visit remote places like Alaska, where seeing a lot on your own is difficult.

Four-wheel-drive trips often entail walking and optional activities such as rafting and horseback riding, but you don't need to be in top physical shape. Vehicles carry the equipment and undertake the heavy-duty travel, which is great if you like wilderness but aren't up for hiking a mountain with a 40-pound pack.

Some companies that offer 4-wheel-drive trips cater to their clients' every whim, with luxurious lodgings and restaurant meals; some use guides who are consummate experts on the area, who can spout Latin names of flora and fauna and explain the significance of prehistoric rock art. Other outfitters design their trips around a special interest, such as geology or photography.

Many of the guides take pride in knowing places their guests would never have found on their own; their ability to take you off the beaten track, away from the herd, and show you spectacular hidden places is one of the best things these trips have to offer. It's worth paying for the enthusiasm and knowledge of someone who is passionate about the area, rather than muddling about on your own.

Costs of 4-wheel-drive trips range widely, but you can expect to spend from $500 for a basic week-long camping trip to $1,500 and more, if you're led by a well-known expert and stay in good hotels. Alaskan trips tend to cost more (everything seems to be expensive there) and can often run to $2,500 for 10 days. A week's trip in Hawaii will cost in the neighborhood of $1,000.

Van trips are common on the East Coast and in the Midwest and the South, all places where 4-wheel-drive trips are almost impos-

---

Sandra Widener, a freelance writer who lives in Denver, takes Jeep trips into the mountains with her family.

sible to find. Van trips use vehicles that comfortably seat a dozen people. Travel is mainly on paved roads, and the tours often cover whole regions visiting cities and famous landmarks, with an emphasis on national parks and natural settings. Over the past 20 years or so, a platoon of van-touring companies has sprung up, aimed at showing groups of mainly foreign young people the United States.

On van tours, everyone contributes to a food kitty and takes turns cooking and cleaning up. Lodging is primarily in fairly civilized campgrounds with hot showers, and most operators supply the tents gratis, though sleeping bags must be rented. The cost, pared down for student budgets, runs about $400 per week: This includes everything but the bill for the moderate hotels where you stay when visiting cities. You're not paying for exquisitely educated guides or attentive service; though often bilingual and even foreign-born, most of the guides are glorified van drivers with guidebooks.

Despite these considerable differences, there are three things that 4-wheel-drive and van trips have in common: Small children often don't do well on them, and many outfitters require participants to be 18 or older. Almost all have no more than 18 people (on most trips, you rub elbows with fewer than 10 people). And for those with a little taste for adventure, both types of trip can make a wonderful vacation.

CHOOSING THE RIGHT TRIP

Here are some questions that will help you pick the right outfitter and the right trip.

How many years has your company been in business? Longevity is evidence that somebody's doing something right.

What are the guides' qualifications? For off-road trips, degrees in botany, zoology, geology, anthropology, and the like are desirable, but local knowledge and experience are a must. For van trips, local knowledge is a frill; what counts is organizational skill and experience in leading groups.

What is the client-to-guide ratio? Will I be expected to do any chores? A client-to-guide ratio of between 10:1 and 13:1 is likely to mean the clients do a lot of the work, but on camping trips that's often part of the fun.

What kinds of people take this trip? How large is the group? It's comfortable to be among your peers, but a little variety adds spice. A small group travels quickly and efficiently, with less waiting around. A larger one offers more possibilities for making friends or just finding congenial companionship. The cost of any trip often determines the age of the participants; the more expensive, generally, the older the clientele.

What are the accommodations like? Find out if you'll be camping or staying in hotels or B&Bs. If camping, ask if there are cabins or tents and if hot showers will be available. If you'll be staying in a B&B, ask if there are private baths.

What are the meals like? Even when you're camping, there's a wide spread between hotdogs and hamburgers cooked over a fire by you and carefully thought-out Dutch-oven dishes prepared by a guide who's a good cook.

What will the weather be like? So you like hot weather—but if you don't ask, you won't know how humid it can be in the South, or how buggy. Or how cold it can get in the mountains, even in July.

What's the cost and what's included? Unless otherwise noted, hotel accommodations (per person, double occupancy), meals, guides, and transportation are included, but participants must get themselves to the trip's jumping-off point. In addition, on camping trips, camp tents and other necessary gear are included, but not sleeping bags (often available for rent). In some cases, you are expected to contribute a set amount to the food kitty. Find out in advance about any hidden costs: meals or hotels or desirable options that cost extra. Will you just have to pay for a bite of lunch, or are you responsible for dinner in a hotel? Is there equipment you must rent?

How much free time will there be? Are any local events happening before or after the

tour? If you find out in advance, you can take advantage of what the area has to offer.

Do you have references from past guests? Sometimes they can articulate important strengths and weaknesses that a tour operator can't or won't point out.

How far in advance do I need to book? You may be able to sign up just a month before departure—or 6 months ahead.

MAJOR PLAYERS

ALASKA WILDLAND ADVENTURES Established in 1977, this company runs natural-history van tours in Alaska. It houses guests in tents at campgounds, in its own rustic riverside cabins, and in its more upscale lodge within Denali National Park. Some members of its staff have been around for years: guides in their forties who love to show off Alaska and college students who have been guiding for several seasons. The guest to guide ratio is about 6:1. The food ranges from campfire cooking and family-style meals on the deck at the cabins to desserts prepared by a pastry chef at the lodge. These tours are at the high end of the scale; the outfitter also offers a trip designed for families and one for seniors (Box 389, Girdwood, AK 99587, tel. 907/783–2928 or 800/334–8730, fax 907/783–2130).

AMERICAN ADVENTURES This van-camping operator runs dozens of low-priced trips throughout the United States, Canada, and Mexico (some even cross borders). Trips range from 6 to 68 days; participants travel in large vans in groups of 11 to 13, and camp in state and national parks, and, occasionally, KOA campgrounds. Everyone helps cook and clean up. Cooking gear and tents for 2 are provided; bring your own sleeping bag. This tour group's guides are exclusively North Americans, which distinguishes them from the competition. Many of them are teachers, others simply have a yen for adventure; their leadership skills are honed by a 6-week training course. Most of the guests are from overseas, and their average age is about 30 (6762A Centinela Ave.,

Culver City, CA 90230, tel. 310/390–7495 or 800/864–0335, fax 310/390–1446).

CAMPALASKA TOURS This company's philosophy is simple: Alaska is a huge, beautiful place where hotels are extremely expensive. The solution? Travel by maxi-van and camp out. Everyone takes a turn with cooking, camp chores, and food shopping, which is done every day or so. Camping is in established campgrounds, although a hot shower may be only an every-third-day event. Participants range in age from 20 to 50, and groups, mixed equally by sex, are never larger than 12. The guides all have at least several years of experience. CampAlaska offers 16 different moderately priced tours throughout Alaska, including a couple with hotel accommodations (Box 872247, Wasilla, AK 99687, tel. 907/376–9438, fax 907/376–2353).

GREEN TORTOISE This outfit appeals to those who never lost their love for the '60s—it's been around since 1972. The mood is togetherness, the mode of transportation is bus-turned-camper, the group size is up to 38, and the meals are vegetarian. The clientele is youngish, poor (a 9-day trip around the Southwest costs $260, including food), obviously gregarious, and doesn't mind not taking a shower every day. Either you fit in or you don't. Each trip has a pair of drivers, who trade off sleeping and driving and whose primary qualification is knowing how to fix the bus. Any guiding expertise they possess comes from a handbook they use to identify the sights. Green Tortoise runs its fleet of buses on trips throughout the United States and to Mexico, Costa Rica, and Guatemala. It runs 8- to 14-day loops around the western national parks, trips that head south from San Francisco to Guatemala and Baja and back, 2-week cross-country trips, and a 35-day trip to Alaska and the Canadian Rockies (Box 24459, San Francisco, CA 94124, tel. 415/821–0803 or 800/227–4766).

NATURE EXPEDITIONS INTERNATIONAL Education is the focus here, with guides trained to a fever pitch in natural history and anthropology. The company, which also runs trips around the world, considers itself an ecotouring pioneer. In the United States it tours Alaska, Hawaii, the Western canyonlands, and the Pacific Northwest. Traveling in vans, groups of about 10 hike between 3 and 5 miles a day. Clients, who are 35 to 70 years old, tend to be as interested as the guides in ecosystems. They also tend to have money; all that expertise can get expensive, and the accommodations and food are generally first-class. The 1- and 2-week tours run about $1,000 per week (Box 11496, Eugene, OR 97440, tel. 503/484–6529 or 800/869–0639, fax 503/484–6531).

PACIFIC QUEST Zane Bilgrav, a research scientist and experienced guide, was a founder of this company in 1980. He was one of the first to design an itinerary for people who come to Hawaii to see the islands instead of the resorts, who want to get past the plastic leis and find the secret waterfalls and rain forests that enchanted the islands' first visitors. Bilgrav runs 1- and 2-week trips—camping trips and lodge trips, trips that concentrate on one island and others that island-hop by plane, putting you up at B&Bs. He uses Hawaiian guides well-versed in local botanical and naturalist lore, and his groups (about 12 people) travel by van to the different activities. You might hike to a historic leper colony or go to a lagoon for swimming and snorkeling. Participants' ages range from the thirties to the sixties; two-thirds are women. The trips cost about $1,000 a week (59–603 Kawoa Pl., Haleiwa, HI 96712, tel. 808/638–8338 or 800/776–2518, fax 808/638–8255).

SOJOURNS OF DISCOVERY Passionate outdoorsman and longtime guide Bill Evans runs unusual western trips. Some of the trips are strictly for hikers, others include canoeing and rafting, and vans are used to carry gear and ferry participants to areas they couldn't reach on foot. Evans limits groups to 10, employs a knowledgeable local guide to back him up for each trip, and retains other guides with years of backcountry experience. On some trips to remote areas, tents and kitchen equipment are supplied (bring your own dishes and sleeping bag); the hearty camping cuisine utilizes both dehydrated and fresh ingredients. Guests can help if they like. Other offerings are on the softer side, with lodgings in B&Bs or in backwoods cabins with baths. The cost for Evans's trips runs from $500 to $750 for 6 days (Box 14057, San Luis Obispo, CA 93406, tel. 805/438–5910 or 800/736–8735, fax 805/543–4295).

SUNTREK This van-camping specialist has been in business since 1974 and runs dozens of trips that range in length from 3 days to 13 weeks and go all over the country—to the Pacific Coast, the western national parks, from San Francisco to New York, down the East Coast, and around the Northwest. You'll stay in campgrounds whenever possible, or in inexpensive hotels, which cost extra. Camping gear is provided, except for sleeping bags, and everyone contributes to a food kitty and takes turns cooking. Two people sleep in each of the company's 4-man tents, so there's plenty of room for gear. Suntrek advertises largely to the European market, and most clients come from abroad. They tend to be 25 to 35 years old, and there's a good mix of men and women, singles and couples (singles get paired with same-sex tentmates), with a maximum of 13 traveling together. The guides—who are as likely to be European as they are American—are usually bilingual. Don't expect detailed knowledge of the terrain. A part of each day is usually spent traveling, and the trips usually include some extras (at extra cost), like whale-watching expeditions or visits to famous sights. Most of the company's trips last at least 2 weeks and cost about $400 per week (Sun Plaza, 77 W. 3rd St., Santa Rosa, CA 95401, tel. 707/523–1800 or 800/292–9696, fax 707/523–1911).

TAG-A-LONG EXPEDITIONS This Utah operator offers Jeep treks with hiking and occasional whitewater rafting. The outfit is based in Moab, a center for 4-wheel-drive trips, and the camping and touring is done in the scenic red rock land of Canyonlands National Park. Tag-A-Long prides itself on the leadership and cooking skills of its guides; it's been in business since 1963 and has been hired by

National Geographic, Walt Disney Productions, and television networks to help them get around the Canyonlands wilderness. Most participants are urban professionals, ranging in age from their thirties to their sixties, and you can expect gourmet camp cooking. (A dinner menu might be a fruit plate, Caesar salad, chicken cordon bleu done in a Dutch oven, wild rice pilaf, and flaming cherries jubilee.) Tag-A-Long's 4-wheel-drive vehicles take you to wilderness trailheads and, on other trips, go into the canyon country to focus on geology, archaeology, and natural history. On the rafting segments offered on some trips you will see the stark, beautiful desert terrain from a different perspective. Trips lasting 5 to 8 days cost between $600 and $1,100. The staff sets up portable restrooms at each camp; you can rent sleeping bags and tents (452 N. Main St., Moab, UT 84532, tel. 801/259–8946 or 800/453-3292, fax 801/259–8990).

TREK AMERICA This outfitter offers 38 trips throughout the United States that last 1 to 9 weeks and cost about $350 per week. Groups of 13, plus a guide, travel in vans around the western national parks, on a southern route across the country, in Alaska, in Florida, and up and down the West Coast: There's not much that Trek America misses. Everyone shares cooking and cleanup duties in camp, and you bring only a sleeping bag; everything else is supplied. Nights are spent in campgrounds with showers and, occasionally, pools. Americans are a rarity on these trips, which draw young visitors (ages 18 to 40) from 35 countries; they're good bets if you want to meet foreign travelers. Guides are at least 25, but they are more drivers than dedicated biologists; most are American and the others are also English-speaking (Box 470, Blairstown, NJ 07825, tel. 908/362–9198 or 800/221–0596, fax 908/362–9313).

FAVORITE TRIPS

THE NORTHEAST

REGION-WIDE **Van Camping Across the Northeast.** Would you like to camp from New York City to Niagara Falls to Maine and back with a group of international travelers? Suntrek's Mayflower, a 2-week loop trip, caters to the 25–35 age group and is informal in style, with group cooking and cleanup. Transport is by maxi-van, which holds up to 13 people (the limit per trip) plus a driver-guide, who is as likely to be European as American (and not an expert on the passing scene). On this trip, starting in New York City, you travel about 4 hours a day, visiting Pennsylvania Dutch country, Niagara Falls (where you take a boat ride), Adirondack Park, White Mountains National Forest, Acadia National Park, Boston, Cape Cod (with a whale-watching trip), and then return to New York. You shop for and cook your own breakfast and dinner (buy your own lunch), and pitch your tents everywhere from KOA campgrounds to those in national parks, most with showers. *Suntrek, Sun Plaza, 77 W. 3rd St., Santa Rosa, CA 95401, tel. 707/523–1800 or 800/292–9696, fax 707/523–1911. Late May–late Oct.: 14 days, $742–$798. Price includes whale-watching and boat ride, but not dinners or $60 for food kitty; sign up 1–2 months in advance.*

THE SOUTH

FLORIDA–NEW YORK **Van Camping Up the Atlantic Coast.** On this 7-day trip, you start in Miami with an international group of 11 to 13 people, most single and in their mid-20s, and travel in maxi-vans up the coast, hitting Cape Canaveral, Daytona Beach, St. Augustine, Charleston, North Carolina, Williamsburg, and Atlantic City, and ending in New York. You camp every night in 2-person tents and help cook and wash the dishes. It's just the thing for those who like togetherness and who want to meet other travelers. The leader-drivers are all Americans or Canadians; they're chosen more for their ability to keep a diverse group together than for their encyclopedic knowledge. Since this trip doesn't go near America's pristine wilderness parks, you can expect fairly pedestrian camping facilities, though they usually have hot showers. *AmeriCan Adventures, 6762A*

Centinela Ave., Culver City, CA 90230, tel. 310/390–7495 or 800/864–0335, fax 310/390–1446. Mid-May–Sept.: 1 week, $359–$419. Price does not include $35 for food kitty; sign up 2–3 months in advance.

THE SOUTHWEST

REGION-WIDE **The National Parks Loop.** On this keep-the-cost-down trip, Green Tortoise's converted bus is not only transportation, but home for up to 38 people. Guests, who are around 25 to 30, are prepared to become very chummy and often sleep in their bunks en route. There are seating areas with tables that convert to bunks, and platforms that become dormitories. On this 16-day trip, half the nights are spent on the bus, the others at campgrounds along the way. Starting in San Francisco, the trip covers a lot of ground, skimming through the cream of the West's national parks and recreation areas: Grand Tetons, Yellowstone, Flaming Gorge, Arches, Canyonlands, the Grand Canyon, and Zion. The bus also makes stops at some hot springs. Food (mostly vegetarian) is communally cooked, the campsites are primitive, and the pair of guides, who trade off on driving, are no scholars, but they know the territory. *Green Tortoise, Box 24459, San Francisco, CA 94124, tel. 415/821–0803 or 800/227–4766. June–Aug.: 16 days, $499. Price does not include $121 food fund, meals eaten in restaurants (about 25%), or camping gear; sign up 1–2 months in advance.*

ARIZONA **Canyons of the Navajo.** The non-profit Canyonlands Field Institute, which exists to promote and protect the Colorado Plateau, runs a 5-day trip on which Navajo Indian guides drive their passengers in open-topped vans down rough roads in the red rock country. Besides visiting the deservedly popular Canyon de Chelly, with its Indian ruins, participants (most 40 to 60 years old) travel to other rarely seen canyons and take guided hikes. There's a sense of splendid isolation in this sun-baked land, and the dust and bumpy roads are a small trade-off for the chance to learn about the Navajos and their

culture, ancient and contemporary, from the members of the tribe themselves. Von Del Chamberlain, an astronomer, is the primary guide, an expert on "star ceilings," a kind of Navajo astronomical rock art. Accommodations are provided at lodges on the reservation, with adequate rooms and meals; singles are paired with one another or pay a single supplement to room alone. Lunches are packed for the day. *Canyonlands Field Institute, Box 68, Moab, UT 84532, tel. 801/259–7750. Oct.: 5 days, $910–$925. Price does not include 4 dinners and 3 breakfasts; sign up 1–2 months in advance.*

ARIZONA **Photographing Waterfalls and Canyons.** Paul Lazarski, a professional photographer from Vancouver, runs this 12-day combination tour and photography workshop. You'll be able to capture the turquoise waterfalls and pools of remote, magical Havasu Canyon and the dry red rock of Sedona; pan across the sweep of the Grand Canyon; and zoom in on the blooming cactus of the desert. A resident of Arizona who's also a photographer comes along as an additional guide, and groups are held to 15. Two vans are used, if needed; you also travel by horseback and helicopter (included in price) to reach some of the remote locations.

For most of the trip the group stays in the Havasupai Lodge, an acceptable motel run by the Indians of the same name. The meals are usually taken in its restaurant, which serves basic American fare. The real attraction at the lodge is its surroundings, which are verdant, tree-filled, and replete with waterfalls—an oasis in an otherwise red rock desert. Participants tend to be 40 to 70 years old, with a deep interest in photography. *Ecosummer, 936 Peace Portal Dr., Box 8014-240, Blaine, WA 98230, tel. 206/332–1000 or 800/688–8605, fax 604/669–3244. Mid-May: 12 days, $1,350. Price does not include food ($40 per day) or lodging (about $60 per night for a double); sign up 4 months in advance.*

UTAH **Rafting and Jeeping in Canyonlands.** For 6 days and 5 nights, you and 7 companions are off the road—either rafting in the famous Cataract Canyon in Canyonlands

National Park or traveling by 4-wheel-drive vehicles on tough roads to see the desert valleys and towering rock monuments of the national park. Two Toyota Land Cruisers are driven by guides who specialize in the natural and human history of the park and provide the running commentary. They also cook the food, which can include everything from pan-fried trout to pineapple upside-down cake. The wilderness campsites are pristine, and everything is set up by the guides, from the portable sanitary facilities to the occasional solar-heated shower. The 3 1/2-day rafting part of the trip sweeps you through 25 significant rapids and whets your imagination for seeing the spectacular, harsh scenery close up. You then fly from Lake Powell to an outpost in Canyonlands. Participants tend to be 30- to 60-year-old professionals. *Tag-A-Long Expeditions, 452 N. Main St., Moab, UT 84532, tel. 801/259–8946 or 800/453–3292, fax 801/259–8990. Apr.–Oct.: 6 days, $1,095. Price does not include tent; sign up 1–2 months in advance.*

UTAH **Prehistoric Rock Art of the Fremont.** Patricia and Gary George, a husband and wife team, deeply love the wild Colorado Plateau where they grew up; they know its history, wildlife, archaeology, and geology, and think showing its beautiful, harsh countryside to others is a blast. They've been leading Jeep tours since 1975, both scheduled and custom-designed, hotel-based or camping, though camping is their specialty. Their favorite is a 5-day tour that takes 6 to 12 people aged 30 to 60 to sites where you see the rock art of the Fremont Indians (ca. AD 700–1300). You are surrounded by gorgeous country: here red rock spires beckoning to powder blue sky, there an oasis of brush green in the valley. Plan on about 6 hours of activity a day, riding and walking. Meals, cooked over the campfire, feature such local fare as trout and Southwestern specialties like deep-dish enchilada pie. The Georges set up camp, with sanitary facilities and camp showers, in isolated, beautiful spots, and they'll help you put up your tent. Take the May trip if possible; August can be gruelingly hot. *Hondoo Rivers and Trails, Box 98, Torrey, UT 84775, tel. 801/*

425–3519 or 800/332–2696. May and Aug.: 5 days, $660. Price includes first nights lodging, but not tent; sign up 1–3 months in advance.

THE ROCKIES

COLORADO **Over the Divide by Jeep.** Burt Green, who holds Colorado Off-Road Scenic Permit No. 1, personifies his company, the Mountain Men. For some 30 years he's been sharing his hidden Colorado—the off-the-asphalt spots with spectacular views; the secrets of gold panning; where to go for great fishing. His is a personalized service: You tell him what you want to do and for how long, and he will create the trip accordingly. One of his favorite itineraries takes you along the catch-your-breath, off-road Jeep trails that crisscross the Continental Divide. Because you design the tour, you decide the level of comfort you want in a lodging and the kinds of meals (and what you want to pay). Remember, though, that you'll be paying for Burt and his guide to eat and sleep where you do, which will set you back $40 to $80 per night for a double and $30 to $40 per person per day for meals. *Mountain Men, 3003 S. Macon Circle, Aurora, CO 80014, tel. 303/750–5200. June–Oct.: $350 daily for groups of up to 14 on custom trips. Price does not include lodging, meals, or staff expenses; sign up 1–2 months in advance.*

COLORADO **To the Switzerland of America.** Ouray, Colorado, has a romantic mining history and equally romantic views of the red mountains that snuggle up against the town. Marv Dimond has been running Jeep tours here for 26 years, and if you ask him why the terrain is special, he gets as enthusiastic as a greenhorn from the East. He'll design multi-day journeys to order, but his choice trip would take his awed guests (7 passengers plus guide in a Jeep Scrambler) on a 5-day outing up and down several rugged 13,000-foot mountains for the 360° views on top, past the remains of old ghost towns, and down passes where riots of wildflowers compete with waterfalls as photographic subjects. Marv and his guides cook sturdy campfire meals such as grilled steak, baked potatoes, green beans, and pudding. You stay in wooded mountain campsites, where the staff sets up sanitary facilities, but not showers. *Switzerland of America, Inc., 226 7th Ave., Box 780, Ouray, CO 81427, tel. 303/325–4484 or 800/432– 5337. Memorial Day–Labor Day: 5 days, $875 ($1,000 if fewer than 4 people). Price does not include tent; sign up 1–2 months in advance.*

MONTANA **Jeeping the Wilds.** This is the less-traveled Rockies, where deer, moose, bear, wolf, bald eagles, and other birds seem more common than people. Although you're surrounded by such wilderness on this package with John and Carma Sinerius, a pair of avid naturalists, it may be just the trip for those whose love for the outdoors doesn't extend to camping out in it. After a day of jeeping, you head for the comforts of home and dinner in the Sinerius's own Virginia City B&B, a main house furnished with antiques, plus a cabin for 6 that's full of the town's Old West atmosphere. The food is "homestyle gourmet," which means barbecued chicken and homemade pie for dinner, and for breakfast, homemade muffins or sourdough pancakes. You travel in 3 vehicles with 3 guides with a group no bigger than 12 (most are smaller). The day's activites might include a trip to pan for gold, a day of mountain biking to see a herd of elk in a meadow, or a walk around a ghost town and mines, hearing echoes of the long-gone gold rush. *Just an Experience, Box 98, Virginia City, MT 59755, tel. 406/843–5402. Memorial Day–Labor Day: 4 days, $560. Sign up 1–2 months in advance.*

MONTANA **Glacier Country: The Land of Shining Mountains.** Glacier is a spectacular park. Its untouched wilderness, the snow on rugged mountains set against piercing blue skies, its lakes of unearthly blue—who could resist? Bill Evans, a longtime Sierra Club trip leader, shares his expertise on this 9-day van trip. Activities include river rafting, canoeing, and guided day hikes with informed commentary about the flora and fauna of the area. This part of Montana has the densest concentration of large mammals in the lower 48

states, with grizzly bears and wolves among them. It is also home to loons, which you are almost certain to see. The group, limited to 10, overnights in B&Bs, a lakefront lodge, a hostel, and campgrounds. You eat some meals at hotels and restaurants, and Evans cooks some in camp—blueberry pancakes and fruit at breakfast, sandwiches at lunch, and vegetables, soup, pasta with chicken, and chocolate mousse at dinner. *Sojourns of Discovery, Box 14057, San Luis Obispo, CA 93406, tel. 805/438–5910 or 800/736–8735, fax 805/543–4295. July: 9 days, $690. Price does not include 5 meals or raft trip; sign up 2 months in advance.*

THE WEST COAST

CALIFORNIA–ARIZONA **Yosemite and the Grand Canyon.** The Explore Company, an English outfitter, runs van tours throughout the United States primarily for Britons. This 20-day tour, as you'd expect, hits the tourist high spots: San Francisco, the Napa Valley, Death Valley, Yosemite, Los Angeles, the winding drive up the coast on Highway 1, Las Vegas, the Grand Canyon, and Zion National Park—a real Western Top 20. A maximum of 12 people travel by van from campground to campground, most of them in national parks; in L.A., San Francisco, and Las Vegas you stay at hotels. Everyone helps cook and clean up. Among various optional excursions, you can take a rafting trip ($60) on the American or the Merced rivers, rent a bicycle ($10 per hour) or a horse ($20 per hour) to cover Yosemite, take a helicopter ride over the Grand Canyon ($75), and explore Lake Havasu by boat ($50). Those who don't take these options can explore a gold-mining town and do more hiking in the Grand Canyon area. The guides, mostly Americans, are chosen more for their ability to keep a group happy than for comprehensive knowledge of the area. Tour participants range in age from their twenties to their sixties, and everyone should be able to handle some serious hiking. *Explore Adventure Center, 1311 63rd St., Suite 200, Emeryville, CA 94608, tel. 510/654–1879 or 800/227–8747, fax 510/654–4200. June–Sept.:*

20 days, $1,795. Price does not include frame backpack, 10 meals, or optional activities; sign up 3 months in advance.

CALIFORNIA–WASHINGTON Up the Pacific Coast. If you have 2 weeks, you can do the Pacific Coast with Trek America, traveling by van, camping out (except in San Francisco, where you stay at a $25-per-night budget hotel), and sampling everything from Disneyland to Yosemite, Mount Rainier to Seattle. The groups are limited to 13, mostly Europeans in their twenties, and cooking and cleaning tasks are shared. Most driver-guides are Americans, with at least 3 years of guiding experience but less botanical or naturalist expertise. You stay at established campsites, most equipped with showers, and many in national parks such as Yosemite. The food depends on the whim—and skill—of that night's guest-chef. *Trek America, Box 470, Blairstown, NJ 07825, tel. 908/362–9198 or 800/221–0596, fax 908/362–9313. Apr.–Aug.: 2 weeks, $635 to $735. Price includes Disneyland admission, but not $60 for food kitty or 2 nights' lodging in San Francisco; sign up 2 months in advance.*

OREGON–WASHINGTON Natural History in the Pacific Northwest. Understanding the ecosystems of the magnificent forests and coasts of Oregon and Washington is the focus on this 16-day trip by passenger van. Nature Expeditions International's guides, all with college-level teaching experience in anthropology, biology, or natural history, explain such arcana as the Native American use of plants, and comment on the local wildlife. You might see moose or elk as you hike through Olympic National Park, take a raft trip down the McKenzie River, or travel from high desert country to rainforest. Accommodations are in lodges, first-class hotels, and inns, where you also eat your meals—except for the occasional barbecue in the woods or salmon bake beside a river. This trip attracts people with an avid interest in natural history, ages 45 to 70, and the average group size is 9. *Nature Expeditions International, Box 11496, Eugene, OR 97440, tel. 503/484–6529 or 800/869–0639,* fax 503/484–6531. July–Sept.: 15 days, $2,290. Sign up 6 months in advance.

ALASKA

CENTRAL From Kenai Peninsula to Denali. "This is a little wilder, a little more Alaskan," says owner Tim Adams, contrasting this 2-week van-camping trip, on little-traveled dirt roads, with others available in the area. Guides with several years' Alaska experience take you into the stunning mountains of Denali National Park. You also see the breathtaking Kenai Peninsula's glaciers and wildlife, visit the towering Wrangell Mountains, and fly to Kodiak Island for 2 days. There's a maximum of 12 people per trip, with an age range of 20 to 50, and half of the clientele is international. Participants take turns cooking and cleaning. Campsites are in state and national parks, and some have showers. *Camp Alaska Tours, Box 872247, Wasilla, AK 99687, tel. 907/376–9438, fax 907/376–2353. June–Aug.: 14 days, $1,175. Price includes flight to and ferry (with cabin) from Kodiak, but not 13 meals and $105 for food kitty; sign up 4 months in advance.*

CENTRAL Cabin Safari to the Fjords and the Bush. Those who want their Alaska wild but like to sleep indoors will be attracted to these tours. Here you're housed in rustic, comfortable cabins with shared baths and in a restored lodge, both run by the outfitter. You're met at the Kenai Airport and taken to the cabins by the Kenai River that are home for the next 5 days. You usually have meals on a riverside deck under a tarp, and salmon is a sure bet. Guides take you by van to trailheads one day; on another you take a raft trip on the Kenai. There's a day trip by yacht to the Kenai Fjords National Park to watch for sea otters, puffins, seals, and sea lions, and then it's on to Talkeetna, a bush town, to stay for a night before heading north for 3 days at a carpeted, just-refurbished lodge in Denali National Park. The lodge has private baths, and the cook specializes in homemade bread and pastries. Groups are never larger than 18, and the 2 or 3 guides are extremely well versed in the natural history of this wild state. Participants are usually 35 to 50. *Alaska Wildland Adventures, Box 389, Girdwood, AK 99587, tel. 907/783–2928 or 800/334–8730, fax 907/783–2130. June–Sept.: 10 days, $2,595. Sign up 4 months in advance.*

HAWAII

THE BIG ISLAND **Fire and Sea.** This tour is designed for those with only a few days to spend on the island of Hawaii and a sneaking suspicion that there's more to it than deluxe resorts. You see both the land and the sea, and taste the bounty of both: You eat lots of fish and tropical fruit and vegetables. On the first 3 days, vans transport you to hikes near jungle waterfalls, down spectacular hidden paths, and to unknown beaches. You stay at a B&B—the former house of a sugar plantation manager—where you wake up in the morning to the smell of Kona coffee. The last day on land you visit Volcanoes National Park, and then you're off for 3 days of sailing in a 42-foot Morgan ketch off the Kona Coast. You spend the days whale-watching, looking for bottlenose dolphins, and inspecting the coral reefs. The average group numbers 10 people, most over 30. *Pacific Quest, 59-496 Pupukea Rd., Haleiwa, HI 96712, tel. 808/638–8338 or 800/776–2518, fax 808/638–8255. June–Dec.: 6 days, $975. Sign up 4 months in advance.*

HAWAII, MAUI, AND KAUAI **Volcanoes, B&Bs, and I'iwi Birds.** On a 10-day trip, Mark Goodoni's company takes small groups (6 to 9 is usual) to Hawaii, Maui, and Kauai, flying between islands and traveling by van to little-visited destinations. His clients hike to volcanoes on Maui, drive to an old fishing village on Hawaii, and snorkel along the Pali coast on Kauai. You spend the nights in off-the-trail B&Bs, whose hospitable owners are as much an attraction as the rooms, most of which have private baths. Both Mark and his wife, Beth, who lead the trips, are trained nat-

uralists with an intense interest in the islands; they can introduce you to such birds as the elepaio, i'iwi, and apapane. Although you eat some meals in the B&Bs and small inns, Mark and Beth cook some in parks and make a point of serving Hawaiian seafood and native produce. Participants tend to be well-educated 35- to 50-year-olds who are in good shape—the hiking is strenuous. *Eye of the Whale, Box 1269, Kapa'au Hawaii, HI 96755, tel. 808/889–0227 or 800/659–3544. Year-round: 10 days, $1,425–$1,575. Price does not include 3 dinners; sign up 2 months in advance.*

SOURCES

ORGANIZATIONS **United Four Wheel Drive Associations** (4505 W. 700 S, Shelbyville, IN 46176, tel. 800/448–3932, fax 317/729–5930) publishes a newspaper 5 times yearly with advocacy information, news about trails, and lists of local associations. For California, contact the **California Association of 4-Wheel Drive Clubs** (c/o Pat Horvath, 3104 O St. 313, Sacramento, CA 95816, tel. 916/332–8890) and the **California Off-Road Vehicle Association** (1500 W. El Camino, Suite 352, Sacramento, CA 95833, tel. 800/422–6782).

PERIODICALS *4-Wheel & Off-Road* magazine (Petersen's Publishing, 6420 Wilshire Blvd., Los Angeles, CA 90048, tel. 800/800–4294) is geared to the do-it-yourself off-road enthusiast. *Off-Road* (12100 Wilshire Blvd., No. 250, Los Angeles, CA 90025, tel. 310/820–3601) is a monthly magazine of general interest to owners of 4-wheel-drive vehicles.

BOOKS Spiral-bound *Backroad Tips & Trips,* by Harry Llewellyn (Glove Box Guides), is available in RV and off-road specialty shops.

ALSO SEE Want other ways to get around in the wilderness without expending too much energy? See Horse Packing and Trail Riding and River Rafting.

Wilderness and Survival Schools

by Naomi Black

ake part in a wilderness skills or survival school and you'll learn how to take care of yourself and feel comfortable in nature. How you get to this point varies considerably. On the one hand, there are so-called survival schools that teach the basics of living outdoors *without* gear, or with a minimum of gear. Everyone gets used to living outdoors without sleeping bags and to build a fire, make a shelter, find food and water, and navigate cross-country.

Then there are outdoor skills schools, which teach a few of these lessons but emphasize minimum-impact recreational camping *with gear* and teach you how to get along in the wilderness well enough that you can avoid survival situations. Either type of program may include a solo—a day or more when you're on your own, alone, in the wilderness, with a minimum of equipment and food. It's a time not so much to practice what you have learned as it is to reflect on who you are and where you're going.

Underpinning all these programs is solid basic instruction in conservation, environmental protection, and safety skills. Most courses teach the rudiments of navigation, food planning and preparation, equipment maintenance, water purification, wilderness first aid, and wilderness safety. Natural history and local history and culture may come up as well. In addition, all the programs encourage some

sort of personal growth; some help you acquire leadership skills, learn teamwork, and build your character. After all, when you're out with a group in an unpredictable environment—and nature is always unpredictable—you have to rely on each other to complete whatever task is given you, whether navigating to a destination or making sure everyone is well fed.

Depending on where the program is held, your development takes place as you're hiking or backpacking, river rafting, whitewater canoeing, sea kayaking, sailing, mountaineering, rock climbing, horse packing, backcountry skiing, even dogsledding. You may be anywhere from Maine to Alaska, and you may spend anywhere from a week to a semester.

Although it helps to be moderately fit, there is just one requirement: You have to be willing to throw yourself into the wilderness life. Some courses are hard-core survival experiences, with no tents, no sleeping bags, no mattress pads, no change of clothes, and no toilet paper. Meals are to fuel the body, not the soul, and you may have only two of them a day. And free time is at a minimum: Whether you learn fire building, shelter building, navigation with a map and compass, and plant lore as you travel or spend a week or more in a single location, you'll be learning every day, practicing what you have learned when you're not being taught; as you will be with instructors or other students almost all the time, and relying on them, there's little room

New York City–based Naomi Black writes frequently about the outdoors. She encountered her first survival skill, making soup in a cow's stomach, as a child in summer camp.

for the kind of privacy you usually encounter in day-to-day living on your own.

The program fees vary considerably, ranging from Reevis Mountain School's rock-bottom rates of about $28 per person per day to Alaskan forays that cost over $150 per person per day.

CHOOSING THE RIGHT PROGRAM

The process of deciding between schools has everything to do with assessing how much you *really* want to leave civilization behind. There are a lot of questions you need to ask the staff at the programs you're considering—and many to ask yourself.

What's the school's safety record and how long has it been in business? Most wilderness skills schools and survival schools have excellent safety records; you don't want to get involved with one that has a history of accidents. A track record is another indication that you'll be in good hands.

What are the leaders' qualifications? At least one instructor in each course should have first-aid training. Wilderness first-aid training, which is slightly different, is an even better qualification. A leader who's an expert on leadership training in desert or mountain or winter conditions may not know in detail the flora and fauna of the area, not to mention the region's history, geology, and ecology. Make sure that your instructor is knowledgeable in areas you care about.

What is the student-to-teacher ratio? To get the most out of a course, look for a small student-to-teacher ratio. Smaller groups are better, not necessarily because they're safer, but because students learn more in a smaller group. In courses that move from point to point, 5 students for each teacher is a good number. For base camp or classroom courses the number can be higher.

What are food and accommodations like, and what's the creature-comfort quotient? Some courses allow more creature comforts than others. Think carefully about what you're willing to give up and make sure the program doesn't ask more of you. Most schools recommend kicking the caffeine habit before you leave home and forbid alcohol as well as drugs. Some courses limit your food intake or give you a diet made up largely of grains and legumes. Such draconian measures are not intended to starve you, but to simulate a camping experience where you're carrying as little as possible or even a survival situation where food is not abundant. Depending on the terrain, weather, insects, and course philosophy, sleeping arrangements vary from wind-tight tents to under the stars without so much as a blanket. Some courses don't allow you to bring a change of clothes and have you use local plants or sand instead of toilet paper.

What is the focus of the school and what is its approach? Some schools teach basic outdoor skills; others emphasize survival skills. Survival skills courses teach you how to get by in the wild without gear and tend to be tougher than outdoor skills courses, which teach you how to camp responsibly with gear. Some schools' core curriculums encourage students to become leaders or team members. If you want to learn the geology or biology of an area, ask in advance if those topics are covered. Some schools have students help out in an orphanage, maintain trails in a national forest, or undertake other service work.

The itinerary of many programs varies from one session to another depending on the weather and participants' fitness levels and skills. Some schools have students work out a plan together with the instructors, while at others the instructors alone know the distances to simulate a survival situation—where, after all, you wouldn't necessarily have someone there to tell you that safety is so many hours or miles away.

What kind of people participate? Some trips bring people of all ages together, and some are age specific, that is, designed for those under 18, over 30, over 50, and the like.

Does the school offer a solo? Not all courses include a solo. This is a period of reflection, abstinence, and consolidating your newly learned skills. You're settled in one spot and monitored regularly by an instructor. If you don't know how you feel about spending time alone in the wild, talk to a staff member from the school. Many people regard the solo as the best part of the trip.

What's the cost and what's included? Prices for these programs, including all of those below unless otherwise noted, include instruction, meals while in the wilderness, and basic camping equipment (including tarps or tents and sleeping bags if you will be using them). Sometimes outdoor clothing can be rented. Transportation to and from the staging area is not included.

How fit do you have to be to participate? Daily exercise and some aerobic activity a few times a week is excellent training for these trips. If you don't exercise regularly, you can still go on most courses; you'll just have to work harder.

Do you have references from past guests? If you have doubts or questions that program spokespeople don't address, there's no substitute for talking to past students.

How far in advance do I need to book? Sign up ranges from a month to a year ahead.

MAJOR PLAYERS

BOULDER OUTDOOR SURVIVAL SCHOOL

This well-regarded school, known informally as BOSS, teaches you to use basic survival crafts to get by in the wilderness without relying on modern gear. As you might expect, BOSS programs are rugged, more primitive than most other programs as well as less expensive (from about $45 to $70 per day). But people come back again and again to hone their skills, and a few students go on to become instructors.

Two types of programs are available: skills workshops and, more demanding, expeditions known as walkabouts. On the skills courses you get by on 2 meals a day; because BOSS does not want to deplete local plant life, the school provides food, including simply processed grains and, to a lesser degree, fresh meat and vegetables. On the walkabouts, diet varies from what you can forage to a more typical (for BOSS) 2-meal day, with no lunch. Courses teach you to light fires without matches, build shelters, identify plants, locate water, fish, trap animals, prepare and preserve food, make tools, and navigate cross-country; you also learn the fundamentals of making things from stone and natural plant fibers. Primitive games add to the curriculum. On walkabouts, you sleep with nothing more than a blanket, which doubles as your pack, except during the acclimatization period, when you have nothing; during the skills courses, sleeping bags and pads are permitted, and you bed down in wickiups or tepees in forest settings and in caves and under overhangs in canyon locations. Instructors teach the basic principles of body heat and encourage you to acclimatize to the weather, whether it's snowing or clear. You learn not to rely on fires for warmth.

BOSS headquarters are in Boulder, Utah, near the western border of Utah, part way between Bryce Canyon and Capitol Reef national parks. The student-to-staff ratio is 4:1 and there are typically about 12 students in a group (Box 3226, Flagstaff, AZ 86003, tel. 602/779–6000).

NATIONAL OUTDOOR LEADERSHIP SCHOOL

People have been hiking, climbing, skiing, and paddling through the wilderness classrooms of NOLS since 1965; the alumni of this school, a nonprofit educational corporation, number more than 30,000. The basic wilderness, water, and mountaineering courses last a month or longer but there are a number of special courses for adults 25 and over who have less time to spend on their vacation. These courses are easier than the longer versions but do not lose the focus for which NOLS is known: minimum-impact camping, outdoor safety, and gear-oriented outdoor skills. Not a survival school, NOLS emphasizes that by learning to camp responsibly, you can avoid a survival situation.

The school's magnificent settings range from Alaska's Gates of the Arctic National Park to Baja California to the Arizonan desert and beyond. The longer courses go even farther afield, both within the United States and to Kenya, India, and Patagonia.

Although the technical skills and safety courses are formal and demanding, there's less structure to the overall expedition than, for instance, Outward Bound or the Boulder Outdoor Survival School walkabouts, whose expeditions have several specific stages. (NOLS courses have no solo or marathon, for example.) In that sense, the NOLS courses may feel more like trips than courses. Most programs, however, do encourage each person to become leader for the day.

Students set up and sleep in 3- to 4-man tents (or tarps) and with their tent mates form a cook group that eats, cleans up, and usually travels together. You eat pasta, lentils, beans, bulgur, and other grains, and cook everything from scratch—bread or cinnamon rolls, pizzas and calzones, *pasta e fagioli, gatogato* (macaroni and cheese in a peanut sauce), salads of wild greens. No freeze-dried or dehydrated prepared foods here.

To sign up, you must usually be at least 16; there are special sessions for 14- and 15-year-olds, educators, and adults 25 years and older. Sign up at least 6 months in advance for the 25 and over courses. Average cost per day is usually a little more than $100, and the student-to-teacher ratio is about 5:1 (288 Main St., Lander, WY, 82520-0579, tel. 307/332–6973, fax 307/332–3631).

OUTWARD BOUND The best known of the wilderness skills schools, Outward Bound is also the oldest: Founded in 1941, it has some 260,000 alumni. Actually, it calls itself an adventure-based education program; the objective is training people as leaders, helping them learn more about themselves, building their self-confidence, and instilling compassion for others. There are Outward Bound schools in Denver, Colorado; Rockland, Maine; Minnetonka, Minnesota; Morganton, North Carolina; and Portland, Oregon. Each is an independent operation, with its own management and roster of courses. But you go through several distinct stages whether you travel to the Cascade Mountains of the Pacific Northwest or the southern Appalachians, and whether you study backpacking, mountaineering, or rock climbing; canoeing, kayaking, or rafting; bicycling or sailing; or dogsledding, skiing, or winter camping.

You spend the course with a group of 8 to 12 other students. Once you've packed your gear and sat in on a period of instruction that includes safety orientation, you set out on an expedition, carrying your own packs, preparing your own food, and bedding down at night in sleeping bags laid out under tarps (or, occasionally, in tents). En route, you learn the skills appropriate to your course. In the wild, you come across situations that the leaders recognize as a goal, and the group works as a team to accomplish it. Then you all separate for your solo, 1 to 3 days in an assigned spot with ample water but a minimum of food; some students choose to fast. Instructors monitor each person at least once a day to ensure their safety. The trip ends with a marathon—either a 26-mile run or some other long, exhausting, and celebratory race that proves how far each student has come. The student-to-staff ratio is 4:1. Like NOLS, OB is a nonprofit educational institution. In addition to its wilderness schools, it has urban centers that reach out to inner-city kids, Vietnam veterans, and substance abusers. The wilderness schools offer special programs for adults over 50, women over 30, 14- to 16-year-olds, parents and their children, couples, and health and corporate professionals. All gear except clothing, boots, and personal items is included in the cost, which averages between $75 and $150 per day. A physical examination is required. Sign up at least 3 months in advance for courses (Rte. 9D, R2, Box 280, Garrison, NY 10524-9757, tel. 914/424–4000 or 800/243–8520, fax 914/424–4280).

TOM BROWN TRACKING, NATURE, WILDERNESS SURVIVAL SCHOOLS

Tom Brown earned a reputation for himself as one of the country's foremost trackers. Simply by looking at the track that a person or animal has left behind, he can tell more about its behavior than most people can by direct observation. He has written 13 books and is considered a guru of ancient Native American outdoor lore although he'd be loathe to accept that title. The school he founded in 1978, now with some 4,000 alumni, is so popular that prospective students sign up 6 months or even a year in advance.

The core of the school's curriculum is comprised of the week-long standard and advanced program. Brown himself teaches about half of the lectures in any given course, and his instructors have all studied with him for years. Once you have taken the Standard Course, you are eligible to sign up for a number of other 7-day courses, including the advanced course as well as Advanced Tracking and Nature Observation and a philosophy course, which covers ancient customs, traditions, and ceremonies such as the vision quest, storytelling, and the sacred pipe. Also available are 10-day winter survival courses and a 7-day course that teaches how an Apache might travel and survive on a mission away from his community. To take these you must have already taken 2 advanced courses.

Brown believes that there isn't time to absorb all the information he covers within the context of an arduous hiking trip, so most courses stay in one place—in many cases the Tracker Farm in Asbury, New Jersey, near the Pine Barrens (though plans are in the offing at press time to move to Colorado). Whether indoors or out, the classes draw everyone together into an almost tribal community in which people look out for others. This group spirit and the oneness with nature that is emphasized are focal points of the school. Learning to rely on your instinct and trained inner vision is as important in the Tracker classes as learning to start a fire with a bow drill. Although you will not test your physical limits, this is hardly a vacation. You'll be rising early and practicing your skills until late at night. Though the minimum age is 18, the school sometimes accepts 15- to 17-year-olds accompanied by a guardian. Average cost per day is between $80 and $95, and the student-to-instructor ratio is usually 12:1 (Box 173, Asbury, NJ 08802, tel. 908/479–4681).

FAVORITE PROGRAMS

THE NORTHEAST

MAINE **Winter Backpacking.** The presence or absence of snow determines the itinerary of this 8-day course in Maine's Mahoosuc Mountains, part of the White Mountain range near the New Hampshire border. No leisurely cross-country ski trip this. Whether or not the ground is white, this is a day-to-day match with the elements, all the more rigorous because almost everyone participating is a neophyte. If there's no snow, the focus is on hiking and winter ecology; you ascend a peak and perhaps do some ice climbing. If you do have snow, you also go cross-country skiing and snowshoeing; the peak ascent goes on as scheduled, though if the snow is deep, you may find yourself climbing up 30 feet and falling back 20.

Heaping portions of oatmeal, pasta with dried spaghetti sauce, real butter, sausage, and other goodies fuel these exertions; your daily caloric intake is a whopping 6,000 calories. You need the extra fats and carbohydrates to manufacture and sustain warmth. To further ensure that everyone is toasty, Outward Bound provides all the winter equipment, from parkas and boots to sleeping bags, and, because this is Outward Bound, tarps instead of tents. You have a typical Outward Bound solo (you may have to break through a stream or melt snow to get more water than you have brought), followed by a marathon—here a 6-mile snowshoe race and 11-mile cross-country ski dash. *Outward Bound, Rte. 9D, R2, Box 280, Garrison, NY 10524-9757, tel. 914/424–4000 or 800/243–8520, fax 914/424–4280. Dec.–Jan.: 8 days, $745. Sign up 3 months in advance.*

THE MID ATLANTIC

NEW JERSEY **The Tracker's Standard Course.** For 7 days, you get up every morning at 5, turn in at 10 or 11, and spend the hours in between listening to lectures and practicing what you've learned. Even the simplest walk between buildings becomes a learning experience: you can practice fox-walking, a balanced gait that should induce a dynamic meditation (like t'ai chi) and that allows you to move soundlessly through the forest.

A typical day includes about 5 lectures and a workshop. Movement and learning how to observe nature take on more importance than philosophy in this beginning course. The rest of the instruction—mostly in the classroom— revolves around how to recognize the plenty that is around you outdoors. You learn how to make a fire with a bow drill, set traps, tan hides, stalk animals, make simple tools out of rocks, and identify edible plants such as stinging nettle, which tastes like spinach. There is also a sweat lodge, a sort of Native American ritual sauna. Because the course is only a week long, however, you are *not* out in the woods: You bundle up in your own sleeping bag in the hay barn at night or bring your own tent and camp.

There's oatmeal for breakfast and vegetarian or meat stew for lunch and dinner, with peanut butter and jelly or spaghetti as special treats. One of the week's culinary highlights is fish you've gutted and cleaned yourself. There are about 80 students in each course. *Tom Brown, Tracker, Inc., Box 173, Asbury, NJ 08802, tel. 908/479–4681. Apr., June–Oct.: 7 days, $615. Sign up 6–12 months in advance.*

NEW JERSEY The Tracker's Advanced Standard Course. Like the Standard Course, Tom Brown's Advanced Standard Course requires its students to rouse themselves before dawn and work until well after nightfall. Out in the sandy-soiled, brushy, pine- and oak-dominated Pine Barrens, all 60 novices build their own debris-hut shelter, a simple, efficient structure that can save lives in a survival situation. All instruction takes place in a group hut or under a tarp.

During this course, you rarely venture far from the base camp. Instead, you spend all your time under the tutelage of Tom Brown, 5 full-time teachers, and any visiting instructors, who coach you in how to make water bowls, utensils, and grass tepees, and other elaborate survival skills. By the end of the week,

you are using chipping stones you've made and blankets instead of the sleeping bags and knives you brought.

Brown advises sleeping in a cooler environment and getting in shape before attending this class, which makes the transition from recreational camping to full survival living. The Standard Course is a prerequisite. *Tom Brown, Tracker, Inc., Box 173, Asbury, NJ 08802, tel. 908/479–4681. Apr.– May, Nov.: 7 days, $665. Sign up 3–4 months in advance.*

THE SOUTH

NORTH CAROLINA Mountain Adventure. In a very short distance, the North Carolina landscape changes from lowland rhododendron forests near gushing waterfalls to 5,000-foot mountain areas above the tree line where it's just rocks and horizon. The state also has some of the nation's best whitewater rafting and rock climbing.

The North Carolina OB School takes advantage of this terrain for its courses. In the 9-day course, the shortest, you do backpacking, ropes work, rock climbing, and canoeing in fall and summer, and caving in winter and early spring.

Just as the terrain changes, so does the weather. Summer, the most consistent season, tends toward daytime highs in the 80s and nighttime lows in the 60s, but it rains. Spring and fall are beautifully clear most of the time but cooler—in the 50s to 70s by day, into the 30s to 50s at night. Flowers are in bloom from late April through early June, and fall puts on its show from mid-September to late October. As for winter, it depends: you could as easily be out in shorts and a T-shirt as buried under 2 feet of snow.

This OB includes a service project, underscoring the program's commitment to helping others. The projects range from trail maintenance, campground cleanups, and other simple tasks to helping return peregrine falcons to the wild. Special courses are also available for couples and other twosomes. *Outward*

Bound, Rte. 9D, R2, Box 280, Garrison, NY 10524-9757, tel. 914/424-4000 or 800/243-8520, fax 914/424-4280. Apr.–Oct.: 9 days, $995–$1,295; 16 days, $1,795; 23 days, $2,095; 28 days, $2,495. Sign up 3 months in advance.

THE SOUTHWEST

ARIZONA **Inner Quest Adventure Trek.** Although the nonprofit Reevis Mountain School, 3½ hours from Phoenix, is small, its reputation extends throughout the world of wilderness skills and survival school teachers. Founder Peter Bigfoot, a Native American, is an expert on medicinal and edible plants.

There are more than 20 weekend courses, everything from felt-hat-making and touch-healing in wilderness emergencies to one called Zen and the Art of Land Navigation. You eat 2 meals a day and camp out or pay $5 extra a night to sleep in Reevis tepees. After taking weekend courses on plant identification, natural healing, and desert survival, or the like, you become eligible to join the Self-Discovery Club ($220). The 8-day Inner Quest Adventure Trek, where you put your skills to the test as you hike along Native American paths or trails dating from America's early mining days, is free to members.

You start each day with meditation before sunrise, then pack up camp and walk several miles before breakfast. You hike from 4 to 14 miles a day (sometimes walking on even after dark), and climb a 5,800-foot mountain pass. Peter, who is always personally on hand, allows a pound of food per person in the communal cache, which includes mainly rice, pasta, oatmeal, and the like; you learn to find sources for water and other food, foraging for prickly pear and hedgehog cactus, small rodents and snakes, agave and onion bulbs in spring, and mesquite tree leaves and cactus fruit in fall. You sleep in sleeping bags under the stars. Most Inner Quest groups number about 10. There is usually one instructor per group. Participants must be in good physical shape. *Reevis Mountain School, HCO2, Box 1534, Roosevelt, AZ 85545, tel. 602/467-2536; writing is preferable, since the phone rings at a neighbor's house 12 miles away from the school.*

Apr., Oct.: 8 days, $220. Sign up 2–3 months in advance.

TEXAS **Whitewater Canoeing and Desert Backpacking.** An indigenous myth tells the story that God made the world and put all the leftovers in Big Bend. The stark southern Texas landscape boasts beautiful combinations of white, yellow, and red volcanic tuff mixed in with basalt. Fossil-filled limestone cliffs and adobe buildings that predate East Coast settlements mark this land that served as a hunting ground for nomadic tribes such as the Comanche and the Apache.

Set against this background is this 14-day course from the Voyageur Outward Bound School, a week of whitewater followed by a week of backpacking. Part of the time, since the river runs alongside a road, cars may be within sight. Sometimes, however, all you'll see is the 500-foot canyon wall or the 8,000-foot Mexican mountains in the background.

The first week, while not physically difficult, demands your attention as you master the art of reading the water and learn to recognize the location of rocks and other obstacles from the patterns on the surface. In this Outward Bound program, the water is the place you confront your fears, so the very first thing your instructor makes you do is to dump your boat and learn to swim in the current.

On the backpacking segment, climbers typically scale a 50- to 80-foot cliff. While exact hiking routes vary, most ascend into high piñon pine and juniper forests or traverse rugged mesas. Packs on this trip are on the heavy side because of the extra water—up to 2 gallons—that you must carry.

Throughout the course, you use tarps, not tents, except when the bugs are out, which is not often, at least while you're backpacking. Weather varies with the season. October can be quite hot, while November might be mild. December and January are usually cold, sometimes chilly enough that the temperature drops below freezing at night. During courses in March and April, the mercury might top 102°F—or you might have a light snow. Some sessions include a service day—when, for example, you help out in a Mexican orphanage. If you're interested in this, make sure you make it clear on your application. *Outward Bound, Rte. 9D, R2, Box 280, Garrison, NY 10524-9757, tel. 914/424–4000 or 800/ 243-8520, fax 914/424–4280. Nov.–Dec.: 14 days, $1,295. Oct.–Jan.: 21 days, $1,595. Sign up 3 months in advance.*

UTAH **Earthskills in Forest and Canyon.** The BOSS Earthskills Course doesn't test your mettle against the elements on an extended trek; instead, it teaches you self-sufficiency out of 2 base camps. The first sits in an aspen forest on a mountaintop, the second among the sage and cottonwood of a low canyon. You sleep in sleeping bags in wickiups in the forest, in caves and under overhangs in the canyon. Staff members do the cooking—2 meals daily of typical BOSS fare, never so much that you're sated but never so little that hunger diminishes your concentration on the lessons at hand: how to set traps, and how to make fires without matches, emergency shelters, and simple tools of bone, stone, and wood. You also learn basic outdoor skills.

Although there's no extensive travel during the 7 days out, you do move about and must be prepared to hike between 3 and 6 miles to gather materials and move from the mountain camp to the canyon. The course is small, with only about 12 participants and 2 instructors. If you want to use your skills on an expedition, sign up for a BOSS walkabout (*see below*). *BOSS, Box 3226, Flagstaff, AZ 86003, tel. 602/779–6000. June–Aug.: 7 days, $475. Sign up 6 weeks in advance.*

UTAH **Primitive Aboriginal Skills Course.** On the first 2 weeks you spend at base camp in this course you acquire the primitive living skills and make the tools and equipment you use during the third week, when you live as a hunter-gatherer on an expedition in the Utah wilderness. There, you and 11 other students plus 2 or 3 instructors have only the stone knives and simple containers that you made the preceding weeks to help you get by. The going can be rough and the food is minimal, so conditions are strenuous. A typical smorgasbord includes parched grains,

sausage, and sprouts that were made earlier. Sleeping bags and pads are permitted, however.

All the basic outdoor skills and earth skills are taught in this course, including, sometimes, the how-to of more complex crafts such as the fashioning of throwing sticks, snares, and darts. A large portion of the course is devoted to the process of turning raw deer hide into soft buckskin and then into various useful items. *BOSS, Box 3226, Flagstaff, AZ 86003, tel. 602/779–6000. May–June: 21 days, $1,025. Sign up 6 weeks in advance.*

UTAH **Rainbow Bridge Hiking.** The food is good on this trip from Earth Treks, a small adventure travel company founded in 1990: You're served bagels with almond butter or cream cheese, granola with fruit, or oatmeal for breakfast; tuna salad, hummus in pita bread, or bean dip with chips and salsa for lunch; udon noodles, burritos, chili, or spaghetti and fruit rolls for dinner. Among wilderness skills schools, whose fare is notoriously basic, this makes Earth Treks a luxury operation.

Still, you get the instruction you need to camp safely and feel comfortable in the wild. Earth Treks proprietor Buck O'Herin, who leads the trips, has been doing this for more than a dozen years and has advanced wilderness first aid and rescue training under his belt. Although you're welcome to pitch in, he is the one to thank for the food, along with his co-cook. Groups usually number only 9 people, most in their 30s and 40s, some of them newcomers to the great outdoors and some simply eager to acquire enough skills to go backpacking on their own.

The group assembles in Phoenix for the long drive into Utah, where you pick up a trail on the Navajo reservation that you follow for 26 miles during the next week. Usually you cover from 3 to 5 relatively level miles; there's normally plenty of time to explore the beautiful sandstone canyons and creek beds en route at a leisurely pace. The ultimate destination is Rainbow Bridge, 300 feet high with a span of about 200 feet, one of the largest natural stone arches in the world. Bring a bathing suit to swim in the lake by the arch or to splash around in one of the area's many small pools. *Earth Treks, RFD 2, Box 785, Thorndike, ME 04986, tel. 207/589–4311. Mar.–Apr.: 8 days, $550. Sign up 3 months in advance.*

UTAH Walkabout. For the indigenous nomadic peoples of Australia, a walkabout is a young man's coming-of-age ritual. The BOSS adaptation of the concept, which may last 7, 14, or 27 days, involves groups of 12 plus 3 instructors, who travel as simply as aborigines, practicing minimum-impact living as they move lightly through southern Utah's rugged canyonlands.

Regardless of its length, each walkabout is highly structured, with 5 components: orientation, impact, survival expedition, quest, and a final expedition or celebration. During the impact phase, students hike together for 2 or 3 days over rugged terrain with only the clothes on their back, sleeping in debris huts or a litter lodge. It's an acclimatization period, a time for getting used to the local alkaline water, natural foods, and the cold. The experience shows every student how well people can survive if they get lost. By the middle of the course, everyone thoroughly appreciates the luxury of having a blanket, but each student will learn first-hand how adaptable the human body can be under high-stress conditions.

During the next phase, the survival expedition, each student carries only a small blanket pack, extra clothing, and a little food. You soon begin to feel a bit run down, just enough to recognize what a little deprivation feels like and how it affects problem-solving abilities. Learning to find solutions to challenges despite the strain builds self-confidence.

Your band travels from food cache to food cache, setting up base camp occasionally on the longer walkabouts. To make the experience feel more like a real-life survival situation, only the instructors know how far away the next cache is. The land is fragile, so you gather food only now and then. BOSS students prepare meals from the 1,500-calorie-per-day food packs that the school supplies—

using rice, wheat flakes, mixed flours, and amaranth, you prepare meals that resemble those consumed by the ancient peoples of the canyons. On the 14- and 27-day treks, you slaughter a sheep, tan its hide, and use all the parts for food, basic material, or tools.

The survival expedition is followed immediately by the quest, similar to Outward Bound's solo except that you're required to spend at least part of your time making a gift for another student: aboriginal earmuffs, leis of aspen leaves, or the like. Participants are monitored using a marker system—you and your instructor leave each other a marker indicating that all is well. On 14- and 27-day walkabouts, the final celebration, at which students present each other with their creations, is preceded by a 24-hour marathon that involves a 12-mile hike and a 12-mile run. On most BOSS programs, the student-to-staff ratio is about 4:1. *BOSS, Box 3226, Flagstaff, AZ 86003, tel. 602/779–6000. June–Aug.: 7 days, $575. July: 27 days, $1,495. Aug.: 14 and 21 days, $935 and $1,295. Sign up 6–8 weeks in advance.*

THE ROCKIES

COLORADO Winter Skills and Simple Comforts in the San Juans. High at 11,500 feet in the San Juan Mountains between Ouray and Silverton, a mile's ski from civilization, sits an 1890s mine building that serves as a shell for a cozy lodge owned by Chris George. It is your base for an Earth Treks trip that's a total immersion in backcountry skiing. The lodge was created using recycled materials; it has composting toilets but no electricity. You do have hot water, a sauna, and private as well as shared rooms. You must also bring your own sleeping bag. Moreover, the chef, who once cooked for Charlie Chaplin, dishes up hearty fare to warm body and soul: breakfasts are hot cereals and eggs and bacon or pancakes; lunches of soups and sandwiches; and dinners, cooked on an antique propane stove, that incorporate fresh vegetables into dishes such as tarragon chicken and lasagna. Whole-grain bread is baked fresh every day. Wine is permitted but its consumption is not recommended, at least early in the program, since it interferes with acclimatization.

Ski outings are scheduled twice daily, one in the morning and one in the afternoon. Tours may go to old mining camps, up to the high passes, or to a summit. The group splits up according to ability, so beginners usually spend the mornings in classes going over basics, while more experienced skiers might learn the nuances of telemark or downhill parallel turns. Every day, after the afternoon outing, leaders Bill Donahue and Dana Densmore offer a different hour-long lecture on wilderness skills. Their 6-part program covers hypothermia and how to treat it, proper clothing and equipment, navigation during white-out conditions, how to build a snow cave, and, if you have time, how to get a fire going in the snow. Chris George, who serves as one of the guides, is also an avalanche expert and discusses the physics of avalanches and avalanche safety, based on the teachings of the Silverton Avalanche School, a well-respected safety school. The price includes use of skis, boots, and poles, as well as food and lodging. *Earth Treks, RFD 2, Box 785, Thorndike, ME 04986, tel. 207/589–4311. Mar.: 7 days, $675. Sign up 3 months in advance.*

WYOMING **Trekking and Wilderness Skills in the Wind River.** Pack animals, either horses or goats, lighten your load on this program, which treks along at 8,000 to 10,000 feet in the spectacular Wind River Wilderness that bridges the Shoshone and Bridger-Teton national forests. The area, known for its glacially sculpted U-shaped valleys, is thick with wildlife, and it's possible to spot deer, elk, pronghorn antelope, marmots, hawks, maybe even moose and bear.

Since you have just 2 weeks, the course concentrates on basic skills such as minimum-impact camping rather than compass work and cross-country travel, which are keystones of most NOLS courses; but you usually learn a few unusual techniques, including the Tyrolean traverse, a thrilling river-crossing method. The trek goes into boulder fields and dense forests, and along some not-so-well-trodden trails. The first days out you average a few miles each day with a lot of ups and downs; by the end of the course, you may cover over 6 miles on an average day. Depending on the group, the season, and the weather, the trip may include the ascent of a peak or you may stick with fly-fishing, rock climbing, or snow travel.

While there's not a lot of free time, the instructors do try to schedule layover days when you can sleep past the usual 6 AM wake up. The layover days also give instructors a chance to coach a morning bird class or help fishermen practice their casts. Most of the leaders know their natural history well and teach wildflower identification, basic geology, tracks, and animal signs.

Lunch and dinners are typical NOLS fare with the occasional freshly caught trout (if you're lucky) and salads of spring beauty, mountain bluebell, or other wild edibles. The weather in the northern Rockies is variable, with occasional great fluctuations between daytime and nighttime temperatures. It can snow at any time or it could be a balmy 80°F out of the wind. In general, weather is wetter for courses earlier in the year, making stream crossings more challenging; the warmer weather later on brings its own problem: bugs. *NOLS, 288 Main St., Lander, WY 82520-0579, tel. 307/332–6973, fax 307/332–3631. June–Aug.: 14 days, $1,750. Sign up 3–4 months in advance.*

THE WEST COAST

CALIFORNIA **Backpacking and Bouldering in Joshua Tree.** Boulder-choked canyons, craggy rock formations, and the eerie, spiky, spare silhouettes of the Joshua tree mark the national monument named for the unusual tree yuccas, a kind of succulent. Because of the solidity of the rock and the reliability of the weather, it's one of the world's best-known climbing sites, and the Pacific Crest Outward

Bound School uses it to good advantage. This exploration course, which follows OB's standard structure, mixes backpacking, rock climbing, and bouldering (climbing over big boulders). Joshua Tree, because its terrain is so unusual, nurtures a profound sense of solitude that's different from that of a forested area. Because the mountains are low, about 5,000 feet, summit ascents are a possibility; alternatively, if the weather's not good, it's easy to drop lower into the desert to stay warm. January, for instance, can be cold—or warm enough to be in short sleeves out of the wind. Because the dates do not coincide with school summer vacation periods, the course attracts an older crowd, and the average age ranges from the mid-20s to late 40s. *Outward Bound, Rte. 9D, R2, Box 280, Garrison, NY 10524-9757, tel. 914/424–4000 or 800/243–8520, fax 914/424–4280. Apr., Oct.–Jan.: 8 days, $795; 14 days, $1,195; 22 days, $1,595. Sign up 3 months in advance.*

ALASKA

NORTHEAST **By Canoe through the Brooks Range.** The Arctic National Wildlife Refuge, the locale of this course, is home to more caribou than canoers and kayakers. On some days, 500 of the animals may loom ahead; on other days, only one or two. And although the group rarely runs into people, there's a noticeable number of small planes droning across the sky: It's the basic method of transportation in this remote area.

Though experienced paddlers do sign up for this 125-mile canoe journey on the Sheenjek River, it is designed to give beginners a jumbo dose of wilderness experience, with a dozen days in the Arctic National Wildlife Refuge. The route, which begins at tree line in the mossy tundra, moves south through the cool boreal forest. Spruce and willows give way to alder, aspen, birch, and poplars. There may be berries by the riverbank: blueberries, cranberries, cloudberries. July usually brings tundra flowers, August the changing of the seasons. Unfortunately, the long nights of twilight don't guarantee summer weather: A calm, sunny 65°F day may be followed by a run of freezing nighttime temperatures. Gentle afternoon showers with rainbows are more common than downpours.

During the first few days, along with basic camping how-to, you learn about bears and basic paddling, equipment care, and paddle signals and communication; and find out how rivers flow and how to pack a boat. The hardest part at first is staying in water deep enough that wading isn't necessary. But then the Sheenjek is joined by tributaries that increase its water volume and transform it from a relatively easy Class I stream into a waterway with some reasonably demanding Class II waters, and the challenges begin. (*See* River Rafting for definitions of classifications.) Wake and sleep times vary with the weather and the group's eagerness to paddle under the midnight sun, and 6-hour day after 6-hour day on the river pushes students to their limit. Layover days offer a chance to hike or fish for grayling. Campfires are permitted in certain places, so unlike many wilderness courses, there's a certain romance intact here. Especially if you hear the wolves at night. *NOLS, 288 Main St., Lander, WY 82520-0579, tel. 307/332–6973, fax 307/332–3631. July–Aug.: 14 days, $2,650. Sign up 5–6 months in advance.*

NORTHWEST **A Backpacking and Rafting Expedition in the Gates of the Arctic.** Lying entirely north of the Arctic Circle in the Brooks Range, the Gates of the Arctic National Park and Preserve boasts hundreds of square miles without trails except animal tracks. It's an area that's as rugged as it is remote. And it's one of the few areas where Outward Bound students routinely sleep in tents, primarily because of bears, insects, and the unpredictability of the weather.

The whole course is modified to the environment, so instead of the standard OB rock-climbing activities or ropes work, students focus on the expedition skills it takes to get from one place to another safely. The solo is also altered: You stay out for only part of a day, in the high country away from known bear territory. There's no standard marathon at the end of the course, either. The food tends to be a little better, too; you'll eat corn-bread biscuits, tortillas, pizza, and other baked goods.

The first 10 days of this 17-day program have you trekking across the tundra, both cross-country and on trails that are used regularly but not marked or officially maintained, into an area of low peaks, where the views are truly amazing. Tree line begins at about 2,500 feet in this part of the world. Because you are so far north, the sun barely dips below the horizon; the nighttime twilight allows you to hike long past the hour that OB students elsewhere have turned in. As the hike ends, you descend to the Koyukuk River to learn river skills and, off-river, natural history. In drier and warmer July, insects can be numerous, but so are the tundra flowers. By August, the flowers thin out and the treed landscape looks like a miniature autumn forest; it can snow at any time. You may spot Dall sheep and wolves in the high country and ptarmigan, moose, caribou, and foxes on the river. *Outward Bound, Rte. 9D, R2, Box 280, Garrison, NY 10524-9757, tel. 914/424–4000 or 800/243–8520, fax 914/424–4280. July– Aug.: 17 days, $2,795. Sign up 3 months in advance.*

SOURCES

ORGANIZATIONS The nonprofit **Wilderness Education Association** (20 Winona Ave., Box 89, Saranac Lake, NY 12983, tel. 518/891–2915, ext. 254) promotes wilderness education at the college level. Membership includes a subscription to "WEA Legend," a quarterly newsletter, among other benefits.

PERIODICALS "Compass: The Outward Bound Alumni Newsletter" (Rte. 9D, R2, Box 280, Garrison, NY 19524-9757, tel. 800/243–8520, fax 914/424–4280), a slim, 16-page newsletter published 2 or 3 times a year and free to alumni, is devoted to alumni news,

instructor profiles, updates on land use, course descriptions, and journal entries. Many wilderness education instructors read the 3-times-a-year *Journal of Experiential Education* (2885 Aurora Ave. #28, Boulder, CO 80303, tel. 303/440–8844, fax 303/440–9581). Its publisher is the Association for Experiential Education (whose members are people involved in wilderness and other outdoor programs).

BOOKS *The New Wilderness Handbook,* second edition, is edited by Paul Petzoldt—founder of NOLS and considered the grand old man of wilderness education. The *Outward Bound Map & Compass Handbook,* by Glenn Randall, teaches you how to get from here to there—and back again. Although it can't substitute for actually taking the course, the *Outward Bound Wilderness First-Aid Handbook,* by Jeff Isaac and Peter Goth, is a good reference guide. Not a guidebook but a thoughtful exploration of the area and its people, *The Pine Barrens,* by John McPhee, is definitely worth reading if you're planning to take one of the Tracker's courses. To get an idea of what you've signed up for, read *Tom Brown's Field Guide to Wilderness Survival,* by Tom Brown, Jr., a good introduction to his philosophy of survival in the outdoors. Its sequel, *Tom Brown's Field Guide to Nature Observation and Tracking,* by Tom Brown, Jr., focuses more on the Tracker's methods. Feeling inspired? *The Tracker, Tom Brown, Jr.,* as told to William Jon Watkins, is Tom Brown's autobiography of his early years, from meeting his mentor, Stalking Wolf, to leaving home.

ALSO SEE Many of the skills you acquire in wilderness and survival schools can be used on trips on your own into the backcountry—or on guided trips of many types. Check out the Canoeing and Kayaking in Flatwater, Canoeing and Kayaking in Whitewater, Climbing and Mountaineering, River Rafting, Sea Kayaking, and Cross-Country Skiing chapters.

Windsurfing Schools

by Melissa Rivers

If you haven't tried windsurfing yet, you haven't been left behind. Also known as boardsailing and sailboarding, windsurfing was invented in California in the late 1960s and is still in its infancy, with new equipment, maneuvers, and teaching methods emerging almost every day. While the sport looks easy, it is actually quite tricky: You need balance and stamina, much as you do in surfing and skiing, and an understanding of wind, current, and wave variables, as in sailing.

Too many sports in one? The easiest, quickest, and least frustrating way to pick up skills from the basics to advanced techniques is through professional lessons at one of the many outstanding schools around the country. Most people who try to teach themselves the sport get frustrated and quickly lose interest. A professional instructor will get the basics across and have you up and sailing in no time so that you get more experience on the water and more enjoyment out of your vacation. That's where inclusive learning packages come in. These packages provide everything from professional instruction to equipment rental, ground transportation, accommodations, dining, and alternative activities to fill those windless days.

Instructors, who have been trained to teach by a variety of equipment companies such as Mistral and Bic, follow different methods, but most break down windsurfing skills into easily understood components learned on a dryland simulator (a sailboard mounted on a swiveling platform that simulates the experience of being on water). You'll get a feel for proper stance and learn to uphaul the sail, tack and jibe, and perform a self-rescue before ever touching the water. And in a very short time, you'll be out there, zipping back and forth on your own, enjoying the thrill of controlling wind in your sail. An average of 3 hours of daily instruction, both on land and water, often includes being videotaped while you're testing your skills in the surf. This is followed by practice, solo, for as long as your strength holds out. Class size is often limited to 4 or 5 participants at the beginning and intermediate levels; advanced techniques are generally taught on a one-to-one basis.

When there is some breeze, you can sail in virtually any body of water, from inland lakes—ideal for learning because of their warm, flat waters—to open ocean, where swells and chop offer bump-and-jump challenges for experienced sailors. In selecting a windsurfing program, most people look for one in a destination that is appealing as a vacation spot and that offers conditions suitable for their particular sailing level. Beginners look for easier areas such as inlets and coves or calmer waters protected by a reef. Inter-

Melissa Rivers is a freelance writer who has covered areas as near as Mexico and Canada and as far as Asia. However, she makes her home not far from one of the world's top windsurfing destinations, The Gorge.

mediate and advanced sailors need the challenges of big winds and waves to increase their knowledge of advanced maneuvers.

In the Columbia River Gorge, mecca of boardheads the world over, there are more than 50 sailing locations and a variety of conditions, from "nuclear" (heavy) winds and large, choppy waves off expert locations like Swell City to calmer, shallower waters such as the Hood River Marina, where beginners will feel comfortable getting their feet wet. The Gorge (as it's known in the windsurfing world) is a research, manufacturing, and production zone for windsurfing equipment, and many school operators there purchase new equipment every season, giving you access to the hottest new boards, sails, and other paraphernalia.

Maui, another world-class windsurfing destination, offers warm waters and strong sideshore winds in a lush tropical setting. Because of rulings prohibiting concessions on the beach, you're generally required to pick up equipment in one location and transport it to the water yourself to meet instructors.

Although the Gorge and Maui top the lists, there are many other windsurfing destinations to choose from. Puerto Rico, one of the best-kept secrets in the industry, has consistent trade winds and clear waters sheltered by barrier reefs. The U.S. Virgin Islands are equally inviting, with similarly conducive conditions suitable for year-round sailing. Hidden surfside locations in Northern Baja that used to be known only to the pros are "in" now; there's an operator who takes intermediate and advanced sailors on week-long journeys to enjoy the tremendously challenging waves and winds. Protected inland lakes and waterways in Florida and California are easier for learning, while the challenging wind and wave conditions of the Atlantic and the Pacific offer something for advanced sailors.

For the most part, instructors are in their 20s or 30s, certified to teach windsurfing, and have had several years of instructional experience, as well as Red Cross lifesaving, first aid, and CPR training. It may be an odd picture to see them teaching the average student, who is a fairly well-to-do professional between 30 and 50, but the enthusiasm that brought them to the sport is contagious and forms a bridge between the generations. They, like their students, are physically active, and usually aficionados of biking, skiing, snowboarding, rollerblading, and other solo outdoor sports.

The cost of a trip like this varies greatly, but on the average a week of windsurfing costs around $700. Ground transportation is usually part of the package: A bus or van is used to carry gear and shuttle students between the learning site and lodgings, out for meals, and to slack-day activities when they are included in the package.

CHOOSING THE RIGHT SCHOOL

In picking a windsurfing school, it's important to ask these questions:

How long has your school been in operation? You want an experienced outfit with a good reputation, not a fly-by-night school with inexperienced instructors. There are no industry regulations for windsurfing schools, but those around for at least 3 years are generally your best bet.

Do you have references from past guests?

What is the location like? Is your lesson site good for beginner, intermediate, or advanced students? Intermediate and advanced students should look for challenging conditions (high winds, big waves) needed to increase skill level. You won't learn new maneuvers on a flat, calm lake. Beginners, however, will do better on flat, calm waters with steady but mild breezes, which are conducive to learning. Warm water and a sandy bottom add to your comfort when just starting out.

Are lessons available for all skill levels?

What are the teacher's qualifications? It's much better to have a professional teacher, rather than the school's temporary summertime helper, instructing you. The professionals are certified, meaning that they have been trained to teach all levels of skill and specifically introductory techniques.

Are land simulators used? Land simulators are boards and rigs set up on land to give you the feel of a particular movement (or set of movements) before you get in the water. Practicing the basics on a simulator cuts the learning time down considerably.

How much time is spent on land and on water learning? Beginners usually spend about a third of the class time on land getting a feel for the basic skills before hitting the water. The time on land is less for intermediate and advanced students. If you've already reached a level of comfort on a windsurfer, then you'll want to spend more time in the water honing your technique. For that reason, intermediate and advanced students should look for a school that emphasizes in-water instruction.

Is the equipment current? Equipment changes frequently—with modifications in designs to make sailing easier and faster—so it's best to learn on the latest gear rather than old gear that will just slow you down.

Must I rig and carry the equipment? This takes time and energy. Several schools pre-rig equipment to get you on the water as soon as possible; others want you to learn to rig and have you do it yourself each time.

What's the cost and what's included? All prices listed are per person, double occupancy, and include lodging, equipment, meals, and airport transfers unless noted otherwise. Every program, however, is run slightly differently, so check carefully before booking your trip. Occasionally, personal gear (harness, wetsuit, gloves, booties or sailing shoes, and so on) is included in the package. Check before purchasing your own.

Is a rental car necessary? Most outfitters transport the gear to the water, but there are those schools that require you to have a car to transport the equipment. Obviously, this will add to the expense of your trip; however, renting a car gives you the flexibility to have a meal on your own or go sightseeing.

Are alternative activities available on windless days? You don't want to waste your vacation just because there's no wind, so pick a school that provides alternative activities to fill those slack days.

Do you have child-size equipment? The special equipment available for children is smaller and easier for them to learn to control. If you plan to travel with children, make sure that the smaller boards are available.

What is the food like? There is a huge variation in the dining options on these trips—from hamburger cookouts to homecooked buffet meals to eating in the local restaurants.

What are the accommodations like? Some schools put you up in tents, others in hotels or bed-and-breakfasts. Each outfitter does things differently so ask ahead so you know what to expect.

Will laundry service be available?

How far in advance do I need to book? All operators will sell space as available up to the last moment, but you should try to book at least 60 to 90 days ahead to make sure you get a spot, especially during peak seasons.

FAVORITE SCHOOLS

THE SOUTH

FLORIDA **The Sailboard School.** Fast tack, flare, carved jibes, water-starts, and beach-starts are covered in this 5-day program that uses 3 types of teaching simulators and extensive video analysis. The school maintains more than 30 current short and long Bic boards and more than 60 UP, North, and Aero Tech sails. Such diverse equipment provides something for every ability level and the chance for experienced sailors to test their skills on equipment they've never tried before.

Since there are only 8 students per session, you receive lots of personal coaching from Burr and Patty Hazen and their assistants, all Mistral-trained instructors, who spend the entire day with you. You learn to rig your own equipment, and before heading out into the shallow waters of Indian River Lagoon, they equip you with a radio receiver so that you can clearly hear instructions and advice while executing turns and other maneuvers. Onshore winds of 10 to 15 knots provide plenty of power for your sails, and as Patty can attest, there are virtually no flat days here.

Burr dropped out of Wall Street banking to open the Sailboard School in Portland, Maine, in 1981. After developing a 6-step teaching process to make learning the sport and its skills easier and quicker, he relocated the school in 1983. By moving to the east coast town of Sebastian near Vero Beach (about an hour and a half southeast of Orlando), the Hazens extended the sailing season.

Burr and Patty completely renovated the Florida Inn, a turn-of-the-century road house, outfitting it as "ground school," where you'll learn skills on land before hitting the water. Some of the guest rooms share a bath, and if you don't come with a partner, you might have to share a room with another student. Most students are professionals (predominantly from the medical field) and are between the ages of 30 and 50; kids under 18 are not accepted.

A Continental breakfast is served each morning before the group reviews videos shot the day before and heads out to practice on dryland simulators. Students then prepare and pack their own lunch to take to the lagoon, where water lessons and free sailing fill the rest of the day. Dinners back at the school are traditional sit-down affairs; London broil, roast turkey, seafoods, and salads galore round out the weekly menu. *The Sailboard School, 9125 U.S. 1, Sebastian, FL 32958, tel. 407/589–2671, fax 407/589–7963. Mid-Feb.–May and Sept.– Dec.: 5 days, $750. Sign up 3 months in advance.*

THE WEST COAST

CALIFORNIA **ABK Rio Vista Camps.** Following the precedent set by ski racing camps, ABK Sports began sending world-class windsurfers around the country in 1982 to teach multiple-day clinics for everyone from novice to expert. The company now runs about 30 very affordable sessions per year. Of those, 6 take place in Rio Vista, a well-known inter-mediate-to-advanced sailing spot about 2 hours north of San Francisco, in rolling delta country, near the historic river towns Locke and Isleton. New sailors may find the river location intimidating because of the winds and currents, but ABK does teach novice courses during the 4-day camp. These cover balance and stance, sail trimming, tacking, and jibing. If you already know the basics, you can learn to sail more confidently in a variety of conditions and work on advanced skills such as jumping, high-wind sailing, carved jibes, and racing techniques. Up to 35 students attend each session.

This really is a camp with everything provided, from tents and meals to instruction and use of up-to-date demo equipment (including Nike Aquasocks, wetsuits, harnesses, and state-of-the-art Bic boards and UP sails). Days can begin early with a warm-up stretch followed by roller blading, running, or mountain biking, or you can choose to sleep in. After a hearty breakfast, you're off to class on a protected grassy area across from the campground just above Windy Cove, a location with constant winds and a gradually dropping sandy floor. Lectures, demonstrations, and rigging practice fill the morning. Students are then divided into small groups (generally 4 per instructor) according to ability level for on-the-water instruction and practice. Afternoon lectures follow lunch, with the topic tailored to the day's conditions, then it's back to the water for practice drills and races. The full day on the water is videotaped so that you can analyze your technique with the instructor after dinner.

There is a tremendous return rate here among students, who come back to hone skills and spend a fun holiday with like-minded friends. Kids are welcome, but those under 14 must be accompanied by a parent and all under 18 must have a signed release form. *ABK Sports, 7 Crescent Rd., Corte Madera, CA 94925, tel. 415/927–8835, fax 415/927–7634. Late June–mid-Aug.: 4 days, $385. Sign up at least 1–3 months in advance.*

OREGON **Camp Surf–The Gorge.** Despite the quaint name, Camp Surf, which offers one of the few all-inclusive windsurfing packages available in the Gorge, is a full-service outfit; no hot dogs and camp outs on this trip. Owned and operated by Tom and Pam Wright, locals who know the Gorge inside and out, Camp Surf is a week-long (Saturday–Saturday) program suitable for all skill levels. The camp accommodates no more than 15 students per week, allowing for plenty of personal attention from certified instructors who are good enough to take you from beginning lessons to water-starts before the week is out. The Wrights provide top-of-the-line equipment, including Bare wetsuits, Gaastra sails, and customized Seatrend and advanced Gorge Animal boards; equipment is replaced every year, so you get to try out the latest designs.

To let you experience the wide variety of conditions in the Gorge, vans transport you to different windsurfing spots each day, including the Hook, the Wall, Maryhill, the Hatchery, and Doug's Beach. Instruction is unlimited—they stick with you until you learn it—and personalized, though you may share an instructor with 3 or 4 other students. Dryland hook-and-foot simulators are used to teach beginners the basics before they enter the water. Once you do get wet, instructors stay right with you. Experienced sailors spend most of their time in the water perfecting techniques and picking up new skills while trying out Gorge Animal boards and other cutting-edge sailboarding equipment. Videos are taken and analyzed to help you learn. Days with little or no wind are filled with other group activities including whitewater rafting, golf, tennis, horseback riding, mountain biking, and visits to top local manufacturing facilities, all covered by the package.

Guests stay at the waterfront Hood River Inn (a Best Western property remodeled in early-1994) in ground-floor, air-conditioned rooms that overlook the water. There's a swimming pool, a grassy area above the beach for land instruction, a storage room for equipment, and easily accessible launch sites. All meals are covered in the package price, from hearty breakfasts at the inn and catered lunches on the road to full-service dinners in a different Hood River restaurant each night. Older teens (usually post-high school) are welcome when accompanied by a parent, but this program is really for adults. While visits to the River City Saloon and popular North Shore on the Washington side aren't included in the package, you might wrangle a van ride to these locations to take in the Gorge's active night scene. *Camp Surf, Box 1526, Hood River, OR 97031, tel. 503/386–9090 or 800/927–3768. June–mid-Sept.: 8 days, $1,195; nonsailor 8-day package, $895. Sign up at least 1 month in advance.*

OREGON **Heavy Air Gorge.** Advanced sailors find their place at Joe and Lucy Field's Heavy Air Gorge. Based in Rowena, their waterfront property is a mile and a half down from the mouth of the Clickitat River, where the world speed-sailing records were set, and a mile and a half up from the swells and expert conditions of Doug's Beach. In other words, there are plenty of challenges here. An array of new, high-end equipment—Neil Pryde and Rush Wind sails, Dynafiber masts, Watson custom and Seatrend epoxy boards—wait pre-rigged for you on Joe and Lucy's private beach, so you can hit the water the moment the wind is up. You can try out a variety of equipment suitable for different skill levels whenever you are ready.

Radar is used to clock your speeds, and a high power video camera puts you on tape, to be played back later on a large screen television. Daily coaching on land is part of the package; Joe will analyze your moves on video and give you pointers each evening, but he doesn't spend time with you on the water. If you want personalized water instruction, it can be arranged, at extra cost. Joe's Zodiac chase boat is on standby if you need a rescue, but advanced sailors seldom do.

Up to 10 guests per week can be accommodated in airy, individually decorated guest rooms in the detached guest lodge or in the main house on the waterfront. Meals are not included in the package (thus the low price), but there is a kitchen for you to use and plenty of fine little restaurants a quick car-ride away in Hood River. Children of all ages are welcome, so this is a viable option for sailboarding families. Those who don't windsurf can hike, relax in the beachside hot tub, or use the mountain bikes to explore the area. Whitewater rafting, horseback riding, and summer skiing and snowboarding outings can be arranged at additional cost. *Joe & Lucy Field's Heavy Air Gorge, 6005 Rowena River Rd., Rowena, OR 97058, tel. 503/298–1513 or 800/544–7211. May and Oct.: 8 days, $619. June and Sept.: 8 days, $719. July and Aug.: 8 days, $819. Prices do not include in-water instruction or meals; sign up 1–4 months in advance.*

OREGON **Vela's Ultimate Gorge Tour.** Established in 1986, Vela Highwind Centers was the first, and is now the largest, windsurfing vacation company in North America, operating windsurfing centers in 5 locations. In 1993, the company joined the ranks in the Gorge, and it now offers 1- and 2-week packages here. These include accommodations, equipment, instruction, and off-water activities. Under the watchful eye of manager Paul Eckert—a former Olympic competitor with 18 years of windsurfing experience—and his 3 instructors, 14 students learn or perfect their skills in the sport using Mistral, Hi-tech, and ASD boards and North sails. Wetsuits are supplied, but the number of harnesses available is limited, so bring your own if you have one.

Morning seminars on land are followed by on-the-water sessions with personal coaching at sites that offer the best wind and conditions for your ability level. Instruction is given 3 or 4 hours each day and is usually followed by 2 to 4 hours of practice. Videos are taken and daily critiques of them accelerate your learning. Because this program is a tour of the Gorge, you hit a variety of top locations throughout your stay. There's at least one whitewater rafting trip per week, and flat days are filled with other group activities, such as wine-tasting tours, a Mt. Hood scenic train ride, hiking, mountain biking, and horseback riding, all included in the package price.

This is a good program for beginning and intermediate sailors, but falls second behind Camp Surf (*see above*) simply because the accommodations aren't as nice. Lodging at the vintage 1913 Hood River Hotel, tasteful-ly appointed with period antiques, is comfortable, but the hotel is not on the water and lacks air-conditioning and a pool. The price includes breakfast at the hotel and lunch on the road each day but only four dinners in local restaurants. Vela accepts kids 14 and older. *Vela Highwind Centers, 125 University Ave., Suite 40, Palo Alto, CA 94301, tel. 415/322–0613 or 800/223–5443. Mid-June–mid-Sept.: 8 days, $1,095; 14 days, $1,995. Prices do not include some meals; sign up at least 2–3 months in advance.*

HAWAII

MAUI **Excursions Extraordinaires on the North Shore.** Keith Nelson and Greg Young, owners of Excursions Extraordinaires, have been organizing windsurfing vacations for seven years at centers in the Gorge, Maui, Baja, Tobago, and other top foreign destinations. Surprisingly, their company is the only operator that provides an all-inclusive windsurfing vacation in Maui. The week-long package includes unlimited use of pre-rigged equipment, a private North Shore launch, ranch-style beachside lodging, breakfast and lunch, daily clinics, and personalized instruction. The program is better suited for intermediate and advanced sailors who want to pick up high wind and short-board skills, but is open to "determined beginners" as well.

The waterfront location between the famous sailing spots of Kanaha and Spreckelsville gives you the opportunity to experience the best of Maui's sailing conditions using the latest Bic Sport and Hi-Tech boards, Windsurfing Hawaii booms, light carbon masts, and Gaastra sails. Afternoon trade winds blow at least 20 knots, especially during the peak months of April, May, and August. Early mornings, fairly calm on Maui, are dedicated to hiking, biking, and snorkeling (rental gear is available). Late mornings and early afternoons are devoted to group instruction, private sessions, and free sailing time. Beginner and high wind simulators are used on land, and instructors join you in the water. Special guest instructors such as Rhonda

Smith-Sanchez, five-time world champion in women's windsurfing, are brought in a few times each season to conduct clinics.

Meals are served al fresco on the large, ocean-view deck of the guest house. There are theme lunches throughout the week with Western barbecue, Polynesian, Thai, Italian, and Mexican specialties; vegetarian options are always available. You sleep in one of the small, private cottages with narrow lanais that look out on the North Shore or one of four simply furnished bedrooms (two with private bath) in the guest house. Just outside is a roomy hot tub to help you relax tired muscles after a long day on the water. Airport pickup is included in the price. Smaller equipment and special kids clinics make this suitable for families. *Excursions Extraordinaires, Box 3493, Eugene, OR 97403, tel. 503/484–0493 or 800/678–2252, fax 503/343–7507. Mid-Apr.–mid-Sept.: 7 days, $899. Price does not include dinners; sign up at least 6–8 weeks in advance.*

MAUI **Vela and Maui Magic.** Unlike its packages in the Gorge, Vela Highwind Center's Maui packages are not all-inclusive. Vela explains your options and puts together the lodging and transportation portions of your trip; the equipment and teaching is left to Maui Magic Windsurfing School, Vela's exclusive center in Maui. Jim Hernandez, owner of Maui Magic, developed his own system of teaching taking into consideration the high-wind conditions of the island and employs a number of high-tech devices to facilitate learning. Lessons are broken down into concise, logical components that are easy to understand, and class size is kept to a minimum of 3 or 4 students per instructor.

Maui Magic has produced a series of instructional videos that are used along with simulators for the on-land lessons. The expert staff (all with five or more years of teaching experience) use instructor-to-student radios to provide simultaneous guidance and feedback in novice sailing classes. Beginners are usually sailing back and forth within the first hour of practice. Instructors join intermediate students in the water for classes in high performance sailing, jibing, and water-starts (the latter guaranteed within 3 days or you continue lessons free of charge). Skilled sailors who rent equipment from Maui Magic can trade off as often as they like to experience all the hottest new boards and rigs that the school carries. The school also teaches children using smaller rigs, but kids must weigh at least 75 pounds and parents must remain on site during the lesson.

First you pick out equipment suitable for your size and ability at the school's headquarters about a half-mile from the beach. The staff there will outfit your rental car with racks and load up the equipment before sending you on to Kanaha Beach Park to meet your instructor. Classes actually take place on Cook's Beach, the longest and most upwind stretch of sand in Kanaha. There is a grassy staging area for rigging and shallow, flat water for learning on the calm side of the reef. Open sea beyond the reef is suitable for polishing wave-sailing techniques. Winds are light each morning (best for beginners) and pick up in the warm afternoon (a challenge for intermediate and advanced sailors). The 3- and 5-day lesson packages include 3 hours of morning or afternoon instruction (1 hour on land, the rest in the water) and unlimited use of equipment. Lessons do not have to be taken on consecutive days, so if you pay for 7 days of lodging, you can take a day off to rest and sightsee. *Vela Highwind Centers, 125 University Ave., Suite 40, Palo Alto, CA 94301, tel. 415/322–0613 or 800/223–5443. Year-round instruction: 3- and 5-day packages, $165–$265; 7 days' lodging from $486. Prices do not include meals; sign up at least 2–3 months in advance.*

BAJA CALIFORNIA

NORTHERN BAJA **Solo Sports Excursions.** Advanced sailboarders looking for a new challenge should get ready for the playful surf of Northern Baja, where Kevin Trejo, owner of Solo Sports Excursions, teaches wave-sailing. For years the sailing spot featured on this trip remained a carefully guarded secret known only to an elite group of top wind-surfers who were drawn to shred and jump in the wind and waves. Word has spread over the years, and now you run into determined sailors from around the world, but the spot's inaccessibility still keeps crowds away—it's a long haul on rough dirt roads, and since there are no services on this remote stretch of Baja Coast, you must bring everything you need with you. Solo Sports Excursions takes the work out of getting here, supplies all the basic necessities (tents, meals, equipment) to keep you in comfort, and offers informal instruction in wave-sailing techniques during 5 full days.

Kevin has been visiting the same Baja location for over a decade; he learned wave-sailing here from pros like Kevin and Matt Pritchard and Bennett Williams. Once or twice a month, one of the top sailors on the professional circuits will take a break from his or her travels to join these trips and help out with instruction. The teaching method is fairly hands on, with dry-land, verbal explanations of the moves followed by work on the waves, where you watch the instructor and copy what he does. Advanced sailors who can already water-start, complete 25% of their jibes, and swim safely in the surf without a personal flotation vest should have no problem picking up several new tricks in the brisk side-offshore winds and long, mellow breaking waves of the site.

The 8-day trip begins and ends in Irvine, California, and includes overnight accommodations at each end of the journey. Airport transfers from Los Angeles and Orange County can easily be arranged. Sturdy shuttle buses are used to haul a maximum of 10 sailors and their equipment to the site; you can either bring your own gear or use the Joe Blair custom boards and wave-sails by Gaastra, North, and UP that Solo Sports Excursions supplies. Tents are set on a desert bluff overlooking the surf, and solar showers are available to rinse off the saltwater. Camp meals are very hearty, from yogurt, cereals, fruit, pancakes, and eggs in the morning to deli-style sandwiches and salads for lunch and chicken, steaks, fish, or pasta dishes with vegetables and breads for

dinner. This is not a trip for kids or beginners. *Solo Sports Excursions, 78 Blazewood, Foothill Rand, CA 92610, tel. 714/837–1396, fax 714/588–8356. Mid-Apr.–Oct.: 8 days, $700 with own equipment, $1,000 without. Price does not include airport transfers; sign up at least 30 days in advance.*

THE CARIBBEAN

PUERTO RICO **Ventolera School.** Eddie Rodriguez, presently ranked among the top three windsurfers in Puerto Rico, runs the Viento y Vela Windsurf Shop and Guest House in Lajas. In 1990, he started the Ventolera Windsurfing School offering instruction and lodging packages from 5 days to one month. Instruction is at all levels, from the basics of rigging, balance, and turns to advanced slalom sailing, jibing, and water-starts. His lessons are easy to understand and his equipment (Mistral boards and Raf and North rigs) is first-rate, but there's no doubt that it's the warm waters and sunny skies of this tropical paradise that are the main draw of this program.

While the shop and accommodations are based in the quaint village of La Parguera in Lajas, actual instruction takes place on the first of three barrier reefs, about a mile off shore. Here steady trade winds blow at 12 to 15 knots across the crest, providing ample wind for sailing away from the reef. The back-reef lagoon, an ideal site for novices, seldom gets large waves and has an average depth of 3 feet of crystal clear water. Eddie and one other instructor teach a maximum of 8 students per session, so personal attention is assured. They follow students by boat, calling out instructions as the group sails along with the wind. Most students are professionals around 35 years old, but the school accepts children 10 and over who can swim (smaller rigs are available). Nonsailors are welcome to join you and can spend the morning watching you sail or snorkeling among the colorful flora and fauna of the reef.

Following morning simulator practice and a critique of your performance on the previous day, you leave the dock with board and rig and head out to the reef by boat. There you receive 3 ½ hours of instruction and practice time before returning for some relaxation. Free-time activities such as scuba diving, snorkeling, fishing, kayaking, and biking (all at additional cost) fill the afternoon. There are numerous seafood restaurants and cafeterias within walking distance of the guest house, but you need a rental car to get from the international airport in San Juan to Lajas and to do any sightseeing. Rooms are simply furnished, but very neat; all have private bath, 3 have air-conditioning (ceiling fans cool the others), and one has a small kitchen and living room. Nightfall brings an impressive display put on by the area's unique bioluminescent organisms, so finish up dinner early and gather with locals and tourists to watch at the nearby bay. *Ventolera Windsurfing School, Box 386, Lajas, PR 00667, tel. 809/899–3030, fax 809/899–4698. Year-round: 5 days, $475; $95 per day, $25–$75 per day for nonsailors. Price does not include meals; sign up at least 1 month in advance.*

SOURCES

ORGANIZATIONS You can write to each of the following organizations for information on the best schools, instructors, and equipment rental shops in the vacation destinations of your choice: **Board Sailing USA** (Box 2157, Citrus Heights, CA 95611), the **International Windsurfer Class Association** (1955 W. 190th St., Box 2950, Torrence, CA 90509), the **National Association of Sailboard Retailers & Instructors** (1000 E. Shore Dr., Ithaca, NY 14850), and the **United States Windsurfing Association** (Box 978, Hood River, OR 97031).

PERIODICALS *New England Windsurfing Journal,* published 11 times a year, covers the sailboarding in the Northeast, with articles on destinations, schools, equipment news, and current events (Buzzwords Publishing, Box 2120, Southbury, CT 06488, tel. 203/264– WIND). *Northwest Sailboard* and *Windsurf California,* both published six times each year, cover the events, destinations, and schools of the West Coast. Subscriptions include a copy of *The Gorge Guide,* a special yearly edition that profiles the many rental and retail shops, restaurants, and lodging that the Gorge has to offer (Gorge Publishing, Inc., Box 918, Hood River, OR 97031, tel. 503/386–7440). *Performance Windsurf Reports,* published six times a year, lists performance ratings on equipment and includes a travel directory for windsurfing schools and resorts throughout the western hemisphere (MBA Publishing, 2710 Belmont Rd., Hood River, OR 97031, tel. 503/386–3522). *WindSurfing Magazine,* formerly *Windrider,* profiles equipment, destinations, and occasionally lists schools. It comes out eight times per year (World Publications Inc., 330 W. Canton Ave., Winter Park, FL 32789-3195, tel. 407/628–4802).

BOOKS *The Complete Guide to Windsurfing* (Facts On File Publications), by Jeremy Evans, is an instructional book on sailing and racing techniques and lists a few top windsurfing destinations. For coverage of sailing techniques, equipment selection, advice on where to go for the sport, even instructions on building your own board, try *The Windsurfing Funboard Handbook* (Barron's Educational Series, Inc.), by Clive Boden and Angus Chater.

ALSO SEE If after getting your feet wet, windsurfing appealed to you, take a dip in the Sailing Schools and Surfing chapters.

Working Farms, Ranches, and Cattle Drives

by Erik Fair

If you picture yourself in a cowboy costume eating country cookin' or in bib overalls wringing milk out of a cud-chewing heifer while spinning yarns at the same time, you want a dude ranch or country inn farm vacation.

But if you want something more—like a sore butt from riding too hard, bleary eyes from waking up with crowing roosters and bellowing cows, or the bone-deep satisfaction of bunking down at night knowing you've worked like hell and had the time of your life doing it—you may be hankering for a more challenging adventure: Like a working farm vacation, a working ranch vacation, or even a real live cattle drive.

Each of the working farms and ranches listed in this chapter produces something for market. And each offers you either the possibility or the guarantee of hard, soul-satisfying work in extraordinarily beautiful surroundings. Most ranches and farms are relatively small family-owned operations run by family members or trusted hands in traditional or semitraditional ways, which means anything from preserving and using their own natural water resources to creating and using their own fertilizer. All of this is more time-consuming and expensive than modern methods, so if the farm or ranch is to remain profitable, something (or someone) has to give.

One of those someones is you. The deal is more or less this: You become a temporary member of a hard-working American family that has at least partially preserved the romance of traditional farm and ranch life in this country. They get some of your honest labor and several hundred of your hard-earned dollars per week—anywhere from $300 to $1,200—to help make ends meet.

The kinds of farms and ranches that can give you a memorable vacation are not to be confused with the ultrabig, ultrascientific farms and ranches that produce the majority of this country's meat, produce, and dairy products. From most vacationers' point of view, there is nothing earthy about fleets of million-dollar farm machines rolling over endless expanses of row crops that have been fertilized by tons of chemicals. There is nothing romantic about the stench of barren feedlots where thousands of cattle drink from metal throughs and consume vast amounts of high-nutrient grain that bring them to market weight as quickly as possible.

Some working farms are in rich agricultural areas like Kansas or Wisconsin. Others are nestled in the beautiful rolling hills of New England. Farmers raise every kind of produce under the sun and may also generate other products such as milk, cream, eggs, chickens, hogs, and wool. Although riding horses is a part of farm life, learning how to drive trac-

---

Adverturer and writer Erik Fair is the author of California Thrill Sports. *He had his share of the farming life after he worked for several summers at High Valley Camp, a working farm near Mount Pisgah in North Carolina.*

337

tors, slop hogs, or use wooling shears is a bigger part. And hands-on exposure to the ageless interaction of land, weather, farm plants, farm animals, and sunup to sundown hard work is the biggest plus of all.

Most working ranches are out West, in valleys near the Great Rocky Mountains, or on the spectacular plains and foothills of Montana and Wyoming. Put most simply: Working ranches raise grass to feed cattle and cattle to feed humans and that's it. But don't underestimate what that entails. Cattle have to be rounded up for inspection, then there's calving, separating into various groups, branding, pregnancy testing, castrating, and other stuff too gross to mention. Riding horses is a huge part of ranch life and mighty useful when it comes time to inspect vast pastures, build or repair fences, or move the herd (or parts of the herd) from one place to another.

Moving cattle from pasture to pasture within the ranch itself is not to be confused with a cattle drive, when ranchers drive cattle to market or—more commonly—between summer and winter grazing areas. Cattle eat tons of grass all year. A rancher has to grow and store enough hay in the summer to feed the whole herd all winter long, but because ranchers can't grow winter feed on land that's being grazed by cattle in the summer, they need a gang of special cowboys called wranglers to drive the herd to a different "summer range" every spring. After the ranchers have grown, cut, and stored enough hay to feed the herd throughout the winter, they need another gang of wranglers to drive the cattle back home to their "winter range" every fall. Cattle drives vary a great deal depending on the distance between the winter and summer ranges and the type of terrain that separates them or the location of the best market.

Almost everything on a ranch or farm is constructed, arranged, and scheduled in accordance with the day-to-day, season-to-season realities of caring for, growing, and delivering a product to market. Everything else has to do with maintaining, improving, or preparing the ranch or farm to assure future production. Consequently, there is always

the anticipation of the next big job at hand. The daily schedule is subject to last-minute changes, depending on the needs of the crop or animals—so there is the excitement of knowing you have to be on your toes, ready for anything. Best of all, there is the right-now intensity of knowing that certain jobs just have to get done no matter how long it takes or how bad the conditions. This is especially true if you've signed up for a multiday cattle drive with overnight camp outs.

The activities that you participate in almost always have a purpose beyond your personal pleasure. You may catch a brilliant sunset on your way back from a late ride to check fences, but odds are good you won't even think about riding out just to see the next sunset after a full day of taking part in the miracle of calving.

The bottom line is that a sense of purpose—a sense of productive participation in an age-old process that is far bigger than yourself—is what ultimately separates working farms and ranches from "farm theme" country inns and "cowboy spa" dude ranches.

Every farm, every ranch, and every cattle drive is different. Some offer basic accommodations and commitment to rugged work, while others offer plush accommodations and the opportunity to take the work or leave it, depending on your mood or preference. Some programs encourage participation by the whole family and provide baby-sitting services and kids' activities to prove it. Others merely tolerate children and leave child care and supervision entirely up to you. Take these choices into consideration when choosing your trip and get a good night's sleep before you go.

CHOOSING THE RIGHT TRIP

By and large, each farm, ranch, or cattle drive reflects the tastes, idiosyncrasies, and personalities of the owners or operators. The only way to know exactly what you're getting into is to ask detailed questions before you sign up.

What do you call yourself? Most places that identify themselves as working farms or working ranches really are, but the variation on the experience is limitless. Ask this question first and you can avoid asking the rest of the questions to places that call themselves dude (or guest) ranch, guest farm (or farm inn), ranch (or lodge) resort, farm (or ranch) bed-and-breakfast, wilderness lodge, or rural hideaway. You might find a wonderful vacation at any of these places but odds are overwhelming that you won't be permitted to soil yourself with honest, productive work.

What do you produce? Potatoes or tomatoes? Hay and 500-pound calves? Chickens and eggs? Hogs and hams? All, some, or none of the above? What you need to know is: What is the specific mission of the farm or ranch (what product does it bring to market)? Once you know the answer you can decide if you want to be an enthusiastic working part of that mission for a week or two.

Season by season, what tasks will I perform as one of your guests? The experience of working the same farm or the same ranch is radically different depending on the season. Let's say you've selected the Hargrave Cattle and Guest Ranch in Montana. If you like the idea of helping out when all the baby calves are born you'll need to schedule your visit for March or April. If you loathe the idea of "burning butts" you'd better stay away from branding season in May. If you want to participate in the spring cattle drives, you're looking at June and part of July. Choose the time of year that you take your trip carefully—your activities depend on it.

Is work required or optional? This question, more than any of the others, will give you clues as to the nature of the farm or ranch, and the personalities, goals, and expectations of your hosts. Some are low key, others are more driven. The ones who can't wait to give you a sore butt from riding too hard say things like "After three days, honey, you can't tell the difference!"

How many head of cattle do you have? Less than 200 head is not an economically feasible unit. If you find a place that advertises itself as a cattle ranch but has just a handful of cattle, odds are great that they're kept around for show only—kind of like pets at a petting zoo.

How many wranglers do you have at one time? If your host makes a big distinction between guest wranglers and real wranglers—and there are more than 20 guests at a time—chances are that you will be treated like part of the herd rather than part of the work force. If you're looking for a working ranch experience, smaller usually means better.

How many horses do you have? Working ranches have nearly two horses for every wrangler. Any fewer means one of two things: overworked, dispirited, or hurt horses or extremely short rides that are more show than function.

How long are the cattle drives? You'll want to find out the answer in miles, days, and nights. A one- or two-day drive covering 10 to 25 miles is a much different experience from a five-day, five-night drive covering 70 miles.

What kind of riding experience do I need to participate? A long ride over rough or hilly terrain requires better horsemanship and tougher buns than a short ride over flat terrain. Also, the amount of experience you need depends on what tasks you participate in.

Do we come back to the ranch at the end of each day or do we camp out? The variations are endless. Some places bring you back to your warm bunk at the ranch every night, even if the drive covers 60 miles. On other drives you'll camp out just one night and on still others you'll sleep under the stars for as many nights as the drive takes.

What are the accommodations like? When you stay on the ranch or farm, your quarters may be a cozy private cottage with a host of modern conveniences, a private room with shared bath in a bunkhouse, or the previous bedroom of an older sister in the main house. When you're away from the ranch or farm (either on the trail, on a cattle drive, or at a distant pasture or feeding area), the roughing it can get a little rougher. Trail accommodations usually mean private tents (possibly with cots), portable outhouses, and primitive bathing facilities. Wood-stove-heated cabins without electricity or running water are sometimes used at distant pastures and other areas away from the main ranch.

What are the dining options? Actually, the better question is **How's the chow?** Home cookin' is the norm, but the location and ambience of where it gets served varies immensely depending on the tasks you're involved in. If you're doing chores in and around the ranch, you can expect home-cooked meals either in the main ranch house where your hosts live or in a central guest dining area. Picnic lunches or outdoor barbecues (usually called steak fries) are common, especially when the work takes you to a distant pasture or a particularly scenic area. If you're camping out on a cattle drive, expect your meals from an old-fashioned chuck wagon or a modern equivalent such as a van.

Will laundry service be available? This could save you a suitcase.

What's the cost and what's included? Prices listed include lodging, meals, and whatever camping equipment is necessary (tents, cots, cooking equipment, and portable toilet), although you'll probably be asked to bring your own sleeping bag and personal items. Most places provide horses and riding equipment as part of the service, but some do charge extra. Be sure to ask.

Pickup and drop-off services usually are available at the airports and bus stations that are closest to the ranch or farm, but beacuse of the remote locations of most ranches and farms, don't be surprised if you are asked to pay a nominal fee for pickup and drop-off—just enough to cover your host's costs.

How long have you been accepting guests? While the farm or ranch has probably been around for a while, having guests along might be a recent addition.

Do you have references from past guests? In this case, straight from the horse's mouth

can give you the exact information you're looking for.

FAVORITE TRIPS

THE NORTHEAST

NEW YORK **Merrills Farm.** New Yorkers looking for a convenient, inexpensive, farm vacation where children are more than welcome need look no farther than the country home of the Merrill family. Just three hours from New York City on the border of the Catskill Forest Reserve near Beaverkill River, Merrills Farm has hosted guests from all over the world for nearly 30 years. The farm has been in the family since 1868 and is currently run as a family corporation with matriarch Vivian Merrill and a number of grown children and grandchildren acting as hosts.

Although the family lost its milk market nearly 15 years ago, patriarch John Merrill still raises "replacement cattle" for sale to the meat market and other dairy farms. The Merrills also produce their own maple syrup. The highlight of the farm, however, is the opportunity to learn how to preserve jams, jellies, and all the vegetables that grow in the garden. The planting starts with frost-resistant onions, peas, radishes, and lettuce, followed by string beans, beets, carrots, corn, potatoes, and—after the last frost in late May or early June—tomatoes.

You can work the garden as much or as little as you wish here. Naturally, all meals, with guests and hosts eating together at a 10-foot dining table, feature homegrown vegetables. Along with the beef, pork, and chicken dishes, Vivian Merrill's famous cinnamon buns and other homemade pastries are always available. Visitors stay in a one-and-a-half-story guest house that has wood-panelled rooms—five with double beds, two with singles—and shared baths. All the rooms have dressers, chairs, and central oil heating that ensures toasty nights.

If you have a car, Cooperstown, New York, with the Farmer's Museum and the Major

League Baseball Hall of Fame, is 70 miles away. Nearby Howe Caverns (an underground cave) also makes an excellent day trip. There are lots of antiques stores, good hiking and fishing, and—with just 10 guests at a time— lots of opportunity to putt around in the Merrills' classic 1924 Dodge. *Merrills Farm, RD 1, Roscoe, NY 12776, tel. 607/498–4212. Early May–mid Oct.: weekly rate, $240 adults, $180 children under 10; daily rate, $40 adults, $30 children.*

VERMONT **Berkson Farms.** "The cows are machine milked at 3:30 AM and 3:30 PM seven days a week, 365 days a year," says the manager of Berkson Farms, Terry Spoonire, "and a surprising number of guests are willing to take turns helping out with the morning milking." Milk is far and away the chief product here. Owner Sidney Berkson's 600-acre dairy farm is in the heart of the small town, quaint covered-bridge section of northern Vermont, just 40 minutes from Stowe, the famous Vermont ski resort, and an hour from downtown Montreal.

The heart of the farm is a century-old farmhouse and a sugarhouse for boiling maple sap into maple syrup; its soul is the 250 head of Holstein dairy cows. You can learn machine-milking or the lost art of hand-milking. Spoonire, who, along with his wife, Susan, runs the farm for owner Sidney Berkson, says "some guests even like to help muck out the stalls but most have more fun with the haying that goes on between June and August." This farm produces all the hay and silage the cows need to get through the winter.

The best time of all to visit may be the period between mid-February and mid-March, and not just because of the excellent opportunities for cross-country skiing, ice-skating, snowshoeing, and snowmobiling right on the farm. "We have our own sugarhouse here," says Spoonire. "We tap four plastic lines into each maple tree and drain off the sap into 300-gallon central tanks. When those fill up we haul them by tractor to the sugarhouse and use a huge wood-burning stove to boil the sap into maple syrup." Spoonire says that 10 to

15 guests at a time can help and most are so amazed that it takes 52 gallons of sap to make one gallon of maple syrup that they don't mind paying $28 a gallon for it. Berkson Farms produces 100 to 150 gallons of syrup a year using this method and also teaches its guests how to gather sap the old-fashioned way, by traditional basket draining.

Chickens, ducks, rabbits, and sheep keep the kids busy, and a large garden, which guests are welcome to work in, produces all the vegetables consumed on the farm. Susan Spoonire cooks custom-tailored meals ranging from Cajun and Mexican dishes to traditional Pennsylvania Dutch recipes and old-fashioned macaroni with Vermont cheddar cheese. There's an apple orchard a mile up the road so the special dessert is homemade apple pie. Guests gather to eat around a huge round dining table on the first floor of the large, two-story, 100-year-old farmhouse. The Spoonire's occupy half of the upstairs and give the other half over to four guest bedrooms, one with private bath and the others sharing two bathrooms.

Hop in your car and take advantage of the nearby auctions, flea markets, antiques stores, theater, boating, riding, tennis, and 9-hole golf course. Best of all are the reasonable rates, which haven't changed since the late 1980s. "I keep trying to get Mr. Berkson to raise his prices," says Spoonire, "but he says he's happy with the way things are." *Berkson Farms, Enosburg Falls, VT 05450, tel. 802/ 933–2522. Year round: weekly rates, $300 adults, $150 children.*

THE MIDWEST

KANSAS **Prairie Star Guest Ranch.** Stan Greene's 6,500-acre ranch is in the Flint Hills of Kansas, a cattleman's paradise with miles of undulating bluestem grass–covered prairie meadows that are ideal for fattening cattle. Stan and his family pride themselves on their top-quality cow horses, horses specially trained to move cattle around. According to Greene, his horses are particularly good at making up for any inadequacies beginning riders have. Which is good because you ride right alongside working cowboys and help them tend to the herd's needs. The ranch typically has 150 cows and 2,200 yearling cattle to look after so there is always plenty to do, most of it on horseback, from moving them from pasture to pasture to inspecting mile after mile of pasture and fences. The prairie comes alive with its prairie chicken, beaver, deer, duck, quail, pheasant, wild turkey, antelope, and eagles. Take your camera along: The wildlife and the vast panoramas of one of the world's richest grazing lands make for some excellent photographic opportunities along the way.

Stan Greene assures that you will get the real old-time experience by eliminating modern distractions such as telephones, televisions, and non-working pets. The goal is to maintain a life-style that, as technology advances and economics becomes burdensome, is becoming less realistic and feasible to practice.

Guests stay in a rustic 3-bedroom cabin with stone fireplace, hot tub, and bathhouse. You can either have meals brought to the cabin or barbecue your own food right outside. Leisure activities include fishing and water sports at nearby El Dorado Lake, hiking along the Teter Nature Trail near the lake, hayrack rides, and old-fashioned barbecues. Groups and organizations are welcome. *Prairie Star Guest Ranch, RR 1, Cassoday, KS 66842, tel. 316/735–4295 or 316/735–4480. Late Apr.–Oct.: daily rate, $175. Price does not include trip from Kansas City Airport.*

NEBRASKA **Meadow View Ranch.** Meadow View Ranch is in northwestern Nebraska in the Sandhills area, particularly well suited for cattle ranching because of excellent grassed-over topsoil and naturally sub-irrigated meadows. "The water table is so high that the roots of the grass are fed by it," says owner Clyde Lefler. "We get excellent grazing and economical hay crops that the cattle do real well on in the winter."

Clyde and wife Billie host one family or group in a 2-bedroom guest house that sleeps seven. As Clyde says, "I can't keep an eye on more

than about six city slickers at a time." New guests join the Leflers between June and September. After they get to know you, they'll let you come around in the spring for calving and branding and for the spring and fall cattle drives.

This 2,000-acre ranch is home to about 400 pair (cow and calf) of cattle. The Leflers drive about 100 pair at a time over the 14 miles between the ranch and the summer range near Batesland, South Dakota. The drives at the end of May and October last the better part of a day and you're back at the ranch at night. The 8-mile-long, 2-mile-wide ranch has 3 lakes (one of them covers a square mile), which can be seen on a 4-wheel-drive tour. Guests love the tour because of the abundant antelope, deer, beaver, blue heron, trumpeter swans, and geese. Rental horses are available for those who want to ride. Lefler agrees that "only about six of our twenty horses are gentle enough for guests and that's the way I like it." *Meadow View Ranch, HC 91, Box 29, Gordon, NE 69343, tel. 308/282–0679. June–Sept. (new guests), Apr.–Oct. (repeat guests): daily rate, $50 per couple, $20 additional adult, $15 children 12–18, $5 children under 12. Horse rentals: $17 per hour, $40 per day.*

THE SOUTHWEST

NEVADA **Cottonwood Ranch.** Horace Smith has spent 41 years raising cattle and hosting guests on 2,000 owned and 5,000 leased acres in the O'Neil Basin of Elko County, Nevada. Smith runs 1,000 head of cattle and horses on the spread, near the beautiful and isolated Jarbidge Wilderness. One of two primary attractions at Cottonwood is the 40-mile, 4- to 7-day cattle drives in mid-May and September, complete with camping out around campfires, cowboy poetry, and sing-alongs. In the summer, you can spend your time working with the cattle, and sleep in the 7-bedroom lodge, which has private and shared baths. But, starting in July after the mountain snows melt, most guests opt for Cottonwood's other attraction—the 4- to 7-day horseback pack trips into the Jarbidge Wilderness.

On these guided trips you take all your food and equipment on packhorses, and ride past dramatic views of mountains with names like Cougar, Matterhorn, and Jumbo Peak. Ride across aspen- and willow-covered hills, and meadows filled with sunflowers and lupine. Photographic and trout-fishing breaks give your sore buns an occasional rest during the day and at night you camp out in the wilderness. These wilderness pack trips, when you just have to look out for yourself and maybe a few pack animals, may be the ultimate trial run for those who are ambivalent about signing up for a working cattle drive.

Whether you go for the cattle drives or the pack trips, all you need to bring is your sleeping bag and personal gear. Food, guides, horses, and tents are provided. Gentle horses are available for children 12 or older. *Cottonwood Ranch, O'Neil Basin, Dept. K, Wells, NV 89385, tel. 702/752–3604. Mid-May–Sept.: daily rate, $100; cattle drive, $1,000; 4-day pack trip, $500; 1-week wilderness pack trip, $850.*

TEXAS   **Y.O. Ranch.** About 100 miles southwest of San Antonio at an elevation of 2,200 feet, Y.O. Ranch is one of the largest working ranches in Texas and one of the largest exotic game ranches in the world. It is famous for its herd of 1,600 Texas Longhorns, the largest such herd in the country. Folks come from all over the world to spend time in the saddle mixing it up with the rare Longhorns and eyeballing the giraffe, wildebeest, scimitar-horned oryx, fallow deer, red sheep, black buck antelope, zebra, and watusi cattle that roam the ranch's 40,000 acres. Over 10,000 animals representing over 35 species are at home on this range.

It's not surprising then that horseback riding is perhaps the biggest pastime on the ranch. Rides go out twice a day for 1 to 3 hours, and experienced riders are allowed to gallop, a rare privilege in the world of ranch vacations. The daily guided wildlife tours are a good way of acquainting yourself with the ranch, and at extra cost there is an excellent photographic safari. Of course, you can always relax by the pool and hot tub. Thirty-four guests stay in five 100-year-old renovated log cabins, each with a fireplace, heat and air-conditioning, and a front porch on which to kick back. There are four additional rooms in the main house, but none of the rooms have telephones and TVs.

Every spring during the last week of April and the first week of May, Y.O. stages a 3-day "cattle drive" and steer-branding involving 60 to 80 Texas Longhorns and 150 to 225 guest wranglers on horseback.

You have plenty of opportunities for hard work with the cattle and sheep, including branding, moving, castrating, and shearing, but because this is not part of the ranch's regular service, it must be pre-arranged with Walter Schriener, manager of Y.O.'s Longhorn division. Schriener will question you to make sure you're up to the work at hand. If you pass muster, you're in for a rare opportunity to work with Texas Longhorns and you'll also gain insight into the care and feeding of the ranch's exotic animals. *Y.O. Ranch, Drawer K, Mountain Home, TX 78058, tel. 210/640–3222. Year-round (except Christmas Eve and Christmas Day): daily rate, $75 adults weekdays, $85 weekends; cattle drive, $300–$350 with your own horse, $400–$450 with horse provided. Pick-up from airport not included.*

UTAH   **Rockin' R Ranch.** Burns Black is the current patriarch of a family that has been raising cattle in Southern Utah for over 100 years. He currently runs about 1,000 head of cattle on 1,000 owned and 50,000 leased acres of grazing land in a beautiful valley surrounded by mountains near the spectacular Rainbow Canyons. Lake Powell, Dixie National Forest, Bryce Canyon, Zion and Capitol Reef National parks are all within striking distance for day trips.

In 1970, Burns and wife, Mona, realized that the best way to survive in the cattle business was to diversify into the guest business. So they did in a way that blows the word *small* out of the old phrase "small mom and pop operation." Rockin' R Ranch can now accommodate over 200 guests in two lodges. The old main lodge has a 3-story fireplace and 38 spacious rooms, all with private baths with either showers or tubs. The new lodge, just opened in 1994, has 62 slightly larger rooms decorated in western decor, also with private baths. These folks are so big they let children under 4 stay free. There are even supervised children and youth activities that make Rockin' R great for families. The ranch's swimming pool, tennis court, and restaurant make it a community within itself with full- and half-day horseback rides, riding instruction, 4-wheel-drive tours, and seasonal elk and deer hunting to make your days fly by. Otter Lake, just 2 miles from the main lodge, offers great fishing, sailboarding, canoeing, sailing, inner tubing, and waterskiing for family members who would rather play in the water than work with cattle.

You are invited to help out with as much summer cattle work as you wish. This includes roundups at the ranch's cow camp 10,000 feet up at the summer range in the mountains. Burns and Mona even have a special coordinator for the 3-, 5-, and 7-day cattle drives that take place between late June and October.

All in all, Rockin' R is the ideal place to get your feet off the ground with cattle work without leaving out family members who would rather spend their vacations enjoying a host of recreational pursuits amidst spectacular Utah scenery. *Rockin' R Ranch, Box 12 K, Antimony, UT 84712, tel. 801/565–8588 or 800/767–4386. Year-round: daily rate, $120 adults, $69 children; cattle drive, $195 per day.*

THE ROCKIES

COLORADO **Focus Ranch.** Aptly named, the focus of this ranch is working with cattle on the ranch itself. Owner Terry Reidy runs 1,000 head of cattle on his spread, which sits at 7,000 feet in the mountains near the northwest corner of Colorado, about 50 miles south of the famous Steamboat Springs ski resort. As a guest on Terry's ranch you are more or less expected to saddle up every morning and ride with him, but you'll want to. You pass through high country, aspen forests, and lush alpine meadows as he rounds up cattle, moves them between forest grazing areas and salt licks, repairs fences, checks irrigation ditches, or busts up beaver dams. Nearby Medicine

Bow National Forest offers unlimited space for pleasure riding and hiking if you want a day off from the work-related rides, and the Little Snake River, dotted with great trout fishing and swimming holes, flows right through Terry's property. At the end of the day you can fry steaks next to the river, play volleyball or baseball, square dance, or just sit back and relax. There's also excellent cross-country skiing in the winter.

Focus Ranch's mission is fattening up yearlings, so there are no cattle drives here. New stock arrives every May and guests help move them among various grazing forests on the ranch until final roundup days in mid-September. This place definitely isn't snooty or luxurious, but accommodations in the lodge with private and shared baths, plus the five rustic log cabins, are homey and comfortable. All the food is homemade. Terry will tell you that this is a meat, potatoes, and vegetables kind of place, but the bread is baked fresh daily—homemade french rolls are a lunchtime favorite—and the desserts are mouthwatering.

Focus Ranch is the place to go if you want to ride along with a devoted and experienced rancher as he goes about the daily business of caring for his herd. Plus, for better or for worse, there's none of that vagabond feeling you'll get on a cattle drive. After a hard day in the saddle, you'll eat like a king every evening, and sleep in the same warm bunk every night. *Focus Ranch, Box A, Slater, CO 81653, tel. 303/583–2410. Year-round: weekly rate, $875 adults, $450 children 12–17, $400 children 4–11.*

MONTANA **Hargrave Cattle and Guest Ranch.** Leo and Ellen Hargrave own 1,400 acres in the Thompson River Valley, 42 miles southwest of Kalispell, Montana. This beautiful mountain valley is shouldered by tall pines with the Thompson River flowing through the ranch's broad green meadows. Bordered by Cube Iron National Forest to the south, it is also only an hour's drive north to Glacier National Park and the Canadian border. The same distance to the southwest is the National Bison Range. There are 6 lakes within 10 miles of the ranch for those who would rather swim, canoe, or fish than work with the cattle. Alpine skiing at Whitefish Mountain Resort and cross-country skiing at Glacier National Park and on the ranch itself make this a great place to come in the winter.

The Hargrave's product is 500-pound calves, which they sell to feed lots. They run 300 pair between their ranch and various grazing areas on 86,000 acres of leased range. This means a lot of horseback riding on the spread, which is always done with a purpose. "If we're not out checking the cows, we're out checking and mending fences," explains Ellen, "or we're out checking the pastures and creeks to make sure they haven't been damaged by the cattle, which tend to trample them." Because so much of your activities involve riding, and the group's riding skills and experience can vary tremendously, the Hargraves routinely provide riding and horsemanship lessons that are tailored to your needs. That means folks with little or no time in the saddle can end up having as much fun as experienced riders.

In addition to all the seasonal work with the cattle, the Hargraves offer five cattle drives per year (three in June and two in July) that are included in the price of your stay. These are one-day drives covering 10–15 miles and, as Ellen Hargrave points out, "our guests come home every night to hot showers and real beds." Alternatively, the Hargraves usually designate one night per week, weather permitting, for camping out somewhere on the ranch. This way you get a taste of chuck wagon cooking (barbecued beef, beans, and biscuits), campfire storytelling, and sleeping out under the stars. *Hargrave Cattle and Guest Ranch, 300 Thompson River Rd., Marion, MT 59925, tel. 406/858–2284 or 800/933–0696. Year-round: weekly rate, $980 adults. Price includes riding lessons, overnight camp out, and tours of Glacier Park and the National Bison Range.*

WYOMING **Two Creek Ranch.** Talk about the real thing. For the past several years Dennis and Nancy Daly have taken guest wranglers on 75-mile spring and fall cattle drives between the winter and summer grazing areas at Douglas Meadows and Laramie

Plains in Wyoming. Now they invite riders to join them throughout the year to find out what cattle ranching is all about. They're not kidding either: Depending on the time of year you go, you'll have completely different experiences. In calving season from mid-February to mid-April you help separate expectant cows and monitor their health and condition as they prepare to calve, then help with the normal births. In late April to early May, you round up 1,000 head of cattle on the winter range and sort them into two groups for the relatively short (17-mile) drive to the spring range. Branding Weekend, the first weekend in May, takes in plenty of riding to gather, brand, and release three separate groups of calves. Keep in mind that branding is hard, dirty work and you've got to be ready for the stench of burning cowhide and the bleating of frightened calves. The spring cattle drive in the last 10 days of May is the big one for wranglers with cabin fever who kinda like the constant bleating of growing calves and nervous mama cows. You trail 1,000 head of cattle 75 miles from the spring range at 5,000 feet to Laramie Peaks, the high-country pasture, at 7,000 feet. You're looking at 11 days and 10 nights with all but 2 nights camping out next to the herd. The fall cattle drive is the same 75 miles in reverse, which takes place in the last 10 days of October. Other activities include anything from pregnancy testing the heifers in early August to separating and weighing the calves for market. *Two Creek Ranch, 800 Esterbrook Rd., Douglas, WY 82633, tel. 307/358–3467. Year-round: daily rate, $65. Late Sept.–Oct.: 11-day cattle drive, $1,100.*

THE WEST COAST

CALIFORNIA **Hunewill Circle H Guest Ranch.** This 4,500-acre spread on the Northeast edge of California's Yosemite National Park has been in the Hunewill (pronounced Honey-will) family since 1861. It sits at 6,500 feet in the Bridgeport Valley North of Mono Lake hard against the eastern slopes of the Sierra Nevada mountain range. The Hunewills opened their white-frame ranch house to guests in 1931 and have such a loyal following that the ranch is usually booked solid in the summer months. That's okay though, because most of the work involving cattle and riding horses takes place in spring and fall.

The highlight from a prospective wrangler's point of view is the November cattle drive from Circle H to the winter range at the Hunewill's other ranch in Nevada, 60 miles to the northeast. The 5-day fall drive starts at Circle H, goes past canyons and piñon-covered mountains to the Bridgeport Reservoir. From there you'll cross the East Walker River and go over Sweetwater Summit on the middle day of the drive. The last leg of the drive into Nevada is past more canyons that eventually open up into a wide, high desert. The bad news is that the weather in November can be anything from bright sun to rain or snow. The good news is that you return to Circle H—and your nice warm bed in a cottage with private bath or in a shared room in the ranch house—every single night of the drive.

Riding horses is the biggest part of life here. There is lots of riding associated with the care, feeding, and moving of the herd, but there are also regular morning and afternoon rides just for fun and practice. The Hunewill's pride and joy are their 100 horses that serve both ranch hands and the up to 40 guests. You get to keep the same horse for your entire stay and you're actually encouraged to ride as much as possible. Ride leaders will show you how to lope with a partner for a mile at a time, perform figure eights, do controlled "serpentine" weaving maneuvers in a group, and perform a timed group crossing maneuver called "thread the needle." Don't worry, there are rides for every age and experience level. The highlights for more experienced riders are the all-day Wednesday rides into the high country in Toiyabe National Forest and special "fall color" rides to view spectacular foliage. Kids over 6 get their own horses and, during the peak summer season, Circle H provides 24 hours per week of free baby-sitting services so you can enjoy your rides too. *Hunewill Circle H Guest Ranch, Box 368, Bridgeport, CA 93517,* *tel. 619/932–7710 (summer) or 702/465–2201 (winter). Mid-June–early Sept.: weekly rate, $795–$856. May–mid-June and Sept.: weekly rate, $731–$792. Nov.: 5-day cattle drive, $600.*

SOURCES

ORGANIZATIONS The Dude Ranchers' Association (Box 471, LaPorte, CO 80535, tel. 303/223–8440) represents more than 100 ranches in the western United States and Canada. The association's annual *Dude Rancher Magazine* is essentially a detailed directory of member ranches, the services they offer, and descriptions of the surrounding areas. The directory costs only $3 and is especially useful because the listings are coded to identify the type of ranch listed—from working ranches to resort dude ranches.

BOOKS *Eugene Kilgore's Ranch Vacations,* by Eugene Kilgore, though somewhat outdated, has detailed listings of hundreds of ranches throughout the United States and Canada. Most are strictly guest or resort ranches, but the ones that do offer work programs are easy to find, thanks to an easily accessible appendix. New editions of *Pat Dickerman's Farm, Ranch & Country Vacations,* by Pat Dickerman, were printed most years between 1949 and 1989. The listings of farms, ranches, lodges, and inns are slightly outdated (especially the prices), but the book has an excellent 6-page introduction. A variety of sections do a great job of conveying the spirit of farm and ranch vacations. Other sections help you with the nuts and bolts of choosing the vacation that's right for you. On the downside, although the working farms and ranches are clearly identified, there are precious few of them buried in a sea of bed-and-breakfasts, guest farms, wilderness lodges, and ranch resorts.

ALSO SEE If your saddle isn't too sore from all this riding, and this hard-working, outdoor life appeals to you, see the Covered Wagon Trains chapter.